The Cultural Life of Intellectual Properties

Post-Contemporary Interve tions

Series Editors: Stanley Fish and Fredric Jameson

The Cultural Life of Intellectual Properties

Authorship, Appropriation, and the Law

ROSEMARY J. COOMBE

DUKE UNIVERSITY PRESS   *Durham and London 1998*

© 1998 Duke University Press
All rights reserved
Printed in the United States of America on acid-free paper
Typeset in Minion by B. Williams & Associates
Library of Congress Cataloging-in-Publication Data appear
on the last printed page of this book.

Contents

Acknowledgments

It would be strange, certainly, if a book about the conceits of authorship and the peculiar powers it confers did not acknowledge the many people, places, occasions, and conversations that went into producing this alchemy we deem a scholarly work. Nonetheless, I feel that I have been uncommonly fortunate to have had so much support and so many lively interlocutors over the (all too many) years this volume has been in preparation. My scholarly itinerary has been itinerant indeed, but the unease of disciplinary homelessness has been more than compensated for by the stimulation of interdisciplinary conversation.

Many friends have read and commented upon the manuscript; many more provided support, inspiration, and critical intervention. I particularly want to thank John Comaroff, Peter Jaszi, Don Brenneis, Harry Arthurs, and Jane Collier for sharing the journey over the long term and helping me face the obstacles with more grace than I might otherwise have managed. Keith Aoki, Lisa Bower, Alan Brudner, Margreta de Grazia, Akhil Gupta, Gail Faurshou, Jim Ferguson, Rob Howse, Willajeanne McLean, Toby Miller, Beth Mertz, Don Moore, Frank Munger, Nel Newton, Kathleen Perry-Adams, Deborah Root, Mark Rose, Diane Rubenstein, Austin Sarat, Susan Silbey, Jean Edward Smith, Terry Smith, Susan Stewart, Paul Stoller, Kath Weston, and Barbara Yngvesson all provided critical and supportive readings of parts of the manuscript. The research assistance of Larry Reimer, Amanda Pask, and Karen Clark was invaluable. A special acknowledgment is due to my former graduate student David Fewer, whose research and editorial assistance went well beyond the call of duty. His enthusiasm for this project buoyed me; he is now a fine intellectual property scholar in his own right and I am very proud of his accomplishments.

There are others whom I wish to thank for early support and guidance. Constance Backhouse introduced me to the interdisciplinary study of law. David Flaherty patiently worked with me on my first ventures into publication and saved my prose from the influence of legal education. Dick Risk and David Sugarman shared and supported my enthusiasm for unconventional theoretical forays into legal contexts. Bob Gordon taught me the power of example. Tom Gray and Barbara Babcock shepherded me through one of this project's more difficult moments with grace and generosity. My parents' love, faith, and determination have made all accomplishments possible.

David Howes, Cheryl Walker, Renato Rosaldo, Michael Roth, the late Mary Joe Frug, Martha Woodmansee, Austin Sarat, Michael Lambek, Jonathan Simon, Alison Young, Brian Goldfarb, Scott Lash, John Urry, Sylvia Yanagisako, Sherry Ortner, Mary Layoun, Pnina and Richard Werbner, Theresa Caldera, Richard Perry, Ioan Davies, Michael Musheno, and David Goldberg all helped to bring together critical audiences for presentations of this work in progress. Parts of the work were presented at the University of Montreal Department of Anthropology, the doctoral programme in the humanities at Concordia University, Concordia University's Department of Communications, the Centre for Critical Cultural Research and the Faculty of Law at Manchester University, the University of Lancaster Social Sciences Faculty and Faculty of Law, the Amherst Seminar in Legal Ideology and Legal Practice, the University of Pennsylvania PARSS Seminar, the University of Wisconsin–Madison Department of Comparative Literature, the American Bar Foundation, the University of Miami School of Law, the School of American Research, the State University of New York–Buffalo Law School, the University of Chicago Humanities Institute, Scripps College Humanities Institute, the Centre for Comparative Legal History Workshop at the University of Chicago, the program in Justice Studies at Arizona State University, the Rockefeller Centre in Bellagio, Italy, the University of California at Irvine Department of Anthropology, and the Media/Generations/Technology Conference sponsored by the New Museum of Contemporary Art.

Generous financial support was provided by the Social Sciences and Humanities Research Council of Canada, the University of Toronto, the Connaught Foundation, the National Sciences Foundation, Washington College of Law at American University, the School of American Research, Amherst College, and the Canadian Bar Association.

Last, but not least, Reynolds Smith, my editor at Duke University Press was a joy to work with, and Judith Hoover provided copyediting of incomparable quality. I thank them both.

Parts of the introduction to this volume were published in "Critical Cultural Legal Studies" 10 *Yale Journal of Law and the Humanities* (1998),

"Contingent Articulations: A Critical Cultural Studies of Law," in Sarat and T. Kearns, eds., *Law in the Domains of Culture* (Ann Arbor: University of Michigan Press, 1998), "Beyond Modernity's Meanings," 11 *Culture* 111 (1991), and "Encountering the Postmodern," 28 *Canadian Review of Sociology and Anthropology* 188 (1991). Chapter 1 is an expanded and updated version of "Objects of Property and Subjects of Politics: Intellectual Property Laws and Democratic Dialogue," 69 *Texas Law Review* 1853 (1991). Chapter 2 elaborates on "Author/izing the Celebrity: Publicity Rights, Postmodern Politics, and Unauthorized Genders," in M. Woodmansee and P. Jaszi, eds., *The Construction of Authorship: Textual Appropriations in Law and Literature* (Duke University Press, 1994) and "Publicity Rights and Political Aspiration," 26 *New England Law Review* 1221 (1992). Parts of chapter 3 appeared in "Tactics of Appropriation and the Politics of Recognition in Late Modern Democracies," 21 *Political Theory* 411 (1993), as "The Demonic Place of the Not-There: Trademark Rumors in the Imaginary Spaces of Postindustriality," in J. Ferguson and A. Gupta, eds., *Culture, Power, Place: Explorations in Critical Anthropology* (Duke University Press, 1997), and in "Sports Trademarks and Somatic Politics: Locating the Law in a Critical Cultural Studies," in T. Miller and R. Martin, eds., *Competing Allegories: Global and Local Cultures of Sport* (University of Minnesota Press, 1998). Part of chapter 4 appeared as "Embodied Trademarks: Mimesis and Alterity On American Commercial Frontiers," 11 *Cultural Anthropology* 202 (1996). Chapter 5 was first published as "The Properties of Culture and the Politics of Possessing Identity: Native Claims in the Culture of Appropriation Controversy," 6 *Canadian Journal of Law and Jurisprudence* 249 (1993), which was abbreviated for inclusion in K. Engle and D. Danielson, eds., *After Identity: Essays in Law and Culture* (Routledge, 1994) and in B. Ziff and P. Rao, eds., *Borrowed Power: Issues of Cultural Appropriation* (Rutgers University Press, 1997). Chapters 6 and 7 are new to the public sphere.

The Cultural Life of Intellectual Properties

Introduction: Authoring Culture

Anthropology is always having an identity crisis. It's like having an intellectual poaching license.—Clifford Geertz, qtd. in Winkler, "An Anthropologist of Influence"[1]

[My] purpose . . . is to make explicit the systems of operational combination . . . which also compose a "culture," and to bring to light the models of action characteristic of users whose status as the dominated element in society . . . is concealed by the euphemistic term "consumers." Everyday life invents itself by *poaching* in countless ways on the property of others.—Michel De Certeau, *The Practice of Everyday Life*[2]

Clint Eastwood doesn't want the tabloids to write about him. Rudolf Valentino's heirs want to control his film biography. The Girl Scouts don't want their image soiled by association with certain activities. George Lucas wants to keep Strategic Defense Initiative fans from calling it "Star Wars." Pepsico doesn't want singers to use the word "Pepsi" in their songs. Guy Lombardo wants an exclusive property right to ads that show big bands playing on New Year's Eve. Uri Geller thinks he should be paid for ads showing psychics bending metal through telekinesis. Paul Prudhomme, that household name, thinks the same about ads featuring corpulent bearded chefs. And scads of copyright holders see purple when their creations are made fun of. Something very dangerous is going on here.—Judge Kozinski, White v. Samsung Electronics[3]

The law seeks to eliminate ambiguity.—Edmund Leach, *Custom, Law and Terrorist Violence*[4]

I'm on my way to the university to teach my class in intellectual property. I decide to walk down Queen Street, into that ever-so-self-consciously hip strip officially (and painfully) known as "The Fashion District" which runs west from the downtown core in Toronto. Parallel to King and Dundas Streets, crosscut by Dufferin, Bathurst, and Simcoe, Queen is central to the city's British colonial topography, overlaid more recently by a municipally imposed multiculturalism. Just to my west, street signs proclaim me to be in "Little Portugal" when all visible evidence suggests that "Little Saigon" might be more appropriate. Identities in such social contexts shift too quickly to be encompassed by official mappings, which, despite the liberal intentions of their cartographers, belie a colonial containment of alterity.

Shifts in relations among spaces, places, and identities are clear in the new uses of old contributions to the cityscape tendered by a now elderly generation of Ukrainian, Polish, and Czech immigrants; orthodox churches, butcher shops, travel agencies, and package services that long specialized in shipping goods into the Soviet Union. Gradually these commercial spaces are being transformed. Rents along this section of the street are lower than they are closer to downtown, but aspiring entrepreneurs still accrue some of the street's cachet. Xeroxed reproductions of Warhol posters, plastic busts of Elvis, Partridge Family gameboards, and Monkees album covers are favored forms of commercial decor in an area where Fredric Jameson's name is often dropped in cafe conversations and paraphrases of Jean Baudrillard litter the alternative press. Nostalgia with respect to histories of marketing and celebrity (and an ironic attitude toward it) creates a shared identity among a generation bound by no more organic traditions. This, social theorists would have us believe, is characteristic of the condition of postmodernity.

To obtain my morning espresso, I am once again compelled to choose between great pastry at the local Ukrainian bakery or better coffee at Starbucks®, the franchised yuppie coffee bar that locals tried hard to resent when it first "invaded" their neighborhood. Priding themselves on their individuality and social distinction, residents rejected the corporate insignia of serial equivalence they saw a "chain" representing. Once the Ukrainian bakery claimed a trademark, standardized its logo, and opened three new locations flying the flag of Futures™, it seemed rather futile to maintain the attitude. It's too early for decisions; characteristically, I decide simply not to decide and visit both. Clutching poppyseed cake and skimming movie reviews, I bump into a dishevelled young man. His shoulder bag proclaims him "Armed and Hammered." I smile at the parody and think about the different ways in which we recode and recycle the detritus of commercial culture.[5]

On the street, hot pink posters stapled to telephone poles inform me that the Nancy Sinatras (a local lesbian band) are again playing the Cameron on Thursday. Huge billboard advertisements for Black Label® beer loom overhead. Populated by nonchalant black-clad youth posing in smoky billiard halls, they seem eerily to echo something of the local mien. In fact, this is exactly what they do. Black Label had been a "dormant brand" for many years. It was precisely this lack of connotation—the mark's minimalist economy—that made the brand a favorite among those associated with the Queen Street counterculture in the late 1980s. Any beer that wasn't associated with suburban barbecues, babes in bikinis, and weekends with the buddies was difficult to find, and this beverage's black label was cooly mnemonic of the anti-lifestyle of the area's artists, actors, students, and cultural workers. Noticing the increase in sales, the manufacturer located the neighborhood taverns doing brisk business and decided to explore its new market. Students "in plain clothes" were sent as detectives to investigate the rites, ethos, and symbols of this lifeworld. Sufficient ethnography was accomplished to renew brand advertising using the signifying styles characteristic of the subculture so discovered. The advertising campaign subsequently won national awards; it was chronicled and celebrated as the creative authorial work of corporate copyrighters. For years, local residents were surrounded by commercial simulacra of their leisure (but tourists were at least assured that they were in the right neighborhood).

A teenager on the streetcar I board shrugs off a leather jacket adorned with a stitch-on emblem, a cameo of the Colonel (you know the one); this genteel Southern gentleman's face is overlaid with skull and crossbones. Food tampering, I wonder? No, too literal—maybe the treatment of the chickens the company purchases. I ask her if she knows why there is a skull and crossbones over the Kentucky Fried Chicken® logo. Glancing quickly and curiously at her jacket she says, "It's my boyfriend's, but I think you can buy them." "Do you know who makes them?" I ask. She looks at me as if I had requested the name of her narcotics source and murmurs something noncommittal.

I wave from the window to a few of my former students selling silk-screened T-shirts. This week they are embossed with the cartoon image of My Favorite Martian™, the insignia of Mattel's Hot Wheels®, and re-productions of popular book jackets. Recently they created T-shirts that featured the cover of anthropologist Emily Martin's book, *The Woman in the Body*, which reproduces Picasso's *Girl Before a Mirror*, and the jacket of Foucault's *Discipline and Punish*, which reproduces a gruesome medieval woodblock. These were sold to local feminists, sadomasochists, and tourists seeking souvenirs to recall their experience of the street's intertextual sophistication. I'm somewhat bemused that these book covers are the most immediately useful resources they derived from my Law and Contemporary Social Theory course. At least in some eyes, I'm uncomfortably aware, my status as professor of intellectual property demands a less reflexive view of their entrepreneurial activities. I'm more concerned that their inventories may at any time be seized without notice by zealous monitors of those private properties that circulate in the public sphere and that criminal charges may be laid by state officials whose sense of the public interest seems shaped primarily by profit-oriented actors. It is difficult merely to wink in their direction.

A young girl I guess to have Salvadorean ancestry walks by carrying a bottle of water marked "Clearly Canadian®." How much easier it is to acquire membership in a national community through the indicia of consumption than through the bureaucracy of immigration tribunals and refugee claims procedures. On the back of the newspaper I'm carrying, a major brewery advertises one of its flagship brands. The slogan "I am Canadian™" surrounds an image of a young white man struggling with his fly in what appears to be a motel room. "Next time, I'll remember to bring underwear," the caption reads. The welfare state is slowly but surely dismantled, and ideologists of free trade sacrifice national traditions of care, shared responsibility, and social commitments for the uncertain benefits of foreign investment and competitive standing in a global economy. A tawdry and exclusionary image of national belonging appears prominently in the press, while others struggle to have the dimensions of their suffering heard in parliaments. Market forces shape the commerce of meanings that citizenship may acquire, ever proclaiming the transparency of the nation-state and the simplicity of its claims upon us.

In a grocery store window incongruously juxtaposed with more fashionable retro façades, the Land O Lakes® Indian princess peeks out from the clutter. Nearby, expensive art deco and '50s modern collectibles are represented by dozens of gleaming chrome objects displayed in the front window of the Red Indian™ store. Such slick nostalgia, marketed with an emblem from an era when "we" were more "innocent" and less "politically correct," sits altogether too smugly across the street from a crafts outlet owned by Native peoples, in which exquisite beadwork sits abandoned on dusty sheets of pegboard. A few yards away, advertisements for Indian jeans adorn the walls of a bus shelter where a man of First Nations ancestry is unconsciously sprawled, suffering the cumulative effects of solvent abuse in a hostile urban environment. More "Clearly Canadian," I wonder? A cheerful Disney film titled *The Indian in the Closet* is advertised through marketing tie-ins promoted by McDonald's®; children are promised their own free "Indian" with every value-meal. In the Magic Kingdom® and under The Golden Arches®, Native peoples are mere toys to fire fantasy. Attempts by First Nations peoples to "come out of the closet" and protest their stereotyping in commercial culture provide poignant reminders of the political stakes in contemporary struggles over commodified representations.

On my way into the subway, I pass the Twiggy restaurant and reluctantly shift my attention to the intellectual property lecture ahead of me. Already I have considered at least thirty-four legally protected cultural texts, run into about a dozen potential intellectual property infringements, and encountered a score of other intellectual properties I didn't reflect upon. Other representations, once commodified but no longer protected by laws of trademark and copyright, are now part of the city's vibrant public domain, while elements of the public domain are constantly appropriated in the proprietary expressions of those whom the law recognizes as authors. Intellectual property issues press upon me in the commercial culture I share with my students, but eighteenth-century philosophical frameworks are deemed the appropriate academic vehicles with which to explore the dusty doctrines of copyright. There are "cases to cover"; get me to the church on time.

My meanderings along Queen Street mirror and compress the major themes of this volume, in the sequence in which I will approach them. The constitutive role of intellectual properties in commercial and popular culture; the forms of cultural power the law affords holders of copyright, trademark, and publicity rights; the significance of celebrity images in alternative imaginations of gender; the commodification of citizenship and the negotiation of national belonging on commercial terrain; the appropriations, reappropriations, and rumors that continually reactivate and reanimate commodity/signs to make them speak to local needs; the colonial categorical cartographies that underlie our legal regimes; and the postcolonial struggles of indigenous peoples to eliminate commodified representations of their alterity are the main themes of the chapters to follow. The limitations of legal frameworks derived from the eighteenth-century (European) bourgeois public sphere for contemplating such phenomena as forms of cultural politics provide the focus for my concluding essays, in which, finally succumbing to the normative impulse, I propose an expanded understanding of the political and advocate an ethics of contingency with respect to the use of commodified social texts. Each chapter is self-contained and reflects a historical moment in an intellectual journey. Although some effort has been made to update chapters to reflect recent contributions by other scholars addressing similar topics, no attempt has been made to revisit theoretical positions held in one moment with later reformulations. My major theoretical convictions are summarized here and will serve to provide the reader with a map of the academic terrain in which this journey was undertaken.

A Critical Cultural Legal Studies

The cultural dimensions of social life and the interpretive nature of human experience have become issues of concern in legal scholarship only in the past decade or so.[6] Rarely, however, does this literature address the legal status of the signifying vehicles with which meaning is made. Intellectual property laws, which create private property rights in cultural forms, afford fertile fields of inquiry for considering social intersections of law, culture, and interpretive agency. The rights bestowed by intellectual property regimes (copyright, trademark, publicity rights, design patents, and associated merchandising rights in particular) play a constitutive role in the creation of contemporary cultures and in the social life of interpretive practice. As the Colonel Sanders image, Nancy Sinatra's nomination, and the appropriation and reappropriation of the Picasso print in my Queen Street saunter suggest, the imagery of commerce is a rich source for expressive activity. In consumer cultures, most pictures, texts, motifs, labels, logos, trade names, designs, tunes, and even some colors and scents are governed, if not controlled, by regimes of intellectual property. These legal frameworks enable the reproduction and repetition of cultural forms as ever the same marks of authorial proprietorship, while paradoxically prohibiting and inviting their interpretive appropriation in the service of other interests and alternative agendas. The law's recognition and protection of some activities of meaning-making under the guise of authorship (the corporate advertising copy) and its delegitimation of other signifying practices as forms of piracy (the shoulder bag parody) create particular cartographies for cultural agency. This dialectical relationship between authorship and alterity is a significant, if overlooked, dimension of contemporary cultural politics.

Scholars in literary theory, communications, film studies, and political theory point to the social importance of media-circulated cultural forms and their political significance in contemporary consumer societies. Most, however, have been oblivious to the legal dimensions of this field of inquiry. Western societies have witnessed a massive expansion of the scope and duration of intellectual property rights since the mid-eighteenth century and an even greater growth and proliferation of legal protections in the twentieth century. The extension of proprietary rights to cultural forms has created immense new fields of potential economic value, engendered new industries, and raised a host of legal and ethical quandaries. There is still, however, a relative paucity of scholarly literature exploring their social and political implications. As my saunter down Queen Street illustrates, the texts protected by intellectual property laws *signify*: they are cultural forms that assume local meanings in the lifeworlds of those who incorporate them into their daily lives. Circulating widely in contemporary public spheres, they provide symbolic resources for the construction of identity and community, subaltern appropriations, parodic interventions, and counterhegemonic narratives.

For years, scholarship devoted to intellectual property merely described legal doctrine, documenting judicial decisions and recording legislative change. This literature chronicled the law but rarely attempted to critically examine its operations. Even today, when the development and expansion of intellectual property protections is justified or criticized, the Western philosophical tradition is generally evoked; appeals to natural rights, Lockean labor theories of property, and Kantian or Hegelian theories of personality abound. Alternatively, economic principles and utilitarian rationales are drawn upon to rationalize or question intellectual property laws as incentive structures that produce a socially optimal supply of intellectual creations. In both these moral and utilitarian arguments, scholars address intellectual property laws purely abstractly, as promoting reified rights in unremarkable and indistinguishable intangibles. Scholars have reflected upon intellectual property protections in terms of incentives to produce abstract goods, without considering *what* is "owned" or *how* rights of possession are exercised for far too long. There has been too little consideration of the *cultural* nature of the actual forms that intellectual property laws protect, the social and historical contexts in which cultural proprietorship is (or is not) assumed, or the manner in which these rights are (or are not) exercised and enforced to intervene in everyday struggles over meaning. The political consequences of expanding intellectual property rights in a democratic society are only now receiving long overdue attention.[7]

Not insignificantly, much of this new academic work is being carried out by younger, female, and minority legal scholars sensitive to the workings of power and the effects of subjection and subjugation that pervade even the most facially neutral areas of legal doctrine. My own work is very much part of this larger critical project; it is distinguished (as works and signatures must be in market economies) from other recent work in the same vein by an ethnographic sensibility, greater attention to the workings of law in everyday life—in local knowledges and local practices—and by greater doubt about the potential of categories derived from Enlightenment traditions to adequately address or resolve contemporary struggles over meaning. Moreover, I believe that controversies over intellectual properties speak to larger debates in the humanities and social sciences about cultural texts and subject-formations, identity and community, hegemony and alterity, democracy and difference, imagery and embodiment, narrativity and nationality. I engage and rework debates in cultural anthropology, cultural studies, and political theory through the medium of struggles around commodified cultural forms.

Laws of intellectual property mediate a politics of contested meaning that may be traced in the creation and appropriation of symbolic forms and their unanticipated reappropriations in the agendas of others. I will focus on practices in which the law of intellectual property disrupts activities of meaning-making as well as instances in which such activities disrupt the positivity of legal meanings. The mass-reproduced, media-circulated cultural form accrues social meaning in a multiplicity of sites, I will suggest, but legally, the meaning of a text is produced exclusively at a mythic point of origin. Thus, the Black Label advertising campaign was, in legal terms, corporately authored, even though the revitalized realm of connotation in which the brand became central was created by the expressive work of consumers.

The law freezes the play of signification by legitimating authorship, deeming meaning to be value properly redounding to those who "own" the signature or proper name, without regard to the contributions or interests of those others in whose lives it figures. This enables and legitimates practices of cultural authority that attempt to freeze the play of difference (and différance) in the public sphere. Emergent social differences are often expressed through the medium of commodified texts —texts that are legally defined as properties. Such differentiations in interpretive practice may, however paradoxically, be inadvertently encouraged even as they are explicitly deterred by regimes of intellectual property. These are the propositions I hope to substantiate by way of example in the studies contained in this volume. First, however, it is necessary to say something about the understanding of law that guides it, before outlining some of the theoretical contexts in which the work figures as both a contribution and a challenge.

The cultural studies of law is in its infancy and the endeavor this volume represents is a venture in largely unmapped territory. With respect to the potential parameters of such an interdisciplinary project, certain convictions have guided my research. There is little purchase, I am convinced, in constructing an ideal bridge to join two autonomous realms of "law" and "culture," insofar as this would reinforce the metaphysics of modernity that enabled their emergence as discrete and naturalized domains of social life.[8] An exploration of the nexus of law and culture will not be fruitful unless it can transcend and transform its initial categories. A continuous mutual disruption—the undoing of one term by the other—may be a more productive figuration than the image of relationship or joinder.

My encounters along Queen Street reflect and refract the major themes of this volume. The lecture that followed this walk—back when I halfheartedly acquiesced in the coverage of doctrine contained in appellate-level judicial decisions as a model for legal pedagogy—will not figure significantly. Although litigated and unlitigated disputes will be referred to, my contribution is not intended as a comprehensive treatise nor as a philosophical tome; it is, rather, a seriously irreverent intervention designed to provoke and stimulate what I will nominate "a critical cultural studies of law." Like other practitioners of cultural studies, my approach is antipositivist. I do not presuppose that the social life of the law can be explored simply in terms of its *logos*, positivities, or presences. It must be seen, as well, in terms of "counterfactuals,"[9] the missing, the hidden, the repressed, the silenced, the misrecognized, and the traces of practices and persons underrepresented or unacknowledged in its legitimations. To embody a sensitivity to the marginalized—absences and inaudibilities in contemporary cultural spheres—I have avoided limiting this study to reported cases or even to litigated disputes. The law's impact may be felt where it is least evident and where those affected may have few resources to recognize or pursue their rights in institutional forums.

Deciphering sometimes almost illegible traces of struggles over signification, I suggest that the law operates hegemonically—it is at work shaping social worlds of meaning—not only when it is institutionally encountered, but when it is consciously and unconsciously apprehended. Hegemonic power is operative when threats of legal action are made as well as when they are actually acted upon. People's imagination of what "the law says" may be a shaping force in those expressive activities that potentially violate it and in those practices that might be considered protected acts of "speech," constitutionally defined. People's anticipations of law (however reasonable, ill informed, mythical, or even paranoid) may actually shape law and the property rights it protects. This is especially the case in areas such as trademark, which, as I discuss in chapter 1, are premised upon legal fictions of public meaning and consumer confusion.

9

The law is a palpable presence when people create their own alternative standards and sanctions governing the use of cultural forms, as I show in chapter 2 in a discussion of the moral economies that regulate the use of images like those of Kirk and Spock in fanzine subcultures shared by middle-class women alienated from mainstream media representations.

The law's ideological effects are also realized when subaltern peoples mimic the modes of communication effected by the commodity form, as I explore in chapters 3 and 4, where I consider the way in which national borders and boundaries of belonging are negotiated through the deployment of the trademark and the form of its authority by lesbian activists, ethnic minorities, and indigenous peoples. The law's hegemonic power is also felt when rumors circulate about the origins of corporate trademarks, as I show in chapter 3, illegible though such fantastic fabulations may at first appear. The Ku Klux Klan rumors that attach to some consumer goods in inner-city black communities reveal both the law's cultural power and some of its more covert social contestations. When an inner-city vendor sells (obviously unlicensed) "Black Bart [Simpson]" T-shirts, the law is at work, as it is when rumors circulate that a twelve-year-old boy has been arrested for selling them.

Relations between legal owners and others—legally authorized texts, their alterations, and ensuing altercations—provide social nexuses for illustrating these propositions; hence my subtitle *Authorship, Appropriation, and the Law*. Practices of authorial power and appropriation, authorized meanings and alternative renderings, owners' interests and others' needs cannot be addressed simply in terms of dichotomies like domination and resistance, however. Romantic celebrations of insurrectionary alterity, long popular in cultural studies, cannot capture the dangerous nuances of cultural appropriation in circumstances where the very resources with which people express difference are the properties of others. Acts of transgression, though multiply motivated, are also shaped by the juridical fields of power in which they intervene. Law provides means and forums both for legitimating and for contesting dominant meanings and the social hierarchies they support.

Although my sensibility is an ethnographic one, an entrenched skepticism toward both law and culture as reified fields of social life animates this anthropological perspective upon issues of intellectual property. It will also orient the theoretical framework provided in this introduction for readers less familiar with debates in anthropology, sociolegal scholarship, and cultural studies. In short, I suggest that the heuristic value of exploring law culturally is a more focused and politicized emphasis upon meaning in disciplinary spaces traditionally preoccupied with questions of power. Similarly, the dividends to be realized from studying culture legally in fields like anthropology and cultural studies are a greater specificity and materiality afforded to understandings of power in disciplines with tendencies toward culturalism.

The social force of signification and the material weight that meanings may bear must both be highlighted in a cultural legal studies simultaneously attentive to issues of power and meaning, structure and agency, symbolic forms and interpretive practice. The law creates spaces in which hegemonic struggles are enacted as well as signs and symbols whose connotations are always at risk. Legal strategies and legal institutions may lend authority to certain interpretations while denying status to others. The multiple connotations contextually created by my students' T-shirts, however significant, bear no weight when up against the crushing pressures of private interests and public power. Such reactivated meanings, however, are only possible given the contingent fixities enabled by the law's proprietary guarantees. Had intellectual property laws not protected such texts in the first instance, they would not have acquired the posterity that makes them such ideal candidates for parodic redeployment. Law's constitutive or productive power, then, as well as its sanctions and prohibitions must be kept continually in mind.

The theoretical exegesis that follows will situate the significance of intellectual property—considered as a field of cultural politics—in anthropology, sociolegal scholarship, and cultural studies. To do so, it will be necessary to engage a decade of debates about the concept of culture that have emerged under the rubric of postmodernism and the perceived crisis of representation that the so-called postmodern turn might be seen to address. The relationship between authorship and alterity—scholarly representation and the others it represents—may then be revisited in another register, more sensitive to the politics of textuality in wider social spheres.

Against Culture(s)

Recent discussions about culture—its heuristic value and political limitations as a term of analysis—reveal a pervasive unease. Misgivings with respect to the heuristic value of studying culture(s) and the powers legitimated by such reifications have generated new perspectives and avenues of research in both the discipline of anthropology and the interdisciplinary field of cultural studies. As anthropologists acknowledged the Orientalizing tendencies of a concept of culture that delineated discrete cultures as formations to be studied in their own terms (cultures with a lowercase *c*), they became increasingly cognizant of the complex relations between power and meaning in everyday life. Similarly, in reaction to the Eurocentrism and elitism of the humanities' privileging of Culture as a canon of discrete works of European art and literature (which I will hereinafter designate with an uppercase *C*), a critical cultural studies was forged. Rejecting modern aesthetic tenets that insisted Culture be approached as a field of self-contained texts to be studied in terms of their own formal relations, practitioners of cultural studies focus on the social power of popular forms of textuality. My theoretical framework is oriented by these two tendencies to write "against culture," and I will relate the significance of my own interventions to these interdisciplinary developments.

These scholarly reactions have parallels in the field of law and social inquiry. Many law and society scholars have turned away from positivist, formalist (doctrinalist or structuralist), and institutionally centered accounts of law to explore law as a more diffuse and pervasive force shaping social consciousness and behavior. Although sociolegal studies has no explicit agenda of writing "against law," such tendencies are nascent, if not fully realized, in a growing body of literature.[10] A similar skepticism with respect to the concepts of law and culture holds promise for a revitalized legal scholarship attentive to issues of might and meaning, signification and interpretation, power and agency.

Whether it is dead[11] or alive, "everyone's favourite *bête noire*,"[12] but nonetheless "a concept in the right place at the right moment,"[13] a term that enables us "to take stock of where anthropology's future lies,"[14] and/ or a concept that has shifted "the paradigms in cultural studies,"[15] debates around the phantom of postmodernity do provide resources with which to reject culture and law as discrete and unitary domains of social life. In contemporary cultural anthropology and in the emergent field of cultural studies, the felt political necessity of writing "against culture" (whether with a lower- or uppercase *c*) has animated new forms of work and new objects of study that have emerged under the rubric of postmodernism, however qualified.

The term *postmodern* is ubiquitous and its referents so various that many scholars are inclined to dismiss it as a rhetorical fashion that addresses no substantive topic or perspective.[16] Those cultural anthropologists who first employed the term were generally concerned with issues of ethnographic representation (to which I will return),[17] whereas legal scholars tend to use the term as if it were synonymous with poststructuralism (as I discuss in chapter 1),[18] and positivist sociolegal scholars deploy it as an insult with which to dismiss most qualitative, interpretive, and culturally oriented work. The term postmodern, however, may inform our scholarship in more diverse and more provocative ways. Annette Weiner, in her 1993 presidential address to the American Anthropological Association, suggested that postmodernism was the sign under which anthropology encountered its own limitations and possibilities; it was a term that attracted the anxieties and desires of scholars challenged by socioeconomic change.[19] In cultural studies, Angela McRobbie sees the postmodern as the conceptual umbrella that afforded shelter for those concerned with issues of media and marginalization.[20] Despite its continuing capacity to make people wince, I will suggest that the term, as it figured in these historical debates, does help us to understand the social life of intellectual properties.

Cultural anthropology, in its "interpretive," "symbolic," or "hermeneutic" guise, was a modernist enterprise challenged both by the theoretical premises of postmodernism and by the historical conditions of postmodernity. The discussion of postmodernism enabled anthropologists to recognize the limitations of the discipline's traditional representational practices and pointed to new avenues for critical cultural research—approaches to considering cultural phenomena that might be considered postmodernist as well as attention to cultural practices characteristic of the condition of postmodernity (which I discuss in greater detail in chapters 1 and 2). Postmodernism has also legitimated a new critical engagement with issues of media, culture, and identity in the field of cultural studies, attentive to the emancipatory as well as the oppressive implications for agency in relation to mass-mediated cultural forms. Tracing these deployments of the term, new fields of inquiry for a critical cultural legal studies become evident.

The postmodern is clearly related historically to the modern or the condition of modernity with which the tradition of cultural anthropology is closely tied. Cultural anthropology posits the linguistic and intersubjective nature of social life and understanding. It is now critical orthodoxy that in the dominant functionalist, structuralist, and interpretive (or hermeneutic) variants of modern anthropology, cultures were depicted as holistic, integrated, and coherent systems of meaning. This depiction of cultures enabled (and was enabled by) the elision of social and political practices whereby meanings and texts were produced. Social relations of production and interpretation were emptied of specificity so that those who produced and interpreted meanings were without class, gender, race, or age characteristics and thus did not occupy social positions or have interests or agendas that might incline them toward alternative interpretations or meaning-making practices. Interpretive processes were represented without reference to cultural differences, social inequalities, and conflicts within communities.[21] The dialogic, contested dimensions of social life were evaded by a focus on dominant interpretations as the univocal voice of legitimate meanings and values. The interpretive approach engaged scholars in the discovery and description of the distinct lifeworlds in which phenomena had significance, as Clifford Geertz put it, the task involved "placing things in local frames of awareness."[22]

In its classical modern form, cultural anthropology recognized and respected differences among cultures but effaced differences within cultures. Defining culture as shared zones of difference—where alternative interpretations are generated and dominant meanings contested—appeared to be areas of deviance and marginality, not central to the culture under study.[23] Anthropologists appeared to divorce culture from creative practice and human agency. Cultural theories, Lila Abu-Lughod suggested, tended to overemphasize coherence and tended to project an image of communities as bounded and discrete.[24] Failing to represent contradictions, conflicts of interest, doubts, or changing motivations and circumstance served to essentialize differences among societies while denying differences within them. In so doing, anthropologists effected a recognition (and legitimation) of certain regimes of power by giving priority to dominant representations and interpretations.

If interpretive anthropologists rejected the universalist pretensions of modernity in order to posit and celebrate the plurality and diversity of human cultural life, they nonetheless maintained a modern aesthetic sensibility. The art museum, suggests Renato Rosaldo, is an apt figure for a field of intellectual endeavor that privileged classic ethnographies—creative works that represented cultures as autonomous, integrated, and formally patterned: "Cultures stand as sacred images; they have an integrity and coherence that enables them to be studied, as they say, on their own terms, from within, from the 'native' point of view . . . [Like the work in an art museum] each culture stands alone as an aesthetic object . . . Once canonized all cultures appear to be equally great . . . Just as [one] does not argue whether Shakespeare is greater than Dante [one] does not debate the relative merits of the Kwakiutl . . . versus the Trobriand Islanders . . ."[25]

Feminist anthropologists showed that the representation of culture as a unified system of meaning was achieved primarily by excluding the cultural meanings that women and other subordinate groups in society attributed to their own experiences. Cultural truths were partial and often based upon institutional and contestable exclusions.[26] Ethnographers too often interpreted native elite male assertions and activities to metonymically represent social reality. Instead, feminists proposed adoption of an analytical attitude that "treats culture as contested rather than shared, and therefore represents social practice more as an argument than as a conversation."[27] They drew attention to the multiple orders of difference existing in any social arena and their intersection in shaping human experience.[28]

Theorists of postmodernism similarly argued that all totalizing accounts of (a) society, (a) tradition, or (a) culture are exclusionary and enact social violence by suppressing continuing and continually emergent differences. One form of cultural critique characteristic of both postmodern anthropology and cultural studies is "to deconstruct modernism . . . in order to rewrite it, to open its closed systems . . . to the 'heterogeneity' of texts"—to challenge its purportedly universal narratives with the "discourses of others."[29] According to Steven Connor, a postmodern consideration of power and value "identif[ies] centralizing principles—of self, gender, race, nation, aesthetic form—in order to determine what those centres push to their silent or invisible peripheries."[30]

Drawing upon feminist work to challenge anthropology's modern predilections, Nicholas Thomas proposes that anthropologists explore local meaning by creating works that convey the politics of producing and maintaining structures of meaning "so as to disclose other registers of cultural difference,"[31] replacing "cultural systems with less stable and more derivative discourses and practices."[32] It is precisely with the politics of producing derivative meanings that I will be concerned, showing how differences within the social fabric are expressed with commodified texts and how differences in meaning are inadvertently encouraged and overtly contained by regimes of intellectual property. Differences between those who disseminate commodity/signs (a sign that is a commodity with an exchange value in its own right as well as a signifier with a field of cultural connotation) and those who consume them animates the legal regulation of cultural forms; such cultural forms simultaneously become mediums for expressions of alterity as they function as expressions of authorial distinction.

Anthropology's Trademark and Its Academic Others

As Annette Weiner notes, "since the beginning of this century, the culture concept has been anthropology's signature symbol and contribution to intellectual discourses. Today, however, 'culture' is increasingly a prized intellectual commodity, aggressively appropriated by other disciplines as an organizing principle."[33] If a critical cultural legal studies might derive resources from anthropological misgivings about culture and the political necessity to write against the grain of those traditions in which the concept has been developed, the emergent field of "cultural studies" provides further strategies for writing against culture. Anthropologist Terence Turner (in response to anthropologists' protests over the propriety of others assuming possession of the culture concept and thus diluting the discipline's trademark) cites a 1991 proposal for a program of specialization in cultural studies at Cornell University: "'Cultural studies' is an interdisciplinary genre of cultural analysis and criticism . . . [that] comprehends work on what has been described as the 'social circulation of symbolic forms,' that is, the institutional and political relations and practices through which cultural production acquires and constructs social meanings . . . Alongside more traditional areas of literary and historical study, [cultural studies is concerned with] cultural forms such as movies, television, video, popular music, magazines, and newspapers, and the media industries and other institutions which produce and regulate them."[34] As Turner points out, culture in this statement is never treated as a reified entity or a bounded, internally consistent domain abstracted from historical forces. The social contextualizations of specific cultural forms as mediators of social processes and resources for social transformation are instead emphasized. So they will be also in my consideration of intellectual property, which will be approached less as a determining structure and more as a field of indeterminate (but overdetermined) practices.

Cultural studies is not "a tightly coherent, unified movement with a fixed agenda, but a loosely coherent group of tendencies, issues, and questions."[35] Emerging from a widespread dissatisfaction with the Eurocentric elitism characteristic of those fields of humanities that traditionally took Culture as their object of inquiry, those practicing cultural studies rejected the modernist insistence upon the integrity and autonomy of the literary or artistic work and the value of studying cultural artifacts as self-sufficient wholes. They connected texts to the specific histories of their production, consumption, reception, and circulation within socially differentiated fields. By connecting the social life of textuality with everyday experience and in drawing attention to the social centralizations and marginalizations realized through rhetorical deployments, this approach shares the inclinations of postmodern anthropology. As Arjun Appadurai suggests: "The subject matter of cultural studies could roughly be taken as the relationship between the word and the world. I understand these two terms in their widest sense, so that *word* can encompass all forms of textualized expression, and *world* can mean anything from the 'means of production' and the organization of life-worlds to the globalized relations of cultural reproduction . . . "[36]

Cultural studies is anticanonical, attentive not to a nominated chain of great works by Great Men (Culture in Matthew Arnold's sense), but to larger social fields of inscription. The strategy is one that connects texts with larger cultural contexts considered as politicized frames of reference.[37] Connecting texts to contexts, however, does not assume holistic systems of meaning—culture in the Romantic or modern anthropological sense. Indeed, cultural studies eschews social organicism, or the idea that the life of a nation may be found embodied in canonized works of cultural expression: "cultural processes are intimately connected with social relations, especially with class relations and class formations, with sexual divisions, with the racial structuring of social relations and with age oppressions as a form of dependency . . . culture involves power and helps to produce asymmetries in the abilities of individuals and social groups to define and realize their needs . . . culture is neither an autonomous nor an externally determined field, but a site of social differences and struggles."[38] Mass culture might, as Xy suggests, be "spread too thin to invite thick description," but lends itself to methodologies adopting multiple and shifting perspectives that consider multiple moments of a cultural form's social life.[39] These would include places in people's daily lives, in the realm of public representations, the contexts and conditions of interpretive reception, the influence and contestations of those readings in private lives and social lifeworlds, the authorization, legitimation, denial, or injunction of those interpretations in institutional forums, and the potential transformation of such readings in new cultural practices.

Multidirectional social circuits of textuality are all too rarely addressed; more often than not, scholars focus on one or two moments in this journey. As Richard Johnson asserted in an influential overview of cultural studies, we cannot know how a text will be read simply from the conditions of its production, any more than we can know which readings of a text will assume salience within people's everyday lives.[40] Scrutinizing texts in terms of their formal qualities tells us nothing about their conditions of production or consumption, the basis of their authority, nor their likely interaction with existing ensembles of cultural meanings in socially specific experiences. These ensembles, "reservoirs of discourses and meanings, are in turn raw material for fresh cultural production. They are indeed among the specifically cultural *conditions* of production."[41]

The proliferation of textuality, is, of course, yet another of the processes to which the term postmodernity refers. It "indicates something of the size and the scale of the new global and local social relations and identities set up between individuals, groups, and populations as they interact with and are formed by the multiplicity of texts and representations which are a constitutive part of contemporary reality and experience."[42] This textually saturated, hypersignificant world needs to be reintegrated with the regimes of law and regulation that govern and shape it if we are to understand the relationship between the word and the world as a dialectical space of governance and praxis as well as one of authorship and readership. Intellectual property protections are central cultural conditions of production, circulation, and reception, providing incentives to produce and disseminate texts, regulating modes of circulation for cultural forms while enabling, recognizing, and enjoining alternative forms of reception and interpretation.

Authoring Alterity

If differences within cultures became more apparent, or were finally articulated by anthropologists with new agendas, differences between cultures were simultaneously scrutinized on both political and empirical grounds. Culture, it seemed, operated conceptually to enable us to separate so-called discrete others from ourselves and to ignore the regimes of power and circuits of exchange that both connected and divided us. Abu-Lughod suggested that culture served to reify differences that inevitably carry a sense of hierarchy; as a discipline built upon the historically constructed divide between the West and the non-West, anthropology "has been and continues to be primarily the study of the non-Western other by the Western self."[43] Culture was a concept that consolidated and naturalized distinctions between self and other, *making* others other; it constructed, produced, and maintained the differences it purported merely to explain.[44] Modern cultural anthropology rested upon an unstated assumption that others *must* be different, from us and from each other (even though those social groups that anthropologists referred to as having cultures were bounded, created, named, and reified in nineteenth-century European colonial struggles and their consequent administrative hegemonies).[45] Even in its more progressive guise as a cultural critique of Western assumptions, anthropology "depended upon the fabrication of alterity, upon a showcase approach to other cultures that is now politically unacceptable."[46]

Anthropology's traditional preoccupation with the other was defined by Michel-Rolph Trouillot as the disciplinary occupation of "the savage slot" in Western epistemology—a space of colonization peopled by others.[47] Trouillot's use of this term is problematic, the savage never occupied a singular or static conceptual space in Western organizations of knowledge, but was constituted historically and dialectically in shifting relationships. Trouillot paints the postmodern anthropologist, moreover, as caricature: "camera and notebooks in hand, he is looking for the savage, but the savage has vanished."[48] Typically, I will suggest, a trademark is chosen to enchant this image: "The world that the anthropologist inherits has wiped out the empirical trace of the savage-object: Coke bottles and cartridges now obscure the familiar tracks. To be sure, one could reinvent the savage, or create new savages within the West itself . . . The very notion of a pristine savagery, however, is now awkward, irrespective of the savage-object . . . At best, they can solve the problem of the empirical object by removing the Cokes and cartridges. At worst they can fabricate an entire new face for savagery. But they cannot remedy the loss of the larger thematic field."[49]

When this essay appeared in 1991, pointing out that the emperor had no clothes was already a tiresome gesture. Few cultural anthropologists felt their disciplinary distinction to rest upon such narrow grounds and many were already exploring the local life of global forces and a multiplicity of modernities forged in diverse locales. Trouillot's proposal that anthropologists read the postmodern situation "as a case for the specificity [and multiplicity] of otherness"[50] in order to "recapture domains of significance by creating strategic points of 'reentry' into the discourse of otherness"[51] is still, however, a sound one.

One strategic point of reentry into realms of significance and registers of alterity is, I suggest, that site too often evoked as a space of colonization: the social place of the commodity/sign. Cultural anthropologists have shown a curious blindness when it comes to legally commodified cultural texts. One might call this "the Coke bottle in the Kalahari syndrome"—as if, with the entry of the Western commodity/sign into the anthropologist's "field," culture ups and leaves. The appearance of "our" signs in "their" lives was long a commonplace of an inverted culture shock in which the anthropologist professed his or her own bemused innocence. Too often the Adidas® T-shirt on the native was figured as the sign of tragic cultural decline, the sure mark of worldly sophistication, or (less frequently) the romantic expression of a resistant agency. The brand name is often evoked to mark a moment of purported first contact: the coming of the West to the Other. On the first page of Gewertz and Errington's article, "First Contact with God,"[52] for example, we find Michael Leahy, leader of the first European expeditions into the hidden valleys of the Papua New Guinea Highlands, described as "a concentrated embodiment of colonial individualism . . . : Mauser slung over one shoulder and Leica over the other,"[53] he arrives as an "intrepid agent of colonial transformation."[54] Trademarks never again figure in the narrative.

The trademark occasionally figures in ethnographic discourse to mark the pending loss of cultural identity, but rarely is it acknowledged to be one of its potential sources. Mere sign of Western hegemony, it is too often treated as a harbinger of homogeneity or irrevocable social transformation rather than as one cultural resource, among others, available for creative expressions of meaning. To engage postmodern conditions, anthropologists have had to transcend concepts of commodities as transparent symbols of Western hegemony and understand them, like other cultural signifiers, as polyvalent, capable of acquiring new meanings in new contexts. It is ethnocentric to believe that when others become involved in cash economies, open to multinational advertising strategies, and engaged in consumer choices, our own commonsense categories then suffice to make sense of their lives.[55] Scholars too often entertain "an imaginary of Capital that consigns it to the demonology of the Other."[56] Reifying it as a monolithic, cunning agent, we fetishize its cultural power and devalue the complex significative work people do while promoting, transforming, and subverting its narratives and its trajectories—a point implicit in Marshall Sahlins's *Culture and Practical Reason* many years ago.[57]

When James Clifford talks about Lévi-Strauss's "refugee" period in New York City, he emphasizes the anthropologist's delight in the "incongruities" the city affords and provides Lévi-Strauss's account of one incongruity he found particularly arresting: "I felt myself going back in time . . . when I went to work every morning in the American room of the New York Public Library. There, under its neo-classical arcades and between walls paneled with old oak, I sat near an Indian in a feather headdress and a beaded buckskin jacket—who was taking notes with a Parker pen."[58] As Clifford acknowledges, this other reader is sited with particular discomfort, because, for Lévi-Strauss, "the Indian is primarily associated with the past, the 'extinct' societies recorded in the precious Bureau of American Ethnology *Annual Reports*"[59] that he himself is reading. The anthropologist feels himself "going back in time"—"an Indian can appear only as a survival or a kind of incongruous parody."[60] But what makes this *particular* Indian a parody for Lévi-Strauss? Not, it would seem, his jacket or his headdress, which might themselves be self-conscious parodies on this Native American's part, but the Parker pen! The trademark functions here in three ways: it is invoked strategically to divide the Indian from his Indianness, to divide him from anything Lévi-Strauss could recognize as a culture. Paradoxically, it also becomes the vehicle through which "the Indian"—who could be a stuffed figure up to this point—is bestowed with agency. For the modern anthropologist, however, such agency may be viewed as a mark of a culture's death, rather than a sign of cultural revitalization. Finally, the trademark might serve here to remark upon the anthropologist's sudden self-consciousness about the disciplinary tendency to deny coevalness,[61] occupation of a shared time and history by the anthropological author and the discipline's others.

It is precisely the full implications of this realization—the shared global space of anthropologists and their others (the inability of subject-object relations to remain constant)—that gives critical purchase to the concept of postmodernism. The "condition of postmodernity" does not refer simply to processes and practices of representation. The breakdown of boundaries between cultures and the implosion of difference within cultures has been discussed. These developments, however, must be related to a global restructuring of capitalism and new media, information, and communications technologies.[62] It is important to remember that if commodified cultural forms are now ubiquitous in contemporary Western societies, this phenomenon is related to massive changes in the rest of the world. Western societies become "reproductive" or "post-industrial"[63] through the movement of production and industry elsewhere and the social spillover effects of exercising global control capacities from urban centers.[64] Inequalities in distribution of wealth are increased, abysmal working conditions become normalized, informal economies proliferate, labor and poverty are feminized and racialized in both urban and rural areas, and traditional communities undergo massive transformations.

Although pink Duracell bunnies and Flintstone® characters appear in Spanish Fiesta parades,[65] cakes are baked in the image of Snoopy in Mexico,[66] Ninja Turtles appear in the place of traditional religious chalk markings in Cairo just as religious icons are mass-reproduced in the fashion of Ninja Turtles,[67] and West African youth use Hindi film characters and dialogue as a form of lingua franca,[68] the significance of this increased flow of cultural imagery is still far from clear. From a superficial perspective, the proliferation of Coca-Cola®, Exxon®, Barbie® dolls, and the Big Mac® around the globe appears as a universalization and homogenization of culture. It is not inevitably the case, however, that these phenomena assume the same meanings in other cultures that they do in our own.[69] It is surely a form of imperialist hubris (and a marketing fantasy) to believe that they do. Anthropologists increasingly recognize that the social dynamics of the cultural indigenization of metropolitan forces are processes worth studying in their own right.

Anthropologists argue that forces of global capitalism have created a situation of late modernity that is "decentered, fragmented, compressed, flexible, refractive,"[70] in which meanings are fashioned with materials from diverse cultural lifeworlds. The Coke bottles that disfigure the modern disciplinary gaze by complicating its subject-object relations and the distinct identities of its alterities may themselves provide an idiom for the expressions of historically specific others—vehicles through which difference finds voice in media of similarity. In Jean and John Comaroff's terms: "capitalism has always been shot through with its own magicalities and forms of enchantment, all of which repay analysis"; the idea that "Western Hegemony is Destiny" belies the incorrigible multiplicity of contemporary global systems.[71] This is no less true of the current stage of capital accumulation, which, for all its vaunted flexibility, must contend with the cultural realities of others: spirit possessions on the factory floor,[72] blessings of money and ritual sacrifices to mines,[73] rumors that surround the trademarks on consumer goods.[74] These phenomena are not merely atavistic residues of some primitive lifestyle, destined to pass with "modernization." Rather, these are new practices—culturally meaningful forms of resistance and accommodation to new forms of wage labor, industrial discipline, consumption practices, and marketing strategies—with which profit-oriented agents and institutions must make accommodation. They reflect the cultural agency and creative interpretive work that inevitably accompanies and challenges social transformation and dislocation.

Promising new points of departure for anthropology may be found in recent ethnographic studies of local cultural interpretations of foreign commodities.[75] Some of this work exhibits less reticence about the local presence and meanings of commodity/signs and the social practices in which they figure. Timothy Burke, for example, explores the social life of commodified toiletries in post–World War II Zimbabwe, the meanings invested in trademarked goods, and the power of these goods and their brand names to provide an expressive idiom for historical reflection and discussion of changing social relations.[76] Ethnographic work among Songhay-speaking migrants in New York City's informal economy indicates that trademarks have become significant cultural vehicles with which new meanings of race, ethnicity, class, and community are negotiated in cross-cultural encounters between Africans and African Americans in Harlem.[77] In the commerce of the black public sphere, Malcolm's trademarked (and much counterfeited) "X," popular sports team logos, brand names that proclaim African American pride, and the commodified indicators of African authenticity are only some of the contested images that saturate local lifeworlds—signs that express and convey conflictual meanings about culture, race, and identity.

Certainly there is significant scholarly work still to be done exploring the significances of Western commodified texts as they are appropriated into the lives of others; but there is no reason to assume that otherness is always elsewhere. The cultural forms of commerce are othered in their readings; others occupy all authorial properties in socially specific ways. It is not simply the case that trademarks, for example, are appropriated differently over there, in some place we could conveniently refer to as another culture. Even those media texts that are always in some sense the same are othered—subjected to claims of difference—in their enculturation, regardless of the geographical contexts of their reception. Gay activists are other to the Olympic body and its politics, as I show in chapter 3. Indigenous peoples, Chicano activists, and Mexican migrants assert alterities and alternative significations to the signs that mark national boundaries and their meanings, as I show in chapter 4. Those of First Nations ancestry reject the insignia of Indian otherness proffered by the entertainment industries and insist upon recognition of their own authorship—to claim expressive practices rather than continue to figure as mere ideas in the expressive works of others, as I explain in chapter 5.

I seek simultaneously to undertake and to undermine modern anthropological authorship—reconfiguring the work of anthropology and resituating the construction of self-other relations—by considering derivative practices of making culture in commercial landscapes. These are practices in which the signifying properties of authors are reappropriated by others, who simultaneously inscribe their *own* authorship of those works the law deems to be *owned* by their corporate disseminators. Culture is contested and created in precisely such instances in which identity is asserted and difference claimed through expressive activities that deploy meaningful forms.

Contested Cultures

To write "against culture" is to focus on practices and problems of interpretation, exploring contradiction, misunderstanding, and misrecognition, being aware of interests, inclinations, motivations, and agendas.[78] Building upon Pierre Bourdieu's insight "that culture commits anthropology to a legalist perspective on conduct,"[79] Abu-Lughod asserted that juridical tropes like rules and models, regimes and structures needed to be replaced with less static and homogenizing configurations that might account for the more creative and improvisational ways in which meaning was produced in everyday life.[80] Such an anthropology would emphasize the social uses by situated individuals of signifying resources and the reinforcements and transformations of dominant meanings thereby accomplished. Refusing to accept modern tendencies to avoid questions of political economy when addressing issues of culture, contemporary ethnographers seek to articulate the complex interrelationships between cultural meanings and social and material inequalities.

Influenced by Gramsci—often mediated through Raymond Williams —anthropologists have become more comfortable with the idea of culture as both the medium and the consequence of social differences, inequalities, dominations, and exploitations: the form of their inscription and the means of their collective and individual imbrication. Culture becomes reconceptualized as activities of expressive struggle rather than symbolic context, involving conflictual signifying practices rather than integrated systems of meaning.[81] To write against culture involves estranging and explaining rather than accepting modernity's metanarratives—shifting emphasis from structure and system to the signifying practices that construct, maintain, and transform multiple hegemonies—as I shall attempt to do throughout this volume.

In accordance with Williams's dictum that "culture is ordinary," British cultural studies centered upon everyday life: the structures and practices within and through which societies construct and circulate meanings and values.[82] Like contemporary ethnographers, practitioners of cultural studies reject the modern focus on the singularity and integrity of authorial works. They study cultural forms, not as timeless statements of value, but as "the real, the occasional speech of temporally and historically situated human beings."[83] Contingency and particularity, affect and ambivalence, iteration and itinerance are emphasized rather than "the eternal and the abstract in language and experience."[84] Again, we see a shift toward the cultural politics of quotidian practice. Rejecting modernity's boundaries between culture and everyday life as well as the related distinction between high and popular culture, cultural studies attends to everyday cultural practices as the locus both of domination and transformation.

Scholars of law and society have more recently turned in the same direction in search of new paradigms with which to model relationships between law and society (and in order to stop conceiving these terms as separate entities that require the exposition of relationship as an adequate term of address). As disillusionment with instrumentalist, functionalist, and structuralist paradigms set in, concerns with law's legitimation functions—its cultural role in constituting the social realities we recognize—were emphasized. Constitutive theories of law recognize law's productive capacities, as well as its prohibitions and sanctions, shifting attention to the workings of law in ever more improbable settings.[85] Focusing less exclusively on formal institutions, law and society scholarship has begun to look more closely at law in everyday life,[86] in quotidian practices of struggle, and in consciousness itself.[87] Austin Sarat and Tomas Kearns suggest that "a focus on law in everyday life can help to bridge the gap between so called 'constitutive' and 'instrumentalist' views of the law, providing a powerful means by which the everyday is understood and experienced, but also a tool that enables people to imagine and effect social change."[88]

Legal forums are obviously significant sites for practices in which hegemony is constructed and contested, providing institutional venues for struggles to establish and legitimate authoritative meanings. The adoption of legal strategies may give meanings the force of material enforcement. Law generates positivities as well as prohibitions, legitimations, and oppositions to the subjects and objects it recognizes. The revitalization of legal anthropology has contributed to our theoretical understandings of power, hegemony, and resistance.[89] Legal discourses are spaces of resistance as well as regulation, possibility as well as prohibition, subversion as well as sanction. Beth Mertz draws our attention to the complexities of legal relations of power: "By contrast with accounts that discuss law as the one-way imposition of power, where lawmakers simply mold social actors and groups like clay, the social constructionist approach . . . understands the subjects of law as agents, actors with at least some ability and power to shape and respond to legal innovations . . . law becomes a form of social mediation, a locus of social contest and construction. And yet, because of its social character, legal mediation does not operate on a level playing field; . . . [we must be] mindful of the effects of differential power and access to resources on the struggle and its outcomes."[90] If law is central to hegemonic processes, it is also a key resource in counterhegemonic struggles. When it shapes the realities we recognize, it is not surprising that its spaces should be seized by those who would have other versions of social relations ratified and other cultural meanings mandated.

Law, then, is culturally explored "as discourse, process, practice, and system of domination and resistance"[91] to be connected to larger historical movements while we remain sensitive to the nuances of "the ontological and epistemological categories of meaning on which the discourse of law is based."[92] Historically structured and locally interpreted, law provides means and forums both for legitimating and contesting dominant meanings and the social hierarchies they support. Hegemony is an ongoing articulatory practice that is performatively enacted in juridical spaces, where, as Susan Hirsch and Mindie Lazarus-Black put it, "webs of dominant signification enmesh at one level even those who would resist at another,"[93] and "hegemonic and oppositional strategies both constitute and reconfigure each other."[94]

Legal regimes shape the social meanings assumed by signifying properties in public spheres. Such meanings are socially produced in fields characterized by inequalities of discursive and material resources, symbolic capital, and access to channels of communication: "if culture is our nature, whatever threatens to shut down, repress, or distort representation through the assertion of some absolute 'presence' threatens also to put an end to both culture and history."[95] Intellectual property rights, as they are currently interpreted and enforced, imagined and asserted, pose precisely such a threat to contemporary signifying practice, freezing forms, deeming denotation, and containing connotation, as I show in chapter 1. The commodification of cultural forms creates new relations of power in contemporary cultural politics. The law legitimizes new sources of cultural authority by giving the owners of intellectual property priority in struggles to fix social meaning. Drawing examples (primarily from the field of trademark law) of the cultural politics that engage commodified cultural signs in the condition of postmodernity, I suggest that the commodity/sign is always simultaneously participating in a poetics and a politics driven by social groups with differential abilities to influence the complexes of signifying forms within which they have agency. Increasingly, holders of intellectual property rights are socially and juridically endowed with monopolies over public meaning and the ability to control the cultural connotations of their corporate insignias (trademarks being the most visible signs of their presence in consumer culture). Intellectual property, then, is an arena for connotative struggle—"contested culture," as Jane Gaines nicely put it.[96]

If we recognize cultural signifiers as multivocal sites of conflict, which bear the traces of social struggles and historically inscribed differences, then laws that prohibit the circulation of these forms—their ironic reproductions and parodic recodings—necessarily intervene in processes of hegemonic articulation, privileging some actors at the expense of others. Moreover, if signifying forms have meaning only within specific trajectories and political practices, the investigation of power and meaning in legal studies must not be permitted to devolve into an "abstract deconstruction of metaphysics but [must involve] a resolutely historical inquiry into the concreteness of the ordinary,"[97] a "return to the terrain of lived experience."[98] Like other practices of cultural studies, a critical cultural legal studies needs to attend to "the important but often unnoticed dynamics of everyday life: the sounds in the kitchen, the noises in the home, and the signs and styles on the street."[99] I will take T-shirts and bumper stickers, billboards, newspaper debates, product labels, neon signs, lapel buttons, and cartoon figures as "signs and styles on the street" that figure in everyday expressive activity and in the articulation of that space we define as the social.

An ethnographic approach to intellectual properties, I suggest, provokes new insights into a cultural politics involving possession and the dispossessed in so-called postindustrial contexts where a proliferation of textuality and mass-reproduced imagery constitutes new realities.[100] This will be illustrated by way of example in my text, where contemporary culture is approached as contested terrain occupied by differentially empowered social agents, who define themselves with commodified cultural texts even as they improvise with and transform those forms in the service of diverse agendas. We need to consider people's active engagement with commodified cultural forms—consumption—as a type of production: a mode of cultural politics contingent upon and necessary to the conditions of postmodernity.

Legal regimes of intellectual property shape (although they do not determine) the ways in which cultural signs are re/appropriated by those who assert difference in the spaces of similarity, imitating and mimicking signs of authority to express relations of alterity. In these studies, I show that intellectual property law does not function simply in a rulelike fashion, nor is it adequately portrayed as a regime of rights and obligations. Although it is constructed through a rhetoric of rights, I seek to go beyond its self-representation to show how it is also simultaneously a generative condition and a prohibitive boundary for hegemonic articulations and subaltern practices of appropriation.

A critical cultural legal studies demands more, then, than an abstract "constitutivism," discursively modeled. It requires consideration of concrete fields of struggle and their legal containment, the legal constitution and recognition of symbolic struggle, and the law's capacity to fix meaning while denying this as an operation of power. It compels a perspective sensitive both to everyday practices of world-making and to their institutional acknowledgment in juridical spaces where material relations between meaning and power are forged. This is to recognize culture as signification, but also to address its materiality: to recognize the symbolic power of law and law's power over signification in concrete struggles over meaning and textuality as well as their daily political consequence.

With such an assertion I seek to move beyond the constitutivist claim that law both enables and constrains by attending to the cultural dimensions of power (as embedded in and expressed by processes of signification) and the politics of signifying practices in which distinction and difference are constructed and contested. Law is an authoritative means and medium of a cultural politics in which the social is itself articulated. By recognizing that the social world must be represented, performatively expressed, and institutionally inscribed, we can avoid a metaphysics of political presence that presupposes a realm of self-evidently "political" practices. Drawing upon poststructuralist, deconstructivist, and psychoanalytic insights,[101] I reject any vision of a social world in which differences exist before the law and law is merely called upon to resolve and legitimate social claims generated elsewhere. Instead, I suggest we see law as providing many, if not most, of the very signifying forms that constitute socially salient distinctions, adjudicating their meanings and shaping the very practices through which such meanings are disrupted. Rather than assert the positivity of any social identity, we might see identities as merely temporary, anxious, and uncertain resting points in quests for recognition, legitimation, and identification.

The actual engagement of the political is a historical moment in which particular cultural forms become meaningful for particular agents. Situations of subordination are transformed into spaces for articulation through identifications with specific signifiers that hold promise for new forms of political recognition. Because meanings expressed through systems of signification are, by definition, perpetually unstable, they are always capable of being deployed against the grain. The ambiguities and traces of cultural forms may be seized upon by those who may well repeat, imitate, and appropriate elements of a dominant cultural order while critically marking differences in social experience. Law is not simply an institutional forum or legitimating discourse to which social groups turn to have preexisting differences recognized, but, more crucially, it is a central locus for the control and dissemination of those signifying forms with which identities and difference are made and remade. The signifying forms around which political action mobilizes and with which social rearticulations are accomplished are attractive and compelling precisely because of the qualities of the powers legally bestowed upon them, as I explore in chapters 2, 3, and 4. Such mobilizations and new articulations may have political consequence when they "provoke a crisis within the process of signification and discursive address."[102]

The enabling power of law, then, is not simply the provision of instruments and discursive resources through which social groups may seek to have their differences legitimated or their needs addressed (although it may be experienced in this fashion). Law also generates the signs and symbols—the signifying forms—with which difference is constituted and given meaning. It provides those unstable signifiers whose meanings may be historically transformed by those who wish to inscribe their own authorial signature on the people, the nation, the state—the official social text. It invites and shapes activities that legitimate, resist, and potentially rework the meanings that accrue to these forms in public spheres. Such processes of intervention and institutionalization are both ongoing and unstable. The disruptions and destabilizations effected by this interchange provide significant sites for considerations of the dynamics of law and culture, identity and difference.

Legalities, Identities, and Mass Media

Considerations of identity and its construction, or subjectivity and its social situation increasingly preoccupy anthropologists and focus work in cultural studies.[103] Individual and collective identities are actively created by human beings through the social forms through which they become conscious and sustain themselves as subjects in communities of similarity. It is now widely acknowledged that law interacts with other forms of discourse and sources of cultural meaning to construct and to contest identities, communities, and authorities.[104] Such approaches to law and society have been deemed by Mertz "a new social constructionism" in sociolegal studies[105] that explores provisional, fluid, strategic, and contested identities constructed in contexts mediated by law.[106] Carol Greenhouse suggests that the idea of cultural construction ties the poetics of identity to the materialities of power.[107] An emphasis on identity is congruent with the contemporary anthropological uneasiness with respect to the reification of culture. Indeed, Turner goes so far as to define culture *as* the process of constructing identity:

> Cultures are the way specific social groups, acting under specific historical and material conditions, have "made themselves." The theoretical contribution of the anthropological approach to culture, in sum, has been the focus on the capacity for culture as a collective power emergent in human social interaction . . . Two features of the anthropological concept of the capacity for culture are particularly relevant in this context: its inherently social character and its virtually infinite plasticity. The capacity for culture does not inhere in individuals as such but arises as an aspect of collective social life . . . Its almost infinite malleability, however, means that there are virtually no limits to the kinds of social groups, networks, or relations that can generate a cultural identity of their own.[108]

The conviction that "the empowerment of the basic human capacity for self-creation (ie, for culture, in the active sense of collective self-production)"[109] is a political accomplishment animates many variants of cultural studies.[110] Identity is a trope that enables us to examine subjectivity ethnographically, in terms of the way senses of self and community are practically expressed and projected through the medium of signifying texts.

Given a predominant concern with contemporary social experience, an engagement with mass-mediated cultural forms was inevitable. Practitioners of cultural studies continually assert that media forms provide the cultural vehicles through which new social meanings are forged and stress their constitutive role in the creation of identity. Less attention, however, is paid to the political economies that enable cultural forms to circulate through the mass media—economies with legal infrastructures. The legal dimensions of cultural production, circulation, and reception have been shamefully neglected.[111] There has been a tendency in cultural studies either to metaphorize law (as in the psychoanalytic Law of the Father)[112] or to fetishize it, according to it a unity and canonical existence that would be rejected were it to be applied to other textual forms.[113] Only at cultural studies conferences, for example, is it possible to hear scholars authoritatively proclaim that "the law says," as if the law had a unified, canonical presence and spoke in a singular, unambiguous voice. It is precisely the formalist emphasis upon texts—even legal ones—as isolated works that a cultural studies of law should, I insist, avoid. Rather than stress isolated decisions, statutes, or treatises, we need to attend to the social life of law's textuality and the legal life of cultural forms as it is expressed in the specific practices of socially situated subjects.[114] The legal status of actual cultural forms, the ability to exercise power over meaning, the denial of ambiguity that law effects, and the resistances such denials engender are central to contemporary fields of cultural politics.

In an early programmatic statement promoting a transnational anthropology, Appadurai claimed that everyday lives are now powered by media forms and possibilities[115] and advocated exploration of "the complex nesting of imaginative appropriations that are involved in the construction of agency in a deterritorialized world."[116] The relation between deterritorialization and territory is likely to be as complex as the relationship between globalization and locality; the conditions and modes of refraction will be as constitutive of agency as anything intrinsic to media itself. As I argue in chapter 2, media representations may indeed link peoples formerly separated by language, class, ethnicity, religion, geography, and generation. To ethnographically explore the complexities of expressive representation, however, requires more than a focus on the social meanings of appropriation. It also compels attention to the political economies of media circulation and the mutual imbrication of domains of consumption and production.[117] Such processes, moreover, must be recognized as taking place; the particularities of interpretation and inscription are intelligible and interlocutory with respect to particular conditions dominant in particular locales, as I emphasize with respect to trademark rumors, resistances, and reiterations in chapter 3.

Cultural studies has devoted great energy to the study of subcultures: genres of media representation consumed, appropriated, resisted, and recoded by groups on the margins of society. Those representations protected by intellectual property (advertising, lyrics, brand names, corporate logos, slogans, indicia of government, and celebrity images, for example) are prevalent and promising cultural forms with which to consider cultural authority, subcultural formations, and hegemonic struggles. The most vibrant, compelling, and ubiquitous of cultural signifiers—those around which marginal groups tend to mobilize—are often the properties of corporate others. Indeed, it is plausible that the protections that intellectual property law affords (and the promise of revenue legal protections offer) induce actors to invest in the widespread dissemination of cultural forms. Media may become "mass" primarily through their juridicalization.

Celebrity names and likenesses protected by laws of publicity and privacy, for example, provide signifying resources for the production of alternative gender identities, as I explore in chapter 2. Judy Garland, Dolly Parton, James Dean, Nancy Sinatra, Luke Skywalker, and Kirk and Spock are a few of the figures in whom libidinal energies are invested and around which identifications emerge and new social identities congregate in relations of community. These are practices that deploy media forms in cultural self-fashionings both engendered and endangered by the law. Intellectual property laws operate to protect the exchange value of media-circulated cultural forms and subcultural practices are both enabled and constrained by legal regimes of commodification. People's relationships to these signifiers are shaped by the knowledge that these signs are both socially shared and individually owned. Those with specific attachments to a star's image or to a fictional character often develop their own moral economies of ownership, proprieties of possession, and ethics of use in the shadow of the law, developing complex attitudes toward the exclusive rights legally held by others.

In a comparison of struggles over "official signifiers" and rumors around corporate trademarks in chapter 3, "Tactics of Appropriation and the Politics of Recognition," I suggest that the forms of signifying power that law enables provoke or invite particular forms of resistance, particular forms of alternative inscription. These appropriations are aw(e)fully appropriate to the forms of legally regulated signification to which they may be seen as forms of response. The public propensity to remark upon dominant forms of signifying power is first explored in a consideration of "official marks": signs held by public authorities in the name of the public interest. These are often key symbols in national and international cultural lexicons with which subaltern groups seek affirmative association. Examining instances involving a gay rights group in the United States and Sikhs in Canada, I argue that the arbitrary exercise of power to control the circulation of a sign or the failure to exercise such discretionary powers may have significant political repercussions for the cultural identities of minority groups. There are both real possibilities and real limitations on political activism posed by practices of appropriation that recode these forms and by the legal regimes of trademark that govern them. The use and abuse of power to control such signs may constitute or reverse perceptions of social devaluation or stigma, articulate alternative narratives of national understanding, and challenge exclusionary imaginaries of citizenship. When "Lesbians Fly Air Canada," a "Gay Olympics" is not prohibited, and Sikh Mounties are seen as representative Canadians (to take a few of the examples that I explore), legal action and inaction will be central to such reinscriptions in the public sphere.

The mass-mediated nature of corporate power is simultaneously recognized and resisted in the bizarre rumors that people spread about the meaning and origins of corporate trademarks. Exploring prominent North American rumors in the 1980s, I consider these as commentaries upon the fetishism of the legally constituted commodity/sign—the meaning of postmodernity and its marginalizations emerging in the fantastic fabulations through which marketing signs are reenchanted—in contexts where processes of production are invisible and the signs of consumption ubiquitous. Rumors, I suggest, mimic the modes of circulation through which trademarks make their way into our daily lives, simultaneously adopting and challenging forms of corporate authorship and legitimation in cultures of commerce.

Intellectual property laws also play an important role in the way histories of imperialism and colonialism, territorial annexation, and political disenfranchisement are socially inscribed across national landscapes. In chapter 4, I engage in a historical genealogy of the emergence of the federally protected trademark form in late-nineteenth-century United States to show how social difference was appropriated by manufacturers as market distinction through commercial adoption of widely recognized indicators of social otherness. These privately held signifiers were publicly circulated to interpellate an American consumer and were then domesticated and consumed by individual Americans who corporeally embodied those same signs of alterity that the national body politic was simultaneously incorporating. In the late twentieth century, we see renewed struggles by formerly (and continually) subjugated groups—particularly by indigenous peoples—as they attempt legally (and illegally) to reclaim the insignia of their former alterity and end the continuing commodification of their names, images, and motifs in mass markets.

Authorship and Alterity

In each of these studies I am concerned with symbolic struggles between owners and others, authors and their alters—an issue of some salience for contemporary anthropology and its reflexive authors. The relationship between authorship and alterity is central to the anthropological debate about the discipline's postmodern future(s). It will also animate my unworking[118] of intellectual property as a regime of private property, and my exploration of it as a cultural and political space of opportunity and constraint. The desire to write "against culture" in both anthropology and cultural studies was motivated by a perceived crisis in representation that has shaped new scholarly agendas in the humanities and social sciences during the past two decades. However overstated or unsubstantiated the crisis in anthropology's disciplinary identity may in fact be, I will address it obliquely to amplify an alternative perspective that views contemporary uncertainties as generative conditions for an interrogation of key concepts and opportunities for a revitalization of research. Retaining anthropology's disciplinary distinction may be less significant than a continued critical engagement with the genealogy of disciplinary identities. Anthropology's key symbols—culture, tradition, tribal and ethnic identities, ritual, myth, and material culture—have indeed lost their distinction. No longer associated simply with a particular disciplinary point of origin, they have become more generic signifiers, deployed in diverse struggles for political recognition and self-determination. Rather than assuming the role of trademark owners by continuing to police public use of such terms, monitoring their circulations and connotations while insisting upon recognition of anthropological authorship and authority, we might instead bring disciplinary expertise to consider the ongoing authorship of new meanings for old works in new contexts.

The much debated (and much maligned) postmodern turn in anthropology emerged with the belated disciplinary consensus that relationships between anthropological authors and their others were neither natural, fixed, nor stable, but contingent subject positions afforded by historical circumstance and modern intellectual conceits. The original debates about postmodernism centered upon problematics of representation (particularly the rhetorical effects of the ethnographic monograph), the propriety of authoring versions of alterity, and the role of anthropological representation in constructing those others (or dominant social understandings of them) whom anthropologists purported merely to describe.

In modern anthropology, the "author-function"[119] was especially pronounced, as Clifford Geertz showed in his aptly titled *Works and Lives*.[120] Anthropologists' proper names were linked to their ethnographic monographs, often titled with the name of the people under study, who became that anthropologist's preserve; it was not uncommon to hear anthropologists authorize their scholarly claims through a rhetoric of possessive relationship to "their" people, further reified in their authorial works. The presence of the ethnographer in "the field" ratified his or her observations and lent authority to a monograph that suppressed all ambiguities in his or her authoring of the society's culture. The notion that the ethnographer could objectively or even aesthetically capture a people within the confines of an ethnography—an authorial work representing the integrated culture of discrete others—marks anthropology's "modernist moment" and its will to power.[121] The monograph was at once the literary property of the anthropologist as the expressive product of his or her authorial activity and a representation of his or her work in the field. It was the singularity or uniqueness of the anthropologist's vision, embodied in the form of his or her expression, that enabled a culture to be represented as an undifferentiated whole. The anthropologist's identity as author rendered others distinctly other and in possession of a culture.

If anthropologists no longer respect the integrity of cultures, the capacity of others to possess cultures has nonetheless assumed new resonances as these tropes have been deployed in new fields. Although contemporary anthropologists recognize the simultaneously contingent, compelling, and contentious character of identity claims in arenas characterized by the resurgence of identity-based politics, they also find that their discipline's modern legacy has assumed a political life of its own. Instances of peoples who, for political purposes, seek out anthropologists to produce authoritative works that define "their culture" and anthropologists finding their authorial works appropriated by their others in political assertions of identity are symptomatic of a postmodern disciplinary moment.[122] The worldly authority of modern ethnography, in other words, may long outlive its credibility within the discipline.

The dynamics of the modern relationship between autonomous authorship and reified culture continue to animate political fields. In chapter 5, "The Properties of Culture and the Politics of Possessing Identity," I suggest that cultures continue to be legally imagined through a collective figuration of the possessive individual property holder. A liberal valorization of cultural difference that beholds the cultural traditions of others as their exclusive properties (often calling forth intellectual property as the relevant analogy) may do a form of violence to the aspirations of subaltern groups seeking to control cultural texts as matters of political self-determination. Failing to attend to the specific social trajectories and contemporary political struggles of those peoples historically othered, liberal discourses of possessive individualism and freedom of expression may operate to sustain contemporary patterns of social inequality. Nonetheless, as the dominant discourses of legitimate entitlement, they may well be strategically adopted by subaltern peoples who claim their "culture" as a means to address contemporary conditions of subordination. By deploying the tropes of intellectual property against the grain—speaking in a double voice—subaltern peoples may well expand our legal categories to recognize new forms of harm and old forms of domination.

Alternative forms of textual practice more sensitive to the power relations between scholars and their informants have been one significant consequence of postmodern concerns with authorship, authority, and alterity. Critics have delegitimated the realist ethnography as the major work of anthropological authorship, a movement concomitant with poststructuralist resistances to the premises of modern authorship and rejections of modernist metanarratives. Although the realist ethnography polemically constructed by postmodern critics was something of a caricature, the critique did pierce the security of at least a few professional conventions. In 1988 James Clifford asserted: "the time is past when privileged authorities could routinely 'give voice' (or history) to others without fear of contradiction."[123] The new audibility in metropolitan centers of various others and their contestations of Euro-American certainties about human universals and cultural difference posed new challenges. Modernist strategies of representational practice, like the discipline's aesthetic preference for singular works that reified societies as authorial expressions, were scrutinized. To evoke experiences of difference, divergences of local meaning, social contradiction, and authorial uncertainty, new forms of ethnographic rhetoric were proposed.

Charges of navel-gazing and self-indulgence in postmodern anthropological practice were perhaps inevitable, given that the undermining of anthropological authority was addressed with most alacrity when it could be met with the heightened creativities of an unrestrained authorship. Collage and montage were suggested as potentially effective vehicles for reflexive ethnography; the shock of juxtaposition of elements from foreign contexts seemed one promising way of avoiding the false integrities of modern representations. Surrealists were valorized over realists,[124] multivocal texts elevated over monologic treatises, and multiple contexts championed to acknowledge coexisting differences among cultural frameworks of interpretation. The summoning of such textual tactics to undermine the modern link between authorship and authority in the anthropological encounter with alterity now seems a bit pompous and somewhat naïve. The anthropologist never controls the ethnographic encounter; his or her authorship of an ethnography is no guarantee of epistemological authority. On the other hand, activities of ethnographic authorship may involve complex processes of compensation, displacement, and projection for precisely this reason. An authorial enablement of multiplicity of voice and venue is no less likely to involve political acts of orchestration that inscribe other relations of power.

My own ethnographic approach to the social life of intellectual properties (and my initial recognition of the potential significance of the topic itself) has been significantly shaped by the postmodern turn in anthropology, along with a recognition of its inevitable complexities. I do juxtapose voices from multiple contexts and competing sources of authority to frame and destabilize authoritative claims about the meaning and value of intellectual properties—illustrating the contradictory dialectics of ideology and practice that simultaneously constitute and undermine relationships between authorship and alterity in commercial public spheres. The ethnographic study of the commodity life of cultural forms is necessarily a study of the social life of particular kinds of textuality and the differences that shape alternative modes of textual interpretation. The discursive properties of my own text—its liberal use of quotation and irreverent "taking(s) out of context," its juxtaposition of and ironic parody upon diverse pretensions of authority, its polyphony of voices from disparate locations in commercial culture, its playful pastiche and passionate polemic—are designed to provoke new insights and recognitions, to compel transformations of identification and empathy. When I let others intervene, both when I seek to avoid speaking on their behalf (in chapter 5 particularly) and when I let others voice what some insist are my "own" ideas, I allude to some of the normative ambiguities produced when economic interests and multiple cultural frames of reference come into unanticipated conjunctures. My idiosyncratic approach to citation (I have chosen law-review-style citations for the endnotes but have provided full titles for journals rather than standard abbreviations likely to confuse nonlegal readers; however, I have refused to engage in the law review editor's beloved practice of parenthetically including a phrase purporting to summarize each work's thesis, as if scholarly books had singular "ratios," and I have included a bibliography to compensate for the lack of publishing details in law review citations adequate to the needs of scholars) acknowledges the problems and ironies of appealing to authority in interpretive communities that cut across disciplinary divides.

This text assumes an ironic reflexivity with respect to its own authorship and to its own alterity to the appropriations it considers and the legal profession in which its author's contested authority has been constituted. I attempt to mimic the textual tactics with which I am concerned, a mimicry that enacts a sympathetic magic and an empathetic identification with those who make meaning on the margins of the mediascapes in which we live. These textual tactics involve instances in which others appropriate the works of authorities in the service of alternative agendas.

So will my own. Moreover, by producing a "billboard effect" of multiple messages and conflicting authorities, I hope to continually remind the reader of the discursive properties of intellectual properties: their sole legal authorship, their ubiquitous proliferation, and their multiple social authorings. I attempt, then, to textually problematize authorial authority both formally and substantively as I explore the way in which mass-reproduced texts—endlessly replicated as the same—are subjected to social difference. Those forms that embody the Western author's authority are othered as they are occupied by the forces of an ever-emergent alterity.

Although such practices may be referred to as postmodern in sensibility, I am not content to formally evoke a world of floating signification, a hyperreality of texts. I also seek to delineate the social worlds in which such practices have political meaning, contexts in which social actors with specific interests, agendas, histories, and social positionings voice their aspirations and irritations, identifications and affiliations, reverences and resentments through the media of commercial culture. Textual strategies alone are insufficient to counter the political dynamics of power and representation that characterize modern anthropological practice. Contemporary concerns with recapturing the discipline's authority are unduly preoccupied with issues of authorship and the proper character of the anthropologist's authorial works. Although an emphasis upon the forms of textuality was necessary, it would be an "idealist conceit"[125] to assume that the work of anthropology is simply the production of literary works or that improved authorship will guarantee the discipline's authority in globalizing cultural contexts. Access to and control over those representations that shape our understandings of the social realities of others pose more ethical challenges and political quandaries.

The activities of reiteration, recoding, and reproduction explored here ultimately pose the challenge of redefining the nature of free speech and the meaning of democracy in so-called postindustrial conditions. The nature of democracy in the condition of postmodernity and the character of dialogue in the cultural conditions of postmodernism are the issues commented upon in chapters 6 and 7. Engaging in dialogue with a few legal theorists who have made cogent contributions to our consideration of free speech in late capitalist contexts, I appeal for an understanding of dialogic practice, a comprehension of cultural politics, and an ethics of contingency alert to the power of commodity/signs in contemporary political struggles. The practices I examine, and the legal regimes with which they are enmeshed, raise significant questions for those concerned with the politics of mass-mediated public spheres. The law presupposes the continued viability of regimes of property and protection, freedom and speech, which privilege a conceptual apparatus appropriate to an eighteenth- and early-nineteenth-century bourgeois public sphere. Engaging the work of political theorists who have challenged the propriety of this model to characterize the space of political practice in conditions of late capitalism, I show how cultural appropriations of the kind explored in this volume challenge the bourgeois model of the public and its politics.

Ultimately, this work is an act of unworking rather than one of deconstruction; it will pose more questions than it will provide answers, disaggregating some of the certainties and identities that provide the currency of modern juridical regimes. This is an effort of reconceptualization, not one of law reform. Too much of the latter is attempted without benefit of the former. The signal contribution of an anthropological approach to law is its characteristic deferral—transforming reflexivity into normativity and normativity into reflexivity in an ongoing dialogical dialectic.[126] Such movements necessarily engage and constitutively transform both forms of knowledge. By engaging in an anthropological interrogation of law's positivity and an exploration of the juridical complications that disrupt anthropological certainties, I hope to provoke an epistemic shift in our understanding of intellectual properties. Small work for an author.

1. Objects of Property and Subjects of Politics

. . . consciousness itself can arise and become a viable fact only in the material embodiment of signs . . . understanding is a response to a sign with signs . . . the individual consciousness is nurtured on signs; it derives its growth from them; it reflects their logic and laws.—V. N. Voloshinov, *Marxism and the Philosophy of Language*[1]

. . . he treats her like a Barbie® doll—overheard

In a civilized nation, much of reality is an artifact. Too broad a set of intellectual property rights can give one set of persons control over how that reality is viewed, perceived, interpreted—control over what the world means.—Wendy Gordon, "Reality as Artifact: From *Feist* to Fair Use"[2]

The storylines make the most universally beloved icon of the twentieth century sound like a rapacious rat. A refugee . . . invites the chairman of the Walt Disney Co. to a Beverly Hills gallery to see his homage to the United States: a painting of Mickey Mouse handing a Campbell's soup can to a Russian. Disney lawyers, decrying copyright infringement, apply enough pressure to get the painting taken off display, and plans to make prints of it dropped . . . During the past three years, Disney counsel estimates they have filed 1,700 copyright suits in U.S. courts. That doesn't count the majority of actions settled early . . . [Caption beneath] an undercover Thai policeman destroying T-shirts . . . "They're burning Bambi in Bangkok . . . and Disney executives couldn't be happier."—Gail D. Cox, "Don't Mess With the Mouse: Disney's Legal Army Protects a Revered Image"[3]

Who authorizes Thumper? I want to express the nature of my disbelief when reading a law review article, I noticed that Pierre Schlag *cited authority* when using the proverb "If you can't say anything nice, don't say anything at all."[4] Perhaps he had his tongue in his cheek. Maybe the editors made him do it (student law review editors are notoriously tyrannical about citations to authority; one cannot say the sky is blue without finding a published source that verifies the fact). Either way, there are readers who no doubt feel that it is entirely appropriate to find authorization before you take the words out of Thumper's mouth. This, despite the fact that a lot of us cried when Bambi's mother died in that fire, that for some of us it's the closest thing we have to a shared cultural memory of childhood,[5] and that we may well share a socialization in which our own mothers were grateful to be able to echo Thumper's words of wisdom. In other words, notwithstanding his role in a collective cultural heritage, Thumper must be authorized. Who authorizes Thumper? Those who own the intellectual property rights in him, of course, and Schlag appropriately cites Walt Disney Studios and the date of their copyright in *Bambi* as the relevant authority with which to credit Thumper's proverbial wisdom. It is the political dimension of this relationship between legal ownership and cultural authority that I address here, as I try to develop what Schlag, in the same article, both implies and denies: the possibility of a normative postmodern vision.

To make this argument, I shall first reiterate social and philosophical commentary made by legal scholars about the inadequacies of the dichotomous understanding of subjectivity and objectivity characteristic of mainstream liberal approaches to legal reasoning and the social life of the law. I attempt to move beyond critique, however, and consider relations among law, culture, and (the commodity) form. For subjects in contemporary consumer societies, I suggest, political action must involve a critical engagement with commodified cultural forms. In the current climate, intellectual property laws often operate to stifle dialogic practice in the public sphere, preventing us from using the most powerful, prevalent, and accessible cultural forms to express alternative visions of social worlds.

I should make it clear from the outset that this chapter speaks simultaneously from several dissonant cognitive frameworks;[6] its polymorphous perversity[7] is intentional, to the extent that authorial intentions are relevant to the rationalist[8] within. As the following discussion will make apparent, I reject the rationalist privileging of the autonomous self and its claims to know an objective social world. Like the modernist, I seek to decenter the subject (in its guise as liberal individual) and its claims to ontological and epistemological primacy, but I reject the modernist insistence that there is a single underlying structure that may be privileged as *the* objective reality underlying the cultural epiphenomena of everyday life and consciousness. I am postmodernist in refusing to believe that we can find solace in any of the totalizing visions that modernism offers us, and in proposing that the social world is constituted only in and through representational relations of difference that are constantly shifting in our all-too-human efforts to give meaning to its terms.

In postmodernist fashion, I feel that form has implications for the issues that we address[9] and that conventional forms of discourse limit and shape the realities we recognize.[10] Like Schlag, I believe that "the typical supposition within the legal community that intellectual endeavour can and must converge in 'solutions' or 'conclusions' has a real tendency to kill thought,"[11] but I am not sufficiently rationalist to believe that it is possible to convey an "is" without imparting an "ought." Although other intellectual property scholars have argued that "normativity" is all that distinguishes academic legal scholarship,[12] I do not find it necessary or even desirable to maintain the authority of such disciplinary distinction. I will leave it to others to monitor our academic trademarks. As suggested earlier, in the movement between normative evaluations and reflexive considerations prompted by an anthropological concern with signifying practice, the normative assumes new nuances. My argument will be made by way of anecdote, appropriation, and dialogue—a tactical pastiche often seen as characteristically postmodern, but, more importantly, a modus operandi that mimics the social practices with which I am concerned. I will also try to cease citing endless authorities in incessant notes,[13] a convention of modern legal scholarship that assumes that an abundance of small typeface will enable us to "speak in the name of the real."[14]

Objects and Subjects

... to understand ourselves as subjects constituted as speaking subjects is to understand ourselves as members of a dialogic community that is not a mere dead weight confronting the individual but rather is both the product and the medium of communicative relations. We transform speech even as we come to ourselves within it.—Drucilla Cornell, "Toward a Modern/Postmodern Reconstruction of Ethics"[15]

A large group of legal scholars[16] have developed and elaborated a critique of the dichotomous understanding of subjectivity and objectivity that characterizes liberal legal thought.[17] Arguing that the objective world is the cultural construction of social subjects and that subjectivity itself is a product of language and cultural practice, this literature draws upon continental philosophy, North American pragmatism, cognitive theory, feminist theory, and cultural anthropology to support its claims. The idea of an objective world that can be known with certainty by a subject whose capacity for knowledge is independent of that world is repeatedly undermined.[18] The world must be understood culturally in terms of the significance it is given by social groups who perceive, categorize, and act upon it according to socially conventional structures of meaning and language. Human beings may never speak in the name of the real, or grasp the world objectively, because the realities we recognize are shaped by the cultural contexts that enable our very cognizance of the world itself. Cultural categories provide the very possibilities for perception. What we experience as social reality is a constellation of cultural structures that we ourselves construct and transform in ongoing practice.

As Steven Winter once put it, legal objectivists treat the world as if it were "filled with determinate, mind-independent objects, with inherent characteristics unrelated to human interactions," understand categorization as inherent in the world or as a human subsumption of objects that have ascertainable properties that independently establish their commonality, and "treat reasoning as about propositions and principles that are capable of 'mirroring' those objects and accurately describing their properties and relations."[19] Many legal scholars now argue that legal categories bear no accurate correspondence to a singular knowable reality, and that language, rather than mirroring or describing an objective state of things in the world, is constitutive of the world itself. Gary Minda, in an overview of "postmodern legal movements," suggests that second-generation critical legal studies scholarship is concerned to show how legal meaning about the world is created by interpreting subjects who are themselves constituted by particular social and cultural environments.[20] These perspectives all emphasize the constitutive role of culture—socially maintained structures of meaning or relations among construable symbols or signs—in constructing the realities we recognize as well as our sense of self, community, and possibility. The imaginative making of meaning is the quintessential human act, and culture is both this practice and its products.[21]

Postmodern legal scholarship—femcrits, critical race theorists, and poststructuralists—adopted social constructionist theses to expose the central ideological role that the autonomous legal subject plays in legal reasoning.[22] These so-called postmodern developments in legal scholarship in fact draw upon understandings of human subjectivity that have deep roots in Western political philosophy and the social sciences. Anthropology, for example, has long distinguished the human subject from the *individual* of bourgeois liberal tradition.[23] This liberal individual was a subject configured for the early modern bourgeois public sphere; the intentional author and the rational reader in this print-mediated public were both individuals, but the term individual has never embraced the full range of beings we now consider human. As Michel Foucault's work showed, "man" was constructed in a matrix of disciplinary surveillance practices that individuated humans in practices of social control that produced new regimes of power and knowledge as well as new forms of human self-consciousness. The priority given to the observing subject, the neutral observer who stands outside of the social world he or she observes, is also a product of such practices and the radical division of subject and object produced by modernity and Enlightenment sensibility. The individual, then, is a mode of being produced in discursive practices that are always simultaneously material and ideal (another crippling distinction inherited from modernity).

The idea of discursive production is crucial to any theory of the human subject; cultural construction is a practice in which the mediation of signifying practices forms both consciousness and the unconscious.[24] Anthropologists, whose discipline was traditionally understood as "the study of man," have, ironically, always been in the vanguard of attempts to challenge the unity of this term and demonstrate the radically diverse ways in which personhood is culturally created and experienced. They contribute to a tradition of thought that recognizes that the individual subject always already finds itself in textualized realities, characterized by signifying systems as diverse as myths, kinship, religion, and commodities, although human language is often seen as the paradigm.

When the subject assumes language, forms belief systems, or develops an imaginary understanding of a "real" social position, enmeshings in realms of signification are realized. One of the central tasks of anthropology, conceived as a form of cultural critique, is to demonstrate the contingency of those things we find natural: to defamiliarize bourgeois culture in order to facilitate an enriched understanding of our human situation as social beings. Traditionally, anthropology accomplished this through the ethnographic rendering of others, but such an endeavor is just as necessary to understand contemporary Western social practices. A focus on cultural signification illuminates both how the subject is constructed in social formations and how human agency is accomplished. To understand contemporary subjects mandates an attention to cultural activities in which identities are forged and transformed, interpellated and resisted, maintained and challenged. It is with such practices that this volume will be concerned.

Drucilla Cornell is one of the more prolific legal philosophers who rejects the notion of a transcendental ego existing prior to its engagement in social and historical context, but she does not thereby view the subject as imprisoned by determining structures or as without capacities for agency. She sees the self as constituted through communicative activity, and consciousness as embedded in language and shared cultural symbols—the same social mediums in which they are realized.[25] Neither self nor community is possible, then, without the social violence of language realized in *writing*:

> Rousseau's originary myth of full speech assumes a linguistic system already in place in which the members come to language. Speech implies "writing." Against Rousseau . . . Derrida argues that there is no innocent community initially free of writing . . . by writing, Derrida means the system of representation that makes communication possible, not just what we mean by writing, a system of graphic signs . . . To back his assertion that there is no community without writing, Derrida argues that the bestowal of the proper name, which no society can avoid, signifies writing in the sense that it implies a system of classification by which people recognize each other. The proper name carries within it the trace of institutional history. In other words, the identity of speech is contaminated by its other, writing.[26]

The speaking subject cannot control the meanings of its speech, then, because the very iterability of signifiers—"the iterability that makes a system of signs a language"[27]—always enables them to exceed the designs of their authors. "Language cannot be *owned* by the subject as her own expression" precisely because of the linguistic character of sociality itself.[28] As we shall see, these understandings of language are routinely denied in laws of intellectual property, and it is the cultural and political consequences of such denials to which I will attend.

If systems of representation constitute both subjects and objects, the identities of subjects and objects are themselves continually disrupted by difference—for systems of signification are also systems of differentiation. The threat of such difference is never fully contained, not even as new identities or positivities are forged to incorporate those differences, for differences continually and contingently manifest themselves. For Cornell, such a decentering of the subject renders subjectivity fundamentally dialogic: "what is most characteristic of our humanity is that we are dialogical or conversational beings in whom language is a reality."[29] The concept of dialogue might and should serve as a powerful regulative ideal with which to orient political life: "If the quintessence of what we are is to be dialogical—and this is not just the privilege of the few—then whatever the limitations of this ideal, it nevertheless can and should give practical orientation to our lives."[30]

Historicizing the Subject

Legal theory tends to render its reconstitution of subjectivity and objectivity in utopian and optimistic gestures, as if legal tendencies to reify and dichotomize subjectivity and objectivity could be reversed with only a modicum of intellectual good faith and political good will. In the Dionysian social worlds they describe, dialogue is always already our state of being and consciousness. If judges and decision makers were simply to recognize this state of affairs as the human condition, better laws and better decisions would further realize this immanent potential. Such scholarship tends to project a purely theoretical subject, far removed from the social, political, and ethical realities in which human agents actually live and the material constraints they encounter.[31] Legal theorists too frequently evade consideration of the social processes at work in everyday life to fix meaning and stifle dialogue. We need to examine the differential power that social agents have to make their meanings mean something, and the material factors that constrain signification and its circulation in contemporary societies. If, as human selves, in human communities, we are constituted by and constitute ourselves with shared cultural vehicles (as many of us are weary of having to assert), then it is important that legal theorists consider the nature of the cultural forms "we" "share" in consumer societies, and the recognition that the law affords them. If both objective social worlds and subjective desires, identities, and understandings are constructed with cultural resources, then legal attitudes toward these resources may have socially significant implications.

Attention to the importance of signification and the law's role in foreclosing access to cultural resources characterizes Carl Stychin's recent work, *Law's Desire*, in which he asserts the need for gay and lesbian subjects to have access to communicative resources so as to construct political identities:

> The constitution of the resistant subject depends upon the ability to formulate cultural meanings from the materials that are available and can be appropriated from the dominant culture . . . cultural appropriation operates not only as a means for the development of an

alternative subjectivity on an individual level, it also opens up cultural space for the formation of collective identities . . . Indeed, how images are consumed, appropriated and deployed depends upon the unique vantage point of the subject located at the conjunction of the matrices of power relationships . . . The implications of a postmodern approach to cultural consumption for a theory of identity are significant. The postmodern view suggests an ongoing struggle, both through the encoding and decoding of texts, to utilise culture for the purposes of individual and collective self-definition . . . The interplay of culture and identity—how culture forms the self and how culture may be subversively utilised for the definition of one's self—becomes a thoroughly political matter with no predetermined outcome. Instead, the process is an ongoing struggle for identity, which itself is a product of culture, or, more accurately, the outcome of a contestation over the meanings of cultural artifacts.[32]

Legal theorizations of the socially constructed subject have proceeded under the rubric of postmodernism—which seems to have entered the legal academy as a generalized umbrella term under which poststructuralist insights are promulgated. Even those legal scholars who seem aware of the use of the term to refer to a sociohistorical periodization linking global capital restructuring, regimes of flexible accumulation, and new communications capabilities rarely permit questions of political economy to impinge upon their discussions of the "decentered subject." In an influential early law review symposium on postmodernism, for example, literary scholar Jennifer Wicke began the discussion with a careful acknowledgment of the ambiguities of the term's current usage that emphasized its association with "the shift to a postindustrial economy" and "broad societal and economic shifts into a media or consumer or a multinational phase": "any serious consideration of postmodernity would have to stem from a historical periodization where the postmodern genuinely described a convergence of historical phenomena, at a specific if loosely chosen time, and second, that postmodernism refers to a congeries of theoretical suppositions about the nature of language, texts, and human subjects within the lens of the social."[33]

After introducing Fredric Jameson's (and later David Harvey's) position that the postmodern is "the logic of the culture of late capitalism," Wicke cautions legal scholars that "None of these changes can be considered without taking into account the material, historical specificity of a vast social change undergone in Western countries, at least, since World War II. Prescient varieties of postmodern thought articulate the political effects of late capitalism and post-industrial society as these inflect all the aspects of modern society and its subjects."[34] Those who articulate theories of the postmodern too often operate as if the socioeconomic, aesthetic, and philosophical dimensions of the field were antipathetic. Within legal scholarship, the philosophical position is clearly the more comfortable space to inhabit. Ultimately, even Wicke chooses to focus her remarks about the relation between law and the postmodern precisely where legal academics are most at home: in philosophical ruminations over the political ramifications of the "decentred subject" and its presence or absence, desirability or dangers in the land of the law. The other contributors to the symposium (with the notable exception of Richard Thomas)[35] followed in her footsteps, largely ignoring the historical, material, and economic dimensions of postmodernity to focus on abstractions about the subject and aesthetic strategies divorced from the very conditions that "prescient varieties of postmodern thought" might seek to articulate.

In "The Postmodernist Subject in Legal Theory,"[36] for example, James Boyle reiterates many of his earlier arguments about the objectivist and subjectivist dichotomizing that pervades liberal legalism.[37] Seeing in postmodernism "a more profitable way to proceed,"[38] he locates a subjectivity that will help legal scholarship out of its liberal, realist, Marxist, feminist, but always modernist theoretical quandaries. This, of course, is the subject propounded by poststructuralist theorists, one that emerges as the nexus of multiple discursive interpellations, which constitutively, if only temporarily, crystallize. Boyle's (admittedly ironic) conclusion, however, is that even if legal theory has been dominated by a modern subject (be it rational, utilitarian, or alienated), "the *legal* subject has seemed distinctly postmodern for a very long time indeed."[39] He insists that the subject is radically and constitutively contextualized, but provides no indication of the social and historical context in which legal practices become postmodern.

I will wander down some inviting tangents: considering language, texts, intertextuality, and subjectivity in a particular social and historical context—the so-called postindustrial consumer society that cultural theorists acknowledge to be the heartland of the postmodern. The intersection of law, postmodernity, and subjectivity I propose compels us to attend to the constitutive role of the law in creating spaces of power and resistance, constructing privileged authors and piratical thieves, distinctions between originals and copies, providing conditions that both promote and prohibit the creative bricolage, pastiche, and parody identified as a postmodern aesthetic. Intellectual property laws play significant roles both in generating and in regulating that prolific intertextuality celebrated as the signature of the postmodern. By creating objects of property, the law simultaneously creates subjects of politics.

Postmodern Culture

In postwar America, media images have dominated our visual language and landscape, infiltrating our conscious thoughts and unconscious desires. In a century that has seen the intrusion of saturation advertising, glossy magazines, movie spectaculars, and television, our collective sense of reality owes as much to the media as it does to the direct observation of events and natural phenomena.—Marvin Heiferman and Lisa Phillips, *Image World: Art and Media Culture*[40]

It is important to focus on the human capacity to engage in imaginative meaning-making, as many legal scholars have done, but it is necessary to go beyond abstract assertions about the nature of subjectivity and objectivity to examine concrete practices of self and world creation. To do so, it is imperative that we acknowledge the politics of making meaning and the conflictual nature of struggles to fix and transform meanings in a world where access to means and media of communication is limited. We need to consider, concretely, what the "optimal material and cultural conditions for participatory dialogue"[41] might be in a world as media saturated as the one in which most North Americans live. As a modest contribution to an "ethics and politics based on the dialogical principle,"[42] I shall indicate how intellectual property laws often function to deprive us of possibilities for dialogic interaction with the cultural reality or lifeworld of postmodernity. (In the next chapter I will illustrate how, paradoxically, they may also invite critical appropriations.) Alongside my first formulation of this proposition in 1991, other intellectual property scholars have elaborated on the dangers to dialogue posed by the expansion of intellectual properties in the economies of late-capitalist communications. In recognition of this collectivity of authorship, I shall authorize Wendy Gordon to begin this discussion:

> In a civilized society, human beings create the reality around them.
> Our direct surroundings are buildings and landscape architecture
> rather than woods and natural water. To be a creative maker of new
> meanings, a rational being needs access to her heritage. Just as land
> is necessary for farmers to bring forth fruit in Locke's imagery, a

common of previously created intangibles is necessary for creators to bring forth new works of the imagination. Too broad a set of intellectual property rights gives one set of persons potential control over how that "created" reality can be interpreted. In other words, it can give them control over what the world *means*. Such control would deny others the understanding, or "naming," that is one crucial way humans interact with the world.[43]

Although the implicit divison between "civilized" and "savage" societies alluded to here is unnecessary (given anthropological and archaeological knowledge of the significant and signifying realities in which all humans live, it would also be inaccurate) and the emphasis upon "rationality" suggests a rather impoverished view of human understanding, Gordon's emphasis upon the social importance of employing cultural resources to interpret social life is well-founded. Interpretive practices, however, do not merely name the world but potentially transform it, through expressive performances of abjection and alienation, displacement and desire, irony and insult, parody and persuasion, metaphor and metonomy, ridicule and rebuke. Intellectual property laws, by prohibiting the reproduction of vital cultural texts, disenable us from subjecting those texts to critical scrutiny and transformative appropriation. Because these texts are constitutive of the cultural milieu in which we live, constructing many of the socially salient realities we recognize, their status as exclusive properties that cannot be reproduced without consent and compensation operates to constrain communication within, through, and about the media that surround us.

Social theorists identify the term postmodern both with a historical era of capitalist development[44] and with particular forms of cultural practice characteristic to it.[45] To simplify things, I will refer to the historical period as the condition of postmodernity, and to its cultural qualities as postmodernism, using the term postmodern or postmodernist to describe practices situated in these contexts.[46] Postmodernity is distinguished by a dramatic restructuring of capitalism in the postwar period, a reconstruction of labor and capital markets, the displacement of production relations to nonmetropolitan regions, the consolidation of mass communications in corporate conglomerates, and the pervasive penetration of electronic media and information technologies. Such processes have coalesced in the Western world in societies oriented toward consumption, which is managed by the capacity of mass media to convey imagery and information across vast areas to ensure the production of

demand. Goods are increasingly sold by harnessing symbols, and the proliferation of mass-media imagery means that we increasingly occupy a
"cultural" world of signs and signifiers that have no traditional meanings
within geographically contiguous communities or organic traditions.[47]

A proliferation of signification seemingly without social contexts,[48]
these signs come at us as if from nowhere—across radio waves, unseen
cables, invisible microwaves, and laser beams, springing up in our living
rooms and over our telephones, bombarding our paths and filling our
horizons wherever we walk. These images, do, however, come from
somewhere, and increasingly they come from fewer and fewer places: "As
the power of media widens, the power base is consolidating. In the U.S. it
is common for a single corporation to control movie studios, publishing
houses, magazine empires, radio and television stations and advertising
agencies. In 1981, forty-six corporations controlled most of the business
in daily newspapers, magazines, television, books, and motion pictures;
by 1986, that number had shrunk to 29. It is estimated that by the year
2000, ownership of the U.S. media industry will be in the hands of only
six conglomerates and global communication will be dominated by
twelve major corporations."[49]

Theorists of postmodernism suggest that we address the "textual
thickness and the visual *density* of everyday life"[50] in societies saturated
with commodified forms of cultural representation. Such images so pervasively permeate all dimensions of our daily lives that they are constitutive of the "cultures" in which most people in Western societies now live.

It's a Small, Small World™

Children have become so sophisticated. Today's five-year-olds always want the
next big thing—and it always has to be more and more complicated . . . They
are our salespeople and their grandparents are our best customers . . . We now
sell virtually the same toys all over the world. So it stands to reason, if all these
kids are playing with the same toys, how could they ever possibly fight with each
other? There's a common thread about how they grow up and what they play
with. I think that's terrific. It makes for one world . . . I was on a trip last week
and I probably spent $50 out of my pocket. That's because everything works
with the American Express® Card . . . —Charles Lazarus, CEO, Toys "R" Us® [51]

A friend tells me about a cross-country plane ride between L.A. and Chicago
with her eighteen-month-old son, Jimmy. There is a little Korean girl two rows
ahead of them. She's about four and speaks no English. She sees Jimmy and

before she waves or smiles, she tries to determine what kind of creature she's dealing with. Bobbing up and down in her seat, she cries, "Ninja, Ninja, Ninja Turtles!" and waits, expectantly. My friend restricts her son's television viewing and tries to protect him from the influence of mass culture. Little Jimmy can't respond, and the girl turns away, disappointed.—All dialogue guaranteed overheard[52]

Five and 6 year-olds at three Florida day-care centers appear on the national nightly news to say how sad they will be if they can't keep Mickey, Minnie, Donald and Goofey on the walls of their playgrounds. But a Disney lawyer who directs anti-piracy efforts out of New York says a nursery school is no less a profit-making enterprise just because little children are involved.—Gail Diane Cox, "Don't Mess With the Mouse"[53]

Our children sleep in Barney® sheets, eat off Aladdin placemats, drink liquids they know only by brand name from plastic cups encircled by Disney characters (protected by copyright laws and character merchandising agreements). "All over the world, more and more of what children eat, drink, wear, ride, play with, and sleep on are influenced by such product promotions, the fruits of corporate licensing departments of Time Warner or Sony or Nintendo and the manufacturers of food, beverages, and toys."[54] A child in the Philippines eats Batman cereal launched by Ralston Purina. Logos like Cabbage Patch Kids, Hot Wheels, and Ghostbusters mark American products as more desirable than local ones in a diversity of markets. When playing in clothing branded with names, images, and logos, children are marked as consumers (and, less obviously, as producers) of an incredible surplus of excess meaning, the value of which accrues to the corporate "authors" of these mass-media texts. The accomplishment of this expropriation of surplus signifying value is effected by intellectual property laws that restrict the right to reproduce these publicly identifiable texts to those who are deemed to "own" them and claim their social meanings under various legal fictions of authorship.

My colleagues Wendy Gordon and Keith Aoki both connect the ever increasing expansion of intellectual property protections ("cultural traffic laws"[55]) and the private enclosure of the public domain of ideas, images, and information (the intellectual commons) to this intensification of the mass-mediation of daily life. Gordon itemizes several developments fueling this trend toward privatization: "the gradual decline in our nation's industrial/manufacturing sectors, the dramatic growth of high-tech information industries, and the perception that our nation's wealth is declining . . . As the economic hopes of a less confident, service-oriented economy have become increasingly dependent on the nation's intangible assets, legislatures and courts seem willing to extend intellectual property protections on the questionable, and surely often unconscious, assumption that protection means prosperity."[56] Margaret Chon resists this assumption and suggests that rather than extend protections on the basis that prosperity will somehow follow, we need to deliberate the social meaning of the concept of "progress" that constitutionally enables the grant of intellectual property protections in the United States and provides its raison d'être.[57] Such dialogic deliberations are particularly necessary in the new capitalist culture of consumption created by information technologies and communications capabilities if we are to avoid having a corporately controlled cultural "commons" made up only of private properties.

The judicial inclination to recognize more and more intangible interests as forms of property corresponds to the high period of postmodernity (from about 1970).[58] Rights to control intangibles, usually signifying texts of one form or another, were increasingly affirmed on the grounds of unjust enrichment (Thou shall not reap where thou has not sown) and the need to provide incentives to creators to produce cultural valuables:

> In some quarters, the traditional suspicion toward intellectual property soon was replaced by its opposite: an eager acceptance of the voracious notion that beneficial products of human effort— works of art, information, computer programs, inventions, designs, ideas, or symbols of celebrity—should yield court-protected rewards for the persons who create them, discover them, or give them popularity. Further, courts seemed to assume that ownership was the most appropriate form for this reward to take . . . In the process, traditional defenses to the creation of such rights based on notions of public interest are sometimes improperly resisted and desirable prerequisites for [bringing] suit ignored . . . decisions construing relevant federal statutes or constitutional clauses showed a similar expansive willingness to grant rights against strangers who would use what others have made.[59]

Other scholars have shown how our intellectual property laws—copyright in particular—have developed without due regard for the public interest, ignoring our social interests in freedom of speech, promoting expressive activity, or protecting the public domain,[60]—issues of considerable importance in societies dominated by mass-media imagery. But to recall Cornell's reading of Derrida, no system of proper names is ever free from the disruption of others, and expressions of difference always emerge to threaten the unitary identity of the authorial voice. Copyright owners, like other holders of intellectual property, continually encounter unforeseen forces of alterity. As we shall see, the author's proper name is always simultaneously enacted and disrupted by the improprieties of others.

A similar expansion of legal rights has accrued to celebrities. Publicity rights enable celebrities (and often their estates) to control the reproduction and circulation of the star's name, image, and other publicly recognizable features. In the next chapter, I will suggest that publicity rights pose particularly acute dangers to expressive activity, but these properties, too, have cultural meanings in the lifeworlds of others. The specter of gendered alterity may compel and resist the celebrity's authorial claims. Trademark laws create proprietary rights in the signs manufacturers use to market their goods, and it is primarily trademarked texts that I shall examine in this chapter (and in chapters 3 and 4, where I consider the activities of those others that alter the manufacturer's signature as it is inscribed across national landscapes).

Postmodern Goods

Jean Baudrillard once theorized the postmodern by extending Marx's critique of the commodity form; in the context of contemporary capitalism characterized by the controlled programming of commodity production and the pervasive penetration of mass media, he suggests, we experience the hegemony of a "signifying culture," in which the social world becomes saturated with shifting cultural signs. The Western world, he asserted, has reached the end of an era dominated by industry and now sustains itself through circulations of image and text (information, in another nomenclature). Baudrillard projected a vision of commodity culture in which the code of marketing signs did not just take priority over or precede commodities, but subsumed the distinction between object and representation altogether.[61] "Instead of a 'real' world of commodities that is somehow bypassed by an 'unreal' myriad of advertising images, Baudrillard discerned only a hyperreality, a world of self-referential signs."[62]

The quintessential self-referential sign or postmodern cultural good, I would suggest, is the product brand name or corporate trademark, as indicated by the slogans that propel them into the public sphere: "What's good for General Motors is good for America," General Electric "brings good things to life," and Coca-Cola is "the real thing." These signifiers serve as the locus of capital's cultural investments and social inscriptions. Through the mass media, the sign increasingly replaces the product itself as the site of fetishism; the focus of commodity fetishism shifts from the product to the sign values invested in products by corporate imagery and marketing's structures of meaning. The value of a product, in other words, lies in the exchange value of its brand name, advertising image, or status connotations: the "distinction" it has, or will acquire, in the market. Monopoly of this trademark or commodity/sign and its meaning is crucial to corporate capital. For today it is no longer the production of goods but the production of consumers to produce demand that is fundamental to profit expansion and a strategic site for corporate investment.[63] The twentieth century has witnessed a massive expansion of the legal protections available for publicly circulating forms of signifying property; in many sectors of the economy, texts deployed to market goods may be more valuable than the physical assets necessary to create the product.

An apocryphal story circulates at marketing conferences: Coca-Cola executives, it is said, routinely visit bottling plants around the globe to monitor the size and proportions of the famous logo to ensure that it does not become distorted on the local product. Gathering together the staff from several plants, a senior Coca-Cola executive is reported to have declared that the company could lose all its plants, lose all its staff, lose its access to the sources of its raw materials, lose its capital and its accounts, but as long as it had this (lights shine on a display board greatly enlarging the famous red and white script), it would be possible to walk into a bank and receive sufficient credit to replace the entire global infrastructure.[64] Corporate trademarks are key symbols in a postmodern signifying culture.

Baudrillard's discussion of the "brand" suggests that the postmodern commodity/sign operates not primarily to signal the product, but to mobilize connotations of affect.[65] Its force is directed, not to use value or utility, but to desire. We speak of emotional attachment to these signifiers as brand "loyalty"—a loyalty not to the product (which can and often does change in its composition) but to its identity and persona. Baudrillard describes this in a manner reminiscent of Althusserian interpellation: "The psychological restructuration of the consumer is performed through a single word—Philips, Olida, General Motors—a word capable of summing up both the diversity of objects and a host of diffuse meanings . . . The lexicon of brands . . . is doubtless the most impoverished of languages: full of signification and empty of meaning. It is a language of signals. And 'loyalty' to a brand name is nothing more than the conditioned reflex of a controlled affect."[66]

A central dimension of the study of postmodernism has, however, been a concern with the ways in which people "live and negotiate the everyday life of consumer capitalism"[67] and the manner in which people use mass culture in their quotidian practices. If society is characterized by pervasive media imagery, and commodified cultural forms permeate all dimensions of our experience, then we must ask what people *do* with these representations. For "one of postmodernism's most provocative lessons is that terms are by no means guaranteed their meanings."[68] Regimes of signification are used in numerous and unexpected ways; people don't use products only as advertised, and they don't necessarily use advertising as it was intended.

The consumption of commodified representational forms is productive activity in which people engage in meaning-making to adapt signs, texts, and images to their own agendas. These practices of appropriation or "recoding"[69] cultural forms are the essence of popular culture,[70] understood by theorists of postmodernism to be central to the political practice of those in subordinate social groups and marginal to the centers of cultural production. It is now evident that mass-media imagery and commodified cultural texts provide important cultural resources for the articulation of identity and community in Western societies where many traditional ethnic, class, and cultural indicia are fading and minority groups organize along alternative lines (commodity texts may also be deployed in reactivating identities).[71]

Despite their pandemic presence in people's daily lives, insufficient anthropological attention has been directed to the use of commercial signs in capitalist cultures. Corporate trademarks are "friends from our childhood," "members of our extended modern family."[72] We grow up with the jolly Green Giant®, Mr. Clean®, the Lucky Charms®' leprechaun, and the Pillsbury Doughboy. Brand names have become so ubiquitous that they provide an idiom of expression and resources for metaphor. With phrases like the Coca-Cola-ization of the Third World, the Cadillac® (or the Edsel) of stereo systems, meeting with the Birkenstock® contingent (or the Geritol® generation), we convey messages easily and economically.

In practices of appropriation we may discern "indexes of the creativity that flourishes at the very point where practice ceases to have its own language."[73] This is especially important in consumer societies where "marginality" is no longer a quality only of minority groups, but is pervasive, in the sense that most of us are nonproducers of the commodified culture within which we live. Cultural activity increasingly involves the recoding of commodified cultural forms. The tactics of subcultural recodings with respect to commodity/signs encompass a range of practices as diverse as children's songs ("Comet. It makes you vomit. It makes your mouth turn green . . ."[74]), through adolescent satire magazines (*Mad* magazine's relentless spoofs on advertising), fanzine writing, graffiti artists' defacement of billboards, bootleg T-shirts parodying media figures for parochial purposes, to more intentionally political practices that appropriate commercialized forms in the visual arts, film, media activism, and community organizing. As Angela McRobbie points out:

> postmodern culture . . . [is] full of jokes; it refuse[s] to take itself seriously and for this reason found itself subject to criticism. Where this playfulness seemed also to penetrate the walls of academia, the response was heavily condemning . . . a playful disposition . . . need not . . . imply a forgetfulness or abandonment of politics. What it can do is force us to reconsider the foundations of our modern thought. It can also force us to think seriously about the trivial . . . the superficial does not necessarily represent a decline into meaninglessness or valuelessness . . . to opt for the superficial can be a deliberate political strategy. Only by theorizing the producers of culture and by paying closer attention to the social practices of consuming culture, can we get a better understanding of how the tinsel and the glitter can produce meaning, in a different, but no less significant kind of way than the great deep works of modernism.[75]

By addressing practices of recoding in an academic manner, I position myself in an attitude of sympathy and respect for practitioners of mass-media appropriations and ally myself with other cultural theorists of the postmodern who insist on blurring or contesting the boundaries between high art and mass culture, the aesthetic and the political, and treating popular cultural practices with the same degree of theoretical sophistication we accord to studies of art and social movements. We need to take these practices seriously as forms of expression emerging from a particular historical matrix of culture and power. It may no longer be possible or desirable to separate the cultural from the social and the political.

Author(iz)ing the Corporate Persona

The author is not an indefinite source of significations which fill a work; the author does not precede the works; he is a certain functional principle by which, in our culture, one limits, excludes, and chooses; in short, by which one impedes the free circulation, the free manipulation, the free composition, decompositon, and recomposition of fiction. In fact, if we are accustomed to presenting the author as a genius, as a perpetual surging of invention, it is because, in reality, we make him function in exactly the opposite fashion.—Michel Foucault, "What Is an Author?"[76]

The signs, symbols, and texts that academic practitioners of cultural studies take seriously as resources for cultural politics are legally defined as properties in which authors are bestowed privileges to preclude reproductions or imitations by others on the basis of their creation under rubrics of originality and distinction. Cultural forms thus become signs with an exchange value enabled and maintained by powers to prohibit uses by others. This was illustrated rather ironically to me while attending a conference on the semiotics of marketing in 1989. Advertising and marketing professionals were offered the theoretical equivalent of fast food—bite-size McNuggets® of Saussure, Pierce, Baudrillard, and Barthes were served up on flowcharts and overhead displays that promised a new science of meaning for the market. Hearing about my interest in trademarks, two marketing consultants eagerly sought me out. They were impatient to let me know that they had obtained federal trademark registration in the term *semiotics*. Although the exclusive protections they obtained pertained only to use of the term in association with marketing consulting services, it was clear that they were bemused by the potentials for exercising their proprietary rights: the possibility of transforming the name of a discipline of linguistic scholarship into an advertising logo. Legally they were enabled to claim royalties and even to enjoin others who might use the term semiotics in association with marketing services or associated wares and goods. The very conference at which we met, with its heavy usage of the term and the preponderence of marketing executives that formed its clientele, was potentially endangered by these preexisting rights. We joked about enjoining the next day's proceedings.

To understand the value and power of the trademark, however, requires some historical consideration of the processes of reification by which the "author-function" was extended to manufacturers and the means by which the consumer's appreciation for business practices became transformed into monopolies over meaning in the public sphere. Contemporary trademark doctrine holds a legally protected mark (which may be a brand name, a distinctive container, a logo, a style of packaging, or even a unique smell or sound) to be a distinguishing marker of origin for the product or service with which it is marketed. It is understood to designate a singular point of dissemination for the commodity (even when the public does not know what the identity of that source is), and to publicly distinguish commodities from this particular source from commodities that have other points of origin:

> the 19th century common law of trademark developed from a general background of seeking to protect the *public* from mistake, confusion, and deception about the source and quality of products purchased in the market. For much of the 19th century, a seller's mark was legally protected because it represented consumer "goodwill" towards the producer of goods to which the mark was affixed—that is, a particular trademark represented an assurance to the buyer that purchased goods were of a consistent quality if bought from the same source. Trademarks also served to lower consumers' "search costs," providing a compact, easily identifiable way for consumers to tell similar products apart—the trademark became an abbreviated informational proxy.[77]

In fact, trademarks have never guaranteed a product's quality, ingredients, or uniformity, but the exclusive right to a trademark and the ability to build consumer goodwill were expected to provide incentives for producers to maintain markets by maintaining product consistency. The trademark provides a consumer with nothing other than the assurance that a good comes from a single source (albeit one whose identity the consumer might not know), or that it comes from someone who has been licensed to use the mark by the original, potentially anonymous, but always singular owner. The social value of such "information" to consumers in mass markets may be negligible, but the symbolic value of such marks—their recognition value—is enormous.

As Jane Gaines demonstrates in her discussion of the legal protection of fictional characters, American trademark law since World War II has developed in a fashion that demonstrates more regard for the exchange value of signifying forms than for the protection of the consuming public.[78] She links this development with television, a communicative medium often seen as quintessentially postmodern in its fragmentation and "its capacity to ingest everything, to repeat infinitely, to stamp its imagery on every conceivable object of everyday life."[79] The motion picture industry, however, has had no difficulty achieving the same saturation of the public sphere with its own imagery, characters, titles, and dialogue, if blockbusters like *The Little Mermaid*, *The Lion King*, and *Jurassic Park* are any indication.

Although trademarks are not conventionally understood to have "authors"[80] because they require no necessary genius, originality, or creativity, the legal recognition that trademark "owners" have a proprietary interest in marketing signs increasingly relies upon a reenactment of the author-function as described by Foucault. This is evident in judicial acceptance of the belief that through investment, labor, and strategic dissemination, the holder of a trademark creates a set of unique meanings in the minds of consumers and that this value is produced solely by the owner's efforts. Sociolinguistics and anthropological scholarship would suggest, instead, that meanings are always created in social contexts, among social agents, in social practices of communication, reproduction, transformation, and struggle: in short, that cultural distinction is socially produced.

Legally, however, the cultural value of a mark generated by such social practices may be expropriated by the owner of that mark and realized as exchange value (thus, companies with rights to trademarks with long histories and a tradition of affirmative advertising are targeted by potential corporate raiders for acquisition or merger). This is justified using rhetoric that mimics the author-function, seeing in the mark's social reproduction, transmission, and reactivation by others only the aura of the corporate persona and its exclusive authorial efforts. Unlike copyright or publicity rights protections, however, the right to control a trademark is potentially perpetual, so long as it continues to be used and retains its distinction in the social imaginary. Unlike human authors or celebrity personas, the corporation may live forever, and its embodied identity in the trademark form shares its potential immortality and, if assigned, will survive even the corporate demise.

As Aoki shows,[81] the focus of trademark law has been progressively inverted in the twentieth century: "the old rationale of preventing consumer confusion over competing market goods has yielded to the current rationale of protecting from 'dilution' or 'misappropriation' the integrity of a set of positive meanings which have been 'created' by the trademark owner's investment. This recent conception of a trademark as property imports 'author reasoning' into trademark law. The trademark owner is viewed as a 'quasi-author' who 'creates' a particular set of meanings attached to a mark by investing time, labor, and money, thereby justifying expansive rights in a mark."[82]

Although some assert that the significance of the author-function has declined in postmodern conditions, as trademark has replaced copyright as the favored form for protecting cultural texts,[83] I would agree with Aoki that the author-function is left substantially unimpeached by this shift in emphasis. Whether the law recognizes an original work understood to embody the personality of a unique creator, as it does when affirming copyright, or acknowledges a signifier and its meanings to be the creations of a singular and unique source of origin, as it does in protecting trademarks, the power of the author is reinforced. Both frameworks depend for their intelligibility upon the assertion of a unitary point of identity—a metaphysics of authorial presence—that denies the investments of others in the commodity/text, and the constitutive history of others in its development, circulation, and significance. As I will suggest in my discussion in chapter 4 of those trademarks that embody images of social alterity, however, the activities and meanings of others (and otherness) may well be constitutive of authorial distinction.

Manufacturing Distinction

Marks can be protected against unauthorized use if they are distinctive or have acquired secondary meaning, terms of art, which, like so many intellectual property doctrines, have meanings that bely commonsense interpretations. Distinctiveness, for example, is legally inscribed with a positivity and fixity of meaning that refers to the signifying mark's linguistic relationship to the goods or services with which it is marketed. Generic words, for example, are not protectable because they are simply the name for the good (the term *safari* is generic for an expedition into African wilderness), whereas certain marks are deemed "inherently distinctive" because they are "suggestive, arbitrary, or fanciful" (words or symbols used in marketing goods or services that do not merely describe the good, such as Ivory® for soap, Citizen® for watch, or Kodak® for camera). The term *inherently distinctive* would seem to imply that a signifier's distinction inheres within it, an impossibility given the fact that distinction necessarily designates the quality of being in a relationship, the product of positioning in a social system of difference. Legally, the term serves as a form of shorthand acknowledging that the signifier occupies a place within the dominant linguistic system which puts it at a formal distance from—and thus more likely to be capable of distinguishing—the goods with which it will be associated. This is no guarantee, of course, that it will actually so function in the social world.

Marks deemed "descriptive" of goods (and thus having no "inherent" distinguishing abilities) can only be protected if they have "secondary meaning"—a quality acquired after a period of time and exclusive use. The marked goods, in other words, are identified with their producer by virtue of the public's recognition that the descriptive term is associated exclusively with a single source of origin.[84] Sources of evidence accepted for establishing the existence of this secondary meaning, however, rely more upon the manufacturer's investments and profits and his or her competitor's activities, than they do upon any actual knowledge or beliefs of the consuming public. Although consumer surveys may be used, they are no more probitive than evidence of a competitor's intentional copying, large advertising expenditures, sales success, or the length of time of exclusive use.[85]

Although *public* meaning is the nominal basis for the granting of the property interest, this understanding may be legally established by a showing of the purported owner's *private* efforts, with no necessity to provide evidence that these were successful in generating any belief on the part of any relevant public. The public is, therefore, often assumed to hold a belief by virtue of publicity efforts that stand in as its surrogate. As Willajeanne McLean suggests, even this doctrine has been superseded in some jurisdictions by "the judicial substitution of the incipient secondary meaning doctrine, also known as secondary meaning in the making."[86] In such instances, the first user of a term or phrase is protected against those who would usurp it on the basis of its *potential* to acquire secondary meaning: "piracy should no more be tolerated in the earlier stage of development of quality than in the later."[87] Findings of "piracy," however, presuppose rights in the entity expropriated. The capacity of a signifier to acquire a particular referent would not seem sufficiently predictable that a right in its realization should be recognized merely on grounds of hopeful anticipation.

The intricacies of the doctrine of secondary meaning in the making and its evaluation and acceptance by courts and commentators are likely to be of little interest to the nonlegal reader, but the underlying assumptions about meaning and its making are significant. Those who renounced the doctrine saw it as "inimical to the purpose of secondary meaning because it did not focus on consumer association, but rather on the attempts of the producer to acquire consumer association."[88] However, as we have just seen, the major evidence accepted for judicial recognition of *actual acquisition* of secondary meaning is precisely this: evidence of attempts by the producer to build consumer association. Both doctrines presuppose that meaning—here reduced simply to an attachment between a signifier and its referent (the progenitor)—is established in a linear and cumulative fashion that can be measured only as more or less evolved. Never at risk, never at play, never carried off in the curiosity or desire of others, such a signifier is legally recognized only to be moving in a singular direction: toward the monumental moment when, prodigal son returning home to the patriarch, it achieves manhood by becoming one with the authority vested in the name of the father. Whatever the traces of the journey, they are simultaneously denied as social experiences in the public realm and surreptitiously embraced as possessions properly part of the paternal domain. In more prosaic terms, whatever connotations a signifier may have acquired along the way are legally irrelevant, but to the extent that they have social value, these values are incorporated under the proper name and realized as exchange value.

Even if a mark is protected by virtue of being "inherently distinctive" or of having "secondary meaning," the holder of a mark traditionally could prohibit reproductions or imitations only if a likelihood of consumer confusion would result from the allegedly infringing use. Here again, however, "likelihood of confusion" is satisfied by a number of criteria, very few of which actually engage any human consumers or attempt to determine the meanings they make of marketing signs. "The factors most commonly used by the courts include similarity of the goods, classes of prospective buyers, actual consumer confusion, and the intent of the defending competitor. These factors, however, are merely a guide in determining whether confusion would be likely."[89] Would consumers upon encountering the allegedly infringing mark believe that it indicated that the goods came from the same source as those bearing the original mark?

In Britain and Canada, at least, the premise that the mark still stands for a set of qualities that the manufacturer has instilled in the product by repeated delivery to the consumer was maintained by rules governing the licensing of trademarks, which required the registration of a "user agreement."[90] Registration could be denied on public interest grounds if the proprietor did not maintain control over the mark's use because it was against the public interest to "traffick in a trade mark."[91] Traditionally, the trademark could not be alienated from the loyalty the business had established (goodwill), for otherwise the public would have a false affection for the new goods based on prior intimacy with the mark—a romance premised upon misrepresentation would be fostered.[92] Such principles, however, have all but collapsed under increasing pressure from industry interests.

Trademarks in the United States, especially, are now recognized as assets that may be independently licensed. Their recognition value may be capitalized upon in ever new fields of enterprise:

> All of these merchandise licensing ventures depend completely on the protectability of the trademark; it is the legal shield around the name, logo, shape, or character image, making it possible for the original proprietor to assign this sign to second and third parties for a limited period of time in exchange for royalties. But it is a shield made possible by the total reversal whereby in trademark law injury to the owner takes precedence over injury to the consumer. Moreover, the theories internal to trademark law seem to have reversed themselves as well; while unfair competition law is based on the prohibition against *palming off* one's goods as the goods of another, licensing itself is essentially a "passing off." If, for instance, RJR Nabisco, through its merchandising agent, Columbia Pictures, licenses the image of Niagara Falls on the Nabisco Shredded Wheat cereal box cover to a manufacturer of beach towels, does Nabisco stand directly behind the towel in the same way it stands behind the box of breakfast cereal?[93]

If actual consumers are more or less ignored in the laws developed to protect them as members of a putative public, their imaginary suspicions about corporate power and concentration are now legally ratified by judicial bestowal of even further powers on those who hold marks to control their circulation. As consumers became aware of corporate licensing arrangements, according to legal argument, it became feasible for them to believe that *all* uses of trademarks must have their "owners'" consent. The fable of public naïveté founded further extensions of property rights. Now a likelihood of consumer confusion is premised on the proposition that consumers will assume that all the iconic indicia of consumer culture must be owned, and thus that *any* appearance of them must be approved by their official owners. The presupposition of a widespread public belief in endorsement is now accepted as legal grounds to further protect the mark's private owner by precluding noncompeting uses of the trademark.[94]

In the name of protecting consumers from the "likelihood of confusion," we now deprive them of the lower prices they might enjoy in a more competitive marketplace. What difference, one might ask, does it make if the towel you buy with the 7UP® logo on it is or is not endorsed by the soft drink manufacturer? (The manufacturer is no less—or more—likely to be licensing the logo to those who subcontract to illegal factories employing child labor than is the infringing distributor; the infringer is no more likely to be contracting for Chinese prison labor than is the mark's registered holder.) The consumer may believe that whoever "owns" 7UP must have some connection to the towel, but it doesn't follow from this that consumers are hurt by their potential confusion if the towel was not actually made by an official licensee with the manufacturer's endorsement. In fact, consumers might be more hurt by the fact that potential legal sanctions preclude many manufacturers from distributing towels emblazoned with this logo, thus creating an artificial scarcity of such towels and an inflated price for them.[95]

Protecting consumers from potential confusion becomes the ruse by which corporations protect themselves from competition and from uncompensated circulation of their cultural indicators.[96] This may also ensure that the public has no access to the signifiers that evoke the positive meanings that their own activities as fans and supporters have created, except at exorbitant prices. Legally it is dangerous to duplicate a sports team's logo as a low-priced cloth emblem that would enable inner-city youth to attach some of the team's allure to their own clothing at a fraction of the price of officially licensed goods. Such activity has been enjoined on the basis that (in judicial recognition of the obvious) consumers will associate the logo with the team—even when it is clear that the public does not believe the emblems came from the team as their source of origin.[97] As Judge Kozinski, so often a dissenting judicial voice in these matters (and a staunch supporter of the legal protection of commercial speech), suggests: "when you don a Mets shirt . . . what you're communicating is your team loyalty, and that loyalty is not something the team owns. Having used the means and methods of advertising to inspire admiration for the home team, the Mets, I would argue, have given you the right to express that admiration in your own way."[98]

Rochelle Dreyfuss helpfully discusses the process as one of reaping the benefits of surplus value. She distinguishes between a mark's signaling functions and its expressive capacities, suggesting that the trademark holder has a right to control the former, but no right to dictate the latter; unfortunately, most contested instances fall between these two poles. She provides a series of examples evoking Barbie, the toy fashion doll marketed by Mattel, to make the point. As well as signaling that a particular doll is made by this company, Barbie has acquired other connotations, including a few perjorative ones, such that the term *Barbie doll* may suggest a bland feminine vacuousness, a woman valued only for her appearance, a prop or accessory for an insecure man. When the term is used in the second sense (imagine a T-shirt with an image or the logo of the doll, with the universal sign for *not* inscribed across it), customer confusion is unlikely. Such usages, Dreyfuss suggests, should be permitted—even if Mattel is unhappy about the association. The case law involving such expressive usages, however, is, in colloquial terms, all over the map.[99] Thus, teenage girls who have used the Barbie name to call attention to home-made protofeminist fanzines, available over the Internet, have been told by Mattel to cease using the name or face legal action. As Dreyfuss suggests: "whatever the reason behind the desire to utilize the mark, so long as the mark is not being used as a signal, traditional trademark law offers no answer to the question of who should garner this value. Not surprisingly, however, trademark owners have expressed a preference in favor of themselves."[100]

Increasingly, investment in a mark's signaling function is recognized to create an entitlement to control and appropriate surplus expressive value. The underlying argument is that trademark owners created this value through their investments and should garner any and all available rewards; to assign the benefit elsewhere would unjustly enrich one who would "reap where he has not sown." This, of course, is simply the Lockean assertion that one should have the benefit of one's own efforts. This affirmation of the trademark holder's investment to create ever more expansive rights over expressive usages represents an unprecedented shift in trademark law; "free speech interests are deeply implicated by this migration."[101] The principle "if value, then right" has no coherent limits and puts holders of trademarks at a decided advantage. As Dreyfuss suggests, the choice for assigning the benefits of surplus signifying value should at least consider public economic and expressive interests. One could argue that if the public creates meanings for *Barbie* in excess of the signifier's capacity to signal Mattel's toy, they have done the sowing, and thus they should do the reaping;[102] in short, authorship of such meanings might be seen to reside in the public sphere.

Fixing the Signifier/Owning the Sign

. . . a signal, entirely rigid and unambiguous in what it signifies, can be liberated and given the fluidity of a symbol by a change of context . . . What is the "context" within which signs exist? First, there is the cultural context created by material objects . . . Second, every material object implies and reflects in itself a set of cultural relationships which explain it or give it purpose . . . Third, an integrated complex of cultural relationships may be said to form a myth . . . myth makes the world immediately self-evident, without contradictions. Bourgeois ideas become the eternal essences of things, they impregnate everyday reality through the mechanism of myth . . . Symbols might be said to become charged with meaning through the use of obsessing techniques . . . The term has its origin in the shaman's incantation . . . Advertisers have gone to great lengths to assure that a product name, its trademark, is highly charged with the desired associations.—Thomas D. Drescher, "The Transformation and Evolution of Trademarks"[103]

[T]he ruling class tries to give an external character to the ideological sign, to extinguish the struggle between social value judgements which occurs in it, to make the sign uniaccentual.—V. N. Voloshinov, *Marxism and the Philosophy of Language*[104]

The transition to seeing connotative value (public associations or cultural meanings) as the property of those who "own" the denotative signifer (the mark) as a marketing proxy is accomplished by the expansion of the theory of "misappropriation" to deal with intangibles, and the idea of trademark "dilution" now accepted by many courts.[105] Both doctrines rely upon normative convictions "that it is 'unjust to appropriate the fruits of another's labor,' and its corollary, that one should not reap where another has sown,"[106] neither of which is subjected to reflexive social scrutiny. As Wendy Gordon suggests: "One might ask why there is a need to trace the restitutionary principle back to any other source, as there is an obvious moral attractiveness to the idea that it is unjust for an entity to reap where it has not sown. The simplest answer is that when taken literally, as a stand-alone prohibition on free riding, the restitutionary claim is drastically overbroad. A culture could not exist if all free riding were prohibited . . . Culture *is* interdependence, and requiring each act of dependency to render an accounting would destroy the synergy on which cultural life rests."[107]

The law constitutes and enforces rights and limitations that govern the relationship between those who claim a proprietary interest in the sign and those who seek to appropriate it, to create other meanings and alternative identities (to turn it to their own ends). We see this process at work in all areas of intellectual property. Postmodern dialogic practices of parody, pastiche, irony, and social critique come into tension with the monologicism of a modern legal discourse that bestows monopolies over meaning under the authority vested in the proper name in the form of property.

The political implications of cultural commodification (and the legal regimes supporting it) were, until quite recently, largely unexplored by critical legal scholars. When the ramifications for the political ideal of democratic dialogic practice are addressed, it is generally in terms of the *material* limitations of access to dialogue that concentrations of capital and mass media monopolies effect. Intellectual property laws, however, may serve to deprive us of the optimal *cultural* conditions for dialogic practice. By objectifying and reifying cultural forms—freezing the connotations of signs and symbols and fencing off fields of cultural meaning with "No Trespassing" signs—intellectual property laws may enable certain forms of political practice and constrain others.

This is most readily apparent in the exercise of trademark rights,[108] but examples of the chilling power of intellectual property are also rampant in the publicity rights and copyright fields. In any case, in an era when characters, phrases, logos, and even names and faces from movies, novels, and television are the subject of merchandising rights and tie-in contracts, these distinctions become less relevant. Humphrey Bogart's estate, for example, could hold general publicity rights and trademark his name and face to sell cigarettes, and perhaps use Sam Spade to market raincoats,[109] while MGM licenses Casablanca to hotel chains and collects royalties for commercial usages of copyrighted dialogue. These figures from our cultural history become private properties that we parody, proliferate, or politicize to our peril.

Let me give a few examples drawn from the trademark field. In 1977, an environmental rights group distributed materials critical of the practices of the electric utility industry. These materials contained a caricature of the Reddy Kilowatt trademark (a stylized cartoon stick figure). Confronted with a motion for an injunction, the Environmental Action Foundation argued that it was exercising its right of free expression.[110] The defense was rejected on analogy to cases affirming the right of private property owners to exclude picketers.[111] In other words, you can't use someone else's property to express yourself. Trademark rights were never designed to bestow "ownership" over a sign or symbol in any and all contexts[112]; judges, however, often authorize such proprietorship. The Manitoba Court of Appeal, for example, allowed the Safeway grocery chain to enjoin picketing workers from using the stylized *S* from the company's logo in its strike literature.[113] Deciding that the insignia was known to the public, the court determined it was an asset connected with the company's goodwill, and thus that the company had proprietary rights in it: "there is no right under the guise of free speech to take or use what does not belong to [you]."[114] It was, of course, precisely because the insignia was publicly linked to the company that the union wished to use it, to let the public know that the sign was associated with unfair labor practices as well as the more cheerful connotations projected by the store's management. They attempted to invest the symbol with another, alternative, set of meanings.

The ability to fix the signifier, because you "own" the sign, has expanded dramatically with increased judicial enforcement of state antidilution statutes.[115] Traditional trademark theory protected rights in the sign only insofar as it was necessary to protect consumers from deception and confusion[116] based upon their recognition of the mark as indicating the source of goods. If the public imagined in this legal arena was, as we have seen, largely one simulated to meet the economic demands of trademark holders, at least the protection of the mark was limited to such contexts, real or projected. Increasingly, however, holders of trademark rights are enabled to prevent "misappropriation" even where the use of the trademark is unlikely to cause public confusion and there is no competition between the goods marketed. Indeed, trademark holders may now enforce their rights to maintain their goodwill against public communicative uses of which they disapprove.

The "dilution rationale" was first suggested by Frank Schechter in 1927 as support for the protection of a mark used in association with non-competing goods: "The real injury in all such cases . . . is the gradual whittling away or dispersion of the identity and hold upon the public mind of the mark or name by its use upon non-competing goods. The more distinctive or unique the mark, the deeper is its impress upon the public consciousness, and the greater its need for protection against vitiation or disassociation from the particular product in connection with which it has been used."[117] Justice Frankfurter put it this way:

> The protection of trade-marks is the law's recognition of the psychological function of symbols. If it is true that we live by symbols, it is no less true that we purchase goods by them . . . The owner of a mark exploits this human propensity by making every effort to impregnate the atmosphere of the market with the drawing power of a congenial symbol. Whatever the means employed, the aim is the same—to convey through the mark, in the minds of potential customers, the desirability of the commodity upon which it appears . . . If another poaches upon the commercial magnetism of the symbol he has created, the owner can obtain legal redress.[118]

According to Schechter, the chief value of the trademark lay in the favorable impressions it imparted, its capacity to convey positive meanings. The use of a similar mark vitiates its unique or distinctive ability to convey meaning, "diluting" its strength in consumer imagination. Although for decades the doctrine was not incorporated into federal trademark legislation (and still remains constitutionally questionable),[119] many states[120] have enacted "antidilution" statutes that provide that "likelihood of injury to the business reputation or of dilution of the distinctive quality of a mark . . . shall be ground for injunctive relief notwithstanding the absence of competition between the parties or the absence of confusion as to the source of goods or services."[121]

Although these statutes initially encountered judicial recalcitrance,[122] courts increasingly accepted the dilution doctrine in the 1970s and 1980s.[123] The dimensions of dilution now extend to include protection against "blurring"[124] a positive image caused by "dissonant"[125] usage, against "erosion"[126] of the "magic"[127] of the status of the mark, "tarnishing"[128] the luster of a trade name, use of the mark in an "unwholesome or unsavoury"[129] context, and the production of "unsavoury mental associations."[130] The trademark owner is invested with authorship and paternity; seen to invest "sweat of the brow" to "create" value in a mark, he is then legitimately able to "reap what he has sown." The imaginations of consumers become the field in which the owner sows his seed[131]—a receptive and nurturing space for parturition—but consumers are not acknowledged as active and generative agents in the procreation of meaning. When positive connotations grow in the promiscuity of social communication, the trademark owner reaps their benefit as goodwill. The generation of new, alternative, or negative connotations are ignored, denied, or prohibited because patrilineal rights of property are recognized as exclusive: no joint custody arrangements will be countenanced.

"Many of our culture's best known and most powerful symbols are trademarks."[132] Moreover, the "owners" of trademarks are some of the most powerful and wealthy actors in North American society. Indeed, the more famous the mark, the more likely judges are to extend it protection against "dilutions" of its commercial aura. The more valuable the mark becomes, the more legal protection it receives, which of course means that it accrues even more value because it is granted further immunity from scrutiny, competition, or denigration. Protected because it is valuable, it is valuable primarily because it is protected.[133] The production operations and management activities of the corporations that hold such powers may be increasingly invisible to us, but their signifiers permeate our senses and surround us with words and images, sights, sounds, and smells.[134] Why should the most prominent symbols of corporate power be enabled to impart an exclusively favorable impression? Why should these symbolic forms be enabled to maintain a pristine innocence, abstracted from the history and the practices of the corporate bodies that produce them? Commodity fetishism is legally endorsed and sanctioned here in a fashion that is rarely so clearly enunciated.

The Coca-Cola Company, which polices its marks assiduously, is often (one could almost say routinely) successful in preventing unauthorized uses of its globally recognized bottles, logos, and trade dress.[135] In 1972 it enjoined entrepreneurs from marketing "ENJOY COCAINE" posters using the famous script employed by the multinational in its "ENJOY COCA-COLA" advertisements.[136] The court found that impermissible damage to Coca-Cola's reputation would be caused by this unwholesome association with an illegal drug.[137] The injunction was granted, the judge commenting that people seeing the posters might "refuse to deal with a company which could seek commercial advantage by treating a dangerous drug in such jocular fashion."[138] The court conveniently overlooked the company's historically established attraction of its early market through its more than symbolic associations with the drug at issue.[139]

General Electric was granted an injunction against the use of "GENITAL ELECTRIC" on T-shirts and briefs in a decision that manipulated the confusion rationale to deal with the threat of tarnishment to the company's image.[140] But what if one were to superimpose the company's advertising slogan, "GE, we bring good things to life," over a drawing of the missiles they produce, or on a photograph of carnage in Iraq (presuming it were established that GE played some role in manufacturing the bombs that inadvertently killed thousands of Iraqi civilians)? Would we be permitted to counter their media message with other mediations? Could we respond to their dissimulations, even if we did have access to the same media channels and the same level of resources? Concepts as vague as loss of distinctiveness and tarnishment have the capacity to escalate into a general power to prohibit all reproductions of a mark and "grow into a powerful vehicle for the suppression of unwelcome speech."[141]

The legal doctrine of dilution provides a potent means for corporate actors to manage their public personas. Perhaps the full implications of this have yet to be realized; it is difficult to know. No one is keeping a record of threatening phone calls and letters received by local parodists, political groups, and other "consumers" of corporate symbols, which are subjectively experienced realities rarely documented by those who quantify objectivities for the official record. The political effects of the exercise of these legal rights may well be (and may remain) invisible to us. In jurisdictions that enforce dilution laws, it would not be advisable to comment upon the sexual objectification of women in a bedding company's ads by way of a feminist film suggesting a rape on a mattress identified with its trademark. Nor could you be sure of your freedom to comment upon multinational capital if you depicted a Nestlé billboard in the midst of Third-World squalor and malnutrition. By controlling the sign, trademark holders are enabled to control its connotations and potentially curtail many forms of social commentary.

Activist Appropriations

The student community at Smith College underwent a fair degree of internal social turmoil in the fall of 1990 as the college dealt with demands for increased commitment to issues of multiculturalism and greater sensitivity to minority experience. In a show of goodwill and solidarity—or ironic recognition— a number of women made, wore, and sold T-Shirts with the internationally-known Bennetton logo parodied for parochial political purpose. "United Colors of Smith" were proudly (or ironically) proclaimed.—Public domain

The reproduction and recoding of advertising (which may contain texts protected by both copyright and trademark as well as potential publicity rights) became a fashionable practice in artworks of the 1970s and 1980s, particularly by artists influenced by poststructuralist currents of thought. These artists were particularly critical of modern ideologies of authorship and originality that emphasized the intentionality and expressivity of the author-work relation. They attempted to illustrate that such premises—upon which contemporary intellectual property laws are based— were ideological and elitist conceptions. "Arts of appropriation" ranged from feminist rewritings of the female body as it appeared in mass-media imagery to advertising adulterations that rehistoricized corporate marketing insignia by placing them back into the trajectories they obscure. Artists like Ashley Bickerton, Mike Bidlo, Sherrie Levine, Barbara Kruger, Cindy Sherman, Elaine Sturtevant, and Hans Haacke reproduced media imagery[142]—prior artworks, film stills, photographs, trademark logos, characteristic advertising layouts, media stills, billboards, and posters— creating new meanings for them by putting them in new contexts or juxtaposing them with other texts that conveyed hidden subtexts.[143] In so doing, they attempted to effect an expressive unworking of the commodity and gender fetishism so characteristic of contemporary public spheres. Not surprisingly, laws of intellectual property were evoked to enjoin such criticism. Although one might debate the political effectivity of critical aesthetic practices that are then appropriated back into the art market as works of art, such activities do provoke new reflections in and upon the public sphere.

Hans Haacke, for example, has deployed his talents to comment on "the ubiquitous cynicism with which multinational corporations use the patronage of art as a form of public relations to promote the appearance of humane, enlightened values while masking suspect political affiliations."[144] In *Metromobilitan*, Haacke imitated the banners upon which major museums advertise exhibitions and their corporate sponsors, using the same form (including the corporate logo, the original layout, and corporate public relations statements) to comment upon the South African investments of Mobil Oil and its sponsorship of African art in the era of apartheid. After threats of legal action (on copyright and trademark grounds) put his catalogue for the exhibit out of circulation for an extensive period, Haacke made the relationship between corporate sponsorship and artistic censorship central to his work. In one instance, he incorporated the lawyers' letters he had received, together with an explanation of the legal defense of fair use, directly into his art (thus effecting yet another act of copyright infringement). Haacke has also received legal threats from the Philip Morris Co. (on copyright and trade dress grounds) for work in which he ensconced a photograph of Jesse Helms on an enlarged package of Marlboro cigarettes that featured Helmsboro as the brand name—a reference, perhaps, to the powerful influence of the tobacco industry in American politics.[145]

The politics of tobacco advertising is also the subject of Dorean M. Koenig's thorough and compelling analysis of "the dark side" of protecting copyright- and trademark-protected icons.[146] A civil liberties attorney, she suggests that intellectual property protections constrain popular cultural forms of resistance and that First Amendment speech protections have been inadequate to deal with increasing corporate control over mass-media-disseminated cultural forms. Koenig creates an imaginary scenario involving an angry mother who attempts to counter the cultural influence of the cartoon figure Joe Camel (associated with cigarettes by 30 percent of three-year-olds and over 80 percent of six-year-olds)[147] on the preteen market (in which the tobacco company has made massive inroads):

> Repairing to her sewing room, Emma embroiders the likeness of Joe Camel and super-imposes upon it the universal symbol of prohibition—a red circle with a red slash through the middle of it. She gleefully notes that this gives the sophisticated Joe a more-than-slightly-sinister look. His look becomes villainous. Underneath the

picture she embroiders a ditty which she composed for her two-year-old: "No, no Joe, not for me. You won't kill me. No. No. No." Entranced by her own cleverness, she writes a whole book of rhymes complete with a portrayal of Joe Camel as a sinister figure. Jean-Pierre wears the clothes to his day-care center and takes his new book of rhymes with him. They are the immediate hit of the school.[148]

Not surprisingly, this fictitious mother goes into business to further disseminate her antismoking message to children attracted to the allure of Joe Camel, soon producing caps, watches, T-shirts—the same items the tobacco giant uses to increase its goodwill. Koenig estimates that RJR Nabisco could allege at least five counts of legal wrongdoing against this militant mother, ranging from violations of federal copyright and trademark laws to state actions alleging interference with contractual relationships and dilution of trademark (as well as potential tort claims, which she does not address).[149] In none of these five areas is our maternal combatant sure to be successful in claiming immunity for her critical missives. There is no guarantee that her appropriation will be seen as a "fair use" under copyright law; a court might well find her use of the trademark confusing; her advertising might be seen as misleading; and parody, although recognized as a possible defense by the United States Supreme Court in the copyright area,[150] has not been definitively legitimated in the field of trademark. Lower courts have occasionally permitted trademark parodies as protected speech, or allowed them because they are not confusing with the original mark, or deemed them protected by the First Amendment, but in other very similar instances, courts have refused to recognize parodies (particularly if they are commercially circulated) as permissable uses.[151]

The fictitious Emma does, of course, have real-life counterparts; in 1996 the *New York Times* ran similar advertisements denouncing Joe Camel placed by antismoking activists:

> sponsorship purchases innocence by association for an industry that *should* be worried about its soul. Philip Morris, in particular, seems almost desperately concerned about its image of moral rectitude. Its "Good People do good things" ad campaign pictured Philip Morris employees who help the handicapped, protect animals, and so on . . . Philip Morris is a great champion of free speech except when it's used to criticize cigarettes. When Dr. Alan Blum of Doctors Ought to Care designed a series of public service announcements satirizing the company's ads, Philip Morris slapped him with

a lawsuit. Philip Morris brought out its big legal guns to silence Peter Taylor, whose documentary film *Death in the West* showed real-life "Marlboro Men"—cowboys dying from lung cancer . . . Philip Morris successfully sued to gain possession of all copies of the film . . . [and] tried to impugn the film's credibility by questioning the men interviewed in the film about whether they were *really* cowboys . . . [152]

It would seem that the "innocence" of the Marlboro Man must be maintained at all costs. Other cigarette advertisement parodies mimic the copy, format, and logos of "the real thing" but replace trademarked slogans with more pointed insinuations. Hence, Newport® becomes Newcorpse and its promise of being "alive with pleasure" becomes the warning "dead with cancer"; Joe Camel, the "Smooth Character," becomes a black-hooded "Smooth Reaper"; and Merit®'s "New crush-proof box" is represented by a coffin in artist/activist Bonnie Vierthaler's mock ads.[153] Artist Robin Shweder asserts that advertising alterations should be considered a form of cultural interrogation; given their ubiquity as public forms of representation that present cultural content, they are also public forums for critique and arenas for cultural contestation.[154] Shweder, however, simply assumes their availability for such appropriations.[155]

Such artistic appropriations are diverse in terms of their intentions and may be politically distinguished by the public sphere domains in which they circulate and have consequence. Legally, however, they are more similarly situated. By subjecting copyright-protected works and trademarks to histories and meanings other than those their "authors" would claim (production processes, working conditions, employment policies, gender disparities, unemployment statistics, investment practices, pollution, and the social costs of military rearmament) and attaching them to an alterity they contain, disembody, and deny (an authorial persona and presence that is other to their publicity values), artists like Haacke, Vierthaler, and Shweder are put at risk. To reduce or avoid this risk they must, ironically, seek corporate consent: an authorial and authorizing signature must be acquired to secure the alterations of others.

Policing Postmodern Precincts

Trademarks have invaded our popular culture in ways never anticipated.—Judge Alex Kozinski, "Trademarks Unplugged"[156]

We are always in a world where some meanings are being fixed while others are changing. A world of free-floating signifiers in which no meanings were fixed would be an impossible one in which to live, as would a world where signification had achieved a state of full closure (even manufacturers would be disadvantaged by this because advertising itself requires that the signifier maintain a surplus that can be tapped). Social actors obviously have diverse capacities and means to fix and to challenge meaning; intellectual property protections are only one form of power in a larger field. We are always engaged in making meaning and attempting to make our meanings mean something. A democratization of access to this practice would give all peoples more equal opportunities to engage in expressive activity, rather than granting already powerful actors even further resources and capacities to dominate cultural arenas than they already possess.

This is a real danger. Fewer and fewer defenses are available in intellectual property infringement actions generally, and free speech defenses are inconsistently interpreted and often dismissed without due consideration. Many parodies and expressive appropriations are enjoined or deemed infringements without any consideration of public expressive interests. Wendy Gordon seeks recourse to the natural rights tradition as a potential means to protect free speech interests that have been routinely ignored or downplayed by judges who suppose "that as long as ideas are free for all to use, no harm to free speech can result from forbidding the copying of expression."[157]

> Legions of commentators have deplored these developments. Lawyers, law professors, and even judges are on record pleading for the law to subject intellectual property to the same free speech principles that limit other assertions of governmental power. Some argue for recognizing an independent First Amendment defense to copyright, right of publicity, and trademark actions, while others marshall free speech principles to argue for strengthening the doctrines within intellectual property, such as fair use in copyright, which exhibit some recognition of free speech interests. But the courts have too often turned a deaf ear to these arguments. The incantation "property" seems sufficient to render free speech issues invisible.[158]

Gordon brilliantly demonstrates that the very natural law principles relied upon to promote, strengthen, and justify intellectual property protections in fact justify *narrower* rather than wider protections for intellectual property owners and provide legitimacy and support to those creative users of intellectual property texts whom the law conventionally damns as pirates for copying the works of others. Her careful reading of Locke is a major contribution to the arsenal necessary to do battle with an ever-expanding cultural field in which more and more private property rights are claimed. Should we find ourselves in the fortunate situation of litigating such issues at an appellate-level court, such arguments may well be invaluable.

More probable, however, is the likelihood that in most cases of politically creative cultural appropriations, freedom of expression arguments will never be asserted, and certainly not publicized. In many instances, the dispute will never be tried on its merits. Faced with the threat of litigation, most local parodists, political activists, and satirical bootleggers will cease their activities. Lawyers advising their clients as to whether to threaten an injunction when they find their copyright or trademarks used in an unwelcome fashion will not be considering the most liberal readings of Lockean natural rights theory, but the most conservative of judicial opinions. The more indigent their opponents, the less likely it is that they will have recourse to counsel sophisticated in intellectual property matters, and the more likely it is that intellectual property holders will be advised to project expansive claims about their own rights and threaten draconian measures of enforcement.[159]

For instance, a local furniture store chain in southwestern Ontario wrote a threatening letter to a Toronto gay nightclub. The bar featured a weekly drag routine in which one performer impersonated and parodied a comical middle-aged female character who was prominent in the furniture store's frequent television advertisements. The letter promised to seek a legal injunction to enjoin the performance on copyright grounds unless the establishment ceased to depict the female character in its entertainments. The copyright and trademark status of fictional characters in Canada is actually quite limited.[160] With the exception of cartoon characters, whose graphic instances are recognized as works in their own rights,[161] to attract legal protection characters must be so central to the work in which they figure, or be so well-known, that consumers associate them with the source of the goods and services for which they serve as marketing vehicles. It is not clear that in permitting the performance the club reproduced any "work" that might even potentially be protected by copyright.[162] In this instance, there was clearly no registration of a trademark,[163] the character had not been used as a trademark, and had not been so extensively employed as to develop secondary meaning. The likelihood of confusion was limited: the furniture store catered to a downscale, suburban clientele, not the urban gay community (although it is plausible that the company's perception of the homophobia of their market niche compelled them to end any suggestion of association with gay nightlife). However, in the absence of a parody defense, fair use provisions, or any judicial consideration of the intersection between intellectual property and freedom of expression in Canada, the furniture store was on fairly safe ground when it asserted its imagined rights.[164]

Canadian courts granting injunctions in such matters rarely examine the niceties of the parameters of the textual properties in which ownership rights are claimed. Those who copy the expressive forms claimed by legally recognized authors may be visited with *ex parte* injunctions and even Anton Piller orders involving raids in which goods and records are seized[165] and confiscated without notice. In circumstances such as these, those visited with accusations of "piracy" are unlikely to have the resources and wherewithal to engage in protracted constitutional litigation.

Xerox® Cultures

Legal doctrines do acknowledge that brand names and trademarks may become part of public discourse, but they do so in a narrow and positivist fashion that understands the public role of signifying forms to be purely referential. In a rule often referred to among lawyers as *genericide*, it is established that if a trademark becomes the generic name for the thing itself—if everyone routinely asks for a Kleenex to blow their nose, for example—then the trademark no longer serves the function of distinguishing the product in the market. The trademark owner loses the exclusive rights to the mark, and thus the signifier devolves to the public domain.[166] In such instances, any and all manufacturers can then use the lost mark to identify their wares because it has become a term of public parlance. Xerox, for example, promotes the concept of the photocopy so that its own trademark does not substitute either for the noun or the verb.[167]

The ubiquity of Coca-Cola and the likelihood that people would use the term *coke* or add the suffix *cola* to refer to soft drinks generally has long been recognized by the manufacturer as a particular danger. The Coca-Cola Co. has a proud tradition of successful trademark litigation produced by its efforts to protect its name, logo, and trade dress. With the passing of the Trademark Law of 1905, the Coca-Cola Co. embarked on a dogged pursuit of imitators that by 1923 had produced a 650-page

"Bible of Coca-Cola law" full of successful defenses of the mark.[168] In 1926, a reporter estimated that Coca-Cola had arranged over seven thousand "burials" of would-be "copy-cat" competitors—a record of success that prompted one commentator to suggest that the Coca-Cola Co. "virtually created modern American trademark law."[169]

Manufacturers must be wary of using their own marks generically—hence the necessity to enjoin consumers not to "Use Kleenex" when they have a cold, but to enjoy the convenience and comfort afforded by "Kleenex® brand tissues"—and routinely advertise their proprietorship over the brand name. The trademark owner is advised to police his or her mark, to guard against its becoming a term of common usage. Large corporations employ clipping services to monitor the use of their marks in the public sphere, maintaining surveillance over journalists, competitors, and novelists. For example, when an interviewer quoted a celebrity who said that she belonged to a cohort of French actresses known as "the Kleenex generation,"[170] both the actress and the magazine's editors might have expected to receive a letter reminding them of the trademark status of the name. Through such correspondence, manufacturers attempt to establish a documentary history of reminding the public that the mark is a private property under their authority, despite its meanings in the worlds of others. If the paper trail demonstrates sufficient diligence, the law will enable the trademark holder to maintain rights to exclusive use. In conditions of postmodernity, then, the proverbial ambulance chaser is likely to be mining the media for the unauthorized use of proprietary images—ascribing alterity by policing mimesis.

Such legal requirements may produce absurd public dialogues and surreal juxtapositions when the cultural meanings of trademarks come up against corporate property interests. A few years back, anthropologist Margaret Visser waxed nostalgically about the "joys of jelly" in her *Saturday Night* magazine column.[171] She explored its decline in status from an elite food that embodied foresight, effort, and elegance to a ubiquitous, mass-produced, and often vulgarly colored substance called Jell-O®, in which fruit and marshmallows were suspended at endless suburban buffets and children's birthday parties. She might also have commented upon the relationship between Jell-O's local status and the spread of the electric refrigerator; in the last areas to receive home refrigerators, Jell-O desserts still displayed the status of the homemaker long after they had been disparaged by sophisticates elsewhere. Despite its current lack of prestige, she suggests, we still retain "an urge to touch jello,"[172] to play with it, even to jump right into swimming pools filled with it. (Some of us also remember blindfolded children's initiation rites in which Jell-O featured prominently.)

The response from Kraft General Foods was swift and to the point. Although amusingly dubbed "Hell-O™ from Jell-O™" by the magazine's editors, the letter to the editor was itself without humor:

> References to JELL-O jelly powder in Margaret Visser's article on jelly ("The Joy of Jelly," September) need to be clarified. Regardless of any common usage of the term, JELL-O is a well-known registered trademark of Kraft General Foods Canada used exclusively by us in Canada to identify jelly powder and other foods we manufacture and distribute. Ms. Visser and your readers should be aware that our company holds all legal and proprietary rights in Canada to the JELL-O mark. The brand name is an asset of substantial value that we vigorously protect. As for those who may ask our advice about using JELL-O products in swimming pools or elsewhere [and just as one is hoping for at least some tongue-in-cheek allusion to an awareness of the mirth this might provoke], our response without exception is [perhaps that one should "keep one's powder dry"?] that such use should not be encouraged. We say this not because large quantities of the product may not set properly but also out of concern for consumer safety, since suffocation in a pool of jelly is a possibility. Furthermore, as a matter of responsible corporate policy, our company deplores the waste of any food [food? jelly is food? does it have *any* nutritional value?] used for purposes other than human consumption. We would hope that you might now see your way clear [no longer clouded by pools of jelly?] to share these further considerations with your readers.
>
> Nada Ristich
> Manager
> Corporate Affairs
> Kraft General Foods
> Don Mills, Ontario[173]

Had I used this letter in its entirety without seeking permission to reprint it (which I did obtain, although my parodic commentary may not be appreciated), I might well be liable under Canadian law for infringing Philip Morris's copyright (the food company is now part of that tobacco company's corporate empire). Neither the context in which I place the text nor the comments I make upon it would necessarily excuse me in a jurisdiction in which "fair use" of copyright texts is not countenanced and "fair dealing" is narrowly defined in favor of those who assert proprietary rights.[174] Other scholars are routinely denied permission to include advertisements in their books, play videos of television commercials in their classrooms, or otherwise engage students in critical commentary on the cultural texts that surround them in any fashion that involves reproducing, displaying, or performing those commodity/signs for critical assessment.[175]

The loss of a mark by genericide assumes only that the mark has become a signifier with a singular referent—which is no longer the mark's originating source, but the product itself. Dreyfuss thoughtfully proposes that if use of the mark is the most economical way to refer to a particular set of connotations—a realm of expressive significance —it should be permitted as an instance of "expressive genericity."[176] Otherwise, expressive communication will be suppressed by the loss of vocabulary—and the capacity of such language to provide the medium for metaphor—that trademark laws effect. Metaphor, however, is generative of meaning even as it calls upon established realms of signification. It is generativity, perhaps, rather than genericity that we might seek to protect.

Dialogics of Postmodern Politics

Gramsci suggested that an integral feature of language was its metaphoricality, and that attempts to eliminate this feature of language-use could in his view only have repressive political consequences. This accords with Bakhtin's stress on the multiaccentual character of the sign and of the threat of monologism to a healthy heteroglossia.—Michael Gardiner, *The Dialogics of Critique*[177]

The concept of dialogue, dialogism, and the dialogical principles of human life were central to the philosophical anthropology of Mikhail Bakhtin (1895–1975), who has been described as "the most important Soviet thinker in the human sciences and the greatest theoretician of literature in the twentieth century."[178] With P. N. Medvedev and V. N. Voloshinov, Bakhtin developed a body of philosophical ethics about the constitutive role of language in human life and the cultural life of democracy that he saw as quintessentially dialogical.[179]

I borrow Bakhtin's authority here because he transcends and rejects the dichotomy of subjectivity and objectivity by understanding culture as the ongoing activity of transformative meaning-making,[180] and he does so without denying either the materiality of signs or the political importance of struggles to fix their meanings.[181] Bakhtin made extensive attacks both on the transcendental ego and on objectivist understandings of self, language, and world. In reaction to the excesses of nineteenth-century positivism and empiricism, Bakhtin saw consciousness not as reflecting an external world, but as bringing historically and socially specific forms to apprehension. Unhappy both with individualism and with abstract epistemologies or formalist explanations, he created a materialist dialogic poetics that took the relation between self and other, socially conceived, as central. The "self" is a dialogic and ethical relation[182] with other selves that is never given, but always dominated by a "drive to meaning." The self authors itself with and through the social signs with which meaning is made: "Meaning comes about in both the individual psyche and in shared social experience through the medium of the sign, for in both spheres understanding comes about *as a response to a sign with signs* . . . 'And nowhere is there a break in the chain, nowhere does the chain plunge into inner being, nonmaterial in nature and unembodied in signs'. . . . the individual is striated by the social."[183]

Bakhtin saw the relation between individual and society not as a binary opposition, but as a continuum, because the contents of the psyche and of culture were the same: signifying forms that simultaneously demand and elude closure as fixed signs with certain meanings. As one commentator has noted: "the nature of the linguistic sign is synergistic, a constant struggle and co-operation between the necessity to be static and repeatable and the opposed but no less imperative necessity of the same material to be open to constantly new and changing circumstances."[184] Meaning must be understood as something always in the process of creation, never completed, for the world itself "is a vast congeries of contested meanings."[185] Communicative acts have meanings only in particular situations or contexts. In their *utterance* meanings are continually "enriched, contested, or annexed."[186] Utterances travel between contingent and historically specific contexts and become "caught up in the complexities and inequities of social life"[187] in different historical periods.

This conceptual framework does greater justice to, or more adequately accounts for, the complexities of the signifying lives of commodified texts protected by intellectual property laws in conditions of postmodernity than either a nominalist-positivist or a structuralist account of language. Rather than a juridical account of language that sees it as a system of rules, it focuses attention upon the historical actuality of its continuous evolution, the particularities of the multiple social contexts in which the signs that surround us are enunciated, the inequalities between those who have resources to speak and those who must speak the languages of others, and the conflicts and antagonisms around meaning that are generated in such conditions. More specifically, it emphasizes that the domain of signs and thus of meaning is always also perforce the realm of ideology:

> Bakhtin manages to conceptualize both the positive (ideology as the central medium in the symbolic constitution of social relations) and the "negative" (ideology as monologism, as an "authorial voice" which suppresses difference and restricts free dialogic intercourse) functions of ideology in an eminently dialectical fashion. And because ideology as a symbolic medium of social interaction is inherently dialogic, this allows for the possibility of actively responding to or even resisting dominant discourses. Hence, Bakhtin's notion that signifying practices are always constituted in and through conflicting social forces—the so-called "struggle over the sign"—helps to open up a vast and relatively unexplored area of social inquiry which could be termed the "politics of signification."[188]

The sign's "multiaccentuality" suggests that it bears within it "different accents, emphases and therefore meanings with different inflections and in different contexts."[189] These differences reflect the different social positionings, interests, values, and attitudes of those who engage the sign in everyday life. Thus, no trademark should be seen to have any singular meaning (secondary or otherwise), nor any singular relationship to either its source of origin nor to the product with which it is associated, nor any necessary teleology of evolution in meaning. So long as the sign is part of a living language, it is continuously caught up in generative processes of struggle. "Dictionaries are the graveyards of language."[190]

As human beings we live an existence of sheer semioticity, "surrounded by forms that in themselves seek the condition of being-there, the sheer givenness of brute nature,"[191] but at the same time we are compelled to invest these forms with new life and meaning so that we may understand. Understanding is responding, answering. "Human being is the *production* of meaning . . ."[192] We are fated to the condition of dialogue, "not only with other humans, but also with the natural and cultural configurations we lump together as 'the world.' The world addresses us and we are alive and human to the degree that we are answerable, to the degree that we can respond to addressivity."[193]

If what is quintessentially human is the capacity to make meaning,[194] challenge meaning, and transform meaning,[195] then we strip ourselves of our humanity through overzealous application and continuous expansion of intellectual property protections. Dialogue involves reciprocity in communication: the ability to respond to a sign with signs.[196] What meaning does dialogue have when we are bombarded with messages to which we cannot respond, signs and images whose significations cannot be challenged, and connotations we cannot contest?

The sign, according to Voloshinov/Bakhtin, is always an arena of social struggle because it embodies the dialectical history of two contending social tendencies: the monologic and the dialogic.[197] Bakhtin often links monologic tendencies with the "official" in cultures, which must always contend with dialogic or "carnivalesque" tendencies, a dynamic momentum between center and periphery. This is a sociopolitical opposition, with those in power attempting to give a brute facticity and singular meaning to the sign and to "extinguish the struggle between value judgements that occurs in it, to make the sign uniaccentual."[198] Bahktin, however, rarely attends to the social and institutional contexts in which such practices take place or the mediums they assume; he addresses few examples outside of those provided by literary and theoretical texts. Intellectual property protections provide one, if only one, example of the way in which authorities "arrest the inherent semantic flux of discourse and . . . impose a rigid code of equivalences between 'language' and reality."[199]

Such centralizing forces of authority (those of the law, the state, the interests of capital) must always contend with alterity—unpredictable, centrifugal forces that find expression in practices like those of satire, parody, irony, quotation, collage, stylization, and polemic.[200] For Bakhtin, the dialogic sphere is a fragile domain that remains in constant peril, threatened by forces of linguistic-ideological closure and centralization. Nonetheless, he continued to believe throughout his life that the carnivalesque tone was deeply embedded in human history and culture and managed to maintain a foothold, however tenuous, in contemporary life. Monologism is always infected by its opposite, the "parodic antibodies" of a transgressive dialogism that promises to rupture this "grey, monotonous seriousness" from within—or, to put it another way, semiotic contestation is immanent within linguistic and cultural practices themselves.[201] These practices, like the appropriative recodings explored earlier, involve a generation of new meanings by unanticipated agencies engaged in metaphorical movements and recontextualizations of the sign.

Attempts to fix the meaning of signifiers or to disarticulate and rearticulate the meaning of texts are the essence of hegemonic struggle, a struggle in which certain social groups periodically *do* manage to fix the meaning of the sign and evoke closure. Because such closure is secured only through discursive practice, however, it is temporary and always open to future disarticulations. The struggles that take place on the terrain of the sign to define its symbolic boundaries are historically specific contentions in which those with divergent social interests strive to establish legitimate meanings for the sign and/or delegitimate the meanings established by others. The sign is dynamic; it maintains the capacity for development—a vitality and a social life—to the extent that it is open to reconfiguration. In postmodernism, I fear, we see fewer and fewer signs of life, but more and more monologic monuments—commercial tombstones marking the demise of the carnivalesque in the condition of postmodernity.

Legal theorists who emphasize the cultural construction of self and world—the central importance of shared cultural symbols in defining us and the realities we recognize—need to consider the legal constitution of symbols and the extent to which "we" can be said to "share" them. I fear that most legal theorists concerned with dialogue objectify, rarefy, and idealize "culture," abstracting "it" from the material and political practices in which meaning is made.[202] Culture is not embedded in abstract concepts that we internalize, but in the materiality of signs and texts over which we struggle and the imprint of those struggles in consciousness.[203] This ongoing negotiation and struggle over meaning is the essence of dialogic practice. Many interpretations of intellectual property laws quash dialogue by affirming the power of corporate actors to monologically control meaning by appealing to an abstract concept of property. Laws of intellectual property privilege monologic forms against dialogic practice and create significant power differentials between social actors engaged in hegemonic struggle. If both subjective and objective realities are constituted culturally—through signifying forms to which we give meaning—then we must critically consider the relationship between law, culture, and the politics of commodifying cultural forms.

Consonant with the "postmodern" turn in cultural anthropology and the disciplinary preoccupation with finding new textual and tactical ways of "writing against culture" (while maintaining emphasis upon quotidian practices of making meaning within relations of power), I adopted collage and montage forms to evoke the experience of living within (and working against) worlds of commodified textuality. To convey a sense of the significance of those cultural forms protected by regimes of intellectual property, I have thus far posed legal enforcement of copyright, publicity, and trademark rights primarily as a source of danger for democratic dialogue. It would be reductionist, however, to see the power of intellectual property in purely prohibitory terms. The law is always simultaneously prohibitive and productive: it creates realities and constitutes possibilities. In this chapter I let the recoding of others show how law enables authorities to stifle the expressive activities of those who would create alternative, ironic, or oppositional meanings for the texts that circulate in the place of the corporate proper name. In the next two chapters, however, I will move beyond the claim that intellectual property laws potentially effect new forms of private censorship and show how intellectual property laws simultaneously constitute fields of signifying practice—shaping fields in which subjectivities are forged, communities and identities are framed, nations negotiated, and resistances to law's power performed and enacted in everyday life.

2. Author(iz)ing the Celebrity:

Engendering Alternative Identities

The white kids had the counter-culture, rock stars and mysticism. The blacks had a slogan which said they were beautiful, and a party demanding power. Middle America had what it always had: Middle America. The hawks had Vietnam, and the doves the Peace Movement. The students had campus politics, and the New Left had Cuba and the Third World. And women had a voice. I had rejection from each of them. I also had Judy Garland.—Drag Queen, a character in *As Time Goes By*, by Noel Grieg and Drew Griffiths[1]

Sex imposes a uniformity upon bodies for the purposes of reproductive sexuality. This is also an act of violence.—Angela McRobbie on Judith Butler, in *Postmodernism and Popular Culture*[2]

. . . new queer spaces open up (or are revealed) whenever someone moves away from using only one specific sexual identity category—gay, lesbian, bisexual or straight—to understand and to describe mass culture, and recognizes that texts and people's responses to them are more sexually transmutable than any one category could signify—excepting perhaps, that of queer.—Alexander Doty, *Making Things Perfectly Queer*[3]

Having categorized the right as property, some courts seem to think that they have little or no choice but to recognize its survivability. After all, an assignable interest that dies with its assignor is a very queer sort of property.—Michael Madow, "Private Ownership of Public Image: Popular Culture and Publicity Rights"[4]

Who authors the celebrity? Where does identity receive its authorization? I shall argue that the law constructs and maintains fixed, stable identities authorized by the celebrity subject but that the celebrity is authored in a multiplicity of sites of interpretive practice. The celebrity image is a cultural lode of multiple meanings, mined for its symbolic resonances. Focusing on cultural practices that appropriate celebrity images in the service of unanticipated agendas, I suggest that in such processes, unauthorized identities are produced, both for the celebrity and for her diverse authors.

In societies characterized by mass production, consumer capitalism, and mass-media communications, the celebrity image[5] holds both seductive power and significant economic and cultural value. Legal regimes simultaneously create, legitimize, and enable the realization of this value through doctrines of personality or publicity rights (and, less directly, through trademark and copyright laws). Celebrity names and images, however, are not simply marks of identity or simple commodities; they are also cultural texts—floating signifiers that are continually invested with libidinal energies, social longings, and, I will argue, political aspirations. The names and likenesses of the famous are constitutive of our cultural heritage and resonate with meanings that exceed the intentions or the interests of those they identify or resemble. I will very briefly summarize the legal doctrine of publicity rights[6] as it has developed in North America and the trend toward increasing the scope and duration of these rights. The social and cultural value of the celebrity image will be situated in the larger historical, political, and economic context of postmodernity and cultural practices characteristic of postmodernism.

In the cultural conditions of postmodernism, the commodification of cultural forms creates both generative conditions and prohibitive obstacles for the formation of alternative subjectivities. Celebrity images provide meaningful resources for the construction of identity and community. The law commodifies the celebrity subject and provides the means through which the celebrity may attempt to fix the identity and meaning of her persona. But in so doing, the law produces the possibility of the celebrity's polysemy. Focusing on a number of cultural practices that engage, reproduce, ironize, and sometimes transform the meaning of celebrity personas in order to produce and assert alternative gender identities for those who are socially marginalized, I argue that through its prohibitions, the law provides the means by which unauthorized identities are both engendered and endangered.

Popular cultural practices that engage celebrity images in innovative fashions illustrate the vibrant role played by these cultural icons in the self-authorings of minority, subaltern, or alter/native social groups. Gay male appropriations of female stars in camp subculture, lesbian refashionings of James Dean, and middle-class women's use of the *Star Trek* characters in the creation of fanzines are practices that recode pervasive images in a subversive but politically expressive manner. Investing celebrity personas with new and often oppositional meanings, subordinate groups assert unauthorized gender identities. They thereby affirm both community solidarity and the legitimacy of social difference by empowering themselves with resources afforded by mass media, which are nearly always the authorial properties of others.

The Value of the Celebrity Persona

What's the difference between Vanna White and a robot? Not much according to White, that woman of letters. The longtime gameshow cubist is suing Samsung Electronics America and its ad agency because of a humorous print advertisement that she claims pirated her celebrity. Several years ago the company ran a vcr ad that depicted a robot with a blonde wig, jewelry and alluring evening gown, turning giant letters on a video board . . . White was not amused . . . she [successfully] argued they had misappropriated her "identity."—*Newsweek*, April 5, 1993

Anglo-American legal jurisdictions recognize the right of individuals to protect publicly identifiable attributes from unauthorized and unremunerated appropriation by others for commercial purposes or economic benefit. In Canada and Britain, this right developed at common law into a distinct cause of action known as the tort of appropriation of personality. Some Canadian provinces also recognize the right in privacy statutes.[7] In the United States, the right of publicity arose as a category of the right of privacy that protects the individual against misappropriations of her name or likeness.[8] Various states have also incorporated these rights in privacy statutes and state constitutional provisions.[9] In both Canada and the United States, federal trademark legislation provides additional protections.[10] The literature detailing the origins and developing scope of these rights is so voluminous that a 256-page *bibliography* of relevant American literature was published in 1987.[11] Today the literature is even more extensive, and I make no effort to summarize the entire field.

Originally developed primarily to deal with an unauthorized use of a person's name or picture in advertising that suggested the individual's endorsement of a product, the right of publicity has been greatly expanded in the twentieth century. It is no longer limited to the name or likeness of an individual, but now extends to a person's nickname,[12] signature,[13] physical pose,[14] characterizations,[15] singing style,[16] vocal characteristics,[17] body parts,[18] frequently used phrases,[19] car,[20] performance style,[21] and mannerisms and gestures,[22] provided that these are distinctive and publicly identified with the person claiming the right. Although most cases still involve the unauthorized advertising of commodities, rights of publicity have been evoked to prohibit the distribution of memorial posters, novelty souvenirs, magazine parodies, and the presentation of nostalgic musical reviews, television docudramas, and satirical theatrical performances.

Increasingly, it seems that *any* publicly recognizable characteristic will be legally legitimated as having a commercial value likely to be diminished by its unauthorized appropriation by others. As we saw in the case of trademarks, recognition by the public is appropriated by the celebrity as intrinsic parts of a personality over which proprietary claims are made; again, *social* knowledge and *social* significance are expropriated as private properties. Some have even recommended that "any distinctive aspect of personality that sets that individual apart in the marketplace and imbues that unique human identity with commercial value" should be protected, such that if tomorrow's rage is "t-shirts sporting a shorthand reference to the DNA makeup of movie box-office idols," a celebrity would be protected against such (ab)use.[23] As other scholars assert, the right of publicity has grown massively in scope in the late twentieth century without clearly articulated grounds that would provide reasonable limitations for its scope and duration.[24] The rationales traditionally offered for recognizing and protecting rights to the celebrity persona cannot be empirically supported and certainly don't justify the extent of the protections legally afforded celebrities, their estates, or their assignees.

The right has been recognized as proprietary in nature[25] and may therefore be assigned and the various components of an individual's persona may be independently licensed. A celebrity could, theoretically at least, license her signature for use on fashion scarves, grant exclusive rights to reproduce her face to a perfume manufacturer, voice to a charitable organization, legs to a pantyhose company, particular publicity stills for distribution as posters or postcards, and continue to market her services as a singer, actor, and composer. The human persona is capable of almost infinite commodification, because exclusive, nonexclusive, and temporally, spatially, and functionally limited licenses may be granted for use of any valuable aspect of the celebrity's public presence. Furthermore, the right of publicity has been extended beyond the celebrity and his or her licensees and assignees to protect the celebrity's descendants or heirs.[26]

Although constitutional protections under the First Amendment privilege certain uses of celebrity names and likenesses, the definition of free speech that has developed in right of publicity cases is both narrow and inconsistently applied.[27] Focusing almost exclusively on the newsworthiness of the alleged appropriation and its ability to disseminate truthful information, courts have failed to consider other values that underlie our commitments to freedom of speech (as I will argue more fully in chapter 6). Freedom of expression is generally understood as essential to democratic self-government and as integral to the self-realization and self-expression constitutive of freedom in liberal societies. The recognition of exclusive proprietary interests in celebrity personas may impose real limits to the self-realization of those with alter/native agendas.

Celebrity Authorship

Cliff and Norm, the buffoon barflies on "Cheers," may have a sense of humor, but apparently the actors playing them don't. John Ratzenberger and George Wendt are suing Host International, which operates a chain of "Cheers" airport bars . . . Each has dark wood panelling, the woodcarving of a Native American near the door—and replicas of Cliff and Norm. While the talking robots are named Bob and Hank, they have physical similarities to the television characters and their conversation is equally insipid. So Ratzenberger and Wendt say they're being ripped off.—*Newsweek*, April 5, 1993

It is impossible to deny the potential value of the celebrity persona. The aura of the celebrity is a potent force in an era in which standardization, rationalization, and the controlled programming of production characterize the creation and distribution of goods. Mass-media communications convey imagery and information across vast distances to produce consumer demand. As mass-market products become functionally indistinguishable, manufacturers increasingly promote them by symbolically associating them with the aura of the celebrity—which may be the quickest way to establish a share of the market.[28] It takes years to establish a brand name but only months to capitalize on celebrity. It is suggested that fame has become the most valuable (and also the most perishable) of commodities[29] and that celebrity will have been the greatest growth industry in the nineties.[30] With its "alchemical power to turn the least promising of raw materials into alluring and desirable artifacts" (designer jeans, sunglasses, deodorants, architects' teakettles and coffee mugs), "fame's economic applications are limitless."[31] Originally a by-product of a successful film or athletic career, we now have celebrities famous simply for being famous (Gloria Vanderbilt, Paloma Picasso, and Vanna White come to mind). The value that a famous name adds to a product may be astronomical; London outworkers knit pullovers for

£6—with a Ralph Lauren tag they sold for $245 in New York—but Lauren had a $17 million annual advertising budget to cover.[32]

Celebrities, then, have an interest in policing the use of their personas to ensure that they don't become tainted with associations that would prematurely tarnish the patina they might license to diverse enterprises. Indeed, a new breed of lawyer has emerged, one who scouts remote corners of metropolitan areas for unauthorized commercial uses of celebrity images. This postmodern ambulance chaser advises the estates of the famous of potential avenues for successful lawsuits, demanding only a portion of eventual damages for a fee. Scouring the urban landscape for signs of renegade Elvis restaurants, unlicensed Marilyn likenesses, and other profitable piracies has become a lucrative occupation made possible by the legal recognition of publicity's value.

This potential commercial value is generally offered as reason in itself to protect the star's control over his or her identity through the allocation of exclusive property rights. Most commentators have defended the recognition and enforceability of exclusive property rights on the grounds of exigent economic necessity: because such interests have market value, they deserve protection.[33] Indeed, until the 1990s it was virtually impossible to find any alternative perspective on the right of publicity. Others, like myself, see this as "a massive exercise in question begging."[34] As Wendy Gordon notes, to propose that a right follows from the existence of potential value is to propound a principle with no coherent parameters.[35]

Market values arise only after property rights are established and enforced; the decision to allocate particular property rights is a prior question of social policy that requires philosophical and moral deliberations[36] and a consideration of social costs and benefits:

> It is sometimes said that the right of publicity rests on the commercial value of the interest itself, but that explanation is nonsense without something more. A claim of this sort will have commercial value only if it also has the protection of the law. In a sense, the value of this property stems from the fact that the law recognizes and protects it. Perhaps the question to be considered, then, is really two questions: first, whether there is a sensible basis upon which a claim can be made to rest beyond the value which protection undoubtedly will confer, and second, whether there is any offsetting consideration which might lead one to conclude that protection ought not be granted even though there is some legitimacy in the claim.[37]

In determining whether there is a sensible basis for granting a property right in a celebrity's persona, we might consider traditional liberal justifications in support of private property. The idea that people are entitled to the fruits of their own labor and that property rights in one's body and its labor entail property rights in the products of that labor derives from John Locke[38] and is persuasive as a point of departure. It does not, however, very far advance the argument in favor of exclusive property rights. As Edwin Hettinger remarks, "assuming that labor's fruits are valuable, and that laboring gives the laborer a property right in this value, this would entitle the laborer only to the value she added, and not to the *total* value of the resulting product."[39]

Publicity rights are often justified on the basis of the celebrity's authorship: his or her investment of time, effort, skill, and money in the development of a persona.[40] Such claims, however rhetorically persuasive, are rarely supported by any empirical data. How much of a star's celebrity and its value is due to the individual's own efforts and investments? Clearly, individual labor is necessary if the persona is to have value, and we could not appreciate celebrities without their expenditure of effort—but it is not usually sufficient for the creation of publicity value. But, as Hettinger argues with regard to intellectual properties more generally, "it does not follow from this that all of their value is attributable to that labor."[41]

Celebrity images must be made, and, like other cultural products, their creation occurs in social contexts and draws upon other resources, institutions, and technologies. Star images are authored by studios, the mass media, public relations agencies, fan clubs, gossip columnists, photographers, hairdressers, body-building coaches, athletic trainers, teachers, screenwriters, ghostwriters, directors, lawyers, and doctors. Even if we only look at the production and dissemination of the celebrity image and see its value as solely the result of human labor, this value cannot be entirely attributed to the efforts of a single person.

Moreover, as Richard Dyer illustrates, the star image is given value by its consumers as well as its producers; the audience makes the celebrity image the unique phenomenon that it is.[42] Selecting from the complexities of the images and texts they encounter, they produce new meanings for the celebrity and find in stars significative values that speak to their own experiences. These new meanings and significations are freely mined by the media producers of the star's image to further enhance its market value. As Marilyn Monroe said, in what are alleged to be her last recorded words in public, "I want to say that the people—if I am a star—the people made me a star, no studio, no person, but the people did."[43]

As Hettinger remarks, "simply identifying the value a laborer's labor adds to the world with the market value of the resulting product ignores the vast contributions of others."[44] The star image is authored by multitudes of persons engaged in diverse activities. Moreover, the star and her fame are never manufactured from whole cloth; the successful image is frequently a form of cultural bricolage that draws upon a social history of symbolic forms. Consider the Marx Brothers. Clearly, the construction of their characters involved creative activity and their characters were successful in the market:

> But what we cannot know in fact, and what I suspect strongly could not be proven now if one set out to do so with the best will in the world, is how much the characters created by the Marx Brothers owe to the work of tens, scores, perhaps hundreds of other vaudeville and burlesque performers with whom they came into contact during their early years in the business. What we do not know, in short, is how much of these characters the Marx Brothers themselves appropriated from others. All that is certain is that they created themselves, individually and collectively, as a kind of living derivative work. That much Groucho himself has told us, but even without his candid admissions, it would be foolish and indeed ignorant of the history of burlesque and vaudeville to doubt that they took what they wanted from what they observed among the performers they grew up with, perhaps adding, in the process, important new material of their own. To be sure, the Marx Brothers became celebrities as most vaudevillians did not. But surely we are not rewarding them on that ground alone. Even in an age as celebrity-haunted as this, we cannot mean to establish dynasties on the memory of fame.[45]

The "authorship rationale" for publicity rights goes beyond the contribution of labor, however, to stress the unique singularity of the individual's efforts in creating a persona. In a recent defense of the right, Roberta Rosenthal Kwall suggests that "fostering creativity" is one of the reasons for extending publicity rights, and asserts that, "whatever the means through which an individual's persona comes to have value, that value should be attributable to the persona of the publicity plaintiff . . . Thus even if others help mold a celebrity's image, the celebrity herself is still responsible for the vast majority of the profit potential of her persona. Those who assist the plaintiff in creating a marketable persona typically are paid for their efforts. Further, when a celebrity borrows from the cultural fabric in creating her persona, it is still the unique combination of the past and the persona's original contributions that give the persona its present appeal."[46]

The attributes that are legally protected as an individual's "persona," however, are those that are *publicly identified* with him or her; it is the degree to which the particular attribute is socially distinctive or publicly recognizable that determines its protection against unauthorized use. It does not follow that that which is most appreciated or distinctive in the public sphere is the attribute in which the celebrity has invested his or her labors, or that the celebrity himself or herself was not paid for efforts in the activities that made him or her famous. There is no guarantee that it is the celebrity's "original" contributions that give his or her image its "appeal" or even its profit potential. It might be an image's conformity to a conventional stereotype and a particular social attachment to that stereotype that give the persona its social meaning and value. Certainly any number of individuals have attempted to achieve celebrity with diligent effort, great investment, and the utmost originality and still failed to achieve any public recognition or social distinction. The social production of meaning and the totally unpredictable generation of public distinction are here neatly attributed to the unique and singular efforts of an author who, in addition to salary and fees, is also ascribed with a new form of cultural authority in the public sphere.

Dynasties established on the memory of fame have also provided sinecures for many who have merely inherited this authority. In Groucho Marx Productions, Inc. v. Day and Night Co., Inc., the successors to rights in the names and likenesses of the Marx Brothers made a successful publicity rights claim against the production company, producers, and authors of the Broadway play *A Day in Hollywood, a Night in the Ukraine*.[47] The authors of that play intended to satirize the excesses of Hollywood in the thirties and evoked the Marx Brothers as characters playfully imagined as interpreting a Chekhov play. The defendants were found liable for appropriating the Marx Brothers' personalities or violating their publicity rights, and their First Amendment privilege was dismissed on the ground that the play was an imitative work.[48]

The Marx Brothers *themselves* might be seen as imitative or derivative works, whose creation and success as popular cultural icons derives from their own creative reworkings of the signifying repertoire of the vaudeville community. Contemporary stars are authored in a similar fashion. How much does Elvis Costello owe to Buddy Holly, Prince to Jimi Hendrix, or Michael Jackson to Diana Ross? Take the image of Madonna, an icon whose meaning and value lie partially in her evocation and ironic reconfiguration of several twentieth-century sex goddesses and ice queens (Marilyn Monroe, obviously, but also Jean Harlow, Greta Garbo, Marlene Dietrich, Gina Lollobrigida, and perhaps a touch of Grace Kelly) that speaks with multiple tongues to diverse audiences. Academic descriptions of Madonna as semiotic montage abound,[49] but the following somewhat hyperbolic extract from a *Village Voice* article appeals to me: "What Madonna served up in the name of sexuality was not liberation as I'd known it, but a strange brew of fetishism and femininity. Only later would I understand that the source of her power is precisely this ambiguity. It's a mistake to think of any pop icon as an individual . . . Madonna is a cluster of signs, and what they add up to is precisely the state of sex in the culture now: torn between need and rage and unable to express one without the other . . . Madonna raids the image bank of American femininity, melding every fantasy ever thrown onto the silver screen and implanting them in the body and voice of every-babe."[50]

In an era characterized by nostalgia for the golden age of the silver screen and an aging baby boom generation's fascination with the television culture of its youth, successful texts and images are often those that mine media history for evocative signifiers from our past. This is not to deny that such appropriations and reconstructions are creative productions; it is to stress emphatically that they *are* and to assert that such creative processes ought not to be frozen, limited, or circumscribed by the whims of celebrities or the commercial caprice of their estates or assignees.

The Marx Brothers scenario illustrates the danger well. The producers of *A Day in Hollywood* used the Marx Brothers characters to speak to our relation to Hollywood in its heyday, much as the Marx Brothers brought the spirit and forms of vaudeville to speak to Depression America. As Lange sees it:

> What they sought to do, by their own account, "was to work a satiric comment on Hollywood movies using a parody of the Marx Brothers movies as one of the literary devices." The work they produced earned substantial public acceptance, and despite the court's opinion, has at least some claim to acceptance as a creative success as well. Yet the result of this litigation is that the work no longer can be performed as written without accommodating the plaintiffs in some fashion. In a case like this, then, what society loses is a right of access amounting to an easement. In at least a preliminary sense, this is always the result of upholding a claim to a right of publicity.[51]

Lange argues forcefully that the proliferation of successful publicity rights claims has occurred at the expense of individual rights in the public domain. The public domain is inadequately considered and rarely conceptually developed in juridical contexts; no one represents the public domain in intellectual property litigation or acts as its guardian, and rules of civil procedure currently prohibit the participation of third parties who will ultimately be affected (other artists, writers, and performers of current and future generations). As a consequence, access to the public domain is choked or closed off, and the public "loses the rich heritage of its culture, the rich presence of new works derived from that culture, and the rich promise of works to come."[52]

If the Madonna image appropriates the likenesses of earlier screen goddesses, religious symbolism, feminist rhetoric, and sadomasochistic fantasy to speak to sexual aspirations and anxieties in the 1980s and 1990s, then the value of her image derives as much, perhaps, from the collective cultural heritage on which she draws as from her individual efforts. But if we grant Madonna exclusive property rights in her image, we simultaneously make it difficult for others to appropriate those same resources for new ends, and we freeze the Madonna constellation itself. Future artists, writers, and performers will be unable to creatively draw upon the cultural and historical significance of the Madonna montage without seeking the consent of the celebrity, her estate, her descendants or their assignees, who may well deny such consent or demand exorbitant royalties.

We might consider whether certain celebrity images are so deeply embedded in the North American psyche and cultural subconscious that they constitute parts of a collective cultural heritage that should not be subject to control by the parochial interests of the celebrity's estate and assigns. Elvis Presley provides an apt example. In the film *Mystery Train*, Jim Jarmusch explored the cultural and psychological significance of Presley in the depressed economy of Memphis, Tennessee, and in the consciousness of those who live on its social margins. The film also addresses his charisma for those in other countries whose fascination with American media images manifests itself in pilgrimages that have turned Memphis into a late-twentieth-century mecca. Even the possibility that Elvis Presley's estate *might* seek to prohibit the production and/or distribution of a film such as this[53] while simultaneously arranging to market cologne designed "for all the King's men"[54] alludes to the parameters of the problem. The opportunity for the celebrity's heirs or assignees to behave in such a manner has, in fact, been seized in similar circumstances. When the city of Memphis decided to erect a bronze statue to memorialize Elvis as part of a city redevelopment scheme, and a nonprofit city corporation offered pewter replicas of the King in return for donations to finance the monument, owners of rights to commercially exploit the Presley likeness were quick to seek and obtain an injunction.[55] Neither Elvis Presley's manager's corporation, Factors, Inc., nor his family can completely control the uses to which his image is put, however. Elvis impersonators and fans create an ever-evolving Elvis folklore and collectively sustain a deep distrust for those mass-media versions of Elvis from which his estate and their official licensees continue to profit. Others author Elvis and forge their own norms of propriety about the use of his image.

A Lockean labor theory justifying property rights in the celebrity image is inadequate to establish a right to receive the full market value of the star persona or to establish exclusive rights to control its circulation and reproduction in society. Although a moral right to the fruits of one's labor must encompass a right to possess and personally use what one develops for one's own benefit and, perhaps, to exchange it on the market, this right need not necessarily be exclusive nor yield the full market value of such exclusivity.[56] Liberal values protecting individual freedom guarantee the possession and personal use of the product of one's labors only insofar as the exercise of this right does not harm the rights of others. As Wendy Gordon argues, deprivation of public domain and loss of access to cultural heritage are forms of harm that might be contemplated.[57] Moreover, rights to possess and personally use the fruits of one's labor do not necessarily entail the imposition of full property rights or rights to perpetually garner the full profits that such a product would yield in the market: "This liberty is a socially created phenomenon; the 'right' to receive what the market will bear is a socially created privilege, and not a natural right at all."[58]

If traditional liberal philosophy appears inadequate to encompass the range of social and cultural considerations that need to be addressed when defining the scope of publicity rights, other fields of intellectual property protection might seem to afford more guidance. However, if we examine traditional rationales for extending property rights to other forms of intellectual property, it becomes clear that the extension of property rights in cultural works is recognized as a socially bestowed privilege granted in exchange for social contributions and the bestowal of public benefits. (To spare the nonlegal reader, I have confined my comparison of the scope of publicity rights with other forms of intellectual property to an extended footnote.)[59] Publicity rights may be loosely analogized to rights granted by copyright, patent, and trademark laws, but none of these doctrines provides a degree of protection against unauthorized appropriation equal to that afforded celebrities. Moreover, all of these other areas of law contain limitations, exemptions, and defenses that recognize competing social and cultural interests.[60] Intellectual property protections were designed to provide limited rights in order to serve community goals and purposes; they make the exercise of individual property rights contingent upon the fulfillment of social responsibilities. Neither traditional liberal theory nor our rationales for recognizing limited property rights in artistic, literary, commercial, and scientific expressions justify the extent of contemporary publicity rights. Moreover, enabling celebrities, their estates, and their assigns to exercise absolute rights to control the celebrity image may have adverse consequences, both for the preservation of our collective cultural heritage and for our future cultural development. Judicial authority (albeit in dissent) is now available to support this claim: "Millions of people toil in the shadow of the law we make, and much of their livelihood is made possible by the existence of intellectual property rights. But much of their livelihood—and much of the vibrancy of our culture—also depends upon the existence of other intangible rights: The right to draw ideas from a rich and varied public domain, and the right to mock, for profit as well as fun, the cultural icons of our time."[61]

The Celebrity Form and the Politics of Postmodernism

The fact that celebrities haul so much semiotic freight in our culture has a number of important consequences.—Michael Madow, "Private Ownership of Public Image"[62]

Systems of mass production and mass-media communications have afforded opportunities for talented, beautiful, and/or charismatic individuals to achieve reknown across unprecedented distances and to have their fame survive for generations. These opportunities have been seized by individuals who seek to maximize their economic return. By recognizing the ability to exploit one's persona as an exclusive property right, the law has created a significant new source of economic value. In the process of developing individual economic rights, the law deprives us of collective cultural resources. The social value and cultural meaning of the celebrity image have their genesis in the same historical conditions that created the possibility of its economic value. In this section, I address the cultural significance of the celebrity image generally, and then explore the specific significance that particular celebrities have to select social groups. As it proceeds, this section becomes more ethnographic as

I submerge the reader in unfamiliar realms of "subculture" (although I might prefer to simply call them queer spaces)[63] before returning to the legal dilemma.

In his illuminating essay "The Work of Art in the Age of Mechanical Reproduction,"[64] Walter Benjamin suggested that technologies of mechanical reproduction and systems of mass production changed modes of human perception and evaluation, fundamentally altering our aesthetic responses. These changes, I would suggest, are integrally related to the cultural value of the celebrity image in contemporary social life. Benjamin argued that our experience of cultural imagery changed dramatically with lithography and photography. The work of art traditionally had a tangible individuated presence in time and space, a singular history, and a situation in a cultural tradition. This notion of the original, necessary to the idea of authenticity and to the work's authority, was maintained during the era of manual reproduction, but increasingly became irrelevant in an age of technical reproduction. Mass reproduction creates copies that possess an independence from the original; they can transcend the spatial and visual limitations of the original's physical tangibility and susceptibility to temporal and material processes of age and deterioration. As the artwork's substantive duration ceased to matter, the art object lost its authority or its *aura*—"the unique phenomenon of distance however close it may be."[65] The aura embodied the work's value by engaging the beholder's affective, reflexive relationship to the cultural tradition in which the work was situated. The artwork was unapproachable; both in its physically unique embodiment and in its tangible history in a cultural tradition, it resisted too intimate an appropriation by the beholder into his or her own physical and cultural lifeworlds.

The work of art's aura was lost in the age of mechanical reproduction because "the technique of reproduction detaches the reproduced object from the domain of tradition."[66] By substituting a plurality of copies for a unique existence it enabled the consumer to position the reproduction in his or her own domestic, social, and historical milieus without any necessary cognizance of an original or its historical situation. The photograph and the film, for Benjamin, represent the culmination of the destruction of the aura because they are designed for reproducibility: "From a photographic negative, for example, one can make any number of prints; to ask for the 'authentic' print makes no sense."[67] The criterion of authenticity ceased to be applicable to artistic reproduction. The uniqueness of a work of art was due to the work's situation in a traditional ritual context, whether that context was magical, religious, or secular. The "contextual integration of art in tradition found its expres-

sion in the cult"[68] that defined its use value. Technologies of mass reproduction enabled copies to transcend the work's historical use value in
social cults of ritual and to become pure objects of exchange value or
commodities.

Benjamin's reflections on the historical development of the work of
art and the decline of its aura may help us to understand the cultural
significance and seductive powers of the celebrity image. Here I want to
go beyond Benjamin's own disjointed observations on the topic. He saw
the screen actor as one whose performance was fragmented by the camera, alienated from the audience, deprived of his corporeality, and dis-
solved into flickering images and disembodied sounds.[69] The effect of
film was to engage the whole living person but to replace the actor's aura
with an artificially produced "personality" that was only the "phony spell
of the commodity."[70] Benjamin alludes to the possibility of another, alternative understanding of the celebrity when he refers to "the cult of the
movie star,"[71] however, an allusion that provokes one to ask whether
celebrities might represent residual vestiges of the "auratic" in contemporary mass culture.

If the work of art's aura derives from its unique, embodied, or tangible
presence in time and space, an individual history, and a situation in a
cultural tradition, then it is difficult to deny the aura of the celebrity.
However often a celebrity's likeness is reproduced, there remains a social
knowledge of the celebrity as an individual human being with an unapproachable or distant existence elsewhere, a life history, and a mortal
susceptibility to the processes of heartache, injury, illness, aging, and, ultimately, death. For example, it is difficult to envisage Elvis Presley without conjuring up images of health, vibrancy, and sexual energy followed
by self-inflicted injury, gluttony, corpulence, and decay. Arguably, celebrities evoke the fascination they do because however endlessly their images are reproduced, their substantive duration—that is, their life—
never becomes wholly irrelevant. They never lose their autonomy from
the objects that circulate in their likeness.

Moreover, the star is historically situated and lives his or her life in social conditions that give his or her image meaning, resonance, and authority. Part of the celebrity image's value might reside in its exemplify-
ing a particular human embodiment of a connection to a social history
that provokes its beholder to reflect upon his or her own relationship to
the cultural tradition in which the star's popularity is embedded. We all
consider celebrities from different social positions; as a feminist and social democrat, for example, I cannot perceive Marilyn Monroe without
reflecting upon my own troubled relationship to male definitions of fe-

male sexuality, the femininity of sexual innocence, the Playboy tradition, the cold war, and Monroe's own left populist politics.[72] Celebrity images, I would contend, always maintain their aura because they bind subjects in affective and historically mediated relationships that preclude their appropriation as pure objects.

Stewart Ewen sees the power of the celebrity image as rooted in photography's simultaneous affinity to reality and fantasy: "As Oliver Wendell Holmes had observed, the power of the disembodied image is that it can free itself from encumbrances posed by material reality and still lay claim to that reality. At the same time that the image appeals to transcendent desires, it locates those desires within a visual grammar which is palpable, which *looks real*, which invites identification by the spectator, and which people tend to trust. According to John Everard, one of the pioneers of commercial photography, it is this trust that makes photography so forceful as an advertising medium."[73]

The personal lives of celebrities, closely monitored and continually represented in the mass media, perform a function similar to that of commercial photography and similarly emerged with the image-making machinery stoked to maintain the perpetuation of contemporary consumer culture.[74] Ewen also sees the celebrity as a cultural response to modern social experiences of alienation and anomie—an icon of the significance of the personal and the individual in a world of standardization and conformity and the embodiment of the possibility of upward mobility from the mass: "Celebrity forms a symbolic pathway, connecting each aspiring individual to a universal image of fulfillment: to be someone, when 'being no one' is the norm."[75] The social potency of celebrity auras and the ubiquity of their presence in contemporary North American society make the celebrity persona a compelling and powerful set of signifiers in our cultural fields of representation. Simultaneously embodying the fantastic and the real, utopian ideals and quotidian practices, and the realization of popular aspirations for recognition and legitimacy, the celebrity form attracts the authorial energies of those for whom identity is a salient issue and community an ongoing dilemma.

But what meaning do particular celebrities have in the cultural lives of specific social groups in North American society? Focusing on a range of practices, engaged in by marginal social groups in nascent constructions of alternative identities, I attempt to make socially concrete the philosophical arguments I asserted earlier about the cultural losses contingent upon the commodification of the celebrity image. Moreover, I shall suggest that this foreclosure on the use of cultural resources has political dimensions. The practices I examine are those of gay male camp subcul-

ture in the preliberation era, lesbian refashionings of pop icons, and finally, middle-class women's engagement in the reading, writing, and circulation of *Star Trek* fan magazines ("fanzines"). These practices involve
the redeployment of celebrity images, an aspect of that rearticulation of
commodified media texts that has been defined as the essence of popular
culture. Many of the people I'll describe here are "fans," and fandom is
often "a vehicle for marginalized subcultural groups to pry open space
for their own cultural concerns within dominant representations . . . a
way of appropriating media texts and rereading them in a fashion that
serves different interests":[76]

> fans enthusiastically embrace favored texts and attempt to integrate
> media representations into their own social experience. Unim-
> pressed by institutional authority and expertise, the fans assert their
> own right to form interpretations, to offer evaluations, and to con-
> struct cultural canons. Undaunted by traditional conceptions of lit-
> erary and intellectual property, fans raid mass culture, claiming its
> materials for their own use, reworking them as the basis for their
> own cultural creations and social interactions. Fans seemingly blur
> the boundaries between fact and fiction, speaking of characters as
> if they had an existence apart from their textual manifestations,
> entering into the realm of fiction as if it were a tangible place they
> can inhabit and explore. Fan culture stands as an open challenge
> to the "naturalness" and desireability of dominant cultural hierar-
> chies, a refusal of authorial authority and a violation of intellectual
> property.[77]

In conditions of postmodernity, cultural consumption is increasingly
understood as an active use rather than a passive dependence upon
dominant forms of signification. As Michel de Certeau[78] and Paul
Willis[79] argue, consumption is always a form of production and people
continually engage in cultural practices of bricolage—resignifying media
meanings, consumer objects, urban spaces, and cultural texts in order to
adapt them to their own interests and make them fulfill their own purposes. The consumer is seen as actively reworking everything from the
design of the shopping mall[80] and the rhetoric of the romance[81] to mass-
marketed toy culture[82] in the articulation of alternative meanings and
identities. Commodified signs become cultural resources with which
new social and political realities are forged.

Hal Foster,[83] for example, views these practices of appropriating or
"recoding" contemporary cultural forms as the essence of popular culture, central to the political practices of those in marginal or subordi-

nated social groups, who construct subcultures with resources foraged from the mediascape.[84] Steven Connor sees postmodernism as (among other things) manifestations of "the central paradox of contemporary mass culture."[85] On the one hand, mass culture has enormous influence due to its global reach and penetration into the daily lives of millions of people, thus posing the possibility (or specter) of cultural unification and homogeneity. On the other hand, it provides resources for and contains the "capacity to tolerate, encourage, and engender a plurality of styles and identities."[86]

Cultural studies theorists defined subcultural practices to involve practices of appropriation and innovation of existing cultural forms in improvisations that provide opportunities for the affirmation of emergent cultural identities.[87] Dick Hebdige, for example, described the manner in which music styles like rap and hip hop deployed available symbolic and material forms using principles of parody, pastiche, and irony to articulate mixed, plural, or transitional identities for social groups at the margins of national or dominant cultures.[88] Angela McRobbie makes a similar case for optimism about the penetration of media imagery and communications into our psychic and social lives, arguing that the frenzied expansion of mass media enables new alliances and solidarities across traditional spatial, racial, and cultural boundaries as well as resources for producing new meanings and new identities.[89]

The constitution of provisional identities through the invocation of mass-media images, texts, and symbols is made possible when an audience is simultaneously absorbed and capable of ironic detachment. Lynda Hutcheon feels that this attitude defines postmodernism, "the name given to cultural practices which acknowledge their inevitable implication in capitalism without relinquishing the power or will to intervene critically in it."[90] This was an attitude Susan Sontag earlier described as the essence of camp, but one that McRobbie sees as shared by many consumers of mass culture in the condition of postmodernity:

> Sontag's linking pastiche with its favoured audience, gay men, is instructive because she shows how a relationship evolved around a social minority making a bid for a cultural form in which they felt they could stake some of their fragmented and sexually deviant identity. The insistence, on the way, on both style and pleasure made the product attractive to those outside as well as inside . . . Sontag's approach is useful because she is talking not so much about pure or original "artistic" invention. Rather she is describing how forms can be taken over, and re-assembled so as to suit the re-

quirements of the group in question. This often means outstripping their ostensible meaning and ostensible function . . . And if media forms are so inescapable . . . then there is no reason to assume that consumption of pastiche, parody or high camp is, by definition, without subversive or critical potential. Glamour, glitter, and gloss should not so easily be relegated to the sphere of the insistently apolitical.[91]

Ours is a world in which spatial and temporary distances can be quickly bridged through instantaneous communications. Ethnic, racial, class, and cultural boundaries are becoming less easily defined as a consequence of mass migration, immigration, transnational flows of labor and capital, and the expansion of mass markets. In this context, allegiances and identities are reconstructed. The breakdown of traditional communities has not resulted in social homogenization, however, but in a proliferation of differences organized along nontraditional lines. As Willis suggests, organic communities and organic communications are breaking down in the late twentieth century, and "proto-communities" are emergent.[92] Proto-communities "start and form not from intentioned purposes, political or other, but from contingency, from fun, from shared desires . . . they form from and out of the unplanned and unorganized precipitations and spontaneous patterns of shared symbolic work and creativity."[93] Such communities may evolve around a "consuming interest" in cultural commodities such as products of the communications media, with which new meanings are minted: "All popular audiences engage in varying degrees of semiotic productivity, producing meanings and pleasures that pertain to their social situation out of the products of the culture industries. But fans often turn this semiotic productivity into some form of textual production that can circulate among—and thus help to define—the fan community."[94]

Mass-media imagery allows people who share similar social experiences to simultaneously express their similarity by emotionally investing in a range of cultural referents to which media communications have afforded them shared access. It also enables them to author(iz)e their difference by appropriating and improvising with these images to make them relevant to their social experiences and aspirations. These images may serve to present these emergent identities in the public sphere in a manner that may be both aesthetically appealing and politically charged; we are culturally drawn to the image because of its presence in our own lifeworlds and, arguably, are therefore more likely to be sympathetic to the legitimacy of the forms of difference and aspirations expressed in its renarrativization by subaltern groups.

Doing Gender

I want to recall Benjamin's critique of the state's techno-fetishization of technologies of reproduction in the context of contemporary lesbian bodies—bodies working under a signifying regime of simulation and within an economy of repetition. Jean Baudrillard has defined postmechanical reproduction as the precession of simulacra, the accession of post World War II, postindustrial culture to a state of hyper-reality . . . The cultural reproduction of lesbian bodies in the age of (post)mechanical reproduction, that is, in an economy of simulacral repetition, has more than ever destroyed any aura of an "original" lesbian identity, while exposing the cultural sites through which lesbianism is appropriated by the political economy of postmodernity.—Cathy Griggers, "Lesbian Bodies in the Age of (Post)Mechanical Reproduction"[95]

Let us turn to specific examples of the cultural politics of authoring social identities through the improvisational use of celebrity images. The phenomenon of projecting new meanings upon celebrity images is no doubt widespread, because, as I suggested earlier, the celebrity is an image that is both fantastic and real and embodies the realization of popular aspirations for recognition and legitimacy. The star persona is especially likely to attract the energies of those in subordinate or marginal groups for whom social recognition and a positively evaluated identity are pressing concerns. Although the recoding of celebrity images is in no way limited to a concern with gender identity, I will focus on practices that question traditional formulations of gender and express desires to construct alternatives.

The social construction of gendered subjectivity is the central premise of an anti-essentialist feminism that understands sexual difference to be "a complex, ever-shifting social practice."[96] If sexual identities are culturally constructed, then we need to explore how specific gendered subjectivities are produced. Feminist poststructuralism has been characterized by a concern with the formation and reformation of gendered social subjectivities in fields of power and knowledge. Earlier I suggested that legal scholars needed to reconceptualize subjectivity in a manner that avoided both liberalism and essentialism and recognized the discursive constitution of subjectivity. I think this is particularly important for feminist legal scholars, for "one of the initial insights of the women's movement and one of the tenets of feminist discourse—that the personal is political—involves a recognition that there is a direct, albeit complex, relation between social life and subjectivity and between language and consciousness. The relation of experience to discourse is central to the very definition of feminism. The parameters of feminism correspond to certain subjective limits, limitations on possible subjectivities imposed by the constraints of language and sociohistorical structures of meaning. Within this range of constraints, however, women find possibilities for new configurations of subjectivity. . ."[97] Feminist historian Joan Scott suggests that we ask *how* categories of gender identity are constructed.[98] I take this question to contemporary domains of popular culture to consider the possibilities for new configurations of gendered subjectivity emergent there.[99] The celebrity icon figures centrally in many constructions of alternative gender identities; the law simultaneously enables and constrains these popular cultural practices. The law both engenders and endangers the production of alternatively gendered subjectivities; fortunately, it can never fully contain or control the direction of this cultural energy.

The concept of alternative gender identities is borrowed from Judith Butler's pathbreaking work *Gender Trouble*,[100] in which she suggested that a feminist politics required an inquiry into the political construction and regulation of gendered identities, a radical critique of the limitations of existing categories of identity, and an exploration of practices in which alternatively gendered worlds are imagined. The practices I explore here are active gender performatives "that disrupt the categories of the body, sex, gender, and sexuality and occasion their subversive resignification and proliferation beyond the binary frame."[101] Before we delve into these, we might ask why Butler believed such practices to be politically significant. One problem that has plagued feminist theory has been the effort to locate a common identity for a feminist politics. Traditionally presupposing "some existing identity, understood through the category of women, who not only initiates feminist interests and goals within discourse, but constitutes the subject for whom political representation is pursued,"[102] feminist theory has been challenged by poststructuralist theorists suspicious of the category of the subject, and by those (women) who refuse the category (woman) as insufficient to represent the complexity of their political identities.

Theoretically, Butler accepted the Foucauldian claim[103] that systems of power *produce* the subjects they supposedly served to represent, and they did so through political practices of domination and exclusion.[104] The feminist subject may "be discursively constituted by the very political system that is supposed to facilitate its emancipation"[105] and may, then, be defined, limited, and restrained by the requirements of these structures of power. Empirically, the insistence on a stable subject of feminism "generates multiple refusals to accept the category"[106] and "feminism thus opens itself to charges of gross misrepresentation."[107] Butler engaged in a genealogical critique to expose the foundational categories of sex, gender, and desire as the artifacts of a patriarchal, heterosexist system of power, invested in the maintenance of an exclusively or primarily reproductive sexuality.

Feminist theory long recognized a distinction between sex and gender, asserting "that whatever biological intractibility sex appears to have, gender is culturally constructed."[108] Even if we assume the stability of binary sex, it does not follow that genders will accrue to sexed bodies in a one-to-one mimetic relationship (i.e., that "women" will interpret only "female" bodies). The recognition of gender as cultural construct enables the possibility of a multiplicity of genders, and also raises the question of whether sex itself may not be produced through the limitations that restrict the performance of gender to a binary economy. In other words, if gender is a cultural or discursive construction, it is perhaps this very act of production that establishes sex as a "natural" fact, and provides the means by which it could be established differently. For Butler, identity is *articulated* from within existing cultural forms; regimes of power institute, maintain, and stabilize naturalistic and causal relations of coherence among and between sex, gender, sexual desire, and sexual practice, but such correspondences are neither "natural" nor inevitable.[109] Other identities that express discontinuous relations between biological sex, cultural gender, and the "expression" or "effect" of these in sexual desire and practice are persistent; their proliferation may provide critical opportunities for subverting and denaturalizing the cultural matrix that supports heterosexual and medicojuridical hegemonies.[110]

Gender, then, is *performative* (but not a performance), a doing and constituting of the identity it is purported to be: "there is no gender identity beyond the expressions of gender; that identity is performatively constituted by the very 'expressions' that are said to be its results."[111] Such enactments must of necessity draw upon existing cultural forms; sexuality and gender are always constructed within the terms of discourse and power, and thus must engage heterosexual cultural conventions:[112] "If sexuality is culturally constructed within existing power relations, then the postulation of a normative sexuality that is 'before,' 'outside,' or 'beyond' power is a cultural impossibility and a politically impracticable dream, one that postpones the concrete and contemporary task of rethinking subversive possibilities for sexuality and identity within the terms of power itself."[113]

Butler is interested in modes of "doing" gender that evoke but do not constitute simple imitations, reproductions, and consolidations of the terms of power but displace, subvert, and confuse the very constructs they mobilize, "displacing those naturalized and reified notions of gender that support masculine hegemony and heterosexist power."[114] The constructed character of sex and gender provides conditions of possibility for their deconstruction; as ongoing discursive practices, they are open to intervention and resignification. For example, "numerous lesbian and gay discourses understand lesbian and gay culture as embedded in the larger structures of heterosexuality even as they are positioned in subversive or resignificatory relationships to heterosexual cultural configurations."[115] The repetition of heterosexual cultural forms *may* also be the site of their denaturalization, bringing "into relief the utterly constructed status of the so-called heterosexual original."[116] As we shall see, celebrity images provide important cultural resources for practices of "doing" gender that subvert and reconstruct dominant forms of gender identity. Such practices, which do not choose, in any voluntarist or intentional way, to resist the normalization of sex/gender,[117] nonetheless pose the promise of an alternatively gendered world that displaces heterosexist cultural conventions even as it ironically evokes their forms.

Respecting Judy

The denaturalization of heterosexual cultural forms is readily apparent in gay camp subculture, a phenomenon I have already alluded to as involving an engagement with media-disseminated celebrity images. Andrew Ross argued that gay camp had a significant influence on changing social definitions of masculinity and femininity from the late 1950s, working "to destabilize, reshape and transform the existing balance of accepted sexual roles and sexual identities."[118] Whatever its ultimate cultural effects, its origins must be understood in the context of gay urban life in the preliberation period. In the 1950s and '60s, a sophisticated gay male subculture evolved around a fascination with classical Hollywood film stars such as Judy Garland, Bette Davis, Mae West, Greta Garbo, and Marlene Dietrich. As Richard Jackson put it, "in an age when their ability to be open about the fact that they were gay was circumscribed, gay men's 'use' of certain star images constituted a kind of 'going public' or 'coming out.'"[119] Camp contained a kind of commentary on the ongoing feat "of survival in a world dominated by the tastes, interests, and definitions of others":[120] "In its pre-Stonewall heyday (before 'gay' was self-affirming) [camp] was part of a survivalist culture which found in certain fantasmatic elements of film culture a way of imaginatively communicating its common conquest of everyday oppression. In the gay camp subculture, glamorous images culled straight from Hollywoodiana were appropriated and used to express a different relation to the experience of alienation and exclusion in a world socially polarized by fixed sexual labels. Here, a tailored fantasy, which never 'fits' the real, is worn in order to suggest an imaginary control over circumstances."[121]

This is explicated by Esther Newton, whose ethnographic study of drag queens and urban camp subculture in the late 1960s indicates that camp humor grew out of the incongruities of living gay and male in a patriarchal and heterosexist society during a period when the stigma of being gay was largely accepted and internalized rather than rejected as illegitimate. Drag queens were homosexual men performing the social character of "women" (that is, the signs and symbols of a socially defined American category) by artificially creating the image of glamorous women (often celebrities publicly affirmed as glamorous). Drag queens were often preeminent "camps," engaging the opposition between inner (subjective) self and outer (social) self in an assertive, theatrical, humorous, and stylized manner that defined a creative strategy for dealing with the homosexual situation.[122] As a practice, drag may perform a subtle social critique:

> the effect of the drag system is to wrench the sex roles loose from that which supposedly determines them, that is, genital sex. Gay people know that sex-typed behavior can be achieved, contrary to what is popularly believed. They know that the possession of one type of genital equipment by no means guarantees the "naturally" appropriate behavior . . . one of the symbolic statements of drag is to question the "naturalness" of the sex role system *in toto*; if sex role behavior can be achieved by the "wrong" sex, it logically follows that it is in reality also achieved, not inherited, by the "right" sex . . . [it] says that sex-role behavior is an appearance [or performance].[123]

Stars who were most popular in the camp pantheon, and the subject of most frequent impersonation, were "glamorous" in highly mannered ways that indicated an awareness of the artifice in which they were engaged: Bette Davis, Mae West, Greta Garbo, Marlene Dietrich, and, to a lesser extent, Marilyn Monroe. The most popular stars were those who acted in subtle ways "against the grain of the sexually circumscribed stereotypes they were contracted to dramatize."[124] This celebration of the personas of those "whose screen identities could not be fixed by the studio machine,"[125] who often fought for their own roles[126] and subtly mocked the "corny flamboyance of femaleness . . . defetishized the erotic scenario of woman as spectacle."[127] Thus, they explored the relation between artifice and nature in the construction of sexuality and gender long before these issues were recognized as part of the political agenda: "To nonessentialist feminism and the gay camp tradition alike, the significance of particular film stars lies in their challenges to the assumed naturalness of gender roles . . . Each demonstrates how to *perform* a particular representation of womanliness, and the effect of these performances is to demonstrate, in turn, why there is no 'authentic' femininity, why there are only representations of femininity, socially redefined from moment to moment."[128]

Greta Garbo, for example, was (and perhaps still is) regarded in the gay community as "high camp," according to Newton; as Parker Tyler put it, "Garbo 'got in drag' whenever she took some heavy glamour part, whenever she melted in or out of a man's arms, whenever she simply let that heavenly flexed neck . . . bear the weight of her thrown-back head . . . it is all impersonation whether the sex underneath is true or not."[129] Just as the covert homosexual must impersonate a "man" (or that social role as defined by the straight world), Garbo playing a "woman" was in drag, and life was theater. (As a performance, rather than a performative, such activities might simply reinforce and reidealize normative sex/gender systems, however.)

Judy Garland had a special place in gay culture as the symbol gay men used in the pre-Stonewall period to speak to each other about themselves.[130] She also symbolizes an important historical era. The period of camp's heyday is punctuated by Garland's repeated suicide attempts (1950–1969), and the Stonewall riots (which inaugurated a new gay political praxis and a rejection of camp) took place on the evening of Garland's funeral. Moreover, Garland occupies a unique role "expressing camp attitudes" because of her repeated shows of resilience in the face of oppression, her strength in the face of suffering, her determination to carry on with the performance no matter how exhausting and debilitating, and the disparity between her ordinariness in film roles and her extraordinary private life.[131] All of this resonated with gay men living on the edge between a stigmatized gay identity and the daily fragile performance of passing for straight.[132] Her failure at femininity and the hints of gender androgyny in her film performances also served to make the Garland image a compelling vehicle for gay men to use as a means of going public or coming out before less heavily coded assertions of identity became possible.[133]

Camp lost its appeal with the arrival of a militant gay politics that asserted the "natural" quality of homosexuality, revived "masculine" styles, and sought to undermine the "effeminacy" of the stereotypical gay image. As Al La Valley noted in 1985, the movement from negotiating gay sexual desire through strong women stars to a more direct appreciation of male celebrities was coincident with Stonewall: "the natural-man discourse with its strong political and social vision and its sense of a fulfilled and open self, has supplanted both the aesthetic and campy discourses."[134] The finale of Michel Tremblay's acclaimed play *Hosanna*[135] well illustrates the new attitude toward camp. Hosanna, an aging drag queen who identifies with and projects her identity upon Elizabeth Taylor, is humiliated and forced to renounce her attachment to the star and disarm herself of her Taylor impersonation. Stripped naked, he declares "I'm a man," and, at long last, it is implied, allows his lover to embrace his "true" "masculine" self. Camp has, however, enjoyed something of a resurgence in the 1980s, confluent, perhaps, with the influence of Foucault, poststructuralism, and a revival of the credibility of the notion of the socially constructed subject and the historical contingency of sexual identities. Judy Garland has survived the vicissitudes of gay politics, continuing as an icon of struggle into the 1990s. As Douglas Crimp writes of his longtime friend, "quintessential gay activist turned AIDS activist"[136] Vito Russo, "a very funny queer": "Reminiscing about Vito's pleasure in showing movies at home to his friends and about his unashamed worship of Judy Garland, Arnie summed up Vito's brand of gay militancy (or perhaps I should say, his gay brand of militancy): 'In Vito's house,' Arnie quipped, 'either you respected Judy . . . or you left.'"[137]

Lesbian engagement with celebrity images is a less documented and more recent phenomenon (although, as we shall see, "Judy" also has a certain significance here). Just as gays dignified and reclaimed Garland from the clutches of the star-making machinery that victimized her, there is some indication of lesbian identification with and resurrection of sixties female pop stars and "girl groups." In Toronto a band called the Nancy Sinatras reworks her songs and in a Queer Culture skit give Sinatra a lesbian identity and the opportunity to strike back at the patriarchal figures who controlled, contained, and ultimately, they suggest, crushed her in the sixties.[138]

In Jean Carlomusto's video, *L Is for the Way You Look*:

> nine women, speaking singly or in groups, tell the story of an evening at the Lower East Side performance space P.S. 122 when lesbian comedian Reno was performing. What made the occasion worth talking about was that someone special was in the audience ... Nancy leaned over to say, "Fran Liebowitz is over there ... " "We're both, you know, we both kinda have a thing for Fran ... there was a commotion on the stairway as the audience was leaving ... and all I see is this giant hair. It's almost like it could have been hair on a stick passing by, this platinum huge thing on this little black spandex." In case we haven't yet figured out what the commotion is about, Zoe adds another little clue: "I turned around, and I saw her breasts, I saw this cleavage, I saw this endowment, and, oh my God, I saw the hair, and it was ... Dolly Parton."[139]

Crimp proposes that the discussion in the video isn't really about Dolly Parton but about gossip and its significance in the construction of lesbian subjectivity and visibility; "Dolly is the absence around which a representation of lesbianism is constituted."[140] Communities are always constructed around identifications of particular kinds. Although Dolly Parton's rumored lesbianism makes her a more likely choice of object,

> the emphasis on signifiers of Dolly's feminine masquerade—huge hair, huge cleavage, tiny spandex miniskirt—by a group of women whose masquerade differs so significantly from hers implicates their identifications and their desire in difference. None of the lesbians visable ... looks femme like Dolly; compared with her absent image, they are in fact a pretty butch bunch. Identification, is, of course, identification with an other, which means that identity is never identical with itself. This alienation of identity from the self it constructs, which is a constant replay of a primary psychic self-alienation, does not mean simply that any proclamation will be only partial, that it will be exceeded by other *aspects* of identity, but rather that identity is always a relation, never simply a positivity ... perhaps we can begin to rethink identity politics as a politics of relational identities formed through political identifications that constantly remake those identities.[141]

Gossip, he suggests, serves important functions in the construction and reconstruction of queer identities. The experience of recognizing oneself when someone else is gossiped about as a fag or a dyke ("So that's what I am") enables identifications to emerge from derogations, confirmed as self-derogations that are then positively nuanced in queer communities through new identifications forged in gossip.[142] Such gossip often involves celebrities; their circulation makes them shared cultural knowledge, and the esteem in which they are generally held, as well as the iconic and semiotic dimensions of their personas, invite such identifications.

Fictionalized Sexualities

There is nothing much deader than a dead motion picture actor, and yet . . .
—John Dos Passos, *Midcentury*[143]

. . . more than any time since the fifties, James Dean now represents *the* coherent icon of our time. He is an American object whose nature is condensed energy, an objectification of attitudes simple and immediate enough to become a brand whose implicit value, like the Coke bottle, is reinforced through repetition . . . In the eighties, Levi Strauss made a series of commercials using James Dean look-alikes . . . one of the commercials features an actress wearing a cowboy hat and Levi jeans, with her boots up in an antique Rolls Royce convertible—imitating the classic James Dean pose in *Giant.*—David Dalton, *James Dean: The Mutant King*[144]

One lesbian challenge to the "truth" of sex, gender, and desire and the restrictions of a binary sexual economy is given voice and celebrated by Sue Golding in her discussion of a performative gender identity she calls lesbian hermaphrodism.[145] This "erotic sensibility," worn, felt, and enacted by a number of lesbians, is a "fictionalized sexuality" that finds its performative significations in mass-media icons that it replicates in ironic, playful, and assertive reconfigurations:[146]

> no tits, no cock, oozing with a kind of vulnerable "masculinity," sheathed in a 50's style black-leather motorcycle jacket. Or to put it slightly differently, it's James Dean, with a clit . . . What emerges is the "virile girl," the butch baby, full of attitude but not of scorn, lots of street smarts and a bit of muscle. This new hermaphrodite embodies forever the image of the destructive adolescent dramatically and in one being, teeming with a creative, raw energy, and beckoning with the possibility of a new era. She's the Peter Pan who reaches puberty and survives—her boyhood and her cunt intact, and ready. Most of all, she's public. But she's public in quite a different sense than meaning simply "out of the closet." For she is the orphan of a people's imaginary; a peculiar offspring of the avant-garde art

world, the butch 50's "diesel dyke," and that kind of feminism which knew above all that sexual difference was ever only a *political* and not biological category. She is public in the most profound sense of the term: a composite copy of a mass invention, a replica of our own societal icons, which are themselves never anything other than a public fiction. She is James Dean over and over again: James Dean with his arrogant hair, James Dean with his tight black denims, James Dean with the bitter brat look, James Dean with the morbid leather boots, James Dean against the whole boring suburban middle class . . . [147]

As Golding makes clear, this is an erotic sensibility or sexual identity that rejects the truth of anatomical sex and goes well beyond the idea of gender as a cultural construction built upon a naturally sexed body that provides a politically neutral surface for multiple significations. Or, as Butler poses it:

> The cultural matrix through which gender identification has become intelligible requires that certain kinds of "identities" cannot "exist"—that is, those in which gender does not follow from sex, and those in which the practices of desire do not "follow" from either sex or gender . . . Indeed, precisely because certain kinds of "gender identities" fail to conform to those norms of cultural intelligibility, they appear only as developmental failures or logical impossibilities from within that domain. Their persistence and proliferation, however, provide critical opportunities to expose the limits and regulatory aims of that domain of intelligibility, and, hence, to open up within the very terms of that matrix of intelligibility rival and subversive matrices of gender disorder.[148]

Demonstrating that gender identity (construed as a causal or natural relationship among sex, gender, sexual practice, and desire) is the effect of a regulatory practice that reproduces medical and juridical hegemonies, this gender rebel without a cause also rejects prior forms of "gender trouble" that accepted and worked within the terms of the natural sex/ cultural gender dichotomy. This hermaphrodism bears no relation to a biological hermaphrodism "connected to some formulaic equation of the x and y chromosome, scientifically tested in relation to the size and shape of the breast and clitoris"[149] (except insofar as nineteenth-century science labeled *all* women hermaphroditic whose sexual orientation was nonheterosexual, insufficiently submissive, or masturbatory). Neither,

Golding makes it clear, is this a '60s androgny that built around an absence or sameness of the sexual organs, nor a '70s sexual aesthetic "born out of an acknowledged irony of the ways in which society enforces gender specific clothing."[150] Rather, this gender rebel performs with her body an erotic identity that is an embodied performative: "'a fiction as "real" as the specific body parts of her hermaphroditic predecessor. Only this time, her "truth," the clues to her sexual transgression will never be found in the physical attributes of her body *per se*, but only in their "look," only in the defiant aesthetic of the erotic masculine shot through with the voluptuousness of the female sexual organs' [and] 'the celebration of female genitalia' that refuses definition as 'a bleeding wound of castrated cock.'"[151] An "erotic mutant," "a fractured playfulness of social icons [like the Dean image, although Elvis Presley offers other possibilities, as k. d. lang might suggest] copied over and over again,"[152] the lesbian hermaphrodite enacts a performative signification that parodies, proliferates, and subverts gendered meanings. To what extent this particular performative engenders communities as well as identifications, however, is never made clear.

"Doing gender" is not the exclusive preserve of gays and lesbians, however more likely the social conditions of their existence are to incline them to contest hegemonic norms of gender identity. This will be clarified by an examination of the activities of certain groups of North American science fiction fans who articulate new gender identities and construct communities by literally rewriting their favorite television series characters into narratives that express their fears and aspirations.

Enterprising Women

The science fiction fan world structures itself around a series of conventions; media fans constitute a distinct fan world and *Star Trek* is one of a number of television and movie series around which a fan community has emerged. *Star Trek* fans constitute a social and cultural network that is international in scope. Within this community itself, there are distinct groups of fans that organize around the production, circulation, and consumption of fan magazines.[153] The fanzine community is almost exclusively female and predominantly heterosexual. It involves middle-class women who work as housewives and in nursing, teaching, and clerical and service occupations.[154] Fans exchange letters, distribute newsletters, create artworks, make videotapes, and produce and circulate fanzines that contain original fiction, poetry, and illustrations by women across North America, Britain, and Australia. I will focus here on the *Star Trek* fanzine community, a subculture explored with great sensitivity by Camille Bacon-Smith in her sparkling ethnography *Enterprising Women*.[155] As well as attending conventions, fanzine community members may belong to clubs that distribute newsletters, and see themselves as members of a larger fan community or interest group (250 to 500 participants) and its constituent parts—local circles (of ten to thirty women) who gather at weekend house parties where they talk, watch videos, read fanzines, work out stories, and establish interpretive norms for their reading and writing activities.[156]

Usually produced out of women's homes, fanzines are generally mimeographed or photocopied productions, but some have become more sophisticated with the introduction of computerized desktop publication technology; most issues are more than a hundred pages long.[157] In 1988, it was estimated that there were 300 publications that enabled fans to explore aspects of television series, 120 of them centered on *Star Trek*,[158] a number that no doubt *underestimates* the production of fan literature because it doesn't include literature circulated only in photocopy circuits or the more covertly circulated publications.[159] These publications are sold at cost, relying on subscriptions and often prepayment to finance production and distribution costs; producers are motivated more by the desire to express identity and establish community than any monetary interest and often operate at a loss.[160] Fans are aware of the copyright status of the source products on which they draw and know that neither writers nor publishers may legally profit from their work.

In their writings and drawings, contributors to the fanzine employ images, themes, and characters from a canonized set of mass-culture texts (the *Star Trek* television series episodes, films, and commercially produced novels) to explore their own subordinate status, voice frustration and anger with existing social conditions, envision and construct alternatives, share new understandings, and express utopian aspirations.[161] In so doing, they force media texts to accommodate their interests, to become relevant to their needs, and thereby empower themselves with mass-culture images. In their creative reworking of *Star Trek* imagery, fanzines create new female communities, new personal identities, and, I will argue, alternative gender identities. These activities create new relationships between those who contribute to fanzines and the larger world, forge a sense of community and extensive social networks, and provide new possibilities for individual expression.[162] Above all, these are shared *social* activities:

Elaine Showalter picks up the metaphor of quilt-making when she describes women writing commercially and her analysis applies equally to fan writers. Using well known communal patterns, the craftsperson creates a work like a quilt top, unique in the way it combines the familiar elements with the distinctly personal statement she makes through her selection of elements . . . Women fan-writers, like the women who wrote gothic romances in the 1850's, value their workmanship in the community, but place little or no emphasis on the concept of "auteur" as solitary creator of an aesthetically unique piece of art. In the fan community, fiction creates the community. Many writers contribute their work out of social obligation, to add to the discourse, to communicate with others. Creativity lies not in how a writer breaks with the tradition of the community's work, but in how she uses the language of the group to shed a brighter light on the truth they work to communicate. Commercial television fits uniquely into this scheme of women's culture . . . television is a readily available source of infinitely combinable but specifically not unique elements. They borrow wholesale from the television sources [to construct fictional "universes" with which they organize their own social worlds].[163]

Star Trek fans characterize their entry into fandom as a movement from the social and cultural isolation imposed on them (both as women in patriarchal society occupying low-paid jobs and as seekers of pleasure within media representations) toward more active participation in a community where cultural creativity is encouraged and appreciated.[164] Star Trek episodes and characters are revised and reworked and new texts are authored to reclaim female interests, experiences, and feelings from a set of common references that women separated by great distances can share. Issues of gender roles, sexuality, and the tension between family obligations and professional ambition are explored. The Star Trek future world holds out the promise of opportunities for nontraditional female pleasures, active involvement in decision making, and a state of sexual equality in which emotional needs and professional responsibilities are taken seriously by men and women alike.[165] Many early stories featured a young, well-educated woman who was desirable, competent, and moral, simultaneously winning the love and respect of the Enterprise crew and ultimately the romantic interest of one of the major male characters. These "Mary Sue" stories, however, produced great discomfort and ambivalence in the community, although most fan writers have written at least one, usually early in their careers.[166]

Contemporary fanzine editors now refuse to publish them. Bacon-Smith suggests that in this writing, women are engaged in re-creating adolescent selves that they may now feel shame or pain in recalling:

> Fans often recount the scorn they experience for their "masculine" interest in science fiction and action adventure. These readers grew up in a period during which active, even aggressive behavior was acceptable for prepubescent girls who were expected to put away their grubby corduroys and baseballs, their books that chronicled the male fantasies of exploration and adventure, when they entered adolescence. With the teen years girls were expected to turn to make up, curlers, and high heel shoes to attract the attention of boys . . . The teenaged girl had to be not just seductive, but non-threatening; she could not challenge the supremacy of the male or in the classroom.[167]

Many women in fandom couldn't successfully make this transition—they were too tall, too "serious," wore glasses, were unable or unwilling to mask their intelligence—and "Mary Sue" reconciles the felt anomalies of their identity. Combining the characteristics of active agent with culturally approved traits of beauty, sacrifice, and self-effacement, she wins the love of the hero: "We can easily see that Mary Sue is a fantasy of the perfect woman created within the masculine American culture. Men are served by Mary Sue, who ideally minimizes her own value while applying her skills, and even offering her life, for the continued safety and ease of men. Even in her superiority Mary Sue must efface her talents with giggles and sophomoric humor. She must deny that her solutions to problems are the result of a valid way of thinking, modestly chalking up successes to intuition."[168] "The writer, become reader, recognizes Mary Sue's childish behavior as a coping mechanism she has used herself or observed in her friends to mask the threat their own intelligence and competence poses to men."[169] But once in fandom, women encourage each other to leave such camouflage behind and construct alternative roles: "Women in the fan community have rejected Mary Sue and the cultural role of precocious child, and in many cases have replaced her with the Matriarch in the genre referred to as "Lay" stories, so named because the alter-ego heroine develops a sexual relationship with the hero. Her adventures are an adjunct to his world and her demeanor is one of matriarchal dignity outside of the bedroom and politically correct sensuality within it."[170]

In "Lay" stories, however, women appear to be more engaged in rewriting the masculine gender than in imagining alternative feminine ones. In particular, the stories teach women how to deal with male sexuality—an uncontrolled or unpredictable internal physical urge coupled with a controlled, emotionless exterior. The female heroine is an intelligent, supportive woman who (often after a period of subjugation and oppression) helps her partner to accept his emotions and recognize that true love and sexual satisfaction grow out of mutual respect and trust. Even these women, however, are being increasingly dismissed as falling into the contemptuous category of Mary Sue, and the lack of strong female characters in most fanzines "signals a continuing dissatisfaction with the options available to women characters and to women in society."[171]

Stories focusing on women represent very few of the stories fanziners read and many more stories involve male friendships. Two significant genres of fanzine fiction are "Slash" (or homoerotic) and "Hurt/Comfort" stories, both of which center on relationships between the male characters in the series. In all of these stories, the links among anatomy, gender, desire, and sexual practice are sundered. In the male friendship stories, the male characters are alternatively engendered; stripping them of a rationalist, ego-centered individualism, the fans imbue them with emotionality and empathy, knitting them into close family and community relationships as well as intimate caring friendships that nurture and support them in their adventures.[172]

In "Slash" fiction, women write erotic stories and draw illustrations depicting a love relationship between Kirk and Spock (erotic fiction is also written about the *Starsky and Hutch, Blake's 7, The Man From U.N.C.L.E, Miami Vice,* and *The Professionals* characters). Fearing social ridicule, loss of employment, and potential legal repercussions, fanzine writers often write such stories under pseudonyms, although within the community most of the authors' identities are known. Some of this literature circulates only through complex subterranean photocopying networks in order to evade exposure outside of the group.[173] So well-hidden is the circuit that only the most experienced readers and writers have access to it. Within this realm of secrecy and risk women explore and express personally painful and significant themes: "Homoerotic fiction addresses some of the most risk-laden questions in the community. It protects the questioner from direct exposure of some of her deeper anxieties, but conserves the risk with a level of metaphor that offers the greatest distance but which itself poses the greatest danger from within and without the community."[174] Some fans oppose these stories on religious or moral grounds, others find them "untrue" to the source or canon, some find them too explicit, and others worry about exposing the original actors to ridicule. Both outside and within the community, writing "Slash" fiction is risky business. Similarly, in the relationships depicted, "romantic love is fraught with risk—of trust broken, of exposure or even loss of the self, of society's disapproval, or of misinterpretation of the intent of the partner—and the prize for risking all is perfect physical and psychic fulfillment,"[175] represented by the mind meld or telepathic union.

Bacon-Smith describes a number of tasks performed by the homoerotic romance in the communication of personal needs and experiences and rejects the idea that the male characters are surrogate women, an idea popularized by Joanna Russ when she argued that because of the overriding importance of touch, to the slow thoroughness and sensitization of the whole body, the sexuality expressed is female.[176] For Russ, "the penis is a sign, literally, behind which the woman can express femaleness free of male domination."[177] Bacon-Smith, however, asserts that these women are writing consciously and deliberately about men,[178] exploring who men are and reconstructing them into people with whom it might be more comfortable to share life, love, and sexual relationships.[179] Certainly, "sexual experiences with men, as they are presently enculturated, can seem intimidating to heterosexual women," and a number of fans "openly express a need for more satisfying sexual relationships."[180] These women also want to explore relationships between powerful equals while tearing "down the very institution of hierarchical power that constructs men as individuals"—reconstructing power itself as an integrated union of mutuality with full and open communication.[181]

In both "Slash" fiction and "Hurt/Comfort" stories,[182] as well as the friendship stories described earlier, the "male" characters are given a combination of gender traits: Kirk's "feminine" traits are matched to Spock's "masculine" ones and vice versa. Each shares aspects of traditional gender roles. In this way, new genders are inscribed on "male" bodies, and new desires, experiences, feelings, and practices may therefore proliferate.[183] Men's suffering, rage, and need for comfort can thus be acknowledged as well as male violence and the need that women feel to be the recipients as well as the bestowers of comfort.[184]

As well as being alternatively engendered, the male characters are freshly embodied; their bodies are inscribed with ranges of sensitivity, zones of erogeneity, and a heightened receptivity to tactile pleasures and physical comfort: "women in the fan community prefer images that reclaim the sensuality of the whole body . . . hands are perceived as sensual, and faces as vulnerable, hands touching a face in an environment of trust symbolize sensuality as protective . . . kisses to the neck, the wrists, the inner arm elicit as strong a reaction as mouth to mouth osculation; women viewers seem to value the rediscovery of some of these more neglected erogenous zones."[185] Their heroes' pain, decontextualized in the mass media, is reunited by fanzine writers with both physical and psychological suffering. The male characters, then, are reconstructed as fully emotional and sentient beings. Perhaps the fanzine writers perform the most thorough practices of "doing gender" that we have examined. Constructing new connections among novel (male?) bodies, new masculinities, erotic desires, and sexual practices, they simultaneously situate these newly engendered creatures in personal and social relationships, empowering themselves and their communities as they do so.

In writing about gender and fanzines as an academic engaged in the production of an authorial work, however, one's authority and one's work are themselves open to the subversion of other authorial energies. Postmodernism is a condition in which genres blur, popular culture and high culture dance seductively, academic commentators can become celebrities, and academic critique can itself become the stuff of parody and fanzine fantasy. One fanzine has turned Judith Butler's own persona into a celebrity image available for the fantastic fabulations of its apparently lesbian graduate student readership. Simply titled *Judy*, the first issue proudly proclaims that all of its texts are anticopyright: "Copy this whole thing if you want; send it to your friends, that's cool—saves me money. Isn't this whole copyright thing out of hand? Go ahead, copy it at Kinko's."[186]

The fanzine features two pictures of Judy Garland with the apology that "it's really hard to find pictures of Judith Butler so here is another Judy."[187] It also features ironic and lusty commentary on several other theorists of gender and sexuality. Declaring itself "a non-academic, sex-oriented, wish-fulfillment magazine,"[188] it includes, in true *Cosmopolitan®* fashion, a special quiz to determine whether you're "a theory-fetishizing biscuithead" or "an illiterate pre-theory peon." This author finds herself guilty, as charged.

Engendering and Endangering Alternative Identities

. . . the very conceptualization of "sex" and "gender" underlying legal categorization creates difficulties that cannot be resolved through resort to static, binary, essentialized approaches. Instead . . . it will be necessary to challenge the system of classification itself in fundamental ways to take account of the ambiguities of homosexual and transsexual identity . . . these identities [are] themselves a challenge to the stable system of identity formulation that lies at the heart of U.S. legal discourse—a challenge that could be destabilizing if not contained. —Elizabeth Mertz on Lisa Bower, in "A New Social Constructionism for Sociolegal Studies"[189]

These subcultural or alter/native practices at first seem distant, if not divorced, from the legal regime of publicity rights, but they do occupy cultural spaces in the social fabric intersected and influenced by relations of law, commodification, and cultural form. We need to think about law not simply as a set of prohibitions, but as an authoritative and pervasive discourse that defines, shapes, and is imbricated within the everyday life of cultural practice. The risks these people run under legal regimes of prohibition *are* certainly significant ones. So are the ethical risks of writing about their practices. Bacon-Smith, Jenkins, and Penley have been very careful not to reveal details about or examples of particular fanzine writing, filming, and drawing practices or the identities of practitioners. I respect their circumspection and similarly will not, as a matter of ethical principle, delineate the precise ways in which fanzine writers or those in gay and lesbian subcultures could be held to violate either publicity rights or the copyright and trademark rights held by the commercial producers of the media products on which they draw. To do so would be to provide the legal resources with which to prosecute them, or with which they might once again be threatened with the prospect of legal action.[190]

It is important, however, to recognize that juridical power is productive as well as prohibitive; the law, as discursive cultural practice, is generative of categories, distinctions, and valuations—of knowledges, spaces, identities, and subjectivities.[191] As Lisa Bower suggests, law simultaneously limits the aspirations and claims of individuals and groups and provides resources for the marginalized to refigure identities; people recreate law in their everyday lives as they draw upon its norms and forms in both conventional and transformative practices.[192] Bower goes beyond such claims, however, to add that law also plays a constitutive role in creating cultural spaces for politicization and community formation.

The law of publicity rights functions in just such a fashion—or at least these are some of its unanticipated consequences. By prohibiting public reproductions of the celebrity image for another's advantage, it promotes the mass circulation of celebrity signifiers by ensuring that they will have a market value; if the image were freely available for mass reproduction, there would, presumably, be less of an incentive to engage in the investments necessary to disseminate it through media channels (the same argument might be made for copyright and trademark). Ironically, then, the law creates the cultural spaces of postmodernism in which mass-media images are authorized and become available for the authorial practices of others. It produces fixed, stable identities authored by the celebrity subject, but simultaneously creates the possibility of places of transgression in which the signifier's fixity and the celebrity's authority may be contested and resisted. Authorized and unauthorized identities are both, therefore, engendered in relation to this juridical regime. The law, however, lends its authority only to those meanings that the celebrity wishes to appropriate, attributing these to his or her own efforts, and denies that legitimate cultural value may be produced elsewhere.

Power may be in a productive relation with forms of resistance, but it does not determine the content of the practices that transgress its strictures. Through its prohibitions, the law may produce the means by which unauthorized identities are both engendered and endangered, but these practices are not simply effects or consequences of juridical regimes. People's interests and inclinations to engage in the construction of alternative gender identities are shaped by multiple hegemonies. Performative enactments of erotic identity are unlikely to be direct or univocal statements of opposition to any singular structure of power; more often they effect diverse forms of cultural "resistance" to multiple sites and forms of power. Through irony, mockery, parody, pastiche, and even alternative modes of appreciation, activities of creative appropriation enable fans to comment indirectly not only on gender ideology, but on law, culture, authorship, authority, and the commodity form.

Such commentary is especially cogent in the fanzine context. Fans don't see *Star Trek* as something that can be reread but as something that must be rewritten in order to make it more responsive to female needs and a better producer of personal meanings and pleasures.[193] According to Henry Jenkins, fans expressly reject the idea that the *Star Trek* texts or the Kirk/Spock characters are a privileged form of exclusive property, but at the same time they have developed a complex moral economy[194] in which they legitimize their unorthodox appropriation of the texts, characters, and personas drawn from the television series. Despite the potential for legal prosecution, they see themselves as loyalists, fulfilling the inherent promise and potential of the series—a potential unrealized or betrayed by those who "own" the intellectual property rights in it. Fans respect the original texts, and regularly police each other for abuses of interpretive license, but they also see themselves as the legitimate guardians of these materials, which have too often been manhandled by the producers and their licensees for easy profits.[195] As one fan writes: "I think we have made Star Trek uniquely our own, so we have all the right in the world . . . to try to change it for the better when the gang at Paramount starts worshipping the almighty dollar as they are wont to do."[196] Fan writers exercise an ethic of care with regard to the characters—a care they fear that more commercially motivated parties frequently do not share.

In *Enterprising Women*, Bacon-Smith also illuminates the complexities of the attitudes fanziners hold with regard to the legal status of the source product. On the one hand, they are aware that the characters, plots, films, television episodes, videos, logos, and dialogues with which they work are the properties of others. On the other hand, they take quite seriously the philosophy of IDIC (Infinite Diversity in Infinite Combination), propogated by Gene Roddenberry, the originator of *Star Trek*. They respect the legal prohibition against selling their writings, videotapes, and artworks for profit, but the possibility that many of their activities might still be enjoined on copyright, trademark, or publicity rights grounds does not appear to operate as a serious deterrent. These women know they assume risks of legal prosecution, but legal risks are only a very few and possibly the most distant of the risks they face; indeed, Bacon-Smith implies that the assumption, management, and shared exploration of risk is the central ethos of the community and constitutive of the construction and reconstruction of culture in which they engage.

Bacon-Smith also discusses the moral economy in which fans operate (although she does not expressly employ the term). She suggests that fans have a respect for the characters and relationships as they are presented in the source product devised by the commercial producers, which serves as "the source of infinitely combine-able but specifically not unique elements. A fan does not change the status of the characters by adding permanent wives or children, or killing or maiming one of the main characters. The writer works hard to create in her stories characters that speak like the ones on television, and whose personalities match the screen product. Consonant with the science fiction assumption that any change from the known history splits off a timeline, or universe ongoing simultaneously to all others, writers who do permanently change the status of a character or characters are said to create a new universe . . . [creating] their own universes, with characters and relationships that exist only in the stories their creators write."[197]

There *are* aspects of the original story and episodes that fans reject, however. For example, fans insist upon seeing characters grow and evolve and engage in relationships that change them as people. They reject linear narratives, aperspectivity, and closure. They don't see either the original episodes or their own stories as a self-sufficient work but as an expression of a continuing experience. At the end of the story characters go on living and changing; later in their lives they may recall the events of the original story differently, or perhaps the events, told from the perspective of another character, tell a different story. There is, then, no final or authoritative account of an event or experience; stories can and must be rewritten according to new perspectives: "The linear story with a single narrative perspective per scene is so alien to this group that they use their fiction to 'correct' the error of linearity in the source products. The fan writers see life as a sea of potentialities, many of which can be realized simultaneously, many of which spread out like ripples across the lives of others, and all of which must somehow be encompassed in the literature if it is to express any kind of truth . . . a worldview that sees every interaction as a multi-layered experience out of which reality is negotiated."[198]

Fans clearly engage in moral deliberation and dialogue when considering the legitimacy of particular activities. These amateur writers and the professional science fiction writers on whose works they have drawn have had to consider the vexed question of what distinguishes the activities of "a community in dialogue" from simple copyright infringement: "Many writers who express concern about the loss of autonomous control of their creation actually embrace the idea of sharing their worlds with their friends—we are not speaking of two groups of professional writers at odds, but of battles being waged within the heart and mind of each individual."[199]

Moreover, the fan community has a relationship with the stars of the various series from which they borrow. Although I know of no publicity rights suits, it is clear that celebrities regard these fan activities with some ambivalence. Stars are often asked to appear at conventions and many of them feel a sense of obligation to the fans for their support. Often they become aware of the fanzines and feel flattered by the attention. Robin Curtis (Saavik in the two *Star Trek* movies) said: "I really had no idea that this all existed . . . I don't know that I'll ever stop being amazed . . . really, the care and the time which people devote to something . . . It is really quite an honor to be the receiver of that kind of appreciation . . . [but] I haven't read it, to be honest with you."[200]

Other celebrities *have* read the literature and responses seem mixed. Constance Penley notes that Shatner and Nimoy have commented appreciatively on fanzines generally and found the homoerotic texts surprising but not inconceivable given what they now see as the "campiness" of some of the old episodes.[201] Other stars have viewed these texts less benignly. One actor in *Blake's 7* encouraged fanzine writing, but upon discovering his fictive presence in homoerotic fiction, withdrew his support and attempted to blackball the writers within the fan community itself.[202] *Starsky and Hutch* fans worried that public exposure of "Slash" literature would hurt the reputations of stars they regarded with respect and affection; they insisted upon keeping the product underground to protect their heroes.[203]

Relations with the corporate producers of their source texts are more complex. Although some program producers and network executives celebrate the ongoing involvement of fans in the production of derivative texts, others see such activities as competitive and as threatening to their goodwill. In extreme cases, producers may try to bring fan activities under control:

> Lucasfilm initially sought to control *Star Wars* fan publications, seeing them as rivals to their officially sponsored and corporately run fan organization. Lucas later threatened to prosecute editors who published works that violated the "family values" associated with the original films. A letter circulated by Maureen Garrett (1981), director of the official *Star Wars* fan club, summarized the corporation's position: "Lucusfilm Ltd. does own all rights to the Star Wars characters and we are going to insist upon no pornography. This may mean no fanzines if that measure is necessary to stop the few from darkening the reputation our company is so proud of . . . You don't own these characters and can't *publish* anything about them without permission."[204]

Jenkins explores the ways in which the fan writing community responded to this threat, regarding it as "unwarranted interference in their own creative activity"[205] that attempted to impose male definitions of correct sexuality and prohibit works that explicitly challenged patriarchal assumptions. "Several fanzine editors continued to distribute adult-oriented *Star Wars* stories through an underground network of 'special friends,' even though such works were no longer publicly advertised or sold."[206]

Although fanziners, gay camps, and lesbian hermaphrodites are not necessarily engaged in practices directly opposing the law (however often they may unintentionally violate it), the law of publicity rights informs their performative activities. The knowledge that the cultural icons with which they express themselves do not belong to them, however affectionately they are adopted, is constitutive of these practices.

The relationship of fans to the commodification of the texts and images whose meanings they simultaneously interpret and create may be one of admiration or antagonism, irony or parody, fear or nurturing, or even complicitous critique.[207] In any case, the law generates spaces for a proliferation of politics as well as identities, ethics as well as expressions, as people forge their own ethical distinctions between expression and theft, collectively negotiating community norms.

Legal forms and norms are socially engaged—embraced and rejected—in practices that do not seek legal recognition but do use legal narratives and forms in counterhegemonic activity. Such practices may coalesce, forging historically contingent (and continually emergent) identities and communities. It is in such activities that "culture" is made and "politics" practiced. Here, as I will elaborate in the next chapter, I am drawing upon an emergent conceptualization of politics that rejects the state as the singular site for identity claims and community coalition and transformation, and incorporates "the everyday enactment of social practices and the routine reiteration of cultural representations"[208] within its purview.

If we recognize the essence of democratic politics to be a dialogic process whereby social identities are actively articulated from contingent cultural or discursive resources, we must be sensitive to the critical role that commodified media texts—mass culture—play in shaping politically salient forms of difference. The subjects produced in popular cultural practice populate the social world with utopian and aspirational articulations. They pose the promise of an "alternatively gendered world" that displaces heterosexist cultural conventions even as it ironically evokes their forms. Those who control intellectual properties must always cope with the presence of others in the cultural spaces they attempt to colonize. In the next chapter, I explore practices in which alterity may consume the trademark in appropriations that escape the surveillance of the manufacturer's gaze, as well as instances where authorial recognition is actively sought by others through a recoding of the proper name.

3. Tactics of Appropriation and the Politics of Recognition

Walking down the street in Toronto one day in 1987, pedestrians were surprised to see a message flashing across an electronic billboard. "Lesbians fly Air Canada" it repeatedly signaled. The next day the message was gone. A gay rights group broadcast the phrase, but their communication terminated abruptly when Air Canada threatened to apply for an injunction to stop the group from using its name.[1]

FILA® brand sportswear became popular among inner-city youth. The high-priced items became status symbols marking local hierarchies. Aware of their products' popularity among minority youth, the manufacturer targeted this market with a new jean carrying the trademark "TAG." Amongst gang members, a kill is called a tag. Accusations circulated that the corporation was promoting violence.[2]

These two anecdotes attest to the lure of trademarks as visual symbols of hegemonic power and as vehicles for alternative articulations in consumer societies. They remind us of the cultural power of those who control commodity/signs as well as the creative activities of those marginal to or excluded from centers of symbolic authority who are nonetheless marked by a relationship to signs they do not author but often alter in their struggles for recognition and voice.

Readers who are not Canadian should be aware that at the time the first message was transmitted (prior to the deregulation of the airline industry), *all* Canadians flying within Canada flew Air Canada. This archetypical "normal" Canadian activity was selected to demonstrate similarities in Canadian lesbians' everyday experiences that were too often overshadowed by fears of sexual difference. A reconfiguration of social identity was thus written over one of the distinguishing signs of the nation-state in a manner that temporarily realigned the forces defining citizenship. The simultaneous identity of this sign—Air Canada—as both a privileged indicator of government power and a legally controlled commodity with an exchange value on the market operated to prohibit this communication from becoming a form of hegemonic articulation. In other words, antagonistic forces that sought to use the mark to authorize their own legitimacy—and thus to alter and disrupt the fixity of "Canadian" identity—were precluded access to a signifier and thus to its performative rearticulation.

The rumor suggesting corporate promotion of violence through the creation, promotion, and circulation of its trademark marks a rather different configuration of power and signification in consumer societies. It betrays an anxious insurgency at the heart of mass culture, which comments indirectly upon the ephemeral and "placeless" nature of commercial power in contemporary public spheres. We need to understand the *affect* of panic that such rumors register, as well as the effects of such agency. These subaltern narratives comment upon the centrality of trademarks in an embodied cultural politics that contests dominant configurations of identity and community. As subjects and objects, selves and others, citizens and consumers, commodified signifiers mark us and our sense of social boundaries. Not surprisingly, they attract the authorial energies of those who would alter the location of these parameters, both to highlight and to challenge the implicit inclusions and exclusions that such social distinctions invariably effect.

Political Articulations

The Air Canada anecdote maps a complex intersection of significations that define a contemporary political space. The tactics of appropriation and processes of identification involved in articulating identity and compelling recognition always invoke and transform fields of power. The polysemic power of the nation, the seductive power of the commodity form, the instrumental power of the state: through the mode in which it signifies, power shapes the political tactics that implicate identities even as they deconstruct difference. The law is central to and constitutive of such productive powers, simultaneously a generative condition and prohibitive boundary for hegemonic articulations.

Politics is a signifying activity in which identities are constructed through transformations of dominant categories of difference that articulate the margins of these categories even as it calls their boundaries into question. Kobena Mercer has suggested that our eagerness to discuss identity is symptomatic of the postmodern predicament of contemporary politics—a politics in which no political subjects are privileged, identities are never essentially fixed (or fixed by any essence), and the signifiers mobilized to achieve recognition have no intrinsically progressive or reactionary character, but are strategically positioned in the signifying chains of dominant discourses.[3] This is politics as articulation, as derived from Gramsci and Voloshinov, both of whom recognized politics as a site of struggle over key symbols whose connotative fields of reference are always at stake.[4]

The politics appropriate to a radical and plural democracy, Chantal Mouffe asserts, requires a new concept of citizenship, one that views the citizen as a subject-position requiring processes of identification.[5] Such a citizen does not merely occupy a position—possession of a legal status —but is defined by her active engagement in practices of social articulation. These presuppose ethicopolitical principles of freedom and equality, but do not presume to fully define their meaning. In seeing citizenship as "a form of identification, a type of political identity, something to be constructed, not empirically given,"[6] Mouffe shares with many political theorists of postmodern or "late modern" politics the desire to reconstruct recognitions of social difference without succumbing to "the liberal logic of difference which tends to construe every identity as positivity."[7] As William Connolly puts it, identities are established in relation to socially recognized differences that have a tendency to emerge discursively as "fixed forms, thought and lived as if their structure established the true order of things."[8] Veiling the elements of contingency in their construction, particular constellations of identities coalesce, privileging particular categories of difference. Against this metaphysics of political presence, theorists of late (or post-) modern politics posit a cultural politics of difference: "We can use the word difference as a motif for an uprooting of certainty. It represents an experience of change, transformation and hybridity . . . an approach to cultural politics . . . for assembling new practices and languages, pulling together a diversity of theories, politics, cultural experiences and identities into new alliances and movements. Such a politics wouldn't need to subsume identities into an underlying totality that assumes their ultimately homogeneous nature. Rather it is a critique of essentialism and mono-culturalism, asserting the unfixed and 'overdetermined' character of identities."[9]

In these political theories pluralism is reconceived. The liberal vision of multiculturalism characterized by an ahistorical multiplicity of discrete and insular cultural identities[10] is rejected in favor of engaged commitments to equality that go beyond mere political alliance to transform the very identities of the social agents involved. The "subject" of this late modern or radical democratic politics, however, remains amorphous precisely because of its lack of fixity and the laudible necessity of avoiding suggestions of closure. But, as Paul Smith argues, although the identities of political agents may be inessential or contingent, there *are* specific material stakes and discernable referents in political articulation. The actual enactment of the political is a historical moment in which a particular signifier in a particular discourse becomes meaningful for the particular agent. Situations of subordination are transformed into articulation through *identifications* with *specific* signifiers that hold promise for new forms of political recognition. The aspiration to identity and recognition is a matter of taking advantage of historically available, historically laden signifieds.[11]

In a diverse democratic society, many discourses signify in the public realm. These include the signifiers of the nation, those of the state, those circulated by capital and the endless lifestyle options it affords, the symbolic traces of imperialism, and the marks of transnational institutions through which the globalization of capital now signifies. The most powerful signifiers are those that compress the connotations of all these forms of power—marketing experts agree that American Express is one of the world's most widely recognized and valuable trademarks.[12] As suggested in previous chapters, the proliferation of signification is one hallmark of the postmodern. Many have theorized the "cultural logic of late capitalism" in terms of the growth of consumer society and modern media technologies. Cultural reproduction or image production effaces production in Western societies, leading to an immense expansion of "culture" throughout society. As Henri Lefebvre much earlier observed, "We are surrounded by emptiness, but it is an emptiness filled with signs."[13] The circulation of images and texts provides new means with which we negotiate the social and our place within it.

The discussion of postmodernism and its regimes of signification tended to swing between two poles. First we had those (like Baudrillard) who see a world saturated with signifiers but bereft of meaning, in which people are inert in the face of "terroristic" modes of signification to which no effective political response is possible. People are no longer historic subjects but "silent majorities," incapable of any significant social action other than a passive "yes/no" response to signals (for Baudrillard), or the creation of new, decontextualized, arbitrary, and ineffective connections among signifiers (for Jameson).[14]

Cultural studies theorists, on the other hand, have insisted that the social deployment of texts always confounds the anticipations of their authors: the connotations of commodified forms exceed those imagined in their inception. Thus, they appeal to us to ethnographically consider the ways in which people use the signifiers of a commercialized society in their quotidian practices—the extent and degree to which consumption practices may be sites of empowerment, contestation, or critique.[15] Increasingly, they suggest that we redefine the political in terms that include local practices of signification and cultural transformation. Influenced largely by Michel de Certeau, they redefined the political to include potentially all practices of cultural appropriation. Remarkably, however, there has been little dialogue between those who propound theories of late modern or radical democratic politics and those who comment upon the cultural manifestations of postmodernity.[16]

If one school of cultural studies posited a univocal world of signs controlled by an abstract force demonized simply as Capital, and the other imagined a Rabelaisian consumer carnivalesque, both have failed to address the logic of the commodity when applied to cultural forms and the politics that this logic engenders. As I have argued in the previous two chapters, intellectual property laws enable such commodification and create conditions for a dialectical cultural politics shaped by the relationship between those who claim proprietary interests and those who seek to appropriate such signifiers for new agendas—to create other meanings, alternative identities, and new forums for recognition.

We have seen how those who lay claim to intellectual property protections may attempt to control both the sign's circulation and its connotations. By creating monopolies in the power of representation, the law inserts signifiers into systems of political economy that "reduce symbolic ambivalence in order to ground the rational circulation of values and their play of exchange in the regulated equivalence of values."[17] Signifiers are progressively (if never completely) stripped of their ambiguity and polyvalence by their commodification under laws that protect their exchange value. As I've argued, "owners" of mass-media signifiers may well permit the social production of significance when it mints meanings with potential market value (indeed, through market research, they may well mine the public sphere for such value). On the other hand, they may also prohibit the circulation of connotations that contest those valences they have propagated in the public sphere. In this way, intellectual property laws play a fundamental role in determining what discourses circulate in the public sphere and how these "languages" are spoken, while providing both enabling conditions and limiting obstacles for those who seek to construct identities and compel recognition.

In chapter 1 I explored the constitutive power of the trademark in contemporary consumer culture and the way it figures in cultural appro-

priations—constructions of subjects and objects in the worlds in which
we live. In this chapter, I will focus specifically on two tactics of appropriation that relate to two forms of signifying power constituted by the
law of trademark. These examples show how commodified marks figure
in the making of imagined communities—the body politic—and in the
making and remaking of minority consumer subjects: the racialized
bodies of a contemporary body politics. The first examples are practices
of articulation that appropriate the signifiers of the nation-state and the
transnational institution—"official marks" controlled by public authorities. The visible and monumental power of these institutions invites particular tactics of appropriation in the service of specific forms of politics.
The second set of examples concerns the palpable but invisible power of
corporate capital in consumer societies which attract other tactics of appropriation—rumors that circulate around trademarks for consumer
products—and a very different form of agency.

Official Signifiers

A large number of statutes bestow upon "public authorities" (which are
often not elected bodies but government agencies, state-owned corporations, or nonprofit organizations) an absolute right to control particular
signifiers. In Canada, for example, there are over three thousand of these
signs.[18] In the United States there are probably millions, given the greater
number of state jurisdictions and operative public authorities.[19] For Canadians, the list of signifiers so protected is indicative of our postcolonial
situation; it includes all symbols of the British monarchy (crowns, crests,
ciphers, arms, and standards) and those signs that indicate the state
(various flags, animals, and flowers), as well as those indicia of Canada's
determination as a nation to avoid U.S. cultural domination (the logo
for the Canadian Broadcasting Corporation and the National Film
Board, for example). For Americans, federally protected signs are iconic
of revolutionary origins, patriotic fervor, and the nationalized landscape:
the Daughters of the American Revolution, the Ladies of the Grand
Army of the Republic, the American Legion, American War Mothers, the
Boy Scouts, the 4-H Club, Future Farmers of America, Little League
Baseball, the Golden Eagle, Woodsy Owl, and Smokey the Bear.[20] Prohi-
bitions on the use of these signs are contained in the same chapter of the
U.S. Code that once imposed penalties for the desecration of the flag.[21]
Fines and imprisonment for unauthorized use of these symbols may be
dictated. The law thus creates the most expansive set of signifying pow-

ers for those authorities that control the signs of the nation, the state, and transnational institutional icons.[22]

Such insignia are seldom the site of explicit political debate, but a recent U.S. Senate controversy over the century-old design patent held by the United Daughters of the Confederacy (UDC) is a rare example of an official signifier becoming the subject of political significance. In the summer of 1993, the Senate voted to deny approval for the routine renewal of a design patent held by the UDC for a graphic logo that featured the original Confederate flag.[23] Although conservative senators contended that the group's members were "delightful gentleladies"[24] merely engaged in charitable endeavors, the first black woman in the Senate's history ultimately convinced others that a sign symbolizing the historic struggle to preserve slavery should in no way receive government sponsorship or be endorsed as a protected property: "In a speech bristling with outrage, [Carol] Moseley Braun, who was elected to the Senate last November, argued that the issue was not the design patent but the symbolism that the Confederate flag conveys, especially for the descendants of slaves. 'The issue is whether or not Americans such as myself who believe in the promise of this country . . . will have to suffer the indignity of being reminded time and time again that at one point in this country's history we were human chattel. We were property. We could be traded, bought and sold.'"[25] Prohibited marks, design patents, and other official signifiers seldom feature so prominently on political agendas, but they do figure politically as cultural targets and as resources in struggles for legitimacy and recognition.

The absolute power of public authorities to prohibit the use of certain symbols is generally justified in terms of public order and safety.[26] A simple example is the red cross; both confusion and danger are avoided by univocally fixing the meaning of this sign and restricting its use to a single organization with defined goals and commitments. Another rationale is consumer confusion; people should not be able to suggest government or crown sponsorship in the market. This power to control signification, however, is not always so easily justified. Once the signifier is adopted, the authority is given complete discretion to singularly determine the "official" meaning of the sign and to prosecute those who give the signifier unsanctioned connotations.[27]

Two examples, the first American, the second Canadian, illustrate the politics of recognition and the limits to freedom that the commodity form enables in the articulatory struggles of minorities. In 1981, San Francisco Arts and Athletics (hereinafter "the Athletics Group"), a nonprofit organization, began to promote the Gay Olympic Games, an event designed to promote a more positive image of the gay community.[28] T-shirts, buttons, and bumper stickers were sold to finance the games. The United States Olympic Committee (hereinafter "the Committee") brought suit to stop the games from occurring and to prevent the use of the term Olympic by the nonprofit group. Congress had granted the Committee exclusive rights to use the word Olympic under the Amateur Sports Act.[29]

A preliminary injunction enjoining the use of the term was issued[30] and affirmed.[31] Eventually, a permanent injunction was imposed and the Athletics Group was forced to pay the Committee's legal fees. Finally, in 1987, the Supreme Court upheld the Committee's exclusive and absolute rights to the word Olympic and decided that it could prohibit any uses of the term Olympic that it found offensive.[32] Trademark legislation thus enabled a public authority to exercise its power over a signifier in a discriminatory manner—to prevent subordination from becoming translated into hegemonic articulation.

The term Olympic has a long history connoting human excellence and achievement. It is a transnational humanist symbol with which dispossessed groups in society seek to identify in order to educate the public and achieve positive recognition. Indeed, the Committee had authorized groups of the disabled to hold Olympic games to encourage their public acceptance and incorporation. Homosexuals, however, were not deemed worthy of the same privilege. As Judge Kozinski, dissenting on the appeal bench, remarked, "It seems that the Committee is using its control over the term Olympic to promote the very image of homosexuals that the [Athletics Group] seeks to combat: handicapped, juniors, police, Explorers, even *dogs* are allowed to carry the Olympic torch, but homosexuals are not."[33] At the U.S. Supreme Court, Justice Brennan, dissenting from the majority opinion, noted over two hundred organizations listed in the Los Angeles and New York phone books *alone* whose names began with the word Olympic. Indeed, the Committee's counsel, nominated by Ronald Reagan in 1987 for the position of District Court judge, was a member of an exclusive, segregated, all-male social club with a history of discrimination against gays and minorities.[34] The name of this elite institution?—The Olympic Club. No legal injunction was launched on that front. Justice Brennan felt that the complete discretion that Congress had given the Committee over public usage of the term threatened freedom of speech.[35]

Although signifiers circulate in social fields and become inflected with new meanings and politically engaged in new articulations, the fields of discourse in which they figure as sites for identification shape and limit tactics of appropriation. Those in marginal groups will continually attempt to put signifiers into arenas of symbolic exchange[36]—activities that do not contribute to capitalist production and accumulation—but they have fewer resources at their disposal than those who maintain the exchange value of the sign.[37] Here, the meaning of Olympic as festival, as a celebration of human excellence and the energizing powers of the body (tied implicitly, of course, to a nonreproductive sexuality), confronted the Olympic signifier as a commodity. Its universalizing and exclusionary values were carefully contained for transnational marketing efforts.

My second example involves a public authority that refused to exercise its rights to control a national signifier and commodified sign. Ironically, this failure to restrict the circulation of the sign had a similar exclusionary effect. In 1989, the Royal Canadian Mounted Police Force (RCMP) commissioner recommended to Parliament that the RCMP relax certain aspects of its traditional dress code to attract women and minorities.[38] In particular, it was suggested that orthodox Sikhs be permitted to wear their turbans as part of their uniform while serving on the force. Nine months of government inaction, public controversy, and racist propaganda ensued.

Despite having obtained legal opinions stipulating that the Canadian Charter of Rights and Freedoms was being violated by the current policy of refusing to permit Sikhs to wear their turbans when in uniform, the government delayed making a policy decision. Conservative members of Parliament from the Western Provinces tabled petitions signed by over 100,000 people who opposed any changes to the dress code. They claimed that the RCMP scarlet tunic, boots, and Stetson hat together constituted a cherished symbol of the nation, part of an honorable and internationally recognized Canadian tradition that should not be jeopardized by minority demands.[39] Sikh leaders and civil liberties groups argued that the RCMP must acknowledge Canada's multiracial and multireligious composition. Moreover, they asserted, the symbols of the nation should reflect Canada's social policy of multiculturalism. Canada's "traditions," it was suggested, were not in the nature of monologic monuments but in practices of pluralism and tolerance. The opposition parties accused the Conservative government of fanning the flames of social hostility by refusing to act. Minority groups claimed government complicity in fueling a racist backlash.

The most ominous signs of racist reaction were the quantities of black market merchandise that proliferated during the government's period of inactivity. In Calgary, a lapel pin appeared, depicting a white man surrounded by an Oriental man in a coolie hat, a Sikh in a turban, and a black man clutching a spear. The caption asked, "Who is the minority in Canada?" An estimated thirteen thousand pins were sold. A poster with a black-faced caricature of a Sikh officer identified as "Sergeant Kamell Dung" was mass-produced. Beneath the officer was the question: "Is this Canadian or does this make you Sikh?" Nearly ten thousand posters were sold. Another button depicted a turbaned, bearded officer with a slash running across his body and through his throat. Around the symbolic decapitation ran the slogan "Keep the RCMP Canadian."

Criminal prosecutions under the hate literature offense were considered, but no charges were laid. The prime minister called the goods racist and analogized their distribution to Ku Klux Klan activity. What the government didn't do, but could have done, was to evoke its powers under the Trade Marks Act to prevent the distribution of this merchandise. Under the act, no one can commercially use any pictorial representation of an RCMP officer without the consent of the public authority.[40]

In seeking to ridicule and reject or to legitimize and accept the turbanned RCMP officer as an official signifier, Canadians participated in those practices of cultural signification that Homi Bhabha delineated in *Nation and Narration*.[41] We construct the field of meanings and symbols we associate with national life in processes of articulation. The cultural boundaries of the nation "contain" thresholds of meaning and are always engaged in a process of hybridity, incorporating new people in relation to the body politic, generating other sites of meaning, and producing new sites of antagonism. To speak of the nation is to speak of "complex strategies of cultural identification and discursive address that function in the name of 'the people.'"[42] The signs and symbols that signify the affective life of national culture are necessarily contingent. The demand for a holistic, representative vision of society can only be made in a discourse that is both obsessively fixed upon—and uncertain of—society's boundaries.[43] The debate about "being Canadian" and the demand that the turbaned RCMP officer be recognized as representative operated to "provoke a crisis within the process of signification and discursive address."[44] The identity of the forces in this negotiation were themselves transformed by these practices of identification and recognition.

The original "lack" (of meaning) that underpins the identity "Canadian" is the source and the site for hegemonic articulations. Canada, a nation anxiously aware of its lack of essential identity, is potentially the first radical democratic polity, due to its openness to the articulation of a diversity of subject-positions that might be encompassed as Canadian.

Any nationalist discourse requires the existence of others against which the nation is defined; alien and disenfranchised, these others struggle for incorporation, and in so doing they alter the frontiers upon which national identity is forged. The national imaginary might be said to be up for grabs, but it is never likely to be fully possessed, even if it is temporarily occupied. The Canadian subject, however contingent, has never been as radically disembodied or abstracted from its corporeality as the U.S. citizen. In chapter 4 I will focus on the consequences of national disembodiment for subaltern groups within the American body politic; here, I want to explore contestations around the political meaning of one hybrid Canadian body: the Sikh Mountie.

Kieran Keohane draws upon Slavoj Žižek's political reading of the psychoanalysis of Lacan[45] to explore Canada's crises of identification and recognition: "the social is constituted as an antagonistic forcefield of relationality between contingent articulations of identities around a basic paradox: that the integrity of identity is contingent upon the identification of elements which are not-the-identity; i.e., a field of Otherness, outside of the identity, which stands in antithetical relation to the identity."[46] The enjoyment of historical identity—the practice, signs, and codes that animate a particular identity—is constantly under threat, vulnerable to the identifications of others. But the dialectical encounter with the other is never only on terms dictated by the master. The encounter with the other is antagonistic; in subjecting the identity to the infinity of difference, the identity itself (the one) is altered.[47] This dialectic between the one and the other is unending because each depends upon the other for its integrity, and their boundaries continually meld as a consequence of historical antagonisms in which old symbolic orders give way to new ones. Keohane sees Mounties' hats and uniforms, oaths of allegiance to the Queen, and official-language barriers as anachronisms—examples of a colonial symbolic order that is transmogrifying into "a sumptuously rich, lusciously fruitful pastiche"[48] that flourishes in an emergent "intercultural" rather than merely multicultural postcolonial context.[49]

Although we might celebrate these new sites of intercultural enjoyment (Thai tapas bars and Mennonite tortilla bakeries are just a few examples from Ontario's consumer sphere), Keohane suggests that we still lack sublime objects of identification to fill the cultural space of this new nation. If "Canadians become aggressive and divisive over Mounties' hats and mug-shots of Her Majesty,"[50] it is because they cling to symbols of national unity in a country where such signifiers are in short supply. But if society or the nation as an intelligible, unitary object is an impossibility, "one might say that Canada doesn't exist, and that the Sikh Mountie is one of its symptoms."[51] Canada exists, in other words, only "insofar as the symptoms of its Lack have a particularity."[52]

Sikhs figured prominently in emergent anxieties about the boundaries of the postcolonial Canadian body politic during the 1980s.[53] The parameters of the political body—its cultural permeability, its vulnerability to political penetration, its potential infiltration by barbaric violence— were discursively negotiated around the figure of the male Sikh in the Canadian social imaginary. Newspaper commentary from the 1980s can be traced to illustrate the development of a nascent postcolonial national consciousness, slowly abandoning the old Orientalist tropes of colonial discourse in favor of a self-consciously enlightened liberal multiculturalism. A complete analysis of the *mise-en-scène* of the Sikh presence in the Canadian public sphere is impossible to embark upon here; a brief characterization of the discursive shifts in journalistic representations of Sikh peoples and their relation to the nation must suffice. The "rhetoric of empire"—recurrent tropes that position the colonized other[54]—is pervasive in 1980s press coverage, but over the course of the decade it gives way to a liberal discourse of pluralism and religious tolerance.

Early discussions of Sikhs position them as phenomenal objects suddenly appearing on the Canadian horizon. They are treated first as primitives, then as children. First they are judged, then spoken to in condescending tones, as they are exhorted to meet "our" standards of civilization and to leave first a bloodthirsty violence and then an oriental despotism "behind" them. Early accounts waver between attributing to them a simple savagery and acknowledging their (despotic) civilization. Much anxiety focuses on and is betrayed by discussions of the Sikh body and its signs and the potential for their incorporation into the institutions of Canadian civil society. Heated discussions of the propriety of "loincloths" and "daggers" in the classroom give way to informative lists and graphic renderings designed to help the reader decipher Sikh religious insignia and its appropriate placement on the template of the Sikh (male) body. During this period, the tone of newspaper articles shifts from one of imperialist judgment and condescending admonishment to encompass an ethnographic gaze before it settles into a space of interlocution in which Sikhs are ultimately recognized (and at last heard from) as fellow British subjects with whom Canadians share a colonial history and postcolonial future. (Sikh publicists were far from passive in this rhetorical enactment of their identity in Canada; indeed, their interventions in deflecting and detourning dominant representations demonstrate remarkable ingenuity.) In any case, it is within this larger discursive context that the national preoccupation with the Sikh Mountie must be situated.

The Canadian state has a longstanding commitment to multiculturalism, even if the meaning of the term has inevitably been the site of political struggle.[55] Canada prides itself on its distinction as a "mosaic" of cultures from the American "melting pot" model of assimilation. The Mulroney government could have used its power over this national signifier positively, promoting new meanings for the RCMP image that envisioned a proliferation of "Canadian" identities and the multivalence of "Canadian" tradition (pregnant Mounties, disabled mounties, mounties of many colors, all represented as proud "Canadians"). It might have evoked its power of prohibition to prevent the univocality of the sign propagated by the racist merchandise. The commodity form, ironically, could have been engaged to encourage symbolic exchange. Instead, inertia on this front enabled this official signifier of the nation-state to become temporarily colonized by fixed and rigid connotations. The most visible image of the RCMP circulating was a monologic image of white supremacy, raising the specter of closure, "which always plays enigmatically in the discourse of the sign."[56] Today, even this option for (re)configuring the Canadian has been foreclosed: the Canadian government has granted all commercial licensing rights in the RCMP image to Disney. Pregnant, disabled, lesbian, and Southeast Asian Mounties are unlikely to pass Disney's legal scrutiny (Disney has already threatened to confiscate wholly innocuous T-shirts featuring Mounties and has told a children's book publisher that it would have to pay Disney a licensing fee to use archival images in an educational book). The image may well be frozen in perpetuity, or at least until opportunities for its profitable and banal animation arise. It has been effectively abandoned as a Canadian political signifier.

The Olympic symbol and the RCMP image are visible, reified signifiers of legitimacy and prestige whose connotations are *legally* contained by powerful structures of prohibition. It is precisely their status as official signifiers of power that makes them attractive to those who seek political recognition and important to those who seek to maintain current hegemonies. They attract efforts of appropriation and rearticulation by those who wish to inscribe their own authorial signature on the people, the nation, the state—the official social text. Tactics of appropriation engage the signifiers of power in a fashion appropriate to their mode of signification, as I will elaborate in the following discussion of trademark rumors.

In the condition of postmodernity, political arenas are often constituted by imagery, and politics may become a cultural practice: the hegemonic struggle to control the meaning of social signifiers and establish the meaning of social difference. As I will suggest in my concluding chapter, many theorists of the contemporary view this as the essence of both a democratic politics and a postmodern ethics. Advances in democratization depend upon processes of symbolic articulation—giving new meaning to old symbols and constructing new social metaphors. When we allow governments to bestow unlimited and exclusive power on select groups to fix the meaning of key signifiers, we nip this process in the bud and dispossess other social groups from participating in hegemonic struggle. Social articulation is only possible when signifiers retain a surplus of meaning—when the given can be contested and the positive shown to be ambiguous.

Postmodernity and the Rumor

In the habitus of death and the daemonic, reverberates a form of memory that survives the sign . . . And then suddenly from the space of the *not-there*, emerges the re-membered historical agency "manifestly directed towards the memory of truth which lies in the order of symbols" . . . the temporality of repetition that constitutes those signs by which marginalized or insurgent subjects create a collective agency.—Homi Bhabha, *The Location of Culture*[57]

From Upton Sinclair's grisly description in *The Jungle* of how workers who fell in vats of fat emerged as Durham's Pure Leaf Lard to the recent belief that McDonald's uses worms in its burgers, one of the most prevalent folk ideas in 20th-century American life is suspicion of big business.—Gary Alan Fine, "The Goliath Effect: Corporate Dominance and Mercantile Legends"[58]

Although Philip Morris manufactures more than 160 other cigarette brands in some 170 countries, Marlboros have been the key to its global success. A succession of marketing entrepreneurs steered the company's phenomenal expansion. But the most valuable figure in the company by far is the mythic billboard idol, the Marlboro man. *Forbes* magazine once estimated that the Marlboro man by himself had a "goodwill" value of $10 billion.—Richard Barnet and John Cavanagh, *Global Dreams: Imperial Corporations and the New World Order*[59]

The bizarre rumors that consumers spread about the origins and meanings of corporate trademarks are phenomena of consumer culture that indirectly articulate social anxieties about the intersections of culture, power, and place in the condition of postmodernity.[60] Demonic rumors, I will suggest, provide a means by which people culturally express commercial power's lack of place, the simultaneously pervasive but incorporeal presence of corporate power. Moreover, such rumors serve to remark upon the consumer's own place—making audible his or her lack of voice—in mass-mediated culture.

To make sense of such practices it is necessary to summarize some of the socioeconomic conditions from which they spring. The corporate trademark is a signifier that proliferates in the mass-media communications of postmodernism. As production moves elsewhere and the industrial landscape fades from public view (emerging, of course, in export processing zones, women's kitchens, and immigrants' garages), the power of the corporation in the imaginary space of postindustriality[61] is most evident in the exchange value of the brand name, the corporate logo, and the advertising lingo—the "distinction" these signifiers assume in the market. Rumors, suggests Bhabha, "weave their stories around the disjunctive 'present' or the 'not-there' of discourse,"[62] and in the "not-there" of production, I propose, we may find new meanings in the devil rumors that circulate in conditions of postmodernity.

As suggested earlier, the proliferation of signification is often understood to be a peculiar characteristic of postmodernity and its hyper-reality of self-referential signs. These signifiers serve as a locus for the cultural investments and social inscriptions of those who manufacture mass-market goods. The intangibles—brand names, images, slogans, and logos—used to market products accrue value in their own right, for in their capacity to attract and promote meaning, future profits increasingly lie. The distinction of such trademarks must be maintained if they are to remain valuable assets.

Corporate trademarks are key symbols in postmodernity. Corporations invest huge amounts monitoring their use in the public sphere. As the examples explored in chapter 1 indicated, a corporation with proprietary rights in a sign may also attempt to control its connotations and to police critical commentary. The more famous the mark, the greater the legal protection that is accorded to it. In practice, this means that the more powerful the corporation's position in the market, the more successfully it can immunize itself against oppositional cultural strategies. But attempts to restrain the tactical appropriations of those signifiers that embody corporate presence in postmodern culture are not always successful.

This is especially evident in the case of rumor. Rumor is elusive and transitive, anonymous and without origin. It belongs to no one and is possessed by everyone. Endlessly in circulation, it has no identifiable source. This illegitimacy makes it accessible to insurgency, whereas its transitivity makes it a powerful tactic, one that Gayatri Spivak calls a truly subaltern means of communication.[63] According to Bhabha, it represents the emergence of a form of social temporality that is both iterative and indeterminate: "Its intersubjective, communal adhesiveness lies in its enunciative aspect. Its performative power of circulation results in the contagious spreading . . . the iterative action of rumour, its *circulation* and *contagion*, links it with panic—as one of the *affects* of insurgency."[64] Rumors, he notes, mark "an infectious ambivalence" of "too much meaning and a certain meaninglessness . . . uncertainty and panic is generated when an old and familiar symbol develops an unfamiliar social significance as sign through a transformation of the temporality of its representation."[65] In rumors, everyday and commonplace forms are transformed in figurations that are archaic, awesome, and terrifying; the circulation of cultural codes is disturbed by new and awful valences.[66]

The ubiquity and the anonymity of trademarks seem to invite such appropriations. When the recoding of corporate signifiers is articulated in the form of rumor, it may be impossible for a manufacturer to stop alien others from speaking its language with their own voices or colonizing its systems of exchange value with their own experiences and lifeworlds. Once again, we see how the authorial voice is disrupted by alter/native murmurings. Procter & Gamble, a company that bombards North America with cleaning products, discovered this phenomenon at quite some cost. First, a word about the sponsor: Procter & Gamble is the largest American corporation producing cleaning and food products[67] and, until quite recently, the single largest American advertiser (its advertising expenditures have been exceeded by Philip Morris, the tobacco giant of Marlboro man fame, who acquired General Foods and Kraft and with them a roster of famous trademarks—Jell-O, Kool-Aid, S.O.S., Maxwell House, Cheez Whiz, and Miracle Whip—and is now the single largest advertiser in the world).[68] Procter & Gamble's daytime radio and television commercials engendered the term *soap opera*, and the marketing of its brands (Tide, Crest, Ivory Snow, Pampers) has been a paradigm case in business school textbooks for years. Yet despite all this public cultural activity, the company itself keeps a remarkably low corporate profile.[69] A survey by *Advertising Age* conducted during the 1980s indicated that 79 percent of the public could not name any specific product made by Procter & Gamble,[70] one of North America's oldest soap companies and owner of some of the oldest and most venerable brand names in American mass markets (Crisco, Folgers, Duncan Hines). Despite the ubiquity of its products, the multiplicity of its brands, and the mass dissemination of its trademarks, few people actually understood the company to be the source of origin for these goods. Like any good corporate citizen, it lets its trademarks do the talking.

Corporate capital, however, cannot always control the conversations in which its trademarks become engaged. From about 1978 until the late 1980s, a rumor campaign linked the company to Satanism. Anonymous social groups ascribed occult significance to the man-in-the-moon logo it used on most if not all its products:[71] the one mark that could be seen to link many of the disparate products and to operate as an authorial signature marking these goods as those of a singular maker. This corporate insignia (which originated in 1851)[72] was seen to be the mark of the devil. One woman, for example, claimed that when you turned the logo to a mirror, the curlicues in the man's beard became 666, the sign of the Antichrist; "I just don't understand the coincidence."[73] An anonymous leaflet asserted that a company official appeared on national television and "gave all the credit for the success of the company to SATAN . . . They have placed their satanist symbol on all their products so that they can get SATAN into every home in America."[74] Others reported hearing that Procter's "owner" appeared on a talk show where he admitted selling his soul to the devil for the company's success.

Procter & Gamble hired private investigators and established a toll-free hotline to deal with twelve thousand to fifteen thousand monthly phone calls from concerned consumers in 1982. As their public relations office put it, "Procter is going after the rumor with all the diligence that it devotes to a new product."[75] The antirumor campaign cost millions; the company hired detectives from Pinkerton and Wackenhut to track down rumormongers, instituted lawsuits against rival Amway distributors who were alleged to be spreading the story, and in Canada enlisted provincial police in their efforts to track down producers of flyers disseminating the story. Yet, in 1985, when the hydra-headed rumor surfaced again, the company acknowledged a form of defeat. It removed the 134-year-old trademark from its products, a decision described by marketing experts as "a rare case of a giant company succumbing to a bizarre and untraceable rumor."[76]

Incredibly, in a decade when the Federal Centers for Disease Control linked the company's tampon with fatal toxic shock syndrome, feminists protested the use of sex in Procter & Gamble's advertisements, fundamentalists boycotted the company for sponsoring violent television shows, and unions urged boycotts to back their struggles for recognition, it was the battle over the meaning of a tiny moon-and-stars symbol that brought the diffident corporation most prominently to public attention. In other words, the biggest threat to the company's benign, if somewhat empty, public image came not from organized groups with expressed political agendas but from the anonymous appropriations of mysterious agents whose interests and motivations remain inscrutable.[77]

Scholarly work on "mercantile legends," although replete with references to well-known trademarks,[78] fails to see such signifiers as anything but referents to the corporations that control them or the products for which they serve as marketing devices. Folklorist Gary Alan Fine, for example, sees trademark rumors as reflecting an American ambivalence toward bigness, manifested in the pervasive portrayal of well-known corporations as distinctly malevolent:

> The popularity of mercantile legends suggests that the public is sensitive to the nuances of corporate capitalism. The legends reveal attitudes within modern capitalism that cannot be easily and directly expressed . . . Most of these narratives are identical thematically: there is danger from corporations and danger in mass-produced and mass-distributed products. In some legends the corporation itself is guilty for producing a shoddy product; in others an employee is to blame . . . In few stories can the corporate entity be considered heroic . . . and even here the stories revolve around the enormous size, power, control, and wealth of the corporation. In American mercantile legends there is a strong undercurrent of fear and suspicion of size and power.[79]

The mistrust of corporations is most fully expressed, he suggests, in mercantile legends that name the firm or product with the largest market share in that product area (or at least market share *as it is perceived* by the public).[80] Fine makes no distinction among legends dealing with prominent corporations (either in terms of market share, advertising saturation, or size of operations), those that identify a manufacturer's products by brand name, and those in which the corporation, the product, and the brand name are linked in public perception. Indeed, he does not address the trademark at all, except to acknowledge that brand names figure as signifiers in the mercantile legends he recounts (often as a means of effacing their corporate authors).[81] Fine makes a more promising suggestion when he remarks:

> the social-psychological rationale of these attitudes seems based on the separation of the public from the means of production and distribution. Corporations are perceived as caring primarily about profits and only secondarily about the needs of consumers . . . Marx was correct in claiming that separating people from the means of

production under capitalism will result in alienation; this alienation provides a psychological climate in which bogey legends can flourish . . . one must accept that the "folk" (in this case the postindustrial public) are capable of conceiving folkloric content in economic terms that reflect the structure of mass capitalist society, feeling constrained, at least subconsciously, by their own lack of control. The resultant sense of constraint and frustration explain this pattern of mercantile legends that is so prevalent under American capitalism.[82]

In later work, Fine suggests that the companies at the center of such rumors are well-known (or at least, it would seem, their trademarks are) and deal almost exclusively in consumer products and services.[83] The management and production operations of such corporations are far more anonymous: "these rumors symbolically mirror the ambivalence between knowledge of the product and ignorance of the individuals who direct the creation and marketing of these products."[84]

Despite references to the "postindustrial state" and the "postindustrial public," Fine does not suggest any reason why people in a postindustrial society would be any more suspicious of corporate power than those of a more obviously industrial age. The content of the rumor drawn from Upton Sinclair's novel—that workers were being cannibalized in the mass-production process—is, however, suggestive. Here, it is the monstrous nature of production itself that figures an unnatural form of human consumption for the sake of maintaining a consumer society. The human fodder consumed by the mechanics of mass production is then literally consumed by those loyal to the brand name.

Let us return to the mark of the devil—the Satanic figuring of the corporation in consumer rumors. In *The Devil and Commodity Fetishism*, anthropologist Michael Taussig explored the significance of devil symbolism to the emergent proletariat in Bolivia and Colombia.[85] He persuasively showed that proletarianizing peasants used the devil, a fetish of the spirit of evil, as a powerful image with which to express an ethical condemnation of the capitalist mode of production, hostility to wage labor, and the unnatural subjection of humans to the commodity form. The maintenance and increase in production under capitalism was understood to result from secret pacts made with the devil.

I shall speculate here upon the role of the devil in the current stage of capitalism and its feverish proliferation of media signifiers in the service of maintaining and increasing consumption (appropriating and detourning Taussig's terms to make them speak to a postmodern context).

The devil contract may be operating in postmodernity as an image with which to indict a system in which consumption is the aim of economic activity, signs circulate without meanings, symbols are divorced from social contexts, the images that convey commodities are abstracted from the sources of their production, and trademarks are held to be their own sources of value. It may be against this obfuscation of power that satanic rumors are directed: the fetishization of evil, in the image of the devil, directed at the fetishism of the commodity/sign. The meaning of late capitalism may be emerging in the fantastic fabulations through which trademarks are given evil reenchantments.

Racial Inscriptions and Iterations

These undecipherable markings on the captive body render a kind of hiero-glyphics of the flesh whose severe disjunctures come to be hidden in the cultural seeing by skin color. We might well ask if this phenomenon of marking and branding actually "transfers" from one generation to another, finding various symbolic substitutions in an efficacy of meanings that repeat the initiating moments.—Hortense Spillers, "Mama's Baby, Papa's Maybe: An American Grammar Book"[86]

The devil in North America may adopt a variety of forms. Demonic others figure in many consumer rumors, but the devil will assume the image of evil most compelling in the subaltern spheres in which it circulates. This is clearly evident in the perpetuation of Ku Klux Klan rumors that circulate among African Americans in a black counterpublic[87] that flourishes in postindustrial enclaves in the United States. Two centuries of official support for the sale of black bodies as chattel, the branding, marking, and wounding of African Americans, official tolerance of white-on-black violence, and an insidious fascination with and fixation on controlling black sexuality have inevitably left legacies of hostility, anger, and distrust. These are registered in rumors—which increasingly target corporate powers. Drawing on the comprehensive accounts furnished by folklorist Patricia Turner, I will elaborate on the particular prevalence of trademarks in the subaltern consumer counterculture she describes.

In her fascinating book *I Heard It through the Grapevine: Rumor in African-American Culture*,[88] Turner links contemporary rumors or legends in African American communities to a provocative corpus of related oral and written lore concerning race relations and the imperiled

black body that can be traced back to the early-sixteenth-century encounters between white European explorers and sub-Saharan Africans.
Similar, if not identical, rumors have circulated back and forth between
black and white communities in mimetic circuits of exchange ever since
this mythic moment of "first contact."[89] As Benjamin might appreciate,
mechanical (and electronic) modes of reproduction have increased the
speed and velocity of these rumors, as corporate control of imagery has
mystified the sources of control over the black body. Turner traces the
continuing operations of the mimetic faculty in the multiple modernities that African Americans have experienced and the demonic others
who populate their appropriations of textual authority. Concerns about
conspiracy, contamination, cannibalism, and castration are repetitively
reiterated; they "run through nearly four hundred years of black contemporary legend material and prove remarkably tenacious."[90]

Historically, as both blacks and whites attempted to fit the other into
their own worldview, they each adopted the figure of the cannibal, with
"flesh-eating representing the epitome of barbaric and uncivilized behavior for both groups during that period."[91] In the slave-trading era,
rumors about the other circulated and were mimicked by their alters, as
evidenced in the continued currency of the trope of man-eating. "New
World cannibalism rumors continued well into the nineteenth century,
as the mutiny on the Spanish slave ship *Amistad* revealed; although the
African men had been subject to all the horrors of experience as cargo in
the Middle Passage, they did not attempt to take over the ship until they
were told by the cook that the white men intended to eat them."[92]

The term *man-eater* had a literal meaning for both the slave traders
and the slaves, the majority of whom were men, and rumors that black
men are particular targets for white animosity and most at bodily risk
have persisted over generations. Although some Europeans began to
question the mark of the cannibal that was used to brand Africans (and
later served as a brand in commercial advertising), the belief that Africans were uniformly cannibalistic remained popular well into the twentieth century. The image of the missionary boiling in a large pot as dancing savages surrounded him repeated itself endlessly in mass-culture
imagery.[93] Africans and Europeans did not have equal access to information about each other. To Africans it was clear that "Europeans maintained a seemingly insatiable appetite for the bodies of their brothers,"[94]
and, in places where the commodification of human labor was unknown, the idea of cannibalism explained a reality: "slave traders kept
coming back for live bodies to satisfy their hunger for human flesh."[95]

The commodification and the vilification of black bodies in the historical American imaginary—their simultaneous status as objects of property and subjects of physical danger and sexual potency, branded as chattel and targeted with violence—have a long and sordid history that lives on in the embodied memories of African Americans. Apologists for slavery in the eighteenth and nineteenth centuries claimed that Africans had been visited with an ancient, if not biblical, "curse" that "marked" them for slavery: "God has placed a mark on the Negro as distinctive as that on Cain."[96] Such marks served to deem those who bore them (blacks, women, natives) subservient to their unmarked (white, male) masters. The witnessing of abuse visited upon black bodies lingers in collective memory and continues to inscribe the bodies of African Americans to the present day. Elizabeth Alexander movingly evokes these corporeally inscribed memories, repetitively inflicted by white-on-black violence, as consolidating "group affiliation by making blackness an unavoidable, irreducible sign which, despite its abjection, leaves creative space for group self-definition and self-knowledge."[97] Ku Klux Klan rumors, I believe, are one example of this memory and creative self-recognition.

After the civil rights struggles, rumors linked reprehensible violence against blacks to the KKK, tying the Klan to consumer goods conspiratorially designed to prohibit black reproduction. "To many African-Americans, the Klan exists as the agency on which whites depend to mitigate or eliminate black access to those rights and privileges that white adults take for granted."[98] The Klan's verifiable abuses of black bodies—lynching, castration, burning, and mutilation—are sufficiently well-documented: "Reconstruction-era Klansmen devised many cruel fates for blacks, which contributed to their emerging reputation as demonically inspired monsters determined to sexually humiliate those who threatened white supremacy. Sexual metaphors abound in stories of KKK violence."[99] In the Reconstruction era, for example, Klan members padded and enlarged their own crotches when pursuing their presumably overendowed victims—a mimicry of the alterity they so fantastically constructed. In many accounts, the desire to destroy or control the victim's sexuality is literally realized,[100] as when black genitalia served as trophies of a successful hunt.

Black engagement in the defense of international democracy during World War I did not bring blacks democratic rights and privileges when they returned home. Wearing uniforms and carrying weapons were privileges that white American men saw as properly their own preserve; black male adoption of these insignia provoked an anxious backlash of white supremacy. Associations between male sexual prowess and military acumen were registered in the lynching, mutilation, and dismemberment of black men in uniform.[101] Later, post–World War II Klan attacks on male genitalia and the bombings and burnings of institutions (such as churches) central to the reproduction of black community life made particularly compelling the rumors linking the KKK to the insidious sterilization of black men.

> The KKK has figured prominently in at least four contemporary legend cycles in which modern corporations are the mechanism by which late-twentieth-century white supremacists pursue the bodies of blacks. The KKK, in other words, has traded its white sheets of yesteryear for the white shirts of corporate America. In one rumor, the KKK, who [*sic*] allegedly owns Church's Fried Chicken, has tainted the chicken recipe so that black male eaters are sterilized after consuming it. In a second, young African-American male consumers are unwittingly supporting the KKK by purchasing overpriced athletic wear manufactured by the "Klan-owned" Troop clothing company. Third, many believe that the KKK owns Marlboro cigarettes, a brand popular among black smokers, and is not only accruing financial benefits from but also deliberately causing cancer in African-American consumers. Finally, the Brooklyn Bottling Company, maker and distributor of a soft drink called Tropical Fantasy, which is said to contain a mysterious ingredient capable of sterilizing black men, is similarly alleged to be a front for the KKK.[102]

In these rumors of KKK manipulation of mass production, the agendas of suspect corporations mimic those traditionally pursued by the Klan—conspiratorial attempts to limit and destroy the reproduction of the black population. Church's Fried Chicken was targeted, Turner suggests, because its persona in the market—its public signature, trademark, and trade name—reminded blacks of houses of worship:

> churches played a pivotal role in the civil rights movement. In many communities houses of worship were the only public spaces in which African-Americans could meet. Moreover, many of the best-known leaders in the civil rights movement emerged from the ranks of the clergy. In its attempts to prevent civil rights advances, the Klan was proven to be responsible for the bombing and burning of numerous black churches throughout the South. This flagrant disregard for the sanctity of churches no doubt left a lasting impression on the African-American mind. The notion that "Church's" [with ownership based in the South] could be responsible for such

destructive behavior as the sterilizing scheme thus gained a perverse, ironic appeal.[103]

Moreover, Church's "product", the "works" for which it was known,
and the work it provided in black communities, involved the preparation
of foods typically associated with the soul food of the folk. Such foods
were sold exclusively in inner-city black areas; Church's was one of the
last fast-food operations to expand into the suburbs.[104] Its retail operations were highly visible in black communities but largely unknown in
white areas, whereas its advertising budget was (contrary to Fine's expec-
tations) the *lowest* in the industry.[105] With few other connotations to attach to its authorial presence, only its disembodied signature remained
for inner-city consumers to invest with meaning. The very anonymity of
the company might have invited rumor, suggests Turner; although the
franchises provided some employment in heating and serving precooked
food, these were jobs that reinforced servile and emasculating images.
Like Kentucky Fried Chicken, Popeye's, and other southern food franchises, moreover, Church's figured in rumors that its fried chicken reci-
pes were stolen from black maids. In such rumors, even the history of
exploitation is further expropriated for white profit when an "imitation
of life" is sold back to blacks under the authorial signatures of southern
white men, descendants of slaveholders, who claim food for the soul as
trade secrets and circulate it by means of trademarks—taking possession
of the literal sustenance of black bodily well-being.

Corporeal Vulnerability

Subjugation in contemporary America is an insidious process because it silences
constituencies even as it gives voice and face to their culture and histories. It
adopts black dress and posture, it facilitates black interpellation without enfran-
chisement, it addresses blacks without providing channels and forums for response and critical engagement; it takes on repertoires of black representation
without respect for the conditions under which the history of that community
is made.—Grant Farred, in "Race and Racism: A Symposium"[106]

In 1985 a company introduced a line of sportswear under the name
Troop, capitalizing on an incipient military aesthetic in the male urban
underclass. It marketed these intimidating combat-style goods almost
exclusively to black and Latino youths in inner cities where the clothing

became incredibly popular. Soon it was reported on community radio stations that the Troop trademark was owned by a company controlled by the Ku Klux Klan; the trademark, in other words, was employed to create the perception of a threatening, oppositional army that would legitimate *and fund* the Klan's own paramilitary operations.[107]

In fact, Troop Sport was a New York firm owned by Korean and American entrepreneurs with production operations based in Korea. It had no Klan affiliations that could be established. Rumor, however, is never error but basically errant,[108] and this one, capturing the public imagination, swept the nation. As the *San Francisco Chronicle* reported in 1989:

> A Chicago variation of the rumor has rap singer L.L. Cool J. ripping off a Troop jacket on the Oprah show and accusing the firm of hating blacks. The singer has never appeared on the talk show . . . In Memphis, the rumor was that the letters in Troop stood for: To Rule Over Our Oppressed People. And in Atlanta some believed that the words "Thank you nigger for making us rich" were emblazoned inside the tread of Troop's tennis shoes . . . Troop's [black] marketing director . . . [claims] that he has gone to great lengths to disprove the alleged Klan connection. "I went to Montgomery, Alabama to a store and cut open five pairs [of shoes] to prove it wasn't like that."[109]

In contrast to Procter & Gamble's defensive countertactics, Troop Sport responded overtly. It decided to "do the right thing" and affirm its allegiance to civil rights. A $200,000 public relations campaign enlisted the aid of Operation Push, the NAACP, and black musicians and athletes. Church rallies were held, black students were publicly awarded scholarships, and anti-Klan posters were distributed. According to Turner, Troop officials in Chicago also engaged the executive secretary of the African American Alpha Phi Alpha fraternity to request that they use their chapter network to dispel the rumors. Despite these efforts, the company fell into dire straits, closed its stores, and filed for bankruptcy in the summer of 1989. Its downfall may have been due to changing fashion trends, but it is difficult to deny the injuries that the rumors visited upon the company's reputation.

The objective falsity of this rumor makes it difficult at first to understand why people found it persuasive; it invites us to speculate upon the nature of truth and how it must be distinguished from objectivity. Although Ku Klux Klan rumors may be empirically false, they articulate compelling truths about the history of black social experience in North

America. In marketing goods to the black population these particular companies were not unusual. But elements specific to these campaigns make them unique. For example, instead of addressing blacks as part of a market in which everyone could now be seen to consume the same goods—an inclusionary gesture—the Troop marketing strategy was designed to mark a difference. The pseudo-military character of the product itself physically interpellated young black men as identifiable targets and marked them (while inviting them to brand or tattoo themselves) as recruitable subordinates. If this seems farfetched, this excerpt from *The Metro Word* ("Toronto's Black Culture Magazine") indicates that such possibilities are never far from consciousness in black urban communities: "On a warm autumn day, Rick is easy to spot wearing his Black leather jacket imprinted with an X along with his Malcolm X cap . . . As Rick turns to catch the bus, the large white X smack dab in the middle of his back takes on an ominous meaning. The X appears almost like a target and Rick appears to have become human prey. From Public Enemy's Rebel Base One in New York, [Harry] Allen says, 'This is why Public Enemy has taken the image of a Black man with his arms crossed defiantly and his head held upward in a rifle sight as their logo. Most Black people see themselves in the same situation—in the sights.'"[110]

The Troop marketing strategy seems to have evoked disturbing associations in black cultural memory and the social unconscious. The disproportionate numbers of young black men recruited to serve as "grunts" in Vietnam was a powerful memory. The experience of serving as capital's reserve army of labor, increasingly mobilized according to the demands of the military-industrial complex, was potentially evoked, along with memories of rewards expected and postponed after serving in two world wars. Indeed, race rumors during these wars demonstrate profound racial distrust. According to Turner:

> The antiblack rumors that circulated during wartime reflect the ambivalence, insecurity, and uneasiness felt during a time of crisis. The dominant culture did not embrace the idea of training black men to shoot, but the idea that they share the risk of being shot at was perfectly acceptable. Blacks were empowered, in short, by America's need for them. A nation that had always tried to limit black access to weapons suddenly needed to train black soldiers. Few roles reinforce masculinity more than that of soldier. Whites knew, moreover, that they could not easily ask blacks to be soldiers while denying them the full rights of citizenship and increased access to the American dream.[111]

Black rumors focused on the second-class treatment of black soldiers. Later, race riots also provoked (and were provoked by) rumors about the relative treatment and marking of black and white bodies by members of the other race.

Michelle Wallace adds further dimension to this emphasis on the black body:

> Afro-Americans, as ex-slaves, are not only permanently exiled from their "homeland" (which now exists most meaningfully only in their imaginations), but also from their bodies. Their labor and their reproduction can be considered to be in a state of postcoloniality—no longer colonized but not yet free. In a manner that may be characteristic of "internal colonization," Afro-American culture has traditionally seemed fully aware of its own marginality to the white American mainstream. Accordingly, it combined (and often cleverly disguised) its political objections to Afro-American "invisibility" with a progressive integration and reinterpretation of those qualities and features that first marked the "racism" of white images of blacks. In other words, black culture continually reincorporates the "negative" or "racist" imagery of the dominant culture.[112]

Manthia Diawara makes a similar point: "Blacks often derive the good life from repressive institutions by systematically reversing the significations of those institutions."[113] With these insights, we might see black male adoption of army surplus, camouflage gear, and military insignia in the service of a "BAD" aesthetic as ironically inverting this symbolism to create and affirm black solidarity. The gesture is one that Henry Louis Gates Jr. might see as a form of "Signifyin(g)"—the employment of figurative rhetorical strategies that repeat and imitate elements of dominant culture while critically marking a difference—that enables blacks to respond indirectly to an exclusionary white culture.[114] Gates discusses literature and the oral tradition, but Wallace argues that Signifyin(g) tactics are even more characteristic of African American popular culture and its mass-culture derivatives.[115]

The conversion of the signs of military conscription and betrayal into a subcultural aesthetic of resistance might be Signifyin(g), but it was as signification that they were rerouted by Troop Sport to serve the endless needs of commerce for new sources of distinction. The appropriation and projection back on blacks of their own Signifyin(g) by anonymous forces of capital—an inversion of their inversion—inevitably sparked racial anxiety about white enmity. This enmity was most aptly represented by the Ku Klux Klan. Black response to the Troop marketing strategy—

the Ku Klux Klan rumor—however false, served to connote historical truths about black male subordination. The Troop marketing strategy stirred something in the political unconscious of African Americans that surfaced in the form of a fantastic recognition of black social identity; the rumor might be understood as a return of the repressed in the black social imaginary.

British Knights and Reebok, both manufacturers of athletic shoes, have also been visited with accusations of Klan affiliation, although in the Reebok case, the funneling of funds to support South African apartheid was the more pervasive theme. As Turner notes, the Knights trademark was easily associated with the knights of the Ku Klux Klan, but the Reebok rumor was more mysterious. The rage for athletic footwear in the 1980s did cause concern within black communities, and the Reebok rumors circulated just as celebrity condemnations of South African apartheid were voiced in the media. Perplexed by these allegations, Reebok marketing personnel chose to interrogate the trademark with which the company purveyed its goods so as to determine if it held any clues to the rumor's origins. Implicitly, they recognized that the authorial mark under which the goods were marketed and with which black consumers marked their bodies might yield meaning as to the nature of African American distrust: "the company's founders, Joe and Bill Foster, turned to the dictionary for a name for the bootmaking company in the late 1950s; they 'picked the name Reebok . . . a light, nimble gazelle'. . . . Coincidentally that species is found almost exclusively in South Africa. [Vice President for Corporate Communications Kenneth] Lightcap, in speculating on the source of the rumor, mentioned . . . the similarity between the words *reebok* and *springbok*—an annual South African rugby match—and the fact that the corporate symbol for the Reebok brand is the British flag."[116]

Turner claims to have found few informants for the rumor who knew anything about the gazelle or the South African rugby team (although informants with a British Caribbean heritage did associate the British flag with a history of racist colonial oppression).[117]

> To the company, its status as the first major U.S. shoe company to withdraw its products from the South African market makes the allegations even more disturbing. Proud of its record on human rights and its support of the African-American community, Reebok has gone to great lengths to dispel the rumor. Kenneth Lightcap spends a great deal of time on the road, pleading Reebok's case to African-American college groups as well as community and political groups.

> Signs disavowing the South African connection are very much in evidence at Reebok outlets. A handsome flyer entitled "Reebok: On Human Rights" contains disclaimers from both African-American athletes and well-known anti-apartheid groups.[118]

The flyer also contained a letter to Reebok employees that reiterated "the company's determination to reproach other American corporations doing business in South Africa, and its commitment to a responsible corporate America."[119] Although it was one of the largest athletic footwear manufacturers in the world, Reebok's vision of American corporate responsibility did not include the provision of any manufacturing jobs for the African Americans who constituted so great a share of its market. Like other corporations, it had adopted strategies of flexible capital accumulation, shifting the places of its production operations to take advantage of low-wage labor and legislative regimes that imposed the least onerous regulatory constraints on its operations.

The effects of global capitalist restructuring have been particularly grave for African Americans: "the shift to a system of flexible accumulation which led to smaller workplaces, more homogenous work forces and the weakening of labor unions, meant that the moderate-waged bases of the Black working and middle classes were eviscerated. Moreover, under the new regimes Blacks were more likely to suffer from racial discrimination in the labor market. Further, the spatial aspects of this transformation left inner-cities economically devastated as their economic base was removed and large sectors of urban minority residents lived in increasingly impoverished neighborhoods."[120] Like Troop and other athletic wear companies, Reebok's manufacturing operations were located in China and Southeast Asia,[121] part of a typical corporate strategy that has moved manufacturing jobs out of the country and, more significantly, out of the areas in which most African Americans live. Providing only low-wage, low-skill, service jobs without benefits or security to those youth able to commute to distant retail outlets, Reebok is typical of a larger pattern of disinvestment in black communities that has prevailed since the 1980s. The shoes sold to young black men might retail for prices that generally exceed $50—sometimes three times that—but are physically produced (largely by women) in minimal-wage sweatshop conditions or subcontracting arrangements to inflate profit margins. These factors are still unknown to many consumers. The invisibility of these conditions of production, or indeed of any places of manufacture for those consumer goods with which African Americans mark status distinctions, makes such rumors more compelling than they might be if African Americans had any role in the goods' manufacture.

Athletic wear has special significance for African American male youth: celebrity sportsmen are role models for many who see their greatest chance for legitimate financial success in the field of professional athletics.[122] Black leaders have accused athletic wear companies of stoking confrontational violence by inspiring lust for expensive goods. In 1990, for example, Reverend Jesse Jackson urged black consumers to boycott products manufactured by Nike because the company had shown so little corporate responsibility toward the black community.[123]

Cigarette companies are also linked in the black popular imagination to the KKK. During the 1960s, rumors circulated about Kool, a cigarette that was a top brand among black smokers. "By misspelling a word prominent in the folk speech of African-Americans to arrive at the product's name," Turner suggests, the manufacturer set itself up for speculation.[124] Again, the trademark, as indicia of authorship and origin, begs questions of authority and authorial intent. Today, the most prominent rumors alleging Klan affiliation are targeted at Marlboro cigarettes, the phenomenally successful brand controlled by the Philip Morris Corporation. Many blacks claimed that the letters KKK could be found in the logo on the cigarette package.[125] One of Turner's informants recalled a caution he received when lighting up a Marlboro:

> The logo design incorporated 3 representations of the letter K . . . So far is plausible, the final "proof" was that if you tore the bottom of the packet open [in a particular way] . . . there would be revealed the head of a hooded klansman, the two spots, in black and gold, standing for eyeholes. To this was added the "fact" that Philip Morris, in person, was a noted Klan member and financier . . . Although I personally never heard or saw the story carried in printed sources or on T.V. . . . Marlboro nevertheless stopped using the two spots on their boxes . . . With the withdrawal of the two spots, this story seems to have died a death, but even so, every now and then somebody will say to Marlboro smokers (there are a lot of us unfortunately), "you shouldn't smoke Marlboro, you know."[126]

The three *K*s on the package that supposedly indicate the Ku Klux Klan "signature" and the efforts in which black consumers engaged to "discover" the Klan's work in the manufacture of the cigarettes display in particularly graphic fashion the dance of mimicry and alterity at play in the market. Out of the trademarks and logos the corporation disseminated, black consumers constructed the signature of the demonic other; they manufactured marks of alterity in the counter-trademarks they created out of the authorial materials afforded them. They detected other authorities behind products that harmed them and did so by conjuring up the figures that most horrifyingly represented their bodily vulnerability in white society.

Philip Morris is not a singular owner of a manufacturing concern but the original English tobacco merchant who achieved success in the mid-nineteenth century (and was a rather minor player in the global tobacco market until the birth of the Marlboro man in the 1950s). The company is now publicly owned by thousands of shareholders. This differentiation of corporate ownership is rarely represented in the public sphere of the commercial marketplace. Brand names that incorporate the names of individuals are far more common on the packages and in the advertising of goods that consumers encounter. Ownership is much more easily conceptualized in individual terms, and the prevalence of patriarchs in consumer culture (Colonel Sanders, Orville Redenbacher, "Mr. Christie," Frank Perdue, Dave Thomas) legitimates a misrecognition of personal control over the manufacture and distribution of goods.

The toxicity of tobacco and the dangers of its consumption require little comment; a product with detrimental effects for black bodies might well attract attention. More, salient, perhaps are historical memories of tobacco harvesting and black exploitation in conditions of forced labor. After emancipation, intimacy with southern tobacco fields continued: "A fancy coffee table book, published in 1979, on the Philip Morris company's commitment to the art world . . . contains several artistically rendered black-and-white photos of African-Americans working in tobacco fields."[127] Today, black and Hispanic communities are particular targets of tobacco company advertising; as wealthier and more educated Americans quit smoking, cigarette companies aim more and more of their marketing at the poor:

> Much of Harlem looks like a war zone, but the ubiquitous billboards featuring scantily clad women advertising Kools, Camels, and Virginia Slims and the fully clothed cowboys welcoming all to Marlboro country are bright and shiny. In early 1990, the *New England Journal of Medicine* published the shocking findings that black men in Harlem were less likely to reach the age of 40 than men in Bangladesh. Six of the top seven killers in Harlem are, according to the great weight of medical opinion, tobacco-related or alcohol-related. According to the Centers for Disease Control, cigarettes and

alcohol are the two most heavily advertised products in African-American and Latino communities. Indeed, about 90 percent of all cigarette and alcohol billboard advertising in the country is located in these communities.[128]

These rumors focus attention on the racial body and its targeting and surveillance in the United States. They mark a suppressed subaltern truth when they stress the vulnerability of those bodies that American industry has controlled, contained, and ultimately abandoned in conditions of postmodernity. Both Fine and Turner view the rumor as a form of resistance—one of the few weapons of the weak in a society where culture is commodified and controlled from indeterminate places. The "folk idioms of late-twentieth-century life" are potent resources with which black consumers contest "ubiquitous billboards, glossy advertisements, coupons, and television commercials."[129] Significantly, the ways in which consumers spread rumors mimic the tactics through which the trademark itself makes its way into daily life: authority seems to provoke its alters to adopt forms of counterpublicity that reproduce patterns of commercial speech, provoking alternative forms of authorship and new sources of authority.

This is particularly evident in the Brooklyn Bottling Company's battle with Klan rumors, which began in 1990. The Tropical Fantasy the company marketed was resisted in communities heavily populated by Caribbean-born blacks and hispanics.[130] Early in 1991 young blacks were handing out photocopied flyers reproducing the rumor and authorizing it with "evidence": an exposé that had supposedly appeared on the television show 20/20. Graffiti artists further perpetuated the rumor. The *Wall Street Journal* describes this scene: "A burned-out building covered with graffiti includes the slogan: 'Oppressors are not our protectors.' Just under the spray-painted warning a chalk-scrawled postscript adds: Tropical Fantasy."[131]

These anonymous others mimic the mass circulation of the commodity sign with whatever means of mass reproduction are accessible, authoring alternative versions to the commodified narratives that mass marketing provides, and claim the authority of the mass media to validate their own authorial assertions. Many rumors contain accounts of their own verification, pointing to the media as authenticating the account. The mediums that interpellate us as mass subjects[132] operate for America's others as authorities that legitimate their own knowledge of their perceived bodily excess and real corporeal vulnerability. Nationally syndicated news and entertainment shows appear to be the vehicles of choice. As one of Turner's African American students put it: "Oh well, I guess that's like what they say about eating at Church's Chicken—you know the Klan owns it and they do something to the chicken so that when black men eat there they become sterile. Except that I guess it isn't really like the one about the Kentucky Fried Rat because it is true about Church's. I know because a friend of mine saw the story on '60 Minutes.'"[133]

In response to the counterpublicity of the Tropical Fantasy rumor, corporate authorities authorized alternative forms of authority—black authorities—to validate their own benign intentions. They sought black authorship, provided black employment, and publicly recognized the specificities of their consumer base:

> While the most potent folklore genres of the postindustrial age—rumor, graffiti, Xeroxlore—were being put to work to spread the notion that Tropical Fantasy was a KKK-inspired aphrodisiac, the company fought back with all the standard damage-control tools. They had their products tested by the FDA and made the results public; they hired a truck to drive around black neighborhoods with a billboard denying the KKK allegation; they hired a black public relations team to propose strategies by which they could reclaim their customer base. Individuals respected in the black community were enlisted for the campaign. The mayor of New York, African-American David Dinkins, guzzled the soda on television; community clergymen denounced the rumor.[134]

Like the Procter & Gamble rumor, these anonymous appropriations had the effect of pulling invisible companies into the public limelight. Rumors may provoke corporations to renounce their lack of public presence and make political commitments. Procter & Gamble, whose implicit motto is that cleanliness is next to Godliness (its products are marketed with biblical referents), may have been compelled only to reaffirm its advertising commitments to purity, cleanliness, and light against the forces of evil, filth, and darkness. Troop Sport, Reebok, and the Brooklyn Bottling Company, however, were pushed into overt political engagement and connection with African American communities and concerns.

Like Fine, Turner does not explore the pervasive significance of trademarks, brands, or trade names in rumors concerning corporately controlled, antiblack conspiracies that threaten black bodies and the fate of the race. Although she recognizes them as "modern motifs" or indicia of "contemporary legends,"[135] we are not told what is peculiarly "modern" about them. I would suggest instead that these are postmodern phenomena, peculiar to late capitalist, post-Fordist, or postindustrial conditions.[136] Trademarks are one contemporary manifestation of the author-function; they mark a unique source of origin for mass-produced goods of identical appearance, but this site can be traced only with great difficulty via its signature postmodernity. The brand name or trademark floats mysteriously; a corporate signature endlessly reproduced by mechanical and electronic means, it marks an invisible and imaginary moment of manufacture, conjuring an invisible source of origin while it magically garners goodwill for its invisible author.

Rumor campaigns such as those directed at Procter & Gamble, Church's, Reebok, Philip Morris, and Troop Sport must be understood in the context of a consumption society in which corporate power maintains silence and invisibility behind a play of media signifiers without referents, a circulation of symbols that are simultaneously overendowed with meaning and essentially meaningless. Such rumors may be understood as cultural guerrilla tactics, "political" in their significance, if not in their self-consciousness. Bhabha phrases a similar insight into rumor: "What articulates these sites of cultural difference and social antagonism, in the absence of the validity of interpretation, is a discourse of panic that suggests that psychic affect and social fantasy are potent forms of political identity and agency for guerrilla warfare."[137]

The nature of signifying power shapes the form of the appropriations it engenders. Arguably, such rumors constitute a "counterterrorism" of sorts to the "terror" of postmodern hyperreality. If the "terror" of hyperreality[138] lies in its anonymity, its fleetingness, its dearth of meaning and excess of fascination, then it is not surprising that it provokes counterterrorist tactics that have the same characteristics (it constitutes an "alter" in its own seductive image).[139] The rumor campaign seems to have the same superficial senselessness and indeterminacy as the media that it combats, into which it simultaneously insinuates itself.

Social psychologist Frederick Koenig no doubt exaggerates when he asserts, "Next to an act of terrorism, what corporations fear most is that they may be targeted with an outlandish tall tale,"[140] but the effect of rumor as an intervention in the public sphere is not insignificant. These rumors certainly challenge visions of the masses as silent majorities capable only of passive yes/no signals in response to power, while they add more subtlety and dimension to claims that people are capable of making only arbitrary and ineffective connections among floating signifiers. Faced with only the signifier, people construct a signified; in a world of empty signification, people may invest their own meanings. The connections people make may well be arbitrary, they may even be absurd, but the massive investments that manufacturers make to counter their influence suggest that they are hardly ineffective.

These rumors mark a popular refusal of a dominant cultural logic that replaces exchange value with sign value to the extent that even the memory of use value is lost. To put this more succinctly, as manufacturers erase and obscure all traces of production through their investments in decontextualized media signifiers, they encounter consumers determined to re-embed these signifiers in myths of origin or narratives of production. These narratives bespeak an anxiety about the abstraction of symbols from lifeworlds and the invisibility of production relations in Western societies, giving voice to a profound suspicion of corporate power.

Devil rumors provide a means by which people culturally express commercial power's lack of place—the simultaneously pervasive but incorporeal presence of corporate power. Moreover, such rumors remark upon the consumer's own place—making audible his or her lack of voice—and the consumer's sense of powerlessness in the ubiquitous but evanescent world of commercial media culture. Rumors give presence to the consumer's cultural absence; they assume power and momentum as they insinuate themselves into the "mediascape."[141] Traveling anonymously, without clear meaning, authority, or direction, rumors colonize the media in much the same way that commercial trademarks do, subversively undermining the benign invisibility of the trademark's corporate sponsor while maintaining the consumer's own lack of authorial voice.

Signifyin(g) Powers

All of the practices of appropriation explored here speak the language of power in a manner that disrupts its discursive address. At the same time, however, these tactics borrow the mode of signification appropriate to the powers they covet, contest, or condemn. Official signifiers represent visible, monumental powers that present themselves as fixed, stable, and immutable. Subaltern seizures of these signs in struggles for recognition involve practices of identification that seek visibility—gays in the United States and Sikhs in Canada sought to publicly inscribe their own authorial signature on the official social text. Commercial trademarks, on the other hand, mark the increasingly invisible presence of capital in post-Fordist conditions of flexible accumulation. These signifiers are in flux, they are unstable and constantly undergoing new media mutations. Rumors are practices that seek to make the power behind the sign both visible and audible; but those circulating these stories remain invisible, evading both detection and authorial presence.

Identities are established in relations of difference that are constantly in articulated circulation. Those who bear difference may invite recognition, tolerance, appreciation, or even anonymity. By constructing fields of signifying power, the law plays a constitutive role in the construction, deconstruction, definitions, and counterdefinitions that define a space of contemporary politics. According to one commentator in a recent symposium on race and racism:

> celebrations of difference, whether in the service of nominalist claims to authentic experience or neoliberal appeals to universalism, elide the complex ways in which differences are articulated, reworked, and indeed, relativized through practices of political and representational rule. As Edward Said and Barbara Hooper noted recently, "hegemonic power does not simply manipulate naively given differences between individuals and social groups, it actively produces and reproduces difference as a key strategy to create and maintain modes of social and spatial division that are advantageous to its empowerment." It is precisely this productive aspect of hegemonic power (what Foucault has called subjectification) that requires close scrutiny . . . [142]

Relations of difference, as we will see in the next chapter, may be legally produced and legitimated by juridical regimes that have as their major purpose the protection of commercial goodwill. I will trace the emergence of U.S. federal trademark law as a hegemonic discourse of social distinctions that served to consolidate emergent subjectivities in the United States and entrenchments of cultural authority that have, in turn, generated a continuing politics of contestation.

4. Embodied Trademarks: Mimesis and Alterity on American Commercial Frontiers

Since 1930, the mascot of Robertson's® Marmalade, England's Golliwog (who looks like Buckwheat, but a bit more nattily attired) has appeared on over 20 million pieces of merchandise—from teapots to toothbrushes to T-shirts . . . When Golly was criticized in 1984 by some of England's "oversensitive" black population, a Robertson's spokesman righteously declared, "the Golly forms part of our national tradition and attacking it is an attack on a part of British culture."—Colson Whitehead, "Review of White on Black"[1]

This anecdote condenses a series of relationships that are relatively unexplored in cultural anthropology and invisible in law and society scholarship. It bespeaks the central role of trademarks in what we might call the visual culture of the nation[2] and points to another politics—of ownership and protest, domination and resistance—that engages intellectual properties in increasingly commodified public spheres. Theoretically addressing the significance of this story, however, is no easy task. It resists easy accommodation within the dominant perspectives on the commodified imagery of late capitalism. Neither a modernist nostalgia for "our" "real" history (now lost in the proliferation of media imagery),[3] nor the increasingly qualified demarcation of consumption as a potential site for critical creativity in the literature of cultural studies[4] does justice to the dilemma posed by the Golly®.

In its reference to the historical images that circulate as floating signifiers in the condition of postmodernity, this story suggests that we attend to the consumption of commodified culture and recognize the signifying politics that embrace mass-media forms—concerns that are central to any analysis of the cultural characteristics of postmodernism.[5] Opposition to the Golly, however, also reminds us of the necessity to acknowledge the historical experiences of specific subjects and the political interests of those who struggle to reinscribe or alter particular commodified images and their meanings. The movement to dislodge the Golly[6] might also, therefore, be seen as a postcolonial practice—as those historically "othered" in imperialist social imaginaries protest the continuing circulation of indicia iconic of their former subjugation. The literature on postcolonialism, however, has not been particularly attentive to practical contentions over the commodification of colonial desire. Academic struggles to define the parameters of postcolonial terrain[7] have yet to incorporate contemporary challenges to the circulation of those commodity/signs that still embody colonialism's others in the mediascapes of mass commerce. Such challenges suggest that one dimension of the relationship between the postmodern and the postcolonial is enacted in the representational exchange of the market.

The Golly is a trademark, a signifier that distinguishes the goods of one manufacturer from those of another. Trademarks may be logos, brand names, characteristic advertising images, or other (usually visual) forms that condense and convey meaning in commerce. The ubiquity of trademarks in national social arenas and their currency both as culture and as private property create generative conditions for struggles over significance; they are simultaneously shared in a commons of signification and jealously guarded in exclusive estates. The visual cultures of national mass markets are often saturated with signs of social difference.[8] When these signs assume the form of marks used in trade, these indicia of cultural difference may be legally recognized as the private properties of those who claim them as marks of their own commercial distinction. I will draw upon both historical and contemporary American examples to show that when—as in the Golly anecdote—trademarks represent an embodied otherness with imperialist precedents, social struggles over their circulation and connotation add more nuanced dimensions to our understandings of contemporary relationships between mimesis and alterity.[9]

Mimicry, Alterity, and Embodiment

Earlier I suggested that most cultural anthropologists have been reluctant to engage the social, cultural, or political role of trademarks in local practices and that in this reticence we may find a tacit acknowledgment of the complications such commodity/signs pose for the disciplinary positioning of the anthropologist. One recent exception to the anthropological tendency to ignore trademarks as cultural forms is Michael Taussig's *Mimesis and Alterity*.[10] Taussig traces the Western preoccupation with the mimetic abilities of savages and the European fascination with being imitated by primitives. He sees in many turn-of-the-century trademarks a link between mimesis, primitivism, and technological development. It is the task of the animal, the child, the black, the primitive Other (however defined), and, of course, women "to register the rediscovery of the naturalness of the mimetic faculty in a technological age of mechanical reproduction."[11] Such social others do indeed figure predominantly in the pantheon of late-nineteenth-century trademarks.[12] Taussig's geographically and historically generalizing observations on mimesis and alterity do not make reference to the cultural influence of national political agendas. Nor do they isolate the local cultural idioms of imperialism in which socially specific relations between mimesis and alterity are articulated. In this chapter, I will be concerned with a particular configuration of this nexus in a particular era of U.S. nation-building.

Taussig's definition of the mimetic faculty is indeed idiosyncratic,[13] but fruitful for considering the power of trademarks. He describes the mimetic faculty as the ability to copy, imitate, yield into, and become other in such a way that the copy draws power from and influences the original.[14] The representation gains or shares in the power of the represented and the image affects what it is an image of. But if imitation or sympathy is one principle of mimesis, sensuousness and contagion is the other. One gets "hold of something by way of its likeness—[mimesis involves] a copying or imitation, and a palpable, sensuous, connection between the very body of the perceiver and the perceived . . . making contact."[15] The fingerprint and "His Master's Voice Talking Dog" (the RCA logo)[16] are the vehicles Taussig uses to show how sympathy and contagion are fused:

> Through contact (contagion) the finger makes the print (a copy). But the print is not only a copy. It is testimony to the fact that contact was made—and it is the combination of both facts that is essential to the use of fingerprinting to the police in detection and by the State in certifying identities. The Talking Dog also interfuses contagion with sympathy, the sensuous with imitation, because it is on account of its sensorium, allegedly sensitive to an uncanny degree, that it can faithfully register—ie. receive the print—and distinguish faithful from unfaithful copies . . . the dog becomes the civilized man's servant in the detection, and hence selling, of [the] good copy.[17]

These principles of imitation and contact are useful for thinking about the role of trademarks in commercial spheres of exchange. A mark must attract the consumer to a particular source that, in mass markets, is often distant and likely unknown. A logo registers fidelity in at least two senses. It operates as a signature of authenticity that the good that bears it is true to its origins—that the good is a true or accurate copy. It is exactly the same as another good bearing the same mark, and different from other goods carrying other marks (these are both fictions, of course, but ones that are legally recognized and maintained). The mark also configures fidelity in a second sense: it registers a real contact, a making, a moment of imprinting by one for whom it acts as a kind of fingerprint: branding. But if the mark figures a fidelity, it also inspires fidelity in the form of brand loyalty. The consumer seeks it out, domesticates it, and provides it with protective shelter; he or she makes a form of bodily contact with it. The mark distinguishes the copy by connecting it to an originator and connecting the originator with a moment of consumption.

The trademark organizes the "magic of the mimetic faculty" in mass-mediated consumer societies; as the mass-reproduced stamp of an author(iz)ed site of origin that authenticates mass-produced goods as bearing the trademark owner's singular distinction, the mark might be seen as channeling the cultural energy of mimesis into the form of the signature—an attempt to appropriate it under the proper name. A commercial surrogate identity, the trademark maintains and garners exchange value in the market, alluring consumers in its endless uniformity with promises of both standardization and distinction.

Laws of intellectual property generally—copyright, trademark, and publicity rights, in particular—constitute a political economy of mimesis in capitalist societies, constructing authors, regulating activities of reproduction, licensing copying, and prohibiting imitation, all in the service of maintaining the exchange value of texts. Such laws, I have argued, provide both generative conditions and prohibitive obstacles, managing mimesis (authorizing true copies and distinguishing between legitimate and illegitimate reproductions) while it polices alterity (prohibiting the resignifications of others).

Such legal forms always invite encounters with alterity: the other that always haunts the proper name,[18] the difference that always already occupies the space of the signature[19] that attempts to keep it at bay. Laws that construct the fiction of the singular, unique, and self-contained work (copyright), the mark of singular meaning and origin for the commodity (trademark), or enable celebrities to control the publicly recognized indicia of their personalities as their autonomous productions (publicity rights) prohibit intertextuality as they simultaneously deny it as a source of meaning and value. In its denial, legal discourse gives voice to the anxiety that authorship always embodies—the anxiety that authors (be they designers of toothpaste labels, advertising copywriters, toy manufacturers, or game show hostesses) might not be the exclusive and originary source of meaning for those signifiers that circulate in their names or embody their personas in the public sphere.

To the extent that the commercial signature itself represents social others in forms that recall their enforced alterity, it is particularly likely to attract the authorial energies of those members of social groups who have an interest in contesting claims that stereotypical images of themselves be considered mere extensions of another's proper name. Ironically, as I will argue in closing this chapter, those persons who continue to bear identities marked by former colonizations, and who find those colonial identities currently commodified as marketing signs, must claim the author-function[20] and trade in the marks of their own cultural distinction if they are to appropriate these as forms to which they can make legally legitimate claims.

Marked and Unmarked Bodies

Scholars developing the concept of the "public sphere"[21] advocate an attention to the quotidian cultural politics that engage commodity/signs.[22] The trademark is both a commodity with an exchange value in its own right and a sign that condenses a relationship between a signifer, a signified, and a referent (linking, for example, a logo, a lifestyle, and a product). Michael Warner,[23] drawing heavily upon the work of Lauren Berlant, asserts the importance of mass media and their characteristic commodity forms in the construction of contemporary publics and subjectivities: "Nearly all of our pleasures come to us coded in some degree by the publicity of mass media. We have brandnames all over us."[24] Trademarks, Warner suggests, are constitutive parts of a public sphere, constructing a common discourse to bind the subject to the nation and to its markets.[25] Some of "us" and "our" ancestors, however, *are*, in fact, brandnames: Cherokee™, Oneida®, Seminoles®, Winnebago®, Crazy Horse®, Aunt Jemima®, Geronimo®, and Uncle Ben's®. Some of "us" may have national trademarks all over our bodies, others of "us" have bodies and nations that are all over the commercial landscape *as* trademarks.

Public sphere scholars suggest that to "think the nation" we must consider the characteristic mass media forms that interrelate collectivities and imagined national communities,[26] while forging corresponding forms of subjectivity. Beginning in the eighteenth century, a bourgeois public sphere and a disembodied and universalized rational subject were created through the medium of print (a configuration of publicity in which the author played a distinct and central role, as I will explore in my concluding essay).[27] Subsequently, mass-mediated consumer capitalism has interpellated a subject (the "consumer") with a more visual orientation and with more corporeal desires—desires met both by material consumption and by visual consumption of embodied others made available through mass media.[28]

To understand the particularities of subjectivity in a mass-mediated public sphere, it is helpful to consider its differences from the eighteenth-century bourgeois public sphere celebrated by writers like Habermas.[29] To be a subject in the bourgeois public sphere required identification with a disembodied public subject. Embedded in the possibility of this public was a promise, "a utopian universality that would allow people to transcend the given realities of their bodies and their status"[30]: "No matter what particularities of culture, race, gender, or class we bring to bear on public discourse, the moment of apprehending something as public is one in which we imagine—if imperfectly—indifference to those particularities, to ourselves."[31] The promise of transcendance has never been fulfilled: "For the ability to abstract oneself in public discussion has always been an unequally available resource. Individuals have specific rhetorics of disincorporation; they are not simply rendered bodiless by exercising reason. The subject who could master this rhetoric in the bourgeois public sphere was implicitly—even explicitly—white, male, literate and propertied. These traits could go unmarked, while other features of bodies could only be acknowledged as the humiliating positivity of the particular."[32]

The bourgeois public sphere claimed no relation to the body, but the particular features of particular bodies did have significance. Access to the public sphere came in the whiteness and maleness that were denied as forms of positivity; "the white male qua public person was only abstract rather than white and male."[33] Such asymmetries of embodiment and demarcation, were, as Nancy Fraser[34] has argued, constitutive of the liberal public sphere itself: "Differences in the social world [always] come coded as the difference between the unmarked and the marked . . . The bourgeois public sphere has been structured from the outset by a logic of abstraction that provides a privilege for unmarked identities . . ."[35] The term *marked* is, of course, a staple of linguistic theory: "It refers to the way language alters the base meaning of a word by adding a linguistic particle that has no meaning of its own. The unmarked form of a word carries the meaning that goes without saying—what you think of when you're not thinking anything special. The unmarked tense of verbs in English is the present . . . to indicate the past, you mark the verb . . . The unmarked forms of most English words also convey 'male.' Being male is the unmarked case. Endings like *ess* and *ette* mark words as 'female.' Unfortunately, they also tend to mark them for frivolousness . . ."[36] Even the use of *he* as the sex-indefinite pronoun is an innovation that we can trace to the emergence of a bourgeois public sphere.[37] Gender, however, is only one form of socially marked difference and those of alternative genders only some of the many others who do not have the option of remaining unmarked. In the United States, the visual display of excessive corporeality marked the other in the national social imaginary—from the noble stoicism of the cigar-store Indian, the sexualized female abundance of the exotic always-elsewhere,[38] to the hyperembodied black mammy of a fictionally reconstructed South.[39] Such imagery became particularly pervasive in the early era of mass-reproduced consumer goods (1870–1910), during which mass subjects and national consumers were constituted in a complex network of hegemonic practices.[40]

If the bourgeois public sphere offered only self-abstraction and disincorporation, the mass-mediated sphere of consumption provides opportunities to reclaim the body. An infinite realm of consumer choice purports to create conditions for a variety of identifications and a seemingly inexhaustible supply of bodily images offered for consumption, seizure, and occupation.[41] The mass subject is visually oriented toward embodied others in acts of consumption that bind him or her to a national market. The visual culture of embodied others who have historically figured as trademarks and instances of their consumption, appropriation, rejection, and reappropriation in negotiating the boundaries of the nation will be drawn upon to illustrate a politics of authorial mimesis coming into contention with assertions of alterity.

Through the use of trademarks the bourgeois subject was able to secure privileges for his otherwise unmarked identity, provided that he marked his prosthetic self[42] with a recognizable sign of distinction; commercial privilege might be marked by the corporeal indicia of publicly recognizable social others. If the bodily images available for identification in the public sphere figure as private properties protected by intellectual property laws, then the politics of identification in mass-mediated public spaces assumes new dimensions of complication. If trademarks are constitutive in the visual culture of mass markets and an orientation to corporeal representation is fundamental to contemporary subject-formation, what political difference does the law make when the bodily images of cultural others circulate as marks of private commercial distinction? I will address this question by way of examples, moving through a century but focusing on two fin de siècle moments that exemplify the politics of social difference and commercial distinction in mass-mediated public spheres. In these examples, we see how advertising produced a sense of belonging to an imagined community of American consumers—a contemporary term of art—as well as contemporary challenges to the forms of inclusion and exclusion these earlier cultural practices effected.[43]

In the late nineteenth century, U.S. trademark laws become federal in markets newly recognized as national. The emergence of trademark laws in the late nineteenth century needs to be understood within the context of mass manufacturing, mass communications, and mass immigration—and the resulting standardization of American culture.[44] The legal protection of imagery as private property provided a means for marrying mass production of goods, mass reproduction of cultural forms, and the mass interpellation necessary to transform a mass of immigrants into similar consumers. In this context, manufacturers, wholesalers, and, to a lesser degree, retailers needed to conjure a particularly American consumer upon which to focus marketing efforts. One way this was culturally accomplished was with marks of trade that all would recognize as binding them across the nation. In precisely the same period, we see preoccupations with the concept of the frontier, the defining features of American civilization, and its distinction from, and annexation and containment of, the savage, the tribal, and the primitive. These processes were linked; the American was constituted in relation to the embodied otherness from which he or she could be distinguished and whose cultural and corporeal distinctions he or she would both recognize and consume.

The nominal disembodiment of the American citizen,[45] I would suggest, was created, in part, by a realm of national signification—mass-advertised trademarks—that denied or downplayed the cultural and ethnic differences of some Americans,[46] while it emphasized the cultural differences of others. It did so literally, through the medium of the (consuming) body and the embodiment, on a national scale, of others whose claims to an American subjectivity were complicated by contemporary relations of subjugation.[47] The "incorporation of America"[48] was integrally related to the corporeality of others.

Recent scholarship asserts that "whiteness" as a social identity must be articulated, and that whiteness and Americanness have been integrally related.[49] Nationalisms may be sexualized,[50] but they may also be (e)raced and (en)gendered in processes in which a "white" subject-position comes to be forged and occupied while unacknowledged as such. In the late nineteenth century, dominant U.S. culture was preoccupied with the nature of civilization and its alters and with the prerequisites of nationhood and its connection to frontiers. The discourse of commerce, advertising, and the law of trademark projected images of barbarism, conquest, and servitude to construct the subject-positions of mass consumer and American citizen. Images and descriptions of African Americans, Indian peoples, Hispanic and mestizo subjects, as well as the perceived "tribal" groups colonized by U.S. imperial expansion (e.g., Filipinos, Hawaiians, and "Eskimos") and references to the corporeal indicators of recent American incorporation (e.g., hula dancers, pineapples, igloos, fur parka bonnets, etc.) were mass-reproduced and projected on a national scale through the medium of trademarks (as well as design patents and label copyrights). Through magazine and streetcar advertising, trade cards, billboards, packaging, and premiums, concepts of savagery and civilization, primitivism and progress were legitimated. In their visual consumption of imagery and their bodily consumption of goods, Americans envisioned and incorporated the same signs of otherness that the national body politic was surveilling and incorporating.

In early federal trademark law, a mark had to be distinctive; it could not be confusing, and it could not be the name of the product itself. It had to be a mark that differentiated one's wares from the goods of others—it distinguished one's product in the market. The legal basis for the claim that such a mark is a form of property is the old mercantile notion of goodwill. The mark that accompanies all of one's goods and makes them recognizable attracts the "loyalty" of consumers, and this loyalty and good feeling is a valuable asset: goodwill. The positive value of one's trade is congealed in the exchange value of the sign. The trademark marks the point of origin of the good—and serves as a surrogate identity for the manufacturer—in a national market in which the distances between points of mass production and points of consumption might be vast.

Not wanting to stifle commerce by allocating exclusive rights to terms that were merely descriptive of goods, their place of origin, or their material qualities, courts would only recognize as marks those indicators sufficiently distant from the goods so that competitors would not be precluded from engaging in the same field of trade. A distributor could not claim "Idaho" as his or her mark for potatoes grown in that state, but "Arctic" might well be seen as sufficiently fantastic to mark one's particular brand of citrus fruits. Marks had to be connotative as well as denotative, but they could not be purely referential. As U.S. markets became national, marks needed to be recognizable to millions of people, from diverse ethnic backgrounds and language groups, many of whom were illiterate. The use of images to mark products was an early development, and manufacturers were taught the semiotics of marketing quite explicitly in numerous manuals. One such manual, intriguingly titled *Trademark Power: An Expedition into an Unprobed and Inviting Wilderness* (1916) by one Glen Buck,[51] lists a series of equivalences that consumers could be expected to know; one of them is a figure of an Indian followed by an equal sign and a picture of a cigar.

Manufacturers were advised to choose marks that were as distant as possible from the nature of the goods they were actually selling. Indeed, an early article in one of the first widely distributed legal periodicals, the *Albany Law Journal*, suggested that foreign words, words in dead languages, and terms and images from areas of the world not empirically (but presumably mythically) known in the local market promised to be the best markers for a manufacturer's wares. Their exoticism was precisely what rendered them "merely arbitrary designations for the sake of distinction."[52] Businesses were advised to establish a "strong mark" that was not "descriptive" nor "suggestive," but "distinctive." In their quest for distinction, it is not at all surprising that producers turned to bodily signs of social difference—those indicia that Americans, via World's Fairs, were coming to recognize as the signs of the primitive other that marked their own civilization. Robert Rydell[53] demonstrates that the midway imposed an evolutionary framework upon the world's peoples in U.S.-based international expositions between 1876 and 1916.[54] The proliferation of American Indian and "Polynesian" imagery and the ubiquity of black servants in the advertising and marketing of consumer goods at the turn of the century is quite remarkable.[55] Thus, publicly recognized signs of social difference created a pool of cultural resources within which manufacturers fished for their own distinction, that is, the distinction they could claim as their own.

Given what Taussig claims to be the "alleged primitivism of mimeticism," it is not surprising that manufacturers should capture the perceived mimetic abilities of others in the magic of the commodity's own mimetic circulation. Those with perceived mimetic capacities—American Indians, Eskimos, children, especially twins, talking birds, animals, and "savages" of every stripe—figure prominently as trademarks. Creatures deemed by a dominant culture to have a "sixth sense"—these creatures served to judge similitude, while simultaneously marking difference. Moreover, such advertising was often "internally referential, an image of the miming of miming,"[56] as, for example, in the ubiquitous imagery of black servants on boxes holding up boxes marked with their image holding up another box, marked with yet another black servant holding a box, and so on (e.g., Cream of Wheat ads). In short, the bodies a mass manufacturing subject might claim were not likely to be his own, but might be recognized as embodying his place in national commerce.

Manufacturers, wholesalers, and retailers were thus legally enabled to make proprietary claims upon such signs against the appropriations of others by virtue of the "distinction" they could claim in the market. To assert such rights, however, one also had to make assertations about the consuming public and its knowledge—the average consumer's likelihood of confusion. One early case is suggestive. In an appeal from the Milwaukee County Court in 1879, one Mr. Leidersdorf brought action against a Mr. Flint to prevent him from using a trademark that imitated his own trademark. Both were tobacco dealers. For thirteen years the plaintiff had manufactured and sold a type of smoking tobacco in paper wrappers stamped with the words and name "Nigger-Hair Smoking Tobacco" and claimed exclusive rights in that mark. The mark, besides the name, included "a representation of the head of a negro surmounted with a copious crop of wool, and having a large ring pending from the nose and another from the ear."[57] The complaint alleged that "the said tobacco is a low-priced tobacco, and is to a large extent bought and consumed by a class of people who cannot read, and whose necessities and manner of living do not require them to practice more than ordinary caution when purchasing the commodities most frequently procured; and to this class of people the said tobacco has become known and is easily recognized, largely by reason of the said peculiar and distinctive trade-mark aforesaid."[58] The plaintiff claimed that the defendant's mark imitated their own proprietary mark and was designed to confuse and deceive customers, divert trade, and steal the goodwill the plaintiff had garnered. Purchasers who thought they were buying the genuine "Nigger-Hair" found themselves with an inferior imitation.

What makes the manufacturer's claim so remarkable today, beyond its obvious racist proprietary (if I may "coin a term"; "coined terms" are the "strongest marks" according to the lore of trademark management), is the fact that the so-called imitation mark was a representation *not* of an African American, but of "the head of an Indian with a ring in his ear, but none in his nose"[59] with the words "Big Indian" under the picture. The judges were asked to permit the ongoing sale of Big Indian tobacco, on the basis that there was no cause of action, but refused to dismiss the claim. Recognizing several points of resemblance between the marks, the court decided it was possible that the public were actually deceived. They therefore decided to let the case go to trial. A public sphere in which the bodily features of a "Nigger" and an "Indian" might be seen as equivalents—one form of alterity mimetic with another, and one mark of distinctive alterity an imitation of the other—was affirmed as both plausible and probable.

To produce an adequate ethnohistory of national commerce, further work will need to be done with respect to the way particular images of alterity were associated with particular products and connotations. No doubt the symbolic field of alterity was both complex and further differentiated within national and regional markets as well as along product lines and points of circulation. The initial point being asserted here is merely that an American identity was simultaneously constituted in racial, ethnic, and commercial terms, using similar strategies to distinguish others and thereby to confer distinction upon the corporate self.

Contemporary Contestations

I want to move my focus forward through a century, to contemporary fields in which embodied distinctions are established and contested on frontiers on which the boundaries of the nation are still very much at stake. Benjamin Lee suggests that the nation-state may no longer be the defining unit for what constitutes a public in contemporary circumstances: "hybrid spaces created by diasporic migrations"[60]—or, I would add, hybrid spaces produced by historic contestations and contingent compromises—may be more significant sites for struggles over publicity. Occupied by "bilingual and bicultural nomads,"[61] these spaces are precisely those in which we see the boundaries of nations narrated and negotiated.[62] Given the historical focus on the "frontier" as defining the space and the possibility of American democracy (and the 1893 World's Fair as the venue at which Frederick Jackson Turner made this thesis famous), I will focus on frontiers as liminal spaces in which nations, citizens, and their differential embodiments were expressed in commercial idioms.

Consider the fantasy colossus, the visual trademark of nineteenth-century fairs that took the body to immense proportions to mark the portals and boundaries of the American horizontal sublime.[63] Indians, black mammies, bison, moose, and suffragettes marked the gateway to those "open spaces"—the frontier that defined the national imaginary of democracy in the late nineteenth century. As Karal Ann Marling shows, even as the frontier "closed" it was recreated as theater and amusement, fun and fantasy for the continuing consumption of Americans.[64] An aesthetic of "surfeit, gigantism, the colossal"[65] is a peculiarly American one that distinguishes a nation and the capacities of its citizenry to deal with the challenges posed by the ever-expanding frontiers of imperial ambition. Even as Turner introduced his famous "frontier thesis" at the American Historical Association meetings, held in conjunction with the 1893 Columbian Exposition, Buffalo Bill's enormously popular Wild West Show was attracting crowds to the midway. The "last" frontier was recreated as theater, adventure, and myth,[66] even as new frontiers, north and south, across the Pacific and the Caribbean, were envisioned.

The spoils of imperial conquest—tepees, wigwams, tropical fruits, icebergs, igloos, and polar bears: magnified images of an alterity claimed in the spirit of national expansion—were first asserted as trademarks in national commerce and then erected in three-dimensional highway sculptures that mark the Midwest. All garnered goodwill but bore no referential relationship to the goods they advertised. Such creatures, from huge plaster buffalo to menacing Indians, still flank the nation's highways. One such roadside colossus, built in Bemidji, Minnesota, in the bitter cold winter of 1937, commemorated a local legend, the great logging hero Paul Bunyan. Used by novelist John Dos Passos "to symbolize the American worker, grown larger-than-life in the strength of collective action, and thus feared by 'the Chamber of Commerce,'"[67] he had achieved national folk-hero status as a workingman's champion, standing firm against both big business and the weather during the Depression. In Bemidji, he was easily appropriated for local commercial needs, attracting tourists to an annual winter carnival. This oversized hero and the twentieth-century myths he inspired are characterized by Marling as "a distilled, collective response to the frontier."[68]

Legend has it that Paul Bunyan was born in Maine but found the East too small, and so headed West "with Babe, his big Blue Ox, whose hoofprints carved the Great Lakes."[69] But he fit the Midwest quite well, and in Minnesota at least three towns claim to be his birthplace, setting up larger and larger Bunyans to mark their hegemony.[70] In fact, Bunyan and his retinue appear to have their origins not in folk tradition, "but [in] the shiny byproducts of modern jazz-age advertising—of popular, mass culture."[71] Lumberjack stories were endowed with a single protagonist (between 1914 and 1922) who became the registered trademark for promoting the products of the Red River Lumber Company of Minnesota. The corporation made the quintessential workingman—its class other—its property and the sign of its distinction. The colossus made him the town's trademark for drawing commerce as well.

Paul Bunyan's trademarked and touristic presence has not, however, gone unchallenged. The national commercial values he so colossally embodies are not universally celebrated, not even in Minnesota. As motorists traverse the northern state, a sign alerts them that they are entering the Red Lake Reservation and subject to the laws of another nation. The respect due the Chippewa peoples and their customs cannot be legislated, but the painted billboard that confronts drivers makes it clear that one is encountering (an)other form of national embodiment. Another huge image of Paul Bunyan appears on yet another highway, but this one is besieged; the Chippewa trickster figure of Nanabozho (elsewhere known as Nanabush) assaults Paul Bunyan with a gigantic walleye, thrashing him over the head with it.[72] Chippewa peoples have longstanding conflicts with local logging concerns; the walleye may be seen as an emblem of their economic independence, arguably an indicia of their own autonomy in commerce. Native peoples borrow the monumentality and mode of publicity of the billboard trademark—its power of assault, as Walter Benjamin[73] saw it—to pitch one mythic figure against another. Asserting a sovereignty that is invisible to most travelers, they use the commodity form to mark the borders of another nation. Borrowing something of the enchantment of the commodity and its characteristic mode of address, they counter it with (an)other form of spiritual embodiment, alter/ing its claim to a singularity of meaning. Paul Bunyan, however, is not insulted, assaulted, or attacked without local resistance. The Red Lake billboard is routinely chopped down in nocturnal forays by local residents outraged by the sacrilege done to their local mascot; people on the reservation resurrect the sign again and again. Mimesis and alterity are embodied on national frontiers. Nanabush laughs.

Move further west, to urban California, and the nationalist politics of Chicano activists, to examine yet another instance of the embodied other meeting the commodity under its own signature. In Jose Antonio Burciaga's work *Drink Cultura: Chicanismo*, the particularities of Chicano social life and identity are explored: "the ironies in the experience of living within, between, and sometimes outside of two cultures."[74] The book's front cover displays an obvious parody of the famous round red Coca-Cola® signs that graced thousands of U.S. streetcorner shops during the mid-twentieth century. The "Drink Cultura" image—a clear satire on the famous trademarked script—was a work that ironically challenged the universalizing and homogenizing pretensions of the multinational corporation ("We'd like to teach the world to sing in perfect harmony") by associating the drinking of the soft drink with the consumption of *cacacan*—Brazilian "white lightning"—simultaneously alluding back to an older "Enjoy Cocaine" parody and giving it a regional twist. The "Drink Cultura" image was widely appropriated, appearing on T-shirted torsos throughout Central and South America in the 1980s. Burciaga's reappropriation of the work, however, is marked by yet another signature, the c/s sign that marks Chicano *placas*, or graffiti, in the southwestern United States. A Mexican American symbol that appears to have originated in South El Paso's Segundo Barrio, it means *con safos*, which translates literally as "with safety": "It was meant as a safety precaution, a barrio copyright, patent pending. No one else could use or dishonor the graffiti. It was an honorable code of conduct, a literary imprimatur. Like saying 'amen' it ended discussion. Above all it meant 'anything you say against me will bounce back to you.' Most kids respected a placa if signed with the c/s. Without that symbol, a placa would sooner or later get scribbled on or erased. Some kids would put a double c/s sign or put xxx after it, or a skull and cross bones, which physically threatened anyone who did not honor and respect the code."[75]

The term originates in *Calo*, the Chicano dialect that combines Hispanicized English, Anglicized Spanish, and the use of archaic fifteenth-century Spanish words that remain in use in isolated pockets of northern Mexico and the Southwest. Although it is derisively called Tex-Mex or Spanglish in the United States, Barciago values it as a "unique multicultural, political, societal and linguistic function and formation."[76]

The sign of the c/s shields from attack, repels insults, and stands for itself. "Chicano artists and writers of the late sixties and early seventies often used the c/s symbol in signing their works, especially when the works were political or cultural in nature."[77] The trademark form is altered to assert a cultural difference, to assert (an)other body in the body politic and challenge the illusion of national homogeneity that might otherwise go unremarked in the public sphere. Even the term *Chicano* was originally considered an insulting imposition, blurring boundaries between distinct forms of essentialist embodiment. Both Hispanic and American Indian, it recognizes an ancestry of both conquerors and conquered, a link to an indigenous past (for many Mexicans it meant a *pochos*, or "spoiled fruit"). Ironically, many of those who first identified themselves as Chicanos forged that identity in opposition to particular trademarks, in boycotts nominated by particular brand names: "the Coors® boycott, the Gallo® wine boycott, the Farah pants boycott, and the Frito Bandito® boycott."[78] Such boycotts were not led by Hispanics—

a government and media term that attempts to unite Latinos from diverse parts of the Americas without regard for racial, class, and political difference—but by Chicanos whose political consciousness was informed by a historical awareness of the exploitation of both Indian ancestors and campesino forebears.

When Burciaga reappropriates the "Drink Cultura" image—itself an appropriation of one of the most ubiquitous trademarks of U.S. global cultural hegemony—with the mark of *con safos*, he effects another signifying intervention into a historical chain of intertextuality marking a series of political realignments. But the power of capital should not be underestimated; when I tried to get Burciaga's permission to reproduce the cover of his book in a description of my own research, I found him reluctant. His publisher has received warnings from Coca Cola that the "Drink Cultura" image is considered a violation and dilution of their trademark. They threaten to enjoin any future imitations of the work; controlling mimesis, they will police alterity.

The newly signed-off "Drink Cultura," appropriated under the mark of Chicanismo, marks only a ceasefire on a particular terrain in which the significations of capital, the nation, and ethnic identity continue to evolve. Burciaga suggests that recent developments in Chicano political identity formation involve "independence from those feelings of shame, hate and guilt that we may have experienced because of Mexico."[79] The embrace of the mother country and the release from shame that Burciaga characterizes as a new aspect of Chicanismo may not be so secure from re-sign(nations) as the *con safos* intimates, however. Chicanos may well find their "return" to Mexico reinscribed with unanticipated signatures: "In Redwood City, California, the Mexican flag was hoisted over the Taco Bell® fast food restaurant . . . the local Mexican-American business community was angered and the flag was taken down. Taco Bell® is determined to make inroads into the Mexican community through its culture and economics."[80]

More recently, the first Taco Bell was established in Mexico City. National borders, bodies politic, and the signs of national belonging are complicated in communities caught up in the global restructuring of capitalism.[81] Redwood City, California, for example, is one end of an unofficial conduit for people, labor, and goods that stretches to the state of Michoacan in Mexico. Home to thousands of documented and undocumented rural Mexican workers and their children, this impoverished area lies adjacent to the wealthy mansions of Atherton, the university community of Palo Alto, the high-tech business developments of Menlo Park, and in the midst of the postindustrial success stories of the Silicon

Valley. Relations between Redwood City and the villages of Michoacan cannot be described either as relations between two "communities" or as center-periphery ties, as dependency and modernization theories would have it.[82] Instead, the movement of Mexicans into and out of the area challenges our spatial images of discretely bounded nations and poses instead what anthropologist Roger Rouse refers to as a "transnational migratory circuit."[83]

Mexicans and Latinos toil in restaurant kitchens, hotel back rooms, nurseries, and in the gardens of the affluent estates they border. They constitute a "postindustrial" proletariat whose relevant communities are constituted within mobile and spatially extended relationships. Their allegiances and commitments are oriented toward the continuation of this circuit rather than to any bounded community or to any nation-state:

> Thus, people in the United States may spend large amounts of time and money trying to obtain papers without ever seeking citizenship because it is as Mexican citizens with the right to "permanent residence" that they will be best equipped to move back and forth between the two countries. And they may send their children back to Mexico to complete their educations or to visit . . . in part because they want to endow them with the bilingual and bicultural skills necessary to operate effectively on both sides of the border . . . [they] see their current lives and future possibilities as involving simultaneous engagements in places associated with markedly different forms of experience.[84]

Rouse suggests we follow Americo Paredes in recognizing borders not simply as lines but as sensitized and productive zones: fractured realities of multiple histories, languages, and traditions come into confrontation or juxtaposition.[85] National borders are mobile and diffuse as immigration officials gain access to workplaces in the United States and U.S. capital interests penetrate ever further into rural Mexico. Working in the service sector and the informal economy, often traveling to their jobs on routes designed to minimize encounters with migration authorities, such Mexican migrants lived for years in fear of deportation (and many still do). Producing fast food (or cleaning up its consumption) in substandard conditions at less than minimum wage is the lot of daily life. At night they retire to Redwood City, where the spaces of Mexican village life are reinscribed on suburban terrain[86] and the food of the mother country may be one form of solace. When the forces of American capital moved into this neighborhood to tender inferior food at an imitation taqueria under the sign of the Mexican flag, annoyance, if not anger, might well have been anticipated.

The prices at Taco Bell simultaneously invite and insult this community. Far lower than those that can be tendered by any local entrepreneur, they attract those whose jobs in this country pay less than minimum wage, teenagers, and large families with parents who work multiple jobs to make ends meet. Empty stomachs and empty pocketbooks convince many to forego the flavors of home, the smell of roasting corn, sizzling carnitas, and the tang of tomatillos, cilantro, and jalapeño in favor of dry, stiff, prepackaged shells filled with flavorless ground beef and mildly doctored ketchup. Such fare is savored in an ambience devoid of irony or sensitivity: "Orders are served in under five minutes and placed on a plastic tray with a paper placemat headlined, 'The Border Run.' It depicts an open highway in the desert leading to a Taco Bell and surrounded by highway signs that tell you to 'Crack It, Bust It, Jump It, Snap It or Cross It.' This, of course, is a subtle reference to crossing the border illegally or jumping a once-proposed fifteen-mile ditch south of San Diego. The hidden message is that eating at Taco Bell can be not only a treat but a real, live *Indiana Jones* adventure."[87] Many of the area's residents risk life and limb to make trips across the border and continue to face serious sanctions if they are found without papers; their daily movements are calibrated to the potential monitoring of those who police the border in the transnational frontiers of the American West. For these migrants, there is little entertainment in the sign of the nation-state tendered as one of the trademarked forms of their own alterity nor in the commodification of national borders as games of chance and amusement.

The Americanization and Anglicization of Mexican culture may well increase under the pressures of the North American Free Trade Agreement, but the signifying forces of U.S. and Canadian capital are by no means guaranteed cultural hegemony. In its daring, the sign of *con safos* does risk erasure when it affixes its signature to the corporate forms that mark commercial space and brand consumer experience, but forces of prohibition and publicity, censorship and censure dance dangerously for proprietors who evoke them, permitting the ongoing promiscuity of appropriation in the spaces of postmodernity. The very form of the *con safos*, the graffiti that operates as a form of signature in late capitalism, is itself an embodied performative. It is both imitative and contagious; it registers sympathy and contact to assert alternative bodies occupying alternative spaces. As a medium, it can be seen as a kind of counterpublicity because it mimics the logic of the trademark's communicative mode; marking distinction while maintaining anonymity, it adopts the utopian promise of the brand name:[88] "by appearing everywhere, it aspires to the placeless publicity of mass print or televisualization. It thus abstracts away from the given body, which in the logic of graffiti is difficult to criminalize or minoritize because it is impossible to locate. Unlike the self-abstraction of normal publicity, however, graffiti retains its link to a body, in an almost parodic devotion to the sentimentality of the signature."[89] As literary theorist Susan Stewart has noted, graffiti seems to claim the imaginary uniqueness promised by commodities but continually deferred and delayed.[90] Marking an individual's past presence at the scene, graffiti re-mark a past point of bodily contact. Their presence on subway cars, high up on walls and under bridges ironically remarks upon the actual *difficulty* of access to mass communication modalities in a public sphere anachronistically attached to an Enlightenment egalitarian logic that purports to be committed to equality of communicative activity. In its emphasis on the individual name, graffiti comments upon the proliferation of the distinctive marks that pass for public speech in a consumer society—the private labels of the powerful that constitute the "culture" of late capitalism.[91] As Stewart points out, contemporary consumer culture contains a tension; consumption is ubiquitously offered by a mass culture that insinuates itself pervasively as social signification in communities where consumption itself is a potential practice. In such social arenas, "graffiti as a phenomenon vividly take on the form and thematic of that tension as graffiti writers or artists address the relation that those cut off from consumption bear to consumerism."[92] Moreover, in Los Angeles, at least, gang graffiti mark territory, the "nations" of youth subculture. Often called "tags," graffiti operate interstitially in a mass-produced consumer sphere. The street becomes an endless billboard for the marks of a nascent counterpublic.

Owners of trademarks must always cope with the presence of the other in the cultural spaces they attempt to colonize. The activities I examine might be seen as forms of counterpublicity, articulations that deploy consumer imagery and the bodily impact of the trademark to make the claims of alternative publics and other(ed) national allegiances. But the *con safos* and Nanabozho operate in different realms of embodiment, commodification, and nationhood. The organized control of mimesis is met with an alter that re-signs it, but in fundamentally distinct ways. The difference of the American Indian nation marked by the trickster is legitimated in a fashion that nationalist sentiments of Chicano activists or inner-city graffiti artists cannot be. The static and monumental bodily icons of the midwestern plains mark fixed and officially recognized boundaries, whereas the stealthily ascribed signatures of mobile bodies mark continually contested territory, both cultural and geographic. The mimeticism of commerce is met, in the first instance, with a counterpublicity of pride that proclaims its own alternative enchantments; in the second, counterpublicity is limited in communicative power by its deliberate indecipherability in a wider public sphere. The Taco Bell incident serves as a cautionary reminder of the power of capital to appropriate the indicia of national difference as exchange value, even as capital accumulation becomes increasingly less constrained by the borders of the nation-state. Some nations, as we shall see, have been significantly erased even as they have been adopted and mass-reproduced as marks of trade.

Fighting Redskins®

The dynamics of relationships between those whose social alterity was specularized and those who profited from its commodification in marks of trade have shifted dramatically as these objects of property have been turned into subjects and sites of politics. Specularizations of alterity have come under the intense scrutiny of civil rights movements since World War II. Peoples historically othered in imperialist social imaginaries protest the continuing circulation of indicia iconic of their former subjugation and contest the propriety of this continuing commodification of colonial desire. The multiple metamorphoses of Aunt Jemima, the abandonment of the Frito Bandito, protests over Sambo restaurants and Robertson's Golly(wog), are but a few of the struggles in which minority groups have focused attention on commodity/signs. Indigenous peoples in Hawaii, for example, seek to rescue such signs of their traditional culture as the hula and the luau from their commercial distortions in a tourist industry founded upon the consumption of their cultural distinction—exotic spoils of an unconstitutional territorial incorporation.[93] Whether these commodity/signs are commodifications of their heritage or stereotypical signs of their alterity, many peoples find "their own" representations legally owned by others.

Of those historically subjugated groups who have demanded an end to the commodification of their cultural difference in North American mass markets, Native Americans have faced the longest struggles. Long after the Frito Bandito has been laid to rest, and black mammies and little black Sambos have ceased to signify on American commercial terrain (although they have returned as a form of collectible nostalgia), Indians are still a privileged form of alterity in advertising.[94] From Red Man® chewing tobacco, Indian Spirit® air freshener, Indian-style™ popcorn, teams of Braves®, Red Indian® jeans, Warrior boxes, and Indian heads on everything from baking soda tins and neon beer signs to children's campgrounds, the corporeality of the "Indian" continues to mark the privileges of the incorporated in commerce.

Contesting legally legitimated claims that stereotypical images of themselves be considered merely the marketing vehicles of others, Native peoples have come up against commercial indifference, animosity, and public ridicule. The movement to end the use of Native American team names, logos, and mascots has been both protracted and politically revealing. Dismissed by some as evidence of "political correctness" gone to ridiculous extremes, the offensiveness of these signs is denied by many bewildered liberals, and they are even considered complimentary by a few team owners, journalists, and zealous fans. Protests about these signs have been greeted with a curious degree of misrecognition. An examination of these controversies reveals a great deal about the trademark as a vehicle for articulatory practice.

The Washington Redskins, Atlanta Braves, Cleveland Indians, Chicago Blackhawks, Kansas City Chiefs, Florida State University Seminoles, St. John University Redmen, Chief Illiniwek of the University of Ilinois Fighting Illini, and Miami of Ohio University Redskins[95] are team names that bind fans across ethnic and generational lines. Along with associated logos and mascots, these names provide steady streams of income. The law bestows on their "owners" exclusive rights to circulate these marks in commercial (and many noncommercial) contexts and powers to enjoin their use by others. As a consequence, team insignia have become valuable properties in their own right. The exploitation of merchandising rights (the right to license one's exclusive rights under trademark laws) provides a significant and autonomous source of revenue.[96]

It is tempting to reduce the reluctance to abandon such marks to economics and sentiment alone. Significant profits will be lost (or dispersed) if these marks are forgone, and there are now long traditions of fan activity associated with them. The cost of conceiving popularly appealing logos, nicknames, and color combinations is not incidental.[97] In earlier chapters, I have discussed the peculiarity of the legal determination that public meaning is a form of private property. Suffice it to say here that to the extent that fans become personally attached to these symbols, the value of such intimacies accrues to the mark's legal holder. To the extent that team owners view public recognition of these symbols as valuable assets in their own right (goodwill), any prohibition on their use is seen as tantamount to an expropriation without compensation.

Neither economics nor emotion, however, fully accounts for the cultural power of such symbols or the almost willful refusal by team owners and fans to entertain Native people's concerns. Stereotypical commercial imagery has been abandoned under minority pressures before, despite predictable economic loss and acknowledged social popularity (the Frito Bandito, for example). The damage to a people's self-esteem effected by stereotypical imagery has been publicly acknowledged with respect to African, Mexican, and Asian Americans and offensive trademarks withdrawn from commerce. After surveying arguments on both sides of this debate, I will suggest that the financial interests and the social sentiments expressed in this controversy are epiphenomena of a deeper convergence of historical, psychosocial, and legal forces.

Native people's opposition to these marks is complex, multifaceted, and far from unanimous in terms of the seriousness accorded the issue or the grounds upon which it is (or is not) condemned.[98] Owners of these marks like to quote Indians who do not object to these marks to support their own reluctance to abandon them. Since the 1991 World Series made the "tomahawk chop" famous, for example, the market for toy "tomahawks" has soared. The Cherokee tribe of North Carolina owns and provides labor for the factory that produces the foam tomahawks used at Atlanta Braves games. Chief Jonathan Ed Taylor is quoted as saying that the Redskin name (and other usages of Indian symbols) "gives our people recognition. The most important thing is that it employs my people. It means our people will get work and not stand in welfare lines. Welfare lines are a lot more degrading than using the name Redskins."[99] Some Native peoples might feel less resentment about the exploitation of Indianness if more of the profits made their way back to Indian peoples to serve their social needs—implicitly suggesting the political propriety of licensing arrangements that might funnel funds back into Native communities.[100] Others, of course, might well view this as a form of cultural prostitution.

The most common basis for antagonism is the conviction that the names, logos, mascots, paraphernalia, and related fan activities represent racist stereotypes of Native Americans and their culture. Historic depictions of Indians as bloodthirsty, warlike savages are racist stereotypes that are perpetuated in these rituals and have the effect of "rendering Native American oppression invisible, justified, or even glorious."[101] More complicated is concern about the negative influence of such imagery upon the already fragile self-image of many Native Americans and especially the self-esteem of youth and children. In communities wracked by alarming rates of youth suicide, alcoholism, poverty, and chronic unemployment, cultural representation is not insignificant. Indian youth see few images of their people in the public sphere except for monstrous caricatures and cartoon figures with painted faces, grunting and whooping unintelligibly, usually savagely preparing for battle or engaged in preposterous or exaggerated rites set in no meaningful context.

The same complexity and range of response characterizes political sympathizers in this field. The use of such symbols may be seen as (unintentionally) disrespectful, demeaning, or discriminatory: an affront to Indian dignity, a mockery of sacred Native American symbols, or quite simply as virulent racism. Types of racism perceived in the athletic field range from the glaring and obvious to the more subtle and complex. Terms like *redskins*, which have historically figured as racial epithets, are more offensive than caricatures that are seen to effect a continuation of social stereotyping, while the appropriation of the names of Indian nations and the trivializing of rituals is felt to have the effect of ridiculing them and demeaning their social significance.

Most of the so-called Indianness drawn upon in sports arenas recalls the Wild West of Buffalo Bill and Hollywood lore—a stereotypical Plains warrior culture now hackneyed to the point that it no longer reflects any particular Indian nation or tradition. This is one reason they are offensive. They reiterate historical stereotypes of the Indian as a monolithic other without internal differentiation in languages, traditions, and ways of life. The Indian as a general category and concept has a long history in North America, as Robert Berkhofer, in his classic study *The White Man's Indian*,[102] delineates. Divided into at least two thousand cultures and more societies at the time of "first contact," the idea and image of the Indian as a singularity is and remains a "white" stereotype, which nonetheless has created its own realities as a result of white power and the necessity of Native Americans to respond to it.[103] Other aspects of this ensemble of signs are more directly offensive. To the extent that feathers were and are used in highly elaborated systems of political honor and prestige and achieve sacred status in particular contexts,[104] peace pipes are significant in wider systems of reciprocity and meaning involving tobacco, and wampum figures in historical political negotiations of great contemporary import, their appropriation as toys and jokes is more than merely insensitive.

Unlike the appropriation of such mascots as the Irish, Native American mascots were not selected by the ethnic group they supposedly represent, nor, like Vikings, Trojans, Spartans, Buccaneers, Pirates, and 49ers, are they mythic figures of the past—except perhaps in popular culture. This is perhaps the most complicated of the injuries effected by such sports fantasies. They make mythic and imaginary images of Native Americans more visible than they are as living peoples with contemporary concerns and pressing political problems, preserving "the crippling myth that Native Americans, their lands, their cultures, their sovereign powers, their very existence, are relics of the past."[105]

Critics of those who oppose the use of these marks and associated practices pose contradictory but revealing arguments. Many, like Paul Tagliabue, commissioner of the NFL, claim to be sensitive to Native American concerns, but simply do not believe these team names are in any way demeaning. Others argue that use of these names and images pay a form of tribute to Native Americans by alluding to their bravery and fighting spirit; in athletic competition, aggressiveness, dedication, courage, and pride are prized, and Indians are recognized to embody these traits. John Cooke, the Redskins' executive vice president (and son of late owner Jack Kent Cooke) goes so far as to say that the team's name "has come to represent the best of the culture—bravery, organization, the whole works. We honor Native Americans. We believe that [it] represents the finest things in Indian culture."[106] Ted Turner, owner of the Atlanta Braves, asserts that the name Braves is "a compliment. Braves are warriors."[107] Ironically, however, many of the same people who believe these are forms of tribute to Native American people simultaneously argue that these names and images don't really refer and were never meant to refer to any particular people at all and that their meanings in the public sphere have entirely to do with the teams and their time-honored traditions.

There is a paradoxical sense in which all of these contradictory assertions are true—in which the use of Native American names and images is both insulting and complimentary, embodies both negative and positive traits, makes reference to Indians but refers to no people in particular, and symbolically has more to do with American audiences than with oppressed nations. To comprehend *how* this might be the case, however, it is necessary to understand the peculiar role of Indians in American colonial discourse and the continuing symbolic role of colonial tropes in the national imaginary. Berkhofer is not the only scholar, sympathizer, or activist to point out that white views of Indians have been inextricably bound up with an evaluation of their own society and culture and reflect ambivalence about European and American attitudes toward their own customs and civilization.[108] The singular space occupied by the generic

Indian was and to a large extent remains a space from which modernity is judged and an image with which to comment upon contemporary social relations. Not surprisingly, the figure of the (imaginary) Indian is internally contradictory:

> Encompassing . . . contrasting modes of performance, the Plains warriors performed complex and contradictory roles of enemies and American heroes, of local specimens and national symbols. With or without their permission, Indians participate in the often violent struggle over what and who is or is not American. In the symbolic economy of Wild West violence especially, American Indians are richly polysemic . . . Indians could signify reckless defiance in the face of oppression and tyranny [as they did for Anglo-Americans cross-dressing at the Boston Tea Party] . . . disenfranchised of a continent, American Indians could also signify holders of legitimate entitlement to either repatriation or revenge. From the time of Plymouth, the Indian appeared in the bad conscience of white mythology as a symbol of savage retribution, the dark agent of God's wrath.[109]

Such a field of contested connotations is particularly apt for the arena of competitive national sport, not least because it reiterates and reinscribes discourses of American cultural colonialism—the American frontier as a contested space testing and consolidating the triumph of a pioneering male "American" spirit, always under threat from races and cultures beyond it.

Here I think Homi Bhabha's understanding of the stereotype as a major discursive strategy of colonial discourse helps us to understand the effectivity of the trademark and the regime of truth it exemplifies.[110] In such discourses, the stereotype of the Indian is both an object of derision and an object of desire, disparaged and admired. From this perspective, the question of whether Native American names and images are positive or negative representations ceases to be the most salient one. Instead, Bhabha suggests that we explore the stereotype in terms of the *processes of subjectification* it makes possible and plausible:

> To judge the stereotyped image on the basis of a prior political normativity is to dismiss it, not to displace it, which is only possible by engaging with its *effectivity;* with the repertoire of positions of power and resistance, domination and dependence that constructs colonial identification[s] [and] subjects (both colonizer and colonized) . . . In order to understand the productivity of colonial

power it is crucial to construct its regime of truth, not to subject its representations to normalizing judgement. Only then does it become possible to understand the *productive* ambivalence of the object of colonial discourse—that "otherness" which is at once an object of desire and derision, an articulation of difference contained within the fantasy of origin and identity.[111]

If colonial discourse fixes otherness in an ideological discourse, it does so in a fashion that requires that that which is already known demands a continual and anxious repetition. The force of ambivalence is what gives the colonial stereotype its currency and longevity,[112] and perhaps this is the heart of the trademark's value. "Indian" trademarks, more obviously than other commodified stereotypes, resonate with an extensive history of national myth making in which both Indians' noble resistance and their ultimate defeat on expanding frontiers are repeatedly imagined and reenacted.[113] They may, therefore, operate more meaningfully and more powerfully than other marks in the forging of "American" allegiances in the political aesthetics of spectator positioning. (Interestingly, Indian sports trademarks have little popularity or presence in either Canada or Australia despite their similar histories of "vanquishing" indigenous populations.)

These are essentially racial dramas in which myths of historical origination are performed. Ideas about modern national foundings—which often stress racial purity or cultural priority—are produced in relation to colonial stereotypes. Recognitions of difference are "disavowed by the fixation on an object that masks the difference and restores an original presence."[114] "The . . . stereotype gives access to an 'identity' which is predicated as much on mastery and pleasure as it is on anxiety and defence . . . The stereotype, then, as the primary point of subjectification in colonial discourse, for both colonizer and colonized, is the scene of a similar fantasy and defence—the desire for an originality which is again threatened by the differences of race, colour and culture . . ."[115] Bhabha focuses on the scopophilic nature of the stereotype as a site (and sight) of subjectification in which identification with the positivity of whiteness is enabled by a disavowal of one's self as other through the fixation upon an other's absolute otherness: "In the act of disavowal and fixation the colonial subject is returned to the narcissism of the Imaginary and its identification of an ideal ego that is white and whole. For what these primal scenes illustrate is that looking/hearing/reading as sites of subjectification in colonial discourse are evidence of the importance of the visual and auditory imaginary for the *histories* of societies."[116]

If, as I have suggested, a mass of immigrants from diverse cultures were interpellated as (white) "Americans" through the commodified specularization of alterity, there is also a sense in which a national childhood is nostalgically reenacted in these scenes of fixity and fantasy in sports arenas. The sentimental attachment that people have to these images may be related to the fantasy of purity of (American) origination they provide in the face of the persistent threat of the disruption of (immigrant, underclass, alien, female?) otherness they hold at bay. Can we resist speculating that perhaps all spectators—regardless of ethnicity, race, gender, sexuality, or generation—become symbolically white, male, and American in these objectifications of the scopic drive?

At any particular moment in the social life of colonial discourse, the differences disavowed and the nature of the subjects produced will be historically specific, but there is no doubt that the figure of the Indian has been central to articulations of Americanness throughout U.S. history and to the racial tragedy that animates them. As theater historian and performance theorist Joseph Roach suggests, from at least the late eighteenth century, Native Americans "play a paradoxically central role in the formation of a self-consciously national drama."[117] The role is paradoxical because they are permitted entry into this history "only as they are represented by white authors and actors. In such roles—cast as effigies—they become integral to the self-invention of 'the American people' but only through artistry and imagination."[118] Americans constantly "seek native authenticity without having to deal with living autochthons"; the function of the surrogated aboriginal is always to vanish.

Walter Benn Michaels provides one example of this in his recent study of American nativist modernism, tracing changing ideas of national identity in literature from the turn of the century to 1925.[119] American culture in this period took on new meanings as a logic of naturalization and assimilation gave way to one of essentialized cultural identities that were racially configured. I cannot do full justice to his nuanced study, but do wish to note his assertion that the nineteenth-century stereotype of "the vanishing race" was redeployed and romanticized when it was feared that "Nordic" peoples were dying out by their failure to reproduce themselves at the same rate as "Mediterraneans" and "Asiatics." The "rhetoric of racial extinction in America was the rhetoric of the vanishing American. To think of Nordics as a vanishing race was inevitably to identify them with the Indians" and to celebrate the Indian's alleged disappearance "as a mark of his racial integrity—better death than crossbreeding."[120] In the aesthetic quest for a pure source for an American culture, American Indians were transformed into Nordic ancestors: "if the Indians had not been perceived as vanishing, they could not have become the exemplary instance of what it meant to have a culture . . . It is because the Indian's sun was perceived as setting that he could become, I want to argue, a kind of paradigm for increasingly powerful American notions of ethnic identity and eventually for the idea of an ethnicity [culture] that could be threatened or defended, repudiated or reclaimed."[121]

The origin of American identity is simultaneously the scene of the extinction of the Indian, and this cultural identity was essentially racial in its contours. Whiteness was rearticulated by an identification with the Indian that no longer functioned, as it did at the turn of the century, "as a *refusal* of American identity, in effect, as a refusal of American citizenship—it would come to function by the early 1920s as the *assertion* of an American identity that could be understood as going beyond citizenship."[122] Indians, unlike aliens and their children who could become Americans, embodied "an Americanism that transcended the state," a purity and aristocracy of an originary Americanism that those of "dark blood" could not achieve. This imaginary Indian was always a male Indian, for the female Indian poses the potential threat of miscegenation. Michaels also explores elite fantasies of carrying on dynasties unthreatened by the deracinating potential of femininity and the eroticizing of relations between men that served as a subliminal model for a racially purified Americanism.

Certainly such fantasies provoke suggestive resemblances and resonances for a consideration of sports spectatorship, but it would be indulgent and historically irresponsible to map this configuration directly onto contemporary athletic arenas without empirical study. Michaels's work does serve, though, as a cautionary example of the complexities of displacement, projection, and desire in the affective life of race so central to the American national imaginary. To the extent that sports spectacles may embody collective social memory, however, it is precisely their performative corporeality that we need attend to. As Roach reminds us, "kinesthetic imagination is a faculty of memory [that] . . . inhabits the realm of the virtual . . . its truth is the truth of stimulation, of fantasy"[123]—although its social effects may be tangible indeed.

Sports trademarks do not stand as abstract icons in the public sphere but focus a kinetic interpellation of spectator/fans that links bodies in the production of esprit de corps—what Americans might call "team spirit."[124] Discussing such performative dimensions of homosocial bonding in sports, Milind Wakankar notes:

at the core of such collective activity is the establishment of the link between the male body and the mass through physio-psycho-socio-logical assemblages of series of actions . . . for the effective interpel-lation of the subject. The proximity of so many uniformed, uni-forming, bodies-in-unison initiates a kind of silent communion . . . Since every action mimes another, collective mimesis sustains the possibility of collective regeneration. As Bourdieu explains, "collec-tive bodily practice," by "symbolizing the social, contribute to somatizing it and . . . by the bodily and collective *mimesis* of a social orchestration, aim at reinforcing that orchestration."[125]

Stereotypical trademarks seem to serve as totemic forms that mark and galvanize bodies in public rituals of homosocial bonding. Not only do fans inscribe these marks on their bodies by donning licensed goods, they engage in corporeal appropriations of alterity—imitations and inti-mations of imaginary indigenes. Surrounding and animating these trademarks are rituals such as the infamous "tomahawk chop," the "war-whoop," the smoking of "peace-pipes," the beating of the "tomtoms," the wearing of "warpaint" and "warbonnets" while on the "warpath," the as-sumption of an alleged Indian ferocity and bloodthirstiness in songs and dances, and even the ritual planting of flaming spears.[126] In addition to clothing and coffee mugs, bath towels, garbage containers, and even toi-let paper are adorned with trademarked caricatures of Indians.[127]

This is not the first instance in U.S. history in which living peoples have been metaphorically erased through appropriations of their alleged alterity in the forging of emergent identities. Indeed, there seems sub-stantial evidence of such activity in working-class popular as well as elite literary culture. Eric Lott's work on blackface minstrelsy is pertinent here, for, like Bhabha, he is concerned with the contradictory impulses at work in stereotypicality, and the dominant racial subjectivities it en-ables. For our purposes, what is especially significant is his exploration of bodily caricature in popular cultural practice. Lott denies that the meanings of popular culture are ever purely reflective of or mimetic with political domination in the social field. The blackface mask "is less a repetition of power relations than a signifier for them—a distorted mir-ror, reflecting displacements and condensations and discontinuities be-tween which and the social field there exist lags, unevennesses, multiple determinations."[128]

Lott explores the simultaneously transgressive and oppressive dimen-sions of this racial cross-dressing that made possible the "formation of a self-consciously white working class"[129] and contributed to ideologies of working-class manhood in the antebellum Northeast. Combining fear and fascination with degraded others in a mimicry of potent masculinity, feelings of racial superiority were indulged while class insecurities were assuaged, class resentments voiced, ethnic conflicts mediated, and a class identity articulated through the occupation of black bodies.[130] Among other things, blackface acts elevated the "black Irish" into white Americans: it was "an 'Americanizing' ritual of whitening through parodic distance."[131] (Michael Rogin similarly finds Jewish assumptions of blackface to symbolically function as markers of assimilation into white America.)[132] Again, this space of cultural cross-dressing is a largely masculine ideological field and not without its misogynist elements.

Cultural appropriation was, of course, central to the minstrel show—although blackface forms involved appropriation of immigrant Irish culture, southwestern humor, and frontier rituals of encounter—which was as significant as anything that might be identified as authentically black or African. Popular culture in America has always been "a site of conflicting interests, appropriations, indeed 'nationalities,' even in its allegedly national forms."[133] In these Americanizing rituals, however, black peoples themselves are absent and, significantly, erased. Lott shows how, from the very beginning of discussions and accounts of the form, the fact of white impersonation was forgotten. The performers became "those amusing darkies" or "the negroes" even in the most serious discussions of blackface and its meaning, as if the originals were in some way lost.[134]

Behaviors that simultaneously involve forgetting and impersonation, or erasure and enactment, are not socially unusual. They mark a relation between surrogacy and effigy central to the creation of circum-Atlantic identities.[135] Roach, for example, argues that "public enactments of forgetting" or "dramas of sacrificial substitution"[136] in spectacles of cultural surrogation were crucial to the self-inventions of modern "cultures." Often the surrogated double is alien to the culture that stages it, and signs of the socially marginal provide the cultural idioms through which a community asserts identity. According to Peter Stallybrass and Allon White, "The result is a mobile, conflictual fusion of power, fear and desire in the construction of subjectivity: a psychological dependence upon precisely those Others which are being rigorously opposed and excluded at the social level. It is for this reason that what is *socially* peripheral is so frequently *symbolically* central."[137] As Roach eloquently phrases it, "the relentless search for the purity of origins is a voyage not of discovery, but of erasure."[138] What is erased, of course, is both the mixtures, blends, and hybridities in the histories of a people, and the contemporary social life of those others whose cultural forms are appropriated in the displacement of memory into more amenable representations through which this collective identity is forged.[139]

The violence instrumental to the creation of America is forgotten, as is the actual life of indigenous peoples, whose return is nonetheless staged by the occupation of their bodies in forms of caricature. Their difference is appropriated, as it were, in effigy: "a general phenomenon of collective memory . . . [t]he effigy is a contrivance that enables the processes regulating performance—kinesthetic imagination, vortices of behavior, and displaced transmission—to produce memory through surrogation."[140] Although as a noun it means a pictured likeness or crudely fabricated image, as a verb "it means to evoke an absence, to body something forth, especially something from a distant past."[141] In sports arenas, then, I suggest that we see "more elusive but more powerful effigies fashioned from flesh. Such effigies are made by performances. They consist of a set of actions that hold open a place in memory into which many different people may step according to circumstances and occasions. I argue that performed effigies—those fabricated from human bodies and the associations they evoke—provide communities with a method of perpetuating themselves through specially nominated mediums or surrogates."[142]

Just as blackface minstrelsy "functioned as a dominant cultural figuration of black people that covered up the people themselves,"[143] holding them captive to representations constructed by others—stereotypes it would take years to loosen—so too are indigenous peoples in North America disguised, dissimulated, and disempowered by representations that have less to do with their culture than a highly mediated set of white responses to it, filtered through racist presuppostions. The enactment of Indianness in athletic arenas, held constant by the totemic power of the trademark form, functions as a form of whiteface minstrelsy.[144] Hence the special disturbance Native peoples voice when African Americans don "Indian" regalia in the contexts of sports events and the hostility registered at the alleged hypocrisy of another historically oppressed and stereotyped minority engaged in such behavior. This disturbance registers an implicit recognition that not only is the black caricaturing the "Indian" in such moments, he is asserting his "whiteness" in so doing.

Blackface minstrelsy's disastrous consequences for black social representation are echoed in the continuing erasure in the public sphere of Native Americans as a living people by virtue of the ubiquity of the popular cultural stereotypes. Just as "black people had little room to contest publicly the social meanings generated out of their culture,"[145] an extended period of Native American political powerlessless has enabled these images and rituals to become ingrained in American memory. Today, many Indian and First Nations peoples feel that their presence as stereotypical images is more pervasive and compelling than the conditions of their lives, their poverty, and their political struggles. Mythic representations of them that are owned by others have greater precedence in the public sphere.

Legally, Native Americans are doubly disenfranchised by virtue of this history of powerlessness and representation, because laws of trademark focus on dominant public meanings in the allocation of rights.[146] Here, critics of Native people's complaints about stereotypical marks unconsciously articulate an underlying legal logic when they assert that whatever the mark might have represented originally (even assuming it was any particular person or people), it no longer has this meaning. Such nicknames, mascots, and rituals are not racist, they suggest, because they have acquired a separate meaning apart from whatever Indian origins they might have had; they are now primarily and most significantly part of the time-honored traditions of the teams they identify. So, for example, John Cooke asserts that the word redskins simply means football in Washington, D.C., and Paul Tagliabue may quite plausibly remark that "fans don't identify, for example, Redskins with Native Americans."[147] Other fans see these team names as attributes of their own familial, regional, or gender identities.

The legal doctrine of secondary meaning supports these claims. To the extent that a descriptive term by extensive use as a mark in commerce has come to be associated with a particular manufacturer, retailer, or service provider, it will be recognized as a signifier to which he or she has exclusive rights, by virtue of the fact that the public now associates the term with his or her wares. For Native peoples, however, these new meanings and their public recognition are products of (and an ongoing source of) the injustices they have historically suffered. Many Native American names, for example, are far more prominent due to their mass reproduction as trademarks than are their original referents. People hear the term Winnebago used to refer to vehicles more often than they do to refer to a people, are more likely to know Oneida as a silverware than as a tribal group in Wisconsin, and recognize a Pontiac as a car, not as a great indigenous statesman in North American history. To tell them that these terms no longer refer to them is not to make a mistake of fact but simply to reiterate the injury. It is just one more of the many ways in which Native Americans are reminded of their symbolic status as an invisible and vanishing peoples,[148] whose images serve primarily as effigies in the national imagination. Victims of the frontier and symbols of its loss in the nation's imaginary, they have figured for so long as a meaningful absence that their contemporary presence struggles to find visibility and voice in the public sphere. Commercial imitations of their embodied alterity—prosthetic selves[149] that belong to others—mark their continuing colonization in mass-mediated culture, precluding full political engagement in the public sphere.[150]

We know, however, that "in the objectification of the scopic drive there is always the threatened return of the look."[151] If the powers bestowed by trademark laws serve primarily to protect the entrenched privileges of those who hold proprietary rights in these stereotypes, the economic and symbolic power of the trademark ironically also provides the site for emergent forms of counterpublicity. The very public recognition that makes a trademark so valuable provides public opportunities to effect a form of detournement,[152] which American Indian media activists and their supporters have exploited. The annual nature of sports spectacles provides regular publicity opportunities and the on-field accomplishments of the teams brings them to media center-stage on an ongoing basis. At such times, the nicknames, mascots, and other marks of their distinction are pervasive, and anything relating to these teams is news that is likely to attract national media coverage. Ironically, then, Native Americans may receive more public attention and media respect (as well as new hostilities) for their grievances and social concerns at precisely the moment when these stereotypes are most prominent. As Vernon Bellecourt, head of the National Coalition Against Racism in Sports and Media, ruefully acknowledges, unlike so many other Native American issues, "a story about the offensiveness of the name of a football team will get coverage from coast to coast."[153] Indeed, Native American activists have engaged in their own form of cross-dressing—as Quakers and Pilgrims—to get their message across. The real challenge for Native activists is to determine how to use the media attention that accrues goodwill for the trademark to dispel old stereotypes and to educate the public about a wider range of Indian concerns and issues.

A quarter century of protest has failed to erase racist stereotypes in professional sports arenas (although reforms at the levels of primary, high school, and college athletics have been effected, state legislatures have shown support, and media sympathy for the issue has grown).[154] Legal grounds are increasingly proffered for challenging the intellectual property rights in such images—including trademark expungement proceedings, defamation suits, passing off litigation, publicity rights claims, and state civil rights actions—the most ambitious of these being the effort to seek cancellation of federal registration for the "Redskins" trademark.[155] Legal challenges to the use of these marks (including congressional intervention that thwarted attempts by the Washington Redskins to have a new stadium built on federal lands)[156] have thus far failed to induce any professional teams to change their names, but they too serve to keep the issue of racism toward Native Americans in the national spotlight. They also create negative publicity for team owners, a form of pressure that might ultimately yield other dividends for Indian peoples.

Consuming Crazy Horse

The law itself affords opportunities for counterpublicity efforts. Indian peoples are now recognizing the potentials as well as the dangers inherent in the proprietary forms of the bourgeois public sphere; mimicking the bourgeois author may prove to be an effective way to counter an enforced alterity and demand respectful recognition of difference. The sovereignty afforded the intellectual property holder in the late twentieth century is a powerful force with which to dispute authorial claims to own images of alterity. Ironically, the most successful way for indigenous peoples to challenge these stereotypical representations of themselves may be to claim them: to claim the misrecognitions of others as their own proprietary products. To do so they must occupy the author-function and seize the commodity form against the grain: to protest inapproriate commodifications and to assert a differential embodiment that is alter to or other than the fetishes of an earlier era of mass cultural enchantment. To counter what Ted Jojola nominates "image injustice" (and to maintain the limited forms of sovereignty they have achieved), Native Americans acknowledge the need to gain control of their own imagery as well as their own image in mass-media environments.[157] Self-determination involves self-definition.

Descendants of the Lakota statesman Crazy Horse, angered to learn of the appropriation of their revered ancestor's name and image as a trademark by a manufacturer of malt liquor, have invoked the legal process to oppose this use of their heritage and to politically assert the legal significance of their own understandings of property and propriety.[158] Consultations in which I engaged in contemplation of this trial may serve to illustrate the ironies faced by those whose cultural distinction attracts the entrepreneurial energies of others. Using legal arguments that included the descending ownership of Tasunke Witko's (Crazy Horse) publicity rights, Sioux peoples and their lawyers discovered that proprietary litigious strategies promised greater success than the more mean-

ingful claim that the Sioux are spiritually injured by the use of an ancestral name to market a substance that continues to poison the lives of
many Native communities. Nonetheless, they have insisted on a recognition of proprietary claims that accord with tribal custom; by making
these claims in tribal court—the forum best able to forge law in accordance with tribal norms—they assert the legitimacy of alternative national needs.

When Crazy Horse Original Malt Liquor was launched in 1992, protests (coming from figures as diverse as President Bush's surgeon general
and the Pine Ridge Tribe's executive director) were first directed to Congress, resulting in federal legislation and state legislative proposals barring the use of the name.[159] Ferolito, Vultaggio & Sons, distributors of the
beverage, countered by successfully challenging the Federal Bureau of Alcohol, Tobacco, and Firearms' labeling prohibition on First Amendment
grounds.[160] Ferolito, Vultaggio & Sons are two Italian Americans from
Brooklyn who create images and promotion campaigns for the beverage
market. Like many postmodern entrepreneurs, they trade in imagery and
symbolism to create new distinctions for goods that have become more
or less functionally indistinguishable. They became particularly infamous for the "target marketing" of beverages with high alcohol content
to African American and Hispanic men (groups that purchase most of
the malt liquor consumed in the United States), a practice that "deliberately employs package designs, images, and phrases the advertisers believe will appeal to racial minorities by playing into fantasies of potency
and conquest."[161]

Crazy Horse was a patriot and a religious leader who denounced the
introduction of alcohol into Indian communities. The use of his name to
market an especially alcoholic malt liquor[162] coupled with a crude picture of an Indian chief and religious symbols was bound to draw outrage. Moreover, the product's label paid tribute to Crazy Horse in a fashion that denied the bloody politics of a history of genocide. Here is the
copy: "The Black Hills of Dakota steeped in the History of the American
West, home of proud Indian Nations a land where imagination conjures
up images of Blue Clad Pony Soldiers and magnificent Native American
warriors. A land still rutted with wagon tracks of intrepid pioneers. A
land where wailful winds whisper of Sitting Bull, Crazy Horse, and
Custer. A land of character, of bravery, of tradition. A land that truly
speaks of the spirit that is America."[163] We might, like Michael Dorris,
wonder whether these were the same blue-clad lads who massacred two
hundred freezing Dakota captives at Wounded Knee.[164] Crazy Horse was

in fact murdered by one of these pony soldiers *after* surrendering to their authority.

Reference to the Black Hills is more than simply geographical; this is the traditional holy place of the Lakota. It is indeed "home of Proud Indian Nations," but it is not merely "imagination [that] conjures up" these soldiers and their antagonists, nor ephemeral "wailful winds [that] whisper of Sitting Bull, Crazy Horse, and Custer." These memories, kept alive through invocations of these historical figures and their narratives, are social practices constitutive of contemporary and continuous "processes of identity-formation by Lakota people."[165] In the malt liquor's trade dress, however, this "land of character, of bravery, of tradition" is stripped of living inhabitants with human agency so that only the land "truly speaks of the spirit that is America." Such tropes work to position "Proud Indian Nations" in the past, a classical period of "magnificent warriors" and "intrepid pioneers." The only tradition deemed relevant today is the one to which "America" lays claim. One of their public relations consultants suggests that it would have been more offensive to celebrate the great American West without including Indians.[166] Indians are included here, however, more as features of landscape than as living peoples with historical memory.

Ferolito & Vultaggio appeared to believe that they had merely taken something from the public domain and turned it into something of value; whatever symbolic value the name had was due to their own authorship of the trademark.[167] They argued that any ban on the mark would be a "confiscatory taking" of private property.[168] Ferolito & Vultaggio went further than simply claiming authorship of the mark. They also staged a protracted dialogue between authorship and alterity that inscribed many of the contradictions we saw to be characteristic of the use of Indian names and mascots in sports arenas. First they denounced the protest as trivial; the chief executive officer of the company suggested that the protesters "get a life."[169] Then they said that the name was chosen without any knowledge that Crazy Horse was a significant historical figure.[170] Later they issued a press release that "maintained that the name was deliberately chosen as a tribute to Crazy Horse,"[171] going so far as to suggest that "they meant to celebrate a man who has been described as 'the greatest leader of his people in modern times,' a man respected for his leadership, pride, discipline, self reliance, and independence."[172] A month later they claimed that "Crazy Horse was and is a true American hero, known and revered not for a spiritual or religious role, but as an independent self-reliant and proud leader."[173] Meanwhile, their public relations firm issued a press release that insisted that "the acceptance of Crazy Horse's role, whatever his role may have been, among Native Americans, was not, and is not, universal."[174] Besides, it was asserted, Native American "attitudes" toward the name were not the only "attitudes" that should count.[175]

Ultimately, they determined that if they could not dictate the meaning of this historical figure and fix his symbolic resonances, they would create another character for publicity purposes. They authored an alternative Crazy Horse and insisted upon a recognition of his legitimacy. Faced with the claims of historical others, they created another history, marking a counterhistory featuring a fictitious "warrior named Curley, who later adopted the colorful nickname Crazy Horse."[176] First an ordinary guy, he became a brilliant warrior who, "although he was religious, was not a spiritual leader in the Pope Paul or Martin Luther King concept."[177]

Despite the personas they authored and authorized, the United States Patent and Trademark Office examiner refused to register their mark, finding that it violated a section of the Federal Trademark Act that bars the registration of marks deemed "immoral . . . or scandalous matter; or matter which may disparage . . . persons, living or dead, institutions, beliefs, or national symbols, or bring them into contempt or disrepute."[178] Given the ambiguity of these terms and the diverging approaches courts have taken to their interpretation, it is highly unlikely that this ruling will go unchallenged or withstand constitutional scrutiny.

The decision to claim proprietary rights in Tasunke Witko's name and image was not one easily made. Crazy Horse refused ever to have his image imprinted by photography and would not even permit his image to be drawn:

> Big Crow along with all other descendants of Crazy Horse had been raised in a tradition of silence that prevented any discussion of the family's relationship to Tasunke Witko. Crazy Horse himself was believed to have instituted this silence, telling his relatives that they must never speak about their relationship to him . . . In an interview in 1994, Big Crow explained why he had decided to break his promise after 42 years: "I'd been listening to people right next to me saying: 'Where are Crazy Horse's descendants? Why won't they stand up for him?' And I couldn't acknowledge who I really was. Finally, after efforts by others failed, I knew I had to stand up."[179]

Named administrator of Tasunke Witko for the purposes of representing his estate in these legal proceedings, Big Crow filed a probate petition in the Rosebud Sioux Tribal Court. But as he himself admitted, "In a spiritual sense, I can never go home again."[180]

From the beginning, this was more than an ordinary publicity rights claim; attorneys working on the case were politically motivated to induce mainstream courts to recognize tribal customary and common law as legitimate sources of law.[181] It has been a longstanding goal of indigenous activists to have tribal court judgments recognized in the federal courts and respected as sources of legal precedent in nontribal tribunals. As indigenous legal activists well understand, this aspiration is fraught with risk; it compels them to speak the languages of dominant others while inflecting the other's categories with unanticipated meanings and stretching them to accommodate injuries suffered by those who bear cultural difference.

The attorneys representing Crazy Horse, for instance, soon recognized that most of their concerns about inappropriate commercial appropriation might be analogized to various forms of property rights recognized outside of the tribal courts. To do so, however, was to assume risks of cultural misunderstanding both within and beyond Sioux reservations. For example, even to appoint an administrator for the Crazy Horse estate for these purposes was, arguably, to privatize an ancestral name of significance to a wider network of extended kin than those likely to be legally recognized as beneficiaries of the estate.[182] Moreover, many of those closely related to Crazy Horse still maintained the pact of silence about their relationship. As a consequence, attorneys directing the suit were compelled to develop their litigation strategy publicly, in meetings that involved collaboration with communities in three reservations and in Rapid City. Elders expressed the pain they felt when encountering the malt liquor, and many refused even to touch the empty bottle when it was handed around at meetings. An emergent consciousness among tribal youth of the harm caused by the commodification of tradition was one outcome of these gatherings.[183]

The use of the tribal court forum was both strategic and symbolic, or to put it another way, signification was part of the strategy. Attorneys made a clearly political statement when they brought an action against two East Coast marketing and manufacturing companies in a venue in the Black Hills—that fabled land of their adversary's advertising lore—in a court system that the defendants (and their lawyers) were almost certain to know nothing about and probably never imagined to have any jurisdiction over them. Moreover, the claim for damages was astutely rendered in traditional Sioux terms: a braid of tobacco, a racehorse, and a four-point Pendleton blanket, for each state and month in which the malt liquor was sold. The image of these two Italian American entrepreneurs leading horses across the plains to show homage due to an Indian ancestral spirit is certainly more striking than the accompanying claim for punitive damages. Finally, by adding two other causes of action to the publicity rights claim—one from Anglo-American law (the intentional infliction of mental distress) and the other derived from tribal custom (defamation of the spirit)—attorneys for the estate compelled the defendants to venture into alien territory and view their own authorship through the lens of alterity. It may well take years for the jurisdictional issues in this case to be resolved,[184] but there is little doubt that it is one of the more fascinating instances of historical others interrogating the claims of postmodern authors.

Mimicking Authors at the Alters of Property

Ironically, proprietary counterclaims may afford more persuasive forms of counterpublicity than assertions that racial stereotyping and derogatory portrayals damage the public estimation of a people and the self-esteem of their children. Assertions of theft seem to have greater rhetorical value in American politics than assertions of harm. It would have been possible, for example, to demonstrate that Crazy Horse was held as a common law mark in trade by tribal peoples long before the malt liquor was put on the market. Both a local tourist monument and its merchandising operations as well as a rifle manufacturer had received tribal authorization for tributory uses of the name that returned revenues to tribal peoples.[185] To make such a claim "stick," however, Sioux peoples would also be obliged to argue that the public was likely to be confused by the use of the mark in the new context because it suggested their endorsement. Given Native people's experience of invisibility in American culture, however, such claims seem rather counterintuitive.

Indian activists concerned with these issues are aware that various intellectual property strategies are available to prevent the commercial exploitation of those "intangibles" that Native Americans regard as their own. Most such strategies, however, involve characterizing their own historical usages of names and symbols as exercises of commercial possession, representing a course of conduct in Anglo-American proprietary terms to assert that these signifiers are marks in trade, service or certification marks, or collective marks that designate a group of producers or service providers. Families, tribal goups, tribal organizations, tribal governments, or Indian-controlled companies may all adopt such tactics to claim preexisting rights in symbols commercially appropriated. Such rights would legally enable them to intervene to prevent cultural others from registering these symbols as trademarks or to cancel existing registrations as wrongfully registered.

When alterity is specularized, the return of the gaze may create alternative spectacles. For instance, trademark expungement proceedings—claims that the nominations of Cherokee, Seminole, Navajo, Oneida, and Winnebago, for example, are already the marks of nations and were held as properties by the governing bodies of national peoples prior to their appropriation in commerce[186]—might provide auspicious avenues of future adversarial strategy. The public presentation to the Trademark Registrar of all signs and symbols that Native Americans hold as indicia of their nations—whose use in commerce disparages a people—has also been considered as a potential political strategy. Given that many of the more significant names, images, and symbols are held secret or in silent forms of guardianship, however, this option has distinct limitations. Sioux peoples might even publicly designate Neil Young to be their first "authorized licensee" and seek his assistance in denouncing disrespectful usages of the Crazy Horse name. Dramatic presentations to the International Trademark Association pose opportunities for a politics of publicity on a more global scale.

Under state statutory and common law dilution provisions, moreover, Native peoples could argue that the offensive commercial usage "diluted" the value and significance of their own marks. To do so, however, would involve characterizing their culture as property, a rhetorical strategy that is not without its risks, as I will argue. The Anglo-American legal system provides a number of spaces within which cultural difference may be asserted and legally recognized as distinction, but it provides little room to suggest that the cultural distinction of some social groups is being diluted by the commerce of others. As one American Indian activist remarked, you can legally protect a mark, but not a peoples' being, against commercial dilution. American tribes and nations find that their own distinction as a people must be established as a property against the proprietary claims of others which otherwise take legal precedence. The ubiquitous generic Indian body in mass advertising will be more difficult to dislodge than specific names and symbols. If the mimetic faculty is the power to copy, imitate, yield into, and become other—and certainly we have seen how many sports arenas seem to provoke the activities of cultural cross-dressers—it is also the case that the copy draws power from and influences the original; the representation gains the power of the represented and the image affects what it is an image of. For Indian peoples, this may mean that their contemporary social needs and political struggles are not recognized because they are publicly identified with (or subsumed by) the warbonneted caricatures first mass-produced in Buffalo Bill's Wild West Show[187] and ever since reproduced in nostalgia and commerce.

Taussig is optimistic about the "reschooling of the mimetic faculty" that contemporary advertising enables. But this is partly because he is generally oblivious to the *content* of the message, so enamored is he with the form. The corporeality of the knowledge he alludes to as being refashioned in late capitalism presupposes a universality and singularity of the human body that denies the ways history has written different bodies differentially, inscriptions that have often taken place in advertising media. The bodily incorporation of the advertising image is different when the image one consumes is a stereotyped version of one's self—when one's mass subjectivity, public subjectivity, and minority subject-position are conflictual. For those whose bodies are marked by a history of commodification (blacks in America) and those whose bodies are marked by alternative histories of fetishism (women and Native peoples), the "reschooled mimetic faculty" may not be the liberator Taussig presupposes. Still, if, as Taussig suggests, the mimicry of the other corrodes the very alterity by which an anthropology of culture was nourished,[188] others may well erode the cultural mimicry of alterity upon which capital continues to thrive.[189]

Embodied distinctions continue to be claimed and contested on emergent national frontiers in those hybrid spaces forged from the histories of others and histories of othering that provoke ongoing struggles over publicity and the parameters of the public sphere. From Paul Bunyon to Crazy Horse, Golly to the Redskins, the instances explored in this chapter call our attention to the contested boundaries of nations and acts of inclusion and exclusion inscribed upon frontiers through the media of commodity/signs. They also testify to new dimensions of what we might deem the politics of mass publicity in a consumer society—strategies of property and impropriety and tactics of publicity and counter-publicity—in which authors and alters engage in dances of mimicry that simultaneously mask and reveal real financial and political stakes.

The modern public sphere presupposes a universality and singularity of the human body that denies the ways history has written different bodies differentially, inscriptions that have often taken place in mass culture itself. The postmodern celebration of pastiche and montage—mimetic juxtapositions of alterity in recodings and reworkings of regimes of signification—must remain cognizant of the imperialist histories in which many commodified forms of available cultural difference were originally forged. Increasingly, it is necessary to attend to the postcolonial claims of those who refuse to put their alterity at the service of a mere mimetic multiplication of possibilities or abandon it to those who would celebrate a merely syncretic hybridity at the expense of historical consciousness and critique.

The mass-mediated public spheres of consumer societies bear traces of the historical trajectories that contain cultural forms; these shape the forms of subjectivity that may be politically recognized therein. The bodily incorporation of the advertising image is not a singular event; it is altered when the image one consumes is a mimetic version of one's self—when one's mass subjectivity, public subjectivity, and minority subject-position are conflictual. For those whose bodies are marked by a history of commodification (blacks in America) and those whose bodies are marked by alternative histories of fetishism (women and Native peoples), the mimesis of mass advertising must be altered in ever new and more imaginative ways. Ultimately, others must interrogate the cultural mimicry of alterity upon which capital thrives. The forms of mass publicity characteristic of late capitalism offer and compel a transformation of the magic of mimesis and its relation to alterity, presenting possibilities for new politics in public spheres.

5. The Properties of Culture and the Politics of Possessing Identity

... there is now a vigorous questioning of the search for the "authentic" indigenous voice that can speak for whole communities or cultures; it appears that more often than not this demand by colonizers for authenticity imposes an approach that simplifies and renders unitary the complexities of local life ... long and labored attempts to delineate the "true" boundaries of a tribe, the "authentic" history of Indian people, or the "real" (singular) identity of particular Native Americans only add to the process of misunderstanding that insistently translates indigenous histories, concepts of identity, and group membership in terms of distinctly nonindigenous categories and forms of thought.—Elizabeth Mertz, "A New Social Constructionism for Sociolegal Studies"[1]

In 1992, a longstanding debate in Canadian arts communities erupted in the national public sphere. For three weeks that spring, Canadians witnessed a remarkable exchange on the pages of the *Globe and Mail*,[2] as controversy raged about the propriety of writers depicting a "culture other than one's own," when or if it was appropriate to tell "someone else's story," and whether it was possible to "steal the culture of another."[3] Although the issues addressed continue to engage critical attention, the *Globe* debate was significant for it brought into sharp relief the limitations of addressing complex issues of culture and identity politics as matters of legal rights. It was also remarkable because of its emotional intensity, the absurdity of the analogies drawn in support of the respective arguments, and the inability of the protagonists to recognize each other's terms of reference.

I was initially drawn to the debate because of its ironic implications for my own work in this volume. For too many years I had been crafting a volume I had provisionally titled *Cultural Appropriations*, and my advance publishing contract specified this as its title. Exploring the ways in which subaltern groups use mass-media texts, celebrity images, trademarks, and other legally protected commodity/signs to forge identities and communities, I focused on the subcultural appropriation of autho-rial forms to construct alternative gender identities, challenge the para-meters of nations and citizenship, express aspiration, and claim recogni-tion. In short, I had developed the concept of *cultural appropriation* as my shorthand for cultural agency and subaltern struggle within media-saturated consumer societies. Imagine my consternation, then, to find the term "officially defined" by the Advisory Committee for Racial Equal-ity in the Arts for no less august a body than the Canada Council. The term was deemed to mean "the depiction of minorities or cultures other than one's own, either in fiction or nonfiction," and designated a serious issue with which Council was compelled to contend.[4]

The ironies of my response to this appropriation and definition of the phrase prompted a reconsideration of the politics of certain knowledges; in this case, academic theory in law and anthropology. At first I was an-noyed; a term I had used to connote progressive, subversive—or at least transgressive—forms of politics on behalf of subordinated social groups had been seized to exclusively denote the invidious practice of white elites stealing the cultural forms of others for their own prestige and profit. I was uncomfortably aware that I had formed a rather proprietary attachment to the term; my own feelings of violation rather too closely mirrored those voiced by corporations who were outraged when *their* trademarks were given unsanctioned meanings by others.

This controversy over cultural appropriation opens up a wider set of concerns. First, I will examine the philosophical premises about author-ship, culture, and property that underlie this controversy and define the legal arena in which it is likely to be evaluated. The West has created cat-egories of property—intellectual property, cultural property, and real property—that divide peoples and things according to the same coloniz-ing discourses of possessive individualism that historically disentitled and disenfranchised Native peoples in North America. Exploring the in-ternal logics of intellectual property and cultural property laws, I will question the exhausted concepts of culture and identity upon which they are based. Although the law rips asunder what Native peoples view as in-tegrally and relationally joined, traditional Western understandings of culture, identity, and property are provoked, challenged, and under-mined by the concept of aboriginal title. The limitations of legal catego-ries for postcolonial struggles, I suggest, are apparent in responses to First Nations peoples' struggles for self-determination. In addressing First Na-tions claims here, I seek to avoid speaking "on behalf of" Native peoples, but to speak alongside First Nations activists who have put this issue on the political agenda, specifically addressing the dangers of receiving these claims in traditional categories. Rather than solve the problem that has been identified as cultural appropriation (which, in any case, is never singular, but specific to particular peoples with particular historical trajectories), I suggest we rethink the terms in which we address the question and the ethical responsibilities entailed in its consideration.

Whose Voice Is It Anyway?

The recent *Globe and Mail* debate began with an innocuous article calling attention to the Canada Council's concern with the issue of cultural appropriation.[5] Government grants, the Advisory Committee suggested, should not be made to writers who wrote about cultures other than their own unless the writer "collaborated" with members of the minority group. Such a strategy was advisable to avoid perpetuating the continuance or proliferation of social stereotypes. Although the choice of language was somewhat peculiar, most scholars were unlikely to find such a suggestion surprising. The public controversy provoked, however, was swift, furious, and quickly polarized upon familiar liberal terrain. I will suggest that these poles—which I will designate as Romantic individualism and Orientalism—operate as dangerous supplements[6] that define an imperialist conceptual terrain that structures our laws of property and may well configure many postcolonial claims for cultural autonomy and political recognition.

As both a law professor and an anthropologist, I found myself conflictually situated with respect to the two discourses that dominated this debate. If my reservations about the proliferation of intellectual property protections made me suspicious of the authorial claims propounded on one side, my training in anthropology made me uneasy with the reification of culture that characterized the other. Struggling to establish political positions on issues of cultural representation that avoid these seductive stances, I found, was virtually impossible within a juridical framework.

In response to the report of the Council's acknowledgment of the issue of cultural appropriation, a series of letters to the editor decried the tyranny of the state over the individual and affirmed the transcendant genius of the Romantic author and his unfettered imagination.[7] Writers wasted no time evoking the totalitarian state, the memory of the Holocaust, and the Gulag. As Timothy Findley forcefully interjected: "Put it this way: I imagine—therefore I am. The rest—believe me—is silence. What has happened here? Does no one understand? In 1933 they burned

10,000 books at the gate of a German university because these books were written in unacceptable voices. German Jews, amongst others, had dared to speak for Germany in other than Aryan voices. Stop. Now. Before we do this again."[8] Joy Anne Jacoby evoked Russian anti-Semitism to urge the Council "to rethink the implications of imposing any policy of 'voice appropriation' lest they find themselves imitating the Russian approach to cultural censorship";[9] Erna Paris titled her intervention in the debate "A Letter to the Thought Police."[10]

Other critics proclaimed the absolute freedom of the author's imagination. Neil Bissoondath affirmed the autonomy of his ego in a passage resplendent with the *I* of Romantic individualism: "I reject the idea of cultural appropriation completely... I reject anything that limits the imagination. No one has the right to tell me who I should or should not write about, and telling me what or how I do that amounts to censorship ... I am a man of East-Indian descent and I have written from the viewpoint of women and black men, and I will continue to do so no matter who gets upset."[11] Richard Outram declared that for the past thirty-five years he had been appropriating the "voices of men, women, dogs, cats, rats, bats, angels, mermaids, elephants . . . [and] salamanders"[12] and that he had no intention of consulting with them or seeking their permission: "In common with every writer worthy of his or her vocation, I refuse absolutely to entertain any argument demanding that I do so, or that I am to be in any way restricted in my choice of subject matter. I will not, in short, submit to such censorship . . . "[13] Russell Smith confidently asserted that "appropriation of voice is what fiction is,"[14] while Bill Driedger lamented that "if cultural appropriation had never been permitted, Puccini could never have written La Boheme, Verdi's Aida would never have been performed, we would never have thrilled to Laurence Olivier in Hamlet and we would have been denied the music of Anna and the King of Siam."[15]

In these constructions of authorship, the writer is represented in Romantic terms as an autonomous individual who creates fictions with an imagination free of all constraint.[16] For such an author, everything in the world must be made available and accessible as an "idea" that can be transformed into his "expression," which thus becomes his "work."[17] Through his labor, he makes these "ideas" his own; his possession of the "work" is justified by his expressive activity. So long as the author does not copy another's expression, he is free to find his themes, plots, ideas, and characters anywhere he pleases, and to make these his own (this is also the model of authorship that dominates Anglo-American laws of copyright).[18] Any attempts to restrict his ability to do so are viewed as censorship and as an unjustifiable restriction on freedom of expression. The dialectic of possessive individualism and liberal democracy is thereby affirmed.

It is, however, somewhat peculiar (and rather anachronistic) to find these affirmations made so forcefully in a context so far removed from the possessive market society in which they arose. The inevitability of market relations under which all writers were equally subjugated was presumably the condition that the Canada Council's subsidization policies were designed to eliminate as the singular social context in which all writers were compelled to toil and all aesthetic evaluations were to be made.

Critical legal scholars have written extensively about the inadequacies of Romantic individualism and its understanding of subjectivity, cultural agency, freedom of speech, and creativity (although usually under the umbrella term of liberalism, a term that is too complex to engage here).[19] The social experiences of authors inevitably shape their voices, and there is no doubt that the voices of people with remarkably similar social experiences continue to dominate the cultural terrain. In a democratic society committed to multiculturalism and to promoting the social equality of diverse groups, it is surely the work of a federal agency allocating public funds to support the work of minority writers and artists who have been marginalized or silenced in the market so that Canadian culture more fully represents the cultural diversity of the country.[20]

The Romantic individualism expounded by writers in this debate obstinately ignored the balance of power in Canadian publishing. In the worldview presented, everyone is implicitly equal in their capacity to write or be written about, to speak or be spoken for. Such a position purports to be apolitical, but manages only to be ahistorical and blind to relations of power. It ignores the very real social lines along which representation has been delineated and the difficulties faced by certain social groups to represent themselves and speak on their own behalf. Cultural representation and political representation are closely linked. It is, for example, inconceivable that a vehicle could be marketed as "a wandering Jew," but North Americans rarely bat an eyelash when a Jeep Cherokee passes them on the road or an advertisement for a Pontiac® automobile flashes across their television screens. More people may know Oneida® as a brand of silverware than as the name of a people and a nation.

For minorities in Canada who have experienced both discrimination and stereotyping, it must be insulting to have your identity analogized to that of mermaids and elephants and cold comfort to know that an author has no intention of speaking to salamanders or angels before he writes about them either. One can only assume that minority groups in Canada occupy the same mythical and inarticulate status in the writer's imagination. In such analogies, many Canadians are denied their humanity. They are not seen as fellow members of a multicultural community whose historical experiences have shaped their current political struggles, but as archetypes and characters; not recognized as human beings to be engaged in dialogue, they are reduced to cultural fodder for the Romantic imagination.[21]

Moreover, the very context in which the debate arose is conveniently elided. Puccini was not, after all, seeking funding from a government committed to multiculturalism when he wrote *La Bohème*, corporate producers would have "thrilled" us with Laurence Olivier in *Hamlet* with or without the Canada Council, and if the Canada Council were asked to fund a musical as blatantly paternalistic and condescending as *The King and I*,[22] there should indeed be questions about the propriety of public funding for such a work. Market forces may dictate that sentimental works nostalgically evoking histories of colonialism will continue to be made, but government subsidization of the arts might well aspire to other criteria for excellence.

But if the fictious being of the Romantic author colored one side of the debate, the essentializing voice of Orientalism dominated the other.[23] The article that began the debate was titled "Whose Voice Is It Anyway?"[24] The question presupposed that a "voice" was both unified and singular and could be possessed by an individual or a collective imagined as having similar abilities to possess its own expressions. This debate was connected to earlier public discussions in which Native writers insisted that white writers refrain from telling stories involving Indians so as to enable Native peoples to tell "their own stories."[25] Questions of "Who's stealing whose stories and who's speaking with whose voice"[26] had been posed by Native cultural activists as "cases of cultural theft, the theft of voice."[27] Canadians were told that "stories show how a people, a culture, thinks,"[28] and such stories could not be told by others without endangering the authenticity and authority of cultural works. The Canadian publishing and broadcasting industries had long been accused of stealing the stories of Native peoples and thus destroying their essential meanings in authentic traditions. Native artists asked if "Canadians had run out of stories of their own"[29] and claimed that the telling of Native stories was theft, "as surely as the missionaries stole our religion, the politicians stole our land, and the residential schools stole our language."[30] As I will suggest later, however, the tropes of cultural essentialism and possessive individualism evoked here are belied by the very expressive forms for which Native peoples seek recognition and the specificity of the historical struggles in which they figure.

As Canadian critical legal theorist Alan Hutchinson suggested, the three-week-long newspaper debate generated more heat than light.[31] He proposes that in the struggle to eliminate invidious social inequalities, we need to hear the voices and understand the experiences of those who have been marginalized to cultivate imaginative means for dealing with domination. In making this argument, however, he too adopts the tropes of possessive individualism, in which authors "have identities" that may or may not ensure "their own work's authenticity" (and Canada has a singular culture, albeit a conversational one): "It does matter who is speaking, but identity is neither entirely dispensable nor completely determinative . . . the hope is that by increasing the membership in the larger community of those who have previously been absent, the overall authority and authenticity of that body of work will be improved."[32]

Most of those who supported the Council and its Advisory Committee rested their arguments on a set of assumptions that, I will suggest, are equally problematic, equally Eurocentric, and employ the same tropes of possessive individualism as those of their opponents. The integrity of cultural identity that grounded their claims effected a reification of alterity that mirrored the reification of authorship effected by their interlocutors. Speaking on behalf of the Canada Council, Director Joyce Zemans claimed that cultural appropriation was a serious issue because "we have a need for authenticity. In our society today, there is a recognition that quality has to do with that authenticity of voice."[33] Susan Crean, chair of the Writers Union of Canada, analogized the issue to a legal claim of copyright, in which any unlicensed use of authorial property is theft.[34]

It seems to be assumed in these arguments that Canada is either a country with its own culture or one in which there are multiple discrete cultures, but that one always has a singular culture of one's own that has a history of its own, and that one possesses an authentic identity that speaks in a univocal voice fully constituted by one's own cultural tradition. Anthropologists and cultural studies theorists today find themselves uneasy in the face of such arguments. It is possible to be simultaneously supportive of First Nations' struggles for self-representation and uncomfortable with the rhetorical strategies employed by many of those sympathetic to this end. For anthropologists today, such propositions about culture, authenticity, and identity are extremely contentious. They urge resistance to the siren call of authenticity, the reification of culture, and the continuity of tradition, arguing that such ideas embody contingent concepts integral to Western histories of colonialism and imperialism.

In the past decade, it has become more intellectually respectable, and certainly more fashionable, to focus on cultural improvisations, productive hybridities, the creative politics and poetics of identity creation, celebrating and affirming cultural conjunctures rather than timeless essences, creolized intercultural processes rather than stable cultural tradition. These culturally creative processes, however, are fabrications, and the cultural resources with which emergent identities are fashioned may be tightly embraced by others in alternative systems of value. This is vividly illustrated in George Lipsitz's otherwise politically sensitive book, *Time Passages*, discussing American memory and popular culture.[35] Lipsitz waxes ecstatic about the emancipatory cultural creativity of the "Mardi Gras Indians"—black youths who dress and dance in Plains Indians costume during elaborately rehearsed street pageantry in New Orleans. Their "Indianness" is drawn from the Buffalo Bill imagery ingrained in American mass culture. They know that they are not "real Indians," but one gets little sense whether they know there are any or believe, as a the young child recently told me (as evidence of her worldly sophistication), that "there are no *real* Indians, just like there are no real witches, trolls, or fairies." In our constant utopian celebration of reinventions of difference, we must be careful not to simply reinscribe the privilege of the Romantic author and his unfettered rights to appropriate all cultural value and deem it his own creative work. As Annie Coombes suggests, hybridity is no guarantee of postcolonial self-determination; it is as available to the colonizing practices of capital as it is to local strategies of resistance.[36]

Maintaining respect for cultural tradition, however, also risks reinscribing the authority of our own cultural categories, albeit in the guise of the liberal property holder. The concepts of culture, authenticity, and identity in the *Globe* debate were posed in proprietary terms, as debates about propriety so often are in contemporary politics. The argument was constructed around the same philosophy of possessive individualism that grounds our legal categories of property. The challenges that postcolonial struggles[37] pose for Canadian society may not be appropriately met by habitual reliance upon categories of thought inherited from a colonial era. To make this argument, I will delineate the conceptual logic that developed in the nineteenth-century colonial context to categorize art, culture, and authorial identity. This European art/culture system continues to mark the contemporary limits of Western legal imaginaries.[38]

The European Art/Culture System

In his influential work *The Predicament of Culture*, historian James Clifford discusses "the fate of tribal artifacts and cultural practices once they are relocated in Western museums, exchange systems, disciplinary archives, and discursive traditions."[39] Clifford delineates an "art-culture system," developed over the nineteenth century in the context of global colonialism and imperialism as a means of categorizing arts and cultural goods. I will suggest that these categories continue to inform our laws of property, and that they may no longer be appropriate in postcolonial contexts.

As many contemporary cultural critics suggest, the concepts of art and culture are mutually constitutive products of the European upheavals and expansions of the early nineteenth century, the ascendancy of bourgeois values, the specter of mass society, imperialist expansion, and colonial rule.[40] To quickly summarize, art in the eighteenth century primarily referred to skill and industry, whereas culture designated a tendency to natural and organic growth, as in sugar beet culture. Only in the early nineteenth century was art as an imaginative expression abstracted from industry as a utilitarian one. The emergence of an abstract, capitalized Art, equated with individual creativity and expressive genius, was developed in the same period as the concept of capitalized Culture, as a noun or the end product of an abstract process of civilization. Tracing this development through the German, French, and English languages, Raymond Williams shows how the term developed three sets of referents:

> (i) the independent and abstract noun which describes a general process of intellectual, spiritual, and aesthetic development . . . (ii) the independent noun, whether used generally or specifically, which indicates a particular way of life, whether of a people, a period, a group, or humanity in general from Herder and Klemm . . . (iii) the independent and abstract noun which describes the works and practices of intellectual and especially artistic activity . . . in English (i) and (iii) are still close; at times, for internal reasons, they are indistiguishable as in Arnold, *Culture and Anarchy* (1867); while sense (ii) was decisively introduced into English by Tylor, *Primitive Culture* (1870) . . . The decisive development of sense (iii) in English was in [the late nineteenth and early twentieth centuries].[41]

It was possible by the end of the nineteenth century to speak of Culture with a capital *C*—representing the height of human development, the most elevated of human expression as epitomized in European art and literature—as well as plural cultures with a small *c*, imagined as co-herent, authentic ways of life characterized by "wholeness, continuity and essence."[42] These two concepts of culture dominate "the limits of [a] specific ideological consciousness marking the conceptual points beyond which that consciousness cannot go and between which it is condemned to oscillate."[43] They may also mark the limits of the legal imaginary.

Clifford begins his discussion of Western classifications with a critical review of a 1984 exhibit at the Museum of Modern Art (MOMA) in New York titled *Primitivism in 20th Century Art: Affinity of the Tribal and the Modern*, which documented the influence of tribal objects in the works of modernist masters such as Picasso, Brancusi, and Miro.[44] In the early twentieth century, the exhibit suggests, these modernists discover that primitive objects are in fact powerful art and their own work is influ-enced by the power of these forms. A common quality or essence joins the tribal to the modern in what is described under the universalizing rubric of "affinity." An identity of spirit and a similarity of creativity be-tween the modern and the tribal, the contemporary and the primitive, is recognized and celebrated (a movement that continues to hold persua-sive power in the Western world, if the television series *Millennium* was any indication).

The humanist appeal of the exhibit, however, rests upon a number of exclusions, evasions, and stereotypes. One could, for example, question the way modernism appropriates otherness, constitutes non-Western arts in its own image, and thereby discovers universal ahistorical human capacities by denying particular histories, local contexts, indigenous meanings, and the very political conditions that enabled Western artists and authors to seize these goods for their own ends. Needless to say, the "imperialist contexts that surround the 'discovery' of tribal objects by modernist artists" just as "the planet's peoples came massively under Eu-ropean political economic and evangelical dominion" is not addressed in the MOMA exhibit. Indeed, the emphasis is on the narrative of European "creative genius recognising the greatness of tribal works,"[45] thereby be-stowing upon these objects the status of "art" in place of their former lowly designation as ethnographic specimans. As Clifford states, "the ca-pacity of art to transcend its cultural and historical context is asserted repeatedly."[46] The category of art, however, is not a universal one, but a historically contingent European category, in which the artistic imagina-tion is universalized in the European image under the name of a puta-tively "human" Culture.

The "appreciation and interpretation of tribal objects takes place," ac-cording to Clifford, "within a modern system of objects which confers value on certain things and withholds it from others."[47] Clifford delineates the "art-culture system" that developed in the nineteenth century as a way of categorizing expressive works of aesthetic value in a context of European imperialist forays in which objects were collected from around the globe.[48] Using a semiotic square or classificatory grid, he demonstrates how two categories have dominated our understanding of expressive works and their proper placement, and two subsidiary categories have encompassed those objects not so easily subsumed by the dominant logic. First, he designates the zone of "authentic masterpieces" created by individual geniuses, the category of "art" properly speaking. Second, he designates the category of "authentic artifacts" created by cultures imagined as collectivities.[49] Objects may, therefore, be exhibited in galleries as examples of a human creative ability that transcends the limitations of time and place to speak to us about the "human" condition; representing the highest point of human achievement, they are regarded as testament to the greatness of their individual creators. Alternatively, objects may be exhibited in museums as the authentic works of a distinct collectivity, integral to the harmonious life of an ahistorical community and incomprehensible outside of "cultural context"—the defining features of authentic artifacts.

For an object to be accepted as an authentic artifact, it must locate itself in an untouched, pristine state that bespeaks a timeless essence in a particular cultural tradition. That which is recognized as authentic to a culture cannot bear any traces of that culture's contact with other cultures; particularly, it may not be marked by that society's history of colonialism that enabled such works to make their way into Western markets. The tribal life from which such objects magically spring are permitted no histories of their own; they are relegated to an ahistorical perceptual present, perceived as essential traditions that are vanishing, being destroyed, or tainted by the forces of modernization. The capacity of "tribal" peoples to live in history and to creatively interpret and expressively confront the historical circumstances in which they live—using their cultural traditions to do so—cannot be contemplated, except under marginalized categories like "syncretism" which suggest impurity and decline. "[A]boriginals apparently must always inhabit a mythic time."[50] Cultural manifestations that signal the creative life rather than the death of societies are excluded as inauthentic or, alternatively, denied cultural, social, or political specificity by becoming incorporated into the universalizing discourse of art.

Tribal objects may transcend their original placement; for example, when African objects become elevated and recognized as art, these "artifacts are essentially defined as masterpieces, their makers as great artists, the discourse of connoisseurship reigns . . . personal names make their appearance, i.e. art has signature."[51] When non-Western objects fully pass from the status of authentic artifact to the status of art, they also escape the ahistorical location of the "tribal," albeit to enter into a "universal" history, defined by the progression of works of great author/artists (the canon of civilization). They become part of a "human" cultural heritage—Culture capitalized—rather than objects properly belonging to the "cultures" defined by the discipline of anthropology in the nineteenth and early twentieth centuries.

These categories of art, Culture, and culture and the domains of authentic masterpieces and authentic artifacts to which they relate are mirrored in our legal categories for the valuation and protection of expressive objects. Laws of intellectual property (copyright in particular) and laws of cultural property reflect and secure the logic of the European art/culture system that Clifford outlines. Laws of copyright, for example, were developed to protect the expressive works of authors and artists—increasingly perceived in Romantic terms of individual genius and transcendent creativity—in the service of promoting universal progress in the arts and sciences. Copyright laws protect works, understood to embody the unique personality of their individual authors, and the expressive component of the original is so venerated that even a reproduction or imitation of it is deemed a form of theft.

Although the history of copyright has been more fully investigated elsewhere,[52] a few points are central to the argument here. The idea of an author's rights to control his expressive creations developed in a context that privileged a Lockean theory of the origin of property in labor in which the expressive creation is seen as authorial "work" that creates an "Original" arising spontaneously from the vital root of "Genius."[53] The originality pertaining to mental labor—as opposed to manual labor or mechanical activity—enabled the author to claim not merely the physical object produced, but the literary or artistic expression itself: the "work" legally defined.

As William Blackstone wrote in the late eighteenth century in the context of literary copyright (although the same ideas were soon extended into other artistic spheres), the work is neither the physical book, nor the ideas contained in it, but the form of the expression that the author gives to those ideas: "The identity of a literary composition consists entirely in the *sentiment* and the *language;* the same conceptions, cloathed in the same words, must necessarily be the same composition; and whatever method be taken of conveying that composition to the ear or the eye of another, by recital, by writing, or by printing, in any number of copies or at any period of time, it is always the identical work of the author which is so conveyed; and no other man can have a right to convey or transfer it without his consent . . ."[54]

Literary or artistic works were incorporeal entities that sprang from the "fruitful mind" of an author,[55] one of many organic metaphors that proliferated in the Romantic ideology of creativity and resonated with Hegelian theories of personality. The work carries the imprint of the author's personality and always embodies his persona, wherever it surfaces, and whatever the sources of its content or the quality of the ideas it expresses; "even the humblest creative effort is protected because personality always contains something unique. It expresses its singularity . . . that which is one man's alone."[56]

If the expressive, inventive, and possessive individual dominates intellectual property laws, legitimizing personal control over the circulation of texts, laws of cultural property protect the material works (objects of artistic, archaeological, ethnological, or historical interest) of culture. Culture may be defined here in either of the two ways established in the nineteenth century: as the universal heritage of humankind—culture with a capital C—or in the plural anthropological sense, in which different cultures lay claim to different properties.[57] These two positions on the nature of the "culture" that can rightfully possess the property at issue define the poles of an ongoing controversy in legal scholarship.

John Henry Merryman, the most prolific of the legal scholars writing in this field, defends a position he defines as "cultural internationalism," which he describes in Enlightenment terms as a commitment to "the cultural heritage of all mankind," to which each people make their contribution and all people have an interest.[58] This attitude toward cultural property emerges from the law of war and the need to cease military activities when cultural objects are endangered, and to treat those responsible for advances against cultural property as having committed a crime against humanity. It is enshrined in *The Convention for the Protection of Cultural Property in the event of armed conflict* enacted in the Hague on May 14, 1954.[59]

The other position on cultural property that Merryman defines and denigrates is "cultural nationalism,"[60] in which particular peoples have particular interests in particular properties, regardless of their current location and ownership. This attitude toward cultural property is embodied in *The Convention on the Means of Prohibiting and Preventing the Illicit Import, Export, and Transfer of Ownership of Cultural Property* of November 14, 1970 (hereinafter UNESCO 1970),[61] in which "the parties agree to oppose the impoverishment of the cultural heritage of a nation through illicit import, export, and transfer of ownership of cultural property, agree that trade in cultural objects exported contrary to the law of the nation of origin is illicit and agree to prevent the importation of such objects and facilitate their return to source nations."[62] As of 1986, fifty-eight nations had become parties to UNESCO 1970; many of these signatories have policies that prevent all export of cultural property, thus making any international trafficking of cultural property "illicit."[63]

Merryman derides cultural nationalism as motivated by "Romantic Byronism," a curiously Eurocentric term that he indiscriminately applies to all nations with an interest in the preservation and repatriation of significant cultural objects.[64] For Merryman, such a position can only be seen as irrational because in the "source nations" who dominate among signatories to UNESCO 1970, the supply of cultural artifacts far exceeds the internal demand—"they are rich in cultural artefacts beyond any conceivable use."[65] Because such nations are relatively poor, he believes they would be better off exporting such objects to locations where they are valued according to free market principles.

In addition to "Romantic Byronism," Merryman cites the notion of national cultural patrimony and political symbolic uses of cultural property as possible reasons for the popularity of cultural nationalism, but he lumps such considerations together with "lack of cultural expertise and organization to deal with cultural property as a resource like other resources to be managed and exploited."[66] The possibility that other peoples may entertain other values is considered no more or less likely than their sheer ignorance and ineptitude in recognizing cultural property as an exportable resource. Merryman seems to find it offensive that source nations have the exclusive voice in determining whether or not cultural objects will be prohibited from export, when dealers, collectors, and museums are deprived of any input into the decision.[67] The interest of dealers, collectors, and museums in such decisions is self-evident; in market terms, they best recognize the value of such objects and are in the best position to see that value realized on the market.

It is not that Merryman fails to recognize any other values than those of the market; rather, it appears that he assumes that the universal human values embodied in such cultural objects are best recognized by those who will pay the market price. A "cosmopolitan attitude" would situate objects where they could be best preserved, studied, and enjoyed. Cultural objects will move to the locus of highest probable protection through the market, because those who are prepared to pay most are most likely to preserve their investment.[68] He makes the case that many source nations retain cultural works that they do not adequately conserve or display and that if such works were removed to another nation, they would be better preserved, studied, and exhibited, or more widely viewed and enjoyed. As Merryman sees it: "cultural nationalism finds no fault with the nation that hoards unused objects in this way, despite the existence of foreign markets for them . . . They forbid export but put much of what they retain to no use. In this way they fail to spread their culture, they fail to exploit such objects as a valuable resource for trade, and they contribute to the cultural impoverishment of people in other parts of the world."[69]

"Cultural internationalism" finds it inconceivable that others might value objects for reasons beyond those of the market, or that there are alternative modes of attachment to objects that do not involve their commodification, objectification, and reification for the purposes of collection, observation, and display. One suspects, however, that "cultural internationalists" would likely object to the movement of Rembrandts from the Netherlands to Lagos, despite the fact that Rembrandt's paintings might be "overrepresented" in their country of origin; the Dutch "fail to spread their culture" to the Third World, and thereby "contribute to the cultural impoverishment" of peoples in Africa and Asia. The existence of vast and seldom displayed holdings in European and North American museums (not to mention private homes) does not appear to have led to any movement among "cultural internationalists" to establish better museums in Niamey, Lima, or Nanjing, despite the vastly larger numbers of people whose "cultural impoverishment" might thereby be alleviated. The "cosmopolitan" attitude espoused here appears more Eurocentric than worldly, more monocultural than respectful of cultural difference, and less concerned with the purported "interests of all mankind"[70] than with the interests of maintaining Western hegemony.

A more sympathetic case for cultural nationalism is made by John Moustakas in a law review note titled "Group Rights in Cultural Property: Justifying Strict Inalienablity." Concerned that Greece has been dispossessed of some of its greatest cultural and artistic patrimony, and that the "looting and pillage of cultural heritage continues wholesale,"[71] as evidenced by thriving black markets, Moustakas argues that neither international conventions nor national laws have recognized that new concepts of ownership must be created to deal with emerging notions of national cultural identity. Existing laws in both national and international arenas presuppose the alienability of all property, including cultural property, according to market principles. Moustakas argues for recognition of strict market inalienability for cultural properties integrally related to group cultural identity, extending legal theorist Margaret Jane Radin's test of "property for personhood"[72] to collectivities conceived as persons.

The nexus between a cultural object and a group, culture, or nation should be "the essential measurement for determining whether group rights in cultural property will be effectuated to the fullest extent possible—by holding such objects strictly inalienable from the group."[73] Just as "property for personhood might describe property so closely bound up with our individual identities that its loss causes pain that cannot be relieved by the object's replacement . . . property for grouphood expresses something about the entire group's relationship to certain property . . . essential to the preservation of group identity and self-esteem."[74]

Against those who would argue that such a position is paternalistic, Moustakas argues that the concept of "communal flourishing" provides an important justification for holding such property inalienable.[75] Using the Parthenon Marbles (the term Elgin Marbles has the effect of ceding legitimacy to British seizure) as his example, Moustakas argues for recognition that some properties can only properly belong to groups as constitutive of group identity, that such properties cannot be alienated because future generations are unable to consent to transactions that threaten their existence as a group, and that commodification and fungibility are inappropriate ways to treat constitutive elements of grouphood and inimical to communal flourishing.

Cultural nationalism, however, also draws upon Western liberal traditions in its support for the rights of groups to claim certain objects as part of their essential identities. Drawing upon C. B. Macpherson's work,[76] anthropologist Richard Handler argues that the logic of possessive individualism—the relationship that links the individual to property as it was initially formulated in Locke's labor theory of value—increasingly dominates the language and logic of political claims to cultural autonomy and legal claims to cultural property.[77] Focusing on sixty years of historic preservation legislation in the province of Quebec, he explicates the tropes used to defend the protection of a unique cultural heritage. In discussing *le patrimoine*, people in Quebec "envision national culture as property and the nation as a property-owning 'collective individual.'"[78]

The modern individual is a self-sufficient and self-contained monad who is complete as a human being: "Not only is one complete in oneself, one is *completely oneself*. By this I mean that we conceive of the individual person as having, as we say, 'an identity.' Identity means 'oneness,' though it is oneness of a special sort . . . 'sameness in all that constitutes the objective reality of a thing.'"[79] The second aspect of modern individualism that Handler points to is its possessive element: in modern culture, an individual is defined by the property he or she possesses and such individuals naturally seek to transform nature into forms of private property. In modernity, these qualities have been extended to nation-states and ethnic groups who are imagined on the world stage and in political arenas as "collective individuals." Like other individuals, these collective individuals are imagined to be territorially and historically bounded, distinctive, internally homogeneous, and complete onto themselves.[80] In this worldview, each nation or group possesses a unique identity and culture that is constituted by its undisputed possession of property. Groups increasingly project images of themselves as individuals prizing their possession of culture and history: "it is our culture and history, which belong to us alone, which make us what we are, which constitute our identity and assure our survival . . . within cultural nationalism a group's survival, its identity or objective oneness over time, depends upon the secure possession of a culture . . . [and] culture and history become synonymous because the group's history is preserved and embodied in material objects—cultural property."[81]

Material objects, therefore, come to epitomize collective identity, as articulated by a 1976 UNESCO panel in the principle that "cultural property is a basic element of a people's identity,"[82] used to legitimate the repatriation of objects of overriding importance to group identity. Being is equated with having (and excluding and controlling):

> This collective individual is imagined like a biological organism to be precisely delimited both physically and in terms of a set of traits (its culture, heritage, or "personality") that distinguishes it from all other collective individuals. The nation is said to "have" or "possess" a culture, just as its human constituents are described as "bearers" of the national culture. From the nationalist perspective, the relationship between the nation and culture should be characterized by originality and authenticity. Cultural traits that come to the nation from outside are at best "borrowed" and at worst polluting; by contrast, those aspects of national culture that come from within the nation, that are original to it, are "authentic."[83]

The rhetoric of cultural nationalism clearly bears traces of the same logic that defines copyright. Each nation or group is perceived as an author who originates a culture from resources that come from within and can thus lay claim to exclusive possession of the expressive works that embody its personality. There is, however, a significant difference in the scope of the claims that can be made on behalf of a culture and those that can be made on behalf of an individual author. Copyright laws enable individual authors not only to claim possession of their original works as discrete objects, but to claim possession and control over any and all reproductions of those works, or any substantial part thereof, in any medium.[84] Cultural property laws, however, enable proprietary claims to be made only to original objects or authentic artifacts. The Western extension of Culture to cultural others was limited to objects of property, not to forms of expression. The full authority of authorship, however, was confined to the Western world.

To make this concrete, consider the Picasso painting. When a primitive statue, produced in a collectivity for social reasons, makes its way into a Picasso painting, the statue itself may still embody the identity of the culture from which it sprang, but any reproduction of it is legally recognized as the embodiment of Picasso's authorial personality. The possession of a culture is profoundly limited, whereas the possession of the author extends through time and space as his work is reproduced. Royalties flow not to the statue's culture of origin, but to the estate of the Western author, where the fruits of his or her original work are realized for fifty years after death.

In his discussion of "possessive collectivism," Handler agrees with the principle of repatriation as a matter of fair play, but suggests that the cultural identity argument used to support it has the insidious effect of reproducing and extending Western cultural ideologies of possessive individualism on a global scale.[85] The problem with restitutionist arguments, he posits, is that they make use of metaphors "borrowed from the hegemonic culture that the restitutionists are attempting to resist."[86] Handler, like most contemporary anthropologists, asserts that cultures are not bounded, continuous over time, or internally homogeneous, that traditions are actively invented, transformed, and reimagined as social agents negotiate their political lives and relationships.[87] The culture to which groups make claims as essentially embodied in particular pieces of property is, he suggests, not an objective thing that has possessed a continuous meaning and identity over time, but the product of current needs and interpretations.[88] It is, however, as politically dishonest to deny the objective identity of those making culturally nationalist claims as it is to assert an internationalism that privileges the nation-building imperialist enterprises of European countries in the name of universal human values or the common heritage of mankind. Both positions are interested human inventions.

Contemporary Properties of Culture and Identity

The European art/culture system and the legal categories that support and sustain it constitute a limited vision of human expressive possibility and a limited understanding of our various modes of cultural attachment to the phenomena that give meaning to our lives. Ultimately, these categories of authorship and alterity serve only to culturally impoverish the Western self, while they Orientalize others. By deeming expressive creations the private properties of authors who can thereby control the circulation of culturally meaningful texts through our intellectual property laws, we deprive ourselves of immense opportunities for creative worldmaking.[89] Denying the social conditions and cultural influences that shape the author's expressive creativity, we invest him with powers of expropriation and censorship in the name of property. Representing cultures in the image of the undivided possessive individual, we obscure people's historical agency and transformations, their internal differences, the productivity of intercultural contact, and the ability of peoples to culturally express their position in a wider world. The Romantic author and the artifacts of an authentic alterity are both fictions of a world best forgone.

Anthropologists have spent well over a decade discrediting the modern disciplinary mode of representing cultures as homogeneous, static, or timeless and as governed by uncontested systems of meaning, codes of conduct, or traditions conceived in juridical terms. Recognizing culture as contested, temporal, and always emergent in worldly political struggle, they have emphasized the invention of tradition and the cultural productivity generated by differences within cultures, at the borders between cultures, and in the ongoing negotiation of situated identities.

The creative negotiation of socially situated identities has also been a theme of contemporary pragmatism, exemplified in legal literature by Martha Minow and in cultural criticism by bell hooks. Minow points out: "As a founding parent of pragmatism, [William] James would reject any approach to the riddle of identity that sought the essence of a person or group. Rather than search for essences or intrinsic qualities of people or concepts, the pragmatists looked to purposes and effects, consequences and functions."[90]

Minow suggests that most legal treatments of identity questions fail to acknowledge that the cultural, gender, racial, and ethnic identities of a person are not simply intrinsic to that person, but emerge from relationships between people in negotiations and interactions with others: "The relative power enjoyed by some people compared with others is partly

manifested through the ability to name oneself and others and to influence the process of negotiation over questions of identity."[91] Thus, "Lawyers and judges who address legal questions of identity should keep in
mind its kaleidoscopic nature. They should examine the multiple contributions given to any definition of identity. They ought to examine the
pattern of power relationships within which an identity is forged. And
they need to explore the pattern of power relationships within which a
question of identity is framed . . . Who picks an identity and who is consigned to it?"[92] As we shall soon see, it is precisely the inability to name
themselves and a continuous history of having their identities defined by
others that First Nations peoples foreground when they oppose practices
of cultural appropriation.

In an effort to create a critical consciousness of racism and its eradication, cultural critic bell hooks also adopts a pragmatic approach to questions of identity. She asserts that cultural critics must confront the power
and control over representations in the public sphere, because social
identity is a process of identifying and constructing oneself as a social
being through the mediation of images.[93] Hence, minority peoples need
to critically engage questions of their representation and its influence on
questions of identity formation. As we have seen, Native peoples are particularly concerned with the ahistorical representations of "Indianness"
that circulate in the public sphere and the manner in which such imagery mediates the capacities of others to recognize their contemporary
identities as peoples with specific needs in the late twentieth century.

Hooks asserts that an identity politics, however necessary as a stage in
the liberation of subordinated peoples, must "eschew essentialist notions
of identity and fashion selves that emerge from the meeting of diverse
epistemologies, habits of being, concrete class locations, and radical
political commitments."[94] A return to "identity" and "culture" is necessary, in hooks's perspective, more as a means of locating oneself in a
political practice than in the embrace of the positivism projected by cultural nationalism.[95] Hooks links this political project to a feminist anti-
essentialism that also links identity to a history and a politics rather than
an essence: "Identity politics provides a decisive rejoinder to the generic
human thesis, and the mainstream methodology of Western political
theory . . . if we combine the concept of identity politics with a conception of the subject as positionality, we can conceive of the subject as non-
essentialized and emergent from historical experience . . ."[96] In the face
of white supremacy, issues of black identity cannot be dismissed, and
critiques of essentialism must recognize the very different positions occupied by oppressed groups in society. Abstract and universalizing criti-

cisms of essentialism may appear to oppressed peoples as threatening, once again preventing "those who have suffered the crippling effects of colonization or domination to gain or regain a hearing . . . It never surprises me when black folks respond to the critique of essentialism, especially when I denied the validity of identity politics by saying, 'Yeah, it is easy to give up identity, when you've got one.'"[97] Critiques of essentialism are useful, hooks suggests, to the extent that they enable African Americans to examine differences within black culture, for example, the impact that class and gender have on the experience of racism. They are also necessary to condemn notions of "natural" and "authentic" expressions of black culture that perpetuate static, ahistorical, and stereotyped images of black people's lives and possibilities.[98] As long as the specific history and experience of African Americans and the cultural sensibilities that emerge from that experience are kept in view, essentialism may be fruitfully criticized: "There is a radical difference between repudiation of the idea that there is a black 'essence' and recognition of the way that black identity has been specifically constituted in the experience of exile and struggle."[99]

First Nations peoples face similar dilemmas in their representation of identity in contemporary Canadian society. When they specify their unique histories, they are often accused of essentialism, but when they write or paint, their work is often criticized for not being "authentic" or sufficiently "Indian."[100] When First Nations peoples make claims to "their own" images, stories, and cultural themes, however, they do not do so as Romantic authors nor as timeless, homogeneous cultures insisting upon the maintenance of a vanishing authenticity. They do not lay claim to expressive works as possessive individuals, insisting on permissions and royalties for the circulation of authorial personas in the public realm.[101] Nor is their assertion of cultural presence made in the name of an ahistorical collective essence, but in the name of living, changing, creative peoples engaged in very concrete contemporary political struggles.[102] The law, however, affords them little space to make their claims.[103] As Amanda Pask explains, Native peoples face a legal system that divides the world up in a fashion both foreign and hostile to their sense of felt need:

> At every level the claims of aboriginal peoples to cultural rights fall
> outside the parameters of Western legal discourse. As neither state
> actors, nor individuals, their claims can be heard neither in the in-
> ternational regimes governing cultural property, nor in the domes-
> tic regimes governing intellectual property. This pattern repeats it-

self internally in each regime: in cultural property law the competing legal values that frame every question are those of national patrimony and the "universal heritage of mankind"; in intellectual property the interests to be balanced are those of "authors" conceived of on an individualistic model and "the public" in their interest in preserving a common public domain. In all cases, aboriginal peoples must articulate their interests within frameworks which obliterate the position from which they speak.[104]

The opposition between private, personal interests and universal ones is understood to cover the field of all possible claims, and, as we have seen, when group rights are entertained, they are often conceived in individualistic terms that freeze and essentialize culture in the name of identity.

Even more debilitating for Native claims, perhaps, is the law's rigid demarcation between ideas and expressions, oral traditions and written forms, intangible works and cultural objects, personal property and real property. The law rips asunder what First Nations people view as integrally related, freezing into categories what Native peoples find flowing in relationships that do not separate texts from ongoing creative production, or ongoing creativity from social relationships, or social relationships from people's relationship to an ecological landscape that binds past and future generations in relations of spiritual significance.

The powerful conceptual framework of the European art/culture system seems so deeply embedded in our legal categories of intellectual and cultural property that they seem immutable, but the claims of non-Western others to objects and representations may well force these Western categories under new forms of scrutiny. As new subjects engaged in postcolonial struggles occupy the categories bestowed upon us by an ignoble past, they may well transform them and eventually perhaps help to crumble the colonial edifice upon which these categories are founded. To understand First Nations claims, we must venture beyond the European categories that constitute the colonial edifice of the law; only by considering Native claims "in context" will we be able to expand "the borders of the legal imagination."[105]

Listening to Native Claims "in Context"

The cultural appropriation debate raises numerous issues and engages many protagonists. I cannot engage all of these arguments here. Rather than attempt to construct a solution to a problem, I will suggest instead that my readers attempt to understand the issues differently. Whereas it may be impossible to delineate formal rules defining, sanctioning, and prohibiting specific acts of "cultural appropriation," it is possible to enact and practice an ethics of appropriation that attends to the specificity of the historical circumstances in which certain claims are made. Only in such contexts can they be adequately addressed.

The moral and political significance of considering claims "in context" has been explored by Martha Minow and Elizabeth Spelman as a conviction that unites philosophical pragmatists, feminists, and critical race theorists.[106] In decision making, an emphasis on context requires a sensitivity to the nuances of the particular historical situation in which a claim emerges and the distinctive needs of the persons involved. Against assumptions of liberal legal and political theory that treat principles as universal and the individual self as the proper unit of analysis, the call to context is a call to consider the structures of power in society and the systemic legacies of exclusion involving the group-based characteristics of individuals.[107] In this sense, "context" is not a reified social totality, like traditional anthropological "cultures," but contingent social fields of agency emergent from specific political trajectories.

Minow and Spelman argue that attention to the contingencies of a situation—the particular cultural and historical backgrounds of the persons involved—neither incapacitates us from making moral judgments nor undermines the possibility of criticism across contexts.[108] Instead, a contextualist approach suggests that all human beings are always in social contexts and make judgments contextually and that any form of abstraction to general principles involves a choice of relevant contexts. Exponents of abstraction who stress the need to develop principles that apply across contexts, like the writers of letters to the editor cited earlier, are themselves situated in ways that limit their understandings, and these limitations must be reflected upon in attempting to understand a context for judgment. Abstract theories, such as freedom of expression, authorship, ownership, and censorship, are "rooted in particular contexts and operate within context with real and particular effects that often benefit some people more than others."[109] Contextualist approaches, moreover, generally do appeal to some more abstract moral or political theory to justify their procedures. Like Cornell West, I point to context here as a means of challenging a political theory that speaks in the name of abstract individual rights with the specific situated experiences of others whose lives bespeak the exclusions effected by those principles.[110]

Native peoples in Canada make specific claims to stories, imagery, and themes based on very specific historical experiences and the specific needs of people engaged in contemporary political struggles in which these stories strategically figure. The claims of First Nations peoples to control the circulation of Native cultural texts cannot be facilely analogized to prohibiting Shakespeare's writing of *Hamlet* or the Third Reich's prohibition of Jewish writing under the rubric of freedom of speech without doing violence to the integrity of Native struggles for political self-determination. Specific historical experiences and current political struggles provide the relevant context for considering claims of cultural appropriation. Only by situating these claims in this context can we understand how supposedly abstract, general, and (purportedly) universal principles (such as authorship, art, culture, and identity) may operate as systematic structures of domination and exclusion. An evaluation and judgment of Native claims of cultural appropriation without this knowledge of context cannot but reinforce these larger patterns of injustice.

> Rather than a weakness or a departure from the ideal of distance and impersonality, acknowledging the human situation and the location of a problem in the midst of communities of actual peoples with views about it, is a precondition of honesty in human judgments . . . The call to make judgments in context often seems misleading if it implies that we could ever make judgments outside of a context; the question is always what context matters or what context should we make matter for this moment . . . in many contemporary political and legal discussions, the demand to look at the context often means a demand to look at . . . structures of power . . . Rather than an injunction to immerse in the unique particularities of the situation, the emphasis on context often means identifying structures that extend far beyond the particular circumstance. But perhaps, it is not so surprising that this should be named a contextual move against the backdrop—the context by default—created by Western liberal legal and political traditions that emphasize as ideals individual freedom, equality, universal reason, and abstract principles. Because persistent patterns of power, based on lines of gender, racial, class and age differences, have remained resilient and at the same time elusive under traditional political and legal ideas, arguments for looking to context carry critical power. In this context, arguments for context highlight these patterns as worthy of attention, and at times, condemnation. Attention to context implies no particular political agenda, but it does signal a commitment to consider and reconsider the meaning of moral and philosophical purposes in light of shifting circumstance.[111]

Representation without Representation: Visibility without Voice

Native peoples discuss the issue of cultural appropriation in a manner that links issues of cultural representation with a history of political powerlessness. In North American commercial culture, imagery of Indians and the aura of "Indianness" is pervasive, but living human peoples with Native ancestry are treated as dead, dying, vanishing, or victimized and—until very recently—in need of others to speak on their behalf. I will try to avoid speaking "on behalf of" Native peoples here, employing direct quotations drawn from articles and public statements by Native authors wherever possible to delineate the context in which claims of cultural appropriation are made. It quickly becomes clear that issues of culture and the proper place of texts cannot be separated from issues of spirituality, political determination, and aboriginal title to traditional lands.

In July of 1990, representatives of 120 Indian nations, international organizations, and fraternal organizations met in Quito, Ecuador, at the first indigenous continental gathering in history, titled "500 Years of Indian Resistance." The Declaration of Purpose that emerged from the meeting set forth "the necessary conditions that permit the complete exercise of our self-determination . . . and autonomy of our Peoples."[112] In the Declaration, territorial rights were deemed the "fundamental demand of the Indigenous Peoples of the Americas," to which end other goals were affirmed. These included: "our decision to defend our culture, education and religion as fundamental to our identity as Peoples, reclaiming and maintaining our own forms of spiritual life and community coexistence, in an intimate relationship with our Mother Nature."[113]

This nexus of ecological, spiritual, cultural, and territorial concerns is central to any understanding of cultural appropriation. Simplistic reductions of Native concerns to trademark or copyright considerations and the assertion of intellectual property rights fail to reflect the full dimensions of Native aspirations and impose colonial juridical categories on postcolonial struggles in a fashion that reenacts the cultural violence of colonization. As many Native writers strive to assert, knowledge of this history of cultural violence is a prerequisite to understanding the issues involved in cultural appropriation. This cultural violence includes the seizure of land, government suppression of Indian religious practice, the prohibition on the speaking of Indian languages in residential schools, the expropriation of ceremonial objects for museum collections, the unauthorized excavation of indigenous graves and the collection of material culture by archaeologists, the definition and description of Native culture by non-Native anthropologists, the loss of Indian status to children of mothers who married non-Natives, the apprehension of aboriginal children from reserves, the separation of families, the withholding from a generation of children their very identity as First Nations people, and a related legacy of sexual abuse.

Central to all of these practices is the experience of having Native cultural identity extinguished, denied, suppressed, and/or classified, named, and designated by others. As Robert Allen Warrior, a member of the Osage nation, writes: "Our primary focus as Indian people must be on establishing our right to a land base and a cultural and political status distinct from non-natives . . . We won't allow Canada to call us ethnic, a minority, or a class . . . Indian people are forever being discovered and rediscovered, being surrounded by thicker and thicker layers of mythology. And every generation predicts our inevitable and tragic disappearance."[114] This history cannot be fully explored here. I will, however, highlight some of those dimensions of Native experience in Canada that figure most prominently in Native discussions of cultural appropriation.

In 1887, Sir John A. Macdonald declared, "The great aim of our civilization has been to do away with the tribal system and assimilate the Indian people in all respects."[115] In 1920, Superintendent-General Duncan Campbell Scott was even more to the point: "I want to get rid of the Indian problem . . . Our objective is to continue until there is not a single Indian in Canada that has not been absorbed."[116]

> After the 1812 War with the United States, British colonizers no longer required aboriginal peoples as allies—or, for that matter, as explorers or traders. Their value rapidly diminished, with the result that aboriginal tribes became stigmatized as obstacles to the progressive settlement of Canadian society. Moreover, by refusing to relinquish their identity and assimilate into higher levels of "civilization," aboriginal peoples were dismissed as an inferior and unequal species whose rights could be trampled on with impunity. Aboriginal lands were increasingly coveted by colonists intent on settlement and agriculture. Policy directives were formulated that dismissed aboriginal peoples as little more than impediments to be removed in the interests of progress and settlement.
>
> A policy of assimilation evolved as part of this project to subdue and subordinate aboriginal peoples. From the early nineteenth century on, elimination of the "Indian problem" was one of the colony's—later the Dominion's—foremost concerns. Authorities rejected extermination as a solution, but focused instead on a

planned process of cultural change known as assimilation. Through assimilation, the dominant sector sought to undermine the cultural distinctiveness of aboriginal tribal society; to subject the indigenes to the rules, values, and sanctions of Euro-Canadian society; and to absorb the de-culturated minority into the mainstream through a process of "anglo-conformity." The means to achieve this outward compliance with Euro-Canadian society lay in the hands of missionaries, teachers, and law-makers.[117]

Aboriginal peoples' relations with the state have been governed for years by the Indian Acts of 1876[118] and 1951[119] and their implementation by the Indian Affairs Department (IAD). The original Victorian Act defined who, legally, was an Indian, and gave the IAD sweeping powers "to invade, control and regulate every aspect of aboriginal life,"[120] curbing constitutional and citizenship rights in the paternalistic guise of Indian protection, while suppressing aboriginal languages, culture, and collective identity.

> The 1876 Indian Act created the legal framework for the paternalistic administration of aboriginal affairs by a federal agency. The Act consolidated existing Indian legislation in the provinces and territories, and delineated the responsibilities of the federal government towards aboriginal peoples as stipulated in the BNA [British North America] Act of 1867. It also established the principle of government control over and responsibilities for managing aboriginal assets (land, funds, and properties). Perception of aboriginal peoples as wards of the state, in need of superior guidance and protection, gave rise to the colonialist/paternalistic character of the Department. Aboriginal people were seen as inferior legal minors who had to be pacified, controlled, managed, and educated in hopes of achieving the ultimate goal of enfranchisement (loss of Indian status) and absorption into society . . . The Department's early policy and administration were consistent with the provisions of the Indian Act. Foremost among its objectives were the protection (guardianship), settlement, and assimilation (through exposure to Christianity and the arts of civilization) of aboriginal peoples, and, through agricultural self-sufficiency, their transformation into productive citizens of the country. The success of the Department's policy was to be measured by the numbers of enfranchised Natives—that is, those who formally renounced Indian status and assumed all the rights, duties, and obligations of citizenship in Canada.[121]

Indian identity has thus been defined and determined by a bureaucracy committed to its disappearance. "Reflecting the commitment to assimilate and 'civilize,' Departmental policy has historically labelled aboriginal peoples a 'problem' whose cultural and social idiosyncracies preclude smooth absorption into society."[122] In other words, Indian cultures were obstacles to Indian people's incorporation into a larger human community as citizens of nation-states. Since World War II the strategy has shifted from cultural assimilation to the eradication of poverty—a process in which "the communal (read 'communistic') aspects of tribal life"[123] were seen as barriers to the process of modernization (which at this time was viewed as a universal process that would inevitably occur in the same fashion for peoples around the world). In both cases, any autonomous Native cultural identity was seen as an obstacle to government objectives.

Although government policies to assimilate aboriginal peoples and undermine their cultural distinction were numerous, the residential school and agricultural work programs, social welfare policies, and religious suppression figure prominently in the memories of First Nations peoples. Most Native peoples were cut off from their traditional land base and consequentially from cultural ways of life by the uprooting and resettlement that these programs entailed. At the residential schools in which aboriginal children were routinely placed, Native languages were prohibited, and many people have memories of severe beatings and punishments for "speaking Indian."[124]

In the 1960s, provincial child welfare agencies were bestowed with increased powers to apprehend aboriginal children from reserves. Now "known as the 60s scoop . . . some reserves lost almost all the children of that generation who were nearly exclusively adopted into white foster homes, many in the United States."[125] Many of these children lost all contact with their relatives and many were adopted into families that withheld information about their Native ancestry. Only years later would they become aware of their personal histories and seek knowledge of the cultural heritage they had been denied.

Another way in which the government controlled Indian identity was through the policy of denying Indian status to the children of Native women married to nonaboriginal men. Some argue that this policy resulted in a social devaluation of aboriginal women and contributed to their negative self-esteem:

> For those without status because of marriage with non-aboriginal males, penalties included deprivation of Indian rights, ostracism

from involvement in band life, and exclusion from housing and jobs. Not even the repeal of the offending [legislation] . . . has eased the barriers for some women. In abolishing the discriminatory sections of the Indian Act that had stripped any Indian woman of status upon marriage to a non-Indian, Bill C-31 reinstated all non-status Indians who had lost status for financial, educational, or career reasons . . . To ensure band control over membership and resources, only women who had lost status because of marriage became eligible to join the band or to partake of reserve land or benefits. Although children of reinstated women were also entitled to band resources, they stand to lose this . . . unless they marry into "status."[126]

This long colonial history of having Indian identity legally defined by a government simultaneously determined to eliminate all vestiges of that identity in Canadian society has left a bitter residue of distrust. Native peoples express great anger at continually having their cultural identity named, defined, and affirmed by others, in a manner that freezes categories of Indianness for bureaucratic purposes both unrelated and oblivious to indigenous values.[127] Many Natives saw the Canadian government policy of not recognizing as Indians any Native women married to white men or their children as particularly imperialist.[128] In a commentary both on Imperial Oil's sponsorship of *The Spirit Sings* exhibition at the Glenbow Museum and on the government marriage policy, Hachivi Edgar Heap of Birds created a work for the Banff Centre in support of the Lubicon Cree. His work incorporated a billboard that read "Imperial Canada Doesn't Make Indians. Native Peoples Recognize Themselves."[129]

The government suppressed aboriginal spiritual practices as a central means to achieve its policies of cultural assimilation and to destroy the social integration of Native communities. For example, the Northwest coast potlatch ceremony was outlawed from 1884[130] until 1951, and sweat lodge and sun dance ceremonies were prohibited until the cultural revivals of the 1960s.[131] As it will become clear, this history of government-directed alienation of Native peoples from cultural traditions is now being repeated. Now, however, First Nations peoples feel themselves alienated from their histories by artists and entrepreneurs who appropriate these same ceremonies as spiritual commodities to be bought and sold on the market. Again, Native peoples' specific histories and experiences of having those ceremonies prohibited is ignored, as New Age entrepreneurs profess spiritual resources to be the fruits of human Culture, freely available to all in need of spiritual sustenance.

Loss of ceremonial objects and reliquiae accompanied the displacement of Native languages and ceremonies. Systematically collected by museums and private collectors, they were valued as authentic artifacts of a dying culture and a vanishing race. When Indian expressive works were appreciated, in other words, it was in terms of their historical value as representative of an anthropological culture, not as the ongoing expressions of peoples engaged in a politics of self-recognition and self-determination. This "imperialist nostalgia"—the longing for the return of something one is engaged in colonizing and destroying—continues today. Witness the controversy over the 1988 Glenbow Museum exhibit, in which Native peoples complained that they were being treated like historical artifacts rather than human contemporaries. As part of the Olympic Arts Festival, the Museum gathered fifteenth-, sixteenth-, and seventeenth-century North American Indian artifacts from around the world for an exhibit titled *The Spirit Sings*. The Lubicon Cree Indians, involved in bitter land claims disputes with the federal and provincial governments for fifty years, launched a boycott against the exhibit. They found it particularly hypocritical that the oil companies sponsoring the exhibit should publicly celebrate Indian material culture while (through their oil drilling activities in northern Alberta) they were actively engaged in decimating Native ways of life. Objectifying, displaying, and glorifying the proud cultural past of peoples whose contemporary lands and livelihoods were being doomed to extinction by those doing the celebrating puts into crude relief the relationship between those who profess a cosmopolitan interest in the preservation of a purportedly universal human Culture and the anthropological cultures it allegedly values.[132]

Joane Cardinal-Schubert argues that the Glenbow exhibit took ceremonial reliquiae out of their contexts in community life, portrayed them as lifeless objects, and "pushed the notion that Native culture was dead, wrapped up, over and collected."[133] Native artists from across the continent participated in protest exhibits at the nearby Wallace and Walter Phillips galleries. In one particularly trenchant authorial "work," Rebecca Belmore sat herself down under a sign that read "Glenbow Museum presents" and titled her self/work "Artifact #671-B."[134] In so doing she drew ironic attention to the relationship between the claims of a "cultural internationalism" to guardianship of all objects having cultural meaning, the claims of Romantic authorship to the ideas they deem human Culture (or public domain), those expressions they claim as properties, and the status of those cultural others who can lay claim only to authentic artifacts as evidence of their specific identities. Relationships between authorship and alterity were put into sharp relief.

The resurgence and revival of Native cultural pride and ceremonial practice in the 1960s by a newly politicized people made the return of expropriated cultural objects imperative, for their presence in these religious practices was felt to give contemporary community life historical meaning and continuity.[135] The development of the idea of *u'mista* among the Kwakiutl people is instructive. Several people were tried under the antipotlatch laws in 1922.[136] In these trials, it was agreed that those charged need not serve jail sentences if the participating villages would forfeit their ceremonial objects: "The federal government paid the owners a total of fourteen hundred and fifty dollars and fifty cents for several hundred objects, which were crated and shipped to Ottawa. There, what came to be known as the potlatch collection, was divided between the Victoria Memorial Museum, later the National Museum of Man and now the Canadian Museum of Civilization, and the Royal Ontario Museum."[137]

Kwakiutl anthropologist and curator Gloria Cranmer Webster is involved in the movement to repatriate these objects that developed momentum after the 1951 repeal of the antipotlatch provisions of the Indian Act,[138] and the revitalization of the potlatch ceremony in contemporary celebrations of cultural identity. For Webster, the need to repossess these ceremonial objects[139] is an integral part of the contemporary political struggle to reconstruct and redefine Native culture and identity:

> We do not have a word for repatriation in the Kwak'wala language. The closest we come to it is the word u'mista which describes the return of people taken captive in raids. It also means the return of something important. We are working towards the u'mista of much that was almost lost to us. The return of the potlatch collection is one u'mista . . . We are taking back from many sources information about our culture and our history to help us rebuild our world that was almost shattered during the bad times [when, she says earlier], "it was believed we were truly the 'vanishing race.'" Our aim is the complete u'mista or repatriation of everything we lost when our world was turned upside down as our old people say. The u'mista of our lands is part of our goal and there is some urgency to do it before the provincial government allows any more clear-cut logging, destroying salmon-spawning streams which effect the livelihood of many of our people.[140]

For Webster, the repatriation of material culture is not the possessive or proprietary claim to the essence of an undivided traditional identity—as cultural nationalists might see it—but part of a larger contemporary struggle for Native self-determination that includes cultural as well as territorial control in the quest for political sovereignty.

But if ceremonial objects have been decontextualized—alienated and removed from the cultural practices of historical communities and collected to be displayed as frozen objects in the museums that document Western imperialism—ceremonial practices themselves are now alienated in a fashion that many Native peoples find just as insidious. New Age religious organizations sell Indian spirituality, marketing participation in "Indian ceremonials" like the sun dance and the sweat lodge ceremonies. Entrepreneurs even offer to turn consumers into shamans if they purchase a weekend-long course of study![141] In some feminist circles, Indian spiritual themes are employed in the name of the essential female.[142] Although many see these appropriations as simple romanticism, many others find them far more insidious. Paul Smith, a Comanche activist, for example, suggests that progressive non-Indians should be prepared "to call romanticism the thuggish racism it really is."[143]

The use of Native motifs, imagery, and themes in the "spirituality" marketed as New Age religion is particularly offensive, both because of its commodification and its distortion of Native traditions. That which is spiritual cannot be sold and must be treated with care and respect. Many non-Native peoples also feel that spirituality should not be "owned," but that it must therefore belong to all people equally, as part of the public cultural domain fully available for the sustenance of all humanity (and as ideas available for reworking into authorial expressions). For Native peoples, however, spirituality is not a thing that can be reified or abstracted from real human communities integrally balanced in a relationship with the earth: "We have many particular things which we hold internal to our cultures. These things are spiritual in nature . . . They are *ours* and they are *not* for sale. Because of this, I suppose it's accurate to say that such things are our 'secrets,' the things which bind us together in our identity as distinct peoples. It's not that we never make outsiders aware of our secrets, but *we* not *they* decide what, how much, and to what purpose this knowledge is to be put. That's absolutely essential to our cultural integrity and thus to our survival as peoples . . . Respect for and balance between all things, that's our most fundamental spiritual concept."[144]

The commodification of Indian spirituality is understood to pose the threat of cultural dissolution.[145] Spiritual knowledge cannot be objectified and exchanged as a commodity or learned as an act of self-discovery:

White people are often eager to learn about our spirituality, apparently seeing it as the latest self-help opportunity. Counter to this notion, however, is the way spirituality in its transference as knowledge and experience is constructed in First Nations cultures. It is based on respect and is meant to be taught in somewhat specific and often personal ways, the meanings of which are ruined by translation into a classroom or mass venue. The same is true for spiritual images that get used in ways wildly out of their cultural context. I can't tell you how hurtful it is to have a sacred image come back to you horribly disfigured by a white artist. If a First Nations artist chooses to use our culture in a new or different way, then that will be a subject for debate within our culture. If a white artist uses and invariably alters our cultural images, then this is an intervention in our culture, another of many.[146]

Ward Churchill argues that representations and misrepresentations of indigenous spirituality are so ubiquitous in academies of higher learning that Native peoples cannot represent their experiences of their religious traditions without being contradicted and corrected by non-Native experts who have assumed the power to define what is and is not truly Indian.[147] Métis filmmaker and videomaker Loretta Todd defines this inability to speak on one's own behalf as constitutive of the experience of cultural appropriation: "For me, the definition of appropriation originates in its inversion, cultural autonomy. Cultural autonomy signifies a right to one's origins and histories as told from within the culture and not as mediated from without. Appropriation occurs when someone else speaks for, tells, defines, describes, represents, uses, or recruits the images, stories, experiences, dreams of others for their own. Appropriation also occurs when someone else becomes the expert on your experience."[148]

The experience of everywhere being seen but never being heard, of constantly being represented but never listened to, being treated like a historical artifact rather than a human being to be engaged in dialogue is a central theme in many complaints of cultural appropriation. As Ojibway poet Lenore Keeshig-Tobias suggests, it is precisely because Native people are so seldom publicly heard or recognized (or rewarded in the market) for recounting their historical experiences that non-Native representation of these themes is so offensive.[149] The Canadian public seems intensely interested in things Indian, but they seem to have no interest in hearing Native peoples speak on their own behalf. When Native writers try to assert that they are better situated to tell these stories, they are accused of trying to shackle the artistic imagination of authors and as advocating censorship. But in making such responses, these critics reinscribe Native peoples as objects of human Culture, rather than authorial subjects in their own right—contributors to Culture, not mere objects of it—capable of the expressive work that defines us as human, rather than merely serving as cultural resources for the expressive works and proprietary claims of others.

After years of having their languages outlawed and their cultural specificity suppressed for the purposes of extinguishing it, First Nations peoples now watch the Canadian government subsidize non-Native citizens (through arts grants and film subsidies) to sympathetically portray Indian culture—and convey the momentous tragedies that Indians historically experienced at government hands—on the basis of their recognized authorial talents. It is as if there were no Natives living in the community who could speak on their own behalf, as if these historical experiences had not left very real psychic scars on real human beings in our communities. As Keeshig-Tobias puts it, "people . . . would rather look to an ideal native living in never-never land than confront the reality of what being native means today in Canadian society."[150] Or, as Gerald McMaster and Lee-Ann Martin ask: "We wish to know and you need to understand why it is that you want to own our stories, our art, our beautiful crafts, our ceremonies, but you do not appreciate or wish to recognize that these things of beauty arise out of the beauty of our people."[151]

Possessive Individualism Revisited: Authorship and Cultural Identity

Earlier I suggested that by considering Native claims of cultural appropriation "in context," the assertions of cultural identity, authenticity, authorial freedom, artistic license, freedom of expression, and censorship in this debate might take on different dimensions. Issues that appeared black and white might emerge cast in very complex shadows. First Nations peoples, I have suggested, are often forced to make their claims using categories that are antithetical to their needs and foreign to their aspirations.

In his discussion of cultural nationalism and the Eurocentric concepts that dominate that discourse, Handler eventually concedes that despite the epistemological bankruptcy of the metaphors of possessive individualism, they have become the dominant metaphors of world political culture. Subaltern groups and less powerful nations must articulate their political claims in "a language that power understands,"[152] and the language that power understands engages the possessive and expressive individualism of the European art/culture system as its conceptual limits. He regrets the fact that "in a world made meaningful in terms of our individualistic moral and legal codes" disputants in the contemporary "culture wars . . . have agreed to a worldview in which culture has come to be represented as and by 'things'"[153] possessed by persons and cultures.

Ultimately, the questions of whose voice it is, who speaks on behalf of whom, and whether one can steal the culture of another are not legal questions to be addressed in terms of asserting rights, but ethical ones to be addressed in terms of manifesting one's moral and political commitments. In contexts of postcolonial struggle, the postmodern claim that cultures are contructed, emergent, mobile, and contested may seem academically abstract and exceedingly empty. Such anti-essentialisms are themselves universalisms that only beg questions of position, perspective, privilege, and power. For whom is culture emergent and contested and in what circumstances? What are the politics of deploying such knowledges alongside the struggles of those for whom possession of a culture may be the last legitimate ground a liberal framework offers for political autonomy and long-delayed self-determinations? From what position can one confidently make such claims, and how and in what circumstances is the privilege of expressive self-fashioning assumed? Ultimately, questions of culture and its appropriation are political rather than ontological ones that will demand continuing identifications rather than formal resolutions—a situational ethics that will continuously compel attention to the dynamics of mimesis and alterity.

Peoples of First Nations ancestry may well be compelled to articulate their claims "in a language that power understands,"[154] but in the substance of their claims they contest the logic of possessive individualism even as they give voice to its metaphors. Native peoples engage in "double voiced rhetoric"[155] when they employ the tropes of a dominant language, simultaneously engaging and subverting these metaphors through the character of the alternative claims they make in the voice of an authorial other.

The perils of making claims in the language of possessive individualism writ large, however, are real, as Native peoples in Canada have discovered. For example, in a presentation on Native cultural autonomy and the appropriation of aboriginal imagery at a meeting of independent filmmakers, Métis videomaker Loretta Todd quoted Walter Benjamin; she was promptly accused of appropriating Western culture![156]

She responded that she was part of Western culture—as a product of colonization, how could she be otherwise?—and Benjamin was part of that culture. Her interlocutors informed her that white use of Native imagery was equivalent to her use of Benjamin, because native imagery was now simply a part of contemporary Culture—with a capital C.[157] Other artists have responded to questions about the propriety of their alleged employment of Native ritual themes in ways that appeared to question the representative status of their aboriginal interlocutors.[158] In speaking for a culture to which one makes a proprietary claim, one always risks allegations that the identity one must possess to make such claims is not the undivided one demanded of the property-holding possessive individual.

The tactic of deeming some people of aboriginal ancestry to be "real Indians" while denying the ability of others to speak on behalf of Native concerns is reminiscent of the historical policies of colonial authorities who arbitrarily conferred and withheld Indian status on spurious grounds that did not recognize indigenous practices defining community membership. There also is embedded in these discussions the notion that all Native peoples must agree for them to have a position that can be recognized as "Native"; but as Paul Smith reminds us, "We have differences in political opinion. After all, we come from hundreds of nations and histories."[159]

Curiously, however, there is an insistence that aboriginal peoples must represent a fully coherent position that expresses an authentic identity forged from an uncomplicated past that bespeaks a pristine cultural tradition before their voice will be recognized as Native. No one, of course, asks white authors what gives them the authority to speak on behalf of artistic license, or what criteria of representativeness they fulfill in order to make claims in the name of the authorial imagination. Nor do we expect uniform positions on the parameters of freedom of speech. The ability to speak on behalf of "universal" values is assumed, even as we argue what their contents might be, whereas people of aboriginal ancestry are often challenged when they name themselves and their experiences. In many ways, this logic mirrors that of the law and its categorizations. In the law's division of intellectual property from cultural property, authors with intellect are distinguished from cultures with property. Those who have intellect are entitled to speak on behalf of universal principles of reason, whereas those who have culture speak only on behalf of a cultural tradition that must be unified and homogeneous before we will accord it any respect. Such arguments are generally used, moreover, to silence and delegitimate particularly unwelcome Native voices, rather than to invite more participants to contribute their viewpoints and join the debate.

In the fashion of a modernist avant-garde, many artists entertain self-conceptions of standing outside the political and economic contexts in which they have artistic agency, and thus as being immune to assertions of representing Western culture. Situating themselves outside of any cultural tradition, they attempt to evade inclusion within the history of Western art and its privileges. Some indigenous critics see this as an "escapist fantasy: Unless whites can acknowledge and respond to their histories of power and racism as it affects all areas of culture, as it inscribes itself in their own minds, an equal and meaningful dialogue is impossible."[160]

Artists have recently demonstrated more concern with issues of cultural appropriation and the colonial histories that inform their work, but they have done so in a manner that focuses more attention on the cultural influences on individual imaginations than on the lives and contemporary circumstances of Native peoples. When Toronto artist Andy Fabo was chastised for his use of the symbolism of the sweat lodge ceremony, he defended his work against the accusation of "cultural plagiarism" on personal grounds: "The first art museum that I ever visited was The Museum of The Plains Indians in Browning, Montana. I was eight years old at the time and for better or worse, the experience had an incredible impact on me."[161]

The museum figures here less as an edifice of imperialism than as the mysterious origin of a personal fetish, as indeed an artist might personally experience it. For a gay artist concerned with questions of AIDS, healing, and otherness, the sweat lodge might indeed constitute a powerful symbolic image, but Fabo's use of it illustrated no knowledge of the legacy of power that enabled him to exploit its symbolic excess.[162] Artists who address such issues seem more concerned with delineating the influence of Native images in their own personal histories and in the dominant culture from which they draw their artistic inspiration than in acknowledging the actual histories of colonization in which those images came to figure as part of the public sphere. When non-Native artists claim that Native images are a part of our Cultural heritage, they are not wrong, but they are incredibly selective. To claim Native spiritual practices, and traditions of motif and design, as part of contemporary Culture—or in the name of one's personal history—while bypassing the history of racism, institutional abuse, poverty, and alienation that enabled its incorporation is simply to repeat the process by which the painful realities of contemporary Native life are continually ignored by those who feel more comfortable claiming the artifacts they have left "behind." Once again the Romantic author claims the expressive power to represent cultural others in the name of a heritage universalized as Culture.

Aboriginal Title

Self-determination and sovereignty include human, political, land, religious, artistic and moral rights. Taking ownership of these stories involves a claim to Aboriginal title over images, culture and stories.—Gerald McMaster and Lee Ann Martin, Introduction to *Indigena: Contemporary Native Perspectives*[163]

In discussions of cultural appropriation, First Nations peoples strive to assert that the relationships that stories, images, motifs, and designs have to their communities cannot be subsumed under traditional European categories of art and culture and the possessive individualism that informs them. It is difficult for Native peoples to even speak about "rights"[164] to cultural practices or creative skills that are passed between individuals generationally through matrilineal inheritance.[165] Some stories are considered so powerful that one storyteller seeks permission before repeating a tale told by another.[166] To equate the need for such permissions to a copyright license is to reduce the social relationship between Native storytellers to one of contract and the alienation of market exchange relationships. These relationships, however, are ongoing ones that bind generations in a spiritual relationship with land, customs, and ancestors based on traditions of respect, not the values of exchange.

When Loretta Todd discusses First Nations concepts of ownership in the context of cultural appropriation, she discusses property in terms of relationships that are far wider than the exclusivity of possession and rights to alienate that dominate European concepts:

> Without the sense of private property that ascended with European culture, we evolved concepts of property that recognized the interdependence of communities, families and nations and favoured the guardianship of the earth as opposed to its conquest. There was a sense of ownership, but not one that pre-empted the rights and privileges of others or the rights of the earth and the life it sustained . . . Ownership was bound up with history . . . Communities, families, individuals, and nations created songs, dances, rituals, objects, and stories that were considered to be property, but not property as

understood by the Europeans. Material wealth was re-distributed, but history and stories belonged to the originator and could be given or shared with others as a way of preserving, extending and witnessing history and expressing one's worldview.[167]

First Nations peoples are engaged in an ongoing struggle to articulate, define, exercise, and assert Aboriginal Title in terms not only of a relationship to territory, but of a relationship to the cultural forms that express the historical meaning of that relationship in specific communities. For Native peoples in Canada, culture is not a fixed and frozen entity that can be objectified in reified forms that express its identity, but an ongoing living process that cannot be severed from the ecological relationships in which it lives and grows. As Winona La Duke expresses this:

> There are many things Cree people have taken for granted over countless generations. That the rivers will always flow, the sun and moon will alternate, and there will be six seasons of the year. The Cree also have assumed that there will always be food from the land, so long as the Eeu—the Cree, do not abuse their part of the relationship to the animals and the land . . . To me this is the essence of culture and the essence of the meaning of life. From where I sit on James Bay, it seems almost trivial to talk about other things—so called religion, literature, spirituality, and economics . . . If [due to the activities of Hydro Quebec and Ontario Hydro] there are no longer six seasons of the year, the waters no longer flow in their order, and places where people have prayed, been buried, and harvested their food cease to exist as "land," is that not the essence of cultural destruction . . . ?[168]

In her language, La Duke indicates how foreign it is to her to divide issues of "so-called" culture—religion, literature, and spirituality—from discussions of "land," whose very position in quotation marks indicates the strangeness of using a noun that alienates it as a thing separate from social and cultural relationships.

As Loretta Todd states, "Aboriginal Title is the term under which we negotiate with the colonizers . . . which asserts a reality that existed before Native peoples were positioned as Other."[169] In coming to acknowledge and affirm this reality, non-Native peoples must begin to recognize the contingency and peculiarity of their own concepts of property and the colonial foundations on which they are built. The abstraction, commodification, and separation of land from people's social lives and from the cultural forms in which we express meaning and value as human beings living in communities represent only a peculiar, partial, and limited way of dividing up the world. The range of Western beliefs that define intellectual and cultural property laws—that ideas can easily be separated from expressions, that expressions are the singular products of the individual minds of Romantic authors, that these expressive works can be abstracted from the meaningful worlds in which they figure to circulate as the signs of unique personality, that cultures have essences embodied in objects that represent unbroken traditions—are not universal values that express the full range of human possibility, but particular, interested fictions emergent from a history of colonialism that has disempowered many of the world's peoples. By listening seriously to claims of cultural appropriation in context and attending to the possibilities afforded by Aboriginal Title, we may better understand the properties of culture(s) and the politics of possessing identity in a contemporary world.

6. Dialogic Democracy I: Authorship and Alterity in Public Spheres

...the blunting of...postmodernism means that it is eighteenth-century conceptions—conceptions of responsibility, or agency, of harm, of language, and meaning itself—that continue to rule the decisions of a late twentieth-century technological society. Such a state of affairs is at once an intellectual embarrassment and a form of violence.—Pierre Schlag, "Missing Pieces: A Cognitive Approach to Law"[1]

If the variously expressed, often contradictory and generally fragmentary sentiments of postmodernity are novel primarily by virtue of their contemporaneity, critical legal studies, which has come latterly in some quarters to be identified in part with postmodernity, is equally both a return to a tradition of resistance or opposition to legal orthodoxy and a novel rewriting of the text or art of law. —Costas Douzinas, Peter Goodrich, and Yifat Hachamovitch, "Introduction: Politics, Ethics and the Legality of the Contingent"[2]

The cultural politics of recoding commodified cultural forms—arts of appropriation, recodings of trademarks, detournements of advertising texts, and improvisations upon the celebrity image—are neither readily appreciated using current juridical concepts nor easily encompassed by the liberal premises that ground our legal categories. Nor, within this Enlightenment framework, may the aspirations of indigenous peoples to protect the cultural indicia of their heritage and the harms experienced by virtue of the circulation of stereotypical representations be adequately acknowledged. The nexus of these difficulties may be located at the heart of liberal legal discourse itself, its contradictions, instabilities, and ambiguities—aporias ever more apparent in late-twentieth-century conditions.

Legal considerations of such issues implicitly presuppose modern social conditions. In so doing, they avoid and evade addressing some of the more salient dimensions of contemporary relations of publicity. Within the law's liberal framework, cultural appropriations certainly pose categorical quandaries. The ability to make representations about self, identity, community, solidarity, and difference or to articulate social aspirations might be considered a matter of freedom of speech. Indeed, one of the chief historical justifications for freedom of expression in modern political philosophy was the self-fulfillment of the individual,[3] now understood to include fulfillment for social groups seeking collective self-determination.[4] Freedom of expression, however, is an area of legal doctrine ill-prepared to cope with postmodern conditions. The doctrinal confusion that results from applying free speech principles in the area of publicity rights will serve to illustrate this point.

Insight into the aporias of modern law may be afforded by a genealogy of literary property and the related emergence of the author. Susan Stewart suggests that both the late eighteenth and late twentieth centuries are periods in which the production of works undergo parallel transformations, and relations among speech, writing, subjectivity, and authority are renegotiated.[5] An anxious recognition (and displaced misrecognitions) of the instability of such relationships characterizes both eras. Law is the means by which these contingencies are denied in both periods of transition, and intellectual property the form and forum through which intertextuality is managed, contained, and obscured. The advent of mass literary production was as fundamental a challenge to traditional social relations in the late eighteenth century as the explosion of multimedia textuality is today, in an era euphemistically nominated the "information age."[6] Digital technologies, for instance, promise to distance disseminators of cultural forms from their reception contexts as thoroughly as widespread print technology detached writers from familiar audiences in the early modern period—a phenomenon described by Bertrand as "one of the most far-reaching influences of modern times in western civilization."[7] The "problems" of rapidity of transmission, deepening anonymities of authorship and readership, the fragmentation of works and their reception—supposedly characteristic of late or postmodernity—were all faced in the transition to modernity. Enduring problems of representation are resurfacing.

The Author in the Modern Public Sphere

To return to the themes of my introduction, the discipline of anthropology and the authorial power of the ethnographer are products of Enlightenment and Romantic idealizations and their political authority.

The traditional anthropological relationship manifests a modern structuration of social relations; anxieties about anthropology's authority are symptomatic of transformations in the public sphere and the exhaustion of modernity's models to comprehend it. To a large extent, this is because traditional models for understanding relationships between authors and others—ideological fictions even in their emergence—can no longer be sustained. The crisis of representation in anthropology and the crisis of representation in liberal legal thought share parallel histories and face similar challenges. It seems appropriate, then, to return to this sense of crisis as a means of framing the debate about the constitutive features of the postmodern public sphere and the civil society enabled by its characteristic forms of publicity.

Modern anthropology approached culture as shared, collectively generated constellations of meaning; its most salient dimensions were realized socially, generally in publicly performed and politically effectual signifying practices. In consumer societies, as we have seen, many of the most accessible, widely known, and compelling of cultural forms around which meanings are forged are not shared in a singular collectivity but are the private properties of corporations with economic interests in preserving their exclusivity. This tense intersection between culture's public space and the commodity's private place—local manifestations of which we have explored in a number of social arenas—challenges conventional Anglo-American legal categories still oriented around social divisions and distinctions characteristic of modern understandings of civil society.

Crucial dimensions of the bourgeois public sphere are revealed by questioning the conditions under which an anthropological perspective on culture is enabled. In an early discussion of the anthropological author-function,[8] Clifford Geertz alluded to the political dimensions of the modern anthropologist's authorial dilemma: "What once seemed technically difficult . . . getting 'their' lives into 'our' works, has turned morally, politically, even epistemologically, delicate . . . The problem has arisen not only amongst anthropologists, nor only among those numerous social scientists who go out to study a 'them' far away. Natives are becoming ethnographers themselves; that is part of the problem—it raises the issue of the boundaries of the public sphere. Who is in the seminar room? At a deeper level, the issue is, What kind of self, person, observer, can collect observations, interpret, and report them to what kind of public?"[9] A perspective that greets the inscriptions of others in contemporary public spheres—the Native's appropriation of the Parker pen—as "part of the problem"[10] presupposes a readership of those who traditionally occupied the privileged position of author—the subjects rather than the objects of anthropological practice. However, the contestations of those othered by historical acts of authorship can be understood as motivating conditions for a perceived crisis of dominant forms of modern representational practice.[11] This may only be a "problem," however, for those authors whose privilege can no longer be assumed. For others, such destabilizations of foundational grounds may have been necessary simply to locate the spaces from which their own subject-positions could be asserted and their own voices acquire public audibility. The concept of culture is now deeply imbricated within a realignment of political forces that challenge the assumptions and authorities of European modernity. The restructuration of subject/object relations poses new challenges for democratic ideals and, significantly, for the nature of expressive activity we deem essential for their articulation and realization. William Reddy asks under what conditions something called a culture may be described and for whom. What kind of self and what kind of public were presupposed by modern anthropological practice?[12] Reddy suggests that the authority of modern anthropology itself grew out of social contexts of communication emergent—if more idealized than realized—in eighteenth-century European societies: "The term modern or 'bourgeois' public sphere refers generally to those institutions open to the public and to those practices, which any member of the public may engage in, that are characteristic of modern societies—it refers, thus, to museums, theatres, libraries, galleries, schools, and universities; cafes, stores, stock exchanges . . . courts, legislatures, town halls . . . The distinctive feature of the public sphere is that any member of the public enters, in principle, on equal terms and that communication and deliberation take place."[13]

This idealized realm privileged a particular subject—a kind of rational self "capable of reading and evaluating modern published texts"[14]—sharing a community with others who wrote and read the same texts. The author, who intentionally conveys his own inner thoughts to others, is central to the communicational life of this public. The belief that "texts are authored by selves with fixed intentions and a definite audience in mind"[15] and that such texts maintain the integrity of authorial intention in all social contexts is a historically specific convention that requires massive misrecognition—and a significant legal architecture—given the nature of language and its use. All writings are at risk of being carried away by others, transcending their agencies of origin, as Rousseau, one champion of writing as an expression of inner self, found to his great detriment.[16] Authors and their publics are fashioned by collective practices that uphold the "arena in which a public 'self' may reflect and address her reflections to other 'selves.'"[17]

Jürgen Habermas's 1962 book, *The Structural Transformation of the Public Sphere*—and critical developments of his ideas in the work of Alexander Kluge and Oskar Negt—provided productive points of departure for theorists of democracy considering culture, identity, and politics in contemporary contexts.[18] Political philosopher Nancy Fraser formulates Habermas's theorization of the public sphere as an "arena conceptually distinct from the state; it is a site for the production and circulation of discourses that can in principle be critical of the state . . . conceptually distinct from the official economy; it is not an arena of market relations but rather one of discursive relations, a theatre for debating and deliberating rather than for buying and selling."[19] Habermas valued a liberal model of the bourgeois public sphere emergent in specific conditions of eighteenth-century Europe. Although mourned by Habermas as no longer viable given late-twentieth-century conditions, the liberal model he delineated is nonetheless easily discerned in contemporary juridical formulations of free speech. This model pictures "a body of 'private persons' assembled to discuss matters of 'public concern'—bourgeois publics that emerged as counterweights to absolutist states. Such publics mediate between 'society' and the state by holding the latter accountable to 'society' via 'publicity' ensured by forms of legally-guaranteed free speech, free press, and free assembly."[20] "Unrestricted rational discussion of public matters that is open and accessible to all in the service of producing consensus about the common good"[21] is anticipated and encouraged. The modern figure of the author emerges concomitantly with this print-mediated public; the very act of publishing implies an appeal to reason, that is, to the reflexive capacities of a readership engaged in relationship to a print-based public sphere. This unitary author who speaks with a single voice and possesses a singular self embodied in unique textual expressions deemed to be his "works," and thus his property,[22] is, as we have seen, the conceptual foundation of copyright, later extended by implication to trademarks, design patents, and rights of publicity.[23]

Historically, the public sphere in which rational selves addressed other rational selves in languages deemed transparent vehicles for the expression of unmediated thought was both partial and exclusionary. Excluding women, children, and various savages, primitives, and barbarous others, the social boundaries between subjects and objects of public discourse were clearly demarcated. Reddy is not alone in suggesting that this public sphere was ethnocentric (and patriarchal) in its very structure.[24] It was also the space in which minute observations of social distinctions and new physical taxonomies were multiplied, catalogued, and publicized (and later iconicized in elite possessions).[25] Critics and historians of the bourgeois public sphere show that it was constituted by a number of significant exclusions along axes of class, race, and gender as well as being premised upon distinctions of public and private that served male bourgeois interests and helped to consolidate bourgeois power.[26]

In *Cultural Rights*, a historical survey of European modes of cultural reproduction, sociologist Celia Lury suggests that the figure of the author functioned to legitimate similar axes of cultural exclusion and political disenfranchisement. Attributions of authorship served to differentiate culturally productive labor using aesthetic ideas of originality and creativity that, when legally institutionalized, "secure special conditions, status and recognisability for the creative worker as author. [Copyright] regimes served to regulate the exploitation of the possibilities of replication which were offered by the new technologies . . . which simultaneously strengthened the aesthetic functions of the author and protected commercial interests."[27] The category of the author reinforced exclusions elsewhere enacted to restrict membership in the public sphere. The distributional systems that made works available to a print-mediated public worked to discriminate among cultural products and to limit the number of cultural producers who might claim authorial privilege. The range of producers enabled to reify their creations as "works"—with an assumed integrity of form denied to other cultural products—was contained by the institutionalization and legitimation of certain modalities of production, circulation, and consumption. Capacities for judgment in the literary field were similarly rarefied and exalted and certain forms of reception cultivated by and for a select readership. Would-be authors came to produce forms that would fit the category; the knowledge and practices of this system of distribution and evaluation came to shape the public sphere itself, such that a shared basis for the collective evaluation of "art" was part of the self-definition of those who made public opinion. As Lury suggests, the "discourses that collectively functioned to construct the object "art" were not distinct from but allied to the determinations of the marketplace which themselves established and confirmed the commodity status of the work of art."[28]

Print technology offered unparalleled opportunities for the reproduction of cultural products, but the capacity for making multiple copies was "counterpointed throughout the history of print by the radical disadvantages of the need for specific training to make use of its potential."[29] The expansion of literacy in European societies over the seventeenth and eighteenth centuries did not necessarily incorporate more people into the public sphere because stratified hierarchies of access, interpretation, and reception were simultaneously effected.[30] This is not to suggest that alternative publics or counterpublics were not emerging. It is to suggest that the dominant culture of authorial works privileged particular textual forms as well as particular forms of distribution and reception which enabled a particular process of commodification "grounded in the privileging of authorial originality defined in relation to an indeterminate public over and above generative copying or standardisation for a targeted market."[31]

The author asserted his autonomy from the market just as his dependence upon it was anticipated.[32] No longer reliant upon the largesse of patrons, men of letters sought to distinguish their creative activities as artists who required freedom from the pressures of employment (or the capricious demands of the buying public) exactly as texts were commodified. As Lury remarks, one might have expected writers to have become literary proletarians, writing for a wage and producing whatever they might be able to sell.[33] Instead, the figure of the author developed as a form of commodity in its own right, through which publishers marketed their wares while denying their status as mere goods in the marketplace. "Capitalist producers and intermediaries including not only publishers, but also printers, booksellers, critics and reviewers,"[34] constituted social networks enabling literary labor to remain relatively unalienated.[35] The bourgeois author produced not commodities but works and created such works in an environment where new relationships between writer and reader—elevated as author and public—were forged.

Elite literary production engendered a very particular type of commodification sustained by the establishment of new forms of reception and new reifications of receptivity.[36] Anonymous as a market, an audience was distinguished as a public by its adoption of an attitude of critical distance and self-reflexivity. Only in a market context could goods acquire value by virtue of their purely aesthetic purposes, Lury notes,[37] but an anonymous public could appreciate the purely formal excellence that defined a writing as an "authored" work of literature only with proper training. A particular self-understanding needed to be cultivated in bourgeois reading habits—an aestheticism of the reflexive personality— that enabled the reader to imagine a privileged relationship to the author's own expressive personality.[38] The imaginary constitution of the audience as an informed and disinterested public operated to displace its potentially larger significance as a mass market for a new commodity. The distinction of the authorial work and the distinction claimed by a discerning public were concomitantly forged.

The rapid expansion of novel writing and novel reading in the late eighteenth century, for example, corresponded with the novel's lessening estimation as a literary form.[39] Viewed as a threat to literature and learning, the novel was attacked in the learned journals of the public sphere precisely on the grounds of its commercial success. The consolidation of the author-function occurs at the same time as anxieties are increasingly voiced by elites "about the perceived vulnerability and lack of discrimination of the mass audience; this contributed to attempts to restrict the circulation of various types of writing on the grounds that the mass audience-as-public required protection from the commercial exploitation of its own demands and desires."[40] The novel became recognized as literature only when rhetorical devices were developed to divorce it from its market origins and deny its status as a popular commodity.[41] The distinction of authorship emerges in a diacritical relationship with indiscriminate and undiscriminating others. The Romantic image of the individuated author as creative genius, autonomously creating works characterized as embodiments of personal originality, provided ideological support for the legal institution of copyright fictions that denied and obscured market forces. However ideological the category of the author might be in terms of the misrecognitions it effected, Lury shows that its institutionalization "had real and important consequences for the range and forms of cultural production."[42]

The figure of the author, or the role of the author-function, might be seen as that of an elite broker for the management of textuality "at a time when the new forms of mechanical reproduction associated with print technology vastly extended the distribution and mobility of cultural goods."[43] An emergent cultural sphere offered unprecedented opportunities both for communication and for commodity-exchange relations in cultural goods, affording an invitation to "multiple forms of appropriation . . . in ways which were potentially disruptive for the existing social and economic order."[44] As Lury's work alerts us, the potential alteration of authorial works for and by others (lower-class audiences, for example) provided generative conditions for the consolidation of the author-function and its associated public.

The social limitation of authorial rights inevitably engendered resistance. Authors and those who had commercial interests in controlling their works were never free from the alterations of others with interests antagonistic to entrenched hierarchies and new privileges. Possibilities for using print were never wholly controllable and the tendencies of textuality to overflow the boundaries of the work never fully containable. Historically, then, the relationship between authorship and alterity was diacritical; the dominant characteristics of the bourgeois author-function were forged in encounters with others (primarily women and the lower classes, although a historical case may also be made for the role of colonized others)[45] who turned textuality to new ends.

A popular reading audience had been growing since the seventeenth century and new methods were constantly sought "to contain the disruptive potential of print."[46] Lury cites press taxes designed to restrict press ownership and readership to the respectable classes, and libel laws and parliamentary privileges as particular enactments (not to mention less formal measures such as subsidies, bribes, and private censorship) that limited participation in the public sphere to a privileged stratum.[47] By the late eighteenth and early nineteenth centuries, the commercial press had developed an autonomy from the landed classes and more overtly commercial mechanisms superseded political ones as means of regulating readership and textuality.[48] Copyright law was critical in normalizing and elevating particular forms of writing and reading and simultaneously delegitimating alternative relations to textuality.

The literary work, Lury reminds us, was rather insignificant commercially; by far the greatest part of publishing output involved reproduction and reiteration, reworking the prior texts of others for an emergent working-class audience.[49] Copying public domain works such as eighteenth-century romances, historical biographies, and erotica, as well as plagiarizing popular bourgeois works for less elite readerships, were popular publishing strategies. Remaindering, rebinding, printing multiple editions, and serializing were other forms of reproductive practice that proliferated texts to another audience understood as a market rather than as a public. Stories, characters, dialogue, and lyrics were also transposed "across popular fiction, drama, ballads and news."[50] Merchandising rights—the extension of authorship into the sphere of mass-produced goods bearing intertextual referents—were clearly slow to develop.[51] In this historical era, as in most others, creative labor was only one of many inputs into cultural production. Most cultural production was formulaic, involving stock characters, predictable styles, variations of routine plots, and standardized narratives revolving around practices that today would be deemed plagiarisms rather than original works. A proliferation of printing technologies and a larger audience for printed goods exacerbated this tendency and intensified both the extent and the degree of indeterminacy at the point of the reactivation of the printed text.

Authorship as a social and legal institution historically originated and was shaped by encounters with others: working-class readers who could not be trusted to receive texts with the proper attitude to be accorded literary works, women whose sentimentality in reading habits did not enable them to maintain the necessary critical distance from print, those whose rationality was clouded by religious superstition, colonial subjects in need of civilizing tutelage, as well as those others who preferred entertainment to enlightenment. Lacking a proper disposition toward art, these people were objects rather than subjects of the bourgeois public sphere and their lifestyles and habits provided constant fodder for the consternation of the reading public. If print technology increased the mobility and proliferation of cultural goods, it simultaneously made them more available for the cultural activities or appropriations of others. Copyright and its aesthetic discursive supports were techniques for managing the subversive potential of print technologies and for maintaining bourgeois hegemonies in the face of the opportunities textuality afforded for the expressive articulations, aspirations, and antagonisms of others.

Free Speech in the Condition of Postmodernity

The liberal print-mediated public sphere shaped an audience with shared orientations. Bourgeois public subjects occupied an "imagined community"[52] of similar readers bound by the technology of print. Novels and newspapers were particularly significant in shaping the sense of similitude and simultaneity linking subjects in eighteenth-century and early-nineteenth-century European societies.[53] Ironically, the division between society and the state—the space of civil society framed in terms of a resistance to government control of speech and the censorship of textual expression—is concomitant with the expansion for a market in textual forms. It gives rise to the

> notion of a public right of access to print technology. It is possible to identify the emergence of an acceptance of a notion of the public good in relation to cultural works with the intensification of cultural commodification. This understanding of the moral and political rights of the public to access to ideas and information, and thus to unconstrained reactivation, has been highlighted in discussions

of the special character of cultural works. Indeed, it is sometimes suggested that they have an intrinsically public status and, while this is true in one sense, at least of media goods, in that such goods are necessarily produced for a diffused large-scale audience, it is important to recognize that this public character is itself socially circumscribed by, for example, forms of regulation and control, including the internalization of specific conceptions of the audience through commodification.[54]

Theoretically, rights of access to print and print capacities were pivotal to the modern public sphere as the site of communication and deliberation; "in actuality this right was defined restrictively in relation to the rights of the individual as either citizen of the bourgeois polis or consumer in a cultural market."[55]

Enlightenment verities continue to animate legal discussions of freedom of expression. In early work, Habermas suggested that under the altered conditions of the late twentieth century the bourgeois model was no longer viable; he seemed to despair of the possibility of theorizing a public sphere appropriate to conditions of postmodernity. An emergent body of critical social theory concerned with democracy and dialogue embraced precisely this challenge. Questioning the propriety of the communicative conditions of the bourgeois public sphere, they showed its constitutive categories of differentiation to be increasingly archaic: "speech v. action, print v. broadcast, political v. nonpolitical. Symbolic expression in its many forms . . . blurs the speech/action cleavage, new forms of technology . . . confuse courts in applying the print/broadcast distinction; arguments over what is and is not political speech have no resolution . . ."[56]

As well as making increasingly untenable distinctions between private property and public speech in an era when so many forms of public speech require the use of private properties, liberal legalism continues to take communication by print as its model and aspiration. A relation between an individual intentional author and a rationally deliberating reader serves as the paradigm for production and reception of communicative forms. Free speech is a doctrinal field that clings tenaciously to Enlightenment concepts and bourgeois ideals in the face of late-capitalist realities. As legal philosopher Owen Fiss asserted over a decade ago, the constitutional tradition of freedom of expression is unable to effectively grasp the salient characteristics or challenges of capitalist mass-communications systems. As a consequence, he suggested, American free speech decisions have "impoverish[ed] rather than enrich[ed] public debate and thus threatened one of the essential preconditions for an effective democracy."[57]

This legal tradition presupposes the state to be the primary threat to expression, and presupposes a dichotomy between state and citizen that equates liberty with limited government.[58] A speaker's autonomy in the modern public sphere is reduced to a mere freedom from government interference.[59] Today, however, threats to the autonomy of speech and to public debate are just as likely—if not more likely—to be posed by so-called private actors in an era in which purportedly private actors (especially media conglomerates) dominate communications. First Amendment doctrine increasingly confronts conflicts between economic and political liberties. One person's right to political speech may easily encroach upon another's right to enjoy her exclusive rights of property. As Fiss and others recognize, the property owner's "No Trespassing" sign generally prevails.[60] For Fiss, the freedom of speech tradition enables these consequences because of its historical presuppositions. The tradition is built around the figure of the individual "street corner speaker" who needs protection against the silencing of the state, an increasingly anachronistic configuration in postmodern conditions.[61]

Mass media, electronic telecommunications, instantaneous communications, and the corporate restructuring and commodification of urban space have made street corners and their speakers invisible, inaudible, and obsolete as forums and agents of political dialogue. It is doubtful that protecting an individual's autonomy to speak will guarantee rich public debate when the forums for speaking and the circuits of communication are privately owned and those who control them have an inordinate capacity to influence the terms of debate.[62] In conditions of scarcity of access, the protection of a certain agent's autonomy to speak may well impoverish public debate because opportunities for effective communication are limited. Markets ensure only that the views of those who are economically powerful will be heard in public debates.[63]

Even many liberal legal philosophers now agree that some form of regulation of media is necessary to achieve democratic political goals.[64] Mass communications controlled by private actors and governed by market forces simply do not permit the diversity of perspectives necessary for the flourishing of dialogic democracy. State regulation of speech is thus supported as necessary to promote free speech. Free speech for those with access to media may limit the speech of those who lack such access. Access to media must be expanded if we are to secure conditions for effective communication to promote recognition of diverse interests in the political process. Fiss, for instance, argued that state intervention might involve regulation of the exercise of private property: limits to the rights of shopping mall owners to control access to their properties, and regulations limiting campaign expenditures, for example.[65]

Critics on the Left assent to the liberal formulation of the problem and support prescriptions for an energized government role in engendering public debate but dispute many of the modern characterizations that underlie them. According to Alan Hutchinson, liberal commitments to state/citizen and public/private dichotomies preclude realization of a truly democratic polity[66] or resolution of free speech dilemmas.[67] The public/private distinction is not so much blurred or amorphous for Hutchinson as it is untenable or simply false:[68] "As sovereign, the government is as responsible for its active decisions not to intervene and regulate as it is for its decisions to act affirmatively... The protection of private property and the enforcement of private contracts by the government attests to the strong and necessary presence of government in private transactions . . . Property and contract are creatures of the state and support for these allocative regimes is neither more or less politically neutral or activist than opposition to them. The question is not whether government should intervene, but when and how . . . "[69]

When public speech interests come up against private interests, the latter almost invariably triumph, ensuring that "the law insulates vast sectors of the social hierarchy from official scrutiny and public accountability."[70] Those who hold private property are not required to consider public interests in expression when exercising their property rights. Once we break down this untenable distinction and admit the state's role in creating and enforcing property rights, "the question of whose entitlements are to be protected from whose interference becomes a contested matter of political choice rather than the correct application of abstract principle."[71]

In popular culture, as we have seen, many of the most prevalent icons of an era may not be reproduced in the expressions of others. The private properties of some prohibit the public speech of others. It would seem that all criticism of the commodity/sign or the creative undoings of the commodity fetishism it effects must assume the form of a written communique to receive legal protection as speech. Commentaries that reproduce the icon and disseminate their messages using means of communication that are as effective as that which communicated the original are nearly always prohibited. Control of speech, not tolerated in other arenas, is achieved through the protection bestowed upon authors, even when these are corporate advertisers engaged in expressions designed to enhance profits.

The modern ideal of intentional authors appealing to the rational deliberation of readers is an embarrassingly inadequate formulation for communication in a promotional culture[72]—like our image- and logo-saturated world—where corporately authored messages, flashing images, and rapid sound bites are dominant signifying modes. Messages conveyed by quickly circulating evanescent signifiers on a multitude of shifting surfaces cannot be effectively countered with written treatises that lie on library and bookstore shelves. As Koenig's Joe Camel examples showed, criticism that deploys the protected symbol is inevitably stronger and more effective than written references to it, especially when the positive connotations associated with a commodity/sign are challenged. Writing or lecturing about the obnoxious use of cartoon imagery to entice children into a health-destroying habit simply does not have the same punch as a parody of the trademarked cartoon character itself: "because graphic advertising can be powerfully seductive, an equally graphic means must be available to counteract the message purveyed in the original."[73]

Owners of commercial texts enable others to use their commodity/signs when positive values are generated (Koenig gives the example of Andy Warhol's reproduction of the Campbell's soup can) but critical usages are enjoined; the silencing of oppositional voices, prohibited when attempted by government, is positively enabled when practiced by commercially oriented actors.[74] Let us examine freedom of expression jurisprudence in an area where we have witnessed alternative gender identities and communities of self-fashioning forged on legality's frontiers: in the informal economy of proprietary signification. Laws commodifying the celebrity image inevitably come up against concerns about freedom of expression, but they do so sporadically, yielding inconsistent and confused rationales that reveal the inadequacies of a modern framework for discourse in the cultural conditions of postmodernism.

It is generally accepted in the United States that rights of publicity must yield to social interests in freedom of expression, "when First Amendment principles outweigh the celebrity's interest in compensation."[75] But when will this be the case? Courts routinely assert that the First Amendment protects publication of news of a celebrity but does not protect commercial uses of celebrity images.[76] Often this is premised on a distinction between fact and fiction: factual accounts about celebrity behavior do not violate their publicity rights because celebrities are the subject of legitimate news.[77] Newspapers, films, and documentaries are not understood to be engaged in commercial purposes when they publish news, notwithstanding that their production, distribution, and exhibition is a large commercial enterprise carried on for private profit.[78] Distinctions between fact and fiction—publishing news about a celebrity and commercially exploiting his or her image—are notoriously difficult to maintain in the promotional culture of postmodernity. The courts' efforts to employ and maintain such distinctions yield contradictory and sometimes ludicrous results, as the following cases, drawn from the same jurisdiction, illustrate.

Ann-Margret sued *High Society* magazine for a violation of publicity rights for the unauthorized use of a seminude photograph taken from one of her films. The court dismissed the action on the basis that the photograph was newsworthy and its use protected.[79] The same year, a model brought legal action for the unauthorized use of a nude photograph in the same magazine. The court rejected the defendant's claim that the First Amendment protected use of the photos because the model was not shown participating in a newsworthy event; the photographs, therefore, were not a matter of public interest.[80] When a couple found their nude photographs in a commercially distributed mass-market guide to nude beaches, however, a court denied them relief and upheld the publisher's right to disseminate information of public interest; the photographs were not being used for commercial purposes.[81]

Law students are trained to rationalize and distinguish such cases to show how categories such as disseminating information in the public interest and commercial exploitation of another's name and likeness are rational, desirable, and necessary. Celebrities and the media industries reward them handsomely for their efforts. Even the most determined law student, however, might have difficulty supporting a decision that held that the unauthorized use of before-and-after photos of a girl in a teen magazine, replete with the brand names of the products used to effect the transformation, was a newsworthy use of her name and likeness rather than a commercial exploitation.[82]

The underlying distinction between fact and fiction that must provide the scaffolding for this conceptual structure becomes increasingly fragile in postmodernity as societies become saturated with signification and the value of the hyperreal accelerates.[83] Courts have found it harder and harder to distinguish truth from falsity and fact from fiction, or to limit First Amendment protection to objective renderings that correspond to some knowable reality. However, they maintain the philosophical edifice of "the mirror of nature"[84] by developing ever more distinctions within distinctions to keep its structure intact.

A defendant is held to forfeit the privilege of disseminating newsworthy information if his or her use is materially and substantially false and he or she has recklessly disregarded its falsity.[85] When a comedian ran a mock campaign for president as a publicity stunt, however, he was unable to prevent an entrepreneur from distributing a poster bearing his photograph with the caption, "For President."[86] The court determined that the poster was newsworthy and thus that the defendant was engaged in spreading information rather than in commercial exploitation. It did not address the issue of whether the "information" the defendant disseminated was to be characterized as materially false (the comedian was not running "For President") or factual information about a fictitious candidacy (a true account of a falsity). When Elvis Presley died, however, those who held his publicity rights successfully stopped an entrepreneur from marketing a picture of Presley "In Memoriam."[87] Perhaps the New York courts, like the weekly tabloids, doubt that the King has truly departed.

Accommodating the immense potential value in fictionalizing the lifestyles of the rich and famous has provoked courts to articulate new distinctions within the fact/fiction dichotomy. A New York court held that a right of publicity will not be recognized where a fictionalized account of a public figure's life is depicted in such a way that the audience knows (truly?) that the events are false.[88] However, another New York bench decided that allowing the publication of a known fictional biography of a (factual) baseball player would take freedom of expression too far given the defendant's "limited research efforts to verify his story."[89] The book was seen as a clear case of "a commercial exploitation."

The efforts of a film producer to verify his findings were not, however, investigated when he represented a deceased pilot's alleged reappearance as a ghost in his mass-marketed movie. The pilot served as captain aboard an Eastern Airlines flight that crashed in 1972. After the crash, people reported that the captain and crew of the fated flight appeared as ghosts aboard other Eastern planes. Relatives of the deceased brought action for unauthorized commercial use of name and likeness against the maker of the film that reconstructed these events.[90] The filmmaker prevailed because of his right to disseminate information "of current and legitimate public interest" under the "newsworthiness" section of the Florida statute.[91] Had the case been considered in New York, the following questions might have to be addressed: Was the information "true"? Was it substantially "false"? Did the filmmaker recklessly disregard its falsity, or was he providing a fictionalized account of a real person's activities? Will a fictionalized version of a real person's activities as imagined by other people be protected? Perhaps it depends how carefully you've verified the falsity of your fabrication and how easily the audience can identify the activities as fictional. What if most of them believe in ghosts? In any case, there is a legitimate public interest in disseminating (true?) information about (actual) ghost sightings in the state of Florida.

Attempting to limit freedom of speech defenses in publicity rights claims to the dissemination of factual information in the name of newsworthiness is conceptually boggling, culturally untenable, and politically pernicious. Similar absurdities permeate trademark law and the legal protection of fictional characters (which, by virtue of the multiplicity of legal regimes that may be invoked to insulate them against public slurs, are far better protected against defamation than real people).[92] Presumed innocent before the law, their authorized owners can shield themselves against the assertions of others by posing as childlike cartoons in the public sphere.[93] As Joe Camel reminds us, the appeal of such characters may well mask more sinister personas and activities.

Objects and Subjects Redux

To return to the issues posed in chapter 1, the basic premises on which the liberal theory of free speech is built have been subjected to thorough criticism because they reinforce inadequate Enlightenment understandings of subjectivity and objectivity.[94] Contemporary free speech doctrine is based on reductionist understandings of human personality and language and their mutually constitutive relationship.[95] Both "freedom" and "speech" require reconceptualization in light of contemporary knowledge about the socially signifying nature of human experience and expressive activity.[96] Like other liberal legal discourses, the liberal theory of free speech "is premised on a social world comprising an aggregation of distinct individuals with a set of pre-social preferences and values"[97] expressed through language. Language is "understood as a neutral medium that is available to all and that stands independently of the ideas and world [and values] it is intended to convey or depict."[98] The objective is to facilitate "free" exchanges of information, values, and knowledge that preexist the medium of their circulation.

Many legal scholars now contest such understandings of freedom, language, and human communication. Drawing upon anthropology, cognitive psychology, linguistics, continental philosophy, and American pragmatism, they reject the liberal notion of language as an instrument with which humans express their prelinguistic selves and/or describe a presocial objective world. Instead, they assert the constitutive world- and self-creating nature of language use. Individual identity and social action are dialectically created and related through signifying activities that must deploy socially available vehicles of significance. Media and cultural studies theorists bemoan the fact that the sophistication of our understandings of language and textuality has not influenced our understanding of politics. As Nicholas Garnham notes, our theories and practices of democratic politics are no longer congruent with our theories and practices of communication (as Hutchinson suggests, the transparency of language as a public medium through which facts and values are communicated is presupposed).[99] Theories of political communication still remain largely trapped within the paradigm of individual face-to-face communication and a nominalist understanding of language. Highly mediated symbolic forms are treated as the unproblematic expressions of singular authors and as unmediated reflections of external realities that preexist (and are uninfluenced by) their circulation.[100] Processes of information production, distribution, and consumption, however, play an ever greater role in contemporary social and cultural theories; mass media is recognized as central.[101]

Moreover, "the modernist separation of social spheres, in particular the separation of culture on the one hand from politics and economics on the other," begs the question of how people endow their lives with the meaning that motivates and legitimates social action.[102] The modern political sphere is defined by open, rational debate, thus "information provision is stressed and entertainment is negatively evaluated."[103] Social theory, on the other hand, suggests that contemporary identity politics are forged within "the institutions of mass-cultural dissemination [which] are seen as providing and structuring the cultural field on which these fragmented and diverse identities are formed and reformed:"[104] "an ever-larger proportion of the cultural goods and services consumed by the world's population are being conceived, produced, and distributed by . . . multinational corporations—not to speak of the consumer goods and their associated advertising that now play such an important role in the creation and maintenance of cultural identities."[105]

As our earlier considerations of subcultural practice illustrated, humans speak with and within historically specific modes of representation. The symbolic resources available for communicative activity shape our ways of knowing even as we use them to express identity and aspiration. We create social realities discursively, through systems of signification we deploy in activities that are simultaneously a politics and a poetics. Discursive social interactions and the opportunities for imaginative meaning-making they yield are paramount to human life and crucial to historical change. Speech is not a means to an end of self-expression or an instrument to convey information, but the marrow of the self one expresses, the social life of intersubjective practice and its potential for transformation. Dialogue is the activity in which people create their selves and their communities—texts and contexts. The interactive conditions for dialogue need to be fostered if we are to give tangible meaning to democracy.[106]

A dialogic theory of human social life provides a means to reconceptualize and reorient the law of free speech or freedom of expression so that it focuses more on the conditions of interaction than on the interacting individuals—freedom not as a lack of all constraints but as an ability to participate in engaged conversations.[107] The autonomy of the speaker from all social constraint is seen as illusory, because social situatedness is the very precondition for human speech. Instead, the conditions for the maximum participation of all people in the ongoing negotiation of the social good must be promoted. For Hutchinson, this implies an expanded role for the state "in order to promote the equality between participants necessary for an effective dialogue . . . In place of the traditional liberal reliance on individual rights to free speech, a dialogic community would rely on social entitlements to open discourse."[108]

In this scenario, private property rights are not understood either as preexisting or as standing in isolation from or in opposition to public rights to speech. Rather, it is recognized that we must collectively negotiate the appropriate combination of state involvement and abstention necessary to facilitate dialogue in all circumstances. The state would constructively affirm the responsibility of all social actors to engage themselves "in providing a positive and empowering freedom" for others.[109] No longer a domain of absolute private rights to exclusive enjoyment in which one is free from government interference, property would have to be recognized as a diverse package of privileges and responsibilities that serve social aspirations for democratic experience.

Many constitutional theorists recognize the dangers of corporate control and concentration of ownership and the effects of free market principles in limiting the cultural resources, information, and modes of argumentation available to us in a consumer society. The free speech principle—or at least contemporary applications of it—tends to favor those in power and those with wealth.[110] Steven Shiffrin shows how the institutional structure of the press effects such tendencies, but suggests that governmental intervention alone is unlikely to improve the market of communications.[111] The Left, he suggests (and it is not at all clear if this includes feminists, minority and immigrant groups, the disabled, and other subaltern populations), is not likely to achieve significant support or change public perceptions from within media: "progressive change is the culmination of grass roots agitation and organizing," and support of free speech is vital to such activities.[112] Shiffrin believes that neither a laissez-faire conception of the First Amendment nor one that invites activist state interventions to promote robust public debate provides an adequate model for the free speech principle. Rather, "the First Amendment serves to encourage and protect those who speak out against established customs, habit, institutions, and authorities—whether or not they inhabit the public sphere. On this understanding, the First Amendment spotlights a different metaphor from that of the marketplace of ideas or the richness of public debate; instead, it supports the American ideal of protecting and supporting dissent . . . it has a political tilt against the powerful."[113] In the dissent model, business corporations and commercial speakers have less of a claim to be at the heart of the First Amendment. To the extent that many of the practices of appropriation I have explored strike out, if not at concentrations of wealth, at least at attempts to concentrate sources of legitimate meaning and consolidate the positivity of corporate imagery, the dissent model would seem to better protect such activities. Indeed, access to media signifiers might well be deemed a requisite to the proliferation of alternative understandings in the public sphere.

When social and communicative relations are inevitably mediated through both time and space, freedom of assembly is no longer adequate to serve the purposes of access to either the channels or means of communication. Such equalities can no longer be guaranteed. More significantly, Garnham points to the fact "that what has also come to be mediated is the content of communication" itself.[114] "Our everyday social relations, our social identities are constructed in complex processes . . . of [media] mediations. We see ourselves . . . in terms of ways of seeing those identities constructed in and through mediated communications . . . and we often express [these] using objects of consumption provided and in large part determined by the system of economic production and exchange."[115]

The denigrations of commercial speech voiced by Hutchinson, Garnham, and Shiffrin, however, may be neither necessary nor appropriate. Currently, critical usages of protected commodity/signs are even less likely to be legally protected if they are disseminated in commerce (and thus circulate in channels as far-reaching as those in which the original message reached an audience). The fair-use provisions of copyright law, for example, devalue commercial usages, and constitutional litigation has established that "commercial speech" is entitled to less protection than fully protected or political speech. Such distinctions, however, are very difficult to draw in any meaningful manner in an increasingly commercial public sphere. Commercial speech has been defined as "expression related solely to the economic interests of the speaker and its audience,"[116] but in other cases individual judges have cautioned against an insistence upon rigid classifications.

Ultimately, "almost any speech involved with any commercial transaction [is] capable of being considered commercial speech."[117] It is the rare defendant whose activities can be characterized as taking place in a totally noncommercial context;[118] to publicize an alternative reading, commercial forms of circulation will almost inevitably be necessary. Legal scholar Keith Aoki points to a case in which a nonprofit public interest group used the term *star wars* to critically comment upon Ronald Reagan's strategic defense initiative in a series of commercial advertisements.[119] The court found the use to be a noncommercial one because the group was nonprofit in nature and expressing a political point of view. Another court, Aoki suggests, could just as easily look to the paid commercial advertising and any fundraising activities of the group that used the phrase (on bumper stickers, promotional literature, buttons, etc.) and find the speech to be commercial in nature, while suggesting that the group could find other ways of expressing its political beliefs that did not involve using the intellectual properties of others.[120]

An ironic consequence of these legal ambiguities is that the corporate messages conveyed through copyright- and trademark-protected commercial forms will be seen as property interests, when they are arguably more appropriately considered forms of commercial speech. The T-shirts worn by Smith College students, Black Bart merchandise, or the fictitious Joe Camel goods, on the other hand, may well be enjoined and/ or devalued as commercial speech despite their expressive political purposes. Few, however, have the resources to have the niceties of these unpredictable constitutional distinctions judicially decided. Ironically, one of the few judicial voices favoring a relativization of private intellectual properties that considers their role in social dialogue is that of Judge Alex Kozinski, whose views are generally more libertarian. He has interpreted trademark protection (using the model of copyright) to allow purely communicative uses of a mark as a form of fair use: "it is often virtually impossible to refer to a particular product for purposes of comparison, criticism, point of reference, or any other purpose without using the mark . . . Much useful social and commercial discourse would be all but impossible if speakers were under threat of an infringement lawsuit every time they made reference to a person, company or product by using its trademark."[121] Judge Kozinski's "nominative fair use defense" in trademark law permits only purely referential usages of the mark, however, and then only when the product or service cannot be identified without use of the mark and no sponsorship or endorsement by the holder of the mark is suggested. The suggestion of endorsement by the holder of the mark is, as we have seen, judicially discovered with alarming alacrity. Trademarks or trade names may be reproduced in "a purely communicational use,"[122] but such nominalist formulations of communication as information transfer deny other, more fundamental facets of human signification.

Kozinski is one of the few judges to speak out against the increasing protection of intellectual properties to the detriment of public expressive activity. A maverick in this area, he has suggested that even outside of First Amendment jurisprudence, trademark law should not be further expanded without consideration for "general communicative interests that should be taken into account—as a matter of *policy*, not constitutional law—when we give wider protection to trademarks."[123] Favorably influenced by Dreyfuss's pathbreaking work developing the doctrine of "expressive genericity,"[124] he suggests that we need these terms *as language*, to describe things and to communicate with others. As linguistic forms, commodified texts have become incorporated into our desires and into consciousness itself, shaping our vision of the world and of ourselves.[125] Clearly, this communicative function is not limited to trademarks, but extends to slogans and celebrities who become resources for the metaphors[126] through which culture is developed:

> any doctrine which gives people property rights in words, symbols, and images that have worked their way into our popular culture must carefully consider the communicative functions those marks serve. The originator of a trademark or logo cannot simply assert, "It's mine, I own it, and you have to pay for it any time you use it." Words and images do not worm their way into our discourse by accident; they're generally thrust there by well-orchestrated campaigns intended to burn them into our collective consciousness. Having embarked upon that endeavor, the originator of the symbol necessarily—and justly—must give up some measure of control. The originator must understand that the mark or symbol or image is no longer entirely its own, and that in some sense it also belongs to all those other minds who have received and integrated it.[127]

This image of consumer consciousness as matter on which symbols and images burn themselves, passively receiving and integrating media messages, is, however, one that I have attempted to dispel. It is (like Habermas's early positions) a perspective that equates media with culture and reifies and freezes culture in the process. As Dana Polan reminds us:

> This slide—from culture to media—is not Habermas's alone. In the age of new forms of culture—of television, of radio, of cable television, of mediatized ideas, of the blurring of all this so that what we know in ourselves of, say, *Teenage Mutant Ninja Turtles,* of what cultural meaning they have for us, is indistinguishable from what television, convenience stores, movies, videos, lunch pails, and so on and on have told us they mean for us—it is easy to assume that culture and media are the same thing. But all too often, the linguistic substitution of one for the other brings with it a semantic shift; in thinking of culture as media we lose some of the things we might take culture to be about.[128]

Significantly, such perspectives deny the social practices through which meanings are generated and transformed. The reactivation of media-activated textuality may be the substance of cultural reproduction and transformation. Lifeworlds are produced through the construction and contestation of meaning. The social and political work such practices of interpreting commodified textuality accomplish cannot be reduced to information transfer. Use of commercial media to make meaning is often a constitutive and transformative activity, not merely a referential or descriptive one. It may create alternative worlds as well as name existing ones. We value freedom of expression not as a means of spreading verifiable information about a world of brute fact, but as the activity with which we culturally construct worlds, create social knowledges, forge ethics, and negotiate intersubjective moral truths whose credence is never established by a measurable correspondence to an objective reality. Self, society, and identity are realized only through the expressive cultural activity that reworks those cultural forms that occupy the space of the social imaginary.[129]

This approach to expressive articulation puts me at odds with much of the Left as well as with liberal and libertarian commentators who hold pessimistic and, I would argue, unduly fatalistic attitudes toward mass media, advertising, and commercial culture. The conditions of postmodernity are often viewed as essentially totalitarian: "the effect of such a commercially-saturated atmosphere is to trivialize and impoverish democratic politics," according to Hutchinson, for example.[130] Thus, protection of commercial speech "threatens to realize a state of affairs in which corporate tyrants indulge in monologues over millions of solitudes."[131]

Such pessimism is unwarranted. Rather than seeing social life and discourse as determined by or merely reflective of the interests of those who disseminate mass-media-circulated representations, I have suggested that we consider the complex, culturally creative manner in which those in subordinate groups interpret, *recode*, or rework media signifiers to express their own identities and aspirations. As gay and lesbian activists, *Star Trek* fanzine writers, and indigenous peoples remind us, signs do not necessarily retain their original meanings when they circulate in social life. The very polysemy of signification—the surfeit of meaning that signifiers always potentially contain—provides the conditions of possibility for social agents to deploy texts, symbols, and images in unforeseen ways in the service of unanticipated agendas. It is, however, necessary to avoid a position of left romanticism that views all forms of local cultural expression as "resistance." Resistance is simply too broad and unnuanced a category to incorporate the diversity of attitudes and practices illustrated by subcultural appropriation of media forms. Furthermore, it may mislead us by elevating relations of antagonism over those of ironic appreciation, complicitous critique, affectionate annoyance, sympathetic intervention, and grudgingly respectful grievances. Culture is created in such activities.

Whereas left pessimism about commercial communication leads many to advocate state regulation to limit or mitigate the impact of corporate speech in the public sphere or to propose lesser protection for the speech of dominant commercial actors, my own guarded optimism about human cultural creativity inclines me in a slightly different direction. In a capitalist society in which mass-media communications systems circulate and disseminate the largest proportion and the most powerful forms of cultural signification, the signs of the economically powerful will always be pervasive, regardless of how closely they are monitored, how assiduously they are regulated, or how much we subsidize nonprofit communications. It is no longer possible to maintain a Romantic opposition between culture as an authentic lifeworld and capitalist market relations as rational systems that alienate us from human meanings.

Commercial speech and public discourse cannot be maintained as pristine categories in the late twentieth century, and the desire to do so bespeaks a seductive but ultimately untenable nostalgia. If dialogue is "the activity *par excellence* through which people constitute and reconstitute themselves" and "an integral part of the democratic good life,"[132] then perhaps we should stop trying to preserve the integrity of a mythic public domain untainted by the stigma of commercial speech and acknowledge the cultural conditions of postmodernity: a historical situation in which identity, tradition, and community are themselves constituted through, and in diverse relations to, commodification and its discourses and practices.

7. Dialogic Democracy II: Alterity and Articulation in the Space of the Political

What is essentially at stake in the debate between modernists and postmodernists is whether the world is best understood as the further working out of that set of social dynamics and thus best understood in terms of the conceptual paradigms and value systems developed within Enlightenment thought to analyze them . . . or whether a new historical epoch, characterized variously as postmodern or postindustrial or post-Fordist or the information society has begun calling for a new set of analytical tools and new value systems.—Nicholas Garnham, "The Mass Media, Cultural Identity, and the Public Sphere in the Modern World"[1]

Political theorists increasingly insist upon the inadequacy of European modern models for critically evaluating public lifeworlds and political activity in contemporary contexts. Their critiques of the liberal assumptions of a "bourgeois public sphere" may enable us to grasp how the conceptual architecture of Enlightenment thought empowers intellectual property holders, operating to privilege authorial speech and silence expressive alterity. Focusing on recent debates about free speech and democracy in consumer societies dominated by mass-media communications, I have suggested that even scholars critical of modern free speech doctrine fail to recognize the full complexities of popular culture and cultural politics. Largely, I believe, this is due to their adherence to a positivist paradigm of the political. The political, however, must be reconceptualized in an era of such pervasive intertextuality. The politics appropriate to democracy in the condition of postmodernity demands a continual critical cognizance, both of the radical contingency of the social and of the expressive activity involved in articulating its parameters.

The institution of literary property purports to tie the work to an authorial location but simultaneously enables it to transcend any such situation; textualizing the author's proper name necessarily projects "the signature" into unanticipated sites for signification.[2] I will suggest that "literary property" is a productive oxymoron in which authorship and alterity are in dynamic tension; the characteristics of the literary are in a relation of some friction with property's conventional qualities, while the proprietary claims of authorship tend to undo the literary character of the work. I will employ the figure of the signature—fundamental to all commodified textualities—to make evident the integral interdependence of authorship and alterity in modern regimes of power. Laws of intellectual property effect a continuing and anxious denial of that relationship when they tenaciously cling to modern categorical frameworks, precluding (among other things) an acknowledgment of the politics of popular culture.

Politics is cultural activity; its practice demands appropriate access to the materiality of means and mediums of expressive communication. A radical democratic politics, however, will involve more than simply a libertarian celebration of regimes of freedom for appropriation. Postcolonial circumstances cut across the grain of postmodern practices and urge upon us a heightened sensitivity to the differential relations of others and their relationship to dominant practices of othering—an ethics of contingency. Such a politics must enunciate an ambivalence with respect to authorship and retain an ironic awareness of the historical contingencies of alignments between authorship and alterity. Such practices alert us to the need to adopt mobile positionings and multiple perspectives if we are to maintain a critical ethnographic distance from the places where authorial power is produced and legitimated and to avoid hypostatizing difference in our attention to alterity. This, at least, is demanded by an anthropology sensitive to the politics of producing and maintaining structures of meaning and emergent registers of cultural difference.

Locating the Politics of the Public Sphere

If distinctions between commercial and noncommercial speech are more and more difficult to draw, determinations of properly "political" expressive activities are even more so. Most legal commentators favor the protection of speech that "is both intended and received as a contribution to public deliberation about some issue."[3] Although those who favor speech rights as necessary incidents to the self-expression of sovereign individuals feel that protection of merely political speech is too restrictive a field of protection, more consequentialist approaches limit protection to speech that contributes to public deliberation of political issues. Both positions, however, presuppose that the political can be defined prior to socially signifying activities and as a category for evaluating them. This predilection, I suggest, can be traced in developing understandings of civil society and the public sphere, both concepts that have been revitalized in debates about their continued relevance.

Critics of the bourgeois public sphere idealized in Habermas's early work suggest that the so-called universal categories of this space of ideal communication—public and private, speech and property, political and nonpolitical—are both exclusionary and elitist. To the extent that a realm designated political may be delineated in advance of social activities of articulation, such parameters will inevitably be perceived from partial perspectives, privilege particular interests, entrench identities, and limit identifications. Many of the underlying premises of the bourgeois public sphere are contested, but some of these are especially significant for a consideration of cultural appropriations: the restriction of political discourse to issues involving the common good, the division between public and private, the normative value attached to the singularity of such a sphere, and the privileging of rationalist forms of communication.

Habermas's early idealization of the bourgeois public sphere was premised on the assumption that discourse in public spheres was properly deliberation about the common good. Iris Marion Young, however, suggests that where existing distributions of symbolic or material goods privilege some, "appeals to a 'common good' are likely to perpetuate such privilege."[4] "Particular" experiences and interests are defined as such from particular vantage points. Seeing political communication as necessarily involving encounters with difference—in meaning, social position, or needs—but not as inevitably or even optimally transcending difference, is necessary to preserve plurality in politics. To speak "across differences of culture, social position, and need"[5] requires respect for embodied and particular expressive practices such as greeting, gesture, humor, wordplay, images, figures of speech, seduction, and narrative. In short, Young argues that models of deliberative democracy ignore or trivialize those cultural forms of communication in which differences are expressed.

A related challenge concerns the line between public and private that informs the boundaries of acceptable deliberation. Such a narrowing of the public sphere might not serve democratic interests if this implies that consideration of "private interests" and "private issues" will be prohibited as inappropriate forms of public discourse. The appropriate boundaries of the public sphere must be part of any process of public negotiation because such boundaries are never naturally given but historically constructed and "are frequently deployed to delegitimate some interests, views, and topics and valorize others."[6] Boundaries exist only in contingent compromises that must be open to the challenges of those who seek "to convince others that so called private matters are subjects of common concern."[7] This, at least, is a criticism of his model that Habermas has accepted[8] and largely taken into account.

Two senses of the term *private* tend to ideologically disenfranchise subordinate groups in public life: that which pertains to private property in a market economy—the private prerogatives of ownership—and that which pertains to intimate, domestic, or sexual life. By deeming such matters private we make them off-limits to public contestation and debate.[9] Habermas's reformulated discourse theory of democracy goes some distance toward meeting these concerns. He has addressed the latter issue, accepting that topics cannot be ruled "out of order" by virtue of some preordained or permanent status as "private issues." On the other hand, the "privacy" of market allocations concerns him less. As we shall see, this is perhaps simply a by-product of his continued insistence that civil society, as the social basis for autonomous public spheres, can be distinguished from both the economic system and public administration.[10]

Throughout this volume we have seen how the logic of turning signifying forms into private properties functions to disentitle expressive uses of texts protected by intellectual property. Not only are trademark and copyright-protected signifiers private properties over which owners may exercise idiosyncratic and discriminatory control, as we saw in the Gay Olympics case, but those who seek to use such texts to express fundamental social differences—to articulate needs, aspirations, and identities in public spheres—are doubly disadvantaged. Gay and lesbian usage of such forms to comment upon social exclusions, for example, may well be seen as the imposition of private concerns into the public sphere. Such articulations are unlikely to be seen as forms of political discourse within a liberal framework; more likely, they will be seen as unauthorized expropriations of private properties by those who seek to publicly express private matters.

The liberal assumption that interlocutors within the public sphere might simply bracket status differentials and deliberate "as if" they were equals has also come under scrutiny. As Fraser elaborates, even the process of discursive interaction in formally inclusive arenas puts some people at a disadvantage; those in subordinate social groups tend to employ styles and idioms of expression denigrated and marginalized by the mainstream.[11] In socially stratified and culturally diverse societies, where deliberative processes tend to silence the contributions of those who are already socially disadvantaged or culturally minoritized, Fraser contends that democracy is better served by a number of competing and conversing publics than a single overarching public sphere. In his discursive theory of democracy, Habermas himself has accepted that "widely diversified and more or less autonomous public spheres"[12] connected by communicative networks provide spaces in which social problems are perceived, identified, and treated. Cultural pluralism, he believes, is thereby protected: "This 'weak' public is the vehicle of 'public opinion.' The opinion-formation uncoupled from decisions is effected in an open and inclusive network of overlapping, subcultural publics having fluid temporal, social, and substantive boundaries. Within a framework guaranteed by constitutional rights, the structures of such a pluralistic public sphere develop more or less spontaneously. The currents of public communication are channelled by mass media and flow through different publics that develop informally inside associations. Taken together, they form a 'wild' complex that resists organization as a whole."[13] Although the hegemony of the bourgeois public sphere can no longer be sustained, this is hardly a crisis, for the historical record shows that the bourgeois public was never *the* public, but only one of many counterpublics with its own characteristic modes of publicity.[14] The norms of this sphere legitimated bourgeois power. Although such norms were dominant, they were never uncontested.

Differentiated "counterpublics" are both necessary and desirable to enable subordinated social groups to circulate counterdiscourses, formulating oppositional interpretations in idioms that might be unwelcome, unacceptable, or simply inaudible in a single dominant public sphere. In this volume, we have explored meanings fashioned by numerous "subaltern counterpublics"[15] in which identities are knit and alternative significations to those proffered in mainstream media culture are woven against the woof. Such counterpublics are not separatist enclaves, however, because they assume a public orientation, disseminating discourse into wider social fields and communicating with wider publics.[16] In many of the examples of appropriation we have explored, forms of counterpublicity deploy popular cultural forms to do so. Their "public" orientation is accomplished through the use of publicly recognized symbols pervasive in commercial media to express particular positions in wider contexts of public consideration.

Debates about contemporary public spheres and whether current conditions are conducive to the development of civil society focus attention on market conditions in shaping the means and forms of communication. Certainly, the legitimating power of the bourgeois author derived to a great degree from his perceived political role in directing expressive works to a readership who would evaluate them and forge public opinion in a space autonomous from both the state and the market. For Habermas, the bourgeois public sphere was possible only in a social order when a sharp distinction between state and market could be made. As the social welfare state collapsed this distinction, it eroded the preconditions for effective publicity; mass-mediated public relations and the manufacture and manipulation of public opinion further destroyed the dialogic dimensions of the bourgeois public.[17]

In *Between Facts and Norms*, Habermas takes a less hostile but still ambivalent attitude toward mass media in a discursive democracy.[18] Primarily this is because he still takes the conveyance of information to reach understanding as the privileged, if not exclusive, form of political communication. Whether what is communicated is needs, interests, or issues, and whether wills or opinions are formulated, he assumes that rational communications are the sole expressive means to accomplish this. The institutional structure and political economy of mass media is relevant to him only to the extent that it may influence the flow of information between the public spheres and the political system: "Furthermore, the unavoidable division of labor in the production and diffusion of knowledge results in an unequal distribution of information and expertise. In addition, the communications media intervene with a selectivity of their own in this social distribution of knowledge. The structures of the public sphere reflect unavoidable asymmetries in the availability of information, that is, unequal chances to have access to the generation, validation, shaping, and presentation of messages."[19]

Like other theorists of deliberative democracy, Habermas restricts his "concept of democratic discussion narrowly to critical argument" and, in so doing, "assume[s] a culturally biased conception of discussion that tends to silence or devalue some people or groups."[20] Young proposes that a truly "communicative democracy" (what I have referred to here as a dialogic democracy) would respect other forms of meaning-making activity than those of rational argument, because the latter contain cultural biases that devalue forms of understanding and expression characteristic of those who are socially marginalized (at least in the "modern West"). They may also facilitate gender bias to the extent that women's use of language may be more "tentative, exploratory, or conciliatory."[21] The speaking styles and rhetorical forms characteristic of subcultural vernaculars put their expressions of social concern beyond the pale of the political in deliberative democracies.

Such a rationalism cannot encompass the range of expressive activity that has political meaning and consequence. There is no doubt that Habermas greatly expanded the scope of communications he considers politically relevant by multiplying the number of operative public spheres in which opinions, interests, wills, and identities are forged. Such publics are privileged precisely because of their intimate relations with meaningful experiences in the contexts of contingent lifeworlds and private lives. Nonetheless, he still believes that lifeworld contexts exist in a pristine integrity from market forces and that "ordinary language" is the authentic vehicle of their maintenance and reproduction.[22] Even as he accepts that public spheres are dominated by the mass media as channels for communication, community formation, and exerting influence, and acknowledges that people actively interpret the media texts they receive, Habermas still sees media as a conduit for communications that are wholly autonomous from market forces.[23] In a nearly complete turnabout from earlier positions, Habermas recognizes the literature on culture industries that delineates the political economy of media ownership, program structuring, and financing and gives long-overdue acknowledgment to reception theories and cultural studies that emphasize the interpretive work that consumers do as audiences. Unfortunately, however, he reads these interpretive strategies as the activity of rational agents whose agencies are in no way influenced by the texts they consume and whose lifeworld resources remain fully autonomous from the cultural forms the media affords them. The possibility that market-driven means, meanings, texts, and forms of communication may actively shape lifeworld contexts and that media texts might themselves become part of "ordinary language" is not envisioned.

Media and communications theorist Nicholas Garnham suggests that we be wary when formulating configurations of a postmodern public sphere to avoid overvaluing "a particular model of rationalist discourse at the expense of disregarding the modes and functions of most media communication."[24] It is no longer possible to pretend that political debates are only carried out in spaces labeled as such or that the entertainment and marketing forms proffered by commercial media are not deployed in the communication of wider social agendas. Nonetheless, Garnham compromises this cautionary claim by attaching another question to it; he wants to know, in advance, whether we can "identify cultural forms or types of media practice that favor the formation of democratic identities and others that undermine such identities."[25] In short, he seeks to ascertain media practices that will develop relations of citizenship rather than intensifications of consumption. To the extent that social consciousness is produced through expressive activities that deploy the forms that dominant modes of communication make available for consumption, however, such a distinction collapses empirically. It is unable to provide any guidance for delineating the parameters of the political because it presupposes the discrete positivity of practices—consumption and citizenship—that are mutually implicated.

Mass Mediation and the Publics of Civil Society

Recent debates about the resurgence and propriety of the concept of civil society and the significance of hegemonic practice emphasize the need to reevaluate market-driven media forms in forging contemporary publics and forms of sociality. As in earlier debates about the public sphere, considerations of civil society have compelled a reexamination of conventional demarcations between public and private spheres, society and economy, culture and the market. "For Habermas, the economy is emphatically *not* part of the public sphere. Habermas's normative, anticommercial view of the public sphere has swallowed up many contemporary treatments of civil society as well, which exclude economics out of a desire to sustain the purity of civil society's ideal or critical function . . ."[26]

Just as theorists of the public sphere pointed to vast changes in markets, media, and consumption in the late twentieth century, critical considerations of civil society address those twentieth-century conditions that challenge the continuing viability of the civil society model. The formation of the corporations and associations of civil society were historically stimulated by market forces and sustained by new forms of communication media; recent debates around civil society, however, have tended to see new technologies of media and information either as providing more intensive structures of domination, or as affording means for the global saturation effects of a "society of spectacle."[27] In both views, the potential force of hegemony has been weakened by contemporary global capitalism. Such perspectives, however, ignore the potential politics of consumption, as both George Yúdice and Bruce Robbins have recently pointed out.

Flexible accumulation strategies, the growth of consumer culture, and the "new world information order" may be global in scope, but this does not necessarily imply any concomitant weakening of those articulatory practices we allude to when we refer to hegemony. It may suggest that the production of a "national popular" should no longer be considered the primary focus of hegemonic activity.[28] Perhaps, however, it is only the Eurocentric conceits of political theorists that have posited the nation-state as the privileged site for such discursive address. Culture has always been produced at transnational and local levels, as its emergence in contexts of global colonial expansion and reifications in local colonial administrations indicate.[29]

Yúdice and Robbins suggest that the concept of civil society will only continue to have critical purchase if it is capable of engaging the global conjunctures of culture and capitalism and the practices through which publics and counterpublics "can maintain significant and even adversarial autonomy within, and even perhaps by means of the market."[30] This requires that we be "willing to rethink relations between commodities and identity, properties and pleasures,"[31] recognizing that "civil society is also the society of consumption and spectacle,"[32] and thus that citizenship and consumer capitalism cannot be absolutely distinguished for analytic purposes. "Politics and culture become intertwined as they traverse the terrain of state, media, and market."[33] It may no longer be possible to think such ideals as citizenship and democracy in the absence of consumption because "most notions of culture . . . will be underwritten by consumer-corporate entities."[34] Both scholars plead for our recognition of a more "creative politics of citizenship"[35] and a greater creativity in conceiving the political, such that it can encompass "all social sites of production and reproduction," which will necessarily include spheres of commerce and consumption.[36] In a world where the media through which views are disseminated are centralized, corporately owned, and operated for profit, subaltern social groups are both culturally disenfranchised and materially deprived of means to public participation.

For a counterpublic to properly express itself it must reach out into a wider public and appeal to a wider audience to recognize its claims. To do so, I have argued, it is especially likely to need to avail itself of widely recognized and publicly meaningful (but privately controlled) cultural forms. As Dana Polan asserted, it is increasingly inaccurate to portray media as a purely corrupting force that distorts a preexisting "pristine realm of rational openness in which citizens once communicated transparently."[37] Assuming that anything other than a singular world of transparent meanings and rational debate represents a fall from modern grace, Habermas offered little by way of conceptual resources with which to think the cultural politics of the public sphere in multicultural and mass-mediated conditions.[38] In his more recent work, and in the productive interlocutions of his critics, however, other possibilities have indeed emerged.

Negt and Kluge's *The Public Sphere and Experience*[39] is proffered by film theorist Miriam Hansen as affording an alternative conceptual architecture to more adequately accommodate contemporary questions about culture and politics. Assuming the dominance of industrially produced and electronically mediated forms of publicity, Negt and Kluge provide a vision of the public sphere that serves as a site for "discursive contestation for and among multiple, diverse, and unequal constituencies" and allows for the uncertainties inherent in a sphere of interaction between "different types of publicity and diverse publics."[40] Postliberal and postliterary public formations pose different questions for democracy and demand different political responses. Hansen, like the contemporary legal philosophers mentioned earlier, recognizes that public spheres in late-capitalist contexts are different from the public cultural realm that legitimated the liberal-bourgeois model because they can "no longer pretend to a separate sphere above the marketplace."[41] Corporate public relations have an increasing presence and influence in public domains, and spaces of leisure, entertainment, and consumption are colonized by "the privately owned media of the consciousness industry."[42] Often, however, their private ownership and the hegemony of the commodity form is invisible or obscured: "Lacking political legitimation of their own, the branches of industrial-commercial publicity, especially the mass media, enter into alliances with the disintegrating classical public sphere . . . industrial-commercial publicity has tended to graft itself onto the remnants of a bourgeois public sphere for cultural respectability and legitimacy . . . These alliances usually work to reproduce dominant ideology and above all, to simulate the fictive coherence and transparency of a public sphere that is not one."[43]

As modes of technology for the transmission of cultural products have proliferated, the author-function has been stretched to accommodate them, as we saw in chapter 1. A comprehensive history is impossible here, but a few examples suffice to reiterate the point. The originating role in cultural reproduction has increasingly become centralized in corporate entities due to the complexities of the divisions of labor and the scale of capital involved in creating new media works for new technologies of dissemination.[44] Legally, however, the bourgeois author-function maintains its hegemony. Drawing upon Edelman's pioneering work, Lury points to the relocation of authorship with respect to cinematographic works. A film is clearly the product of highly differentiated labor and a multiplicity of creative processes not easily accommodated by the legal fictions of individuated creation, singular personality, and juridical subjecthood that copyright law crystallizes in the figure of the author as first owner of copyright. By vesting legal rights of authorship "in the collective subject constituted by the representatives of the capital used to produce the film,"[45] the attributes of the creative author are extended to capital itself: "the 'original' moment here is thus that of investment. By contrast, the 'creative' labour of others involved in the process of film production is proletarianised (it is standardised to the point of interchangeability) in order to deprive them of such a right."[46]

Romantic ideologies of authorship justify copyright protections and the commodification of cultural texts. Modernity's legitimating rhetorics—based on democratic dialogical ideals—now protect corporate hegemony over increasingly monologic domains of mass culture.[47] Fictions of creativity, personality, and originality are preserved to legitimate the rights of investors to control the circulation of corporately produced textuality and its reworkings by others. As we have seen, this establishes rights not merely to a continuing return on investment but to control of the cultural activities of those others who, like their eighteenth- and nineteenth-century forebears, re-create textual tendencies to make them better expressions of their own lives and aspirations. Today, however, those cloaked with authorial privilege maintain little pretense to enlightenment but proclaim the mantle of authorship for the avowed purpose of maintaining the exchange value of entertainment. They do so in the name of property, pure and simple.

Public dialogue about the greater good once encouraged by the activities of publicly responsible authors is no longer even considered to be a social goal that might be accomplished through corporately authored, mass-media commerce in promotional texts, but the exclusive rights of authors nonetheless still attach to those who invest in their dissemination. With all of the privileges and none of the responsibilities of authorship, important forms of capital formation and return on investments in textuality are secured, but the social anima of meaning is denied. As literary theorist Peggy Kamuf puts it, the modern notion of the author denies the eidetic law of *writing*, a resolutely social space where subjective intentionality cannot be secured, where the positivities of original identity are lost, and where inscriptions are dislodged from authorial origins to become part of the social life of language itself.[48]

The Space of the Signature

The signature [may serve as] an instrument with which to unnerve discourses about textual authorship . . . The institution of authorship has shown a remarkable capacity to return even after being pronounced dead. —Peggy Kamuf, *Signature Pieces: On the Institution of Authorship*[49]

One of the more influential sources for the development of a postmodern attitude toward authorship and textuality is Roland Barthes's brief essay "The Death of the Author."[50] Barthes suggests that literature's modern history can be divided between the age of the author and the age of the text. Dominant understandings of literature remain "tyrannically centred on the author . . . The *explanation* of a work is always sought in the man or woman who produced it, as if it were always in the end, through the more or less transparent allegory of the fiction, the voice of a single person, the *author* confiding in us."[51] Seeing the author-work relationship as "the epitome and culmination of capitalist ideology," Barthes sowed seeds for a poststructuralist agenda that undermines the ideological supports that enable authors to be the owners of their texts.[52] "To give a text an Author," he asserted, was "to impose a limit on that text, to furnish it with a final signified, to close the writing."[53] Throughout this volume, we have seen how the law engages in this process, seeing in all practices of meaning and interpretation only the efforts of the author-owner of the protected text, often a corporate "individual" who is viewed as the singular point of origin for the meanings of those legally protected works that circulate in its name.

Rather than the Romantic expression of an author—the literary work that embodies his unique personality—the (post)modern text "has no other origin than language itself."[54] A text is recognized to be "a tissue of quotations drawn from the innumerable centres of culture [in which] the writer can only imitate a gesture that is always anterior, never original."[55] The text, unlike the work, is fabricated from a multiplicity of activities of writing or signification, which enter into mutual relations of dialogue, parody, and contestation.[56] Barthes looks to the activities of certain late-nineteenth- and early-twentieth-century writers who sought to loosen the hold of the author on writing. Aesthetic modernists (like the surrealists and their successors in postmodern anthropology) sought to undo the modern author's stranglehold on the play of signification in artistic works, allowing them to function textually.

The so-called death of the author affords little anxiety in the humanities or social sciences, but it is greeted less sanguinely in legal studies, where entire regimes of property hinge upon the author's unquestioned positivity. Although it is not my purpose to provide an overview of the critical scholarship addressing the origins of modern authorship that has appeared in the past decade,[57] a few points pertinent to the power of intellectual property protections must be made. Postmodernity is at once the condition in which the author-function is fundamentally challenged by new ideas about subjectivity, language, communication, and difference—delegitimated in many cultural arenas—and concomitantly the description given to a public sphere saturated by an unprecedented proliferation of corporately authored (commodified) texts. In Hansen's words, "the media of industrial-commercial publicity... [is] an inescapable horizon, and the most advanced site of struggle over the organization of everyday experience ..."[58]

Significantly, Hansen sees contemporary media practices of cultural appropriation and social acts of reappropriation as posing some of the most pressing contemporary political questions. How and under what circumstances, she asks, "can such cultural 'hybridity' be mobilized in the political fight for social and economic equality?"[59] Here, Hansen alludes to a central paradox of postmodernity: just as cultural difference and alterity is appropriated by capital in the authorship of new commodity forms that circulate publicly through mass-media communications, the proliferation of publicly disseminated commodity/signs simultaneously enriches the realm of cultural resources with which counterpublics may be forged. Such alternative public spheres, however, remain vulnerable to the legal power that authorship confers upon commercial-industrial forces of publicity. Mass-media flows are controlled by maintaining tortuous distinctions between public and private, property and speech, fact and fiction, commercial and noncommercial forms of expression. Intellectual property, therefore, serves to privilege the appropriations, decontextualizations, and commodification of lifeworlds by capitalist interests as acts of authorship, while it simultaneously invites and delegitimates those creative reappropriations around which counterpublics form as acts of illicit piracy.

The rapid proliferations of intertextuality afforded by communications technologies have not resulted in any decline in the rhetorical appeal of the author-function. Instead we have witnessed a steady expansion of the fields in which authorship and new forms of cultural authority are claimed. When IBM can refer to itself as a "binary bard,"[60] companies claim properties in seeds they engineer—denying any value to generations of cultivation by Third-World peasants because they don't fit Western notions of authorship[61]—the inscription of sequences of human DNA codes are asserted as authorial acts,[62] and every reading of a digital text on the information highway is deemed a theft of authorial property,[63] the author is alive and well and doing pervasive ideological work. Massive evidence of collaborative authorship, intercultural borrowings, collective writings, institutional teamwork in producing texts, and the ubiquitous intertextuality of late-capitalist contexts must be denied to maintain a modern vision of culture as a field of protected works—monologic monuments of authorial authority. Contemporary conditions of electronic reproduction afford massive potentials for a proliferation of textual agency. Nonetheless, the modern concept of the author exhibits a remarkable capacity for revitalization, even in contexts that would seem least hospitable to its colonization.

To disrupt assumptions of authorship, Kamuf employs the figure of the signature as a means to explore that place between writer and writing, the difference between the writer and the work, the ambivalent and productive space in which the signature both divides and joins life and letters. While the signature, as the personal mark of an individual creator, affords the basis for the legitimacy of authorial power, it functions simultaneously to reveal a constitutive vulnerability: "At the edge of the work, the dividing trait of the signature pulls in both directions at once: appropriating the text under the sign of the name, expropriating the name into the play of the text."[64] This "double-jointedness of signatures" is lost, Kamuf suggests, if we "posit an essential exteriority of subjects to the texts they sign."[65] In short, she addresses the distinctive mark of the author not simply as an ideological trope of authority but as a productive space of cultural possibility, as I have done throughout this volume.[66]

The figure of the signature is potentially a useful one with which to comprehend the social circulation of trademarks, protected indicia of celebrity personas, and marks of governmental authority. Each signature form presupposes the presence of an author—the subject of an agency that engaged in the original act of signing.[67] The subject who properly claims the proper name may be singled out; it is assumed to have a unique being (the originating creator in copyright law, the single source in trademark law, the autonomously created personality or identity in the field of publicity rights, to reiterate relevant examples). Because the signs of this distinction circulate within a linguistic public sphere, however, they can always be altered, borrowed, duplicated, and changed. The truth of the authenticity of the author's mark always requires supplementary guarantees of its singularity—its differentiation or distinction. The very distinction "it assumes, however, cannot be absolute; on the contrary, verifiability or authentication relies on its reproducibility by the subject named."[68] If the mark were not each time, in some important sense, the same, there would be no evidence of its singular origin: "By a seeming paradox, then, the singularity of the signature's mark depends upon its limitation within recognizable parameters of reproducibility or iterability, which is to say of generalizability. The signature, therefore, is always detachable from the singular instance it supposedly designates."[69]

In conditions of mass reproduction, the signature is vulnerable to the fragmentation of its singularity; the mark of the author is always at risk of chance encounters with others who would create new connotations and alternative values.[70] It is impossible to sign fully an intent, or to sign what one means, because one's meanings are always beyond the space of the signature.[71] Provocatively, Kamuf asserts that the signature "occurs" in a space of difference: in a difference from itself and an address to the other.[72] The modern concept of authorship lies within an idealist exclusion of writing from the material worlds of meaning and social difference, in the name of the subject's distinctive identity (which the law of intellectual property purports merely to acknowledge, but in fact creates and maintains). A signature, however, is not an author nor even simply the proper name of an author; it is the mark of an articulation that both joins and divides identity with/from difference.[73] "As part of a text, however, whose regime is precisely not that of property or ownership, the signature detaches from the functioning of proper name, or rather joins that function to the other textual function of producing meaning without strictly determinable intentions . . . signatures demand first to be *read* before any law can assign their meaning, whereas it is precisely the possibility of assigning a certain meaning or intention which reading puts into question."[74]

This space, between the law of the proper name and the space in which the name is subject to interpretive practice, Kamuf describes as the space of alterity.[75] We have seen how works and marks accrue benefits for their owners in the market, while their textuality invites the production of alternative meanings that in turn may activate activities of censorship. At the same time, the commodity/sign still retains the capacity to dissimilate into anonymity (genericide) and to become caught up in the impropriety of rumor.[76] The trademark rumors examined in chapter 3 emerge from spaces of social exclusion where "the search for an 'innocent' signature encounters its limit in the crime of representation, where vindication takes the form of repetition. The impossibility that arises here is that of signing from the place of the excluded other."[77] Such practices are indicative of the traces of an insistent alterity "in the very place of identity's signature."[78]

Positivity of meaning and certainty of authorial identity are constituted through deference and deferral, an ongoing denial of the constitutive force of alterity. The signature cannot maintain proprietary borders when it is swept up in textual (or literary) activities; it is disarticulated by "the work of writing, whose real 'properties' must finally return to no one."[79] Hence, the signature must be propped up by law. Through the enforcement of intellectual property protections, the signature is rearticulated in order simultaneously to deny and to appropriate the creative energies emergent in the expressive activities of others. For Kamuf, the eradication of the voice of alterity is necessary to any understanding of society as a whole; to give the social positivity, difference—that which cannot claim its propriety in the name of property—can only be recognized as a lack, a place where the whole is not.[80] Within the whole—that space of positive signification determined by the order of the proper name—difference is rendered and recognized as distinction, whereas outside of this order alterity is a space of silence, inaudibile until it demands recognition within the realm of proprietary claims.[81] So, for example, as we saw in chapter 5, Native peoples find themselves represented as signs of alterity that are protected as properties within cultures of commerce, while they find their own voices inaudible in the public sphere. The stereotyped representation is more visible than their own social existence; only by making proprietary claims to own their cultural distinction will intellectual property laws legitimate their difference.

Stewart and Kamuf show us that the integrity of the system of proper names is integrally related to a denial of the radical otherness that constantly threatens to disrupt its positivity; the specter of alterity always haunts the proper name. This, of course, is a property of language more generally—of the capacity of signifiers to differ from their referents— but to the extent that the social world itself is rendered textually, "to deny or disregard this difference between language and its referents is . . . to risk the suppression of all the nonlinguistic eruptions of otherness,"[82] and, it might be added, the expressive forms through which such emergences assume public presence.

The iterability of the sign and the actual impossibility of a text's being the "same" in all contexts—that is, to function solely as a "work"—is denied by intellectual property laws based on the founding conceit of the authorial personality and its embodiment in expressive form. But I would also suggest that it is the encounter with otherness and its potential destabilization that makes it necessary to construct the idea of the work and the author and their integral relationship in the first instance. It is the work of the work, if you will, to deny the voice of the other and the other's articulation of meaning in the name of the author's authority or paternity, and it is the undermining of this authority with which intellectual property operates in dialectical and diacritical relationship— "dancing with a stranger," so to speak.

Sometimes the work we encounter is an advertisement, a fictional character, or an image, or it may take the form of a celebrity likeness, a marketing symbol, or a brand name. The author may be a corporation or a person, an organization or a government agency. The other may be other culturally or racially, occupy an alternative sex/gender positioning, or simply challenge the logic of equivalence upon which intellectual property laws depend with a form of difference that upsets that logic. As Trouillot remarks, there is no singular savage slot; the other has no specific properties and its "identity" cannot be predetermined.[83] Otherness is a contingent social product and ever emergent in the continual work of social differentiation. Gay caricatures of John Wayne provide alternative meanings for dominant significations of masculine hyperbole, for instance. Society's others may feel compelled to visualize their presence in the realm of the proper name, adopting the authority of the signature and the indicia of its propriety, to make themselves audible and credible, laying claim to legitimacy. Borrowing the stature of the Olympic body or the recognition accorded the Mountie, insisting that the signs of Indian nations have fixed social referents, and making possessive claims to certain fictional characters on the basis of a history of prior use and care— these are all strategies that partake of such logic.

To the extent that such activities call into question the positivity of the social, the parameters of community, the borders of the nation, or the objectivity of sex and gender, they have political dimensions. If, as both Stewart and Kamuf suggest, the privileges of authorship are bound to the legitimation of a contingently forged social contract, the identities it affords, and the relations of alterity it denies, then practices that reactivate the immanent textuality of the signature may be fundamental to democratic dialogue. As Stewart puts it, laws of literary property (and their derivative extensions in consumer cultures) reify an economy of social life and contain these reifications as well as their inevitable transgressions in the public sphere.

The Unworked Community

The voice of community is articulated in the interruption . . .
—Jean-Luc Nancy, *The Inoperative Community*[84]

If we are to encourage a more fully dialogic democracy, it may be imperative *not* to isolate a sphere of political activity when assessing the effects and affect of expressive activity. To do so is to entrench a model of membership or citizenship that freezes what might more appropriately be considered a contingent vision of community. Visions of community as a process that positively values its own contingent formation—rather than a product that values its own essential identity as a positivity—are offered by a number of political theorists, including Areh Botwinick, David Carroll, Drucilla Cornell, Claude Lefort, Jean-François Lyotard, Ernesto Laclau, Chantal Mouffe, and Jean-Luc Nancy.[85] In Carroll's terms, "the so-called postindustrial, postmodern, hyperreal age of information in which we supposedly live"[86] demands the articulation of a critical sense of the political formulated without Enlightenment certainties about the boundaries of public and private, culture and politics, commerce and art.[87] What makes a contemporary political community common cannot assume the form of an identity or image of collectivity but must remain indeterminate.[88] An undetermined notion of community is necessary to animate a postmodern public and to enable the full range of activities we might recognize as political: "The critical demand we make of the political should also challenge what is accepted or acceptable as 'practical politics' by constantly making possible other forms of political practice than those practiced as politics. Culture in this sense could be seen as the manifestation of the heterogeneous public spaces in which alternative 'products' and practices of art and politics are produced."[89]

Carroll draws upon Lyotard's critique of the desire for community and Jean-Luc Nancy's view that the inability to conceptualize an indeterminate community paralyzes Western political thought to suggest that community be rethought in terms of a constitutive relation to alterity.[90] Art is central to the possibility of such a politics of community, and literature—conceived of as writing or ecriture—is that "voice of interruption"[91] which enables "community to resist and exceed its own limits and ends, to be constantly undone by an alterity it cannot and should not attempt to contain or incorporate."[92] As both Stewart and Kamuf have explained, the most significant quality of the literary is "that which escapes being";[93] unfortunately, the law takes on the endless task of restoring qualities of positivity to the social space of literature by its allocation of authorial rights. In so doing, it reifies communities and precludes politics.

Community exists "in a tremor of 'writing' wherein the literary work mingles with the most simple public exchange of speech."[94] Throughout this volume, we have seen how authorial works in social contexts resist being reduced to closed textual forms, cannot be limited to the expressive intentionality of singular authorial voices, and invite the appropriations of others. "Literature" (and this would include all textual forms commodified by intellectual property laws) is literary to this extent.[95] The critical political force of the literary is precisely this force of resistance, or, to rephrase this, a practice is political to the extent that it has literary qualities. Nancy uses this notion of literature or writing to rethink the very concept of political practice: "the political . . . the site where what it means to *be* in common is open to definition and politics . . . the play of forces and interests engaged in a conflict over the representation and governance of social existence."[96]

Community, then, exists only in its communication, and what is communicated is the articulation of difference, not as an identity but as "an opening to alterity."[97] Writing or literature seems to function as an agency or immanent force that opens community to itself. Significantly, Nancy does not attempt to delimit the traits of such writing or dictate the form such literary activities will assume; presumably any human signifying activity could fulfill this political function. Community is always of language but is articulated at its limits; politics is the act of writing at the margins of the social text and community the site where the meaning of collectivity is reopened at its edges.

Literature is undoubtedly a problematic term with which to refer to this voice of interruption or "immanence of alternity,"[98] insofar as its own bourgeois mythology (institutionalized in intellectual property laws) identifies it in discrete and limited forms—in literary works—and denies its social indeterminacy. The idea of the literary work stresses originality, creation, and a unified authorial voice, thus literature—as a noun—is awkward to deploy here. The mythology of literature inconveniences us here in yet another sense. Whereas a community requires (literary and other) works, community is properly realized not in their interpretation—the creation of an authoritative meaning—but in the shared experience of their interruption or unworking.[99] In other words, community is realized in practices that reactivate immanent textualities. Community no longer constitutes a work in its own right, nor can it be understood through its works (canons, institutions, symbols, constitutions) because this would presuppose that its common being were objectifiable. Hence, there are two senses in which politics, for Nancy, presupposes acts of unworking. First, to the extent that a community represents itself essentially as a work, politics calls the essence, parameters, and completion of that work into question. Moreover, to the extent that any community will offer works (of literature, art, state-making) as authoritative representations of the social or as embodying finite meanings, politics involves the imperative to an "unworking" of such fixities from the perspective or in the space of the differences such positivities would occlude.[100] In any work, "there is a share of myth and a share of literature or writing . . . the latter interrupts the former."[101] Although I am less than satisfied with a lack of social agency in Nancy's formulation of interruption, I agree that the possibilities for such interruption or unworking are made available within works themselves, although they do not themselves provide conditions or motivations for their activation. The conditions of intertextuality that Nancy alludes to as making literature the potentially political force that it is have historical conditions of emergence and social particularities of existence.

The notion of an unworked community, "displaced at and as its limit"[102] (also central to the jurisprudence of Drucilla Cornell), is less obscurely developed in the political philosophy of Ernesto Laclau. Laclau's formulations, which emphasize the fundamental role of constitutive alterity in the politics of authoring community, bring us back to the centrality of cultural appropriations as vehicles for cultural politics. In a 1988 interview, Laclau observed that social order was only able to affirm itself as a positivity "insofar as it represses a 'constitutive outside' which negates it." A society never entirely succeeds, therefore, in constituting itself objectively.[103] This position is one that appropriates for political theory Derrida's central notion of *différance*, the idea that determinate meaning is accomplished only in relation to specific orienting horizons. Principles of positive social organization and systems of difference "are endowed with a determinate identity—through contrast with unstable constellations of 'others'—of what differs from themselves."[104] Democracy, then, is understood as the continual tendency toward the affirmation of the "constitutive outside."[105] Challenges to the boundaries of the public sphere from those formerly excluded from making public claims, for example, creates a potentially far greater realm of and for political activity.

The reasons for this lie in the lack of our capacities to fully represent the social world. This is not to suggest that society is meaningless, but that its meaning is never fully transparent to us. The declining faith in reason, in objectivism and positivism, enables us to acknowledge the contingent character of those articulations that gave full meaning to Enlightenment concepts and the categories of modern politics.[106] The most obvious of these are equality and freedom, but public and private, property and speech also present themselves as distinctions ripe for the political projections of others. As spaces for such contestations become open to other, equally contingent articulations, we expand the field we regard as political.

The deconstructivist intervention here is clear: the fulfillment of meaning for any particular category is deferred; rather than an intervention from the level of a social ground that preexists the articulation, "a contingent intervention taking place in an undecidable terrain is exactly what we have called a hegemonic intervention."[107] The social is neither a ground nor a foundation, but precariously constituted in those activities through which it is given expressive and contested meaning. Neither the social nor the subject is ever fully forged and each is constituted through fragile identifications compelled by the absent fullness shared by both subjects and social structures. If "social relations are discursive relations, symbolic relations that constitute themselves through processes of signification,"[108] the constitution of even contingent relations requires expressive activity to create the temporary effects of positivity.

The absent fullness of society, Laclau suggests, manifests itself through "the discursive presences of floating signifiers that are constitutively so."[109] Political forces provide the concrete content for them at any given time, but such signifiers are "not fully exhausted by any of these alternative concrete contents."[110] As one example, he offers "the unity of the British people," but Laclau provides us with no criteria by which we could designate the signifiers that have this socially constitutive quality. Perhaps this is appropriate. Although he seems to imply that the political is forged by the signifying investments of antagonistic social groups in a privileged group of floating signifiers, the implications of his own theory suggest that it would be unwise and impossible to predetermine *which* constellation of cultural forms afford such potential. Only with hindsight do we see how social agents, through expressive practice, invest alternative meanings in particular cultural forms. The Air Canada name, the image of the Mountie, the Olympic logo, the Bart Simpson cartoon, the figure of Paul Bunyan, the body of James Dean, the characters of Kirk and Spock—none of these could have been reliably anticipated as key symbols likely to attract alternative energies. We have seen that particular signs have particular value for particular groups with particular histories and that mass-media-circulated and legally protected signifiers *do* have particular properties that make them especially amenable to such appropriations. We cannot, therefore, delineate the full parameters of a category of speech acts that should be protected because the political *is* fundamentally a force field of expressive activity pushing its own parameters. Just as Sikh mounted police stretched Canadian understandings of the body politic and its defense, so did gay activists expand the Olympic body of human excellence. The arbitrariness of social order "periodically—contingently—prods different groups to call the social order into question and to detach it from the particular 'constitutive outside' that previously defined it."[111]

The parameters of the public sphere as a space of deliberation and recognition are only ever contingently forged. Moreover, they are continuously challenged by the expressive activities of others who may be deemed without standing in political arenas, making appeals with respect to issues first understood to be the private concerns of those who occupy particularistic spaces. Contemporary public spheres must continually incorporate new social developments that press political boundaries. These include both the contestations of those whose specificities had previously excluded them from the bourgeois public sphere (whose particular needs were rendered private issues) and the transformation of relations of representation and reception in a world of globalized media communications.[112] The result of such an engagement is a more inclusive understanding of the political that extends beyond the influence of state policy to potentially include all sites of cultural production and reproduction—to incorporate, in Kirsty McClure's terms, "the politics of direct address."[113]

Laclau's discussion of the political, however, lacks any consideration of the institutions of civil society and the materiality of forces that restrict and shape hegemonic articulations. In this respect his work and his work with his partner and collaborator Chantal Mouffe, departs rather significantly from Gramsci's emphasis on the institutional sites of civil society, which were distinguished both from the economy and from what was called "political society."[114] Rejecting these as absolute distinctions may be empirically appropriate in contemporary conditions, but a refusal to address the materiality of discursive activity, the media of communicative practice, and the logic of commodity relations is less defensible. As Robert Miklitsch puts it, "what escapes their theory is the concept *and* practice of culture."[115] Although Laclau would seem to accept that the logic of the commodity form now infiltrates, if not dominates, lifeworlds, this conceptualization of articulation remains at a level of theoretical abstraction. Articulation, in this view, would seem to require no media nor mediums of communication, and no material obstacles intervene to pose any barriers to access, production, and dissemination. We have seen throughout this volume, however, that cultural forms do have institutional conditions of existence that limit their availability for articulatory practices and powerfully, if incompletely, freeze fields of connotation and protect partial meanings. As Miklitsch explains, such fixations are anticipated but never given significative weight in this theory of articulatory praxis:

> The impossibility of what Laclau and Mouffe call an "ultimate fixity of meaning" presupposes the existence of partial fixations, such as

Laclau and Mouffe themselves observe, even in order "to differ, to subvert meaning, there has to be meaning"... they recognize the necessity of signification ... hence the indispensability, for Laclau and Mouffe, of Lacan's notion of the *points de capiton*, which constitute the privileged discursive points of the partial fixations. But what is the status of these nodal points ... [the] emphasis is firmly on the fictional and differential nature of these partial fixations ... [116]

Laclau stresses the infinite force of the excess in language, rather than the structural limits or institutional obstacles to dislocation or the state's bestowal of particular legal capacities upon market agents to effect partial fixations of social meaning and to shape and contain the articulatory agencies of others. These limits, institutions, and capacities are at the heart of civil society in capitalist cultures.

The social and political orders in which we live are contingent creations that we ourselves discursively construct. It is through creative cultural practices of articulation that the social world is given meaning and, hence, it is always contestable and open to rearticulations. Practices of articulating social difference are central to democratic politics. All knowledges of social identity presuppose symbolic systems of difference, and representational structures of difference are, by their very nature, incapable of achieving closure. No structure of differential identity is ever final; new forms of difference are always emergent, and new social identities continually assert their legitimacy and presence. Indeed, advances in the democratization of Western societies are dependent upon "autonomous initiatives starting from different points within the social fabric,"[117] as new groups constitute themselves politically.

A democratically inclusive political community is one in which "the public sphere recognizes the [indeterminate] diversity of identities people bring to it":

Identity formation needs thus to be approached as a part of the process of public life, not something that can be fully settled prior to it in a private sphere. The liberal model of the public sphere needs reexamination insofar as it depends on disqualifying discourse about the differences among actors ... because if it is impossible to communicate seriously about basic differences among members of a public sphere, then it may be impossible also to address the differences of communication across lines of basic difference ... In a basic and intrinsic sense, if the public sphere has the capacity to alter civil society and to shape the state, then its own democratic practice must confront the questions of membership and the identity of the

> political community it represents ... participation always holds the possibility not just of settling arguments or planning action but of altering identities.[118]

In a postmodern context, there is no reason to privilege a priori any particular subject positions. Rather, we need to consider the contemporary political world as one of multifaceted struggles among peoples continually articulating new social identities from discursive resources. Democratic politics is essentially a dialogic process whereby social identities are continually emergent in political articulation. A radical and plural democracy must maintain optimal conditions for encouraging such articulations. Democracy is endangered by forces that impose closure upon language and when groups close around fixed positivities of identity. Any universal or preordained concept of the subject must therefore be relinquished. Continually emergent social groups gather facts *and* fictions into "identities"—partial and contingent constellations that are bases for recognition and legitimation, aspirations for and alterations of social structurations.

Articulations of identity, challenges to social positivities, and transformative identifications are possible only in conditions of polysemy and symbolic ambiguity where cultural resources for contesting meaning and asserting identity are open to transformation. In conditions of postmodernity, however, our cultural resources are increasingly the properties of others, and many meanings are monopolized by elites who control the commodified texts that pervade our social lives. These are the cultural images with which politically salient forms of difference may increasingly be shaped. Whose identities will be authorized and whose authorship will be recognized? As the cultural cosmos in which we live becomes increasingly commodified, we will need to define and defend the cultural practices of articulation with which we author the social world and construct the identities we occupy within it.

Democratic dialogue will also, therefore, require more than equal access to the forums and channels of communication, the material conditions for conversation. It will require consideration of appropriate access to the symbolic means of communication, the cultural conditions for conversation. If the most powerful signifiers and those most widely disseminated are the private properties of an elite—if their meanings are controlled and their polysemy exclusively possessed—it becomes impossible to engage in dialogic interaction with and within the historical lifeworld in which we are situated. The social systems of signification through which a dialogic democracy constitutes itself must be available not merely to convey information—an unduly reductivist understanding of human communication—but to express identity, community, and social aspiration in the service of imagining and constructing alternative social universes. Regardless of those who assert them, such dialogic practices may be of larger social benefit, for they provide conversational means for new allegiances and affiliations, the basis for recognizing the other in one's self and one's identification with others. Dialogic practices must be public and widely visible to serve these purposes; this is only possible when they can be mass-disseminated. In a market economy this will necessarily involve mass reproduction and distribution processes linked to the commerce that increasingly constitutes relations of communication. No pristine space of noncommercial dialogic exchange need be insisted upon, nor is it appropriate to privilege particular discursive sites, cultural mediums, or signifying vehicles as posing the parameters of the properly political. Politics can assume no proper name(s).

An Ethics of Contingency

Ethical alternity is not just the command of the Other, it is also the Other within the *nomos* that invites us to new worlds and reminds us that transformation is not only possible, it is inevitable.—Drucilla Cornell, *The Philosophy of the Limit*[119]

For those whom history has denied access to dialogue, and those whose social positioning as objects for the self-definition of subjects in modern public spheres still colors their public representations, the political articulation of identity may require further measures. To the extent that Native peoples, for example, still occupy the space of specularized alterity in mass-mediated public spheres, freedom of access to signification is unlikely to provide them with political voice. The continuing proliferation of commodities that circulate in their purported image may socially foreclose the space for the literary: the inscription of less mythical identities and the soundings of more politically audible subjectivities. A truly dialogic democracy might be one in which we respect a prohibition on the commodification of some signifiers as commodities, to the extent that recognizing authorial possession of the signs of alterity may well suppress the ability of others to articulate social identity. Just as the sacrifice of images of blacks as properties in commerce was seen as necessary to create cultural space for the creation of African American identities, so too the imagery of Indian alterity must be abandoned (or gifted) to create political room in the public spheres of mass commerce.

Participatory democracies confronting postcolonial struggles in postmodern conditions cannot rely upon abstract, universalist principles of conversation inherited from the modern era. Neither an abstract commitment to some universal access to cultural forms—a commons of signification—nor the vigilant protection of private estates will serve as the basis for an ethics or politics with relation to commodity/signs. In some instances, as we have seen, to enforce property rights is to avail corporate censorship; in others, free access to signifiers will effect forms of social disenfranchisement. The issue here is not one of absolute access or absolute prohibition. Rather, we need to ask what forms of social relationships with respect to commodified representation will facilitate the expansion of spaces hospitable to expressive articulations that call the social into being by calling it into question. Within such spaces the political is emergent.

The resistances, imaginative strategies, and creative reappropriations enacted by subjects alienated from networks of public expression and representation are potentially political practices to the extent that relations of social production and cultural reproduction are thereby challenged. Forged "in a collective experience of marginalization and expropriation," the activities of such counterpublics may offer "forms of solidarity and reciprocity," but "these forms are inevitably experienced as mediated."[120] Lesbian hermaphrodites, *Star Trek* fanziners, and Native activists reclaiming the signifiers of their subjugation under nineteenth-century imperialist expansion are all united as communities of self-fashioning by experiences expressed in relation to media forms that they neither possess nor control but can and do make their own in specific ways. Our legal institutions must abandon universalisms that prohibit the emergence and expression of alterity. Only a legality attentive to an ethics of contingency can accommodate such proliferations of difference.

As political theorist William Connelly suggests, such an ethical sensibility "opens up new uncertainties within established terms of judgment"[121] by drawing attention to the "ambiguity and arbitrariness in cultural norms that have become naturalized."[122] Rather than give priority to any given systems of identity and their internal boundaries, the cultivation of a postmodern ethical sensibility draws sustenance from contingency in identities, recognizing that the abundance in human cultural capacities exceeds any particular organization of it.[123] By exposing the "artifice in hegemonic identities and the definitions of otherness through which they propel their self-certainty," we may also "destabilize codes of moral order within which prevailing identities are set."[124] Such an ethical sensibility accords with the requirements of an ethos of democracy[125] that would encourage "disturbances of sedimented identities that conceal violence in their terms of closure, practices that permit multifarious styles of life to coexist in the same territory, and a plurality of political identifications that extend beyond the state" and de-emphasize state-centered politics.[126] An interrogation of authorship and the alterities it produces is but one step in bringing such a sensibility to bear upon considerations of legal practice. It is, however, one that is crucial given the massive growth of communications technologies and the distributional effects contingent upon the maintenance of modern fictions of authorship and their pre-judgments of alterity: "a postmodern theory of justice allows otherness to survive and become a theoretical space through which to criticize the operations of the law's ceaseless repetitions . . . Justice returns to ethics when it recognizes the embedded voice of the litigant, when it gives the other in her concrete materiality a *locus standi* or place of enunciation. The law is necessarily committed to the form of universality and abstract equality; but a just decision must also respect the requests of the contingent, incarnate and concrete other, it must pass through the ethics of alterity in order to respond to its own embeddedness in justice."[127] An "ethically committed politics of law," suggest British critical legal scholars Douzinas, Goodrich, and Hachamovitch, must acknowledge "the symbolic and substantive domains and implications of legal practice" and the exclusions, inequalities, and injustices that are routinely effected in the law's name.[128] "Ethics precedes law, it is the precondition and horizon of the political—the making of law—while justice is the precondition of legality . . . the critical concern with the ethical is a return to the political and an embrace of responsibility: for the other, for the stranger, the outsider, the alien or underprivileged who needs the law, who needs, in the oldest sense of the term, to have a hearing, to be heard."[129]

An ethics of contingency in the field of intellectual properties must be cultivated if we are to do justice in a world where new communications technologies enable ever greater flows of cultural goods and new possibilities for communities, identities, and solidarities to be forged, and to afford cultural opportunities for social transformation. Global circulations of texts provide enormous political opportunities, but these may well be foreclosed if we insist upon preserving and expanding intellectual property protections appropriate to an earlier era. An ongoing interrogation of authorship, an opening to alterity, and an ethics of contingency pose pressing challenges as we create conditions conducive to dialogic democracy.

Notes

Introduction: Authoring Culture

1   Quoted in K. Winkler, "An Anthropologist of Influence: Clifford Geertz Relishes Experimentation and Refuses to Be Pigeonholed," *The Chronicle of Higher Education* 5 May 1995, at a16, a23.
2   M. de Certeau, *The Practice of Everyday Life* xi–xii (1984).
3   White v. Samsung Electronics America Inc., 989 F.2d 1512, 1512-13 (9th Cir. 1993).
4   E. Leach, *Custom, Law, and Terrorist Violence* 19 (1977).
5   Standing in line amid the predictable layout of the coffee bar (it's probably a legally protected form of trade dress), I notice the lovely graphics of the early-twentieth-century cigarette advertisements, now enlarged and framed to hang on walls. Their availability for this purpose is a consequence of the expiry of copyright protection for the advertisements, but savvy marketers know only too well that you need only provide them with a new format to set the royalties flowing once again. Although the original image may not be protected as an exclusive property, the new presentation of it will be. In any case, the copyright notice will scare off a good number of competitors regardless of its legitimacy or the extent of its coverage. (Witness, for instance, the number of old fruit crate labels and Southern racist product logos that have been purportedly revived as exclusive properties in the form of copyrighted postcards.) I glance at the display of merchandise in the coffee shop. "Old" "colonial" trademarks have been newly reproduced to stick on bags of coffee and adorn overpriced mugs, while "new" varieties of expensive Colombian beans are marketed with narratives of imperialist nostalgia. Scorning the brand-name coffees embraced by our parents, we are nonetheless eager to embrace ever-emergent symbolic distinctions in "unbranded" goods.

  The social passages from advertisement to ambience, distinction to genericity, labor to logo to libertinism (the Armed and Hammered parody), or standardization to sophistication that are congealed in these encounters are complex but typical of relationships of symbolic exchange (as well as capitalist patterns of manufacturing difference and consumer behaviors of social differentiation).

  In the window of a Latin American import shop I recognize a familiar logo, but I can decipher no more—the rest of the label is in Spanish. Jars of Nescafé® are imported from Latin America to sell to immigrant families from Ecuador and Colombia, nostalgic for the tastes of home. In mass markets, I muse, "the real thing" must be authenticated by figures of standardization; somehow the trademark embodies the security and comfort afforded by familiar distinctions. This speculation is only slightly complicated when I find Jacob's Krim Krakers from Malaysia in an Asian grocery—next to the more familiar Jacob's Cream Crackers offered at a lower price. The cost of importing the pidgin packaging is clearly substantial. Also on display are varieties of tinned beans, canned by Mr Gouda's. Once the main source of mass-marketed Caribbean foodstuffs in Toronto—the only source of ackee, for example—the company now markets garbanzo, pinto, and kidney beans under the banner "Multicultural." How long, I wonder, before they claim the trademark rights in the use of this term for the marketing of dry goods?

6   Those concerned with interpretive issues, however, focus primarily on the interpretation of legal texts, with some lesser attention to the interpretation of legal facts. For an overview of the field of "law and interpretation" see R. J. Coombe, "Same as It Ever Was: Rethinking the Politics of Legal Interpretation," 34 *McGill Law Journal* 603 (1989) (*hereinafter* Coombe, "Same as It Ever Was"). For the interpretation of legal fact see C. Geertz, *Local Knowledge* (1983); K. L. Scheppele, "Facing Facts in Legal Interpretation," in *Law and the Order of Culture* 42 (R. Post, ed., 1991); K. L. Scheppele, "Manners of Imagining the Real," 14 *Law and Social Inquiry* 995 (1995).

7   For representative examples see K. Aoki, "Authors, Inventors, and Trademark Owners: Private Intellectual Property and the Public Domain," Parts I and II, 18 (1,2) *Columbia-VLA Journal of Law and the Arts* 1, 191 (1993, 1994); K. Aoki, "(Intellectual) Property and Sovereignty: Notes Toward a Cultural Geography of Authorship," 48 *Stanford Law Review* 1293 (1996); M. Chon, "Postmodern 'Progress': Reconsidering the Copyright and Patent Power," 43 *Depaul Law Review* 97 (1993); M. Chon, "New Wine Bursting from Old Bottles: Collaborative Internet Art, Joint Works, and Entrepreneurship," 75 *Oregon Law Review* 257 (1996); R. C. Dreyfuss, "Expressive Genericity: Trademarks as Language in the Pepsi Generation," 65 *Notre Dame Law Review* 397 (1990); R. Cooper Dreyfuss, "We Are Symbols and Inhabit Symbols, So Why Should We Be Paying Rent? Deconstructing the Lanham Act and Rights of Publicity," 20 *Columbia-VLA Journal of Law and the Arts* 123 (1996); D. M. Koenig, "Joe Camel and the First Amendment: The Dark Side of Copyrighted and Trademark-Protected Icons," 11 *T. M. Cooley Law Review* 803 (1994); A. Kozinski, "Trademarks Unplugged," 68 *New York University Law Review* 960 (1993); A. Kozinski, "Mickey and Me," 11 *University of Miami Entertainment and Sports Law Review* 465 (1994); D. Lange, "At Play in the Fields of the Word: Copyright and the Construction of Authorship in the Post-Literate Millennium," 55 *Law and Contemporary Problems* 139 (1992); J. Litman, "The Public Domain," 39 *Emory Law Journal* 965 (1990); J. Litman, "Mickey Mouse Emeritus: Character Protection and the Public Domain," 11 *University of Miami Entertainment and Sports Law Review* 429 (1994); J. Litman, "The Exclusive Right to Read," 13 *Cardozo Arts and Entertainment Law Journal* 29 (1994); J. Litman, "Revising Copyright Law for the Information Age," 75 *Oregon Law Review* 19 (1996); M. Madow, "Private Ownership and Public Image: Popular Culture and Publicity Rights," 81 *California Law Review* 125 (1993).

8   Law and culture(s) emerge conceptually as autonomous realms of being in Enlightenment and Romantic imaginaries; they share a parallel historical trajectory in ideologies that legitimate and naturalize bourgeois class power and global European hegemonies. To ask how it became possible to frame questions in these terms—under what conditions it became conceivable to comprehend law as something that regulates culture or culture as something that helps us to understand law—is to in-

quire into a history of mutual implication in European modes of domination. Recognition of the Eurocentric, racist, and colonialist provenance of these categories does, however, open up conceptual space for new avenues of inquiry. Whether this interdisciplinary opportunity is deemed a cultural studies of law, a critical legal anthropology, and/or a genre of cultural studies matters less than a continuing rejection of reified concepts of law and culture. I develop this point at more length in R. J. Coombe, "Contingent Articulations: A Critical Cultural Studies of Law," in *Law in the Domains of Culture* 21 (A. Sarat and T. Kearns, eds., 1998). See P. Fitzpatrick, *The Mythology of Modern Law* (1992), and R. Young, *Colonial Desire: Hybridity in Theory, Culture and Race* (1995), for discussions of the histories of the emergence of law and culture as discrete and autonomous realms.

9 P. Brantlinger, *Crusoe's Footprints: Cultural Studies in Britain and America* 64 (1990).

10 Most scholars of law and society write against law as a body of self-sufficient doctrine or law as an autonomous set of institutions and also reject the abstractions of structuralist analysis of law or liberal legal discourse, even when such practices are allegedly critical, as they are in critical legal studies and critical race theory. These might be seen as propensities to write "against law" in the sense that these scholars are writing against its dominant self-representations.

11 See M. Rosenthal, "What Was Postmodernism?," 22(3) *Socialist Review* 83 (1993). Actually, "dated," "tired," and "passe" are the terms he uses, ironically and unconsciously evoking the same sense of arbitrary, market-based fashion cycles as determinative of significance that critics cited as their reason for rejecting the term in the first place.

12 A. McRobbie, *Postmodernism and Popular Culture* 1 (1994).

13 *Ibid.*

14 A. B. Weiner, "Culture and Our Discontents," 97(1) *American Anthropologist* 14 (1995).

15 McRobbie, *supra* note 12, at 1.

16 Most early dialogue employing the concept of the postmodern was concerned with the continuing social value of Enlightenment philosophical traditions. Lyotard, Rorty, Derrida, and Foucault engaged in critiques of the Cartesian or Kantian tradition, asserting the pernicious impossibility of grandiose European desires to define foundational truths that would guarantee the legitimacy of political and intellectual practices. In debates with Jürgen Habermas, who seeks to preserve the project of modernity, they disseminated the term postmodern as a reproof of universal reason and a challenge to the legitimating myths of modernity. They posited, instead, an antifoundationalism that described the simultaneity of plural teleologies and violent ruptures (against the idea of a linear historical evolution of progress toward a state of universal reason) and the inescapable heterogeneity of contemporary cultural life.

To cultural anthropologists, for whom the diversity of language games, plurality of worldviews, multiplicity of cultural histories, and incommensurably of forms of life are staples of the discipline, this is not a particularly novel observation. The hermeneutic tradition acknowledged this as its point of departure. What distinguishes a postmodern approach is the insistence upon the incommensurable within cultures, forms of life, or language games. As an example, Lyotard sees participation in language games as a struggle or conflict, involving agonistic play. See J.-F. Lyotard, *The Postmodern Condition* (1984), *Explaining the Postmodern* (1992), and *The Postmodern Explained* (1993).

17 The literature exploring the political problematic of representation in ethnographic writing is now quite extensive. For representative discussions of the topic, see J. Clifford, *The Predicament of Culture: Twentieth-Century Ethnography, Literature, and Art* (1988) (*hereinafter* Clifford, *The Predicament of Culture*); *Writing Culture: The Poetics and Politics of Ethnography* (J. Clifford and G. Marcus, eds., 1986); G. Marcus and M. Fischer, *Anthropology as Cultural Critique: An Experimental Moment in the Human Sciences* (1985); P. S. Sangren, "Rhetoric and the Authority of Ethnography: Postmodernism and the Social Reproduction of Texts," 29 *Current Anthropology* 405 (1988); *Fieldnotes: The Makings of Anthropology* (R. Sanjek, ed., 1990); P. Stoller, *The Taste of Ethnographic Things: The Senses in Anthropology* (1989); S. Tyler, "The Poetic Turn in Postmodern Anthropology," 86 *American Anthropologist* 328 (1984); S. Tyler, "Postmodern Anthropology," in *Discourse and the Social Life of Meaning* (P. P. Chock and J. R. Wyman, eds., 1986).

18 See J. Boyle, "Is Subjectivity Possible? The Post-Modern Subject in Legal Theory," 62 *University of Colorado Law Review* 489 (1991); M. Frug, "Law and Postmodernism: The Politics of a Marriage," 62 *University of Colorado Law Review* 483 (1991); D. Patterson, "Postmodernism/Feminism/Law," 77 *Cornell Law Review* 254 (1992); P. Schlag, "The Problem of the Subject," 69 *Texas Law Review* 1627 (1991); P. Schlag, "Foreword: Postmodernism and Law," 62 *University of Colorado Law Review* 439 (1991); J. Wicke, "Postmodern Identity and the Legal Subject," 62 *University of Colorado Law Review* 455 (1991), for some examples. One recent exception is *Legal Studies as Cultural Studies: A Reader in (Post) Modern Critical Theory* (J. D. Leonard, ed., 1995), although, as the title would indicate, the editor is reluctant to deploy the term.

19 For Weiner, this is a politicized view of postmodernism. It differs from the literary mode of entry through which the discipline first encountered the term, where the issue was one of anthropology's modes of representation: "the postmodern focus on how power is generated and diffused through dislocation and difference and through space-time disjunctures is essential for understanding the global transformations that are rapidly unfolding. To reject postmodernism out of hand as if all its positions are antithetical (or heretical) is to return to an anthropology of the past that only can alienate us from the major Western and non-Western discourses of this and future decades" (Weiner, *supra* note 14, at 15).

20 McRobbie, *supra* note 12.

21 R. Rosaldo, *Culture and Truth: The Remaking of Social Analysis* 30–38 (1989).

22 Geertz, *supra* note 6, at 6.

23 See Rosaldo, *supra* note 21, at 27–30; W. Roseberry, *Anthropologies and Histories: Essays in Culture, History, and Political Economy* 24–25 (1989); and Stoller, *supra* note 17, at 56–68.

24 L. Abu-Lughod, "Writing against Culture," in *Recapturing Anthropology: Working in the Present* 137, 139 (R. J. Fox, ed., 1991) (*hereinafter Recapturing Anthropology*).

25 Rosaldo, *supra* note 21, at 43.

26 J. Clifford, "Introduction: Partial Truths," in Clifford and Marcus, *supra* note 17.

27 R. Lederman, "Contested Order: Gender and Society in the Southern New Guinea Highlands," 16 *American Ethnologist* 230 (1989). Lederman criticizes a dominant tendency in ethnographic work on the New Guinea Highlands that represents these societies in terms of male-dominated clan relationships, giving the exchange networks in which women are prominently involved secondary or negligible significance. Such an emphasis does not represent these societies as effectively as it echoes

and gives legitimacy to a specific, interested indigenous perspective—an ideology of male dominance—that is contested by women and disputable even among men.

28 See H. Moore, *A Passion for Difference: Anthropology and Gender* (1994).

29 *The Anti-Aesthetic: Essays on Postmodern Culture* ix, x (H. Foster, ed., 1983).

30 S. Connor, *Postmodernist Culture: An Introduction to Theories of the Contemporary* 228 (1989).

31 N. Thomas, "Against Ethnography," 6 *Cultural Anthropology* 306, 312 (1991).

32 *Ibid.* at 312.

33 Weiner, *supra* note 14, at 15.

34 T. Turner, "Anthropology and Multiculturalism: What Is Anthropology That Multiculturalism Should Be Mindful of It?," 8(4) *Cultural Anthropology* 411, 420 (1993).

35 Brantlinger, *supra* note 9, at ix. A good history is provided in I. Davies, *Cultural Studies and Beyond* (1995). Summary overviews of cultural studies abound; metatheories of the field's coverage and import are now almost as ubiquitous as examples of the genre. Toby Miller provides an irreverent overview of the overviews and a copious bibliography in "Introducing *Screening Cultural Studies*," 7(2) *Continuum* 11 (1994). Aware that no state-of-the-art summary would be complete, or completely satisfy those who identify with the practice, I think that the admittedly partial trajectory in my text is likely to find wide assent.

36 A. Appadurai, "Global Ethnoscapes," in *Recapturing Anthropology, supra* note 24, at 196. See also A. Appadurai, *Modernity at Large: Cultural Dimensions of Globalization* (1996).

37 "These passages beyond the text [in the formalist sense] or even beyond literature by supposedly literary critics are clear challenges to traditional ways of understanding the humanities disciplines. They are all also movements in the direction of a cultural politics that aims to overcome the disabling fragmentation of knowledge within the discursive structure of the university, and in some cases, to overcome the fragmentation and alienation in the larger society that that structure mirrors. In these ways most versions of literary theory point in the direction of a unified, inter- or antidisciplinary theory and practice" (Brantlinger, *supra* note 9, at 16).

38 R. Johnson, "What Is Cultural Studies Anyway?," 16 *Social Text* 38, 39 (1987).

39 The phrase is borrowed from J. D. Peters, "Seeing Bifocally: Media, Place, Culture," in *Culture, Power, Place: Explorations in Critical Anthropology* 75 (A. Gupta and J. Ferguson, eds., 1997).

40 *Ibid.*

41 *Ibid.*, at 47.

42 McRobbie, *supra* note 12, at 26. See also G. Marcus, "Past, Present and Emergent Identities: Requirements for Ethnographies of Late Twentieth-Century Modernity Worldwide," in *Modernity and Identity* 309 (S. Lash and J. Friedman, eds., 1992), and G. Marcus and F. R. Myers, "The Traffic in Art and Culture: An Introduction," in *The Traffic in Culture: Refiguring Art and Anthropology* 1 (G. Marcus and F. Myers, eds., 1995).

43 Abu-Lughod, *supra* note 24, at 139.

44 *Ibid.*, at 143.

45 Thomas, *supra* note 31.

46 *Ibid.*, at 310.

47 M. R. Trouillot, "Anthropology and the Savage Slot: The Poetics and Politics of Otherness," in *Recapturing Anthropology, supra* note 24, at 17.

48 *Ibid.*, at 35.
49 *Ibid.*
50 *Ibid.*, at 38.
51 *Ibid.*, at 39.
52 D. B. Gewertz and F. K. Errington, "First Contact with God: Individualism, Agency, and Revivalism in the Duke of York Islands," 8 *Cultural Anthropology* 279 (1993).
53 *Ibid.*, at 279.
54 *Ibid.* See, however, D. B. Gewertz and F. K. Errington, "On Pepsico and Piety in a Papua New Guinea 'Modernity,'" 23 *American Ethnologist* 476 (1996).
55 Rosaldo, *supra* note 21, at 199.
56 A. Ross, Introduction, in *Universal Abandon?* (A. Ross, ed., 1988) at xiv.
57 M. Sahlins, *Culture and Practical Reason* (1976).
58 J. Clifford, *The Predicament of Culture, supra* note 17, at 237, citing C. Lévi-Strauss, "New York in 1941," in C. Lévi-Strauss, *The View from Afar* 258, 266 (1985).
59 *Ibid.*, at 237.
60 *Ibid.*, at 245.
61 The classic discussion of this is found in J. Fabian, *Time and the Other: How Anthropology Makes Its Object* (1983). A more historically nuanced context is provided by E. Wolf, *Europe and the People without History* (1982). A recent overview may be found in B. McGrane, *Beyond Anthropology* (1989).
62 For influential discussions, see *Cultural Politics in Contemporary America* (I. Angus and S. Jhally, eds., 1989); A. Appadurai, "Disjuncture and Difference in the Global Cultural Economy," 2 *Public Culture* 1 (1990); D. Harvey, *The Condition of Postmodernity* (1989); J. Hinkson, "Postmodernism and Structural Change," 2 *Public Culture* 82 (1990); F. Jameson, *Postmodernism, Or, the Cultural Logic of Late Capitalism* (1991). A more comprehensive and recent discussion of the relationship between postindustrialism and postmodernism may be found in K. Kumar, *From Post-Industrial to Post-Modern Society: New Theories of the Contemporary World* (1995). Interesting case studies in cultural studies may be found in *Global/Local: Cultural Production and the Transnational Imaginary* (R. Wilson and W. Dissanayake, eds., 1996), and in anthropology in *Siting Culture* (K. Olwig and K. Hastrup, eds., 1996) and *Culture, Power, Place* (A. Gupta and J. Ferguson, eds., 1997).
63 Both Grant Kester and Neil Lazarus make significant interventions questioning the propriety and political effects of using the term *postindustrial* to refer to the increasing significance of information and its management in new forms of capital accumulation. Obscuring the real labor done both at home and abroad, it further devalues those who are already increasingly marginalized in so-called global economies. See G. H. Kester, "Out of Sight Is Out of Mind: The Imaginary Space of Postindustrial Culture," 35 *Social Text* 72 (1993); N. Lazarus, "Doubting the New World Order: Marxism, Realism, and the Claims of Postmodernist Social Theory," 3(3) *Differences* 94 (1991).
64 This is a very complex process. I refer the reader to S. Sassen, *Cities in a World Economy* (1994); S. Sassen, *The Global City: London, Tokyo, New York* (1991), and *World Cities in a World System* (P. L. Knox and P. Taylor, eds., 1995).
65 Conversation with Sally Merry at the Law and Society Association Meetings in Toronto, 1995.
66 I honestly don't remember where I heard this.

67 G. Starret, "The Political Economy of Religious Commodities in Cairo," 97 *American Anthropologist* 51 (1995).

68 Conversation with Mamadou Diouf at the Conference on Globalization, University of Chicago Humanities Institute, February 1995.

69 See D. Morley and K. Robins, *Spaces of Identity: Global Media, Electronic Landscapes and Cultural Boundaries* (1995), for an extensive if not exhaustive discussion of debates over cultural homogenization and heterogeneity in media and communications studies. The work, however, draws upon few ethnographic studies of local interpretive practice, except in the area of television viewing. More ethnographic studies may be found in *Cross-Cultural Consumption: Global Markets, Local Realities* (D. Howes, ed., 1996); D. Miller, *Modernity: An Ethnographic Approach* (1994); D. Miller, *Capitalism: An Ethnographic Approach* (1997); *Worlds Apart: Modernity through the Prism of the Local* (D. Miller, ed., 1995); and *Acknowledging Consumption* (D. Miller, ed., 1995).

70 R. Fox, Introduction, in *Recapturing Anthropology, supra* note 24, at 6.

71 J. Comaroff and J. Comaroff, *Ethnography and the Historic Imagination* (1992). See also *Modernity and Its Malcontents: Ritual and Power in Postcolonial Africa* (J. Comaroff and J. Comaroff, eds., 1993); *Global Modernities* (M. Featherstone et al., eds., 1995); M. Featherstone, "Localism, Globalism, and Cultural Identity" in *Global/Local: Cultural Production in the Transnational Imaginary* 46 (R. Wilson and W. Dissanayake, eds., 1996); A. Pred and M. J. Watts, *Reworking Modernity: Capitalism and Symbolic Discontent* (1992); and Appadurai, *Modernity at Large, supra* note 36.

72 A. Ong, *Spirits of Resistance and Capitalist Discipline: Factory Women in Malaysia* (1987).

73 M. Taussig, *The Devil and Commodity Fetishism in South America* (1980); J. Nash, *We Eat the Mines and the Mines Eat Us: Dependency and Exploitation in Bolivian Tin Mines* (1979); J. Clark, "Gold, Sex, and Pollution: Male Illness and Myth at Mt. Kare, Papua New Guinea," 20 *American Ethnologist* 742 (1993).

74 M. Crain, "Poetics and Politics in the Ecuadorian Andes: Women's Narratives of Death and Devil Possession," 18 *American Ethnologist* 67 (1991); L. Hirschkind, "Dedevilled Ethnography," 21(1) *American Ethnologist* 201 (1994); M. Crain, "Opening Pandora's Box: A Plea for Discursive Heteroglossia," 21(1) *American Ethnologist* 205 (1994).

75 See J. Tobin, "Introduction: Domesticating the West," in *Re-Made in Japan: Everyday Life and Consumer Taste in a Changing Society* 1 (J. Tobin, ed., 1992), for an alternative reading of the ways in which American trademarks have been "read" in Japan. See also A. Masquelier, "Encounter with a Road Sign: Machines, Bodies and Commodities in the Imagination of a Mawri Healer," 8 *Visual Anthropology Review* 56 (1992); A. Stambach, *Curl Up and Dye*, paper presented at the conference The Struggle for Civil Society in Postcolonial Africa at the University of Chicago, 31 May–2 June 1996; B. Weiss, *The Making and Unmaking of the Haya Lived World: Consumption, Commoditization, and Everyday Practice* (1996); L. White, "Cars out of Place: Vampires, Technology and Labor in East and Central Africa," 43 *Representations* 27 (1993); and the books and anthologies by Daniel Miller, cited *supra* note 69.

76 T. Burke, *Lifebuoy Men, Lux Women: Commodification, Consumption, and Cleanliness in Modern Zimbabwe* (1996).

77 R. Coombe and P. Stoller, "X Marks the Spot: The Ambiguities of African Vending in

the Commerce of Black Public Spheres," 7 *Public Culture* 249 (1994), reprinted in *The Black Public Sphere* 253 (The Black Public Sphere Collective, ed., 1995).

78 Abu-Lughod, *supra* note 24, at 147.

79 See discussion of P. Bourdieu, *Outline of a Theory of Practice* (1977), in R. Brightman, "Forget Culture: Replacement, Transcendence, Reflexification," 10 *Cultural Anthropology* 509, 513 (1995).

80 Abu-Lughod, *supra* note 24, at 147. The ethnographic representation of Mediterranean societies as unified by the cultural honor/shame complex, for example, is similarly affected by a failure to acknowledge the differential meanings given to these values by those in different social positions. See R. J. Coombe, "Barren Ground: Reconceiving Honour and Shame in the Field of Mediterranean Ethnography," 32(2) *Anthropologica* 221 (1990). Along the same lines, Nicole Polier and William Roseberry assert that among the Solomon Islands Kwaio, ancestral custom is an arena of ongoing negotiation, in which women question authoritative definitions within a field of meaning traditionally understood as the legitimate preserve of male elders. See N. Polier and W. Roseberry, "Tristes Tropes: Postmodern Anthropologists Encounter the Other and Discover Themselves," 18 *Economy and Society* 245 (1989). Janice Boddy suggests that women simultaneously reproduce and rework dominant Islamic meanings in *tsar* possession cults; she contests the erroneous but common assumption that culture in northern Sudan is a monolithic, masculine preserve. She explores differential female and male readings of infibulation in Hofreyat, indicting the reductionism of accounts that merely recount those meanings that the powerful bestow upon culturally salient practices. See J. Boddy, "Anthropology, Feminism and the Postmodern Context," 11 *Culture* 125 (1991). Many more examples could be cited.

81 Postmodernist approaches may also be distinguished from hermeneutic ones by a discomfort with modernity's surface/depth metaphors that "interpreted" cultural life as a mere manifestation of some underlying, deeper structure of reality such as desire, the unconscious, social structure, or the economy. (Marx, Freud, and Lévi-Strauss look equally modern from this vantage.) There are various critiques of the "hermeneutics of suspicion," ranging from the peculiarly celebratory despair of Jean Baudrillard to the humanism of Renato Rosaldo and Paul Stoller. What they have in common is a conviction that representations of cultural phenomena that privilege deep structures do a form of violence to lived experience and usually fail to grasp the meaning of cultural activity to those engaged in it. Drawn to activities (such as ritual and ceremony) most likely to yield recurrences of structure, ethnographers may not consider the more meaningful, if extemporaneous, practices of everyday life.

82 Brantlinger, *supra* note 9, at 37.

83 Connor, *supra* note 30, at 120.

84 *Ibid.*, at 121.

85 F. Munger, "Sociology of Law for a Postliberal Society," 27 *Loyola of Los Angeles Law Review* 89 (1993). See also A. Hunt, *Explorations in Law and Society: Toward a Constitutive Theory of Law* (1993), and S. Lees, "Lawyers' Work as Constitutive of Gender Relations," in *Lawyers in a Postmodern World: Translation and Transgression* 124 (M. Cain and C. Harrington, eds., 1993). For a discussion of the constitutive perspective, see A. Sarat and T. R. Kearns, "Beyond the Great Divide: Forms of Legal Scholarship and Everyday Life," in *Law in Everyday Life* 21 (A. Sarat and T. R. Kearns, eds., 1993).

86 See *Law in Everyday Life, supra* note 85. See also C. McEwen, R. Maiman, and L.

Mather, "Lawyers in Everyday Life: Mediation in Divorce Practice," 28 *Law & Society Review* 149 (1994).

87 S. E. Merry, *Getting Justice and Getting Even: Legal Consciousness among Working-Class Americans* (1990); S. E. Merry, "Resistance and the Cultural Power of Law," 29 *Law & Society Review* 11 (1995); A. Sarat, "'. . . The Law Is All Over': The Legal Consciousness of the Welfare Poor," 2 *Yale Journal of Law and the Humanities* 243 (1990); A. Sarat, "Lawyers and Legal Consciousness: Law Talk in the Divorce Lawyer's Office," 98 *Yale Law Journal* 1663 (1989); *The Rhetoric of Law* (A. Sarat and T. R. Kearns, eds., 1994); A. Sarat and W. Felstiner, *Divorce Lawyers and Their Clients: Power and Meaning in the Legal Process* (1995); S. Silbey and P. Ewick, "Conformity, Contestation, and Resistance: An Account of Legal Consciousness," 26 *New England Law Review* 731 (1992); M. Musheno, "Legal Consciousness on the Margins of Society," 2 *Identities* 102 (1995).

88 Sarat and Kearns, *supra* note 85, at 21. But see L. Nader and T. Plowman, "Anthropology and Everyday Scholarship," 98 *American Anthropologist* 624 (1996).

89 J. L. Comaroff, Foreword, in *Contested States: Law, Hegemony and Resistance* (M. Lazarus-Black and S. Hirsch, eds., 1994) (*hereinafter Contested States*).

90 E. Mertz, "A New Social Constructionism for Sociolegal Studies," 28 *Law & Society Review* 1243, 1246 (1994).

91 S. Hirsch and M. Lazarus-Black, Introduction, in *Contested States*, *supra* note 89, at 1–2.

92 P. Just, "History, Power, Ideology, and Culture: Current Directions in the Anthropology of Law," 26 *Law & Society Review* 373 (1992).

93 Hirsch and Lazarus-Black, *supra* note 91, at 8.

94 *Ibid.*, at 9.

95 Brantlinger, *supra* note 9, at 66.

96 J. Gaines, *Contested Culture: The Image, the Voice, and the Law* (1991).

97 Brantlinger, *supra* note 9, at 66.

98 McRobbie, *supra* note 12, at 40.

99 *Ibid.*, at 41.

100 See J. Fiske and K. Glynn, "Trials of the Postmodern," 9(3) *Cultural Studies* 505 (1995).

101 Theoretical underpinnings for this approach may be discerned in A. Botwinick, *Postmodernism and Democratic Theory* (1993); D. Carroll, "Community after Devastation: Culture, Politics and the 'Public Space,'" in *Politics, Theory and Contemporary Culture* 159 (M. Poster, ed., 1993); *Politics, Postmodernity and Critical Legal Studies: The Legality of the Contingent* (C. Douzinas, P. Goodrich, and Y. Hachamovitich, eds., 1994); E. Laclau, "Power and Representation," in *Politics, Theory and Contemporary Culture* 277 (M. Poster, ed., 1993), and the essays in *The Making of Political Identities* (E. Laclau, ed., 1994); *Community at Loose Ends* (Miami Theory Collective, 1991); D. Scott, "A Note on the Demand of Criticism," 8 *Public Culture* 41 (1995); and J. L. Nancy, *The Inoperative Community* (1991). Judith Butler's work *The Psychic Life of Power* (1997) became available too late to incorporate into my theoretical paradigm, but clearly provides some important insights into the workings of law, power, and identification relevant to the considerations in this volume.

102 *Nation and Narration* 291, 297 (H. Bhabha, ed., 1990). Similar insights into law and

politics may be found in M. McCann, *Rights at Work: Pay Equity Reform and the Politics of Legal Mobilization* (1994), and in L. Bower, "Queer Acts and the Politics of Direct Address: Rethinking Law, Culture and Community," 28 *Law & Society Review* 1009 (1994).

103   The intellectual history behind this agenda is complex; it involves a working through of issues of consciousness, ideology, interpellation, subject-formation, and psychoanalysis, engaging the theoretical work of Marx, Althusser, Gramsci, Foucault, and Lacan.

104   See R. J. Coombe, "Contesting the Self: Negotiating Subjectivities in Nineteenth-Century Ontario Defamation Trials," 11 *Studies in Law, Politics, and Society* 3 (1991), Bower; *supra* note 102; and the essays in the issue edited by J. Collier, B. Maurer, and L. Suarez Navaz, *Sanctioned Identities: Legal Constructions of Modern Personhood*, 2(1, 2) *Identities* 1 (1995).

105   Mertz, *supra* note 90.

106   In so doing, proponents question the tendencies of legal doctrine and statutory dictates, which understand identities in static and fixed terms, embodying a unity and coherence that can be ascertained. Although the term *social constructionist* is an inadequate nomination for the tendencies of this range of scholarship (it harkens back to a sociological phenomenology that was less than cognizant of inequalities in power and in access to and control over discursive resources), this work does portend the dawning of a cultural materialist study of law. I speculate that the term is used to make such work appear less threatening to social science empiricists who would at least recognize this scholarship as stemming from a recognizable lineage that includes scholars such as Shutz, Berger, and Luckman.

107   C. J. Greenhouse, "Constructive Approaches to Law, Culture, and Identity," 29 *Law & Society Review* 1231 (1995).

108   Turner, *supra* note 34, at 426.

109   *Ibid.*, at 427.

110   For McRobbie, identity has been the trope that has transformed cultural studies into a truly critical form of inquiry: "Identity could be seen as dragging cultural studies into the 1990s by acting as a kind of guide to how people see themselves, not as class subjects, not as psychoanalytical subjects, not as subjects of ideology, not as textual subjects, but as active agents whose sense of self is projected onto and expressed in an expansive range of cultural practices, including texts, images, and commodities" (McRobbie, *supra* note 12, at 58).

111   Works addressing intellectual property by James Boyle, Celia Lury, Jane Gaines, and Tom Streeter are welcome exceptions. In *Shamans, Software, and Spleens: Law and the Construction of the Information Society* (1996), Boyle provides a characteristically elegant structuralist analysis of the liberal legal discourses that legitimate new forms of property in the information age under the rubric of authorship. The collapsing of cultural questions into issues of information circulation, however, obscures the worlds of human significance in which cultural forms have social consequence. Moreover, by accepting the entertainment industry position that copyright is a means of managing information in a postindustrial world, the historically fundamental limitation upon copyright—the restriction of protection to prohibitions upon the reproduction of expressive works—is forgone. In my view, this is simply too central—both to copyright's ideology and to any principled boundary to the copyright monopoly—to be ignored, glossed over, or effaced. I make this ar-

gument in more detail in R. J. Coombe, "Left Out on the Information Highway," 75 *Oregon Law Review* 237 (1996), and in "Authorial Cartographies: Mapping Proprietary Borders in a Less-Than-Brave New World," 48(5) *Stanford Law Review* 1357 (1996). In *Selling the Air: A Critique of the Policy of Commercial Broadcasting in the United States* (1996), Streeter shows the pervasive resurgence of the figure of the author in the allocation of property and the attribution of revenue in the wake of new communications technologies. In *Cultural Rights: Technology, Legality and Personality* (1993), Lury provides a historical sociology of the development of various forms of intellectual property, their role in changing forms of social reproduction and in constituting modes of cultural authority. She accords little specificity to the legal frameworks she sees as having such social and cultural significance, however, and the work evinces no concern with the deployment and interpretation of law. In perhaps the first and most original cultural studies volume on the topic, Gaines provides astute readings of significant cases that figure as turning points in American law and transformations in the logic upon which intellectual property protections were based. Insightful as these readings are, however, the work does not always resist the tendency to reify doctrine, adopting a formalist understanding of law as existing primarily and most substantially in its authoritative tomes and reported disputes. See *Contested Culture, supra* note 96. See also the historical studies reviewed in R. J. Coombe, "Contesting Paternity: Histories of Authorship," 6 *Yale Journal of Law and the Humanities* 397 (1994). All of these scholars provide important historical overviews of the evolution of legal structures to which my own work is greatly indebted. None, however, shares the emergent emphasis in cultural studies upon the everyday life of textuality and its imbrication in struggles over identity and community.

Ironically, as Toby Miller reminds us, the British school of cultural studies was initially focused on legal questions, and the Birmingham school was funded with the settlement of a legal struggle involving issues of literature and censorship. Commenting on William Hoggart, Miller remarks: "The oldest of the three men conventionally catalogued as the founding parents of cultural studies, and the first director of the Birmingham Centre, he is oft-listed alongside Raymond Williams and Stuart Hall, but rarely made the subject of equivalent exegetical projections. It is worth remarking that, in Hoggart's phrase, cultural studies always had a significant engagement with the bureaucratic public sphere (also known as the law). Hoggart it was who gave the crucial testimony at the Lady Chatterley trial. Penguin Books it was that subsequently made the endowment-in-gratitude which was used to establish the Centre. And Hoggart it was that served on the United Kingdom's Pilkington Committee on Broadcasting" (T. Miller, "Culture with Power: The Present Moment in Cultural Policy Studies," 22 *Southeast Asian Journal of Social Science* 264, 270 [1994] [notes omitted]).

112   G. Rose, *Dialetic of Nihilism* (1984). For a critical exploration, see A. Pottage, "The Law of the Father," in *The Legality of the Contingent, supra* note 101, at 147.

113   See discussion of Gaines, *supra* note 111.

114   See R. J. Coombe, "Room for Manoeuver: Toward a Theory of Practice in Critical Legal Studies," 14 *Law and Social Inquiry* 69 (1989), for a more elaborated outline of the parameters of such a perspective.

115   Appadurai, "Global Ethnoscapes," *supra* note 36, at 198.

116   *Ibid.*, at 205.

117   What Appadurai does not mention is that all those forms of media experienced by his new cosmopolitans are intellectual properties in their own right; they are not merely forms to be consumed, but forms that are globally policed by their author-owners to protect their economic value. Their availability for the self-fashionings of others is limited by the Eurocentric premises of modernity upon which laws of intellectual property are based and the local life of legal interpretation. For recent work considering the relationship among communications, communities, and identities, see *Cultural Studies and Communications* (J. Curran, D. Morley, and V. Walkerdine, eds., 1996).

118   The concept of "unworking" is borrowed from J.-L. Nancy, *supra* note 101. I discuss his work more fully in my final chapter.

119   M. Foucault, "What Is an Author?," in *The Foucault Reader* 101 (P. Rabinow, ed., 1984).

120   C. Geertz, *Works and Lives: The Anthropologist as Author* 7–8 (1988).

121   M. Manganero, Introduction, in *Modernist Anthropology: From Fieldwork to Text* (M. Manganero, ed., 1990) at 6. For critical discussions of the conditions of possibility for anthropology as a science of "the field" and the misrecognitions thereby availed, see *Anthropological Locations: Boundaries and Grounds of a Field Science* (A. Gupta and J. Ferguson, eds., 1997).

122   See, e.g., V. Adams, *Tigers of the Snow and Other Virtual Sherpas: An Ethnography of Himalayan Encounters* (1996); D. B. Gewertz and F. K. Errington, *Twisted Histories, Altered Contexts: Representing the Chambri in a World System* (1991); R. Keesing, *Custom and Confrontation: The Kwaio Struggle for Cultural Autonomy* (1992); *When They Read What We Write: The Politics of Ethnography* (C. Brettell, ed., 1996), for discussions of how peoples come to rely upon (and reject and transform) anthropological representations of themselves in political self-fashionings and/or seek to have modern ethnographic works created to meet needs for political legitimacy and cultural self-preservation. Anthropology's others may have significant interests in anthropological authorship and its representation of their alterity.

123   Clifford, *The Predicament of Culture, supra* note 17, at 7.

124   Manganero, *supra* note 121, at 23.

125   R. Fox, "For a Nearly New Culture History," in *Recapturing Anthropology, supra* note 24, 101 at 111.

126   See A. Riles, "Representing In-Between: Law, Anthropology, and the Rhetoric of Interdisciplinarity," [1994] *University of Illinois Law Review* 597.

1. Objects of Property and Subjects of Politics

1   V. N. Voloshinov, *Marxism and the Philosophy of Language* 11–13 (L. Matejka and I. R. Titunik, trans., 1973).

2   W. Gordon, "Reality as Artifact: From *Feist* to Fair Use," 55 *Law and Contemporary Problems* 93, 101 (1992).

3   G. D. Cox, "Don't Mess with the Mouse: Disney's Legal Army Protects a Revered Image," *The National Law Journal* (31 July 1989) at 1, 26–27.

4   P. Schlag, "Normative and Nowhere to Go," 43 *Stanford Law Review* 167, 175, and n.23 (1990).

5   Well, of course there's Santa. Santa has long been with us as a European saint named

Nicholas. What few people realize, however, is that until 1931, the old saint was a thin, dark man dressed in drab green or brown. His reincarnation as a plump, twinkling, jolly, white-bearded old chap in a red suit originated in a Coca-Cola advertising campaign (if pressed, I'll provide N. Cornell, "Collecting Christmas," *Sky*, December 1990, at 67, 72, as authority for this. I found this magazine in the seat pocket of an airplane). The artist Haddon Sundblom who received his first commission from the company in 1931 is credited with creating the North American image of Santa Claus. See S. Godfrey, "It May Be the Real Thing but Is It the Right Thing," *The Globe and Mail* 9 November 1991, at C1. Fortunately for North American children and commercial culture, the Coca-Cola Company did not claim trademark rights or copyright in the figure. Had they done so, to produce Santa's likeness might also require authorization. The Royal Ontario Museum held an exhibition entitled *Santa: The Real Thing at the* ROM (November 17, 1991–January 5, 1992), sponsored by the Coca-Cola Company, who provided the Santa memorabilia that documented this history. Thus, authority from the citadels of high culture is now available.

6   The term *dissonant cognitive framework* is borrowed from Schlag, who argues that dissonance among incomprehensible cognitive frameworks characterizes legal thought, legal argument, and legal texts (but that to characterize incommensurability as dissonance itself implies a rational belief in a unified ego). See P. Schlag, "Missing Pieces: A Cognitive Approach to Law," 67 *Texas Law Review* 1195, 1228–1236 (1989).

7   Schlag says that postmodernists believe that all legal texts are polymorphously perverse (*ibid.*, at 1209).

8   Schlag defines the rationalist worldview as one that asks for the redemption and justification of all descriptive and normative claims and that privileges the individual rationalist self and its ability to make normative recommendations about the law's ideal structure through ego-centered reason (*ibid.*, at 1208, 1210–1212).

9   *Ibid.*, at 1217–1220. "Postmodernists breach rules of discourse [because] they believe that form has implications and conventional forms of discourse may be inadequate to express alternative visions. The postmodernist voice is irreverent and typically bent on irony." See, e.g., Schlag, "Normative and Nowhere to Go," *supra* note 4, at 167–177 (comparing normative legal thought to the Top 40 radio charts).

10 "Normative legal thought is in part a routine—our routine. It is the highly repetitive, cognitively entrenched, institutionally sanctioned and politically enforced routine of the legal academy—a routine that silently produces our thoughts and keeps our work channelled within the same old cognitive and rhetorical matrices" (*ibid.*, at 179).

11 Schlag, "Missing Pieces," *supra* note 6, at 1243.

12 M. Chon, "Postmodern 'Progress': Reconsidering the Copyright and Patent Power," 43 *DePaul Law Review* 97, 106, n.26 (1993).

13 Well, I did try.

14 I have appropriated this phrase from P. Stoller, "Speaking in the Name of the Real," 29 *Cahiers d'Etudes Africaines* 113 (1989), who borrowed it from I. Brady, "Introduction to Speaking in the Name of the Real: Freeman and Mead in Samoa," 85 *American Anthropologist* 908 (1983), who appropriated it from M. de Certeau, "History: Ethics, Science and Fiction," in *Social Science as Moral Inquiry* (N. Haan et al., eds., 1983), who discusses reading and writing as textual poaching in *The Practice of Everyday Life* (S. Rendall, trans., 1984).

15   D. Cornell, "Toward a Modern/Postmodern Reconstruction of Ethics," 133 *University of Pennsylvania Law Review* 291, 299 (1985) at 362 (footnote omitted). See also R. J. Coombe, "Room for Manoeuver: Toward a Theory of Practice in Critical Legal Studies," 14 *Law & Social Inquiry* 69, 88–99 (1989), for a discussion of the simultaneously constraining and enabling qualities of signification.

16   For early examples, see S. Brainerd, "The Groundless Assault: A Wittgensteinian Look at Language, Structuralism, and Critical Legal Theory," 34 *American Law Review* 1231 (1985); Coombe, "Room for Manoeuver," *supra* note 15; R. Coombe, "'Same as It Ever Was': Rethinking the Politics of Legal Interpretation," 34 *McGill Law Journal* 603 (1989); M. Minow, *Making All the Difference* (1990); G. Peller, "The Metaphysics of American Law," 73 *California Law Review* 1151 (1985); Schlag, "Missing Pieces," *supra* note 6; Schlag, "Normative and Nowhere to Go," *supra* note 4; P. Schlag, "Fish v. Zapp: The Case of the Relatively Autonomous Self," 76 *Georgetown Law Journal* 37 (1987); S. L. Winter, "Transcendental Nonsense, Metaphoric Reasoning, and the Cognitive Stakes for Law," 137 *University of Pennsylvania Law Review* 1105 (1989); S. L. Winter, "Bull Durham and the Uses of Theory," 42 *Stanford Law Review* 639 (1990). This list is by no means exhaustive of legal theorists who have addressed these issues. Indeed, given the proliferation of scholarship that now works with such premises, it seems rather pointless to continuously attempt to compile such compilations.

17   For two influential early examples, see G. E. Frug, "The Ideology of Bureaucracy in American Law," 97 *Harvard Law Review* 1276 (1984), and J. Boyle, "The Politics of Reason: Critical Legal Theory and Local Social Thought," 133 *University of Pennsylvania Law Review* 685 (1985) (*hereinafter* Boyle, "The Politics of Reason").

18   Coombe, "Same as It Ever Was," *supra* note 16, at 605–610.

19   Winter, "Transcendental Nonsense," *supra* note 16, at 1108.

20   G. Minda, *Postmodern Legal Movements: Law and Jurisprudence at Century's End* 117 (1995).

21   S. L. Winter, "Foreword: On Building Houses," 69 *Texas Law Review* 1595, 1607 (1991); see also S. Winter, "The Cognitive Dimension of the Agon between Legal Power and Narrative Meaning," 87 *Michigan Law Review* 2225, 2230 (1989).

22   For example, some legal feminists have argued against the so-called universality or neutrality of the legal subject, showing how such concepts as the "reasonable man" are fundamentally gendered and reflect the perspectives of the privileged. Others have challenged "the modern concept of the self as the subject that controls discourse and analysis, by exposing how the identity of the subject is an artifact produced by discourse." Critical race theorists reject the objectivity of conventional legal scholarship and deploy narratives that express the felt experiences of subordinated peoples in order to challenge the neutrality of the legal subject with the situated stories of others. See discussions in Minda, *supra* note 20, at 116–148, 155–156, 159–161, 167–174, and the numerous sources cited therein.

23   The following discussion draws upon R. Sullivan, "Marxism and the 'Subject' of Anthropology," in *Modernist Anthropology: From Fieldwork to Text* 243 (M. Manganaro, ed., 1990). More recent anthropological treatments of the varieties of and means of human subject-formation may be found in *Rhetorics of Self-Making* (D. Battaglia, ed., 1995), and *Embodiment and Experience: The Existential Ground of Culture and Self* (T. J. Csordas, ed., 1994).

24   Sullivan, *supra* note 23, at 244. For a fine study of modern subject-formation, atten-

tive to the interplay of discipline and discursivity in creating subjects "before the law," see T. Miller, *The Well-Tempered Self: Citizenship, Culture, and the Postmodern Subject* (1993).

25 Cornell, "Reconstruction of Ethics," *supra* note 15, at 297–298. For a recent overview of Habermas's understanding of subjectivity, which takes the view that the paradigm of knowledge of objects needs to be replaced with a communicative or intersubjective paradigm of mutual understanding by subjects and rejects the self-objectification of a philosophy dominated by the self-reflecting subject, see P. Dews, *The Limits of Disenchantment: Essays on Contemporary European Philosophy* (1995).

26 D. Cornell, *The Philosophy of the Limit* 51 (1992).

27 *Ibid.*, at 52.

28 *Ibid.*

29 Cornell, "Reconstruction of Ethics," *supra* note 15, at 365, quoting R. J. Bernstein, *Beyond Objectivism and Relativism* 162 (1983).

30 *Ibid.*

31 P. Smith, *Discerning the Subject* (1988); P. Smith, "Laclau and Mouffe's Secret Agent," in *Community at Loose Ends* (Miami Theory Collective, ed., 1991).

32 C. F. Stychin, *Law's Desire* 31–32 (1995).

33 Wicke, *supra* note 18 at 457.

34 *Ibid.*, at 458. For perspectives on the postmodern subject in law that are less provincial in their considerations of political economy (although no less utopian), see B. de Sousa Santos, "Three Metaphors for a New Conception of Law: The Frontier, the Baroque, and the South," 29 *Law & Society Review* 569 (1995); R. J. Coombe, "Finding and Losing One's Self in the Topoi: Placing and Displacing the Postmodern Subject in Law," 29 *Law & Society Review* 599 (1995); and the other essays commenting upon Santos contained in that issue.

35 R. M. Thomas, "Milton and Mass Culture: Toward a Postmodernist Theory of Tolerance," 62 *University of Colorado Law Review* 525 (1991). Using elements of Milton's *Areopagitica* as his starting point, Thomas seeks to engage radical democratic postmodernism with the philosophy of freedom of expression to construct a postmodernist theory of tolerance. Thomas points to Milton's anti-essentialist epistemology, his belief in expressive complicity and appropriation, his acceptance of pluralism, and the proximity of Milton's vision of Christian liberty to the postmodernist premise of the decentered self to articulate a postmodernist vision of tolerance for free speech. In developing this position, Thomas examines contemporary speech issues such as hate speech, appropriational art, and pornography, and contrasts the postmodernist position with the attacks against tolerance raised by both leftist and conservative critics of mass popular culture.

36 J. Boyle, "Is Subjectivity Possible? The Post-Modern Subject in Legal Theory," 62 *University of Colorado Law Review* 489 (1991).

37 Boyle, "The Politics of Reason," *supra* note 17.

38 Boyle, "The Post-Modern Subject in Legal Theory," *supra* note 36, at 500.

39 *Ibid.*, at 521 (emphasis is mine). In legal practices, he suggests, we find numerous examples in which the subject is constructed in mutually contradictory ways and occasionally transformed by practices that draw upon the ambiguities of legal precedent and tradition. One might question the distinction Boyle's argument is founded upon—between the subject in legal theory and the subject in legal practice—given its implicit premises about the law's location.

315

40 M. Heiferman and L. Phillips, *Image World: Art and Media Culture* 13 (1989).

41 Cornell, "Reconstruction of Ethics," *supra* note 15, at 365.

42 *Ibid.*

43 W. Gordon, "A Property Right in Self-Expression: Equality and Individualism in the Natural Law of Intellectual Property," 102 *Yale Law Journal* 1533, 1556 (1993) (*hereinafter* Gordon, "A Property Right in Self-Expression").

44 See F. Jameson, *Postmodernism, or, The Cultural Logic of Late Capitalism* (1991), and D. Harvey, *The Condition of Postmodernity: An Enquiry into the Origins of Cultural Change* (1989).

45 See Jameson, *supra* note 44, at xx–xxii, L. Hutcheon, *The Politics of Postmodernism* 1 (1989); S. Connor, *Postmodernist Culture: An Introduction to the Theories of the Contemporary* (1989); A. Ross, Introduction, in *Universal Abandon? The Politics of Postmodernism* viii (A. Ross, ed., 1988); and the papers collected in 5 (2, 3) *Theory, Culture and Society* (1988).

46 For further elaboration of the distinction, see M. Featherstone, "In Pursuit of the Postmodern: An Introduction," 5 *Theory, Culture and Society* 195 (1988).

47 Every day, according to the Association of American Advertising Agencies, the average person is exposed to 1,600 advertisements. Heiferman and Phillips, *supra* note 40, at 18.

48 See D. Kellner, *Jean Baudrillard: From Marxism to Postmodernism and Beyond* (1989), for an extended discussion of Baudrillard's musings on this topic.

49 B. H. Bagdikian, *The Media Monopoly* 4 (3d ed., 1987). See also H. I. Schiller, *Culture, Inc.: The Corporate Takeover of Public Expression* (1989), and H. Schiller, *Information Inequality: The Deepening Social Crisis in America* (1996).

50 A. McRobbie, *Postmodernism and Popular Culture* (1994) (emphasis added).

51 "Five-Year-Olds Make Ruthless Customers," Advertisement for American Express® Card in the inside cover of *Ambassador Magazine*, June 1993. The copy and layout of the advertisement itself is protected by copyright, and the slogan "Don't Leave Home Without It"® is a registered trademark. Indeed, American Express enjoined the use of this slogan to market condoms in 1989. See American Express Co. v. Vibra Approved Laboratories Corp., 1989 U.S. Dist. LEXIS 4377, 10 U.S.P.Q. 2d (BNA) 2006 (S.D.N.Y. 1989).

52 This slogan sometimes accompanies "Stan Mack's Real Life Funnies," a cartoon that appears in the *Village Voice*. It may well be copyrighted.

53 Cox, *supra* note 3.

54 R. Barnet and J. Cavanagh, *Global Dreams: Imperial Corporations and the New World Order* 166 (1994).

55 K. Aoki, "Authors, Inventors, and Trademark Owners: Private Intellectual Property and the Public Domain, Part I," 18(1) *Columbia-VLA Journal of Law and the Arts* 1, n.1 (1993), citing Crosley Bendix and noting the litigation surrounding the unauthorized sampling of the band U2 by a rap band Negativland, who then released a 96-page publication protesting the use of intellectual property laws to prohibit media appropriations in an environment of "canned ideas, images, and sounds" in which artists live and upon which they must comment.

56 W. Gordon, "On Owning Information: Intellectual Property and the Restitutionary Impulse," 78 *Virginia Law Review* 149, 156–157 (1992).

57 Chon, *supra* note 12.

58 Gordon, "Intellectual Property and the Restitutionary Impulse," *supra* note 56, at 151.

59   *Ibid.*, at 153–154 (citations omitted). Gordon rightly notes that the decision of the Supreme Court of the United States that a noncreative compilation of facts should not receive copyright protection seems to tend in the other direction. See Feist Publications v. Rural Tel. Serv. Co., 111 S. Ct. 1282 (U.S.S.C. 1991). But, as she astutely points out, "the very decision that so restrained federal copyright protection for facts, however, unfortunately may have opened the door to *state*-granted private ownership rights in information."

60   See Aoki, "Part I," *supra* note 55; Chon, *supra* note 12; Gordon, "A Property Right in Self-Expression," *supra* note 43; Gordon, "Reality as Artifact," *supra* note 2; E. C. Hettinger, "Justifying Intellectual Property," 18 *Philosophy & Public Affairs* 31 (1989), K. E. Kulzick and A. D. Hogue, "Chilled Bird: Freedom of Expression in the Eighties," 14 *Loyola of Los Angeles Law Review* 57, 77–78 (1980); J. Hughes, "The Philosophy of Intellectual Property," 77 *Georgetown Law Journal* 443 (1988). The unwillingness of the judiciary to consider the creative, productive, and culturally transformative ways in which copyrighted works may be used (and to insist on a bright line distinction between "authors" and "users" that privileges and overestimates the creativity of the former) is also discussed in P. Jaszi, "Towards a Theory of Copyright: The Metamorphoses of 'Authorship,'" [1991] *Duke Law Journal* 455; P. Jaszi, "On the Author Effect: Contemporary Copyright and Collective Creativity," 10 *Cardozo Arts and Entertainment Law Journal* 293 (1992). The increasing lack of consideration for the public interest is explored in P. Jaszi, "Caught in the Net of Copyright," 75 *Oregon Law Review* 299 (1996); P. Jaszi, "Goodbye to All That—A Reluctant (and Perhaps Premature) Adieu to a Constitutionally-Grounded Discourse of Public Interest in Copyright Law," 29 *Vanderbilt Journal of Transnational Law* 595 (1996); Note, "Copyright Infringement and the First Amendment," 79 *Columbia Law Review* 320, 320–321 (1979); L. R. Patterson, "Copyright and the 'Exclusive Right' of Authors," 1 *Journal of Intellectual Property Law* 1 (1993); D. Vaver, "Intellectual Property Today: Of Myths and Paradoxes," 69 *Canadian Bar Review* 98 (1990); D. Vaver, "Rejuvenating Copyright," 75 *Canadian Bar Review* 69 (1996); M. Woodmansee, "On the Author Effect: Recovering Collectivity," 10 *Cardozo Arts and Entertainment Law Journal* 279 (1992); J. Litman, "The Public Domain," 39 *Emory Law Journal* 965 (1990). The increasing expansion of private copyright interests, the diminished arena of cultural forms that constitute the public domain, and the concomitant threat to the public interest in progress in the arts and sciences is explored in A. Yen, "Restoring the Natural Law: Copyright as Labor and Possession," 51 *Ohio State Law Journal* 517 (1990), and R. Stallman, "Re-evaluating Copyright: The Public Must Prevail," 75 *Oregon Law Review* 291 (1996). Jessica Litman argues that copyright law is inhospitable to actual processes of authorship precisely because it maintains untenable distinctions between (romantic) authors and (suspect) users, and misunderstands the nature of creative authorship: "All authorship is fertilized by the work of prior authors, and the echoes of old work in new work extend beyond ideas and concepts to a wealth of expressive details. Indeed, authorship *is* the transformation and recombination of expression into new molds, the recasting and revision of details into different shapes. What others have expressed, and the ways they have expressed it, are the essential building blocks of any creative medium" (J. Litman, "Copyright as Myth," 53 *University of Pittsburgh Law Review* 235 [1991]). For a discussion of state use of copyright, see R. M. Gellman, "Twin Evils: Government Copyright and Copyright-like Controls over Government Information," 45 *Syracuse Law Review* 999 (1995).

David Lange argues that both publicity rights and trademark protections have expanded to the detriment of those engaged in creative authorship and at a significant cost to the public in "Recognizing the Public Domain," 44(4) *Law and Contemporary Problems* 147 (1981). See R. C. Dreyfuss, "We Are Symbols and Inhabit Symbols, So Why Should We Be Paying Rent? Deconstructing the Lanham Act and Rights of Publicity," 20 *Columbia-VLA Journal of Law and the Arts* 123 (1996), for a discussion of recent tendencies in trademark, unfair competition, and publicity rights law.

61 J. Baudrillard, *Simulations* (1983).

62 See discussion in M. Poster, Introduction, in *Jean Baudrillard: Selected Writings* 1 (Mark Poster, ed., 1988).

63 Thomas Drescher suggests that the "multi-billion dollar trademark" is not unusual: "Some of the biggest 'brand-driven deals' ever were made in 1988, among them, the following: the $25 billion buy-out of RJR Nabisco and with it the trademarks CAMEL, RITZ, BENSON & HEDGES, WINSTON and NABISCO; the purchase of Kraft whose trademarks include KRAFT cheese, MIRACLE WHIP, and BREYERS ice cream, for $12.9 billion or four times Kraft's tangible assets; Nestlé's takeover of Rowntree, the owner of KIT KAT, AFTER EIGHT, QUALITY STREET, and ROLO marks, for more than five times book value." Drescher takes these examples from "The Year of the Brand," *The Economist* 24 December 1988, at 95–100, and also cites M. Landler, Z. Schiller, and L. Therrien, "What's in a Name?," *Business Week* 8 July 1991, at 66–67. See T. Drescher, "Article and Report: The Transformation and Evolution of Trademarks—From Signals to Symbols to Myth," 82 *Trademark Reporter* 301, 302 (1992).

Dorean Koenig suggests:

Current government protection of corporate imagery reflects the commercial value of the images. The value added to the [U.S.] Gross National Product (GNP) from copyrighted and trademark-protected tobacco icons is powerful economic stimulus; for example, in 1992, Philip Morris was the seventh largest industrial corporation in the United States, with $50 billion in sales. When these corporations were ranked according to profits, however, Philip Morris made more money in 1992—$4.9 billion—than any other company in the United States . . . Cigarette advertising and promotion, despite some government restrictions, have undergone unbridled expansion in the past 30 years . . . From 1975 to 1990, annual expenditures on cigarette advertising and promotional events grew from $500 million to $3.9 billion. In constant 1975 dollars this represents more than a threefold increase. In 1989, Philip Morris had the largest advertising budget of any company in the United States, spending $2 billion to promote its products. In 1988, cigarettes were the most advertised product on billboards and the second most advertised product in print media. (D. M. Koenig, "Joe Camel and the First Amendment: The Dark Side of Copyrighted and Trademark-Protected Icons," 11 *Thomas M. Cooley Law Review* 803, 811–812, n. 56 [1994] [citing T. MacKenzie et al., "The Human Costs of Tobacco Use," Pt. 2, 330 *New England Journal of Medicine* 975 (1994)].)

64 I heard the story at the 1989 International Semiotics Institute for the Marketing of Meaning. Another version of the story is provided by a quotation from Julius R. Lunsford Jr., who in 1986 estimated that although the Coca-Cola Company's hard assets were valued at only $7 billion, the other $7 billion of the company's estimated value was attributed to the value of the trademark: "The production plants and inventories of The Coca-Cola Company could go up in flames overnight . . . Yet, on

the following morning there is not a bank in Atlanta, New York, or anywhere else, that would not lend this Company the funds necessary for rebuilding, accepting as security only the inherent goodwill in its trademarks 'Coca-Cola' and 'Coke'" (cited in Drescher, *supra* note 63).

65   See J. Baudrillard, "The System of Objects," in *Jean Baudrillard: Selected Writings*, *supra* note 62, at 17.

66   *Ibid.*

67   Ross, *supra* note 45, at *xv*.

68   *Ibid.*, at *xx*.

69   H. Foster, *Recodings: Art, Spectacle, Cultural Politics* (ed., 1985). See also *The Anti-Aesthetic: Essays on Postmodern Culture* (H. Foster, ed., 1983).

70   Connor, *supra* note 45; Hutcheon, *supra* note 45, at 8; D. Hebdige, *Cut 'n' Mix: Culture, Identity, and Carribean Music* (1987); McRobbie, *supra* note 50; P. Willis, *Common Culture* (1990).

71   Rumor has it that gangs in many inner cities mark their identities, communities, and turf with particular brands of athletic shoes. See R. Wilkerson, "Challenging Nike, Rights Group Takes a Risky Stand," *New York Times* 25 August 1990 at A10, and A. Kozinski, "Trademarks Unplugged," 68 *New York University Law Review* 960 (1993).

72   D. Carlisle, "The Museum of Modern Mythology," *The Last Issue* 8, 9 (autumn 1987).

73   Certeau, *The Practice of Everyday Life*, *supra* note 14; at xi–xii.

74   I am grateful to a fellow anthropologist (who will be grateful not to be named) for singing this out loud after my first presentation at an academic conference on an intellectual property topic.

75   McRobbie, *supra* note 50, at 3–4.

76   M. Foucault, "What Is an Author?," in *The Foucault Reader* 101, at 118–119 (J. Harari, trans., 1979, P. Rabinow, ed., 1984).

77   K. Aoki, "Authors, Inventors and Trademark Owners: Private Intellectual Property and the Public Domain. Part II," 18 *Columbia-VLA Journal of Law and the Arts* 191, 236 (1994), and sources cited therein.

78   J. Gaines, *Contested Culture: The Image, the Voice, and the Law* (1991).

79   *Ibid.*, at 208.

80   Trade-mark Cases, 100 US 82, 92 (1879) at 94.

81   Aoki, "Part II," *supra* note 77, at 234–257.

82   Aoki, "Part I," *supra* note 55, at 4. Staffin is somewhat less conclusive:

In essence, dilution law attempts to provide the trademark owner with direct protection against the misappropriation of its mark's selling power. Because this attempt is fully congruent with the Lanham Act's secondary purpose [allegedly, "to protect the trademark owner's investment of 'energy, time and money in presenting to the public the product' from the misappropriation of its trademark 'by pirates and cheats.'" Unfortunately, this is to give the lobbying efforts of the United States Trademark Association a rather elevated status], it should not automatically be concluded that dilution law conflicts with the goals of traditional federal trademark law. However, because of the central, "misappropriation protection goal of dilution law, there is a danger that federal adoption of an overly broad dilution doctrine could elevate the Lanham Act's secondary purpose to its primary one [which has traditionally been "to protect the public from deceptive and misleading trademark practices, without fostering unnecessary monopolization of language that would impede free competition"], thereby swallowing up all competition in the claim of protection against trademark infringement. (E. B. Staffin, "The Dilution Doctrine: Towards a Reconciliation with the Lanham Act," 6 *Fordham Intellectual Property, Media, and Entertainment Law Journal* 105, 110–111 [1995] [internal cites omitted].)

83 See Gaines, *supra* note 78.

84 An extensive review of the term *secondary meaning* and the mass of supporting legal authorities may be found in W. F. McLean, "The Birth, Death, and Renaissance of the Doctrine of Secondary Meaning in the Making," 42 *American University Law Review* 737 (1993), and in the extensive secondary literature cited therein.

85 See *ibid.*, at 749–750, for a discussion of the wide variety of judicial decisions and the incoherence of the tests judicially employed.

86 *Ibid.*, at 753.

87 R. Callman, *The Law of Unfair Competition, Trademarks and Monopolies* 356 (3d ed., 1969).

88 McLean, *supra* note 84, at 757.

89 *Ibid.*, at 752.

90 Trade Mark Act 1938, s.28. Until 1993, Canada adhered to a "registered user" system in which uses of trademarks by persons other than their owners were permitted only insofar as a registered user agreement was filed with the Registrar of Trademarks, which indicated what control the trademark owner was exercising over the quality of the goods to which the mark would attach. The onus was on the trademark holder to demonstrate that provisions were in place such that consumers would not be confused and could anticipate continuity in product quality despite the transfer of the trademark to a new entity. These provisions were abandoned in 1993 pursuant to the Intellectual Property Law Improvement Act and replaced with licensing arrangements under which it is presumed, unless the contrary is proven, that if the trademark has been licensed the character and quality of the goods with which it is used are under the control of the owner. The onus thus shifts away from the owner and licensee to prove that steps have been taken to protect the public and is placed upon those who would challenge the licensing arrangement, who, arguably, are least able to obtain such information. Once again, the owner's proprietary rights take precedence over public interests. Although it would seem that theoretically the restraints against trafficking in marks have been maintained, such practices are more easily enabled and subject to less scrutiny under the new provisions. See Intellectual Property Law Improvement Act, Statutes of Canada 1993, c.15, s.69.

91 Trade Mark Act 1938, s.28(6). The House of Lords considered this provision of the Trade Mark Act in the *Hollie Hobby* case. There, Lord Brightman "groped" for a definition of trafficking in a trademark context, and emerged with the following: "To my mind, trafficking in a trade mark context conveys the notion of dealing in a trade mark primarily as a commodity in its own right and not primarily for the purpose of identifying or promoting merchandise in which the proprietor of the mark is interested. If there is no real trade connection between the proprietor of the mark and the licensee or his goods, there is room for the conclusion that the grant of the license is a trafficking in the mark. It is a question of fact and degree in every case whether a sufficient trade connection exists" *Hollie Hobby* Trade Mark, [1984] R.P.C. 329, 356-7 [H.L.].

92 The trademark holder's rights in the trademark were defined by its use of the mark in commerce. Thus, it could not sell the trademark apart from the goodwill in com-

merce that that mark represented. See Bi-Rite Enterprises, Inc., v. Button Master, 555 F. Supp. 1188, 1193-94 (S.D.N.Y. 1983). "Character merchandising" has challenged this principle. In the *Hollie Hobby* case, the holder of the mark was clearly engaged in character merchandising. As Lord Bridge of Harwich wryly noted: "the phrase 'trafficking in a trade mark'. . . (is a) precisely apt description of the commercial activity now widely known as 'character merchandising'" (*Hollie Hobby* Trade Mark, [1984] R.P.C. 329, 350 [H.L.]). The "trafficking" provisions meet the traditional function of trademark law: protecting consumers. The commercial practice of character merchandising subverts the purposes of trademark doctrine; instead of protecting the public by signifying origin, the law is called upon to protect the proprietor from unauthorized and unremunerated uses in contexts where his or her mark would not otherwise be protected under traditional principles. Commercial use of trademarks has evolved in a fashion than exceeds the intentions of Parliamentary legislation. However, the simultaneous copyright protection of such images provides an alternative basis for licensing agreements that might otherwise transgress trademark limitations. Lord Bridge of Harwich concluded his brief treatment of the case by noting that the statutory prohibition on trafficking "seems likely to generate a mass of difficult and expensive litigation which cannot be in the public interest . . . I do not hesitate to express my opinion that it has become a complete anachronism and that the sooner it is repealed the better" (*Hollie Hobby* Trade Mark, [1984] R.P.C. 329, 351 [H.L.]). Indeed, a recent review of English trademark law has recommended just that ("Reform of Trade Marks Law," Cm. 1203; para. 4.40). One might, however, ask why courts are so eager to capitulate to commercial practice instead of exploring the social costs and benefits of activities in light of established principles of public interest.

In Canada, judicial discussion of trafficking is both terse and confusing. In the 1988 case of Kamercorp Holdings Inc. v. 624564 Ontario Ltd. 23 C.P.R. (3d) 262 (F.T.D.), Justice Joyal stated that "trafficking" in a mark *might* be considered in Canada as contrary to the public interest, but did not find it to have occurred given the facts of the case at bar (assignment of trademarks between related companies). On the other hand, he stated that (then) s. 47(1) of the Act specifically provided that a trademark was transferable separately from the goodwill of the business, which, he noted, was "an inherent condition, in my view, to the application of the trafficking rule." Thus he appears also to suggest that the Canadian statute expressly permits trafficking of trademarks, in which case it is not clear why he believes it might be considered contrary to public interest.

93   Gaines, *supra* note 78, at 214.

94   In Anheuser-Busch, Inc. v. Balducci Publications, 28 F.3d 769, 31 U.S.P.Q. 2D (BNA) 1296 (8th Cir. 1994), an advertising parody used a beer company's trademarks in a humor magazine to comment upon a recent oil spill in the river from which the plaintiff derived water for its production ("One taste and you'll drink it Oily"; "Michelob Oily" with an oil-soaked eagle and fish beneath the Shell Oil logo). The parody was not enjoined at the District Court level because there was no likelihood of confusion and the court acknowledged a "special sensitivity" to First Amendment concerns. On appeal to the Eighth Circuit, the decision was reversed, and the court used "an expansive interpretation of likelihood of confusion," extending "protection against use of (plaintiff's) mark on any product or service which would reasonably be thought by the buying public to come from the same source, or thought to be affiliated with, connected with, or sponsored by, the trademark owner" (*ibid.*, at 774,

citing J. T. McCarthy, *McCarthy on Trademarks and Unfair Competition* s.24.03 at 24–13 [3d ed., 1995]). The court determined that "There is a distinct possibility that a superficial observer might believe that the ad parody was approved by Anheuser-Busch" (*ibid.*, at 775). The plaintiff asked open-ended questions in a survey in a St. Louis mall that indicated that over half of those surveyed thought that the publisher would need Anheuser-Busch's approval to run the parodic advertisement. Despite ambiguities in the way the survey was conducted, the court found it a strong indication of actual consumer confusion. The First Amendment's "protection of social commentary generally and parody in particular" was not seen to outweigh "the public interest in avoiding consumer confusion" (*ibid.*, at 776). To the extent that the court enjoined the parody, of course, it further reinforces public belief that parodies must have the authorization of the trademark holder, and thus makes future parodies more likely to be seen by future courts as creating a likelihood of confusion. Hence, a further extension of rights to holders of trademarks at the expense of other expressive and critical usages is accomplished in the name of protecting the public. As Rochelle Dreyfuss rightly notes, "as courts have increasingly handled the consumer confusion requirement with the assumption that consumers are very unsophisticated, confusion has come to serve as a rather minor impediment to according plenary control to purveyors of images . . . Courts deciding § 43 (a) cases have shown a willingness to believe in an astonishingly stupid consumer" (Dreyfuss, *supra* note 60, at 131 and 133).

95 M. Madow, "Private Ownership and Public Image: Popular Culture and Publicity Rights," 81 *California Law Review* 125 (1993); R. C. Dreyfuss, "Expressive Genericity: Trademarks as Language in the Pepsi Generation," 65 *Notre Dame Law Review* 397 (1990); Aoki, "Part I," *supra* note 55, and Aoki, "Part II," *supra* note 77, all provide similar scenarios.

96 One of the strategies trademark holders use for reaping surplus value from their marks involves stretching traditional trademark principles. "Thus . . . 'likelihood of confusion' now includes protection against usages that may tend to injure the trademark owner's reputation, imply sponsorship, limit expansion opportunities, and erode or tarnish advertising values" (see Dreyfuss, *supra* note 95, at 403, and cases cited therein).

97 Boston Professional Hockey Ass'n v. Dallas Cap & Emblem Mfg., Inc., 510 F.2d 1004, 1032 (5th Cir. 1975).

98 Kozinski, *supra* note 71, at 976. Kozinski, however, is less permissive about allowing those with "brand loyalty" to status goods to express their admiration with low-priced substitutes for "the real thing" because the producers of such copies are not engaged in creative activity, nor are they advancing the originator's interests. An image based on exclusivity, he suggests, should be protected against those who would make it less exclusive: "whatever pleasure people get from wearing an image-enhancing product is diminished if everyone else can get the same thing at a discount store . . . Allowing unrestricted copying of the Rolex trademark will make it less likely that Rolex, Guess, Pierre Cardin and others will invest in image advertising, denying the image-conscious among us something we hold near and dear" (*ibid.*, at 970). Unfortunately, this argument is somewhat tautalogical; it freezes and privileges connotations at a particular point in time without reference to any principled criteria for choosing one moment in time rather than another. Presumably *all* trademark

holders attempt to create an image, but the image will convey exclusivity only to the extent that cheaper copies deploying the mark are prohibited. The exclusivity that Judge Kozinski seeks to protect, rather than being the *ground* upon which legal protection is premised, is an *effect* of earlier legal protection.

99 Dreyfuss, *supra* note 95. But, as Dreyfuss recently ackowledged when commenting on case law in the last decade, "there is, apparently, an irresistible impulse to give the original purveyor of an image the right to control it" (*supra* note 60, at 135).

100 Dreyfuss, *supra* note 95, at 403–404, and case law cited therein. As Dreyfuss states in her more recent article, "courts are too quick to equate value with right; to leap from recognizing that consumers attach value to trademarks to concluding that trademark holders ought to capture that value for themselves" (*supra* note 60, at 124). Moreover, "demonstrating the power of signifiers does not get us very far, for to those who equate value with right, the more important the symbol, the clearer is the case for private ownership" (*ibid.*, at 140).

101 Dreyfuss, *supra* note 95, at 405. See also A. Langvardt, "Trademark Rights and First Amendment Wrongs: Protecting the Former without Committing the Latter," 83 *Trademark Reporter* 633 (1993).

102 Dreyfuss, *supra* note 95, at 407. Although Dreyfuss initiated use of the term *surplus value,* and Aoki added the Marxian *expropriation,* I would add *signifying,* so that "the expropriation of surplus signifying value" would clearly refer to the semiotic dimensions of this appropriation of social meaning.

103 Drescher, *supra* note 63, at 305–307.

104 Voloshinov, *supra* note 1, at 23.

105 Keith Aoki provides case law and historical citation as well as a list of relevant legal commentary in "Part II," *supra* note 77, at 193–195. See also Staffin, *supra* note 82, at 109–111, particularly his discussion of how state law doctrine of misappropriation supplements a rapidly expanding dilution action (e.g., Deere & Co. v. MTD Products Inc., 41 F. 3d 39, 44–45 [2d Cir. 1994]) to protect holders of trademarks even when trademark infringement cannot be found.

106 Gordon, "Intellectual Property and the Restitutionary Impulse," *supra* note 56, at 166. Dreyfuss agrees that "the more fundamental problem is that there is no normative principle that equates value and private right. To the contrary, black letter law is that everyone is free to copy. Now it is true that there are laws that depart from this baseline, but the justification for them is not 'if value then right.' Usually, it is not even a principle of just desserts or a theory of natural rights. Rather, departures occur for instrumental reasons, when the creation of private rights is seen to further important social goals" (Dreyfuss, *supra* note 60, at 141–142). For a defense of the "if value, then right" proposition by two lawyers who believe that "the positive associations that comprise a brand—a brand's equity—can rise to the level of a property right entitled separately to protection irrespective of confusion or the existence of a dilution statute," see J. B. Swann and T. H. Davis Jr., "Dilution, an Idea Whose Time Has Gone: Brand Equity as Protectable Property, the New/Old Paradigm," 1 *Journal of Intellectual Property Law* 219 (1994).

107 Gordon, *supra* note 56, at 168.

108 Dreyfuss, *supra* notes 60 and 95, and the numerous cases cited therein.

109 See Lugosi v. Universal Pictures, 603 P.2d 425, 160 Cal. Rptr. 323 (L.A. County Ct. 1979). Bela Lugosi's heirs sued a movie company for using Lugosi's likeness in pro-

moting new Dracula movies. Although the company owned the copyright to the film, the court found that during his lifetime, Lugosi could also have created a "right of value" in his name or likeness (*ibid.*, at 428).

110   Reddy Communications, Inc. v. Environmental Action Foundation, Inc., 199 U.S.P.Q (BNA) 630, 631–32 (D.D.C. 1977) (denying preliminary injunction. A permanent injunction was also denied: see 477 F.Supp. 936 [D.D.C. 1979]).

111   Reddy Communications, Inc. v. Environmental Action Foundation, Inc., 199 U.S.P.Q. (BNA) 630, 633-34 (D.D.C. 1977). The Court concluded that the plaintiff's "property" had not "assume[d] . . . the functional attributes of public property devoted to public use," thus the enforcement of plaintiff's private rights was not considered state action (see *ibid.*, at 633–634). In other words, because the private action was not inherently governmental, it was not subject to constitutional limitation. See R. C. Denicola, "Trademarks as Speech: Constitutional Implications of the Emerging Rationales for the Protection of Trade Symbols," [1982] *Wisconsin Law Review* 158 at 190–191 and n.146 for a critique of this reasoning.

112   See 3 McCarthy, *supra* note 94, § 24.01–24.04 at 24-1-28.

113   Canada Safeway Ltd. v. Manitoba Food and Chemical Workers, Local 832, 73 C.P.R.(2d) 234 (Man.C.A. 1983).

114   *Ibid.*, at 237. This logic was accepted and reiterated in another Canadian case involving the parody of a corporate trademark by striking union members. See Cie generale des establissements Michelin-Michelin & Cie v. National Automobile, Aerospace, Transportation and General Workers of Canada (CAW-Canada), [1996] F.C.J. No. 1685 QL (*hereinafter Michelin*).

115   State antidilution statutes are a relatively recent phenomenon. Massachusetts adopted the first antidilution statute in 1947. See H. J. Shire, "Dilution versus Deception—Are State Antidilution Laws an Appropriate Alternative to the Law of Infringement?," 77 *Trademark Reporter* 273, 278 (1987). Today, at least twenty-five states have antidilution statutes. See *infra* note 120 for a list of state antidilution statutes. See R. J. Shaughnessy, "Trademark Parody: A Fair Use and First Amendment Analysis," 72 *Virginia Law Review* 1079, 1088–1092 (1986), and 3 McCarthy, *supra* note 94, § 24.15[3]–24.16[4] at 24-127-138.5, for examinations of increasing judicial acceptance of dilution statutes. As Staffin explains, "in the last decade or so, the role of dilution theory in U.S. trademark law has dramatically increased in importance . . . In finding that dilution occurred despite the absence of federal trademark infringement, these federal courts have indirectly expanded the scope of trademark protection available under U.S. law" (*supra* note 82, at 108).

Canada does not, as yet, have a judicially developed dilution doctrine and, given judicial interpretations of its *Trademarks Act*, R.S.C. ch. T-10, § 22(1) (1985), is unlikely to develop antidilution protections unless there are statutory amendments.

However, the tendency of those with distinctive trademarks to register them as copyrights augers in the same direction, as does a judicial tendency to see them as properties. Unlike the United States, Canada has no fair use defense for copyright infringement and only an anachronistic fair dealing defense to permit limited quotation for the purposes of news reporting, criticism (of the work), private study, and review. See *Copyright Act*, R.S.C. c.C-42, § 27(2)(a)–c (1985). Canadian courts have been routinely hostile toward expressive and transformative usages of copyright protected works.

116   See, e.g., Waterman Co. v. Gordon, 72 F.2d 272, 273 (2d Cir. 1934); Yale Electric Corp.

v. Robertson, 26 F.2d 972, 974 (2d Cir. 1928); Aunt Jemima Mills Co. v. Rigney & Co., 247 F.407, 410, 412 (2d Cir. 1917). As Denicola described the traditional approach:

> At a rhetorical level there is a certain convenience in speaking of a trademark "owner"; as the symbol of the goodwill enjoyed by an enterprise, the mark is indeed a valuable commercial asset capable of exploitation and assignment. Yet as a description of the legal consequences attaching to the adoption of a particular symbol as an indication of origin, the property conception is largely inadequate. Traditional trademark doctrine does not establish the general right to exclude others implied by the property designation. Protection is normally limited to instances in which there is a threatened appropriation or injury to goodwill arising through customer confusion. The danger in utilizing a property conception of trademark . . . [is that it has a tendency to preclude] rational consideration of competing social, economic, and occasionally, constitutional interests. (Denicola, *supra* note 111, at 165)

More recently, Elliot Staffin reiterated the traditional principles when he asserted: "It is a truism of U.S. federal trademark law that there can be no trademark rights in gross. Unlike a patent or copyright owner, under current federal law, a trademark holder cannot control all uses of its mark. The Lanham Act only protects a trademark holder against unauthorized, subsequent use of the same or similar mark that is likely to result in public confusion" (Staffin, *supra* note 82, at 105).

117 F. I. Schechter, "The Rational Basis of Trademark Protection," 40 *Harvard Law Review* 813, 825 (1927).

118 Mishawaka Rubber & Woolen Mfg. Co. v. S.S. Kresge Co., 316 U.S. 203, 205 (U.S.S.C. 1942).

119 An antidilution provision was incorporated into the Lanham Act only in January 1996, allegedly to make U.S. federal trademark law compliant with the requirements of GATT. It applies only to famous marks and only to "commercial use in commerce," and there is a fair use defense as well as an exception for all forms of news reporting. We have yet to see if "commercial" will be more narrowly interpreted than it has been in state courts. See Federal Trademark Dilution Act of 1995, Pub. L. No. 104-98, 109 Stat. 985 (to be codified at 15 U.S.C. SS 1125 (c), 1127). It appears that the so-called minimum requirements of the 1994 Agreement on Trade-Related Aspects of Intellectual Property Rights (TRIPS) were designed under the pressure of industry lobbyists who wished to ensure that antidilution provisions could be globally enforced. In this area, as in others, transnational capital interests were able to use international trade law to exact concessions that they had been unable to achieve domestically and effectively do an end run around elected bodies, national governments, and inconvenient judicial concerns with larger social interests. Ironically, then, the U.S. federal government was pushed into passing legislation that it had resisted for decades on the basis of international "requirements" that enacted on a global level what had been frustrated by a consideration of wider interests at the domestic level. There are good arguments to be made that, in fact, TRIPS did not mandate dilution protection; see P. J. Heald, "Trademarks and Geographical Indications: Exploring Contours of the TRIPS Agreement," 29 *Vanderbilt Journal of Transnational Law* 635 (1996), and E. A. Prager, "The Federal Trademark Dilution Act of 1995: Substantial Likelihood of Confusion," 7 *Fordham Intellectual Property, Media and Entertainment Journal* 121 (1996). Thanks to Melanie Sharman for bringing these arguments to my attention.

120 See Ala. Code § 8-12-17 (1993); Ark. Stat. Ann. § 4-71-113 (Michie 1993); Cal. Bus. & Prof. Code § 14330 (West 1987); Conn. Gen. Stat. Ann. § 35-11i(c) (1993); Del. Code Ann. tit. 6, § 3313 (1993); Fla. Stat. ch. 495.151 (1995); Ga. Code Ann. § 10-1-451(b) (1995); Idaho Code § 48-512 (1994); Ill. Ann. Stat. ch. 765 § 1035/15 (1995); Iowa Code Ann. § 548.11(2) (1995); La. Rev. Stat. Ann. § 55:223.1 (West 1995); Mass. Gen. Laws Ann. ch. 110B, § 12 (West 1995); Me. Rev. Stat. Ann. tit. 10, § 1530 (West 1994); Mo. Rev. Stat. § 417.061(1) (1994); Mont. Code Ann. § 30-13-334 (1994); Neb. Rev. Stat. § 87-122 (1994); N.H. Rev. Stat. Ann. § 350-A:12 (1994); N.M. Stat. Ann. § 57-3-10 (Michie 1995); N.Y. Gen. Bus. Law § 368-d (1994); Or. Rev. Stat. § 647.107 (1989); Pa. Cons. Stat. Ann. tit. 54 § 1124 (1995); R.I. Gen. Laws § 6-2-12 (1994); Tenn. Code Ann. § 47-25-512 (1995); Tex. Bus. & Com. Code Ann. § 16.29 (West 1995); Wash. Rev. Code § 19.77.160 (1995). The state of Ohio has adopted the dilution doctrine as part of its common law. See Ameritech, Inc. v. American Info. Technologies Corp., 811 F. 2d 960, 965 (6th Cir. 1987).

121 Model State Trademark Bill § 12 (United States Trademark Association 1964), reprinted in 3 McCarthy, *supra* note 94, § 22.04[2] at 24-25-37.

122 See discussion in 3 McCarthy, *supra* note 94, at § 24.15[1-3] pp. 24-126-130; B. Pattishall, "The Dilution Rationale for Trademark–Trade Identity Protection, Its Progress and Prospects," 71 *Northwestern University Law Review* 618, 621–624 (1977).

123 See Note, "Copyright Infringement and the First Amendment," *supra* note 60, at 1088–1089. For a recent overview, see E. Staffin, *supra* note 82.

124 See, e.g., Mead Data Central, Inc. v. Toyota Motor Sales, U.S.A., Inc., 875 F.2d 1026, 1030 (2d Cir. 1989) (defining "dilution as either the blurring of a mark's product identification or the tarnishment of the affirmative associations a mark has come to convey").

125 See, e.g., Exxon Corp. v. Exxene Corp., 696 F2d 544, 550 (7th Cir. 1983) (explaining that similar names may cause dissonance in the minds of consumers: "It is the same kind of dissonance that would be produced by selling cat food under the name 'Romanoff,' or baby carriages under the name 'Aston Martin'").

126 See, e.g., Jordache Enterprises, Inc. v. Hogg Wyld, Ltd., 625 F. Supp. 48, 52 (D.N.M. 1985) (stating that there is a risk of "erosion of the public's identification" of a trademark, diminishing its distinctiveness, uniqueness, effectiveness, and prestige" [quoting Tiffany & Co. v. Boston Club. Inc., 231 F. Supp. 836, 844 (D. Mass. 1964)]).

127 See, e.g., Augusta National, Inc. v. Northwestern Mutual Life Ins. Co., 193 U.S.P.Q. (BNA) 210, 214 (S.D. Ga. 1976) ("[T]here is reasonable certainty that the value of [Augusta National's Masters] mark will be eroded; a little now, more later, until the 'magic' of the Masters will be mortally dissipated if not completely dispelled").

128 See, e.g., Mead Data Central, *supra* note 124 (stating that dilution has been defined as "the tarnishment of the affirmative associations a mark has come to convey").

129 See, e.g., Mutual of Omaha Ins. Co. v. Novak, 648 F. Supp. 905, 912, 231 U.S.P.Q. (BNA) 963, 967 (D. Neb. 1986) ("Trademark disparagement can be found where the defendant has used the same or a confusingly similar mark in a way that creates an undesirable, unwholesome or unsavoury mental association with the plaintiff's mark").

130 *Ibid.*

131 This metaphor was borrowed from Keith Aoki and accords with the metaphors of paternity that are ubiquitous in the history of intellectual property laws. For historical examples, see M. Rose, *From Paternity to Property: The Remetaphorization of*

Writing (unpublished manuscript), and M. Rose, "Mothers and Authors: Johnson v. Calvert and the New Children of Our Imaginations," 22 *Critical Inquiry* 613 (1996).

132 Shaughnessy, *supra* note 115.

133 F. S. Cohen, "Transcendental Nonsense and the Functionalist Approach," 35 *Columbia Law Review* 809 (1935).

134 The United States Patent and Trademark Office determined on September 19, 1990, that a distinctive smell could be registered as a trademark, thereby opening up a whole new realm of the senses to commodification. In re Clarke, 17 U.S.P.Q. 2d (BNA) 1238, 1239–40 (1990) (holding fragrance added to applicant's yarn functions as a trademark for the yarn). For a discussion of the commercial use of scent and the new science of "olfactory management," see *Aroma: The Cultural History of Smell* (C. Classen, D. Howes, and A. Synott, eds., 1994). Certain sounds added to particular brands of cassettes at the end of the tape also function as trademarks, and colors have been judicially recognized as having secondary meaning. It has been suggested that the flavor of pharmaceutical capsules should also accrue trademark protection.

135 See, for example, Coca-Cola Co. v. Alma Leo U.S.A., Inc., 719 F. Supp. 725, 726 (N.D. Ill. 1989) (granting injunction against the sale of "Mad Scientist Magic Powder" bubble gum to children because their gum container resembled a Coca-Cola bottle).

136 Coca-Cola Co. v. Gemini Rising Inc., 346 F. Supp. 1183, 1193 (E.D.N.Y. 1972).

137 *Ibid.*, at 1191.

138 *Ibid.*

139 See E. Kahn, *The Big Drink: The Story of Coca-Cola* 54–55, 101–103 (1960). See also M. Schatzman, A. Sabbadini, and L. Forti, "Coca and Cocaine: A Bibliography," 8 *Journal of Psychedelic Drugs* 95, 97 (1976).

140 General Electric Co. v. Alumpa Coal Co., 205 U.S.P.Q. (BNA) 1036, 1037 (D. Mass. 1979). The "expansive confusion analysis" is discussed in Note, "Copyright Infringement and the First Amendment," *supra* note 60, at 1094–1096, and Denicola, *supra* note 111, at 186.

141 Denicola, *supra* note 111, at 190.

142 For discussions of this art and its various motivations, see Foster, *Recodings, supra* note 69; R. E. Krauss, *The Originality of the Avante Garde and Other Modernist Mysths* (1985); G. Marcus and F. R. Myers, "The Traffic in Art and Culture: An Introduction," in *The Traffic in Culture: Refiguring Art and Anthropology* (G. Marcus and F. R. Myers, eds., 1995) at 1–51; P. Marincola, *Image Scavengers: Photography* (1992); C. Owens, "The Discourse of Others: Feminists and Postmodernism," in *The Anti-Aesthetic, supra* note 69; J. A. Walker, *Art in the Age of Mass Media* (1994). The journals *Artforum* and *Artnews* both commented extensively on the practice in the 1980s.

143 The most notorious case of artistic appropriation to receive sustained legal attention was Rogers v. Koons, 960 F.2d 301 (2d Cir. 1992), a case involving an artist notorious for his appropriation of the vulgar commercial forms of contemporary American society. In his *Banality* exhibition, he displayed a work, "String of Puppies," that appropriated a rather saccharine postcard image of a middle-American white couple surrounded by puppies in a sculpted form that further emphasized the vacuousness of the image. The original photographer successfully claimed copy-

right infringement, and Koons's parody defense was rejected because his work was not recognizably a parody of the original work itself. Given Koons's history of commercial publicity stunts, he was arguably not the artist best able to make a credible case for the politically expressive value of appropriation in art as social critique. For legal discussions of arts of appropriation and the Koons case, see J. Carlin, "Culture Vultures: Artistic Appropriation and Intellectual Property Law," 13 *Columbia-VLA Journal of Law & the Arts* 103 (1988); L. A. Greenberg, "Art of Appropriation: Puppies, Piracy, and Post-Modernism," 10 *Cardozo Arts & Entertainment Law Journal* 1 (1992); W. F. McLean, "All's Not Fair in Art and War: A Look at the Fair Use Defense after *Rogers v. Koons*," 59 *Brooklyn Law Review* 373 (1993); E. H. Wang, "(Re)Productive Rights: Copyright and the Postmodern Artist," 14 *Columbia-VLA Journal of Law & the Arts* 261 (1990); G. J. Yonover, "The 'Dissing' of Da Vinci: The Imaginary Case of Leonardo v. Duchamp: Moral Rights, Parody, and Fair Use," 29 *Valparaiso University Law Review* 935 (1995). See also M. Buskirk, "Commodification as Censor: Copyrights and Fair Use," 60 *October* 92, 101–103 (spring 1992).

144   J. Fisher, "Corporate Muse," 25 *Artforum* 108, 109 (March 1987).

145   I am grateful to my former student Julia Schatz for her research exploring the issue of Haacke's work in a paper written for my Intellectual Property course. Her discussions with him in 1991 about the legal challenges he has faced are the basis of these comments.

146   Koenig, *supra* note 63 .

147   *Ibid.*, at 807 n.21. The Joe Camel figure is copyright- and trademark-protected by R. J. Reynolds Nabisco, Inc.

148   *Ibid.*, at 806–807.

149   *Ibid.*, at 808.

150   Campbell v. Acuff-Rose Music, Inc., 114 S. Ct. 1164 (U.S.S.C. 1994).

151   Most cases litigated involve the use of trademarks in commercial parodies that the trademark holder finds to be noxious and offensive, and courts tend to uphold the property right. Some recent case law suggests that judges are beginning to recognize the First Amendment implications of prohibiting parodies in contexts where consumers are unlikely to believe the product to have originated with the trademark's source, but even extremely recent cases have been decided in favor of the trademark holder's rights to maintain only positive associations with its mark. For discussions, see Aoki, "Part II," *supra* note 77, at 251–256, and numerous cases cited therein. For a more optimistic reading of judicial tendencies, see Note, "Trademark Parodies and Free Speech: An Expansion of Parodists' First Amendment Rights in L.L. Bean, Inc. v. Drake Publishers, Inc.," 73 *Iowa Law Review* 961 (1988). But see Koenig, *supra* note 63 for a more up-to-date and pessimistic view. A recent review of the case law on parody in intellectual property is found in T. A. Gauthier, "Fun and Profit: When Commercial Parodies Constitute Copyright or Trademark Infringement," 21 *Pepperdine Law Review* 165 (1994) who remarks upon the inconsistency and unpredictability of the case law and the availability and applicability of First Amendment defenses. See also S. M. Perez, "Confronting Biased Treatment of Trademark Parody under the Lanham Act," 44 *Emory Law Journal* 1451 (1995), for an analysis of the case law and the tendency toward an erosion of First Amendment freedoms. A recent overview of parody in U.S. intellectual property doctrines more generally is found in B. Keller and D. Bernstein, "As Satiric as They Wanna Be:

Parody Lawsuits under Copyright, Trademark, Dilution and Publicity Laws," 85 *Trademark Reporter* 239 (1995).

Certainly the dangers of corporate censorship posed by state antidilution laws are now far more readily acknowledged than they were five years ago (when I first addressed the topic). Mounting case law indicating the alacrity with which corporations pounced upon the potentials for silencing others inherent in such statutes has drawn the attention of the American Law Institute. In its *Restatement of the Law (Third) Unfair Competition* (1995), use of state antidilution laws to enjoin "tarnishing" nontrademark usages of a mark are recognized to pose substantial free speech issues:

> Use of another's trademark, not as a means of identifying the user's own goods or services, but as an incident of speech directed at the trademark owner, however, raises serious free speech concerns that cannot be easily accommodated under traditional trademark doctrine. The expression of an idea by means of the use of another's trademark in parody, for example, will often lie within the substantial constitutional protection accorded noncommercial speech and may thus be the subject of liability only in the most narrow circumstances. Although such nontrademark uses of another's mark may undermine the reputation and value of the mark, they should not be actionable under the law of trademarks. (*Ibid.*, at 273)

Not surprisingly, this raised the ire of trademark holders; for a discussion of the contested relationship between parody and the dilution doctrine of the law of unfair competition, see M. J. Alexander and M. K. Heilbronner, "An Analysis of the Dilution Section of the Restatement (Third) of Unfair Competition," 47 *South Carolina Law Review* 629 (1996).

152 M. F. Jacobson & L. A. Mazur, *Marketing Madness: A Survival Guide for a Consumer Society* 158–159 (1995), citing P. Taylor, *The Smoke Ring: Tobacco, Money, and Multinational Politics* (1984). Joe Camel came under scrutiny by the Clinton government in August 1996 when it ordered the Food and Drug Administration to introduce regulations that would curb underage smoking. As Clinton proclaimed, "With this historic action that we are taking today, Joe Camel and the Marlboro Man will be out of our children's reach forever" (cited in the *Hartford Courant* 24 August 1996). The regulations included a prohibition on billboard advertisements near children's schools, limit other billboard advertisments (and advertising in publications with more than 15 percent youth readership) to black-and-white text, and ban brand-name sponsorship of sporting events and logo merchandising of caps, gym bags, and T-shirts. Reynolds denied that Joe Camel was targeted at youth or that advertising played a role in promoting smoking among teens. Such regulations will be subject to First Amendment scrutiny. Although commercial speech is entitled to lesser protection, tobacco industry interests have good reason to believe that these regulations may be deemed unconstitutional, particularly those that restrict advertising content. Given the $6 billion that tobacco companies spent on advertising and promotion in 1993, for example, it will not be surprising if the advertising and publishing trade associations join the tobacco industry to block the implementation of these rules. The Federal Trade Commission declined to ban Joe Camel ads in 1994, saying there was insufficient evidence to prove that the advertising campaign caused underage smoking; the issue will no doubt continue to be revisited.

153 Both parodies/satires are reproduced *ibid.*, at 158–159.

154 R. Shweder, "Ad-Alterations as a Form of Cultural Interrogation," 1(2) *Public Culture* 80, 83 (1989).

155 In *Public Culture* (*ibid.*), Shweder explains her earlier publication in the February 1989 issue of *Zeta Magazine* of what she deems a "commercialism": a satire on corporate advertising, in which she "alters" a full-page commercial advertisement that appeared in the Sunday *New York Times* on November 27, 1988:

> The original advertisement has the image of a man and a woman signing their names onto a large scroll filled with other signatures. On the top of the scroll is written, "Total Quality on the B-2 Begins With Me." In the middle of the scroll there is a seal with a star and the words, "United States Air Force Northrup B-2 Team" surrounding it. On the bottom of the scroll the names of each company involved in the project are listed. In the ad itself, in bold large print, it reads, "The B-2. We Take it Personally." The text goes on to say, "We're 34,000 people who have each signed this scroll to mark our personal commitment to quality production of America's newest strategic deterrent . . . the Air Force B-2 Bomber. It says 'Total Quality on the B-2 Begins with Me.' And it does. For all of us who work on the B-2 at Northrup, the prime contractor, and at Boeing, LTV, Hughes Aircraft Company and General Electric, major members of the B-2 industrial team. Our work here may still be secret. Our commitment is not." The ad ends with the names of the companies involved in the project, listed again in larger and bolder print.

Shweder's "alteration" was to insert, in the form of collage, multiple photographs of human skulls where the original signatures appeared on the scroll. As a form of social commentary, she suggests that the ad-alteration works "to reveal and make evident the hidden meaning, subtext, or absences in a text." Advertisements, however, are works subject to copyright protection, and their reproduction in entirety opens one to liability for infringement in many jurisdictions. Moreover, they generally feature the trademarks of those on behalf of whom they seek a market. Even if we question the success of Shweder's appropriative critique, it is important to recognize that both to engage in her original "work," and later to explain its political meanings (which she does in more interesting detail than I can reiterate here), Shweder must reproduce the advertisement and the trademarks it contains. In so doing, she opens herself to potential injunction, damages, fines, a criminal record, an accounting of (albeit unlikely) profits to the author of the advertisement (most probably the Northrup corporate body), and an antidilution action from the four corporations whose trademarks act as "signatures" at the bottom of the work. (In explaining it here, I too must reproduce much of the text if not the imagery of the original advertisement.)

156 Kozinski, *supra* note 71, at 965.

157 Gordon, "A Property Right in Self-Expression," *supra* note 43, at 1537.

158 *Ibid.*

159 If authority needs to be claimed for this proposition, it comes from personal communications with Toronto lawyer Joseph Conforti. Thanks also to Eugene Cipparone.

160 Fictional characters receive copyright protection only to the extent that a character's expression is a component of a preexisting work, is "distinctly delineated," and

is elaborately developed. For discussions of the legal protection of fictional characters in Canada, see R. G. Howell, "Character Merchandising: The Marketing Potential Attaching to a Name, Image, Persona, or Copyright Work," 6 *Intellectual Property Journal* 197–223 (1991), and R. G. Howell, *Recent Developments in Character Merchandising: Ewoks, Crocodile Dundee in Ontario and Ninja Turtles in the United Kingdom*, paper presented at the Canadian Association of Law Teachers Intellectual Property Section, Charlottetown, P.E.I., 3–6 June 1992. In the United States, the character must be the central significance of the work. See Nichols v. Universal Pictures Corp., 45 F. 2d 119 (2d Cir. 1930). The "scènes à faire" doctrine bars stereotypes, character types, and stock characters from copyright protection because too much of their composition is culled from the public domain. See Atari Inc. v. North Am. Philips Consumer Elecs. Corp., 672 F. 2d 607 (7th Cir. 1982). Fictional characters appropriated outside of the works in which they originally figured will not be protected if they are merely vehicles that move the plot: the character must be so integral to the work as to constitute the very "story being told." See Warner Bros. Pictures, Inc. v. Columbia Broadcasting System, Inc., 216 F.2d 945 (9th Cir. 1954). In the United States, the "convergence" of copyright, trademark, and publicity rights protections (which many argue has resulted in an overprotection) is discussed in M. T. Helfand, "When Mickey Mouse Is as Strong as Superman: The Convergence of Intellectual Property Laws to Protect Fictional Literary and Pictorial Characters," 44 *Stanford Law Review* 623 (1992).

161 See, e.g., Walt Disney Productions v. Air Pirates, 870 F. 2d 40 (2d Cir. 1989). Courts have also begun to consider the "look and feel" of the environments in which visual characters are cast in considering a copyright infringement actions. See Sid & Marty Kroft Television v. McDonald's Corp., 562 F. 2d 1157 (9th Cir. 1977); Warner Bros., Inc. v. American Broadcasting Co., 530 F. Supp. 1187 (S.D.N.Y. 1982); Ideal Toy Corp. v. Kenner Products, 443 F. Supp. 291 (S.D.N.Y. 1977).

162 In the nightclub instance, an infringement action is unlikely to succeed. A series of thirty-second commercials does not provide the character a sufficient medium to develop sufficient delineation to merit copyright protection, nor would the milieu of a gay club seem likely to mimic the "look and feel" of the commercial.

163 Trademarks serve to publicly indicate the source of goods or services; the appropriation of a character registered as a mark functions to falsely designate origin and gives rise to an infringement action. The test for determining trademark infringement in the context of fictional characters is two-pronged: first, has the character developed "secondary meaning"? In other words, does the public associate the fictional character with a particular source? Second, has the claimant shown a likelihood of consumer confusion?

164 The only case to date to consider the Canadian Charter of Rights and Freedoms in a trademark and copyright infringement dispute is Michelin, *supra* note 114, which clearly favored property rights over free speech interests. For a more nuanced analysis in the copyright context see D. Fewer, "Constitutionalizing Copyright," 55 *University of Toronto Faculty of Law Review* 175 (1997). For a recent decision recognizing that the tort of appropriation of personality may implicate speech protections, see Gould Estate v. Stoddart Publishing Co. [1996] O.J. NO. 3288 (Ont. Ct. Gen.).

165 Matt Groening's allusion to Twentieth Century Fox's "busts" no doubt referred

to officials carrying out the authority given them under an Anton Piller order or temporary restraining order. Such operations are often ominously Kafkaesque, as armies of officials across wide regions simultaneously surround and enter premises, seizing merchandise and business records as evidence for a forthcoming trial that is unlikely to take place once the alleged infringer has lost his or her inventory. Recently, the FBI has become involved in raiding and seizing the goods of those suspected of being involved in the trading of "counterfeit T-shirts showing Mickey Mouse and other copyrighted characters" as part of "a three month investigation by a private investigator hired by Warner Bros. to root out unauthorized sales of T-shirts bearing its copyrighted Looney Tunes® characters, according to an affidavit filed with a U.S. magistrate judge in Alexandria" (quoted from *The Washington Post* 31 July 1993, at C-5).

166 See D. E. Clarke, "On Trade-marks Becoming Invalid," in *Trade-Marks Law of Canada* (G. F. Henderson et al., eds., 1993), and R. Hughes, *Hughs on Trademarks* (1992) at § 27, for an overview on the Canadian law relating to "genericide," and McCarthy, *supra* note 94, at § 12.09–12.11 pp. 12-60-70 for the equivalent American law.

167 Dreyfuss, *supra* note 95, at 417.

168 M. Pendergrast, *For God, Country and Coca-Cola* 105 (1993). In the years since, Coca-Cola has accumulated enough favorable case law to fill two more volumes. The company has circulated these volumes to lawyers and libraries, with the goal of "educating" the public and the legal community. I thank Peter Jaszi for sharing his "Coke" library with me.

169 *Ibid.*, at 105. Despite the willingness of the Coca-Cola Company to litigate to protect its trademark, the company ultimately lost its right to exclusive use of the word *cola* in the 1941 settlement to the first of many heated battles with the Pepsi-Cola Company (*ibid.*, at 195–196).

170 See *Mirabella* (July 1993) at 23.

171 "The Joy of Jelly," *Saturday Night* (September 1992) at 38.

172 *Ibid.*

173 N. Ristich, "Hell-O™ from Jell-O™," [Letter to the Editor] *Saturday Night* (December 1992) at 5, 14.

174 Copyright law's fair use doctrine, along with the idea/expression dichotomy, represents an attempt by the law to accommodate free speech principles in its analytical framework. However, the articulation of that doctrine has taken very different forms in the United States and Canada, with the U.S. codification providing the broader protective mantle to prospective users of copyright materials. The U.S. fair use exception to copyright infringement, as codified in the Copyright Act, 1976, 17 U.S.C., s.107 (1988 & Supp. V 1993) provides:

> Notwithstanding the provisions of sections 106 and 106A, the fair use of a copyrighted work, including such use by reproduction in copies or phonorecords or by any other means specified by that section, for purposes such as criticism, comment, news reporting, teaching (including multiple copies for classroom use), scholarship, or research, is not an infringement of copyright. In determining whether the use made of a work in any particular case is a fair use the factors to be considered shall include—
>
> (1) the purpose and character of the use, including whether such use is of a commercial nature or is for nonprofit educational purposes;

(2) the nature of the copyrighted work;

(3) the amount and substantiality of the portion used in relation to the copyrighted work as a whole; and

(4) the effect of the use upon the potential market for or value of the copyrighted work.

The fact that a work is unpublished shall not itself bar a finding of fair use if such finding is made upon consideration of all the above factors. In contrast, Canada's fair dealing provision as revised by Bill C-32, S.C. 1997, C-24, s.18(1) declares that:

fair dealing for the purposes of criticism, review, or news reporting does not infringe copyright if (and only if) the source, author, performer, maker, or broadcaster are mentioned.

There are two major structural differences between the two statutory treatments of allowable dealings with copyright materials. First, the Canadian "fair dealing" exception is exhaustive: if an activity is not catalogued in the statute, it cannot be a dealing which is fair under the Act and will infringe copyright, unless covered by limited specified exemptions elsewhere contained in the Act. In contrast, the U.S. treatment describes those activities listed as merely inclusive of those activities which may be considered fair uses of a work. Accordingly, the U.S. fair use provisions are much less restrictive than their Canadian counterparts. Second, Canada's Copyright Act does not set out a list of factors to be considered in a fair dealing analysis, whereas the U.S. Copyright Act provides factors that should be taken into account when determining if a use is a fair one (for example, the effect of the use on the market for the original work). Canadian courts are under no obligation to attend to such matters, and in fact rarely do. A third manner in which Canada's fair dealing exemption differs from the U.S. fair use defense is in its state of development: Canada simply has not generated any considerable amount of infringement defense jurisprudence, whereas more extensive American experience in this area has enabled fair use to develop in more nuanced ways. For example, the United States Supreme Court has recently laid to rest a controversy over the status of parody as fair use. See Campbell, *supra* note 150. Canada, in contrast, has yet to see fair dealing successfully invoked as a defense to copyright infringement in a parody case. For what might have been such an attempt, see Michelin, *supra* note 114. Although Canadian judges have both British fair dealing jurisprudence and U.S. fair use principles to draw upon should such a dispute arise, the paucity of Canadian jurisprudence leaves the law in an uncertain state and makes the overreaching of intellectual property holders inevitable.

175   Sut Jhally, a professor at the University of Massachusetts, received a letter from MTV threatening to sue for violation of copyright laws after he used the MTV logo and clips from 165 videos he taped at home to produce an educational video. The video, titled *Dreamworlds: Desire/Sex/Power in Rock Videos*, shows how rock videos depict women as sex objects and reaffirm the hegemony of the masculine gaze. Professor Jhally responded to the threat by faxing letters to several reporters, detailing MTV's attempts to censor his work. See "A Professor's Class Video Runs into an MTV Protest," *New York Times* 18 May 1991, at I46. See also Joseph Roach's account of his attempts to get permission to use a reproduction of the U.S. Post Office's "Elvis" stamp in *Cities of the Dead: Circum-Atlantic Performance* (1996).

176 Dreyfuss, *supra* note 95.

177 M. Gardiner, *The Dialogics of Critique: M. M. Bakhtin and the Theory of Ideology* 186 (1992).

178 T. Todorov, *Mikhail Bakhtin: The Dialogical Principle* ix (W. Godzich, trans., 1984). Much of Bakhtin's work is still untranslated, and it is necessary to refer to secondary sources to get a sense of the full range of his thought.

179 K. Hirschkop, "Introduction: Bakhtin and Cultural Theory," in *Bakhtin and Cultural Theory* 1–2 (K. Hirschkop and D. Shepherd, eds., 1989).

180 See M. Holquist, *Dilogism: Bakhtin and His World* 41 (1990).

181 *Ibid.*, at 49.

182 *Ibid.*, at 19; see also M. Bakhtin, *Problems of Dostoevsky's Poetics* 311–312 (C. Emerson, trans., 1984).

183 Holquist, *supra* note 180, at 49 (quoting Voloshinov, *supra* note 1, at 11) (emphasis in original); see also Todorov, *supra* note 178, at 30. There is a vociferous debate about whether the works allegedly authored by Voloshinov were in fact written by Bakhtin. See Holquist, *supra* note 180, at 8. I think Bakhtin would be amused.

184 Holquist, *supra* note 180, at 175.

185 *Ibid.*, at 23–24; see also Todorov, *supra* note 178, at 175.

186 S. Dentith, *Bakhtinian Thought: An Introductory Reader* 3 (1995).

187 *Ibid.*

188 *Ibid.*, at 192.

189 *Ibid.*, at 23.

190 *Ibid.*, at 24.

191 Holquist, *supra* note 180, at 66.

192 *Ibid.*, at 158 (emphasis in original).

193 *Ibid.*, at 29–30.

194 "To be human is to seek coherence, constantly to engage in an 'effort after meaning'" (Winter, "The Cognitive Dimension," *supra* note 21, at 2230, quoting Bruner, Foreword to D. Spence, *The Freudian Metaphor: Toward Paradigm Change in Psychoanalysis* xii [1987]).

195 We constantly use our imaginative capacities "to recast what we find and reconstruct our context by reconceptualization" and our "power of imagination to create new meanings not already shaped by what we believe" (Winter, "Bull Durham," *supra* note 16, at 674–676). "Freedom consists not in an unrestricted capacity to define meaning, but in an ability to modulate meanings" (*ibid.*, at 684, quoting K. Whiteside, *Merleau-Ponty and the Foundation of an Existential Politics* 68–69 [1988]).

196 Voloshinov, *supra* note 1, at 11.

197 See G. Pechey, "On the Borders of Bakhtin: Dialogisation, Decolonisation," in *Bakhtin and Cultural Theory, supra* note 179, at 43–52.

198 Voloshinov, *supra* note 1, at 23.

199 Gardiner, *supra* note 177, at 177.

200 See M. M. Bakhtin, "Discourse in the Novel," in *The Dialogic Imagination: Four Essays by M. M. Bakhtin* 259, 298–299 (M. Holquist, ed., C. Emerson and M. Holquist, trans., 1981).

201 Gardiner, *supra* note 177, at 173.

202 For example, Winter says that his conception of "culture" does not reify it into some monolithic, determinate "thing," but he never explores any social negotia-

tions of meaning nor any conflictual practices or struggles to define meaning, rele-gating the politics of meaning to a single phrase in a single footnote when he tersely notes that "people in power get to impose their metaphors" (Winter, "Tran-scendental Nonsense," *supra* note 16, at 1135 n.101, quoting G. Lakoff and M. John-son, *Metaphors We Live By* 157 [1980]). For a longer discussion of the tendency of legal theorists to avoid issues of power when discussing "culture," see Coombe, "Same as It Ever Was," *supra* note 16, at 630–652.

203   But if legal theorists concerned with "culture" have a tendency toward idealism, those concerned with free speech tend toward an undue materialism in their con-siderations of dialogism. I discuss the left critique of the public-private dichotomy in the penultimate essay in this volume.

2. Author(iz)ing the Celebrity: Engendering Alternative Identities

1   A character in N. Grieg and D. Griffiths, *As Time Goes By* (1981), cited in R. Dyer, *Heavenly Bodies: Film Stars and Society* 141 (1986).

2   A. McRobbie, *Postmodernism and Popular Culture* 70 (1994).

3   A. Doty, *Making Things Perfectly Queer: Interpreting Mass Culture* xviii–xix (1993).

4   M. Madow, "Private Ownership of Public Image: Popular Culture and Publicity Rights," 81 *California Law Review* 127, 173, n.229 (1993).

5   Throughout this chapter, I will use the term *celebrity image* to designate not only or exclusively a celebrity's visual likeness but rather all elements of the complex con-stellation of visual, verbal, and aural signs that circulate in society and constitute the celebrity's recognition value. The term *persona* will also refer to this configuration of significations.

6   I use the umbrella term *publicity rights* to encompass the tort of appropriation of personality as it has developed at common law, the proprietary right of publicity that has developed in U.S. law, and rights to prevent the appropriation of (*inter alia*) names and likenesses that have been enacted in provincial and state statutes as well as federal trademark legislation.

7   D. Vaver, "What's Mine Is Not Yours: Commercial Appropriation of Personality un-der the Privacy Acts of B.C., Manitoba and Saskatchewan," 15 *University of British Columbia Law Review* 241 (1981).

8   See American Law Institute, *Restatement (Second) of Torts* § 652A–652I (1977). Also, American Law Institute, *Restatement of the Law (Third) Unfair Competition* (1995) S. 46–49. As Christopher Pesce points out, the right of publicity is "a hybrid of privacy's tort of appropriation, the law of unfair competition, and the law of prop-erty" (C. Pesce, "The Likeness Monster: Should the Right of Publicity Protect Against Imitation?," 65 *New York University Law Review* 782, 792 [1990]).

9   See F. M. Weiler, "The Right of Publicity Gone Wrong: A Case for Privileged Appro-priation of Identity," 13 *Cardozo Arts & Entertainment Law Journal* 223, 224–225, n. 14–17 (1994), for a list of state name-and-likeness statutes, a list of those states that have codified the right of publicity and recognize an independent common law right of publicity, a list of states that recognize the right only at common law, and the varying periods of protection afforded to the right in different American jurisdictions.

10   Trade Marks Act, R.S.C. 1985, c.T-13; Lanham Act, 15 U.S.C.A. § 1052.

11   L. Lawrence, "The Right of Publicity: A Research Guide," 10 *Hastings Communica-*

tions and Entertainment Law Journal 143 (1987). See also F. Houdek, "The Right of Publicity: A Comprehensive Bibliography of Law-Related Material," 7 *Hastings Communications and Entertainment Law Journal* 505 (1985), and F. Houdek, "Researching the Right of Publicity: A Revised and Comprehensive Bibliography of Law Related Materials," 16 *Hastings Communications and Entertainment Law Journal* 385 (1994). Unfortunately, the latter author's summaries of the materials he includes are both inadequate and misleading.

12 Hirsch v. S. C. Johnson & Son, 90 Wis.2d 379, 280 N.W.2d 129 (1979) (athlete has right of publicity in his nickname "Crazylegs" and could sustain action against shaving gel manufacturer).

13 Cepeda v. Swift & Co., 291 F.Supp. 242 (E.D. Mo. 1968), aff'd, 415 F.2d 1205 (8th Cir. 1969); U.S. Life Insurance Co. v. Hamilton, 238 S.W.2d 289 (Tex. Civ. App. 1951).

14 Athans v. Canadian Adventure Camps Ltd., 34 C.P.R.(2d) 126 (Ontario High Court 1977).

15 (1979) Lugosi v. Universal Pictures, 160 Cal. Rptr. 323.; Price v. Worldvision Enters., Inc., 455 F.Supp. 252 (S.D.N.Y. 1978) aff'd, 603 F.2d 214 (2d Cir. 1979); Price v. Hal Roach Studios, Inc., 400 F.Supp. 836 (S.D.N.Y. 1975).

16 Midler v. Ford Motor Co., 849 F.2d 460 (9th Cir. 1988) (singer awarded damages for television commercial's use of a "sound-alike" to imitate her voice and singing style).

17 In Lahr v. Adell Chemical Co., the court noted that Lahr had achieved stardom due to his "style of vocal delivery which, by reason of its distinctive and original combination of pitch, inflection, and comic sounds has caused him to become widely known and readily recognized." A television commercial using a similar voice was "stealing the thunder" of the performer (300 F.2d 256 (1st Cir. 1962) at 257).

18 Joseph v. Daniels, 11 C.P.R.(3d) 544 (B.C.S.C. 1986).

19 Carson v. Here's Johnny Portable Toilets, Inc., 698 F.2d 831 (6th Cir. 1983) (portable toilet manufacturer violated Johnny Carson's right of publicity by using phrase "Here's Johnny" with the slogan "The World's Foremost Comodian"); Ali v. Playgirl, 447 F.Supp. 723, 3 *Media Law Reporter* (BNA) 2540, 206 U.S.P.Q. (BNA) 1021 (S.D.N.Y. 1978) (illustration depicting nude black male with caption "The Greatest" violated plaintiff's right of publicity because the phrase was known to be a common reference to the plaintiff).

20 Motschenbacher v. R. J. Reynolds Tobacco Co., 498 F.2d 821 (9th Cir. 1974) (plaintiff racing car driver had identifiable attributes appropriated because unique and distinctive decorations on his car were recognizable in cigarette commercial).

21 Lahr v. Adell Chemical Co., 300 F.2d 256 (1st Cir. 1962) (comic delivery style); Booth v. Colgate Palmolive Co., 362 F.Supp. 343 (S.D.N.Y. 1975) (imitation of Shirley Booth's voice and style of portraying television character Hazel).

22 Lombardo v. Doyle, Dane & Bernbach, Inc., 58 A.D. 2d 620, 396 N.Y.S. 2d 661 (N.Y. App. Div. 1977).

23 H. L. Hetherington, "Direct Commercial Exploitation of Identity: A New Age for the Right of Publicity," 17 *Columbia-VLA Journal of Law & the Arts* 1, 43 (1992).

24 See, e.g., J. R. Braatz, "White v. Samsung Electronics America: The Ninth Circuit Turns a New Letter in California Right of Publicity Law," 15 *Pace Law Review* 161 (1994); S. C. Clay, Note: "Starstruck: The Overextension of Celebrity Publicity Rights in State and Federal Courts," 79 *Minnesota Law Review* 485 (1994); R. C. Dreyfuss, "We Are Symbols and Inhabit Symbols, So Why Should We Be Paying Rent? Deconstructing the Lanham Act and Rights of Publicity," 20 *Columbia-VLA Journal*

of Law and the Arts 123 (1996); P. B. Frank, Note: "White v. Samsung Electronics America Inc.: The Right of Publicity Spins Its Wheels," 55 *Ohio State Law Journal* 1115 (1994); W. M. Heberer, Comment: "The Overprotection of Celebrity: A Comment on White v. Samsung Electronics America, Inc.," 22 *Hofstra Law Review* 279 (1994); Hetherington, *supra* note 23; J. F. Hyland and T. C. Lindquist III, "White v. Samsung Electronics America, Inc.: The Wheels of Justice Take an Unfortunate Turn," 23 *Golden Gate University Law Review* 299 (1993); D. R. Kelly and M. E. Hartmann, "Parody (of Celebrities, in Advertising), Parity (between Advertising and Other Types of Commercial Speech), and (the Property Right of) Publicity," 17 *Hastings Communications and Entertainment Law Journal* 633 (1995); Madow, *supra* note 4; G. A. Pemberton, "The Parodist's Claim to Fame: A Parody Exception to the Right of Publicity," 27 *University of California-Davis Law Review* 97 (1993); S. M. Perez, "Confronting Biased Treatment of Trademark Parody under the Lanham Act," 44 *Emory Law Journal* 1451 (1995); T. F. Simon, "Right of Publicity Reified: Fame as Business Asset," 30 *New York Law School Law Review* 699 (1985); L. J. Stack, "White v. Samsung Electronics America, Inc.'s Expansion of the Right of Publicity: Enriching Celebrities at the Expense of Free Speech," 89 *Northwestern University Law Review* 1189 (1995); Weiler, *supra* note 9. Most of these articles review the history of the doctrine and make suggestions for limiting the right of publicity and recognizing First Amendment concerns; I find many of the recommendations plausible and potentially effective, but my interest here does not center on law reform, but on the celebrity as a medium for the creation of alter/native identities. The slash here is meant to indicate that in the creation of such new identities, that which is "native" is altered. I prefer this to the term *subaltern*, for it suggests the potentially transformative effects that the margins may have upon the center and dominant understandings of what is natural or native to human being.

25 Canadian and British courts have not gone so far as to recognize the right as proprietary and continue to deal with it as a tort. This has not prevented celebrities from entering into licensing contracts and conveying merchandising rights, however.

26 American courts are divided on the issue of whether a right of publicity survives the individual's death and in what circumstances. Some courts have refused recovery for the relatives or assignees of a decedent where the name or likeness has been appropriated for commercial purposes on the grounds that an individual's personal right of privacy does not survive his or her death. Others have allowed recovery for invasion of privacy in similar circumstances. Decisions predicated upon rights of publicity range from those that hold that the right survives death in all circumstances, those that require the celebrity to have engaged in some form of commercial exploitation during his or her life before the right will be descendible, and those that unconditionally oppose descendibility in any circumstances. The tendency, however, has been toward greater recognition of the descendibility of publicity rights, and state legislatures have also inclined toward statutory recognition of the descendibility of such rights. The issue has yet to be determined or even seriously addressed in Canadian or British courts.

27 See discussion and cases cited in J. Gross, "The Right of Publicity Revisited: Reconciling Fame, Fortune, and Constitutional Rights," 62 *Boston University Law Review* 965 (1982), and R. T. E. Coyne, "Toward a Modified Fair Use Defense in Right of Publicity Cases," 29 *William & Mary Law Review* 781 (1988). In the case of celebrity images employed in commercial advertising, there are conflicting lines of authority.

Historically, U.S. law accorded commercial advertising little or no value when it conflicted with an individual's privacy or publicity rights. Before 1976, this was consistent with the low constitutional value placed on commercial speech. As T. F. Haas, "Storehouse of Starlight: The First Amendment Privilege to Use Names and Likenesses in Commercial Advertising," 19 *University of California Law Review* 539 (1986) argues, however, the extension of limited First Amendment protection to commercial speech suggests that many of the cases involving appropriations of name and likeness in commercial advertising would now have to be decided differently.

28 D. Sudjic, *Cult Heroes: How to Be Famous for More than Fifteen Minutes* (1989). See also R. Schickel, *Intimate Strangers: The Culture of Celebrity, Where We Came In* (1985).

29 Sudjic, *supra* note 28, at 10.

30 *Ibid.*, at 15.

31 *Ibid.*, at 19.

32 *Ibid.*, at 83.

33 H. Gordon, "Right of Property in Name, Likeness, Personality and History," 55 *Northwestern University Law Review* 553, 555–557 (1960); Comment, "The Right of Publicity: Premature Burial for California Property Rights in the Wake of Lugosi," 12 *Pacific Law Journal* 987, 995–997 (1981).

34 D. Lange, "Recognizing the Public Domain," 44(4) *Law and Contemporary Problems* 147 (1981).

35 W. Gordon, "On Owning Information: Intellectual Property and the Restitutionary Impulse," 78 *Virginia Law Review* 149 (1992).

36 See M. Radin, "Market Inalienability," 100 *Harvard Law Review* 1859 (1987); M. Radin, *Contested Commodities* (1996); and E. Anderson, "Is Women's Labor a Commodity?," 19 *Philosophy and Public Affairs* 71 (1990), for philosophical discussions of the factors we need to weigh in determining if commodification is an appropriate mode of valuation.

37 Lange, *supra* note 34, cites S. J. Hoffman, "Limitations on the Right of Publicity," 28 *Bulletin of the Copyright Society* 111, 116–133 (1980), as asking a similar question. See also A. M. Weisman, "Publicity as an Aspect of Privacy and Personal Autonomy," 55 *Southern California Law Review* 727, 729–751 (1982).

38 J. Locke, *Second Treatise of Government*, ch. 5 (1978), [1690].

39 E. C. Hettinger, "Justifying Intellectual Property," 18 *Philosophy and Public Affairs* 31, 37 (1989).

40 For example, "the celebrity has invested time, money, and effort to develop a high level of public recognition. Therefore, the unauthorized use of the celebrity's persona . . . deprives the celebrity of the economic gain he or she deserves, unjustly enriches the user and reduces the celebrity's ability to control his or her public image" (A. Cifelli and W. McMurray, "The Right of Publicity—A Trademark Model for Its Temporal Scope," 66 *Journal of the Patent Office Society* 455, 462 [1984]).

41 Hettinger, *supra* note 39.

42 Dyer, *supra* note 1; and R. Dyer, *Stars* (1979).

43 D. MacCannell, "Marilyn Monroe Was Not a Man," 17 *Diacritics* 114, 115 (1987).

44 Hettinger, *supra* note 39, at 38.

45 Lange, *supra* note 34, at 162.

46 R. R. Kwall, "The Right of Publicity vs. the First Amendment: A Property and Liability Rule Analysis," 70 *Indiana Law Journal* 47 (1994). Professor Kwall's support of an

"authorship rationale" for publicity rights is also shown in her belief that American copyright law in practice is inordinately concerned with pecuniary as opposed to personal interests and is to that extent incompatible with publicity rights protection. She suggests that *copyright theory*, to the extent that it acknowledges and protects an individual's authorial presence in his or her work and recognizes the personal interests of creators in their works, is compatible with publicity rights: "If copyrighted property can be said to represent the embodiment of a creator's heart, mind, and soul, this is even more true for attributes such as an individual's name and likeness that are protected by the right of publicity" (*ibid.*, at 59–60). The extent to which one's labor is embedded in one's name or likeness is questionable (except for some obvious examples), and a right to privacy, protection against defamation, and consumer protection laws would cover most objectionable usages of these attributes. Unfortunately, other attributes protected by rights of publicity go well beyond those that are most "personal" to include all attributes that are *publicly* recognized and hence, by virtue of mass exposure, the *least* intimate aspects of one's persona. The right, after all, does not protect one from alienation inasmuch as it fosters one's ability to engage in self-commodification.

47 523 F.Supp. 485 (S.D.N.Y. 1981), 689 F.2d 317 (2d Cir. 1982).

48 *Ibid.*, 523 F.Supp. 485, 492–494.

49 See T. Podlesney, "Blondes," in *The Hysterical Male: New Feminist Theory* 82 (A. Kroker and M. Kroker, eds., 1991), who argues that "the blonde" is the perfect post–WWII product and the ultimate sign of U.S. global supremacy, white patriarchy, and the triumph of American mass media and mass production. Madonna, she suggests, is the blondest blonde ever, "with forty years of the blonde phenomenon informing her every move." As Podlesney notes, Madonna has frequently been "heralded for mis(re)appropriating the iconography of the blonde bombshell in a cynical defiance of the rules of sexuality codified by patriarchy" (*ibid.*, at 84). On January 16, 1991, the *Washington Post* reported that Florida State University professor Chip Wells was writing a doctoral dissertation on Madonna as a "postmodern social construct." For a recent academic study, see S. P. Baty, *American Monroe: The Making of a Body Politic* (1995).

50 R. Goldstein, "We So Horny: Sado Studs and Super Sluts: America's New Sex 'Tude," *Village Voice* 16 October 1990, at 35, 36.

51 Lange, *supra* note 34, at 163.

52 *Ibid.*, at 165.

53 I have no idea whether Jarmusch sought the consent of the Presley estate or the corporate owners of his publicity rights and, if so, what royalties he agreed to pay. Nor do I know whether the Presley estate ever sought to enjoin the film's production or to demand royalties. The very possibility of such an injunction and its desirability is what is at issue here. Celebrities or their estates are not obliged to grant licenses for the use of their image regardless of the artistic or social merit of the works in which these are deployed, and may withhold consent on any pretext. In this hypothetical scenario, *Mystery Train might* be privileged under the First Amendment, but then again, it might not, given the difficulties contemporary courts face in distinguishing between fact and fiction in consumer markets.

54 A party launching "Elvis Presley" cologne was held at the New York club Hot Rod in early October of 1990 (reported by M. Musto, "La Dolce Musto," *Village Voice* 26 October 1990, at 44). Wine is now marketed as "Marilyn Merlot," with the actress's

likeness on the label (her image also adorns lingerie), and "Rebel" cologne is marketed with an image of James Dean's face, which, in Canada at least, is registered as a trademark. I am grateful to lawyers at Gowling & Henderson in Toronto for bringing this to my attention.

55 Memphis Development Foundation v. Factors Etc., Inc., 441 F.Supp. 1323 (W.D. Tenn. 1977). On appeal, the Sixth Circuit reversed and remanded, holding that the right of publicity was not descendible under Tennessee law 616 F.2d 956 (6th Cir. 1980). The Tennessee legislature responded by statutorily recognizing a descendible exclusive property right in an individual's name or likeness, terminable only upon two years of commercial nonuse (Tennessee Code Annotated [1988] § 47-25-1101-1108). The Tennessee Court of Appeals has since determined that Presley's right of publicity survived his death in 1977 and expressly rejected the Sixth Circuit's opinion on Tennessee law (Elvis Presley International Memorial Foundation v. Crowell 733 S.W.2d 89 [Tenn. Ct. App. 1987]). The Sixth Circuit then declared itself bound by the Court of Appeal's ruling in Elvis Presley Enterprises v. Elvisly Yours 817 F.2d 104 (6th Cir. 1987). For a discussion of some of the alternative moral economies in which Elvis figures in the American Midwest, see L. Spigel, "Communicating with the Dead: Elvis as Medium," 23 *Camera Obscura* 177 (1990).

56 Hettinger, *supra* note 39, at 39–40.

57 W. Gordon, "A Property Right in Self-Expression: Equality and Individualism in the Law of Intellectual Property," 102 *Yale Law Journal* 1533 (1993).

58 Hettinger, *supra* note 39, at 40.

59 Commentators seem eager to extend publicity rights using analogies to copyright, patent, and trademark, but they rarely carry such analogies through to the point of imposing either temporal limits on the right or permitting a range of defenses, exemptions, and opportunities for cancellation equal to those afforded the public in these other areas of law. In both copyright law and patent law, the grant of a property right is part of a socially beneficial bargain between the creator of the work and the public. Because we deem progress in the arts and sciences socially beneficial, we wish to encourage creative efforts and innovations. To induce individuals to invest their efforts in these areas, we grant such individuals exclusive property rights in their works and inventions for a limited period of time in order to recoup their investment costs. In exchange, the creator is obliged to disseminate these works and make them available to the public (sometimes by way of compulsory license) while the patent or copyright is in force, and bequeath the work to the public domain after the monopoly expires.

The reasons we bestow property rights in literary, artistic, and scientific works, and the reasons we put limitations upon those rights, emerge from a history of social deliberation that is manifestly absent in our creation of publicity and personality rights. For example, if we extend property rights in the products of intellectual labor as an incentive to encourage socially desirable activities, then we need to address three questions: Is fame or celebrity a socially desirable product whose cultivation we wish to encourage? Are incentives necessary to encourage this activity? Does the necessity for incentives require the granting of exclusive property rights? The first question is the most difficult to answer; the celebrity phenomenon does appear to serve certain social needs and desires. However, to the extent that the celebrity aura is harnessed to develop wholly symbolic market distinctions among functionally indistinguishable goods (and may, therefore, concomitantly decrease incentives to improve product quality or encourage innovative product research and design), its social utility may be doubted. Such a qualification, however, already presupposes the answers to the second and third questions; only when exclusive rights to the image are granted will licenses of such rights have value in the market.

If we decide that the development of celebrity is socially desirable, then we need to determine if incentives are necessary to encourage these creative endeavors. Clearly the potential for financial reward afforded by the commercial exploitation of one's persona must glimmer on the horizon as a tantalizing possibility for some celebrities, especially those, like sports stars, whose professional lives are temporally limited. But again, this possibility begs the question. Those stars most likely and able to exploit their personas are those with successful careers in acting, singing, athletics, or politics who receive media recognition for their achievements. In the course of their careers they have been compensated with large salaries, lucrative bonuses, valuable perks, fees for public appearances, and fame itself. Arguably, they are already so well compensated (some would say overcompensated) for their activities that no additional incentives are necessary. Legal recognition of an exclusive right of publicity does not serve to induce, protect, or compensate the celebrity's achievements, but serves instead to give an additional and collateral economic value to the benefit of fame itself.

It seems doubtful that any further economic incentive is required to encourage the achievements of media and sport stars, and even more dubitable that such incentives should take the form of exclusive property rights. If required, such incentives might just as well take the form of higher salaries, public subsidies, reduced taxes, or free housing. But even if we *had* determined that an exclusive property right was a necessary incentive to have a celebrity bestow his or her fame upon us, the logic of intellectual property rationales would demand that the celebrity give us something in return. Copyright and patent laws insist that the work be made publicly available, whereas celebrities may insist upon seclusion and refuse to let their image circulate or price its use on the market so high that no one else can possibly have access to it.

Moreover, copyright laws enable fair uses to be made of a work, whereas we have no criteria or legislation enabling appropriators of a celebrity's image to claim that their use was a fair one. See K. E. Kulzick and A. D. Hogue, "Chilled Bird: Freedom of Expression in the Eighties," 14 *Loyola of Los Angeles Law Review* 57 (1980); K. S. Marks, "An Assessment of the Copyright Model in Right of Publicity Cases," 70 *California Law Review* 786 (1982); R. Kwall, "Is Independence Day Dawning for the Right of Publicity?," 17 *University of California-Davis Law Review* 191 (1984); Hoffman, *supra* note 37; Simon, *supra* note 24, and Coyne, *supra* note 27, for arguments in favor of a fair use defense in publicity cases. See Pemberton, *supra* note 24, and Weiler, *supra* note 9, for other potential copyright-based exemptions.

Copyright, furthermore, is limited to works of authorship fixed in a tangible medium of expression on the policy grounds that although expressions can be owned, ideas should be freely accessible to promote further creative endeavor. Many of the attributes protected by the right of publicity are intangible attributes of an individual that have become associated with that individual in the public mind. These associations are ideas in the public realm. By designating these public ideational associations the private property of individuals, we create individual monopolies in ever more ephemeral attributes and preclude these ideas from contributing to new creative works and the social goal of progress in the arts. Some commentators suggest that the copyright model is inadequate precisely *because* it cannot fully protect all aspects of the celebrity image, given that "the myriad of quirks and nuances that comprise the persona are not capable of being fixed in a tangible medium of expression" (B. Singer, "The Right of Publicity: Star Vehicle or Shooting Star?," 10 *Cardozo Arts & Entertainment Law Journal* 1 [1992]).

Moreover, not all of the elements that make up a copyrightable work are protected by copyright. Many components of the work are deemed to be in the public domain. See J. Litman, "The Public Domain," 39 *Emory Law Review* 965 (1990). Use of standard plot lines and stock characters, for example, are not considered copyright infringement because such devices are considered part of the public domain that must be available to future creators. We have more conceptual difficulty recognizing any recognized attribute of a persona to be in the public domain because these are understood to be bound up in the person, but if we think of celebrities as works we wish to promote, then some famous attributes will have to enter the public domain to provide resources for others. Otherwise, models such as Claudia Schiffer would have to receive licenses and pay royalties to ancestresses like Bridget Bardot and their estates and assigns.

Copyright and patent laws grant a limited term of exclusive rights on the basis that a temporarily limited monopoly satisfies the need for economic incentive and that the fruits of humanity's intellectual labors thereafter fall into the public domain and become the collective resources of humankind. The descendibility of publicity rights, however, raises the specter of human creative works owned and controlled in perpetuity by avaricious assignees ever more distant from the original creator, concerned only with a continuing stream of royalties and license fees. (For a longer discussion of the inaccuracies and inadequacies of comparing publicity rights to copyright, see Simon, *supra* note 24.)

Some have argued that a right of publicity is more akin to a trademark than to copyright and patent, and, to a limited degree, the analogy holds. Few, however, have pushed the analogy to its logical conclusions. For trademark law, too, has social purposes, grants limited rights, and affords reasonable defenses, all of which serve to contain the property right in a manner that contrasts with the absolute nature of proprietary publicity rights. Trademark law is concerned with the protection of words and symbols as indicators of the source or sponsorship of commercial goods and services. Trademark rights arise through the extensive and continuous use of a brand name, image, or symbol in marketing particular goods or services. Once the trademark serves to distinguish a group of goods or services from other goods or services, the holder of the mark is given exclusive rights to use that mark in conjunction with that particular class of wares. He or she can then prevent others from using the mark on the same or similar goods on the basis that potential customers are likely to be confused as to the source of those goods and that the reputation of the trademark owner may be diminished by the use of the mark on inferior goods.

The value of a trademark is integrally related to the goods and services it represents. Rights to trademarks are never absolute property rights but exclusive rights to use the sign or symbol in conjunction with a particular class of goods or services. Thus, it is not a violation to use a mark in association with unrelated goods or services where there is no competition between the parties, no likelihood of customer confusion, and no suggestion in the public mind that the original trademark owner endorses the second group of goods. Trademark rights are linked to a certain line of goods and services; they cannot, for example, be assigned except in conjunction with the goodwill of the goods or services to which they pertain. Hence the rule that it is the trade and not the mark that trademark law serves to protect. Neither the common law nor trademark legislation recognizes a property right "in gross" (although, as the discussion in chapter 1 alerted us, this may well be the *effect* of enforcing antidilution provisions and stretching the doctrine of confusion). To maintain a dilution claim, however, the symbol must at least serve as a trademark or trade name, whereas celebrities are enabled to enforce rights to icons even where these icons do not serve distinguishing roles in commodity markets. Even when trademarks are licensed, licensors were traditionally obliged to maintain control over the quality of the goods and services being rendered under the mark, because trademarks were intended to prevent the deceit of the public as to the source and quality of goods. Where there is no likelihood of confusion of sponsorship, and hence no possibility of public deception, the use of a mark would not be enjoined. Although consumer confusion is increasingly found by judges with alarming alacrity, these principles at least provide some guidance and limitations. Trademarks, moreover, must be monitored; they may be deemed abandoned, and they may be challenged for lack of use and loss of distinction.

Trademark rights, then, are limited rights, designed to serve social purposes—not absolute or exclusive property rights in a sign or symbol that can be evoked by a trademark "owner" in any context. Some aspects of publicity rights might be justified by analogy to trademark law. A celebrity might well use his or her name or likeness to market a particular class of goods or services. If the name or likeness came to identify and distinguish particular wares to consumers, a trademark right would be justified. However, the doctrine of publicity rights extends to celebrities a property right to their name and likeness before any marketing use of the celebrity image has been made and whether or not the public has come to recognize the image as distinguishing a group of goods or services. Moreover, a celebrity may attempt to prevent the use of his or her image even where there is no competition between the parties, no evidence that the defendant intended to pass off goods as those endorsed by the celebrity, and no evidence that the public was in any way confused by the use of the persona.

Indeed, whereas trademark laws (theoretically) attempted to prevent deceit in the marketplace, publicity rights may be exercised in a manner that contributes to consumer confusion. A celebrity can assign and license the attributes of his or her persona without having any relationship to the manufacture, production, and distribution of the merchandise to which he or she has linked his or her image, and he or she assumes no responsibility to the public for the quality of those goods. A well-known architect can license his name for use in the marketing of tea kettles, and the estate of an artist may collect royalties for the use of his name on perfume. If the public comes to associate certain attributes of quality with goods bearing these names, they may well be confused and disappointed when the architect's or the artist's estate later licenses these names to totally unrelated manufacturers who use them to market shoddy merchandise of inferior quality.

Celebrities may do nothing more than make a few carefully orchestrated public appearances every year to command a steady return of royalties from the licensing of their merchandising rights. They need invest no money of their own or have any involvement in the design, production, or dissemination of the products that bear their names. Once a famous designer, Pierre Cardin now earns a small fortune merely by capitalizing on his name. In 1987 he made $125 million from licenses to eight hundred licensees in ninety-three countries who sell merchandise worth more than $1 billion a year, from which he earns royalties of about $75 million. The Cardin name adorns products as diverse as cigarettes, clocks, and deodorants, but neither Cardin nor his company maintains much involvement in their design or production; Cardin's director of licensing admitted that "even we don't know all the products we license." (See discussion of Cardin in Sudjic, *supra* note 28, at 61.) Consumers were given no guarantee of source or quality; the goods bearing the Cardin name might have come from a Filipino factory or the former Soviet Union's Ministry of Light Industry (one of the hundreds of Cardin licensees), but still legitimately carried the celebrity's name. The recent controversy over celebrities' licensing their names to goods produced in sweatshop conditions makes it clear that such activities are only illegitimate in the court of public opinion and that publicity provides the only form of censure. For a longer discussion, see R. J. Coombe, "Sports Trademarks and Somatic Politics: Locating the Law in a Critical Cultural Studies," in *Competing Allegories: Global and Local Cultures of Sport* (R. Martin and T. Miller, eds., 1998).

Trademark law also incorporates a recognition that no sign or symbol can be taken out of public discourse except insofar as it actually continues to distinguish a particular range of goods. As the discussion of genericide in the previous chapter indicated, if a mark ceases to distinguish particular goods, a trademark holder may lose his or her exclusive rights to the mark unless he or she can show evidence of behavior indicating an intent not to abandon it. If the mark ceases to be used in connection with those goods with which it was acquired, or ceases to be distinctive in that it becomes a name in common parlance used to designate all goods of a particular class, then the mark holder will no longer have exclusive rights to it and the mark will be consigned to the public domain. A trademark owner is therefore obliged to police his or her mark in order to retain the rights to it. A celebrity or his or her estate is under no such obligation. A deceased star's estate or assignees, for example, might decide to use the star's likeness to market shoes years after his or her death, even though the likeness doesn't distinguish the shoes from others in the public mind, the celebrity's image has never been used to distinguish goods before, and the celebrity's image has become part of the popular culture used for a variety of entertainment and/or commercial purposes. Assignees may have done nothing to police the use of the likeness in the past yet suddenly claim exclusive rights to an image commonly understood to be part of a cultural heritage available to us all.

60 As Judge Kozinski put it in his acute dissent in White v. Samsung Electronics, 971 F.2d 1395 (9th Cir. 1992) at 1516:

Intellectual property rights aren't free: They're imposed at the expense of future creators and of the public at large . . . This is why intellectual property law is full of careful balances between what's set aside for the owner and what's left in the public domain for the rest of us: The relatively short life of patents; the longer, but finite life of copyrights; copyright's idea-expression dichotomy; the fair use doctrine; the prohibition on copyrighting facts; the compulsory license of television broadcasts and musical compositions; federal preemption of overbroad state intellectual property laws; the nominative use doctrine in trademark law; the right to make soundalike recordings. All of these diminish an intellectual property holder's rights. All let the public use something created by someone else. But all are necessary to maintain a free environment in which creative genius can flourish.

The evocation of the Romantic "creative genius" aside, Kozinski's outrage with the unprecedented expansion of publicity rights effected by the decision (that a celebrity could claim damages and demand royalties from anyone who in any way *reminded* the public of his or her celebrity or evoked the celebrity's image in the public mind) was a welcome departure from judicial proclivities.

61 *Ibid.*, at 1521.

62 Madow, *supra* note 4, at 128.

63 Doty suggests that the term *subculture* reinforces marginality:

we queers have become locked into ways of seeing ourselves in relation to mass culture that perpetuate our status as *sub*cultural . . . By publicly articulating our queer positions in and about mass culture, we reveal that capitalist cultural production need not exclusively and inevitably express straightness. If mass culture remains by, for, or about, straight culture, it will be so through our silences, or by our continued acquiescence to such cultural paradigms such as connotation, *sub*-cultures, *sub*cultural studies, *sub*texting, the closet, and other heterocentrist ploys positioning straightness as the norm. Indeed, the more the queerness in and of mass culture is explored, the more the notion that what is "mass" or "popular" is therefore "straight" will become a highly questionable given . . . (*supra* note 3, at 104).

64 W. Benjamin, "The Work of Art in the Age of Mechanical Reproduction," in *Illuminations* (H. Arendt, ed., 1969).

65 *Ibid.*, at 221.

66 *Ibid.*, at 221.

67 *Ibid.*, at 224.

68 *Ibid.*, at 223.

69 *Ibid.*, at 228–229.

70 *Ibid.*, at 231.

71 *Ibid.*

72 See G. McCann, *Marilyn Monroe* (1988), for an extended elaboration of a male feminist's reflections on his relationship to her image, and Dyer, *Heavenly Bodies, supra* note 1, for an insightful discussion of her position in newly emergent discourses of sexuality in the 1950s. Monroe's ongoing dynamic presence in contemporary sexual politics is addressed by MacCannell, "Marilyn Monroe Was Not a Man," *supra* note 43, in a perceptive and scathing review of biographies written by Norman Mailer, Gloria Steinhem, Anthony Summers, and Roger G. Taylor. See also Baty, *American Monroe, supra* note 49.

73 S. Ewen, *All-Consuming Images: The Politics of Style in Contemporary Culture* 90 (1988).

74 *Ibid.*, at 91.

75 *Ibid.*, at 95–96.

76 H. Jenkins III, "Star Trek Rerun, Reread, Rewritten: Fan Writing as Textual Poaching," 5 *Critical Studies in Mass Communication* 85, 87 (1988).

77 H. Jenkins III, *Textual Poachers: Television Fans and Participatory Culture* 18 (1992).

78 M. de Certeau, *The Practice of Everyday Life* (1984).

79 P. Willis, *Common Culture* (1990).

80 See especially the studies in J. Fiske, *Reading the Popular* (1989), and J. Fiske, *Understanding Popular Culture* (1989).

81 *Loving with a Vengeance* (T. Modleski, ed., 1983); *Studies in Entertainment* (T. Modleski, ed., 1986); J. Radway, *Reading the Romance* (1984).

82 Conversations with Brett Williams. See also *The Politics of Culture* (B. Williams, ed., 1991).

83 H. Foster, *Recodings: Art, Spectacle, Cultural Politics* (1985).

84 The concept of the mediascape is borrowed from A. Appadurai, "Disjuncture and Difference in the Global Cultural Economy," 2 *Public Culture* 1 (1990), who asserts that we need to consider the complexity of the global flow of cultural imagery as producing new fields he defines as ethnoscapes, technoscapes, finanscapes, mediascapes, and ideascapes. For an overview of postmodernism and popular culture, see J. Docker, *Postmodernism and Popular Culture: A Cultural History* (1994).

85 S. Connor, *Postmodernist Culture: An Introduction to Theories of the Contemporary* (1989).

86 *Ibid.*, at 186.

87 *Ibid.*

88 D. Hebridge, *Cut 'n' Mix: Culture, Identity and Caribbean Music* (1987).

89 McRobbie, *supra* note 2.

90 L. Hutcheon, *The Politics of Postmodernism* (1989).

91 McRobbie, *supra* note 2, at 174–175.

92 Willis, *supra* note 79.

93 *Ibid.*, at 141–142.

94 J. Fiske, "The Cultural Economy of Fandom," in *The Adoring Audience: Fan Culture and Popular Media* 30 (L. Lewis, ed., 1992). See also H. Jenkins, "Strangers No More, We Sing: Filking and the Social Construction of the Science Fiction Fan Community," in *The Adoring Audience: Fan Culture and Popular Media* 208 (L. Lewis, ed., 1992).

95 C. Griggers, "Lesbian Bodies in the Age of (Post)Mechanical Reproduction," in *Fear of a Queer Planet* 178 (M. Warner, ed., 1993) at 180.

96 M. J. Frug, *Sexual Equality and Sexual Difference in American Law*, talk presented at the Symposium on Sexual Equality, Sexual Difference and Law at West Virginia University College of Law, Morgantown, West Virginia, 8 April 1988. See generally M. J. Frug, *Postmodern Legal Feminism* (1992).

97 T. de Lauretis, "Feminist Studies/Critical Studies: Issues, Terms, and Contexts," in *Feminist Studies/Critical Studies* 1 (T. de Lauretis, ed., 1986).

98 J. W. Scott, *Gender and the Politics of History* (1988).

99 An alternatively gendered world was one that I imaginatively shared with the late Mary Joe Frug, a legal scholar and feminist who was shaping a postmodern feminist legal theory that recognized the iterative quality of gender identity and the significant role played by law in constructing a variety of gendered subjectivities. We shared a belief that legal scholarship and legal thought should be characterized by a far greater variety of voice and a surfeit of style(s) that could evoke the irony, humor, rage, and sensuality that characterize everyday life and everyday struggle. We both regretted that commercial culture was so quickly dismissed and denigrated in academic circles. Mary Joe hoped that the voices of lesbian hermaphrodites and *Star Trek* fanziners might be heard, and that the cultural energy of the streets might one day invigorate legal debate. May her memory, her work, and her spirit continue to engender such utopian possibilities in the law.

100 J. Butler, *Gender Trouble: Feminism and the Subversion of Identity* (1990) (*hereinafter* Butler, *Gender Trouble*).

101 *Ibid.*, at *xii.*

102 *Ibid.*, at 1.

103 This argument is elaborated in M. Foucault, *History of Sexuality, Vol. 1: An Introduction* (R. Hurley, trans., 1980).

104 In earlier work, I attempted to demonstrate how juridical systems of power produce the subjects they claimed only to represent. For a historical discussion and elaboration of the juridical production of gender and class subjectivities through representational practices in the adjudication of defamation claims, see R. J. Coombe, "Contesting the Self: Negotiating Subjectivities in Nineteenth-Century Ontario Defamation Trials," 11 *Studies in Law, Politics, and Society* 3 (1991) (*hereinafter* Coombe, "Contesting the Self").

105 Butler, *Gender Trouble, supra* note 100, at 2.

106 *Ibid.*, at 4.

107 *Ibid.*, at 5.

108 *Ibid.*, at 6.

109 *Ibid.*, at 17.

110 *Ibid.*, at 17–23.

111 *Ibid.*, at 25. For an elaboration of the meaning of performativity as used here, see J. Butler, "For a Careful Reading," in *Feminist Contentions: A Philosophical Exchange* 127 (S. Benhabib et al., eds., 1995), and J. Butler, "Critically Queer," 1 *Gay and Lesbian Quarterly: A Journal of Lesbian and Gay Studies* 17, 21–24 (1993).

112 Butler, *Gender Trouble, supra* note 100, at 25–30. Butler's position here is congruent with my stance in "Room for Manoeuver," 14 *Law and Social Inquiry* 69 (1989), where I argue that subjectivity is always constructed within the discursive forms of prevailing structures of power, through the creative process of bricolage—cultural practices that deploy existing cultural forms in ever-emergent new fashions that may transform structures of power even as they evoke its significations.

113 Butler, *Gender Trouble, supra* note 100, at 30.

114 *Ibid.*, at 33.

115 *Ibid.*, at 121.

116 *Ibid.*, at 31.

117 Butler clarifies the nonliberal character of the subject and the reiterative and rearticulatory (rather than original or intentional in any Romantic or modern sense) nature of the agency involved in *Bodies That Matter* (1993) at 15.

118 A. Ross, *No Respect: Intellectuals and Popular Culture* 159 (1989).

119 R. Jackson, *Modernist and Postmodernist Inscriptions of Camp*, paper presented at the Popular Culture Association meetings (7–10 March 1990).

120 Ross, *supra* note 118, at 157–158.

121 E. Newton, *Mother Camp: Female Impersonators in America* 3 (1979).

122 *Ibid.*, at 103.

123 *Ibid.*

124 Ross, *supra* note 118, at 159.

125 *Ibid.*, at 160.

126 *Ibid.*

127 *Ibid.*, at 159.

128 *Ibid.*, at 161.

129   P. Tyler, "The Garbo Image," in *The Films of Greta Garbo* 28 (M. Conway et al., eds., 1968); cited in Newton, *supra* note 121, at 108.

130   Dyer, *Heavenly Bodies, supra* note 1, at x.

131   *Ibid.*, at 148–154.

132   *Ibid.*, at 154, 160.

133   See Jackson, *supra* note 119.

134   A. La Valley, "The Great Escape," 10(6) *American Film* 71 (1985).

135   M. Tremblay, *Hosanna* (J. Van Burek and B. Glassco, trans., 1974).

136   D. Crimp, "Right On, Girlfriend!," 33 *Social Text* 2, 4 (1993).

137   *Ibid.*, at 3.

138   Lesbian identification with Sinatra does not appear to be limited to Toronto, judging from the New York "Lookout" Downtown Community Television's second annual Gay and Lesbian Video Festival. There, a video titled *Cruisin' the Rubyfruit Jungle* contained "a tribute to Nancy Sinatra that would make Irving Klaw blush" according to M. Dargis, "Being on the Lookout," *Village Voice*, 16 October 1990, at 51.

139   Crimp, *supra* note 136, at 12.

140   *Ibid.*

141   *Ibid.*

142   *Ibid.*, at 13.

143   J. Dos Passos, *Midcentury* (1960).

144   D. Dalton, *James Dean: The Mutant King* (1983).

145   S. Golding, "James Dean: The Almost-Perfect Lesbian Hermaphrodite," in *Sight Specific: Lesbians and Representation* 49 (D. Brand, ed., 1988).

146   *Ibid.*, at 50.

147   *Ibid.*, at 52.

148   Butler, *Gender Trouble, supra* note 100, at 17.

149   Golding, *supra* note 145, at 50.

150   *Ibid.*

151   *Ibid.*, at 52.

152   *Ibid.*

153   For a discussion of the social and institutional structures of particular fan communities, see C. Bacon-Smith, *Enterprising Women: Television Fandom and the Creation of Popular Myth* (1992) at ch. 2. See also C. Penley, "Brownian Motion: Women, Tactics, and Technology," in *Technoculture* 135 (C. Penley and A. Ross, eds., 1991).

154   Bacon-Smith, *supra* note 153, at 322; Jenkins, "Star Trek Rerun, Reread, Rewritten," *supra* note 76; C. Penley, *To Boldly Go Where No Woman Has Gone Before: Feminism, Psychoanalysis, and Popular Culture*, lecture delivered at the Public Access Series CAPITAL/CULTURE, Toronto, 24 April 1990.

155   Bacon-Smith, *supra* note 153, at 26–28.

156   *Ibid.*, at 16–31.

157   *Ibid.*, at 45.

158   Jenkins, "Star Trek Rerun, Reread, Rewritten," *supra* note 76, at 89.

159   In 1991, Constance Penley, *supra* note 154, estimated that there are 300 to 500 publishers of homoerotic fanzines alone. This number has no doubt increased with the ease of electronic communications.

160   Bacon-Smith, *supra* note 153, at 45.

161   Jenkins, "Star Trek Rerun, Reread, Rewritten," *supra* note 76, at 104.

162   Fanzine writers face ridicule and hostility both in "mainstream" society and among

other (predominantly male) science fiction fans who see them as less than intelligent and as an embarrassment to fandom (Bacon-Smith, *supra* note 153, at 7–43, 77). For a more extensive discussion of their vilification in academia, the mainstream press, and the larger science fiction community, see Jenkins, *Textual Poachers*, *supra* note 77, at 1–24.

163 Bacon-Smith, *supra* note 153, at 56–57.

164 Jenkins, "Star Trek Rerun, Reread, Rewritten," *supra* note 76, at 88.

165 *Ibid.*, at 93–97.

166 Bacon-Smith, *supra* note 153, at 94–98.

167 *Ibid.*, at 100.

168 *Ibid.*, at 101–102.

169 *Ibid.*, at 102.

170 *Ibid.*, at 102–103.

171 *Ibid.*, at 141–143.

172 *Ibid.*, at 145–147.

173 *Ibid.*, at 209–216.

174 *Ibid.*, at 334.

175 *Ibid.*, at 230.

176 J. Russ, "Another Addict Raves about K/S," 8 *Nome* 28 (1985), cited in Bacon-Smith, *supra* note 153, at 371.

177 Bacon-Smith, *supra* note 153, at 245.

178 *Ibid.*, at 247.

179 *Ibid.*, at 246–249.

180 *Ibid.*, at 246.

181 *Ibid.*, at 249–250.

182 Hurt/Comfort stories are those in which one male character is hurt and suffers and the other comforts and nurses him (see discussion in *ibid.*, ch 10, at 255–281).

183 This would help to explain why fans don't necessarily see the sexual relationship between Kirk and Spock as a homosexual one (Penley, *supra* note 154). As some fans see it, there are forms of love that defy description; the sexual orientation of Kirk and Spock is irrelevant because their love is a matter of cosmic destiny (*ibid.*). For similar reasons, fans don't see even the most sexually graphic material as pornographic (Bacon-Smith, *supra* note 153, at 243). Such categories are simply inappropriate in these alternative universes.

184 Bacon-Smith, *supra* note 153, at 270–277.

185 *Ibid.*, at 195–196.

186 1(1) *Judy!* 1 (spring fever 1993) (unpaginated fanzine, P.O. Box 121, Iowa City, IA 52245-0121).

187 *Ibid.*

188 *Ibid.*

189 E. Mertz, "A New Social Constructionism for Sociolegal Studies," 28 *Law & Society Review* 1243, 1257 (1994).

190 It will undoubtedly be argued that if the individuals engaged in these subcultural practices were to be threatened with legal action, they could claim a defense under the First Amendment. Such responses evince an incredible naïveté about the obstacles that confront most people in even reaching a legal forum in which a constitutional challenge could be made. Moreover, First Amendment defenses in this area are rarely upheld and often dismissed out of hand. The case law in this area, more-

over, is extremely confusing and often contradictory, as I will discuss in my concluding essay.

191   This insight finds its clearest articulation in the work of Michel Foucault. Although he dealt with the law as primarily repressive in his early work, he also argued that regimes of power were productive rather than merely prohibitive: they produce what they purport merely to represent. Others have extended this insight into the juridical domain. Clifford Geertz makes similar observations in *Local Knowledge: Further Essays in Interpretive Anthropology* (1983). These ideas are developed in G. Peller, "The Metaphysics of American Law," 73 *California Law Review* 1151 (1985), and elaborated in C. Harrington and B. Yngvesson, "Interpretive Social Research," 15 *Law & Social Inquiry* 135 (1990). For a discussion of the juridical production of class and gender subjectivities in the transition to industrial capitalism, see Coombe, "Contesting the Self," *supra* note 104.

192   L. Bower, "Queer Acts and the Politics of Direct Address," 28 *Law & Society Review* 1009 (1994).

193   Jenkins, "Star Trek Rerun, Reread, Rewritten," *supra* note 76, at 100.

194   This concept is developed in E. P. Thompson, "The Moral Economy of the English Crowd in the 18th Century," 50 *Past and Present* 76 (1971). The development of moral economies with respect to celebrity images—informal modes of regulation and sanction that grow up in the shadow of the law and with knowledge of the policing activities of those with legally recognized rights in the text—is not limited to the fanzine context. For example, it would appear that Elvis impersonators and fans are not deterred by the Presley estate's policing efforts (which have attempted to control and/or prohibit activities as diverse as black velvet art featuring "the King," computer games featuring Elvis as street fighter, and at least one lesbian Elvis impersonator). However, some impersonators feel that they themselves have acquired rights by virtue of their transformative appropriations and, in at least one case, the law has supported the claim. In Flying Elvi v. Flying Elvises (unreported), one team of skydiving Elvis impersonators successfully sued another on grounds of potential consumer confusion. The defendants attempted to counterclaim "on behalf of anyone who wants to hit the silk in the name of the King" but lost. See M. Neill and A. M. Otey, "All Shook Up: Two Skydiving Groups Try To Chute Each Other Down," *People* (27 February 1995) at 50; "Look Up in the Sky. It's the Flying Elvises, er, Elvi," *The National Law Journal* (17 April 1995) at A27. For a discussion of the maintenance and social transformations of the Elvis image, see D. S. Wall, "Reconstructing the Soul of Elvis: The Social Development and Legal Maintenance of Elvis Presley as Intellectual Property," 24 *International Journal of the Sociology of Law* 117 (1996).

195   Jenkins, "Star Trek Rerun, Reread, Rewritten," *supra* note 76, at 100.

196   *Ibid.*, citing Schnvelle, 4 *Sociotrek* 8–9.

197   Bacon-Smith, *supra* note 153, at 58.

198   *Ibid.*, at 66.

199   *Ibid.*, at 40.

200   *Ibid.*, at 33.

201   Penley, *supra* note 154.

202   Bacon-Smith, *supra* note 153, at 35.

203   *Ibid.*, at 223.

204   Jenkins, *Textual Poachers, supra* note 77, at 30–31. Constance Penley told me in con-

versation that Lucasfilm threatened legal action on copyright grounds when they discovered that fanzine writers had depicted Luke Skywalker and Han Solo in an erotic relationship. Bacon-Smith, *supra* note 153, at 251, n.6, also notes that fandom has had an uneasy relationship with Lucasfilm but does not elaborate. A copyright claim would not require that the use be commercial to succeed and is thus a more flexible instrument for producers to use than trademark and more economically feasible than backing publicity rights claims by all of the individual actors to achieve the same ends.

205 Jenkins, *Textual Poachers*, *supra* note 77, at 31.

206 *Ibid.*

207 For a discussion of complicitous critique as an attitude symptomatic of postmodernism, see Hutcheon, *supra* note 90.

208 K. McClure, "On the Subject of Rights: Pluralism, Plurality and Political Identity," in *Dimensions of Radical Democracy: Pluralism, Citizenship, Community* 123 (C. Mouffe, ed., 1992).

3. Tactics of Appropriation and the Politics of Recognition

1 The story circulates in Toronto and was mentioned to me by a sociology professor in the form quoted. I later learned that the sign had been conceptualized as part of a citywide progressive art exhibit by Public, a nonprofit arts organization. Before it was broadcast, lawyers advised the group of their potential liability and the likelihood of injunction. A decision was made not to convey the message, but the story circulates as if the event had taken place—an apocryphal rumor that bespeaks a truth about gay and lesbian citizenship in Canada. Given the significance I attribute to rumor in this chapter, it seemed an especially apt anecdote with which to begin.

2 Rumor reported to me by Nick De Genova, a doctoral candidate in the University of Chicago Department of Anthropology, who has done extensive fieldwork relating to inner-city popular culture, at the Society for Cultural Anthropology meetings in May 1994.

3 K. Mercer, "Welcome to the Jungle: Identity and Diversity in Postmodern Politics," in *Identity: Community, Culture, Difference* 43 (J. Rutherford, ed., 1990).

4 A. Gramsci, *Prison Notebooks* (1971); V. N. Voloshinov, *Marxism and the Philosophy of Language* (1973). The concept of key symbols was first developed in S. Ortner, "On Key Symbols," 75 *American Anthropologist* 1338–1346 (1973), and further developed in a manner more consistent with my usage here in S. Ortner, "Theory in Anthropology since the Sixties," 26 *Comparative Studies in Society and History* 126–169 (1984). See also S. Golding, *Gramsci's Democratic Theory: Contributions to a Post-Liberal Democracy* (1992).

5 C. Mouffe, "Democratic Citizenship and the Political Community," in *Community at Loose Ends* 70 (Miami Theory Collective, ed., 1991). Reprinted in *Dimensions of Radical Democracy* (C. Mouffe, ed. 1992).

6 Mouffe, "Democratic Citizenship," *supra* note 5, at 75.

7 C. Mouffe, "Pluralism and Modern Democracy: Around Carl Schmitt," 14 *New Formations* 1 at 14 (1991).

8 W. Connolly, *Identity/Difference: Democratic Negotiations of Political Paradox* 64 (1991).

9   J. Rutherford, "A Place Called Home: Identity and the Cultural Politics of Difference," in *Identity: Community, Culture, Difference* 9 at 10 (J. Rutherford, ed., 1990).

10 For an excellent critique of the liberal politics of diversity as instantiated in the academy, see C. Mohanty, "On Race and Voice: Challenges for Liberal Education in the 1990s," 14 *Cultural Critique* 179 (1990).

11 P. Smith, "Laclau and Mouffe's Secret Agent," in *Community at Loose Ends* 99 (Miami Theory Collective, ed., 1991).

12 S. J. Levy, *Product and Brand Symbol Systems*, paper presented at The Marketing of Meaning: Toward a Better Understanding of Business Signs and Symbols, Eleventh International Summer Institute for Semiotic and Structural Studies, Indiana University–Purdue University at Indianapolis, 16–21 July 1989.

13 Cited in H. Foster, *Recodings: Art, Spectacle, Cultural Politics* 165 (1985).

14 See especially J. Baudrillard, *In the Shadow of Silent Majorities* (1983), F. Jameson, "Postmodernism or the Cultural Logic of Late Capitalism," 146 *New Left Review* 59 (1984), and F. Jameson, *Postmodernism, or, The Cultural Logic of Late Capitalism* (1991).

15 For an early example, see L. Grossberg, "Putting the Pop Back into Postmodernism," in *Universal Abandon?* (A. Ross, ed., 1988).

16 Recent exceptions include the work of those reconsidering the paramaters of the public sphere and the meaning of civil society, which I address in my concluding essay.

17 Baudrillard, *For a Critique of the Political Economy of the Sign* (1981), at 146–147.

18 Listed under s.9 of the Trade Marks Act R.S.C. 1985, c.T-13 are sixteen categories of prohibited marks, including a category that includes "any . . . mark . . . adopted and used by any public authority in Canada as an official mark for wares and services, in respect of which, the Registrar . . . has given public notice of its adoption and use." *Trademark Journal*, in which such notices are advertised to the public, lists an increasing number of such marks annually. The number of marks so claimed increased tenfold from 1980 to 1985 alone.

19 It is impossible to know how many marks are protected in the United States. In his treatise *Trademarks and Unfair Competition*, Vol. 2 (2d ed.) 869–872 (1984 and 1990 Supp.), J. Thomas McCarthy includes a list of many *federally* protected names, characters, and designs, but specifies that the list is neither complete nor exhaustive. (The third edition of McCarthy's work does not contain an updated list.) The exorbitant cost of doing searches precludes compiling a complete list of marks protected in either the Canadian or the U.S. context.

20 The list is drawn from the larger list contained in McCarthy, *Trademarks and Unfair Competition, supra* note 19 at 869–872. States have also granted exclusive use of words and symbols to nonprofit groups. See, for example, A. E. McKinney, *New York General Business Law* 8397 (1984, and 1988 Supp.).

21 USCA c.33, §700 and Title 36.

22 Whereas the use of other trademarks may be enjoined only when such a use is confusing to the consumer or depreciates the trademark holder's goodwill, public authorities have unlimited power to prevent (or charge exorbitant royalties for) the use of their registered marks in any and all circumstances. In Canada this has led to situations of grave abuses of power that have alarmed the practicing bar. As R. Brant Latham wrote in 1985, "Section 9(1)(n) of the Canadian *Trade Marks Act* is an unjustifiable abhorition [*sic*] creating unconscionably broad rights in special class per-

sons." See "Explosion of Section 9(1)(n) Notices," *Patent and Trademark Institute of Canada Review* 74 (1985). Many lawyers have called s.9 an anachronism and called for amendments to the section. See G. F. Henderson, *Intellectual Property: Litigation, Legislation, and Education* (1991). Amendments to the Trade Marks Act have not yet included a repeal or any narrowing of s.9 rights, despite their ongoing abuse and anticompetitive character.

23 "The UDC patent had been approved without controversy every 14 years since it was first granted nearly a century ago" *The Washington Post* 23 July 1993 at A10.

24 Senator Jesse Helms, quoted in *The Washington Post* 23 July 1993 at A1.

25 *Ibid.*, at A10.

26 "Section 9 supports public order and as such places the Crown and public authorities in a position of virtual invulnerability. An official mark is virtually unexpungeable . . . " (R. Hughes, *Hughes on Trademarks* 453 [1992]).

27 "Section 11 of the *Trade Marks Act* now prohibits the use in connection with a business, *as a trademark or otherwise,* of any mark adopted contrary to ss.9 and 10 of the *Trade Marks Act* . . . no penalty is provided in the statute for the adoption and use of any such marks and s.107 of the Criminal Code, therefore, becomes applicable" (H. G. Fox, *The Canadian Law of Trademarks and Unfair Competition* [1972]).

28 According to the SFAA's president, the Games would "provide a healthy recreational alternative to a suppressed minority," "educate the public at large towards a more reasonable characterization of gay men and women," and "attempt, through athletics, to bring about a more positive and gradual assimilation of gay men and women, as well as gays and non-gays, and to diminish the ageist, sexist and racist divisiveness existing in all communities regardless of sexual orientation" (San Francisco Arts & Athletics, Inc., v. United States Olympic Comm., 107 S. Ct. 2971, 2976, 2980 n. 13 [1987]).

29 36 U.S.C. §371–396 (1988). In particular Section 110 of the Act, set forth in 36 U.S.C. §380 (1988) provides that (a) without consent of the USOC "any person who uses for the purpose of trade, to induce the sale of any goods or services, or to induce the sale of any goods or services to promote any theatrical exhibition, athletic performance, or competition . . . the words 'Olympic,' 'Olympian,' . . . tending to cause confusion, to cause mistake, to deceive, or to falsely suggest a connection with the [USOC] or any Olympic activity shall be subject to suit in a civil action by the [USOC] for the remedies provided in [the Lanham Act]" and that (c) "the [USOC] shall have exclusive right to use . . . the words 'Olympic,' 'Olympian,' [etc.] subject only to lawful uses of these words established prior to 1950."

30 219 U.S.P.Q. 982.

31 International Olympic Committee v. San Francisco Arts & Athletics, 707 F.2d 517 (9th Cir. 1983).

32 Moreover, it was determined that there were no defenses available to anyone who used the term without authorization. San Francisco Arts & Athletics, Inc., v. United States Olympic Committee 107 S. Ct. 2971 (1987).

33 International Olympic Committee v. San Francisco Arts & Athletics, 789 F. 2d 1319 at 1323 (per Kozinski, J.).

34 See Philip Shenon, "Battle Looming over a Nominee for U.S. Court," *New York Times*, 14 January 1988 at A14, and Craig McLaughlin, "The Walker Nomination: A Bork Style Battle in San Francisco," *The San Francisco Bay Guardian* 20 January 1988 at 7.

35 San Francisco Arts & Athletics, Inc. v. United States Olympic Comm., 107 S. Ct. 2971 (1987) at 2998 and n.32. He classified the SFAA's use of the Olympic trademark as primarily charitable solicitation and political advocacy worthy of full First Amendment protection (*ibid.* at 2995 and n.24). In the majority opinion written by Justice Powell, however, it was held that prohibition of the word Olympic did not prohibit the Athletic Group's political speech about the status of homosexuals in society but only the manner in which it could convey its message (*ibid.* at 2981). The statute was held to apply primarily to commercial speech, which, in any case, receives only a limited form of First Amendment protection, and only incidentally restricted expressive speech (*ibid.* at 2980–2981). For more extensive commentary on the freedom of expression analysis engaged in by the court, see R. N. Kravitz, "Trademarks, Speech, and the *Gay Olympics* Case," 69 *Boston University Law Review* 131 (1989).

36 Symbolic exchange is explored in Baudrillard, *For a Critique of the Political Economy of the Sign, supra* note 17, and in Baudrillard, "Symbolic Exchange and Death," in *Jean Baudrillard: Selected Writings* (M. Poster, ed., 1988). See also D. Kellner, *Jean Baudrillard: From Marxism to Postmodernism and Beyond* 42–46, 65–66, 87, 103–107 (1989).

37 Another trademark suit has been filed against the Pink Panther Patrol, a group formed to deter gay bashing in Manhattan's West Village. The company that owns the rights to the *Pink Panther* movies claims that the group's use of the name with an emblem consisting of a paw print inside a pink triangle "diminish[es] the identity and reputation" of their trademark. The group considers this to be a necessarily homophobic argument (C. Hays, "Gay Patrol and MGM in a Battle over Name," *New York Times* 27 May 1991 § 1 at 21).

38 RCMP Commissioner Norman Inkster had first made the recommendation to Solicitor-General Pierre Blais in a letter written on 10 April 1989. My account of the controversy is drawn from a number of Canadian newspapers that presented and participated in producing the controversy in the public sphere.

39 Ironically, the Stetson had been borrowed from the American forest rangers to replace the British pillbox that colonial officers had originally worn.

40 *Trade Marks Act,* R.S.C. 1985, c.T-13 s.9(1)(o). Phone calls made to the Minister of Justice and the Solicitor-General's Office were unsuccessful in convincing them to use this provision of the *Trade Marks Act* as an expedient course of action to stem this tide of merchandise. It might have been possible for the government to seek and obtain an Anton Piller order from a court of law that would enable them both to get an interlocutory injunction without notice to the manufacturers and vendors of the goods and to seize the merchandise from unknown vendors as evidence likely to disappear before the trial. The practice of seizing goods that bear counterfeit trademarks or infringe copyright from unidentified defendants named only as John and Jane Doe is a common one in Canada. It tends to be employed by representatives controlling the merchandising rights of rock bands, sports teams, and other popular entertainers, especially to prevent the sale of "bootleg" T-shirts in conjunction with local concerts and sporting events.

41 Homi K. Bhabha, "Dissemination: Time, Narrative, and the Margins of the Modern Nation," in *Nation and Narration* 291 (Homi K. Bhabha, ed., 1990).

42 *Ibid,*. at 292.

43 *Ibid.,* at 296.

44 *Ibid.* at 297.

45 See S. Žižek, *For They Know Not What They Do* (1991).

46 K. Keohane, "Symptoms of Canada: National Identity and the Theft of National Enjoyment," 28 *Cineaction* 20, 23 (1992).

47 *Ibid.*, at 25.

48 *Ibid.*

49 The concept of the intercultural is similar to that of hybridity, in that it retains the possibility of the dynamism inherent in cultural meetings or transgressions and does not rely upon an idea of singular fixed identities that are merely juxtaposed or synthesized; possibilities for challenging and transforming preexisting categories while acknowledging their continued historical weight are here recognized.

50 K. Keohane, *supra* note 46, at 26.

51 *Ibid.*, at 28.

52 *Ibid.*, at 29.

53 Canada can be seen to become "postcolonial" only in the 1980s. Only then is the Canadian constitution repatriated and only then does the country get its own Charter of Rights and Freedoms which delineate the contours of citizenship and an emergent jurisprudence that gives content to the specific nature of Canada as a "free and democratic society." The nominal independence from the colonial motherland, however, may result in the instantiation of relations better described as neocolonial than postcolonial. Further discussion of postcolonialism in Canada will be found in chapter 5.

54 D. Spurr, *Rhetorics of Empire: Colonial Discourse in Journalism and Travel Writing* (1993). Spurr suggests that colonial discourse in journalistic contexts displays recurrent tropes that position the colonized other. Alterity is repetitively confirmed in a series of predictable configurations, which he delineates in detail.

55 See E. Mackey, "Postmodernism and Cultural Politics in the Multicultural Nation: Contests over Truth in the *Into the Heart of Africa* Controversy," *Public Culture* 7(2): 403–432 (1995), and K. Mitchell, for an excellent discussion of recent controversies over multiculturalism in the Canadian public sphere.

56 H. K. Bhabha, "Introduction: Narrating the Nation," in *Nation and Narration*, *supra* note 41, at 2.

57 H. Bhabha, *The Location of Culture* 199–200 (1994).

58 G. A. Fine, "The Goliath Effect: Corporate Dominance and Mercantile Legends," 98(387) *Journal of American Folklore* 63 (1985).

59 R. Barnet and J. Cavanagh, *Global Dreams: Imperial Corporations and the New World Order* 188 (1994).

60 I should make it clear at the outset that I don't believe it is possible to adopt the position of a detached, omniscient scientist for whom the rumor is an observable object of study. In a mass-mediated society and culture, the practices involved in spreading a rumor, reporting it, commenting upon it, and analyzing it necessarily collapse into one another, imploding boundaries between fact and fiction.

61 The term *postindustrial* should be approached with great caution; the idea that we are now in a postindustrial society is part of an ideological structure—one that many see postmodern social theory as being complicit with—that denies the real labor being done in the world "out of sight." I use the term here to refer to a *felt sense* of industrial production's disappearance and some of its cultural manifestations. See G. Kester, "Out of Sight Is Out of Mind: The Imaginary Space of Postindustrial Culture," 35 *Social Text* 72 (1993), and N. Lazarus, "Doubting the New World Order:

Marxism, Realism, and the Claims of Postmodernist Social Theory," 3(3) *Differences* 94 (1991).

62 Barnet and Cavanagh, *supra* note 59, at 200.

63 G. C. Spivak, "Subaltern Studies: Deconstructing Historiography," in *Selected Subaltern Studies* 23 (R. Guha and G. C. Spivak, eds., 1988).

64 Bhabha, *supra* note 57, at 200.

65 *Ibid.*, at 202.

66 *Ibid.*

67 G. A. Fine, "Among Those Dark Satanic Mills: Rumors of Kooks, Cults, and Corporations," 47 (2) *Southern Folklore* 133, 137 (1990).

68 Barnet and Cavanagh, *supra* note 59, at 197, 221. By acquiring General Foods and Kraft, Philip Morris now controls about 10 percent of the entire array of food products on U.S. supermarket shelves. Thanks to relationships with 165 banks, more than $19 billion was offered in loans in a twenty-four-hour period to accomplish this hostile takeover. Accountant Storr refers to himself as a shaman: "at a meeting in Nigeria for senior managers, he put on an African mask and waved a wooden snake to make the point. He knows that when he telephones for money, he is certain to get it because his request is backed by the full faith and credit of the Marlboro man" (*ibid.* at 229).

69 See discussion in "Procter and Gamble Lifts Veil a Little," *The Globe and Mail*, 15 March 1982 at B1.

70 Cited in "Fine, The Goliath Effect," *supra* note 58, at 72.

71 Fine suggests that even though the trademarks belonging to Procter & Gamble were unknown, rumors suggesting that the company was controlled by Satanists, a witches' coven, or the Unification Church were believed, because "the psychological dominance of the corporation as a whole made such beliefs credible . . . Such rumors need not be grounded in knowledge, but only in general emotions about the corporation" (*ibid.*, at 72). Interestingly, this begs the question of how a company becomes "psychologically dominant" and ignores the very signifier around which the rumor circulated: the medieval stylization and religious resonance of the moon-and-stars logo, which no doubt suggested the association with the devil, witches, and "Moonies" in a fashion that a more streamlined or modern logo would not.

72 It underwent refinements and federal registration in 1882 and 1930 and is "among the most intricate and artistic corporate trademarks" (Fine, "Among Those Dark Satanic Mills," *supra* note 67, at 138).

73 Quoted in "Procter and Gamble's Battles with Rumors," *New York Times* 22 July 1982 at D1 and D10.

74 *Ibid.*

75 *Ibid.*

76 "P & G Loses Campaign for the Moon and Stars," *The Globe and Mail* 26 April 1985 at B6.

77 Threats to a company's public image are necessarily based on perceptions of perceptions and therefore cannot be measured in quantitative terms. Press surveys for the 1980s, however, indicate that the rumor campaign received more press coverage than Procter & Gamble's other difficulties and suggest that their public relations department devoted more energy and resources to publicly deflecting the rumor than to meeting other challenges that the company simultaneously faced. Most recently, the company seems to have focused upon rival Amway distributors for fueling the ru-

mor. See D. Canedy, "Advertising: After Two Decades and Counting, Procter & Gamble Is Still Trying to Exorcise Satanism Tales," *New York Times* 29 July 1997 at C7.

78 See for example, J. Brunvand, *The Choking Doberman and Other "New" Urban Legends* (1984), and *The Mexican Pet: More "New" Urban Legends and Some Old Favorites* (1986).

79 Fine, "The Goliath Effect," *supra* note 58, at 79.

80 *Ibid.*, at 65–66.

81 According to Fine:

> Some companies so dominate their product areas that their names are almost generic. We refer to Xerox machines rather than copiers, Jell-O rather than flavored gelatin, Kleenex rather than facial tissues, or Oreos rather than sugar cream sandwiched between two chocolate wafers. People use these names even when they refer to other brands because these corporate names symbolize the products. In legends and rumors dealing with these products ("Xerox machines cause cancer") we use the corporate name without necessarily claiming that the corporation named is the only corporation involved. When informants talk about "Jell-O" hardening into rubber and being indigestible, the target of the story may not be General Foods. However, the mention of such corporate names reflects psychological dominance. If asked directly which corporation was involved, informants typically confirmed that it was the corporate leader even though the source for the account might have used the product reference generically. (*Ibid.*, at 71)

Fine does not explore the possibility that there may be social significance to and distinctions made among the name of the corporation, a legally protected trade name (which may also be the name of the corporation), a brand name legally protected as a trademark, and the product itself, conflating all of these when he decides "for ease of reference" to "use 'corporation' to refer to corporations and products." Thus it becomes impossible to determine whether particular rumors manifest distrust of known corporations, surround trademarks of particular reknown in their own right (through advertising, for example), attach to brand names known to have particular corporate owners, or are associated with particularly popular products that are most easily referred to by a mark that is becoming generic.

Fine does allude, however, to an anxiety that might be understood as a reaction to corporate patriarchy. Fast-food operations, he suggests, attract rumors, especially when they have prominent male owners or figureheads. The founder and late president of McDonald's, Roy Kroc, was the personal subject of rumors (that he was a member of the Church of Satan), while "Colonel Sanders" is well-known in his own right and "Kentucky Fried" is often rumored to be something other than chicken. Food is still, in popular perception, best when it is "homemade" by a woman to whom one is connected by bonds of kinship and affection; food not made at home is better when made in individualized portions for discerning patrons than when mass-produced for indistinguishable customers waiting in lines. The personalized patriarchal owner of a company who does not "make" but manufactures depersonalized food for mass consumers is categorically suspect, and the food itself a likely site for suspicion. It is also difficult for Fine to explain why, in the anxiety surrounding certain technological innovations (e.g., microwave ovens), rumors do not attach to a certain manufacturer or any particular brand name, but to the product itself, yet with others (e.g., soft bubble gum), a brand name (Bubble Yum) figures prominently (except to suggest that perhaps in the microwave field no one brand is publicly perceived as dominant, whereas in the bubble gum field, the new brand became the best-seller; we have no way of knowing if the rumormongering public were aware of this). Only by examining the particular products, their consumers, and the corporate marketing strategies that accompanied their introduction into the market, would any rationale emerge. To the extent that children form the penny candy market, and perhaps the most mystified segment of the consuming population when it comes to recognizing and distinguishing corporate ownership, production processes, marketing strategies, trademarks, and the products to which they refer, their rumors are the most likely to name products exclusively by trademark (Pop Rocks and Bubble Yum are examples Fine cites).

82   *Ibid.* at 80.

83   Fine, "Among Those Dark Satanic Mills," *supra* note 67.

84   *Ibid.* at 144.

85   M. Taussig, *The Devil and Commodity Fetishism in South America* (1980).

86   H. J. Spillers, "Mama's Baby, Papa's Maybe: An American Grammar Book," 17(2) *Diacritics* 65, 77 (1987).

87   As I will discuss in greater detail in the next chapter, the ideal of a singular public sphere for civil society has come under critical scrutiny. In the context of a discussion of the possibility of a black public sphere, Steven Gregory evokes Nancy Fraser:

Fraser notes that members of subordinated groups, such as women, people of color, lesbians and gays have found it politically important to constitute alternative, or "subaltern counterpublics"; that is, "parallel discursive arenas where those excluded from dominant discourses, invent and circulate *counter*discourses," so as to formulate oppositional interpretations of their identities, interests, and needs. The proliferation of such counterpublics allows issues that were previously shielded from contestation to be publicly argued . . . The presence of a counterpublic can direct attention to the public arenas where micro-level discursive interactions are shaped by wider institutional power arrangements and discourses. (S. Gregory, "Race, Identity, and Political Activism: The Shifting Contours of the African American Public Sphere," 7 *Public Culture* 147, 153 [1994])

Although Gregory clearly has a more articulate and rational discussion in mind, a *counter*discourse is no more likely to adopt a rationalist tone than the discourses it counters. Hence, in the case of the subaltern practices I shall discuss, the rumor adopts a mode of address and circulation that simultaneously mimics and disrupts the mass-market media significations to which it might be seen to be responding.

88   P. A. Turner, *I Heard It through the Grapevine: Rumor in African-American Culture* (1993).

89   My use of mimesis and alterity as related to moments of "first contact" and what might be deemed the phenomenology of primitivism draws extensively from M. Taussig, *Mimesis and Alterity: A Particular History of the Senses* (1993). A longer discussion of Taussig's theory of mimesis and alterity and its relevance for considering the cultural power of trademarks is contained in the next chapter.

90   Turner, *supra* note 88, at xv.

91   *Ibid.*, at 9.

92   *Ibid.*, at 14.

93   *Ibid.*, at 22, citing J. N. Pieterse, *White over Black: Images of Africa and Blacks in Western Popular Culture* 114 (1992).

94   *Ibid.*, at 30.

95   *Ibid.*

96   Harriet Schoolcraft (1860) quoted in D. Roberts, *The Myth of Aunt Jemima: Representations of Race and Region* 58 (1994).

97   E. Alexander, "Can You be BLACK and Look at This?: Reading the Rodney King Video(s)," 7 *Public Culture* 77, 78 (1994).

98   Turner, *supra* note 88, at 58.

99   *Ibid.*, at 64.

100 *Ibid.*

101 *Ibid.*, at 71.

102 *Ibid.*, at 82–83.

103 *Ibid.*, at 85.

104 *Ibid.*, at 86.

105 *Ibid.*

106 G. Farred, Untitled contribution to "Race and Racism: A Symposium," 42 *Social Text* 21, 26 (1995).

107 I am grateful to Kathleen Pirrie Adams for her insights into this issue and for helping to give linguistic shape to my inchoate sense of inequity upon learning of the Klan's purported involvement in the marketing of these goods.

108 Spivak, "Subaltern Studies," *supra* note 63, at 23.

109 "Klan Rumor Helped Ruin Sport Clothing Firm," *San Francisco Chronicle* 22 July 1989.

110 Heather Beaumont, "The X Factor," 1(9) *The Metro Word* 7 (8 November–9 December 9, 1992). Margaret Russell also describes how California police use certain brand-name clothing to target minority youth. They are seen as de facto indicators of gang status in "gang profiles" that are used to justify the harassment, interrogation, and detainment of minority youth and as grounds for denying Latinos and African Americans entry into public amusement parks or ejecting them if they are inadvertently admitted. See M. Russell, "Entering Great America: Reflections on Race and the Convergence of Progressive Legal Theory and Practice," 43 *Hastings Law Journal* 749 (1992).

111 Turner, *supra* note 88, at 45.

112 M. Wallace, *Invisibility Blues: From Pop to Theory* 2 (1990).

113 M. Diawara, "Malcolm X and the Black Public Sphere: Conversionists versus Culturalists," 7 *Public Culture* 35, 42 (1994).

114 H. L. Gates Jr., *The Signifying Monkey: A Theory of African-American Literary Criticism* (1988).

115 Wallace, *supra* note 112, at 2.

116 Turner, *supra* note 88, at 129.

117 *Ibid.*, at 129.

118 *Ibid.*, at 130.

119 *Ibid.*, at 131.

120 M. C. Dawson, "A Black Counterpublic? Economic Earthquakes, Racial Agenda(s), and Black Politics" 7 *Public Culture* 195, 209 (1994).

121 Barnet and Cavanagh, *supra* note 59.

122 Turner, *supra* note 88, at 173.

123 According to Patricia Turner: "Although African-American consumers purchase 30 percent of all Nike shoes, blacks had no Nike executive positions, no subcontracting arrangements, and no seats on the company's board of directors; moreover, the

footwear giant did not advertise with black-owned media outlets. With the possible exception of such celebrity spokesmen as film director Spike Lee and basketball superstar Michael Jordon, both of whom received large sums in exchange for product endorsements, Nike simply was not sharing its profits with blacks" (*ibid.*, at 173).

124 *Ibid.*, at 98.
125 *Ibid.*, at 100.
126 *Ibid.*
127 *Ibid.*, at 102.
128 Barnet and Cavanagh, *supra* note 59, at 196–197.
129 Turner, *supra* note 88, at 178.
130 *Ibid.*, at 142.
131 *Ibid.*, at 169.
132 See the discussion of the concept of the mass subject, in chapter 4.
133 *Ibid.*, at xii and 84.
134 Turner, *supra* note 88, at 169–170.
135 *Ibid.*, at 5.
136 For further discussion of the role of the trademark in the configuration of African and African American identities and the politics of the black public sphere in globalizing conditions, see R. J. Coombe and P. Stoller, "X Marks the Spot: The Ambiguities of African Trading in the Commerce of Black Public Spheres" 7 *Public Culture* 249 (1994).
137 Bhabha, *supra* note 57, at 203.
138 The concept of hyperreality as developed by Jean Baudrillard and Umberto Eco is ably summarized in B. Woolley, *Virtual Worlds* 190–210 (1992).
139 The concept of the seduction used here is drawn from Jean Baudrillard, "On Seduction," in *Jean Baudrillard: Selected Writings* 199 (M. Poster, ed., 1988).
140 Cited in Turner, *supra* note 88, at 166.
141 The concept of the mediascape is borrowed from A. Appadurai, "Disjuncture and Difference in the Global Cultural Economy," 2(2) *Public Culture* 1 (1990).
142 S. Gregory, Untitled contribution to "Race and Racism: A Symposium," 42 *Social Text* 16, 18 (1995).

4. Embodied Trademarks: Mimesis and Alterity on American Commercial Frontiers

1 C. Whitehead, "Review of White on Black," *Voice Literary Supplement* October 1992, at 25. Cited in "Miscellany," 5 *Public Culture* (1993).
2 See V. R. Dominguez, "Visual Nationalism: On Looking at National Symbols," 5 *Public Culture* 451 (1993); U. Hannerz and O. Lofgren, "Defining the National: An Introduction," 58(3–4) *Ethnos* 157 (1993); S. Hegeman, "Shopping for Identities: 'A Nation of Nations' and the Weak Ethnicity of Objects," 3(2) *Public Culture* 71 (1991); O. Lofgren, "Materializing the Nation in Sweden and America," 58(3–4) *Ethnos* 161 (1993).
3 See, e.g., F. Jameson, *Postmodernism, or, The Cultural Logic of Late Capitalism* (1991).
4 For early and influential examples, see J. Fiske, "Cultural Studies and the Culture of Everyday Life," in *Cultural Studies* (L. Grossberg, C. Nelson, and P. Treichler, eds., 1992); J. Fiske, "The Cultural Economy of Fandom," in *The Adoring Audience: Fan*

Culture and Popular Media 30 (L. A. Lewis, ed., 1992); J. Fiske, *Understanding Popular Culture* (1989); J. Fiske, *Reading the Popular* (1989); A. McRobbie, *Postmodernism and Popular Culture* (1994); P. Willis, *Common Culture* (1990); S. Willis, "Hardcore: Sub-culture American Style," 19 *Critical Inquiry* 365 (1993); S. Willis, *A Primer for Every-day Life* (1992).

5   S. Connor, *Postmodernist Culture: An Introduction to Theories of the Contemporary* (1989); M. Featherstone, *Consumer Culture and Postmodernism* (1991); H. Jenkins III, *Textual Poachers: Television Fans and Participatory Culture* (1992); B. Jules-Rosette, "Simulations of Postmodernity: Images of Technology in African Tourist and Popu-lar Art," 6 *Society for Visual Anthropology Review* 29 (1990); S. Lash, *Sociology of Postmodernism* (1990); D. Kellner, "Popular Culture and the Construction of Post-modern Identities," in *Modernity and Identity* 141 (S. Lash and J. Friedman, eds., 1992); McRobbie, *supra* note 4.

6   Several town councils in Britain have addressed the matter, and at least one, Isling-ton, voted to ban the trademark as a racist stereotype. Artist David Bailey's work has incorporated images of "the Golly" in a critical consideration of the character's role in British culture.

7   D. Bahri, "Coming to Terms with the 'Postcolonial,'" in *Between the Lines: South Asians and Postcoloniality* 137 (D. Bahri and M. Vasudeva, eds., 1996); D. Bahri and M. Vasudeva, "Pedagogical Alternatives: Issues in Postcolonial Studies: Interview with Gauri Viswanathan," in *Between the Lines* (D. Bahri and M. Vasudeva, eds., 1996); H. K. Bhabha, "Postcolonial Authority and Postmodern Guilt," in *Cultural Studies* 56 (L. Grossberg, C. Nelson, and P. Treichler, eds., 1992); A. Coombes, "In-venting the 'Postcolonial': Hybridity and Constituency in Contemporary Curating," 18 *New Formations* 39 (1992); R. Frankenberg and L. Mani, "Crosscurrents, Crosstalk: Race, 'Postcoloniality' and the Politics of Location," in *Displacement, Diaspora and the Geographies of Identity* 273 (S. Lavie and T. Swedenburg, eds., 1996); L. Hutcheon, "Circling the Downspout of Empire: Post-Colonialism and Postmodernism," 20(4) *Ariel* 149 (1989); A. McClintock, "The Angel of Progress: Pitfalls of the Term 'Post-Colonialism,'" 31/32 *Social Text* 84 (1991); A. P. Mukherjee, "Whose Post-Colonialism and Whose Post-Modernism?," 30(2) *World Literature Written in English* 1 (1990); D. Scott, "Criticism and Culture: Theory and Postcolonial Claims on Anthropological Disciplinarity," *Critique of Anthropology* 12 (4): 371–394 (1992); P. Seed, "Colonial and Postcolonial Discourse," 26 *Latin American Research Review* 181 (1991); E. Shohat, "Notes on the 'Post-Colonial,'" 31/32 *Social Text* 99 (1991); E. Shohat and R. Stamm, *Unthinking Eurocentrism* (1994); H. Tiffin, "Post-Colonialism, Post-Modernism, and the Rehabilitation of Post-Colonial History," 23 *The Journal of Commonwealth Lit-erature* 169 (1988); Colonial Discourse and Post-Colonial Theory: A Reader (P. Will-iams and L. Chrisman, eds., 1994).

8   See, e.g., R. W. Stedman, *Shadows of the Indian: Stereotypes in American Culture* (1982); P. Van Nederveen, *White on Black: Images of Africa and Blacks in Western Popular Culture* (1992).

9   M. Taussig, *Mimesis and Alterity: An Alternative History of the Senses* (1993).

10   *Ibid.*

11   *Ibid.*, at 210.

12   For examples, see A. McClintock, *Imperial Leather: Gender, Race and Sexuality in the Colonial Contest* (1995), and T. Jackson Lears, *Fables of Abundance: A Cultural History of Advertising in America* (1994).

13 M. Jay, "Unsympathetic Magic," 9(2) *Visual Anthropology Review* 79 (1993); P. Stoller, "Double Takes on Jay on Taussig," 10(1) *Visual Anthropology Review* (1994).

14 Taussig, *supra* note 9, at xiii.

15 *Ibid.*, at 21.

16 Actually, the dog is listening, not talking, as Jim Laski and Sean Cubitt pointed out to me.

17 Taussig, *supra* note 9, at 220.

18 H. K. Bhabha, *The Location of Culture* (1994).

19 P. Kamuf, *Signature Pieces: On the Institution of Authorship* (1988); S. Stewart, *Crimes of Writing: Problems in the Containment of Representation* (1991).

20 M. Foucault, "What is an Author?," in *The Foucault Reader* (P. Rabinow, ed., 1984).

21 See *The Phantom Public Sphere* (B. Robbins, ed., 1993).

22 N. Garnham, "The Mass Media, Cultural Identity, and the Public Sphere in the Modern World," 5 *Public Culture* 251 (1993); D. Polan, "The Public's Fear: or, Media as Monster in Habermas, Negt, and Kluge," in Robbins, *supra* note 21, at 33; M. Warner, "The Mass Public and the Mass Subject," in Robbins, *supra* note 21, at 234.

23 Warner, *supra* note 22.

24 *Ibid.*, at 242.

25 *Ibid.*, at 243.

26 B. Lee, "Going Public," 5 *Public Culture* 165 (1993).

27 N. Fraser, "Rethinking the Public Sphere: A Contribution to the Critique of Actually Existing Democracy," in Robbins, *supra* note 21, at 1, and C. Calhoun, "Civil Society and the Public Sphere," 5 *Public Culture* 267 (1993).

28 Lee, *supra* note 26.

29 J. Habermas, *The Structural Transformation of the Public Sphere: An Inquiry into a Category of Bourgeois Society* (T. Berger and F. Lawrence, trans., 1992).

30 Warner, *supra* note 22, at 239. For a discussion of bodily differentiation in Enlightenment thought, particularly in the French Revolutionary context, see J. B. Landes, "The Performance of Citizenship: Democracy, Gender, and Difference in the French Revolution," in *Democracy and Difference: Contesting the Boundaries of the Political* 295 (S. Benhabib, ed., 1996).

31 Warner, *supra* note 22, at 235.

32 *Ibid.*, at 239.

33 *Ibid.*

34 Fraser, *supra* note 27.

35 Warner, *supra* note 22, at 240.

36 D. Tannen, "Wears Jumpsuit. Sensible Shoes. Uses Husband's Last Name," *New York Times Magazine* 20 June 1993 at 18.

37 *Ibid.*, at 54.

38 C. Bongie, *Exotic Memories: Literature, Colonialism, and the Fin de Siècle* (1991).

39 L. Berlant, "National Brands/National Body: Imitation of Life," in Robbins, *supra* note 21, at 173; P. A. Turner, *Ceramic Uncles and Celluloid Mammies: Black Images and Their Influence on Culture* (1994). See D. Roberts, *The Myth of Aunt Jemima: Representations of Race and Region* (1994), for a discussion of the discursive relation between the South and the grotesque body.

40 S. Strasser, *Satisfaction Guaranteed: The Making of the American Mass Market* (1989), and R. S. Tedlow, *New and Improved: The Story of Mass Marketing in America* (1990).

41 Lee, *supra* note 26.

42 Berlant, *supra* note 39.

43 These examples are drawn from an ongoing study of the cultural politics of federal trademark law in the United States between 1870 and 1920.

44 G. Jowett, "The Emergence of Mass Society: The Standardization of American Culture 1830–1920," 7 *Prospects* 207 (1982). Although I recognize the political difficulties involved in the use of the term *American* to refer to things pertaining only to the United States, the term was the indigenous term of national belonging in the period under examination. I have chosen to avoid using scare quotes around the term in every instance that I evoke it, on the understanding that I only evoke it insofar as it figures in national rhetoric, and do not endorse a political position in so doing.

45 Berlant, *supra* note 39.

46 See, e.g., A. R. Heinze, *Adapting to Abundance: Jewish Immigrants, Mass Consumption, and the Search for American Identity* (1990).

47 See, e.g., E. Lott, *Love and Theft: Blackface Minstrelsy and the American Working Class* (1993).

48 A. Trachtenberg, *The Incorporation of America: Society and Culture in the Gilded Age* (1982).

49 T. W. Allen, *The Invention of the White Race, Vol. 1: Racial Oppression and Social Control* (1994); *Critical White Studies* (R. Delgado and J. Stefancic, eds., 1997); R. Frankenberg, *The Social Construction of Whiteness* (1992); D. R. Roediger, *The Wages of Whiteness: Race and the American Working Class* (1991); C. Harris, "Whiteness as Property," 106 *Harvard Law Review* 1709 (1993); S. M. Wildman, *Privilege Revealed* (1996).

50 *Nationalisms and Sexualities* (A. Parker et al., eds., 1992).

51 G. Buck, *Trademark Power: An Expedition into an Unprobed and Inviting Wilderness* (1916).

52 "Trade-Marks," *Albany Law Journal* 171 (1875), reprinted in 9 *Irish Law Times and Solicitor's Journal* 171.

53 R. Rydell, *All the World's a Fair: Visions of Empire at American International Expositions, 1876–1916* (1984).

54 See also R. R. Badger, *The Great American Fair: The World's Columbian Exposition and American Culture* (1979), and B. Benedict, *The Anthropology of World's Fairs* (1983).

55 The same goods are now collectibles that carry a hefty price. See Turner, *supra* note 39.

56 Taussig, *supra* note 9, at 213.

57 B. Price and A. Steuart, *American Trade-Mark Cases Decided by the Courts of the United States, Both State and Federal and by the Commissioner of Patents, and Reported Between 1879 and 1887* 428 (1887).

58 *Ibid.*, at 429.

59 *Ibid.*

60 Lee, *supra* note 26, at 174.

61 *Ibid.*

62 *Nation and Narration* (H. Bhabha, ed., 1990).

63 K. A. Marling, *The Colossus of Roads: Myth and Symbol along the American Highway* (1984).

64 *Ibid.*

65 *Ibid.*, at 6.

66 *Ibid.*, at 20.

67 *Ibid.*, at 1.

68 *Ibid.*, at 9.

69 *Ibid.*

70 According to Marling:

> In the 1930s, everybody knew Bemidji's mythical tales of the stupendous logging boss named Paul Bunyan. Novelist John Dos Passos appropriated the legend to symbolize the American worker, grown larger-than-life in the strength of collective action, and thus feared by "the Chamber of Commerce" and the business establishment. His *Nineteen Nineteen*, published in 1932, described . . . a martyred sawmill organizer . . . as like Paul Bunyan:
>
>> The i.w.w. put the idea of industrial democracy in Paul Bunyan's head; wobbly organizers said the forests ought to belong to the whole people, said Paul Bunyan ought to be paid in real money instead of in company scrip . . . When Paul Bunyan came back from making Europe safe for democracy . . . he joined the lumberjack's local to help make the Pacific slope safe for the working stiffs.
>
> In 1936, Carl Sandburg devoted a canto of *The People, Yes* to an investigation of this populist hero . . . not an emblematic figure, a heroic individual . . . so while he delineated Bunyan in all his singularity—his gargantuan flapjacks, his titanic dinner table, his . . . campaigns against a monstrous species of mosquito— Sandburg cared less for the unique protagonist of the stories than for their smalltown storytellers. Who made Paul Bunyan? asked the poet . . . who invented a woodland hero mighty enough to challenge . . . the wintry wrath of nature itself . . . The people did, he declared. The anonymous folk concocted Paul Bunyan out of the genial humor of their collective imagination and mutual resilience of spirit. The Blue Snow tales were Depression-time parables, fables testifying to the force of the American will. Paul Bunyan got his massive stature from the frontier savvy and the native grit of a nation, from the energy of a whole people endowed with the indomitable legacy of the westering pioneers. (*Ibid.*, at 1–2)

71 *Ibid.*, at 15.

72 I am very grateful to Brenda Child for bringing this to my attention.

73 See Taussig's discussion of Walter Benjamin, *supra* note 9.

74 J. A. Burciaga, *Drink Cultura: Chicanismo* 5 (1993).

75 *Ibid.*, at 6–7.

76 *Ibid.*, at 7.

77 *Ibid.*, at 8.

78 *Ibid.*, at 26.

79 *Ibid.*, at 55.

80 *Ibid.*, at 21.

81 For a discussion of the economic polarizations effected by global capital restructuring and the emphasis on information technologies see S. Sassen, *The Global City: London, Tokyo, New York* (1991); S. Sassen, *Cities in a World Economy* (1994); M. Castells, *The Informational City* (1984); and *World Cities in a World System* (P. L. Knox and P. Taylor, eds., 1995). Keith Aoki and I have both been engaged in the effort to draw connections between the role of intellectual property in these new forms of capital formation and the social consequences engendered thereby. See R. J. Coombe, "Left Out on the Information Highway," 75 *Oregon Law Review* 237 (1996); K. Aoki, "(Intellectual) Property and Sovereignty: Notes toward a Cultural Geogra-

phy of Authorship," 48 *Stanford Law Review* 1293 (1996); R. J. Coombe, "Authorial Cartographies: Mapping Proprietary Borders in a Less-than-Brave New World," 48 *Stanford Law Review* 1357 (1996); R. Coombe, "The Cultural Life of Things: Anthropological Approaches to Law and Society in Conditions of Globalization," 10 *American University Journal of International Law and Policy* 791 (1995).

82 See R. Rouse, "Mexican Migration and the Social Space of Postmodernism," 1 *Diaspora* 8 (1991).

83 R. Rouse, "Making Sense of Settlement: Class Transformation, Cultural Struggle, and Transnationalism among Mexican Migrants in the United States," 645 *Annals of the New York Academy of Sciences* 25 (1992).

84 Rouse, *supra* note 82, at 14.

85 *Ibid.*, at 15.

86 These constructions of space are explored in an unpublished manuscript by Roger Rouse titled "Men in Space." I thank him for sharing it with me.

87 Burciaga, *supra* note 74, at 24.

88 Stewart, *supra* note 19.

89 Warner, *supra* note 22, at 254. Warner overstates graffiti's placelessness, or perhaps simply generalizes as a characteristic of all graffiti such an abstraction from place. Graffiti in many contexts may bear very specific relationships to space and its occupation. For one example, see J. Peteet, "The Writing on the Walls: The Graffiti of the Intifada," 11 *Cultural Anthropology* 139–159 (1996).

90 Stewart, *supra* note 19, 206–233.

91 For an extended discussion of the expressive politics of the trademark in one inner-city venue, see R. J. Coombe and P. Stoller, "X Marks the Spot: The Ambiguities of African Trading in the Commerce of Black Public Spheres," in *The Black Public Sphere* 253 (The Black Public Sphere Collective, ed., 1995).

92 Stewart, *supra* note 19, at 209.

93 For one discussion, see H.-K. Trask, "Lovely Hula Lands: Corporate Tourism and the Prostitution of Hawaiian Culture," 23 *Border/lines* 22 (winter 1991–92). See also H.-K. Trask, *From a Native Daughter: Colonialism and Sovereignty in Hawai'i* (1993).

94 See e.g., W. Churchill, *Indians Are Us? Culture and Genocide in Native North America* (1994). For a discussion of the rage to collect the racist kitsch of the early twentieth century, see Turner, *supra* note 39.

95 After using the name for sixty-eight years, Miami University's Board of Trustees voted to discard the name out of respect for the Miami Indian Tribe of Oklahoma in September 1996 as a response to a resolution passed by the Tribe (which reversed earlier resolutions in which the Tribe had endorsed the name). However, the Tribe did urge the university to keep using an image of an Indian chief as the team logo. See "Miami U. Abandons 'Redskins' Name," *The Chronicle of Higher Education* 4 October 1996 at A8.

96 Licensing revenues from trademarked merchandise are an increasing source of profit in both professional and college sports:

> This phenomenon has transformed sports into a $12 billion market. In 1992, analysts estimate that within the four professional leagues, Major League baseball sold about $2.4 billion in licensed merchandise, the National Football League sold about $2.1 billion, the National Basketball Association reached $1.4 billion, and the National Hockey League sold about $600 million. Also benefitting from the growing public demand for sports merchandise, colleges

and universities have experienced a boom in sales of products bearing their logos. The Collegiate Licensing Company, which coordinates licensing agreements for 126 colleges and universities, estimates that college merchandising has reached nearly $1.5 billion in sales during 1992. (B. C. Kelber, "'Scalping the Redskins:' Can Trademark Law Start Athletic Teams Bearing Native American Nicknames and Images on the Road to Racial Reform?," 17 *Hamline Law Review* 533, 549–550 [1994]). In 1992 it was also estimated that the Washington Redskins logo alone had a value to the team of more than $1 million—through the year's sale of licensed merchandise after the Super Bowl triumph. See *ibid.*, and sources cited therein.

97 A report in *USA Today* estimated a cost of $25,000 to $100,000 in marketing and research efforts. See G. Mihoces, "Trying to Get a Handle: Possible Merchandise Bonanza Hinges on Selection," *USA Today* 17 September 1993 at 6c.

98 For an excellent survey of the arguments put forth on both sides of the controversy in a discussion of the likelihood of success of trademark expungement proceedings, see Kelber, *supra* note 96. Mr. Kelber cites a wealth of press reports on the issue. Another article, more exclusively concerned with the potential for canceling the Washington Redskins trademark registration, and which contains up-to-date media coverage of the controversy, is K. A. Pace, "The Washington Redskins Case and the Doctrine of Disparagement: How Politically Correct Must a Trademark Be?," *Pepperdine Law Review* 22: 7–55 (1994). Ward Churchill is one of the more vocal and prolific activists who argue that the commercialization of Native culture and tradition and its caricature is one of the most pernicious forces undermining Indian and First Nations' political self-determination. His writings on the topic are collected in Churchill, *supra* note 94. My own understanding of the issue was greatly enlightened by indigenous activists who attended the conference The Commercial Appropriation of Tradition: Legal Challenges and Legal Remedies, which I co-organized with Nell Newton and Peter Jaszi at the Washington College of Law, American University, April 15–18, 1994. I thank Vernon Bellecourt, Sam Deloria, Robert Gough, Michael Haney, Suzan Shown Harjo, Ted Jojola, Stuart Kaler, Chad Smith, Brian St. Laurent, Jonny Bearcub Stiffarm, and Charlene Teeters for the education.

99 In L. Shapiro, "Offensive Penalty Is Called on 'Redskins': Native Americans Protest the Name," *Washington Post* 3 November 1992 at D1.

100 James Billie, chairman of the Seminole Tribe of Florida, feels that Florida State University's use of the name "reflects a pride in Florida Seminole history." Oklahoma Seminoles are not nearly so happy, and it has been suggested that a licensing agreement could provide revenues to fund tribal needs for youth education programs. See J. Wheat, "Real Seminoles Resent the Profits FSU Makes off Their Tribal Name," *Miami Herald* 11 February 1993 at 7B. The licensing arrangement was mentioned to me by activists from the National Coalition Against Racism in Sports and Media in the spring of 1992.

101 Kelber, *supra* note 96, at 545.

102 R. F. Berkhofer Jr., *The White Man's Indian: Images of the American Indian from Columbus to the Present* (1979).

103 *Ibid.*, at 3.

104 Tim Giago, editor in chief of *Indian Country Today*, says that the use of feathers in sports arenas is another example of how those things Indians hold sacred are in-

sulted: "The turkey feathers protruding from [sports spectators'] heads insult another spiritual practice of most Plains Indians. The eagle feather is sacred. It is given to the recipient in a religious ceremony, usually to honor, to thank, or to bless" (T. Giago, "Drop the Chop! Indian Nicknames Just Aren't Right," *New York Times* 13 March 1994). Feathers, however, have alternative meanings in the histories and imaginaries of European domination. Joseph Roach suggests that feathers historically figured as signs of abundance and excess or nonproductive expenditure. Like face painting (also associated with Indianness), it designated "a physical incorporation of excess expenditure, a luxurious emblem of distinction" (J. Roach, *Cities of the Dead: Circum-Atlantic Performance* 156 [1996]). The violent disappearance of the excessive other is a national mise-en-scène.

105   D. Pierson, "Redskins Nickname Will Be Protest Target," *Chicago Tribune* 19 January 1992 at C2, cited in Kelber, *supra* note 96, at 545.

106   Cited in Shapiro, *supra* note 99, at D1.

107   Cited in D. Burkhart, "Turner Won't Change Braves' Name, but Wouldn't Mind Stopping the Chop," *Atlanta Journal* 3 December 1991 at F8.

108   See also D. Francis, *The Imaginary Indian: The Image of the Indian in Canadian Culture* (1994); R. H. Pearce, *Savagism and Civilization: A Study of the Indian and the American Mind* (1988 [1953]); D. Root, *Cannibal Culture: Art, Appropriation, and the Commodification of Difference* (1996).

109   Roach, *supra* note 104, at 205.

110   Bhabha, *supra* note 18, at 66–84.

111   *Ibid.*, at 67.

112   *Ibid.*, at 66.

113   For an extensive history of this trope as it repeats itself across the continent and eventually into the Philippines, the Caribbean, and Indochina, see R. Drinnon, *Facing West: The Metaphysics of Indian-Hating and Empire Buliding* (1980).

114   Bhabha, *supra* note 18, at 74.

115   *Ibid.*, at 75.

116   *Ibid.*, at 76.

117   Roach, *supra* note 104, at 187.

118   *Ibid.*

119   W. B. Michaels, *Our America: Nativism, Modernism, and Pluralism* (1996).

120   *Ibid.*, at 12.

121   *Ibid.*, at 38.

122   *Ibid.*, at 45.

123   Roach, *supra* note 104, at 27.

124   P. Bourdieu, "Programme for a Sociology of Sport," in *In Other Words: Essays Towards a Reflexive Sociology* 156, 167 (P. Bourdieu, ed., 1990).

125   M. Wakankar, "Body, Crowd, Identity: Genealogy of a Hindu Nationalist Ascetics," 14(4) *Social Text* 45, 59 (1995), citing Bourdieu, *ibid.*, at 167.

126   This is a composite of the many ritualized behaviors that accompany games played by teams with "Indian" names (by both fans and fans of opposing teams). No single event would encompass all of these, and some of these performances are specific to particular teams.

127   See illustrations in Churchill, *supra* note 94, at 71.

128   Lott, *supra* note 47, at 8.

129   *Ibid.*

130   *Ibid.*, at 68–69.

131   *Ibid.*, at 96.

132   See "Blackface, White Noise: The Jewish Jazz Singer Finds His Voice," 18 *Critical Inquiry* 425, 431–434 (spring 1992).

133   *Ibid.*, at 92.

134   *Ibid.*, at 98. For example, the expressed fear that American culture might be a slave culture that owed too much to "Ethiopia" conveniently forgot that the forms of blackness this cultural form evoked were all fictions constructed by white impersonators.

135   Roach, *supra* note 104.

136   *Ibid.*, at 3.

137   P. Stallybrass and A. White, *The Politics and Poetics of Transgression* 5 (1986).

138   Roach, *supra* note 104, at 6.

139   To elaborate: "the vast scale of the project of whiteness—and the scope of the contacts among cultures it required—limited the degree to which its foils could be eradicated from the memory of those who had the deepest motivation and the surest means to forget them. At the same time, it fostered complex and ingenious schemes to displace, refashion, and transfer those persistent memories into [more amenable] representations ... In that sense, circum-Atlantic performance is a monumental study in the pleasures and torments of incomplete forgetting" (*ibid.*, at 6–7).

140   *Ibid.*, at 36.

141   *Ibid.*

142   *Ibid.*

143   Lott, *supra* note 47, at 99.

144   There is a long history in North America of cultural cross-dressing of which the Boston Tea Party, with its howling "Indians" and "blacks," is perhaps the most famous example. Masked bands of "Indians" were part of nineteenth-century charivaris in which contemporary social mores and behaviors were commented upon. There are also many instances of whites representing themselves as Indian sages, translating Indianness for white audiences while fulfilling stereotypical anticipations of authentic Indianness (getting far more attention in the public sphere than actual Native activists struggling for their people's political rights and economic survival). New Age shamanism and some ecofeminisms provide recent examples.

145   Lott, *supra* note 47, at 102.

146   In addition, legal doctrines of laches and estoppel (which preclude one from exercising one's rights if too long a delay has occurred after one's rights have been violated) serve, at least in this area, to ensure that the disempowered remain that way and that the advantages that one group exercises at the expense of another, by virtue of its political powerlessness, become entrenched as property rights.

147   Cited in Kelber, *supra* note 96, at 548.

148   In *Cannibal Culture, supra* note 108, Deborah Root's "attempt to construct a topography of the West's will to aestheticize and consume cultural difference" (at xiii), the author identifies a variety of sites where the cannibalization of difference is manifested. Although sports arenas are not addressed, her general comments on cultural appropriation and cultural cross-dressing are apropos. Most so-called appreciation of cultural difference is "done with mirrors ... what is usually available are the morphological forms that connote difference ... difference in effigy, as it

were" (*ibid.*, at 69). She relates this "appreciation" to "an insidious salvage paradigm, which assumes such cultures to be dying or dead" (*ibid.*, at 96). Because of
their supposedly inevitable disappearance, all adoption of their forms may seem
like a form of favor—a eulogy of sorts. But "the desire to appropriate meaning
from another cultural tradition is not just another romanticized nostalgia for supposedly dead cultures but can also be a way of marking death and conquest and
doing so on the bodies and communities of living people." *Ibid.*

Root also points to the importance of the Indian as victim in this narrative and
its Christian underpinnings. It is Indians' inevitable victimization that makes them
heroic, but such heroism presupposes that issues of land and conquest have all, already, been settled. Never entirely abject, the victim in Christian tradition also suggests a certain moral and spiritual superiority connected with virtuous struggle. It
is virtuous, however, only because it is doomed; such ways of "honoring" Native
peoples imply no connection with actual Native peoples or any political connection to their contemporary social needs or political struggles (*ibid.*, at 99–101).

Joseph Roach sees this emphasis on vanishing as part of a larger project of legitimating manifest destiny, "in which the inevitability of Anglocentric displacement
of indigenous peoples and rival colonial interests takes on the golden penumbra of
a creation myth," in "which the expanding frontier and 'America' emerged as coex-
tensive imaginative spaces" (Roach, *supra* note 104, at 188, citing R. Slotkin, *Regeneration Through Violence: The Mythology of the American Frontier* [1973], and W. H.
Truettner, *The West as America: Reinterpreting Images of the Frontier* [1991]). He
also mentions the ongoing exploitation in popular entertainment of a sentimental
fascination with "the last of" stories as part of a genealogy of popular Indian death
scenes that he sees as a form of "national wish fulfillment in genocidal fantasies"
(*ibid.*, at 189).

149 See Berlant, *supra* note 39, for the development of the concept of the trademark as
prosthesis in mass culture.

150 One particularly amazing example of this occurred in Canada. After the barricades
had been dismantled in the Mohawk territories besieged by the Canadian Armed
Forces (and the Quebec provincial police) in the Oka standoff of 1990, it was reported that a white entrepreneur in Quebec was seeking to market a "Mohawk
Warriors" board game and to trademark the monikers (e.g., Lasagne) of the central
First Nations' agents in the standoff for licensing purposes. Even contemporary
politics involving Native peoples, it would appear, are quickly appropriated as the
stuff of play and fantasy. See L. Roth, "Media and the Commodification of Crisis,"
in *Media, Crisis and Democracy: Essays on Mass Communications and the Disruption of Social Order* (M. Raboy and B. Dafenais, eds., 1992).

151 Bhabha, *supra* note 18, at 81.

152 I borrow this term from the Situationists. For a brief discussion of the concept, see
S. Plant, *The Situationist Internationale* (1993).

153 Cited in D. Grow, "The Way to Redskins Owner's Heart Is through His Wallet," *Star
Tribune* (Minneapolis) 11 September 1992 at 3B.

154 For an overview of reform efforts and achievements at state, local, and federal levels, see Kelber, *supra* note 96.

155 If successful, the action would end the exclusive rights that the Washington team
has in this appellation. This will not, however, preclude others from using the term,
but will only prevent the team's ability to enforce its rights against others (and thus

diminish licensing revenues), but it is assumed that the loss of these rights would devalue the trademark so dramatically that the term would be voluntarily abandoned. This raises the real possibility that more teams will use the term, at least locally, and for this reason, some supporters have opposed the proceeding. Ironically, any prohibition upon the logo would massively increase the value of the remaining licensed merchandise as these become collector's items. The action is likely to be held up in constitutional wrangling for years; one of the defenses to the suit is that the section of the Federal Trademark Act upon which the expungement proceeds is an unconstitutional restriction on commercial speech. For an analysis rejecting this legal argument, see Kelber, *supra* note 96. For an argument in support of this argument, see Pace, *supra* note 98. For more general discussions of the use of trademark law for political purposes, see S. R. Baird, "Moral Intervention in the Trademark Arena: Banning the Registration of Scandalous and Immoral Trademarks," 83 *Trademark Reporter* 661 (1993), and P. E. Loving, "Native American Team Names in Athletics: It's Time to Trade These Marks," 13 *Loyola of Los Angeles Entertainment Law Journal* 1 (1992).

156   As a consequence, the team announced their intentions to move the stadium to Maryland and build it on private lands. Because nearly all stadium construction requires public funding or the posting of bonds, state legislatures are in positions to deny funds and make such bonds difficult to obtain by prohibiting discrimination against Native Americans, use of disparaging images, and mockery of Native American symbols. State civil rights powers also create opportunities to control such imagery in association with public schools and other publicly funded institutions.

157   See T. Jojola, "Negative Image Exploited to Undercut Indian Self-Government," *Albuquerque Journal* 27 June 1993 at B3.

158   Acting on behalf of the estate of Crazy Horse, Seth Big Crow and his activist attorneys have deliberately constructed the legal case as part of a multiple strategy: to educate and to build opposition to the marketing of the malt liquor among Lakota people; as a vehicle to engender cohesion and community pride; as part of a broader effort to gain greater legitimacy for tribal courts within tribes, in part by encouraging greater use of tribal customary law in tribal courts; and to strengthen tribal court systems as centers of resistance to the jurispathic influence of state and federal laws. More generally, this case is part of a multivocal, multilocal struggle of Indian people in the late twentieth century to destabilize the stereotypes that make up the dominant society's image of "Indianness" and replace these ahistorical, timeless, static, passive, decontextualized, Orientalized images with the multilayered, multipurposive, individual and collective identities claimed by Indian people and tribes in the late-twentieth century. (N. J. Newton, "Memory and Misrepresentation: Representing Crazy Horse," 27 *Connecticut Law Review* 1003 [1995])

159   See *ibid.*, at 1019 n.63. for citations to these public laws and state bills. Legislation was introduced in Minnesota and California, and in Washington sales were banned on the basis of that state's restriction upon the use of religious figures in alcohol promotion.

160   The justification used for banning the name was the high incidence of alcoholism on Indian reservations. However, because the product was not marketed on reservations, the use of the name was considered a protected form of commercial

speech and the barring of the name on the product not seen to be directly related to the purpose of preventing alcohol abuse among Native Americans. See Hornell Brewing Co. v. Brady, 819 F. Supp. 1227 (E.D.N.Y. 1993).

161 See Newton, *supra* note 158, at 1025, nn.85–93, for a survey of sources that describe the controversies over target marketing in inner cities, including efforts by public interest groups concerned with the health consequences and racial and sexual stereotyping effected by these practices.

162 A single bottle of the high-octane malt liquor contains as much alcohol as a six-pack of more conventional beers. Hornell Brewing Company has a history of marketing especially high-alcohol-content beverages in minority communities. In 1991 it withdrew Powermaster from the shelves after protests from the black communities in which it was most heavily marketed. Crazy Horse replaced it on the shelves in March 1992.

163 No doubt this copy is legally protected by the copyright rights of the G. Heileman and Hornell Brewing Company. In the United States, the fact that I have reproduced it in a noncommercial context for the purposes of criticism and commentary would bring it under the defense of fair use. In Canada, the fact that I had used it in its entirety would count against my claim that this was a fair dealing for the purpose of criticism, but because it is necessary to reproduce the whole to make the criticism and I have acknowledged the source (a beer bottle), I am probably safe from liability for infringement.

164 M. Dorris, "Noble Savages? We'll Drink to That." Op-Ed. *New York Times* 21 April 1992 at A23.

165 Newton, *supra* note 158, at 1018.

166 Jim Mattox, interviewed by Catherine Crier, *Crier and Company*, CNN transcript #62 (27 May 1992).

167 Letter from Hank Shafran of Ferolito, Vultaggio, & Sons to Hon. Frank Wolf (6 November 1992) at 2. On television, communications lawyer Diane Zipursky declared that because Crazy Horse is dead, there are no rights to the name, and "so it is out there, free for anybody to want to use" (in interview by Catherine Crier, *Crier & Company*, CNN transcript #62 [27 May 1992]). This shows a remarkable ignorance of publicity rights, but one, I would argue, that is symptomatic of a national tendency to regard all things "Indian" as public domain—phenomena for fantasy. I discuss this further in the next chapter.

168 Shafran, *supra* note 167.

169 Quoted in G. W. Prince, "Tall Order: The Making and Marketing of Arizona Iced Tea," *Beverage World*, June 1994.

170 D. Grow, "Relative of Crazy Horse Questions Brewer's 'Honor,'" *Star Tribune* (Minneapolis) 21 April 1995 at B3, notes that in a deposition and testimony at a hearing protesting state bans on malt liquor, Mr. Vultaggio said that he was unaware that Crazy Horse had been an honored Dakota chief. This does not explain why, then, it was corporately determined that the malt liquor would not be marketed in the Black Hills or in areas with substantial Indian populations. At the Commercial Appropriation of Tradition conference, Robert Gough, attorney for Seth Big Crow, shared with us a series of press releases prepared by Beverage Distribution Consultants, who became the public author for Ferolito & Vultaggio, and the Hornell Brewing Company. In one of these, it is claimed that the Original Crazy Horse Malt Liquor is not marketed in South Dakota, North Dakota, Minnesota, Montana, Ne-

braska, Arizona, and eight other states with substantial numbers of Indian residents. See *Backgrounder, Is Socially-Acceptable Marketing in America Changing? Products and Marketing Considered Tasteful by Some, Are Decried as Offensive by Others. Whose Attitudes Should Count?* (undated press release prepared by Hank Shafran and Mark Rodman, associates of Beverage Distribution Consultants; *hereinafter Whose Attitudes Should Count?*).

171 Newton, *supra* note 158, at 1027, citing press release dated 19 May 1992 prepared by Beverage Distribution Consultants.

172 *Ibid.*

173 Press release, *Statement of the Marketers of the Original Crazy Horse Malt Liquor* 20 June 1992, prepared by Beverage Distribution Consultants.

174 *Whose Attitudes Should Count? supra* note 170.

175 *Ibid.*

176 Newton, *supra* note 158, at 1018.

177 Memorandum to Sen. Alfonse D'Amato, from John Ferolito and Don Vultaggio (24 September 1992) (addendum to press release, prepared by Beverage Distribution Consultants dated 26 September 1992).

178 15 U.S.C. & 1052 (a) (1988).

179 Newton, *supra* note 158, at 1021.

180 Quoted in M. Vaillancourt, "Big Crow's First Stand: Descendant of Crazy Horse Goes Public to Keep Legendary Warrior's Name off High-Octane Beer," *Boston Globe* 4 December 1994 at A85.

181 Newton, *supra* note 158, at 1022.

182 As Newton notes: "Relatives of Tasunke Witko live on the Pine Ridge, Cheyenne River, and Rosebud Reservations as well as in the large Rapid City, South Dakota, off-reservation Indian community . . . Although there was some objection to the appointment of Mr. Big Crow as the sole administrator by the Pine Ridge Council, family members from Pine Ridge and Rosebud who attended the hearing did not object to the appointment; family members from Cheyenne River did not attend but had communicated with Big Crow (the Cheyenne River Sioux Tribe has subsequently entered the case as an amicus) . . . The [tribal] court dismissed the Pine Ridge Council's objections on the grounds that only family members could contest the appointment" (*ibid.*, at 1020 and 1022).

183 *Ibid.*, at 1023.

184 In re Tasunke Witko, Civ. No. 93-204 (Memorandum decision, October 25, 1994). In the Tribal District Court, it was determined that the court had no jurisdiction over the defendants. However, the decision was appealed to the Rosebud Sioux Supreme Court, which determined that the tribal court did have jurisdiction if the jurisdictional facts were true: the claim arose on the reservation, the defendant purposefully directed conduct at the forum by committing intentional torts, and the defendant by virtue of marketing the product in forty states could not be said to be unduly inconvenienced by having to travel to the reservation. See Law Professors Amicus Brief on Behalf of Petitioners, In re Tasunke Witko, Civ. No. 93-204 (Ct. App. Rosebud Sx. Tri., March 10, 1995) (submitted by Joseph William Singer and Nell Jessop Newton). Thus, the case was remanded to the trial court to engage in the necessary fact finding. Meanwhile, the federal court agreed that fact finding was necessary, but opined that it was unlikely that a tribal court had jurisdiction over non-Indians. As Nell Newton maintains, even a victory in the tribal court on the

merits is fraught with risk; the tribal court's jurisdiction will undoubtedly be challenged in federal court, and there "the case may be used as a vehicle to deny *all* tribes civil jurisdiction over non-Indians" (Newton, *supra* note 158, at 1052).

185 The historical disenfranchisement of Native peoples in North America, however, has made it impossible for them to monitor those signifiers they consider their own and thus for them to demonstrate the history of policing that both common law and statutory law require of mark holders. For instance, at the time of the Crazy Horse litigation, there were at least thirty-three commercial usages of his name that had been found by the attorneys, including for nightclubs and restaurants in Paris and Washington, D.C. Given that tribal peoples were politically disenfranchised from using civil courts to make trademark and unfair competition claims as legally designated "wards of the state" until the 1960s, however, it seems hardly just to expect them to have threatened to exercise rights they could not possibly enforce. Moreover, the isolation of reservations from most mainstream media, their relative poverty, the poor communications infrastructures that link reservations to the rest of the country, and residents' lack of access even to law libraries that would inform them of their rights until relatively recently all militate against maintaining the same standards for trademark management and policing that commercial entities must meet. Even at the time of this litigation the lawyers working on the reservation did not have published law reports, access to computerized legal databases, or even a fax machine with which to help prepare themselves for trial. People living on reservations do not know when others are attempting to register Native American symbols as trademarks; fortunately, many American Indian law students do have access to the relevant databases and might assume the role of monitoring attempted registrations.

186 Newton locates 94 names of products that use the term *Cherokee* in a 1995 Trademarkscan-U.S. Federal database search, 35 references to *Navajo*, and 208 appropriations of Sioux peoples' nominations (which include the Dakota and the Lakota). *Supra* note 158 at 1008, n.19.

187 See D. Trotter, "Colonial Subjects," 32 (3) *Critical Quarterly* 3 (1990).

188 Taussig, *supra* note 9, at 8.

189 Taussig discusses the appropriation of the "talking dog" in Cuna molas (traditional works of appliqué and embroidery) and how it brings "intense pleasure—the catching of the breath, the delighted laugh, the stirring of curiosity—that this particular mola brings to Western viewers today, including myself, all the more so when held side by side with its Western original" (*supra* note 9, at 225). Why, he asks, this laugh?—"the (not so) simple fact that observing mimesis is pleasurable. And just as surely there is an element of colonialist mastery in this laughter . . . how difficult it is to pry mimesis loose from pervasive intimations of primitiveness. But there is also the possibility that this sudden laugh from nowhere registers a tremor in cultural identity, and not only in identity but in the security of Being itself" (*ibid.* at 226). Taussig asks why the existence of "our" signs in "their" worlds fascinates us so. Rejecting explanations that point simply to an unusual juxtaposition or the effect of surreal pastiche, and similarly suspicious of those who see in every local use of the Western sign an act of "resistance to a dominant order," he finds in these moments some potential for humanity (that he rather wishes to universalize). I would suggest a more culturally specific possibility; it is perhaps the power of the trademark in our own culture, its ability to interpellate us as mass

subjects, that creates the "flash of recognition" that Taussig alludes to. In other words, we so rarely recognize this power *as* power, these properties *as* properties, that it is only when these marks are in the possession of others that we recognize our own routine misrecognitions of the nature of "culture" in late capitalism.

5. The Properties of Culture and the Politics of Possessing Identity

1   E. Mertz, "A New Social Constructionism for Sociolegal Studies," 28 *Law and Society Review* 1243, 1254 (1994).

2   Between 21 March and 14 April 1992, articles, editorials, and letters to the editor considered the issue of "cultural appropriation" or "appropriation of voice" in fictional and nonfictional writing.

3   Although the controversy died down, references and allusions back to it can be found throughout 1992, as, for example, in a books column by Philip Marchand titled "When Appropriation Becomes Inappropriate," *The Toronto Star* 23 November 1992 at B5. I have not pursued the debates in the Canadian press since 1992.

4   S. Godfrey, "Canada Council Asks Whose Voice Is It Anyway?," *Globe and Mail* 21 March 1992 at C1 and C15.

5   *Ibid.*

6   The term *dangerous supplement* is borrowed from Jack Balkin, who borrows it from Jacques Derrida, in "Deconstructive Practice and Legal Theory," 96 *Yale Law Journal* 743 (1987).

7   I use the gendered pronoun deliberately here because I am referring to a cultural concept—the Romantic author—rather than any actual authors. The author in Western European history is a figure who occupies a decidedly male-gendered position. For further discussion, I refer the reader to S. Gilbert and S. Gubar, *The Madwoman in the Attic* (1979).

8   T. Findley, Letter to the Editor, *Globe and Mail* 28 March 1992 at D7. Reprinted in *OUT Magazine: Canada's National Gay Arts/Entertainment Monthly* (June 1992). Canada's gay and lesbian communities have been disproportionately affected by the Supreme Court of Canada's decision to uphold Canada's obscenity laws. See (1992) R. v. Butler, 89 D.L.R. (4th) 449 (S.C.C.). A victory for mainstream feminists has become an opportunity for federal officials to seize and confiscate gay and lesbian erotica. This has created a climate of opposition to state censorship among gay and lesbian activists that perhaps accounts for the reprinting of Findley's letter in a gay journal. As I will suggest, however, opposition to repression of alternative representations of minority groups cannot be maintained solely in the name of "freedom of expression" without thereby becoming complicit with the relations of power at work in the contemporary deployments of the term.

9   Jacoby, Letter to the Editor, *Globe and Mail* 28 March 1992 at D7.

10 *Globe and Mail* 31 March 1992 at A16.

11 Godfrey, *supra* note 4, at C15.

12 Outram, Letter to the Editor, *Globe and Mail* 28 March 1992 at D7.

13 *Ibid.*

14 Smith, Letter to the Editor, *Globe and Mail* 3 April 3 1992 at A3.

15 Driedger, Letter to the Editor, *Globe and Mail* 28 March 1992 at D7.

16 For discussions of the relationship between Romanticism and imperialism in the nineteenth century, see *Macropolitics of Nineteenth-Century Literature: Nationalism, Exoticism, Imperialism* (J. Arac and H. Ritvo, eds., 1991). The relationship between copyright and colonialism as forms of governance is explored in my, *Copyright, Colonialism, and the Evangelical Impulse* (forthcoming from the University of Minnesota Press).

17 For a discussion of the similar and simultaneous logic of European colonialism, see T. Mitchell, *Colonising Egypt* (1988).

18 For a discussion of the difficulties of maintaining the stability of the idea/expression distinction in copyright law, see A. B. Cohen, "Copyright Law and the Myth of Objectivity: The Idea-Expression Dichotomy and the Inevitability of Artistic Value Judgements," 66 *Indiana Law Journal* 175 (1990).

19 J. Balkin, "Ideology as Constraint," 43 *Stanford Law Review* 1133 (1991); J. Boyle, "The Politics of Reason," 133 *University of Pennsylvania Law Review* 685 (1985) J. Boyle, "Is Subjectivity Possible? The Post-Modern Subject in Legal Theory," 62 *University of Colorado Law Review* 489 (1991); P. Chevigny, *More Speech: Dialogue Rights and Modern Liberty* (1988); R. J. Coombe, "Room for Manoeuver: Toward a Theory of Practice in Critical Legal Studies," 14 *Law and Social Inquiry* 69 (1989); R. J. Coombe, "Same as It Ever Was: Rethinking the Politics of Legal Interpretation," 34 *McGill Law Journal* 604 (1989) (*hereinafter* Coombe, "Same as It Ever Was"); D. Cornell, "Toward a Modern/Postmodern Reconstruction of Ethics," 133 *University of Pennsylvania Law Review* 291 (1985); D. Cornell, *Beyond Accommodation: Ethical Feminism, Deconstruction and the Law* (1991); D. Cornell, *The Philosophy of the Limit* (1992); D. Cornell, *Transformations* (1993); S. Fish, *Doing What Comes Naturally: Change, Rhetoric, and the Practice of Theory in Literary and Legal Studies* (1989); O. Fiss, "Free Speech and Social Structure," 71 *Iowa Law Review* 1405 (1986); O. Fiss, "Why the State?," 100 *Harvard Law Review* 781 (1987); M. J. Frug, *Postmodern Legal Feminism* (1992); M. Minow, "Identities," 3 *Yale Journal of Law & the Humanities* 97 (1991); D. Patterson, "Postmodernism /Feminism /Law," 77 *Cornell Law Review* 254 (1992); G. Peller, "The Metaphysics of American Law," 73 *California Law Review* 1152 (1985); P. Schlag, "Fish v. Zapp: The Case of the Relatively Autonomous Self," 76 *Georgetown Law Journal* 37 (1987); P. Schlag, "The Problem of the Subject," 69 *Texas Law Review* 1627 (1991), and other sources cited therein. I cannot claim that this list is exhaustive.

20 Allan Hutchinson makes similar points in his article, "Giving Smaller Voices a Chance to Be Heard," *Globe and Mail* 14 April 1992 at A16.

21 It has been suggested that the term multiculturalism is inappropriate as an umbrella term within which to consider Native claims to self-determination or cultural autonomy:

> The principle of aboriginality may be defined in essentially political terms, as a statement of power that acknowledges the special status of the original occupants of a territory and aims at restoring rights and entitlements that flow from recognition of this unique relationship with the state . . . This politicized view of aboriginality has several implications. There is a sense in which the aboriginal people retain their original, inherent sovereignty, because the Canadian Constitution does not necessarily apply to them, because they are exempt from federal/provincial laws, and because treaties are viewed as nation-to-nation agreements specifying separate jurisdictions. Programs and policies that apply to other Cana-

dian minority groups are dismissed as inapplicable—even counterproductive—to aboriginal ambitions. Any move to integration as one ethnic component in a Canadian multicultural mosaic is rejected as diminishing entitlement as "first among equals"... In rejecting an ethnic or immigrant dimension, aboriginal people prefer to define themselves as a "sovereign" entity within the federal state, with collective rights guaranteed by virtue of their ancestral occupation and arising from first principles. (A. Fleras and J. L. Elliott, *The "Nations Within": Aboriginal-State Relations in Canada, the United States, and New Zealand*, 30 [1992])

This would suggest that respect for and recognition of Native cultural autonomy must rest upon different grounds than the mere value of cultural diversity.

22 Many Thai people consider this film a blatant example of Western imperialism that is condescending in its attitudes toward Thais and perpetuates many stereotypes about Oriental peoples.

23 The term Orientalism is drawn from Edward Said's pathbreaking work of the same title (1979). Although Said's work was concerned to explicate the rhetorical strategies and informing tropes of late-eighteenth- and early-nineteenth-century Orientalist scholars, the term has come to stand for a mode of representing the other that projects upon non-Western peoples qualities and characteristics that are mirror opposites of the qualities the West claims for itself. Moreover, such approaches have a tendency to deny other societies their own histories, to present them as internally homogeneous and undifferentiated, "timeless," defined and subsumed by unchanging "traditions," and unable to creatively deal with outside influences or interpret the impact of external forces. Often, to "Orientalize" also means to represent others as both feminine and childlike and in need of representation by Western authorities.

24 Godfrey, *supra* note 4.

25 L. Keeshig-Tobias, "Stop Stealing Native Stories," *Globe and Mail* 26 January 1990 at A8.

26 *Ibid.*

27 *Ibid.*

28 *Ibid.*

29 *Ibid.*

30 *Ibid.*

31 Hutchinson, *supra* note 20, at A16.

32 *Ibid.*

33 Godfrey, *supra* note 4, at C1.

34 *Ibid.*, at C15.

35 G. Lipsitz, *Time Passages: Collective Memory and American Popular Culture* (1990).

36 A. Coombes, "Inventing the 'Postcolonial': Hybridity and Constituency in Contemporary Curating," 18 *New Formations* 39 (1992).

37 I have deliberately chosen to use the term *postcolonial* rather than the term *multicultural*, and the language of struggle rather than the currently fashionable discourse of cultural diversity, because these alternative terms emphasize rather than obscure the very real histories of colonialism from which all peoples in Canada are still emerging, and the very real relations of power and domination inherited from our diverse colonial pasts that continue to shape social relations of difference in this country. Multiculturalism seems to assume a social field of equivalent differences that can be subsumed under a single policy of tolerance, without regard for the very

real psychic, social, economic, and cultural damage done by histories of Western imperialism. For critical discussions of multiculturalism, see K. Moodley, "Canadian Multiculturalism as Ideology," 6 *Ethnic and Racial Studies* 320 (1983), and C. Mohanty, "On Race and Voice: Challenges for Liberal Education in the 1990s," 14 *Cultural Critique* 179 (1990). The literature discussing postcolonialism is vast. There is general agreement that the reception and interpretation of two texts—E. Said, *Orientalism, supra* note 23, and F. Fanon, *Black Skin, White Masks* (1967)—mark the beginnings of the development of the discourse, but it has now expanded across several disciplinary fields. For a fine overview, see P. Seed, "Colonial and Postcolonial Discourse," 26 *Latin American Research Review* 181 (1991). For recent criticisms of the term and its range of extension, see D. Bahri, "Coming to Terms with the 'Postcolonial,'" in *Between the Lines: South Asians and Postcoloniality* 137 (D. Bahri and M. Vasudeva, eds., 1996); A. P. Mukherjee, "Whose Post-Colonialism and Whose Postmodernism?," 30(2) *World Literature Written in English* 1 (1990); E. Shohat, "Notes on the 'Post-Colonial,'" 32 *Social Text* 99 (1991); H. Tiffin, "Post-Colonialism, Post-Modernism, and the Rehabilitation of Post-Colonial History," 23(1) *Journal of Commonwealth Literature* 169 (1988); R. Frankenberg and L. Mani, "Crosscurrents, Crosstalk: Race, 'Postcoloniality' and the Politics of Location," in *Displacement, Diaspora and the Geographies of Identity* 273 (S. Lavie and T. Swedenburg, eds., 1996). A collection of influential essays is contained in *Colonial Discourse and Post-Colonial Theory: A Reader* (P. Williams and L. Chrisman, eds., 1994). Lynda Hutcheon has written that "Canada [i]s still caught up in the machinations of Empire and colony, imperial metropolis and provincial hinterland," a context in which the debates about postcolonialism have historically specific relevance, given the experience and ongoing manifestations of British Empire, and the arrival of immigrants from other postcolonial nations. Furthermore, she suggests that when Canadian culture is called postcolonial today, the reference is very rarely to the Native culture, which might be the more accurate historical use of the term. Native and Metis writers are today demanding a voice (Cuthand, Armstrong, Campbell), and perhaps, given their articulations of the damage to Indian culture and people done by the colonizers (French and British) and the process of colonization, theirs should be considered the resisting, postcolonial voice of Canada. See L. Hutcheon, "Circling the Downspout of Empire: Post-Colonialism and Postmodernism," 20(4) *Ariel* 149 at 156 (1989).

38 I use the term *imaginary* in the Lacanian sense to refer to an agent's compulsion to seek "an identificatory image of its own stability and permanence (the imaginary)" in "the order of images, representations, doubles, and others" (E. Grosz, *Jacques Lacan: A Femist Introduction* [1990]).

39 J. Clifford, *The Predicament of Culture: Twenthieth-Century Ethnography, Literature, and Art* 215 (1988).

40 See P. Brantlinger, *Crusoe's Footprints: Cultural Studies in Britain and America* (1990); Clifford, *ibid*; R. J. Coombe, "Beyond Modernity's Meanings: Encountering the Postmodern in Cultural Anthropology," 11 *Culture* 111 (1991) (*hereinafter* Coombe, "Beyond Modernity's Meanings"); R. Rosaldo, *Culture and Truth: The Remaking of Social Analysis* (1989); R. Williams, *Culture and Society 1780–1950* (1983), R. Williams, *Keywords: A Vocabulary of Culture and Society* (1983) (*hereinafter* Williams, *Keywords*).

41 Williams, *Keywords*, at 90–91.

42 Clifford, *supra* note 39, at 233.

43 *Ibid.*, at 223, citing F. Jameson, *The Prisonhouse of Language: Narrative as a Socially Symbolic Act* 47 (1981).

44 *Ibid.*, at 189–214.

45 *Ibid.*, at 196.

46 *Ibid.*, at 195.

47 *Ibid.*, at 198.

48 *Ibid.*, at 215–251.

49 Clifford's other two categories are inauthentic masterpieces (counterfeits and illicit copies), which would seem to include all works that infringe copyright, and inauthentic artifacts (mass-produced objects and crafts), which would fall into the realm of items not protected by law, such as crafts, or given a lesser degree of protection due to their status as commercially produced objects (as industrial design) (*ibid.*, at 223). Clifford points out that objects often pass from one zone to another, in terms of the way that they are socially valued. Hence, works that deliberately copy other works in artistic statements, such as those of the anti-art or anti-aesthetic movement in the 1980s, are sought as original works of art by collectors, thus moving from the zone of inauthentic to the zone of authentic masterpieces as their artists achieve renown. See *The Anti-Aesthetic: Essays on Post-Modern Culture* (H. Foster, ed., 1983), and *Recodings: Art, Spectacle, Cultural Politics* (H. Foster, ed., 1985) for discussions of artistic work in this tradition. Similarly, examples of early commercial packaging may cease to be seen as inauthentic artifacts and become valued as authentic artifacts that embody the culture of a particular era in history. Some commercialized mass-produced painting from the Third World may become valued either as the work of a culture or, eventually, as the work of an individual artist, as is currently the case with barbershop signs from West Africa. It is important to note here that the law assigns works a category and a degree of protection at the time of origin, not at shifting points of public reception. Hence, an artistic work that copies the work of another, regardless of the social critique or political point the artist believes he or she is making, is a copyright infringement and remains one even if the art world comes to regard the work/copy as an authentic masterpiece. Works do not move through legal categories as quickly as they are revalued in the social world. Elsewhere I suggest that this works to the detriment of Third-World peoples.

50 Clifford, *supra* note 39, at 201–202.

51 *Ibid.*, at 205–206.

52 J. Feather, "Publishers and Politicians: The Remaking of the Law of Copyright in Britain 1775–1842," 25 *Publishing History* 45 (1989), argues that the centrality of authorship in copyright and the belief that the author should be the main beneficiary of literary work was not fully established in Britain until 1814 and reflects the ascendency of Romantic reconceptualizations of the creative process. For further historical studies of "authorship," see the entirety of 10(2) *Cardozo Arts and Entertainment Law Journal* 279–725 (1992), reprinted in *The Construction of Authorship: Textual Appropriation in Law and Literature* (M. Woodmansee and P. Jaszi, eds., 1994).

53 I am paraphrasing E. Young, *Conjectures on Original Compostion* (1759). The essay may be found in B. Kaplan, *An Unhurried View of Copyright* 27 (1967).

54 W. Blackstone, *Commentaries on the Laws of England* 405–406 (1765–69).

55 W. Enfield, *Observations on Literary Property* 21 (1774).

56 Bleistein v. Donaldson Lithographing Co., 188 U.S. 239, 250 (1903) interpreting the

nineteenth-century artist John Ruskin, a central figure in the Romantic movement. These Romantic and preindustrial concepts continue to dominate copyright doctrine even in a postindustrial age in which individual Romantic authors are increasingly difficult to find in the bureaucratic and corporate structures of today's culture industries.

57 An overview of the treaties that define the parameters of the international law of cultural property may be found in J. F. Edwards, "Major Global Treaties for the Protection and Enjoyment of Art and Cultural Objects," 22 *Toledo Law Review* 919 (1991).

58 J. H. Merryman, "Two Ways of Thinking about Cultural Property," 80 *American Journal of International Law* 831 (1986) (*hereinafter* Merryman, "Two Ways of Thinking"), and J. H. Merryman, "The Public Interest in Cultural Property," 77 *California Law Review* 339 (1989) (*hereinafter* Merryman, "The Public Interest").

59 249 U.N.T.S. 240.

60 It would appear that Merryman equates nationhood with statehood and is not prepared to recognize the existence of more than one nation within a sovereign state. Hence he finds demands for the repatriation of objects from cultural groups rather than nations to be "awkward" and "embarrassing" events. See Merryman, "The Public Interest," *supra* note 58, at 351. He also sees one of the major values of cultural objects to be their embodiment of truth, envisioned as a source of certainty about the authenticity of the human cultural past, not in terms of an object's role in the ongoing lives of peoples and communities. See R. Clements, "Misconceptions of Culture: Native Peoples and Cultural Property under Canadian Law," 49 *University of Toronto Faculty of Law Review* 1 (1991), for a good discussion of the possibilities afforded to First Nations peoples for the repatriation of sacred objects under cultural property laws.

61 823 U.N.T.S. 231, reprinted in 10 *International Legal Materials* 289 (1971), as cited in Merryman, "Two Ways of Thinking," *supra* note 58, at 833.

62 Merryman, "Two Ways of Thinking," *supra* note 58, at 843.

63 *Ibid.*

64 *Ibid.*, at 833.

65 *Ibid.*, at 832.

66 *Ibid.*, at 832 n.5.

67 *Ibid.*, at 844–845.

68 *Ibid.*, at 849.

69 *Ibid.*, at 847.

70 *Ibid.*, at 850.

71 J. Moustakas, "Group Rights in Cultural Property: Justifying Strict Inalienability," 74 *Cornell Law Review* 1179, 1182 (1989). Ironically, Greece, the country of origin for classical Western or European culture, now is often portrayed as a nation that has degenerated from its classical origins such that it is no longer an appropriate custodian for those objects that define classical European Culture. For a discussion of Greek nationalism that defines the cultural struggles of Greek peoples in terms of these historical perceptions, see M. Herzfeld, *Anthropology through the Looking Glass* (1989).

72 M. Radin, "Property and Personhood," 34 *Stanford Law Review* 957, 959ff. (1982).

73 Moustakas, *supra* note 71, at 1184.

74 *Ibid.*, at 1185, citing Radin, *supra* note 72, at 959.

75 *Ibid.*, at 1185.

76 C. B. Macpherson, *The Political Theory of Possessive Individualism: Hobbes to Locke* (1962).

77 See R. Handler, "Who Owns the Past? History, Cultural Property, and the Logic of Possessive Individualism," in *The Politics of Culture* 63 (B. Williams, ed., 1991) (*hereinafter* Handler, "Who Owns the Past?"); R. Handler, "On Having a Culture: Nationalism and the Preservation of Quebec's Patrimoine," in *Objects and Others: Essays on Museums and Material Culture* 197 (G. W. Stocking, ed., 1985) (*hereinafter* Handler, "On Having a Culture"). Others who have pointed out the peculiarity and contingency of Western individualism include L. Dumont, *From Mandeville to Marx: The Genesis and Triumph of Economic Ideology* (1977); L. Dumont, *Essays on Individualism: Modern Ideology in Anthropological Perspective* (1986); and, of course, A. de Tocqueville, *Democracy in America* (H. Reeve, trans., 4th ed., rev. and corrected from 18th Paris ed., 1841).

78 Handler, *On Having a Culture, supra* note 77, at 194.

79 Handler, "Who Owns the Past?," *supra* note 77, at 64.

80 Cultural property laws are not the only laws that envision culture in terms of monolithic traditions. Kristin Koptiuch writes movingly of the way the "cultural defense" has been constructed in criminal law as a means of espousing cultural relativism and a politically sensitive response to the dilemmas of cultural difference, but has done so using the tropes of a colonial discourse on the Orient that deems it ahistorical and essentializes Western constructions of racialized gender difference that permit sexual violence against Asian women. See K. Koptiuch, "Cultural Defense and Criminological Displacements: Gender, Race, and (Trans)Nation in the Legal Surveillance of U.S. Diaspora Asians," in *Displacement, Diaspora, and Geographies of Identity* 215 (S. Lavie and T. Swedenburg, eds., 1996). Like Koptiuch, I think it is important to excavate the colonial past stratified in Western forms of knowledge.

81 Handler, "Who Owns the Past?," *supra* note 77, at 66.

82 Cited in *ibid.*, at 67.

83 Handler, *On Having a Culture, supra* note 77, at 198.

84 These basic premises form part of all copyright regimes, and there is no particular reason to privilege any specific statutory enactment of these principles here.

85 Handler, "Who Owns the Past?," *supra* note 77, at 67.

86 *Ibid.*, at 68.

87 *Ibid.*

88 *Ibid.*, at 69.

89 I borrow this term from N. Goodman, *Ways of Worldmaking* (1978).

90 Minow, *supra* note 19, at 97–98.

91 *Ibid.*, at 98–99, citing A. Harris, "Race and Essentialism in Feminist Legal Theory," 42 *Stanford Law Review* 584 (1990).

92 *Ibid.*, at 112.

93 b. hooks, *Yearning: Race, Gender, and Cultural Politics* (1990), at 5.

94 *Ibid.*, at 19.

95 *Ibid.*, at 20.

96 *Ibid.*, citing L. Alcoff, "Cultural Feminism vs. Poststructuralism: The Identity Crisis in Feminist Theory," 13 *Signs* 405 at 433 (1988).

97 *Ibid.*, at 28.

98 *Ibid.*

99 *Ibid.*, at 29.

100 On accusations of essentialism, see L. Todd, "What More Do They Want?," in *Indigena: Contemporary Native Perspectives* 71–79 (G. McMaster and L. Martin, eds., 1992). Lee Maracle notes that publishers are absolved of charges of censorship when they choose not to publish Native works (often returning works to writers with "Too Indian" or "Not Indian enough" written on them by non-Native editors who presume the authority to judge the works' authenticity), while she is accused of "being a fascist censor" for objecting to non-Native use of Native themes and stories. See L. Maracle, "Native Myths: Trickster Alive and Crowing," *Fuse* 29 (fall 1989).

101 I do not wish to suggest here that artists and authors of First Nations ancestry do not wish to have their works valued on the market, or that they would eschew royalties for works produced as commodities for an exchange value on the market. That would be essentialist indeed! Instead, I am suggesting that in the debates surrounding cultural appropriation, Native peoples assert that there are other value systems than those of the market in which their images, themes, practices, and stories figure and that these modes of appreciation and valuation are embedded in specific histories and relationships that should be accorded respect. Copyright laws, of course, protect only individual authors against the copying of their individual expressions, and do not protect ideas or cultural themes, practices, and historical experiences from expropriation by cultural others.

102 The best demonstration of this is to be found in Native art and literature where issues of identity are engaged in innovative fashions that often employ European cultural forms to examine the specificity of First Nations history as it figures in contemporary political struggles and the need to forge alliances with other subordinated groups. The Romantic notion of art for art's sake is often challenged, as is the art/culture system that relegates Native expressive forms to an ethnographic realm or, alternatively, claims them as art, but only to deny their claims to political statement. For discussions, see the various artists whose work is featured in *Indigena, supra* note 100, and the essay by Cree art instructor A. Young Man, "The Metaphysics of North American Art," in *Indigena, supra* note 100, at 81–99.

103 I do not wish to suggest that intellectual property laws hold no potential for protecting some of the interests of Native peoples. Individual Native artists may well avail themselves of copyright protections, but collective authors and claims of intergenerational creation cannot be entertained. Trademark law, were it to be diligently enforced, might afford protection against false representations of "Indian" or "Native" production in the market. Section 9 of the Trademark Act could be amended to prohibit representations of Native peoples and motifs in commercial contexts, unless the consent of band councils were obtained. Collectives of Native peoples might well use the common law tort of passing off to prevent misrepresentations of Native origins in advertising and sales. More general themes, narratives, and artistic styles, however, cannot be protected because they are likely to be viewed as ideas rather than expressions. Doctrines of consumer confusion might be deployed, however, to prevent representations that suggest First Nations origins to the average consumer. Peter Weinrich, executive director of the Canadian Crafts Council, for instance, found the issue of adopting the stories of others to be less aptly named "cultural appropriation" than the very real ongoing practice of "nonnative people stealing traditional designs of the Haida and reproducing them for economic gain." In the absence of copyright protections, he asks, "what are we going to do about providing a community with rights over its own traditions?"

104 A. Pask, "Making Connections: Intellectual Property, Cultural Property, and Sovereignty in the Debates Concerning the Appropriation of Native Cultures in Canada," 8 *Intellectual Property Journal* 57, 64 (1993).

105 I borrow this phrase from P. Macklem, "First Nations Self-Government and the Borders of the Canadian Legal Imagination," 36 *McGill Law Journal* 382 (1991).

106 M. Minow and E. V. Spelman, "In Context," in *Pragmatism in Law and Society* 247 (M. Brant and W. Weaver, eds., 1991).

107 *Ibid.*, at 248–249.

108 *Ibid.*, at 249–255.

109 *Ibid.*, at 258.

110 See discussion of West, *ibid.*, at 257.

111 *Ibid.*, at 269–270.

112 "Declaration of Quito, July 1990: Indigenous Alliance of the Americas on 500 Years of Resistance," 23 *Borderlines* 23 (1991/92).

113 *Ibid.*, at 3.

114 "The Sweetgrass Meaning of Solidarity: 500 Years of Resistance," 23 *Borderlines* 35, 37 (1991/92).

115 As quoted in J. R. Miller, *Skyscrapers Hide the Heavens: A History of Indian-White Relations in Canada* 189 (1989).

116 As quoted in *ibid.*, at 207.

117 Fleras and Elliott, *supra* note 21, at 41 (citations omitted).

118 Act to Amend and Consolidate the Laws Respecting Indians, Statutes of Canada, 39 Victoria Chapter 18, 1876.

119 An Act Respecting Indians, Statutes of Canada 15 George VI Chapter 29, (1951).

120 Fleras and Elliott, *supra* note 21, at 74.

121 *Ibid.*, at 76–77.

122 *Ibid.*, at 79.

123 *Ibid.*

124 J. Cardinal-Schubert, "In the Red," *Fuse* 20, 21 (fall 1989).

125 R. Hill, "One Part per Million: White Appropriation and Native Voices," 15 *Fuse* 12 (winter 1992).

126 Fleras and Elliott, *supra* note 21, at 19.

127 As Comanche activist Paul Smith notes, Native peoples in North America are always being asked "How much Indian are you?" No one, however, "asks a black how much black blood she has." Such racist notions of Indian identity are colonial impositions; they have nothing to do with Native understandings of community membership and belonging. See P. Smith, "Lost in America," 23 *Borderlines* 17 (1991/92).

128 "Hachivi Edgar Heap of Birds," 23 *Borderlines* 19 (1991/92).

129 *Ibid.* Hachivi Edgar Heap of Birds is assistant professor of painting at the University of Oklahoma and headsman of the Tsistsistas (Cheyenne) Elk Warrior Society.

130 An Act to Further Amend the "Indian Act, 1880" Statutes of Canada, 47 Victoria, Chapter 27 (1884).

131 Cardinal-Schubert, *supra* note 124, at 21.

132 See the discussion in "Appropriation: When Does Borrowing Become Stealing?," 5(1) *Last Issue* 20, 30–33 (1987). Further background may be found in M. M. Ames, "Free Indians from Their Ethnological Fate: The Emergence of the Indian Point of View in Exhibitions of Indians," 5(2) *Muse* 14 (1987). Many international museums

did eventually refuse to lend objects to the museum in support of the Lubicon boycott, and there is certainly evidence that museums are beginning to take the claims of subaltern peoples with regard to objects and representations far more seriously. See, e.g., *Turning the Page: Forging New Partnerships Between Museums and First Peoples* (Assembly of First Nations and the Canadian Museums Association, 1992) (*hereinafter Turning the Page*), and of course, the "recent" Royal Ontario Museum exhibit *Fluff and Feathers*, which is actually five years old, first opening in Brantford at the Woodlands Cultural Centre in 1988.

133   Cardinal-Schubert, *supra* note 124, at 23.

134   A photograph of this performance/work may be found on the last page of *Turning the Page, supra* note 132, at 19.

135   See Cardinal-Schubert, *supra* note 124, and Clements, *supra* note 60.

136   The case is discussed in great depth in D. Cole, *An Iron Hand upon the People: The Law against the Potlatch on the Northwest Coast* (1990). The case does not appear to have been reported.

137   "From Colonization to Repatriation," in *Indigena, supra* note 100, at 25–38.

138   Act Respecting Indians, Statutes of Canada, 15 George VI, Chapter 29 (1951).

139   To quote Webster: "In the late 1960s we still remembered what had happened more than forty years earlier. We began to work towards the return of our treasures from the museums. The National Museum of Man agreed to repatriate its part of the collection on the condition that museums were built in Alert Bay and Cape Mudge which were to divide the collection. The Kwagiutl Museum opened in Cape Mudge in 1979 and the U'mista Cultural Centre opened in Alert Bay a year later. A request to the Royal Ontario Museum for the return of its part of the collection was not met until 1988 and we're still waiting for the balance of the collection to be returned from the Museum of the American Indian, that is in New York" (*supra* note 137, at 37). For a recent discussion of repatriation efforts and legal frameworks in the United States, see S. Platzman, "Objects of Controversy: The Native American Right to Repatriation," 41 *American University Law Review* 517 (1992).

140   *Ibid.*

141   Referred to in Smith, *supra* note 127.

142   See Cardinal-Schubert, *supra* note 124.

143   Smith, *supra* note 127, at 18.

144   B. Owl, a White Earth Anishnabe, cited in W. Churchill, "Colonialism, Genocide and the Expropriation of Indigenous Spiritual Tradition in Contemporary Academia," 23 *Borderlines* 39, 41 (1991/92).

145   American Indian Movement leader Russell Means suggests that this appropriation is a form of cultural genocide. *Ibid.*, at 41.

146   Hill, *supra* note 125, at 17–18.

147   Churchill, *supra* note 144. Churchill makes several unsubstantiated claims about the reception of Castaneda and Andrews in universities and an incomprehensible attack on ethnomethodology that give me pause, but the sincerity of the conviction that Native peoples have continually been misrepresented by non-Native academics cannot be doubted.

148   L. Todd, "Notes on Appropriation," 16 *Parallelogramme* 24 (1990).

149   Keeshig-Tobias, *supra* note 25, at A8.

150   *Ibid.*

151   G. McMaster and L. Martin, Introduction, in *Indigena, supra* note 100, at 17.

152 Handler, "Who Owns the Past?," *supra* note 77, at 71.

153 Handler, "On Having a Culture," *supra* note 77, at 215.

154 Handler, "Who Owns the Past?," *supra* note 77, at 71.

155 For a discussion of this phenomenon in literary works by First Nations authors, see B. T. Godard, "The Politics of Representation: Some Native Canadian Women Writers," in *Native Writers and Canadian Writing* 183–205 (W. H. New, ed., 1990).

156 L. Todd, "Notes on Appropriation," *supra* note 148, at 24.

157 *Ibid.*

158 See, e.g., Cardinal-Schubert, *supra* note 124; D. Skuse et al., Letter to the Editor, 13(3) *Fuse* 2 (1989–90); Hill, *supra* note 125; D. Skuse and K. Kozzi, Letter to the Editor, 15(6) *Fuse* 4 (1992). I make absolutely no comment on the substance of any allegations made in these articles and correspondences.

159 Smith, *supra* note 127, at 18.

160 Hill, *supra* note 125, at 14.

161 A. Fabo, Letter to the Editor, 13 *Fuse* 2,4 (1989–90).

162 Liz Magor, another artist whose work has figured prominently in debates about appropriation, foregrounded the issue in her photography. Richard Hill describes his experience of viewing her show:

> I notice the photographs on the nearby wall in black and white that depicted a man paddling a canoe, a blond hippie looking woman in a headband, people camping on the beach, etc. . . . the title of the photo of the blonde woman was called "Cheyenne type". . . This must be done ironically but how can I say for sure whether Magore's work was ironic? Maybe she was trying to point out the overlap of cultures, or the richness of First Nations culture as a resource for white artists. I left the work not knowing quite what was going on . . . Perhaps it was merely another case of white people talking about themselves using First Nations culture as their medium? Sometime later I read a statement by Magore about the photographs mentioned above. She said that she wanted to deal with her personal history of appropriating from First Nations cultures "slowly and gently," and indeed she does. So slowly and gently, in fact, that the work loses any serious claim to criticality. In effect, it seems to do more to prop up old stereotypes than to aggressively call them into question. This is especially true when the work is shot in the context of a national gallery which inevitably lends its authority to the piece . . . She defends her project on the grounds that although the photos are embarrassing, a disavowal of my own history is equally uncomfortable . . . (Hill, *supra* note 125, at 20)

163 McMaster and Martin, *supra* note 151, at 17.

164 David Alexis writes that rights are a further imposition upon Native peoples: "Indian people do not think in terms of rights but in terms of responsibility. Whatever flows from the fulfillment of those responsibilities are the gifts in life. The demanding of status from one's mere existence is ludicrous. The so-called fishing rights won by Indian people are not a gift bestowed by white people because of recognition by white people of those rights. Those so-called 'rights' are the result of traditional people fulfilling responsibilities to fisheries through traditional ceremony and lifestyle . . . a gift from creation [that results from] a fullfillment of responsibilities through Indian belief" (D. Alexis, "Obscurity as a Lifestyle," 23 *Borderlines* 15 [1991–92]).

165 Cardinal-Schubert, *supra* note 124, at 20.

166 Keeshig-Tobias, *supra* note 25.

167 Todd, "Notes on Appropriation," *supra* note 148, at 26.

168 W. La Duke, "The Culture of Hydroelectric Power," 23 *Borderlines* 42–45 (1991–92).

169 Todd, "Notes on Appropriation," *supra* note 148, at 32.

6. Dialogic Democracy I: Authorship and Alterity in Public Spheres

1 P. Schlag, "Missing Pieces: A Cognitive Approach to Law," 67 *Texas Law Review* 1195, 1248 (1989).

2 "Introduction: Politics, Ethics and the Legality of the Contingent," in *Politics, Postmodernity and Critical Legal Studies: The Legality of the Contingent* 3 (C. Douzinas, P. Goodrich, and Y. Hachamovitch, eds., 1994).

3 P. Chevigny, *More Speech: Dialogue Rights and Modern Liberty* 4 (1988), citing F. Schauer, *Free Speech: A Philosophical Enquiry* (1982). Increasingly it seems that arguments in favor of the preservation of democracy are preferred. See O. Fiss, "Free Speech and Social Structure," 71 *Iowa Law Review* 1405 (1986), reprinted in O. Fiss, *Liberalism Divided: Freedom of Speech and the Many Uses of State Power* (1996).

4 Dom Caristi is one contemporary scholar who finds "self-fulfillment" to merit the greatest weight of the various first principles that have been proffered for freedom of speech and deems access to media an important means to achieve it. See D. Caristi, *Expanding Free Expression in the Market Place: Broadcasting and the Public Forum* (1992).

5 S. Stewart, *Crimes of Writing: Problems in the Containment of Representation* 4 (1991).

6 My misgivings about the political consequences of the pervasive rhetoric of information in digitalized environments are further elaborated in "Authorial Cartographies: Mapping Proprietary Borders in a Less-than-Brave New World," 48(5) *Stanford Law Review* 1357 (1996).

7 Cited in Stewart, *supra* note 5.

8 In my view, Geertz is insufficiently sensitive to the consequences that representations of a people may have in those people's lives. Struggles over representations of difference implicate anthropologists who are positioned to present authoritative renderings of difference in diverse arenas.

9 W. M. Reddy, "Postmodernism and the Public Sphere: Implications for an Historical Ethnography," 7(2) *Cultural Anthropology* 135, 140 (1992), citing C. Geertz, *Works and Lives: The Anthropologist as Author* 130 (1988).

10 *Ibid.*

11 For a critical discussion of the language of crisis and postmodernity, see R. J. Coombe, "Finding and Losing One's Self in the Topoi: Placing and Displacing the Postmodern Subject in Law," 29(4) *Law and Society Review* 599 (1995).

12 Reddy, *supra* note 9, 135–136.

13 *Ibid.*, at 136.

14 *Ibid.* (I use the masculine pronoun deliberately when discussing the author and the bourgeois subject.)

15 *Ibid.*, at 143.

16 See P. Kamuf, *Signature Pieces: On the Institution of Authorship* (1988), for a discussion of Rousseau's struggles to control and contain his signature in the late eighteenth century.

17　Reddy, *supra* note 9, at 143.

18　J. Habermas, *The Structural Transformation of the Public Sphere* (1992); O. Negt and A. Kluge, *The Public Sphere and Experience* (P. Labanyi, J. Daniel, and A. Oksiloff, trans., 1993).

19　N. Fraser, "Rethinking the Public Sphere: A Contribution to the Critique of Actually Existing Democracy," in *The Phantom Public Sphere* 1, 2–3 (B. Robbins, ed., 1993).

20　*Ibid.*, at 4.

21　*Ibid.*

22　I explore the historical emergence and consolidation of these ideas in a review of historical literature on copyright in R. J. Coombe, "Contesting Paternity: Histories of Authorship," 6 *Yale Journal of Law and the Humanities* 397 (1994).

23　See *ibid.*, and the sources cited therein, for an overview of some of the developing literature on the history of literary property in the eighteenth century. See also *The Construction of Authorship: Textual Appropriation in Law and Literature* (M. Wood-mansee and P. Jaszi, eds., 1994) for an excellent collection of essays on historical and contemporary dimensions of authorship and copyright.

24　Reddy, *supra* note 9, at 144. See also C. Calhoun, "Civil Society and the Public Sphere," 5 *Public Culture* 267 (1993); P. Cheah, "Violent Light: The Idea of Publicness in Modern Philosophy and in Global Neocolonialism," 43 *Social Text* 163 (1995); Fraser, *supra* note 19; B. Robbins, "The Public as Phantom," in *The Phantom Public Sphere*, *supra* note 19; M. Warner, "The Mass Public and the Mass Subject," in *The Phantom Public Sphere*, *supra* note 19, at 234; M. Warner, "The *Res Publica* of Letters," in *Revisionary Interventions into the Americanist Canon* 38 (D. Pease, ed., 1994).

25　Reddy, *supra* note 9, at 144.

26　There is certainly a large literature to suggest that the author-function was concep-tualized as a gendered subject-position—the space of a patriarch whose works were regarded as his progeny. See F. Ayala, "Victorian Science and the 'Genius' of Women," 38 *Journal of the History of Ideas* 261 (1977); C. Bender, *Gender and Genius* (1989); M. Griffin, *The Disappearing Woman Writer and the Gendering of the Idea of Author-ship*, paper presented at the conference Cultural Agency/Cultural Authority: Politics and Poetics of Intellectual Property in a Postcolonial Era, in Bellagio, Italy, 8–12 March 1993; S. Gilbert and S. Gubar, *The Madwoman in the Attic* (1979); J. McGann, "My Brain Is Feminine: Byron and the Poetry of Deception," in *Byron: Augustan and Romantic* 26 (A. Rutherford, ed., 1990); P. Parker, *Literary Fat Ladies: Rhetoric, Gen-der, Property* (1987); M. Rose, *From Paternity to Property: The Remetaphorization of Writing* (unpublished manuscript); M. Ross, *The Contours of Masculine Desire: Ro-manticism and the Rise of Women's Poetry* (1989); R. G. Swartz, "Patrimony and the Figuration of Authorship," 7(2) *Works and Days* 29 (1989). This is by no means a comprehensive list of sources.

27　C. Lury, *Cultural Rights: Technology, Legality and Personality* (1993), at 26–27.

28　*Ibid.*, at 30.

29　*Ibid.*, at 101.

30　*Ibid.*, at 101–102.

31　*Ibid.*, at 119.

32　For a longer discussion of this process in the German context, see M. Woodmansee, *The Author, Art and the Market* (1994).

33　Lury, *supra* note 27, at 108.

34　*Ibid.*

35 *Ibid.*

36 Martha Woodmansee makes similar arguments with respect to the historical development of authorship and the aesthetic category of literature in the German context. See Woodmansee, *supra* note 32.

37 Lury, *supra* note 27, at 113.

38 For scholarship that historicizes German and English Romanticism and links them to global and domestic social forces, see *Macropolitics of Nineteenth-Century Literature* (J. Arac and H. Ritvo, eds., 1991); *The Invention of Tradition* (E. Hobsbawm and T. Ranger, eds., 1983); *Rethinking Historicism: Critical Readings in Romantic History* (M. Levinson et al., eds., 1989); J. McGann, *The Romantic Ideology* (1983); T. Pfau, "The Pragmatics of Genre: Moral Theory and Lyric Authorship in Hegel and Wordsworth," 10 *Cardozo Arts & Entertainment Law Journal* 397 (1992); Ross, *supra* note 26; Rutherford, *supra* note 26; C. Siskin, *The Historicity of Romantic Discourse* (1988); R. Williams, *Culture and Society, 1780–1950* (1983).

39 Lury, *supra* note 27, at 109.

40 *Ibid.* Similar arguments are made by Martha Woodmansee, in *The Author, Art and the Market, supra* note 32.

41 T. Lovell, *Consuming Fiction* (1987).

42 Lury, *supra* note 27, at 112.

43 *Ibid.*, at 118.

44 *Ibid.*

45 This is the theme of my forthcoming book, *Copyright, Colonialism and the Evangelical Impulse: The Work and the Word in Early English Empire, 1750–1850.*

46 Lury, *supra* note 27, at 105.

47 The "emergence of a radical press under working-class control" should not be discounted here (*ibid.*, at 106).

48 *Ibid.*

49 *Ibid.*, at 115, citing J. Sutherland, *Fiction and the Fiction Industry* (1978).

50 *Ibid.*, at 118.

51 M. Madow, "Private Ownership and Public Image: Popular Culture and Publicity Rights," 81 *California Law Review* 125, 149–151 (1993).

52 Lury draws heavily upon Benedict Anderson's notion of "imagined community" in his study of nationalisms. See B. Anderson, *Imagined Communities* (1993).

53 As Lury puts it: "Through the manipulation of the mass simultaneity of reception made possible by technologies of replication, newspapers act as a technical means for 'creating that remarkable confidence of community in anonymity which is the hallmark of modern nations'" (Lury, *supra* note 27, at 32, citing B. Anderson, "Apprehensions of Time," in *Popular Fiction: Technology, Ideology, Production, Reading* 79 [T. Bennet, ed., 1990]).

54 *Ibid.*, at 107.

55 *Ibid.*

56 R. Trager, "Entangled Values: The First Amendment in the 1990's," 45 *Journal of Communication* 163, 169 (1995). Garnham makes a significant point about the shortcomings of the liberal model in contemporary conditions: "While the rights of free expression inherent in democratic theory have been continually stressed, what has been lost is any sense of the reciprocal duties inherent in a communicative space that is physically shared . . . the social obligations that participation in the public sphere involves . . . duties to listen to others . . . to alternative versions of events . . . to take

responsibility for the effects of actions that may result from that debate . . . A crucial effect of mediated communication in a context of mediated social relations is to divorce discourse from action and thus favour irresponsible communication." See N. Garnham, "The Mass Media, Cultural Identity, and the Public Sphere in the Modern World," 5 *Public Culture* 251, 261 (1993).

57 Fiss, "Free Speech and Social Structure," *supra* note 3, at 1407.

58 *Ibid.* For a recent discussion in the Canadian context, see R. Moon, "The Supreme Court of Canada and the Structure of Freedom of Expression Adjudication," 45 *University of Toronto Law Journal* 419 (1995).

59 Fiss, "Free Speech and Social Structure," *supra* note 3, at 1414.

60 *Ibid.*, at 1407. See C. E. Baker, "Advertising and a Democratic Press," 140 *University of Pennsylvania Law Review* 2097 (1992); J. Balkin, "Some Realism about Pluralism: Legal Realist Approaches to the First Amendment" [1990], *Duke Law Journal* 375; M. Becker, "The Politics of Women's Wrongs and the Bill of Rights," 59 *University of Chicago Law Review* 453 (1992); M. Becker, "Conservative Free Speech and the Uneasy Case for Judicial Review," 64 *University of Chicago Law Review* 975 (1993); Chevigny, *supra* note 3; R. Delgado and J. Stefancic, "Images of the Outsider in American Law and Culture: Can Free Expression Remedy Systemic Social Ills?," 77 *Cornell Law Review* 1258 (1992); M. Horowitz, "Rights," 23 *Harvard Civil Rights–Civil Liberties Law Review* 393 (1988); A. Hutchinson, "Talking the Good Life: From Free Speech to Democratic Dialogue," 1 *Yale Journal of Law & Liberation* 17 (1989); D. Kairys, *With Liberty and Justice for Some* (1993); F. Schauer, "The Political Incidence of the Free Speech Principle," 64 *University of Colorado Law Review* 935 (1993); S. H. Shiffrin, "The Politics of the Mass Media and the Free Speech Principle," 69 *Indiana Law Journal* 689 (1994); C. R. Sunstein, *Democracy and the Problem of Free Speech* (1993); S. L. Winter, "Fast Food and False Friends in the Shopping Mall of Ideas," 64 *University of Colorado Law Review* 965 (1993).

61 Fiss, "Free Speech and Social Structure," *supra* note 3, at 1408. See also O. Fiss, "In Search of a New Paradigm," 104 *Yale Law Journal* 1613 (1995). For an extensive discussion of the ways in which freedom of expression jurisprudence ignores fundamental facets of communication in late-twentieth-century contexts and dominant principles of protection are at odds with the realities of a mass-mediated "amusement-centred culture," see R. K. L. Collins and D. M. Skover, *The Death of Discourse* (1996).

62 Fiss, "Free Speech and Social Structure," *supra* note 61, at 1410–1411; O. Fiss, "Why the State?," 100 *Harvard Law Review* 781, 786 (1987), reprinted in Fiss, *Liberalism Divided*, *supra* note 3.

63 Fiss, "Free Speech and Social Structure," *supra* note 61, at 1413.

64 See, e.g., *The Bill of Rights in the Modern State* (G. Stone, R. Epstein, and C. Sunstein, eds., 1992), and Sunstein, *supra* note 60. For an overview of recent scholarship, see Trager, *supra* note 56.

65 Fiss, "Free Speech and Social Structure," *supra* note 3, at 1417–1418.

66 Hutchinson, *supra* note 60, at 19–20.

67 *Ibid.*, at 20.

68 *Ibid.*, at 21.

69 *Ibid.*

70 *Ibid.*, at 22.

71 *Ibid.*

72 The concept of promotional culture is developed in A. Wernick, "Promotional Cul-

ture," 15 *Canadian Journal of Political & Social Theory* 260 (1991), and A. Wernick, *Promotional Culture: Advertising, Ideology and Symbolic Expression* (1991). Wernick says that North American culture has come to present itself at every level as an endless series of promotional messages, and advertising, besides having become a most powerful institution in its own right, has been effectively universalized as a signifying mode.

73 D. M. Koenig, "Joe Camel and the First Amendment: The Dark Side of Copyrighted and Trademark-Protected Icons," 11 *T. M. Cooley Law Review* 803, 814 (1994).

74 *Ibid.*, at 804–806.

75 L. Lawrence, "The Right of Publicity: A Research Guide," *Hastings Communications and Entertainment Law Journal* 10: 143, 246 (1987).

76 See, e.g., Grant v. Esquire, Inc. 367 F. Supp. 876 (S.D.N.Y. 1973); Rinaldi v. Village Voice, 79 Misc. 2d 57, 359 N.Y.S. 2d 176 (1974), modified 47 A.D. 2d 180. 365 N.Y.S. 2d 199, cert. denied 423 U.S. 883 (1975); Garner v. Triangle Publications, 97 F. Supp. 546 (S.D.N.Y. 1951).

77 Garner v. Triangle Publications, 97 F. Supp. 546 (S.D.N.Y. 1951).

78 University of Notre Dame v. Twentieth Century Fox, 22 A.D. 2d 452, N.Y.S. 2d 301 (N.Y. App. Div. 1965).

79 Ann-Margret v. High Society Magazine, 498 F. Supp. 401, 6 Media Law Reporter (BNA) 1774 (S.D.N.Y. 1980).

80 Hansen v. High Society Magazine, 5 Media Law Reporter (BNA) 2398 (N.Y. Sup. Ct.), rev'd, 76 A.D. 2d 812, 429 N.Y.S. 2d 552, 6 Media Law Reporter (BNA) 1618 (N.Y. App. Div. 1980).

81 Creel v. Crown Publishers, 115 A.D. 2d 414, 496 N.Y.S. 2d 219, 12 Media Law Reporter (BNA) 1558 (N.Y. App. Div. 1985).

82 Lopez v. Triangle Communications, 70 A.D. 2d 359, 421 N.Y.S. 2d 57, 5 Media Law Reporter (BNA) 2039 (N.Y. App. Div. 1979).

83 For discussions of hyperreality, see *U. Eco, Travels in Hyperreality* (1989), and Baudrillard's work, *Simulations* (1983).

84 The phrase, of course, is borrowed from *R. Rorty, Philosophy and the Mirror of Nature* (1979), who no doubt derives it from "To hold, as 'twere, the mirror up to nature . . ." (*Hamlet* III, ii, 25).

85 Lerman v. Flynt Distributing Co., 745 F. 2d 123, 10 Media Law Reporter (BNA) 2497 (2d Cir. 1984), cert. denied 471 U.S. 1054.

86 Paulsen v. Personality Posters, 59 Misc. 2d 444, 299 N.Y.S. 2d 501 (N.Y. County Ct. 1968).

87 Factors Etc., Inc. v. Creative Card Co., 444 F. Supp. 279, 3 Media Law Reporter (BNA) 1290 (S.D.N.Y. 1977).

88 Hicks v. Casablanca Records, 464 F. Supp. 426, 4 Media Law Reporter (BNA) 1497, 204 U.S.P.Q. (BNA) 126 (S.D.N.Y. 1978).

89 Spahn v. Julian Messner, Inc., 43 Misc. 2d 219, 250 N.Y.S. 2d 529 (N.Y. County Ct. 1964).

90 Loft v. Fuller, 408 So. 2d 619 (Fla. Dist. Ct. App. 1981).

91 Section 540.08, Florida Statutes (1977).

92 M. T. Helfand, "When Mickey Mouse Is as Strong as Superman: The Convergence of Intellectual Property Laws to Protect Fictional Literary and Pictorial Characters," 44 *Stanford Law Review* 623 (1992); Koenig, *supra* note 73, at 803; A. Kozinski, "Mickey & Me," 11 *University of Miami Entertainment & Sports Law Review* 465 (1994); L. Kurtz,

"The Methuselah Factor: When Characters Outlive Their Copyrights," 11 *University of Miami Entertainment & Sports Law Review* 437 (1994); J. Litman, "Mickey Mouse Emeritus: Character Protection and the Public Domain," 11 *University of Miami Entertainment & Sports Law Review* 429 (1994). The protection afforded fictional characters under English and Canadian law differs only slightly from U.S. law; see H. Carty, "Character Merchandising and the Limits of Passing Off," 13 *Legal Studies* 289 (1993); S. Chong, "The Teenage Mutant Ninja Turtles Case [Mirage Studios v. Counter-Feat Clothing Co., Ltd., (1991) F.S.R. 145]: 'Zapping' English Law on Character Merchandising Past the Embryonic Stage," 13 *European Intellectual Property Review* 253 (1991); M. Elmslie, "Passing Off and Image Marketing in the United Kingdom," 14 *European Intellectual Property Review* 270 (1992); M. Leaffer, "Character Merchandising in the U.K., A Nostalgic Look," 11 *University of Miami Entertainment & Sports Law Review* 453 (1994). For an examination of the protection available to fictional characters in Canada, see R. G. Howell, "Character Merchandising: The Marketing Potential Attaching to a Name, Image, Persona, or Copyright Work," 6 *Intellectual Property Journal* 197 (1991), and R. Howell, *Recent Developments in Character Merchandising: Ewoks, Crocodile Dundee in Ontario and Ninja Turtles in the United Kingdom*, paper presented at the Canadian Association of Law Teachers Intellectual Property Section, Charlottetown, P.E.I., 3–6 June 1992.

93 Helfand, *supra* note 92.

94 See R. J. Coombe, "Room for Manoeuver: Toward a Theory of Practice in Critical Legal Studies," 14 *Law and Social Inquiry* 69 (1989).

95 Hutchinson, *supra* note 60, at 23.

96 For an excellent example of legal scholarship that attempts to do just this, see Chevigny, *supra* note 3.

97 Hutchinson, *supra* note 60, at 23.

98 *Ibid.*

99 *Ibid.*

100 Garnham, *supra* note 56, at 261.

101 *Ibid.*

102 *Ibid.*, at 253.

103 *Ibid.*

104 *Ibid.*

105 *Ibid.*, at 256.

106 Hutchinson, *supra* note 60, at 24–25.

107 *Ibid.*

108 *Ibid.*, at 25–26.

109 *Ibid.*

110 See sources cited *supra* note 60.

111 Shiffrin, *supra* note 60.

112 *Ibid.*, at 715.

113 *Ibid.*, at 719.

114 Garnham, *supra* note 56, at 260.

115 *Ibid.*, at 260–261.

116 Koenig, *supra* note 73, at 834, quoting Central Hudson Gas & Electric Corp., 447 U.S. 557, 561 (1980), rev'd on other grounds, 51 N.Y.2d 816 (N.Y. 1980). The Supreme Court of Canada has also accepted commercial speech as within the scope of the Charter guarantee of freedom of expression: "[Freedom of expression] plays a sig-

nificant role in enabling individuals to make informed economic choices, an important aspect of individual self-fulfilment and personal autonomy" (Ford v. Quebec [Attorney General] [1988] 2 S.C.R. 712). See also Irwin Toy v. Quebec (Attorney General) [1989] 1 S.C.R. 927; Rocket v. Royal College of Dental Surgeons [1990] 2 S.C.R. 232; R.J.R. MacDonald, Inc. v. Canada (Attorney General) [1995] 3 S.C.R. 199. See also Robert Sharpe, "Commercial Expression and the Charter," 37 *University of Toronto Law Journal* 229 (1987).

117   Koenig, *supra* note 73, at 832–835, and cases cited therein.

118   K. Aoki, "Authors, Inventors and Trademark Owners: Private Intellectual Property and the Public Domain. Part II," 18 *Columbia-VLA Journal of Law and the Arts* 191, 256 (1994).

119   Lucasfilm Ltd. v. High Frontier, 622 F. Supp. 931 (D.D.C. 1985).

120   Aoki, *supra* note 118, at 256–257. This is precisely what occurred in the Gay Olympics case, discussed in detail in chapter 3.

121   New Kids on the Block v. News America Publishing Inc., 971 F. 2d 302, 306-7 (9th Cir. 1992).

122   *Ibid*; see also D. Westberg, "Intellectual Property Law: New Kids on the Block v. News America Publishing, Inc.: New Nominative Use Defense Increases the Likelihood of Confusion Surrounding the Fair Use Defense to Trademark Infringement," 24 *Golden Gate University Law Review* 685 (1991); "News Gathering, Intangible Property Rights and 900-Line Telephone Services: One Court Makes a Connection, 11 *Loyola of Los Angeles Entertainment Law Journal* 535 (1991); R. Frisch, "New Technologies on the Block: New Kids on the Block v. News America Publishing, Inc.," 10 *Cardozo Arts & Entertainment Law Journal* 51 (1991).

123   A. Kozinski, "Trademarks Unplugged," 68 *New York University Law Review* 960 at 973–974 (1993).

124   R. Dreyfuss, "Expressive Genericity: Trademarks as Language in the Pepsi Generation," 65 *Notre Dame Law Review* 397 (1990). See also R. Dreyfuss, "We Are Symbols and Inhabit Symbols So Why Should We Be Paying Rent?," 20 *Columbia-VLA Journal of Law and the Arts* 123 (1996).

125   Kozinski, *supra* note 123, at 974.

126   For a longer discussion of the constitutive role of metaphor in shaping social worlds and legal practice, see Coombe, *supra* note 94, at 91–111.

127   Kozinski, *supra* note 123, at 975.

128   D. Polan, "The Public's Fear: or, Media as Monster in Habermas, Negt, and Kluge," in *The Phantom Public Sphere, supra* note 19, at 35.

129   The concept of the social imaginary is developed in C. Castoriadis, *The Imaginary Institution of Society* (1987).

130   Hutchinson, *supra* note 60, at 27–28.

131   *Ibid.*

132   *Ibid.*, at 30.

7. Dialogic Democracy II: Alterity and Articulation in the Space of the Political

1   N. Garnham, "The Mass Media, Cultural Identity, and the Public Sphere in the Modern World," 5 *Public Culture* 251, 252 (1993).

2   See discussion in S. Stewart, *Crimes of Writing: Problems in the Containment of Representation* 15 (1991).

3   *The Bill of Rights in the Modern State* 304 (G. Stone, R. Epstein, and C. Sunstein, eds., 1992).

4   I. M. Young, "Communication and the Other: Beyond Deliberative Democracy," in *Democracy and Difference: Contesting the Limits of the Political* 120 (S. Benhabib, ed., 1996).

5   *Ibid.,* at 127.

6   *Ibid.,* at 22.

7   *Ibid.,* at 20.

8   See discussions in J. Habermas, *Between Facts and Norms: Contributions to a Discourse Theory of Law and Democracy* 306, 309, 314 (W. Rehg, trans., 1996).

9   G. Yúdice, "Civil Society, Consumption, and Governmentality in an Age of Global Restructuring," 14(4) *Social Text* 19, 22 (1995).

10   Habermas, *supra* note 8, at 299. In this view, each sphere—the public sphere, the economic sphere, and the sphere of public administration—rather neatly has its own mechanism of social integration. Just as administrative power is the coordinating force in public administration (a rather tautological proposition), money is the co-ordinating motor of the economic system (a reductionist position that discounts the various social conventions and cultural belief systems that enable markets to function), and language is the medium that integrates the public spheres that comprise civil society. Although Habermas would seem to acknowledge that ordinary language communications can be distorted, he provides no mechanisms for avoiding this danger. In none of these spheres are possibilities for aggregations of wealth or concentrations of power adequately attended to.

11   N. Fraser, "Rethinking the Public Sphere: A Contribution to the Critique of Actually Existing Democracy," in *The Phantom Public Sphere* 10 (B. Robbins, ed., 1993).

12   Habermas, *supra* note 8, at 299.

13   *Ibid.,* at 307.

14   Fraser, *supra* note 11, at 7.

15   *Ibid.,* at 14.

16   *Ibid.,* at 15.

17   *Ibid.,* at 5.

18   As Peter Dews puts it:

> He [Habermas] does not conceal the mass of evidence suggesting the extent to which the manipulated, media-saturated public sphere destroys the potential for an effective democratic opinion to form . . . One could also argue that Habermas' enthusiasm for the post-Marxist category of "civil society," already tarnished by the latest developments in Eastern Europe, seriously underplays the continuing role of social class as a factor in determining access to channels of political influence. In *Faktizitat und Geltung* he is obliged to appeal, rather weakly, to the "normative self-understanding of the mass media," as informing and facilitating public discussion, in order to convince his readers that issues of sufficient common concern will eventually obtain a hearing. Even then, however, he stresses that only crises are capable of mobilizing people successfully. Can such sporadic movements really be said to constitute "communicative practices of self-determination"? (P. Dews, *The Limits of Disenchantment: Essays on Contemporary European Philosophy* 199 [1995])

For an informative discussion of how we might rethink class relations in a postmodern context characterized by concentrations of media power and monopolies over information, see J. C. Rowe, "The Writing Class," in *Politics, Theory, and Contemporary Culture* 41 (M. Poster, ed., 1993).

19   Habermas, *supra* note 8, at 325.

20   Young, *supra* note 4, at 120.

21   *Ibid.*, at 123.

22   See discussions in Habermas, *supra* note 8, at 352–364.

23   See *ibid.*, at 376–380.

24   Garnham, *supra* note 1, at 252.

25   *Ibid.*, at 264.

26   B. Robbins, "Some Versions of U.S. Internationalism," 14(4) *Social Text* 97 (1995).

27   George Yúdice credits Cohen and Arato with the first view, and Michael Hardt and Antonio Negri with the second. See Yúdice, *supra* note 9.

28   *Ibid.*, at 4; Yúdice draws upon L. Sklair, *Sociology of the Global System* (1991), to make this point.

29   See N. Thomas, *Colonialism's Culture: Anthropology, Travel and Government* (1994).

30   Robbins, *supra* note 26, at 112.

31   *Ibid.*, at 112–113.

32   Yúdice, *supra* note 9, at 5.

33   *Ibid.*, at 12–13.

34   *Ibid.*, at 22.

35   *Ibid.*

36   Robbins, *supra* note 26, at 113.

37   D. Polan, "The Public's Fear: or, Media as Monster in Habermas, Negt, and Kluge," in *The Phantom Public Sphere* 33, 36 (B. Robbins, ed., 1993).

38   *Ibid.*, at 40.

39   O. Negt and A. Kluge, *The Public Sphere and Experience* (P. Labanyi, J. Daniel, and A. Oksiloff, trans., 1993). First published in 1972, the book was not published in English translation until twenty years later.

40   M. Hansen, "Unstable Mixtures, Dilated Spheres: Negt and Kluge's *The Public Sphere and Experience*, Twenty Years Later," 5 *Public Culture* 179, 199 (1993).

41   *Ibid.*, at 200.

42   *Ibid.*

43   *Ibid.*

44   C. Lury, *Cultural Rights* 34–35 (1993)

45   *Ibid.*, at 35.

46   *Ibid.*

47   Thomas Streeter shows how the author-function was continually extended to maintain the fiction of individual authors and readers in relations of direct contractual exchange in the development of television broadcasting in the United States. See T. Streeter, *Selling the Air* (1996).

48   P. Kamuf, *Signature Pieces: On the Institution of Authorship* 8–9 (1988).

49   *Ibid.*, at 16.

50   R. Barthes, "The Death of the Author," in *Image-Music-Text* 142 (S. Heath, trans., 1977).

51   *Ibid.*, at 143.

52   *Ibid.*

53   *Ibid.*, at 147.

54   *Ibid.*, at 146.

55   *Ibid.*

56   *Ibid.*, at 148.

57   For an overview of some of the more recent additions to this literature, and citations to the bulk of it, see R. J. Coombe, "Contesting Paternity: Histories of Authorship," 6 *Yale Journal of Law and the Humanities* 397 (1994).

58   Hansen, *supra* note 40, at 211.

59   *Ibid.*, at 182.

60   A. Clapes et al., "Silicon Epics and Binary Bards: Determining the Proper Scope of Copyright Protection for Computer Programs," 34 UCLA *Law Review* 1493 (1987) (Anthony L. Clapes is assistant general counsel for International Business Machines Corporation).

61   J. Boyle, *Shamans, Software, and Spleens: Law and the Construction of the Information Society* 125–128 (1996).

62   For a longer discussion of the many fields in which authorship functions to legitimate these and other new forms of property and authority, see *ibid.*

63   See *Roundtable on the Whitepaper: Intellectual Property and the National Information Infrastructure,* unpublished collection of essays distributed by American University, Washington College of Law, 13 October 1995; P. Samuelson, "The Copyright Grab," 4(1) *Wired* 134 (January 1996); J. Litman, *Revising Copyright Law for the Information Age,* paper presented to the twenty-third annual Telecommunications Policy Research Conference, 2 October 1995, reprinted in 75 *Oregon Law Review* 19 (1996); E. Lifer and M. Rogers, "NII White Paper Has Libraries Concerned about Copyright," *Library Journal News,* 12–13 (1 October 1995).

64   Kamuf, *supra* note 48, at 13.

65   *Ibid.*, at viii.

66   Stewart makes a similar point, noting that law reifies an economy of social life which creates certain relations and identities in the public sphere, regulating and containing transgressions. Alterity, or the fundamental character of the literary, however, always threatens to erupt and disrupt this order of proper names. Literature as social action, in other words, always threatens to displace literature as the artifact that law contains. See Stewart, *supra* note 2, at 280.

67   Kamuf, *supra* note 48, at ix.

68   *Ibid.*

69   *Ibid.*

70   *Ibid.*, at 3.

71   *Ibid.*, at 5.

72   *Ibid.*, at 18.

73   *Ibid.*, at 39–40.

74   *Ibid.*, at 59–66.

75   *Ibid.*, at 66.

76   Kamuf sees these as two necessary functions of the signature (*ibid.*, at 119).

77   *Ibid.*, at 120.

78   *Ibid.*

79   *Ibid.*, at 119.

80   *Ibid.*

81   *Ibid.*, at 117–118.

82   *Ibid.*, at 118.

83   M. R. Trouillot, "Anthropology and the Savage Slot: The Poetics and Politics of Otherness," in *Recapturing Anthropology: Working in the Present* 33 (R. Fox, ed., 1991).

84   J. L. Nancy, *The Inoperative Community* 63 (1991).

85   A. Botwinick, *Postmodernism and Democratic Theory* (1993); D. Carroll, "Community after Devastation: Culture, Politics and the 'Public Space'," in *Politics, Theory, and Contemporary Culture, supra* note 18, at 159; D. Cornell, *The Philosophy of the Limit* (1992); D. Cornell, *Transformations* (1993); E. Laclau, "Power and Representation," in *Politics, Theory, and Contemporary Culture, supra* note 18, at 277; C. Lefort, *Democracy and Political Theory* (1988); J.-F. Lyotard, *The Postmodern Condition: A Report on Knowledge* (G. Bennington and B. Massumi, trans., 1984); J.-F. Lyotard, *Explaining the Postmodern* (1992); C. Mouffe, "Democratic Citizenship and the Political Community," in *Community at Loose Ends* 70 (Miami Theory Collective, ed., 1991); C. Mouffe, "Pluralism and Modern Democracy: Around Carl Schmitt," 14 *New Formations* 1 (1991); Nancy, *supra* note 84. For an introduction to the range of Nancy's work, see *The Sense of Philosophy: on Jean-Luc Nancy* (D. Sheppard, S. Sparks, and C. Thomas, eds., 1997).

86   Carroll, *supra* note 86, at 160.

87   *Ibid.*, at 164.

88   *Ibid.*, at 166.

89   *Ibid.*, at 172–173.

90   *Ibid.*, at 183.

91   Nancy, *supra* note 84, at 63.

92   Carroll, *supra* note 85, at 187.

93   Stewart, *supra* note 2, at 16. She adds: "the oxymoron of 'literary property' continually appears as the site in which the law works out all that it is *not* as a form of writing: the unlocalizable, the excess of the signifier, the nondeclarative in syntax. The idealized conditions of codification—authority, genealogy, precedence, application, specificity, and transcendence—are established as qualities of a literary realm that it becomes the task of the law—as writing that is *other*—to regulate."

94   *Ibid.*, at 40.

95   Christopher Fynsk glosses Nancy's term as "writing," a formulation that at least has the virtue of reference to a practice rather than an entity. See C. Fynsk, "Foreword: Experiences of Finitude," in Nancy, *supra* note 84, at vii–xxxv.

96   *Ibid.*, at xxxvi, commenting on J.-L. Nancy, Preface, in Nancy, *supra* note 84.

97   *Ibid.*, at xxiii.

98   The phrase is that of Emmanuel Levinas and is deployed by Drucilla Cornell in *The Philosophy of the Limit, supra* note 85, at 110 ("Derrida . . . can be understood to more successfully displace the dichotomy of transcendence and immanence through the exposure of the 'immanence' of ethical alternity in the iteration").

99   Nancy, *supra* note 84, at 39.

100 The politics of community is found "in the unworking and as the unworking of all its works" (*ibid.*, at 72). David Carroll, elaborating upon Nancy's insights, enigmatically suggests:

> Nancy proposes fundamental links between literature and (nonworked) community that parallel the nondetermined links, which . . . exist between the aesthetic and the political . . . Nancy argues that the unworkness of literature is in

fact "offered to the infinite communication of the community" but not as *a* communication as such . . . Quite simply, there is no common space in which the work (or community) can be located, for "only the limit is common and limit is not a place but a partition/sharing of places.". . . What is common and thus "public" for Nancy is not space but spacing, not identity but difference or differentiation, not an identical historical destiny and direction that one shares with others but an alterity from self and an openness to others . . . (Carroll, *supra* note 85, at 189; emphasis in original; internal cites omitted)

101 Nancy, *supra* note 84, at 63.

102 *Ibid.*

103 Strategies Collective, "Building a New Left: An Interview with Ernesto Laclau," 1 *Strategies* 10 (1988).

104 Botwinick, *supra* note 85, at 12.

105 *Ibid.*

106 E. Laclau, *The Making of Political Identities* 1–8 (1994). For similar arguments, see Botwinick, *supra* note 85, and Lefort, *supra* note 85, who argues that "democracy is instituted and sustained by the dissolution of the markers of certainty. It inaugurates a history in which people experience a fundamental indeterminacy as to the basis of power, law and knowledge, and as to the basis of relations between self and other, at every level of social life" (*ibid.*, at 17–19).

107 Laclau, *supra* note 85, at 282.

108 *Ibid.*, at 287.

109 *Ibid.* See also E. Laclau, *Emancipations* 36–46 (1996).

110 *Ibid.*

111 Botwinick, *supra* note 85, at 13.

112 Hansen, *supra* note 40.

113 See K. McClure, "The Subject of Rights," in *Dimensions of Radical Democracy: Pluralism, Citizenship, Community* 108 (C. Mouffe, ed., 1992).

114 See R. Miklitsch, "The Rhetoric of Post-Marxism: Discourse and Intentionality in Laclau and Mouffe, Resnick and Wolff," 14(4) *Social Text* 167, 176 (1995). As Miklitsch puts it: "Though the concept of civil society has, it is true, an ambiguous status in Gramsci's work, I understand it here as that domain of social hegemony which *mediates* between the economy and political society. (Hence the accent in Gramsci on the institutions of civil society as '*cultural intermediations*.') As Gramsci puts it: 'Between the economic structure and the State with its legislation and its coercion stands civil society . . .' In other words, while a determinate dialectical relation obtains among these various spheres or structures, civil society retains . . . a semi-autonomy from both the economy *and* political society" (*ibid.*, at 178–179).

As Michael Hardt puts it: "Civil society is proposed as the essential feature of any democracy: the institutional infrastructure for political mediation and public exchange." See M. Hardt, "The Withering of Civil Society," 14(4) *Social Text* 27 (1995). He reminds us: "the standard German translation of the English 'civil society' that Hegel used was 'bourgeois society'. . . the conception of the civilizing process contained in market exchange and capitalist relations of production" (*ibid.*, at 28).

Although the plural institutions of civil society (social, cultural, and economic) provide possibilities for democratic representation at the level of the state, these institutions were also the locus for "disciplinary deployments, producing normalized subjects" (*ibid.*, at 31). What Hardt might also have mentioned is that Hegel's conceptualization of civil society was integrally related to European colonial expansion, which he saw as necessary to absorb the negative social consequences that the growth of civil society was bound to foster. See T. Serequeberhan, "The Idea of Colonialism in Hegel's Philosophy of Right," 29 *International Philosophical Quarterly* 301 (1989).

115   Miklitsch, *supra* note 114, at 177.

116   *Ibid.*, at 181.

117   E. Laclau and C. Mouffe, "PostMarxism without Apologies," 166 *New Left Review* 79, 105 (1987).

118   C. Calhoun, "Civil Society and the Public Sphere," 5 *Public Culture* 267, 279 (1993).

119   Cornell, *The Philosophy of the Limit, supra* note 85, at 111.

120   *Ibid.*, at 207.

121   W. E. Connolly, "Beyond Good and Evil: The Ethical Sensibility of Michel Foucault," 21 *Political Theory* 365 (1993).

122   *Ibid.*, at 367.

123   *Ibid.*, at 371. Connolly uses the term *post-Nietzschean*, to describe such an ethics, but I find the determination of any particular thinker or body of thought as that which we are "after" too limiting. Moreover, his description of a post-Nietzschean sensibility accords nicely with what has elsewhere been propounded within the framework of postmodernism in law and anthropology and my own delineations of the postmodern in this volume.

124   *Ibid.*, at 372.

125   *Ibid.*, at 379.

126   *Ibid.*

127   C. Douzinas. P. Goodrich, and Y. Hachamovitch, "Introduction: Politics, Ethics and the Legality of the Contingent," in *Politics, Postmodernity and Critical Legal Studies: The Legality of the Contingent* 24 (C. Douzinas, P. Goodrich, and Y. Hachamovitch, eds., 1994).

128   *Ibid.*, at 7.

129   *Ibid.*, at 22.

References

Abrams, Floyd (1987) "First Amendment and Copyright: The Seventeenth Donald C. Brace Memorial Lecture," *Journal of the Copyright Society* 35: 1–12.

Abu-Lughod, Lila (1991) "Writing against Culture," in R. J. Fox (1991a), pp. 137–162.

——— (1995) "Movie Stars and Islamic Moralism in Egypt," *Social Text* 42: 53–67.

Adams, Vincanne (1996) *Tigers of the Snow and Other Virtual Sherpas: An Ethnography of Himalayan Encounters.* Princeton: Princeton University Press.

Alexander, Elizabeth (1994) "Can You Be BLACK and Look at This?: Reading the Rodney King Video(s)," *Public Culture* 7: 77–96.

Alexander, Miles J. and Michael K. Heilbronner (1996) "An Analysis of the Dilution Section of the Restatement (Third) of Unfair Competition," *South Carolina Law Review* 47: 629–656.

Alexis, David (1991–92) "Obscurity as a Lifestyle," *Borderlines* 23: 15.

Allen, Theodore W. (1994) *The Invention of the White Race, Vol. 1: Racial Oppression and Social Control.* London: Verso.

American Law Institute (1977) *Restatement (Second) of Torts.* St. Paul: American Law Institute Publishers.

——— (1995) *Restatement of the Law (Third), Unfair Competition.* St. Paul: American Law Institute Publishers.

American University, Washington College of Law (1995) *Roundtable on the Whitepaper: Intellectual Property and the National Information Infrastructure* Unpublished collection of essays distributed by the American University, Washington College of Law 13 October.

Ames, Michael M. (1987) "Free Indians from Their Ethnological Fate: The Emergence of the Indian Point of View in Exhibitions of Indians," *Muse* 5(2): 14–19.

Amin, Ash, ed. (1994) *Post-Fordism: A Reader.* London: Basil Blackwell.

Anderson, Benedict (1993) *Imagined Communities: Reflections on the Origin and Spread of Nationalism.* New York: Verso.

Anderson, Elizabeth (1990) "Is Women's Labor a Commodity?," *Philosophy and Public Affairs* 19: 71–92.

Angus, Ian and Jhally, Sut, eds. (1989) *Cultural Politics in Contemporary America.* New York: Routledge, Chapman and Hall.

Aoki, Keith (1993) "Authors, Inventors, and Trademark Owners: Private Intellectual Property and the Public Domain. Part I," *Columbia-VLA Journal of Law and the Arts* 18: 1–73.

——— (1994) "Authors, Inventors, and Trademark Owners: Private Intellectual Property and the Public Domain. Part II," *Columbia-VLA Journal of Law and the Arts* 18: 191–267.

———— (1996) "(Intellectual) Property and Sovereignty: Notes toward a Cultural Geography of Authorship," *Stanford Law Review* 48: 1293–1355.

Appadurai, Arjun (1990) "Disjuncture and Difference in the Global Cultural Economy," *Public Culture* 2: 1–24.

———— (1991) "Global Ethnoscapes: Notes and Queries for a Transnational Anthropology," in R. J. Fox (1991a), pp. 191–210.

———— (1996) *Modernity at Large: Cultural Dimensions of Globalization.* Minneapolis: University of Minnesota Press.

Apter, Emily and Pietz, William, eds. (1993) *Fetishism as Cultural Discourse.* Ithaca, NY: Cornell University Press.

Arac, Jonathan and Ritvo, Harriet, eds. (1991) *Macropolitics of Nineteenth-Century Literature.* Philadelphia: University of Pennsylvania Press.

Arato, Andrew and Cohen, Jean, eds. (1992) *Civil Society and Political Society.* Cambridge, MA: MIT Press.

Asch, Timothy (1991) "The Story We Now Want to Hear Is Not Ours to Tell—Relinquishing Control over Representation: Toward Sharing Visual Communication Skills with the Yanomamo," *Visual Anthropology Review* 7(2): 102–106.

Assembly of First Nations and The Canadian Museums Association (1992) *Turning the Page: Forging New Partnerships between Museums and First Peoples.* Ottawa: Assembly of First Nations and Canadian Museums Association.

Atwan, Robert, McQuade, Donald and Wright, John (1979) *Edsels, Luckies, & Frigidaires: Advertising the American Way.* New York: Dell Publishing Co.

Ayala, F. (1977) "Victorian Science and the 'Genius' of Women," *Journal of the History of Ideas* 38: 261.

Bacon-Smith, Camille (1992) *Enterprising Women: Television Fandom and the Creation of Popular Myth.* Philadelphia: University of Pennsylvania Press.

Badger, R. Reid (1979) *The Great American Fair: The World's Columbian Exposition and American Culture.* Chicago: Nelson Hall.

Bagdikian, Ben H. (1987) *The Media Monopoly.* 3d ed. Boston: Beacon Press.

———— (1992) *The Media Monopoly.* 4th ed. Boston: Beacon Press.

Bahri, Deepika (1996) "Coming to Terms with the 'Postcolonial,'" in Bahri and Vasudeva (1996b), pp. 137–164.

———— and Vasudeva, Mary (1996a) "Pedagogical Alternatives: Issues in Postcolonial Studies: Interview with Gauri Viswanathan," in Bahri and Vasudeva (1996b).

————, eds. (1996b) *Between the Lines: South Asians and Postcoloniality.* Philadelphia: Temple University Press.

Baird, Stephen R. (1993) "Moral Intervention in the Trademark Arena: Banning the Registration of Scandalous and Immoral Trademarks," *Trademark Reporter* 83: 661–800.

Baker, C. Edwin (1992) "Advertising and a Democratic Press," *University of Pennsylvania Law Review* 140: 2097–2243.

Bakhtin, Mikhail M. (1981) "Discourse in the Novel," in Michael Holquist ed. *The Dialogic Imagination: Four Essays by M. M. Bakhtin.* Caryl Emerson and Michael Holquist, trans. Austin: University of Texas Press, pp. 259–422.

———— (1984) *Problems of Dostoevsky's Poetics.* Caryl Emerson, trans. Austin: University of Texas Press.

Balkin, Jack (1987) "Deconstructive Practice and Legal Theory," *Yale Law Journal* 96: 743–786.

———— (1991) "Ideology as Constraint," *Stanford Law Review* 43: 1133–1169.

———— (1990) "Some Realism about Pluralism: Legal Realist Approaches to the First Amendment," *Duke Law Journal* [1990]: 375–430.

Barnet, Richard and Cavanagh, John (1994) *Global Dreams: Imperial Corporations and the New World Order.* New York: Simon & Schuster.

Barnett, Stephen R. (1996) "The Right of Publicity Versus Free Speech in Advertising: Some Counter-Points to Professor McCarthy," *Hastings Communications and Entertainment Law Journal* 18: 593–614.

Barthes, Roland (1977) *Image-Music-Text.* Stephen Heath, trans. New York: Hill and Wang.

Battaglia, Debbora, ed. (1995) *Rhetorics of Self-Making.* Berkeley: University of California Press.

Battersby, Christine (1989) *Gender and Genius: Towards a Feminist Aesthetics.* Bloomington: Indiana University Press

Baty, S. Paige (1995) *American Monroe: The Making of a Body Politic.* Berkeley: University of California Press.

Baudrillard, Jean (1975) *The Mirror of Production.* St. Louis: Telos Press.

———— (1981) *For a Critique of the Political Economy of the Sign.* St. Louis: Telos Press.

———— (1983a) *In the Shadow of Silent Majorities.* New York: Semiotext(e).

———— (1983b) *Simulations.* New York: Semiotext(e).

———— (1988a) "Consumer Society," in Poster (1988b), pp. 29–56.

———— (1988b) "On Seduction," in Poster (1988b), pp. 149–165.

———— (1988c) "Symbolic Exchange and Death," in Poster (1988b), pp. 119–148.

———— (1988d) "The System of Objects," in Poster (1988b), pp. 10–25.

Bauman, Zygmunt (1992) *Intimations of Postmodernity.* New York: Routledge, Chapman and Hall.

Beam, Carl (1992) Untitled contribution in McMaster and Martin (1992a), pp. 119–121.

Beaumont, Heather (1992) "The X Factor," *The Metro Word* 1(9): 7.

Becker, Mary (1992) "The Politics of Women's Wrongs and the Bill of Rights," *University of Chicago Law Review* 59: 453.

———— (1993) "Conservative Free Speech and the Uneasy Case for Judicial Review," *University of Chicago Law Review* 64: 975.

Benedict, Burton (1983) *The Anthropology of World's Fairs.* Berkeley: Lowie Museum of Anthropology and Scholar Press.

Benjamin, Walter (1969) "The Work of Art in the Age of Mechanical Reproduction," in Hannah Arendt, ed. *Illuminations.* New York: Schocken Books, pp. 217–253.

———— (1986) *Reflections: Essays, Aphorisms, Autobiographical Writing.* Edmund Jephcott, trans. New York: Schocken Books.

Berg, Jeff (1991) "Moral Rights: A Legal, Historical and Anthropological Perspective," *Intellectual Property Journal* 6: 341–371.

Berger, Peter and Luckman, Thomas (1966) *The Social Construction of Reality.* New York: Doubleday.

Berkhofer, Robert F., Jr. (1979) *The White Man's Indian: Images of the American Indian from Columbus to the Present.* New York: Vintage.

Berlant, Lauren (1993) "National Brands/National Body: Imitation of Life," in Robbins, pp. 173–208.

Bernstein, Richard J. (1983) *Beyond Objectivism and Relativism.* Philadelphia: University of Pennsylvania Press.

Bhabha, Homi K. (1990a) "DissemiNation: Time, Narrative, and the Margins of the Modern Nation," in Bhabha (1990c), pp. 291–322.

——— (1990b) "Introduction: Narrating the Nation," in Bhabha (1990c), pp. 1–7.

———, ed. (1990c) *Nation and Narration*. New York: Routledge, Chapman and Hall.

——— (1992) "Postcolonial Authority and Postmodern Guilt," in L. Grossberg, C. Nelson, and P. Treichler, eds., *Cultural Studies*. New York: Routledge, Chapman and Hall.

——— (1994) *The Location of Culture*. New York: Routledge, Chapman and Hall.

——— and Burgin, Victor (1992) "Visualizing Theory," *Visual Anthropology Review* 8(1): 71–81.

Blackstone, William (1765–69) *Commentaries on the Laws of England*. 4 vol. Oxford: Clarendon Press.

Boddy, Janice (1991) "Anthropology, Feminism and the Postmodern Context," *Culture* 11: 125–133.

Bongie, Chris (1991) *Exotic Memories: Literature, Colonialism, and the Fin de Siècle*. Stanford: Stanford University Press.

Borofsky, Robert (1989) *Making History: Pukapukan and Anthropological Constructions of Knowledge*. Cambridge: Cambridge University Press.

Botwinick, Aryeh (1993) *Postmodernism and Democratic Theory*. Philadelphia: Temple University Press.

Bourdieu, Pierre (1977) *Outline of a Theory of Practice*. Cambridge: Cambridge University Press.

——— (1990) *In Other Words: Essays towards a Reflexive Sociology*. Stanford: Stanford University Press.

Bower, Lisa (1994) "Queer Acts and the Politics of Direct Address: Rethinking Law, Culture and Community," *Law and Society Review* 28: 1009–1033.

Boyle, James (1985) "The Politics of Reason: Critical Legal Theory and Local Social Thought," *University of Pennsylvania Law Review* 133: 685–780.

——— (1991) "Is Subjectivity Possible? The Post-Modern Subject in Legal Theory," *University of Colorado Law Review* 62: 489–524.

——— (1992) "A Theory of Law and Information: Copyright, Spleens, Blackmail and Insider Trading," *California Law Review* 80: 1413–1540.

——— (1996) *Shamans, Software, and Spleens: Law and the Construction of the Information Society*. Cambridge, MA: Harvard University Press.

Braatz, John R. (1994) "White v. Samsung Electronics America: The Ninth Circuit Turns a New Letter in California Right of Publicity Law," *Pace Law Review* 15: 161–222.

Brady, Ivy (1983) "Introduction to Speaking in the Name of the Real: Freeman and Mead in Samoa," *American Anthropologist* 85: 908–909.

Brainerd, Stephen (1985) "The Groundless Assault: A Wittgensteinian Look at Language, Structuralism, and Critical Legal Theory," *American Law Review* 34: 1231–1262.

Brantlinger, Patrick (1990) *Crusoe's Footprints: Cultural Studies in Britain and America*. New York: Routledge, Chapman and Hall.

Bredice, Steven A. (1995) "Media Hybrids and the First Amendment: Constitutional Signposts along the Information Superhighway," *Emory Law Journal* 44(1): 213–266.

Brenkman, John (1987) *Culture and Domination*. Ithaca: Cornell University Press.

Brennan, Tim (1990) "The National Longing for Form," in Bhabha (1990c), pp. 44–70.

Brettell, Caroline B., ed. (1996) *When They Read What We Write: The Politics of Ethnography*. Westport, CT: Bergin & Garvey.

Brightman, Robert (1995) "Forget Culture: Replacement, Transcendence, Reflexification," *Cultural Anthropology* 10: 509–546.

Browning, Janisse (1991) "Self Determination and Cultural Appropriation," *Fuse* (fall) 15: 31–35.

Brunvand, Jan (1984) *The Choking Doberman and Other "New" Urban Legends.* New York: Norton.

——— (1986) *The Mexican Pet: More "New" Urban Legends and Some Old Favorites.* New York: Norton.

Buck, Glen (1916) *Trademark Power: An Expedition into an Unprobed and Inviting Wilderness.* Chicago: Monroe and Southworth.

Burciaga, Jose Antonio (1993) *Drink Cultura: Chicanismo.* Santa Barbara: Capra Press.

Burke, Timothy (1996) *Lifebuoy Men, Lux Women: Commodification, Consumption, and Cleanliness in Modern Zimbabwe.* Durham, NC: Duke University Press.

Burton-Carvajal, Julianne (1994) "'Surprise Package': Looking Southward with Disney," in Smoodin (1994a), pp. 131–147.

Buskirk, Martha (1992) "Commodification as Censor: Copyrights and Fair Use," *October* 60: 83–109.

Butler, Judith (1990) *Gender Trouble: Feminism and the Subversion of Identity.* New York: Routledge, Chapman and Hall.

——— (1992) "Contingent Foundations: Feminism and the Question of Postmodernism," in J. Butler and J. W. Scott, eds., *Feminists Theorize the Political.* New York: Routledge, pp. 3–21.

——— (1993a) *Bodies that Matter.* New York: Routledge, Chapman and Hall.

——— (1993b) "Critically Queer," *Gay and Lesbian Quarterly: A Journal of Lesbian and Gay Studies* 1: 17–32.

——— (1995) "For a Careful Reading," in Seyla Benhabib et al., eds., *Feminist Contentions: A Philosophical Exchange.* New York: Routledge, pp. 127–144.

——— (1997) *The Psychic Life of Power: Theories of Subjection.* Stanford: Stanford University Press.

Byram, Tamara (1990) "Digital Sampling and a Federal Right of Publicity: Is It Live or Is It MacIntosh?," *Comparative Law Journal* 10: 365–393.

Cain, Maureen and Harrington, Christine, eds. (1993) *Lawyers in a Postmodern World: Translation and Transgression.* New York: New York University Press.

Cairns, J. W. (1984) "Blackstone, an English Institutist: Legal Literature and the Rise of the Nation State," *Oxford Journal of Legal Studies* 4: 318–360.

Calhoun, Craig (1993) "Civil Society and the Public Sphere," *Public Culture* 5: 267–280.

Callman, Rudolph (1969) *The Law of Unfair Competition, Trademarks and Monopolies,* 3d ed. Mundelein, Il: Callaghan.

Caputo, John D. (1987) *Radical Hermeneutics: Repetition, Deconstruction, and the Hermeneutic Project.* Bloomington: Indiana University Press.

Cardinal-Schubert, Joane (1989) "In the Red," *Fuse* 13 (1, 2): 20–28.

——— (1992) Untitled contribution in McMaster and Martin (1992a), pp. 130–135.

Cardoso, Ferdinand Henrique and Falleto, Enzo (1979) *Dependency and Development in Latin America.* Berkeley: University of California Press.

Caristi, Dom (1992) *Expanding Free Expression in the Market Place: Broadcasting and the Public Forum.* Westport, CT: Greenwood Press.

Carlin, John (1988) "Culture Vultures: Artistic Appropriation and Intellectual Property Law," *Columbia-VLA Journal of Law & the Arts* 13: 103–143.

Carlisle, David (1987) "The Museum of Modern Mythology," *The Last Issue* 5(1): 9.

Carnoy, M. et al., eds. (1993) *The New Global Economy in the Information Age*. University Park: Pennsylvania State University Press.

Carrier, James (1990) "The Symbolism of Possession in Commodity Advertising," *Man* (Journal of the Royal Anthropological Institute) 25: 693–705.

Carroll, David (1993) "Community after Devastation: Culture, Politics and the 'Public Space,'" in Mark Poster, ed. *Politics, Theory, and Contemporary Culture*. New York: Columbia University Press, pp. 159–196.

Cartwright, Lisa and Goldfarb, Brian (1994) "Cultural Contagion: On Disney's Health Education Films for Latin America," in Smoodin (1994a), pp. 169–180.

Carty, H. (1993) "Character Merchandising and the Limits of Passing Off," *Legal Studies* 13: 289.

Casebeer, Kenneth (1989) "Work on a Labor Theory of Meaning," *Cardozo Law Review* 10: 1637–1664.

Castells, Manuel (1989) *The Informational City: Information Technology, Economic Restructuring, and the Urban-Regional Process*. Oxford: Basil Blackwell.

Castoriadis, Cornelius (1987) *The Imaginary Institution of Society*. Kathleen Blamey, trans. Cambridge, MA: MIT Press.

Certeau, Michel de (1983) "History: Ethics, Science and Fiction," in N. Haan et al., eds., *Social Science as Moral Inquiry*. New York: Columbia University Press, pp. 125–152.

———— (1984) *The Practice of Everyday Life*. Berkeley: University of California Press.

Cheah, Pheng (1995) "Violent Light: The Idea of Publicness in Modern Philosophy and in Global Neocolonialism," *Social Text* 43: 163–190.

————, Fraser, David and Grbich, Judith, eds. (1996) *Thinking through the Body of Law*. New York: New York University Press.

Chevigny, Paul (1988) *More Speech: Dialogue Rights and Modern Liberty*. Philadelphia: Temple University Press.

Chon, Margaret (1993) "Postmodern 'Progress': Reconsidering the Copyright and Patent Power," *DePaul Law Review* 43: 97–146.

———— (1996) "New Wine Bursting from Old Bottles: Collaborative Internet Art, Joint Works, and Entrepreneurship," *Oregon Law Review* 75: 257–276.

Chong, S. (1991) "The Teenage Mutant Ninja Turtles Case: Zapping English Law on Character Merchandising Past the Embryonic Stage," *European Intellectual Property Review* 13: 253.

Churchill, Ward (1991/92) "Colonialism, Genocide and the Expropriation of Indigenous Spiritual Tradition in Contemporary Academia," *Borderlines* 23: 39–41.

———— (1994) *Indians Are Us? Culture and Genocide in Native North America*. Toronto: Between the Lines Press.

Cifelli, Armand and McMurray, Walter (1984) "The Right of Publicity—A Trademark Model for Its Temporal Scope," *Journal of the Patent Office Society* 66: 455–474.

Clapes, A. et al. (1987) "Silicon Epics and Binary Bards: Determining the Proper Scope of Copyright Protection for Computer Programs," UCLA *Law Review* 34: 1493.

Clark, Jeffrey (1993) "Gold, Sex, and Pollution: Male Illnes and Myth at Mt. Kare, Papua New Guinea," *American Ethnologist* 20: 742.

Clarke, David E. (1993) "On Trade-marks Becoming Invalid," in Gordon F. Henderson et al., eds., *Trade-marks Law of Canada*. Toronto: Carswell.

Classen, Constance, Howes, D. and Synott, A., eds. (1994) *Aroma: The Cultural History of Smell*. London: Routledge.

Clay, Steven C. (1994) Note: "Starstruck: The Overextension of Celebrity Publicity Rights in State and Federal Courts," *Minnesota Law Review* 79: 485–517.

Clayson, A. and Leigh, S. eds. (1994) *Aspects of Elvis*. London: Sidgwick and Jackson.

Clements, Rebecca (1991) "Misconceptions of Culture: Native Peoples and Cultural Property under Canadian Law," *University of Toronto Faculty of Law Review* 49: 1–26.

Clifford, James (1986) "Introduction: Partial Truths," in Clifford and Marcus (1986), pp. 1–26.

———— (1988) *The Predicament of Culture: Twentieth-Century Ethnography, Literature, and Art*. Cambridge, MA: Harvard University Press.

———— and Marcus, George, eds. (1986) *Writing Culture: The Poetics and Politics of Ethnography*. Berkeley: University of California Press.

Clifton, James A., ed. (1990) *The Invented Indian: Cultural Fictions and Government Policies*. New Brunswick, NJ: Transaction Publishers.

Cohen, Amy B. (1990) "Copyright Law and the Myth of Objectivity: The Idea-Expression Dichotomy and the Inevitability of Artistic Value Judgements," *Indiana Law Journal* 66: 175–232.

Cohen, Felix S. (1935) "Transcendental Nonsense and the Functionalist Approach," *Columbia Law Review* 35: 809–849.

Cole, Douglas (1990) *An Iron Hand upon the People: The Law against the Potlatch on the Northwest Coast*. Vancouver: Douglas & McIntyre.

Collier, Jane, Maurer, Bill and Suarez Navaz, Lilliana (1995) "Sanctioned Identities: Legal Constructions of Modern Personhood," *Identities* 2: 1–27.

Collins, Jim (1989) *Uncommon Cultures: Popular Culture and Postmodernism*. New York: Routledge, Chapman and Hall.

Collins, Ronald K. L. and Skover, David M. (1993) "Commerce and Communication," *Texas Law Review* 71: 697–746.

———— (1996) *The Death of Discourse*. Boulder, CO: Westview Press.

Comaroff, Jean (1985) *Body of Power, Spirit of Resistance*. Chicago: University of Chicago Press.

Comaroff, Jean and Comaroff, John (1991) *Of Revelation and Revolution: Christianity, Colonialism, and Consciousness in South Africa, Vol.1*. Chicago: University of Chicago Press.

———— (1992) *Ethnography and the Historical Imagination*. Boulder, CO: Westview Press.

————, eds. (1993) *Modernity and Its Malcontents: Ritual and Power in Postcolonial Africa*. Chicago: University of Chicago Press.

Comaroff, John L. (1994) Foreword, in Lazarus-Black and Hirsch (1994), pp. ix–xiii.

———— (1996) "Ethnicity, Nationalism and the Politics of Difference in an Age of Revolution," in E. Wilmsen and P. McAllister, eds., *The Politics of Difference: Ethnic Premises in a World of Power*. Chicago: University of Chicago Press.

Comment, "The Right of Publicity: Premature Burial for California Property Rights in the Wake of Lugosi" (1981) *Pacific Law Journal* 12: 987–1011.

Conforti, Joe (1989) "Copyright and Freedom of Expression: A Privilege for News Reports," *Intellectual Property Journal* 5: 103–135.

Conley, Diane (1991) "Author, User, Scholar, Thief: Fair Use and Unpublished Words," *Cardozo Arts and Entertainment Law Journal* 9: 15–60.

Connolly, William E. (1991) *Identity/Difference: Democratic Negotiations of Political Paradox*. Ithaca: Cornell University Press.

———— (1993) "Beyond Good and Evil: The Ethical Sensibility of Michel Foucault," *Political Theory* 21: 365–389.

Connor, Steven (1989) *Postmodernist Culture: An Introduction to Theories of the Contemporary.* London: Basil Blackwell.

Coombe, Rosemary J. (1989a) "Room for Manoeuver: Toward a Theory of Practice in Critical Legal Studies," *Law and Social Inquiry* 14: 69–121.

———— (1989b) "Same as It Ever Was: Rethinking the Politics of Legal Interpretation," *McGill Law Journal* 34: 603–652.

———— (1990a) "Barren Ground: Reconceiving Honour and Shame in the Field of Mediterranean Ethnography," *Anthropologica* 32: 221–234.

———— (1991a) "Contesting the Self: Negotiating Subjectivities in Nineteenth-Century Ontario Defamation Trials," *Studies in Law, Politics, and Society* 11: 3–40.

———— (1991b) "Beyond Modernity's Meanings: Encountering the Postmodern in Cultural Anthropology," *Culture* 11: 111–124.

———— (1994) "Contesting Paternity: Histories of Authorship," *Yale Journal of Law and the Humanities* 6: 397–422.

———— (1995a) "The Cultural Life of Things: Anthropological Approaches to Law and Society in Conditions of Globalization," *American University Journal of International Law and Policy* 10: 791–836.

———— (1995b) "Finding and Losing One's Self in the Topoi: Placing and Displacing the Postmodern Subject in Law," *Law and Society Review* 29(4): 599–608.

———— (1996a) "Left Out on the Information Highway," *Oregon Law Review* 75: 237–248.

———— (1996b) "Authorial Cartographies: Mapping Proprietary Borders in a Less-than-Brave New World," *Stanford Law Review* 48: 1357–1366.

———— (1997) "Identifying and Engendering the Forms of Emergent Civil Societies: New Directions in Political Anthropology," *Political and Legal Anthropology Review* 20: 1–12.

———— (1998a) "Contingent Articulations: A Critical Cultural Legal Studies," in Sarat and Kearns (1998), pp. 21–65.

———— (1998b) "Sports Trademarks and Somatic Politics: Locating the Law in a Critical Cultural Studies," in Randy Martin and Toby Miller, eds., *Competing Allegories: Global and Local Cultures of Sport.* Minneapolis: University of Minnesota Press, 1998.

———— and Stoller, Paul (1994) "X Marks the Spot: The Ambiguities of African Trading in the Commerce of the Black Public Sphere," *Public Culture* 7: 249–274, reprinted in The Black Public Sphere Collective, ed. (1995) *The Black Public Sphere.* Chicago: University of Chicago Press, pp. 253–278.

Coombes, Annie (1992) "Inventing the 'Postcolonial': Hybridity and Constituency in Contemporary Curating," *New Formations* 18: 39–52.

Cornell, Drucilla (1985) "Toward a Modern/Postmodern Reconstruction of Ethics," *University of Pennsylvania Law Review* 133: 291–380.

———— (1991) *Beyond Accommodation: Ethical Feminism, Deconstruction and the Law.* New York: Routledge, Chapman and Hall.

———— (1992) *The Philosophy of the Limit.* New York: Routledge, Chapman and Hall.

———— (1993) *Transformations.* New York: Routledge, Chapman and Hall.

Cornell, N. (1990) "Collecting Christmas," *Sky* (December) 67.

Cox, Gail Diane (1989) "Don't Mess with the Mouse: Disney's Legal Army Protects a Revered Image," *The National Law Journal* 11 (31 July): 1, 26–27.

Coyne, Randall T. E. (1988) "Toward a Modified Fair Use Defense in Right of Publicity Cases," *William & Mary Law Review* 29: 781–821.

Crain, Mary (1991) "Poetics and Politics in the Ecuadorian Andes: Women's Narratives of Death and Devil Possession," *American Ethnologist* 18: 67–89.

——— (1994) "Opening Pandora's Box: A Plea for Discursive Heteroglossia," *American Ethnologist* 21(1): 205–210.

Crimp, Douglas (1993) "Right On, Girlfriend!," *Social Text* 33: 2–18.

Cronon, William, Miles, George and Gitlin, Jay, eds. (1992a) *Under an Open Sky: Rethinking America's Western Past.* New York: Norton.

——— (1992b) "Becoming West: Toward a New Meaning for Western History," in Cronon, Miles, and Gitlin (1992a), pp. 3–27.

Cruz, Jon and Lewis, Justin, eds. (1994) *Viewing, Reading, Listening: Audiences and Cultural Reception.* Boulder, CO: Westview Press.

Csordas, Thomas J., ed. (1994) *Embodiment and Experience: The Existential Ground of Culture and Self.* Cambridge: University of Cambridge Press.

Curran, James, Morley, David and Walkerdine, Valerie, eds. (1996) *Cultural Studies and Communications.* London: Arnold.

Dallmayr, Fred R. (1988) "Hegemony and Democracy: On Laclau and Mouffe," *Strategies* 1: 29–49.

Dalton, David (1983) *James Dean: The Mutant King.* New York: St. Martin's Press.

Danielsen, Dan and Engle, Karen, eds. (1995) *After Identity: A Reader in Law and Culture.* New York: Routledge.

Davies, Ioan (1995) *Cultural Studies and Beyond: Fragments of Empire.* London: Routledge.

Davis, Laurel (1993) "Protest against the Use of Native American Mascots: A Challenge to Traditional American Identity," *Journal of Sport and Social Issues* 17: 9–22.

Davis, Mike (1990) *City of Quartz: Excavating the Future in Los Angeles.* London: Verso Books.

Davis, Theodore H., Jr. (1993) "Registration of Scandalous, Immoral, and Disparaging Matter under Section 2(a) of the Lanham Act: Can One Man's Vulgarity Be Another's Registered Trademark?," *Ohio State Law Journal* 54: 338–364.

Dawson, Michael C. (1994) "A Black Counterpublic?: Economic Earthquakes, Racial Agenda(s), and Black Politics," *Public Culture* 7: 195–224.

"Declaration of Quito, July 1990: Indigenous Alliance of the Americas on 500 Years of Resistance" (1991/92) *Borderlines* 23: 2–3.

de Cordova, Richard (1994) "The Mickey in Macy's Window: Childhood, Consumerism, and Disney Animation," in Smoodin (1994a), pp. 203–213.

Deetz, Stanley A. (1992) *Democracy in an Age of Corporate Colonization.* Albany: State University of New York Press.

de Lauretis, Teresa (1986) "Feminist Studies/Critical Studies: Issues, Terms, and Contexts," in Teresa de Lauretis, ed. *Feminist Studies/Critical Studies.* Bloomington: University of Indiana Press, pp. 1–19.

Delgado, Richard (1982) "Words That Wound: A Tort Action for Racial Insults, Epithets, and Name-Calling," *Harvard Civil Rights–Civil Liberties Law Review* 17: 133–181.

——— and Stefancic, Jean (1992) "Images of the Outsider in American Law and Culture: Can Free Expression Remedy Systemic Social Ills?," *Cornell Law Review* 77: 1258–1297.

——— (1993) "A Shifting Balance: Freedom of Expression and Hate-Speech Restriction," *Iowa Law Review* 78: 737–750.

———, eds. (1997) *Critical White Studies.* New York: New York University Press.

Denicola, Robert C. (1982) "Trademarks as Speech: Constitutional Implications of the Emerging Rationales for the Protection of Trade Symbols," *Wisconsin Law Review* 158: 190–207.

Dentith, Simon (1995) *Bakhtinian Thought: An Introductory Reader.* London: Routledge.

Dews, Peter (1995) *The Limits of Disenchantment: Essays on Contemporary European Philosophy.* London: Verso.

Dezaley, Yves and Garth, Bryant (1995) "Merchants of Law as Moral Entrepreneurs: Constructing International Justice from the Competition for Transnational Business Disputes," *Law & Society Review* 29(1): 27–64.

Diawara, Manthia (1994) "Malcolm X and the Black Public Sphere: Conversionists versus Culturalists," *Public Culture* 7: 35–48.

Dissanayake, Wimal and Wilson, Rob, eds. (1995) *Global/Local: Cultural Production in the Transnational Imaginary.* Durham, NC: Duke University Press.

Docker, John (1994) *Postmodernism and Popular Culture: A Cultural History.* Cambridge: Cambridge University Press.

Dominguez, Virginia R. (1993) "Visual Nationalism: On Looking at National Symbols," *Public Culture* 5: 451–456.

Doolittle, L., Elton, H. and Laviolette, M. (1987) "Appropriation: When Does Borrowing Become Stealing?," *Last Issue* 5(1): 20.

Dorfman, Ariel (1983) *The Empire's Old Clothes: What the Lone Ranger, Babar, and Other Innocent Heroes Do to Our Minds.* New York: Pantheon Books.

—— and Matteltart, Armand (1975) *How to Read Donald Duck: Imperial Ideology in the Disney Comic.* New York: International General.

Doty, Alexander (1993) *Making Things Perfectly Queer: Interpreting Mass Culture.* Minneapolis: University of Minnesota Press.

Douglas, Lawrence (1995) "The Force of Words: Fish, Matsuda, MacKinnon, and the Theory of Discursive Violence," *Law & Society Review* 29(1): 169–190.

Douzinas, Costas, Goodrich, Peter and Hachamovitch, Yifat, eds. (1994) *Politics, Postmodernity and Critical Legal Studies: The Legality of the Contingent.* London: Routledge.

Douzinas, Costas, McVeigh, Shaun and Warrington, Ronnie (1991) *Postmodern Jurisprudence: The Law of Text in the Texts of Law.* London: Routledge.

Drahos, Peter (1996) *The Philosophy of Intellectual Property.* Aldershot: Dartmouth.

Drescher, Thomas (1992) "Article and Report: The Transformation and Evolution of Trademarks—From Signals to Symbols to Myth," *Trademark Reporter* 82: 301–340.

Dreyfus, Hubert and Rabinow, Paul (1983) *Michel Foucault: Beyond Structuralism and Hermeneutics.* Chicago: University of Chicago Press.

Dreyfuss, Rochelle Cooper (1990) "Expressive Genericity: Trademarks as Language in the Pepsi Generation," *Notre Dame Law Review* 65: 397–424.

—— (1995) "A 'Wiseguy's' Approach to Information Products: Muscling Copyright and Patent into a Unitary Theory of Intellectual Property," *Supreme Court Review* [1995]: 195–234.

—— (1996) "We Are Symbols and Inhabit Symbols, So Why Should We Be Paying Rent? Deconstructing the Lanham Act and Rights of Publicity," *Columbia-VLA Journal of Law and the Arts* 20: 123–156.

Drinnon, Richard (1980) *Facing West: The Metaphysics of Indian-Hating and Empire Building.* Berkeley: University of California Press.

Duff, Gerald (1995) *That's All Right, Mama: A Novel.* Dallas: Baskerville Publishers.

Dumont, Louis (1977) *From Mandeville to Marx: The Genesis and Triumph of Economic Ideology.* Chicago: University of Chicago Press.

—— (1986) *Essays on Individualism: Modern Ideology in Anthropological Perspective.* Chicago: University of Chicago Press.

Durang, Simon (1990) "Literature: Nationalism's Other? The Case for Revision," in Bhabha (1990c), pp. 138–153.

Durone, Anthony J. and Smith, Melissa K. (1995) "The First Amendment and Private Property: A Sign for Free Speech (City of Ladue v. Gilleo, 114 S. Ct. 2038, 1994)," *Missouri Law Review* 60: 415–443.

Dyer, Richard (1979) *Stars.* London: British Film Institute.

———— (1986) *Heavenly Bodies: Film Stars and Society.* New York: St. Martin's Press.

Eagleton, Terry (1984) *The Function of Criticism.* London: Verso/New Left Books.

Eco, Umberto (1989) *Travels in Hyperreality.* San Diego: Harcourt, Brace Jovanovich.

Edwards, Joseph F. (1991) "Major Global Treaties for the Protection and Enjoyment of Art and Cultural Objects," *Toledo Law Review* 22: 919–953.

Ehrenreich, Barbara and Fuentes, Annette (1983) *Women in the Global Factory.* Boston: South End Press.

Elliott, Jean Leonard and Fleras, Augie (1992) *The "Nations Within": Aboriginal-State Relations in Canada, the United States, and New Zealand.* Toronto: Oxford University Press.

Elmslie, M. (1992) "Passing Off and Image Marketing in the United Kingdom," *European Intellectual Property Review* 14: 279.

Enfield, William (1774) *Observations on Literary Property.* London: Joseph Johnson.

Enloe, Cynthia (1989) *Bananas, Bases, and Blue Jeans: Making Feminist Sense out of International Politics.* Berkeley: University of California Press.

Epstein, R., Stone, G. and Sunstein, C. (1992) *The Bill of Rights in the Modern State.* Chicago: University of Chicago Press.

Errington, Shelly (1989) "Fragile Traditions and Contested Meanings," *Public Culture* 1(2): 49–59.

Escobar, Arturo (1992) "Culture, Practice and Politics: Anthropology and the Study of Social Movements," *Critique of Anthropology* 12(4): 395–432.

Espeland, Wendy (1994) "Legally Mediated Identity: The National Environmental Policy Act and the Bureaucratic Construction of Interests," *Law & Society Review* 28: 1149–1179.

Ewen, Stuart (1976) *Captains of Consciousness.* New York: McGraw Hill.

———— (1988) *All-Consuming Images: The Politics of Style in Contemporary Culture.* New York: Basic Books.

———— and Ewen, Elizabeth (1982) *Channels of Desire.* New York: McGraw Hill.

Ewick, Patricia and Silbey, Susan (1992) "Conformity, Contestation, and Resistance: An Account of Legal Consciousness," *New England Law Review* 26: 731–749.

Fabian, Johanes (1983) *Time and the Other: How Anthropology Makes Its Object.* New York: Columbia University Press.

Fabo, Andy (1989–90) Letter to the Editor, *Fuse* 13(3): 2, 4.

Fanon, Frantz (1967) *Black Skin, White Masks.* New York: Grove Press.

Farred, Grant (1995) Untitled contribution to "Race and Racism: A Symposium," *Social Text* 42: 21–26.

Feather, John (1989) "Publishers and Politicians: The Remaking of the Law of Copyright in Britain 1775–1842," *Publishing History* 25: 45.

Featherstone, Mike (1988) "In Pursuit of the Postmodern: An Introduction," *Theory, Culture and Society* 5: 195–215.

———— (1991) *Consumer Culture and Postmodernism.* Newbury, CA: Sage Publications.

———— (1996) "Localism, Globalism, and Cultural Identity," in Wilson and Dissanayake (1996), pp. 46–77.

———— et al., eds., (1995) *Global Modernities*. London: Sage.

Ferguson, James (1988) "Cultural Exchange: New Developments in the Anthropology of Commodities," *Cultural Anthropology* 3: 488–513.

Fewer, David (1997) "Constitutionalizing Copyright," *University of Toronto Faculty of Law Review* 55: 175–240.

Fine, Gary Alan (1985) "The Goliath Effect: Corporate Dominance and Mercantile Legends," *Journal of American Folklore* 98(387): 63–84.

———— (1990) "Among Those Dark Satanic Mills: Rumors of Kooks, Cults, and Corporations," *Southern Folklore* 47: 133–146.

Fish, Stanley (1980) *Is There a Text in this Class? The Authority of Interpretive Communities*. Cambridge, MA: Harvard University Press.

———— (1989) *Doing What Comes Naturally: Change, Rhetoric, and the Practice of Theory in Literary and Legal Studies*. Durham, NC: Duke University Press.

Fisher, Jean (1987) "Corporate Muse," *Artforum* (March) 25: 108.

Fisher, William W., III (1988) "Reconstructing Fair Use Doctrine," *Harvard Law Review* 101: 1659–1795.

Fiske, John (1989a) *Reading the Popular*. Boston: Unwin, Hyman.

———— (1989b) *Understanding Popular Culture*. Boston: Unwin, Hyman.

———— (1992a) "Cultural Studies and the Culture of Everyday Life," in Grossberg, L., Nelson, C. and Treichler, P., eds., *Cultural Studies*. New York: Routledge, Chapman and Hall, pp. 30–49.

———— (1992b) "The Cultural Economy of Fandom," in L. A. Lewis (1992a), pp. 30–49.

———— and Glynn, Kevin (1995) "Trials of the Postmodern," *Cultural Studies* 9(3): 505–521.

Fiss, Owen (1986) "Free Speech and Social Structure," *Iowa Law Review* 71: 1405–1425.

———— (1987) "Why the State?," *Harvard Law Review* 100: 781–794.

———— (1995a) "Building a Free Press," *Yale Journal of International Law* 20: 187–202.

———— (1995b) "In Search of a New Paradigm," *Yale Law Journal* 104: 1613.

———— (1996) *Liberalism Divided: Freedom of Speech and the Many Uses of State Power*. Boulder, CO: Westview Press.

Fitzpatrick, Peter (1992) *The Mythology of Modern Law*. London: Routledge, Chapman and Hall.

———— (1995) "Passions out of Place: Law, Incommensurability and Resistance," *Law and Critique* 6(1): 95–112.

Fleras, Augie and Elliott, Jean Leonard (1992) *The "Nations Within": Aboriginal-State Relations in Canada, the United States and New Zealand*. Don Mills, Ont.: Oxford University Press.

Fog Olwig, Karen and Hastrup, Kirsten, eds., (1996) *Siting Culture: The Shifting Anthropological Object*. London: Routledge.

Foster, Hal (1983a) *The Anti-Aesthetic: Essays on Postmodern Culture*. Seattle: Bay Press.

———— (1983b) "Postmodernism: A Preface," in H. Foster (1983a), pp. ix–xvi.

———— (1985a) "The Expressive Fallacy," in H. Foster (1985b), pp. 59–115.

————, ed. (1985b) *Recodings: Art, Spectacle, Cultural Politics*. Seattle: Bay Press.

Foster, R. J. (1991) "Making National Cultures in the Global Ecumene," *Annual Review of Anthropology* 20: 235–260.

Foucault, Michel (1980) *History of Sexuality, Vol. 1: An Introduction.* Robert Hurley, trans. New York: Vintage.

———— (1984) "What Is an Author?," in Paul Rabinow, ed. *The Foucault Reader.* New York: Pantheon, pp. 101–120.

Fox, David L. (1995) "'What's This I See, She's Walking Back to Me . . . Oh, Pretty Woman!' 2 Live Crew Leads Us Back toward Greater Clarity and Predictability in the Doctrine of Copyright Fair Use," *Loyola Law Review* 40(4): 923–953.

Fox, Harold G. (1972) *The Canadian Law of Trademarks and Unfair Competition.* Toronto: Carswell.

Fox, Richard J., ed. (1991a) *Recapturing Anthropology: Working in the Present.* Santa Fe, NM: School of American Research Press.

———— (1991b) "Introduction: Working in the Present," in R. J. Fox (1991a), pp. 1–16.

Francis, Daniel (1994) *The Imaginary Indian: The Image of the Indian in Canadian Culture.* Vancouver: Arsenal Pulp Press.

Frank, Patricia B. (1994) Note: "White v. Samsung Electronics America Inc.: The Right of Publicity Spins Its Wheels," *Ohio State Law Journal* 55: 1115–1142.

Frankenberg, Ruth (1992) *The Social Construction of Whiteness.* Minneapolis: University of Minnesota Press.

———— and Mani, Lata (1996) "Crosscurrents, Crosstalk: Race, 'Postcoloniality' and the Politics of Location," in Smadar Lavie and Ted Swedenburg, eds., *Displacement, Diaspora and the Geographies of Identity.* Durham, NC: Duke University Press, pp. 273–293.

Fraser, Nancy (1993) "Rethinking the Public Sphere: A Contribution to the Critique of Actually Existing Democracy," in Robbins, pp. 1–32.

Friedman, Jonathan (1991) "Consuming Desires: Strategies of Selfhood and Appropriation," *Cultural Anthropology* 6: 154–163.

———— (1992) "Narcissism, Roots and Postmodernity: The Constitution of Selfhood in the Global Crisis," in Lash and Friedman (1992), pp. 331–366.

Friedman, Monroe (1985) "The Changing Language of a Consumer Society: Brand Name Usage in Popular American Novels in the Postwar Era," *Journal of Consumer Research* 11: 927–938.

Frisch, R. (1991) "New Technologies on the Block," *Cardozo Arts & Entertainment Law Journal* 10: 51.

Frobel, Heinrichs (1980) *The New International Division of Labor.* Cambridge: Cambridge University Press.

Frohmann, Lisa and Mertz, Elizabeth (1994) "Legal Reform and Social Construction: Violence, Gender, and the Law," *Law and Social Inquiry* 19: 829–852.

Frug, Gerald E. (1984) "The Ideology of Bureaucracy in American Law," *Harvard Law Review* 97: 1276–1388.

Frug, Mary Joe (1988) "Sexual Equality and Sexual Difference in American Law," talk presented at the Symposium on Sexual Equality, Sexual Difference and Law, West Virginia University College of Law, Morgantown, WV 8 April.

———— (1991) "Law and Postmodernism: The Politics of a Marriage," *University of Colorado Law Review* 62: 483–488.

———— (1992a) "A Postmodern Feminist Legal Manifesto (An Unfinished Draft)," *Harvard Law Review*, 105: 1045–1075.

———— (1992b) *Postmodern Legal Feminism.* New York: Routledge, Chapman and Hall.

———— (1992c) "Progressive Feminist Legal Scholarship: Can We Claim 'A Different Voice?,'" *Harvard Women's Law Journal* 15: 37–64.

Fynsk, Christopher (1991) "Foreword: Experiences of Finitude," in Nancy (1991), pp. vii–xxxv.

Gaines, Jane (1991) *Contested Culture: The Image, the Voice, and the Law.* Chapel Hill, NC: University of North Carolina Press.

———— (1993) "Bette Midler and the Piracy of Identity," in Simon Frith, ed. *Copyright and Music.* Edinburgh: Edinburgh University Press.

Gardiner, Michael (1992) *The Dialogics of Critique: M. M. Bakhtin and the Theory of Ideology.* London: Routledge.

Garnham, Nicholas (1993) "The Mass Media, Cultural Identity, and the Public Sphere in the Modern World," *Public Culture* 5: 251–265.

Gates, Henry Louis, Jr. (1988) *The Signifying Monkey: A Theory of African-American Literary Criticism.* Oxford: Oxford University Press.

Gauthier, Tammi A. (1994) "Fun and Profit: When Commercial Parodies Constitute Copyright or Trademark Infringement," *Pepperdine Law Review* 21: 165–205.

Geertz, Clifford (1983) *Local Knowledge: Further Essays in Interpretive Anthropology.* New York: Basic Books.

———— (1984) "Anti-Anti-Relativism," *American Anthropologist* 86(2): 263–279.

———— (1988) *Works and Lives: The Anthropologist as Author.* Stanford, CA: Stanford University Press.

Geller, Paul Edward (1994) "Must Copyright Be For Ever Caught Between Marketplace and Authorship Norms?," in Brad Sherman and Alain Strowel, eds., *Of Authors and Origins.* Oxford: Oxford University Press, pp. 159–202.

Gellman, Robert M. (1995) "Twin Evils: Government Copyright and Copyright-like Controls over Government Information," *Syracuse Law Review* 45: 999–1072.

George, Diana and Sanders, Susan (1995) "Reconstructing Tonto: Cultural Formations and American Indians in 1990's Television Fiction," *Cultural Studies* 9(3): 427–452.

Gewertz, Deborah B. and Errington, Frederick K. (1991) *Twisted Histories, Altered Contexts: Representing Chambri in a World System.* Cambridge: Cambridge University Press.

———— (1993) "First Contact with God: Individualism, Agency, and Revivalism in the Duke of York Islands," *Cultural Anthropology* 8(3): 279–305.

———— (1996) "On Pepsico and Piety in a Papua New Guinea 'Modernity,'" *American Ethnologist* 23: 476–493.

Giffin, Mary (n.d.) "The Disappearing Woman Writer and the Gendering of the Idea of Authorship." Unpublished manuscript.

Gilbert, Sandra and Gubar, Susan (1979) *The Madwoman in the Attic.* New Haven, CT: Yale University Press.

Gilroy, Paul (1993) *The Black Atlantic: Modernity and Double Consciousness.* Cambridge, MA: Harvard University Press.

———— (1994) "'After the Love Has Gone': Bio-Politics and Etho-Poetics in the Black Public Sphere," *Public Culture* 7: 49–76.

Gilson, Jerome (1974) *Trademark Protection and Practice.* New York: Mathew Bender.

Ginsburg, Jane C., Goldberg, David and Greenbaum, Arthur J. (1991) *Trademark and Unfair Competition Law: Cases and Materials.* Charlottesville, VA: Mitchie Company.

Ginsburg, Jane C. and Litman, Jessica (1993) *Trademark and Unfair Competition Law: Cases and Materials. 1993 Cumulative Supplement.* Charlottesville, VA: Mitchie Company.

Godard, Barbara Thomson (1985) *Talking about Ourselves: The Literary Productions of Native Women of Canada.* Ottawa: Criaw/Icref.

——— (1990) "The Politics of Representation: Some Native Canadian Women Writers," in W. H. New, ed. *Native Writers and Canadian Writing*. Vancouver: University of British Columbia Press, pp. 183–225.

Goldberg, David Theo, ed. (1994) *Multiculturalism: A Critical Reader*. London: Basil Blackwell.

Golding, Sue (1988) "James Dean: The Almost-Perfect Lesbian Hermaphrodite," in Dionne Brand, ed. *Sight Specific: Lesbians and Representation*. Toronto: A Space, pp. 49–52.

——— (1992) *Gramsci's Democratic Theory: Contributions to a Post-Liberal Democracy*. Toronto: University of Toronto Press.

Goldman, Lee (1992) "Elvis Is Alive, but He Shouldn't Be: The Right of Publicity Revisited," *Brigham Young University Law Review* [1992]: 597–628.

Golwag, Celia (1979) "Copyright Infringement and the First Amendment," *Columbia Law Review* 79: 320–340.

Gomery, Douglas (1994) "Disney's Business History: A Reinterpretation," in Smoodin (1994a), pp. 71–86.

Goodman, Nelson (1978) *Ways of Worldmaking*. Hassocks: Harvester Press.

Gordon, Harold (1960) "Right of Property in Name, Likeness, Personality and History," *Northwestern University Law Review* 55: 553–613.

Gordon, Robert W. (1984) "Critical Legal Histories," *Stanford Law Review* 36: 57–125.

Gordon, Wendy (1989) "An Inquiry into the Merits of Copyright: The Challenges of Consistency, Consent, and Encouragement Theory," *Stanford Law Review* 41: 1343–1469.

——— (1990) "Toward a Jurisprudence of Benefits: The Norms of Copyright and the Problem of Private Censorship," *University of Chicago Law Review* 57: 1009–1049.

——— (1992a) "On Owning Information: Intellectual Property and the Restitutionary Impulse," *Virginia Law Review* 78: 149–281.

——— (1992b) "Reality as Artifact: From *Feist* to Fair Use," *Law & Contemporary Problems* 55: 93–106.

——— (1993) "A Property Right in Self-Expression: Equality and Individualism in the Law of Intellectual Property," *Yale Law Journal* 102: 1533–1609.

Gottlieb, Alma (1992) *Under the Kapok Tree: Identity and Difference in Beng Thought*. Bloomington: University of Indiana Press.

Gramsci, Antonio (1971) *Prison Notebooks*. New York: International Publishers.

Greenawalt, Kent (1990) "Insults and Epithets: Are They Protected Speech?," *Rutgers Law Review* 42: 287–307.

Greenberg, Judi, Minow, Martha and Schneider, Elizabeth (1992) "Contradiction and Revision: Progressive Feminist Legal Scholars Respond to Mary Joe Frug," *Harvard Women's Law Journal* 15: 65–77.

Greenberg, Lynne A. (1992) "Art of Appropriation: Puppies, Piracy, and Post-Modernism," *Cardozo Arts & Entertainment Law Journal* 10: 1–33.

Greenhouse, Carol J. (1995) "Constructive Approaches to Law, Culture, and Identity," *Law & Society Review* 28: 1231–1241.

Gregory, Steven (1994) "Race, Identity, and Political Activism: The Shifting Contours of the African American Public Sphere," *Public Culture* 7: 147–185.

——— (1995) Untitled contribution to "Race and Racism: A Symposium," *Social Text* 42: 16.

Grider, Sylvia Ann (1973) "Con Safos: Mexican-American Names and Graffiti," *American Journal of Folklore* 83: 132–142.

Grieg, Noel and Griffiths, Drew (1981) *As Time Goes By*. London: Gay Men's Press.

Griffin, Mary (1993) *The Disappearing Woman Writer and the Gendering of the Idea of Authorship*, paper presented at Cultural Agency/Cultural Authority: Politics and Poetics of Intellectual Property in a Postcolonial Era, Bellagio, 8–12 March.

Griffith, Gareth (1987) "Imitation, Abrogation, and Appropriation: The Production of the Post-Colonial Text," *Kunapipi* 9: 13–20.

Griggers, Catherine (1993) "Lesbian Bodies in the Age of (Post)Mechanical Reproduction," in Warner (1993a), pp. 178–192.

Gross, Joan (1982) "The Right of Publicity Revisited: Reconciling Fame, Fortune, and Constitutional Rights," *Boston University Law Review* 62: 965–1001.

Grossberg, Lawrence (1988) "Putting the Pop Back into Postmodernism," in Ross (1988), pp. 167–190.

Grosz, Elizabeth (1990) *Jacques Lacan: A Feminist Analysis*. New York: Routledge, Chapman and Hall.

Gupta, Ahkil (1997) "The Song of the Nonaligned World: Transnational Identities and the Reinscription of Space in Late Capitalism," in Gupta and Ferguson (1997b), pp. 179–202.

———— and Ferguson, James (1997a) "Beyond Culture: Space, Identity, and the Politics of Difference," in Gupta and Ferguson (1997b), pp. 33–51.

————, eds. (1997b) *Culture, Power, Place: Explorations in Critical Anthropology*. Durham, NC: Duke University Press.

———— (1997c) *Anthropological Locations: Boundaries and Grounds of a Field Science*. Durham, NC: Duke University Press.

Haas, Theodore F. (1986) "Storehouse of Starlight: The First Amendment Privilege to Use Names and Likenesses in Commercial Advertising," *University of California Law Review* 19: 539–595.

Habermas, Jürgen (1984) *The Theory of Communicative Action, Vol. 1: Reason and the Rationalization of Society*. Boston: Beacon Press.

———— (1988) *The Theory of Communicative Action, Vol. 2: Lifeworld and System: A Critique of Functionalist Reason*. Boston: Beacon Press.

———— (1992) *The Structural Transformation of the Public Sphere: An Inquiry into a Category of Bourgeois Society*. Thomas Berger and Frederick Lawrence, trans. Cambridge, MA: MIT Press.

———— (1996a) *Between Facts and Norms: Contributions to a Discourse Theory of Law and Democracy*. Cambridge, MA: MIT Press.

———— (1996b) "Three Normative Models of Democracy," in Seyla Benhabib ed., *Democracy and Difference: Contesting the Boundaries of the Political*. Princeton: Princeton University Press, pp. 21–31.

Hachivi, Edgar Heap of Birds (1991/92) Untitled contribution, *Borderlines* 23: 19.

Halpern, Sheldon W. (1995) "The Right of Publicity: Maturation of an Independent Right Protecting the Associative Value of Personality," *Hastings Law Journal* 46: 853–873.

Hammond, Joyce (1988) "Visualizing Themselves: Tongan Videography in Utah," *Visual Anthropology* 1: 379–400.

Handler, Richard (1985) "On Having a Culture: Nationalism and the Preservation of Quebec's Patrimoine," in Stocking (1985), pp. 192–217.

———— (1991) "Who Owns the Past? History, Cultural Property, and the Logic of Possessive Individualism" in B. Williams (1991b), pp. 63–74.

Haney Lopez, Ian (1996) *White by Law: The Legal Construction of Race*. New York: New York University Press.

Hannerz, Ulf (1989) "Notes on the Global Ecumene," *Public Culture* 1(2): 66–75.

———— (1992) *Cultural Complexity: Studies in the Social Organization of Meaning.* New York: Columbia University Press.

———— and Lofgren, Orvar (1993) "Defining the National: An Introduction," *Ethnos* 58 (3–4): 157–160.

Hansen, Miriam (1993) "Unstable Mixtures, Dilated Spheres: Negt and Kluge's *The Public Sphere and Experience*, Twenty Years Later," *Public Culture* 5: 179–212.

Hardt, Michael (1995) "The Withering of Civil Society," *Social Text* 45: 27–44.

Harrington, Christine and Yngvesson, Barbara (1990) "Interpretive Social Research," *Law and Social Inquiry* 15: 135–148.

Harris, Angela (1990) "Race and Essentialism in Feminist Legal Theory." *Stanford Law Review* 42: 584.

Harris, Cheryl (1993) "Whiteness as Property," *Harvard Law Review* 106: 1709–1791.

Harrison, T. (1992) *Elvis People: The Cult of the King.* London: Harper Collins.

Harvey, David (1989) *The Condition of Postmodernity: An Enquiry into the Origins of Cultural Change.* Oxford: Basil Blackwell.

Hayden, Robert (1994) "When Woodchips Become Shrapnel: The Reifications of 'Culture' by Law," *Law and Social Inquiry* 19: 243–252.

Heald, P. J. (1996) "Trademarks and Geographical Indications: Exploring Contours of the TRIPS Agreement," *Vanderbilt Journal of Transnational Law* 29: 635.

Hebdige, Dick (1987) *Cut 'n' Mix: Culture, Identity and Caribbean Music.* London: Methuen.

Heberer, William M. (1994) Comment: "The Overprotection of Celebrity: A Comment on White v. Samsung Electronics America, Inc.," *Hofstra Law Review* 22: 729–772.

Hegeman, Susan (1991) "Shopping for Identities: 'A Nation of Nations' and the Weak Ethnicity of Objects," *Public Culture* 3(2): 71–92.

Heiferman, Marvin and Phillips, Lisa (1989) *Image World: Art and Media Culture.* New York: Whitney Museum of American Art.

Heinze, Andrew R. (1990) *Adapting to Abundance: Jewish Immigrants, Mass Consumption, and the Search for American Identity.* New York: Columbia University Press.

Helfand, Michael Todd (1992) "When Mickey Mouse Is as Strong as Superman: The Convergence of Intellectual Property Laws to Protect Fictional Literary and Pictorial Characters," *Stanford Law Review* 44: 623–674.

Henderson, Gordon F. (1991) *Intellectual Property: Litigation, Legislation, and Education.* Ottawa: Government of Canada, Department of Consumer and Corporate Affairs.

Herrera, Jessica R. (1994) "Not Even His Name: Is the Denigration of Crazy Horse Custer's Final Revenge?," *Harvard Civil Rights–Civil Liberties Law Review* 29: 175–195.

Herzfeld, Michael (1989) *Anthropology through the Looking-Glass: Critical Ethnography in the Margins of Europe.* Cambridge: Cambridge University Press.

Hetherington, H. Lee (1992) "Direct Commercial Exploitation of Identity: A New Age for the Right of Publicity," *Columbia-VLA Journal of Law and the Arts* 17: 1–49.

Hettinger, Edwin C. (1989) "Justifying Intellectual Property," *Philosophy & Public Affairs* 18: 31–52.

Hill, Richard (1992) "One Part per Million: White Appropriation and Native Voices," *Fuse* 15(6): 12–22.

Hinkson, John (1990) "Postmodernism and Structural Change," *Public Culture* 2: 82–101.

Hirsch, Susan F. (1995) "Interpreting Media Representations of a 'Night of Madness': Law and Culture in the Construction of Rape Identities," *Law and Social Inquiry* 19: 1023–1056.

——— and Lazarus-Black, Mindie (1994) "Introduction: Performance and Paradox: Exploring Law's Role in Hegemony and Resistance," in Lazarus-Black and Hirsch (1994), pp. 1–34.

Hirschkind, Lynn (1994) "Bedevilled Ethnography," *American Ethnologist* 21(1): 201–204.

Hirschkop, Ken (1989) "Introduction: Bakhtin and Cultural Theory," in Hirschkop and Shepherd (1989), pp. 1–38.

——— and Shepherd, D., eds. (1989) *Bakhtin and Cultural Theory.* Manchester: Manchester University Press.

Hoban, R. (1988) *The Medusa Frequency.* New York: Summit Books.

Hobsbawn, Eric and Ranger, Terence, eds. (1983) *The Invention of Tradition.* Cambridge: Cambridge University Press.

Hodge, Robert and Kress, Gunther (1988) *Social Semiotics.* Ithaca: Cornell University Press.

Hoffman, Steven J. (1980) "Limitations on the Right of Publicity," *Bulletin of the Copyright Society* 28: 111–145.

Hollister, Paul (1994) "Genius at Work: Walt Disney," in Smoodin (1994a), pp. 23–41.

Holquist, Michael (1990) *Dialogism: Bakhtin and His World.* New York: Routledge.

hooks, bell (1990) *Yearning: Race, Gender and Cultural Politics.* Toronto: Between the Lines Press.

——— (1992) *Black Looks: Race and Representation.* Boston: South End Press.

Horowitz, Morton (1988) "Rights," *Harvard Civil Rights–Civil Liberties Law Review* 23: 393–406.

Houdek, Frank (1985) "The Right of Publicity: A Comprehensive Bibliography of Law-Related Material," *Hastings Communications and Entertainment Law Journal* 7: 505–525.

——— (1994) "Researching the Right of Publicity: A Revised and Comprehensive Bibliography of Law Related Materials," *Hastings Communications and Entertainment Law Journal* 16: 385–423.

Howell, Robert G. (1986) "The Common Law Appropriation of Personality Tort," *Intellectual Property Journal* 2: 149–200.

——— (1991) "Character Merchandising: The Marketing Potential Attaching to a Name, Image, Persona, or Copyright Work," *Intellectual Property Journal* 6: 197–223.

——— (1992) *Recent Developments in Character Merchandising: Ewoks, Crocodile Dundee in Ontario and Ninja Turtles in the United Kingdom,* paper presented at the Candian Association of Law Teachers Intellectual Property Section, Charlottetown, P.E.I., 3–6 June.

Howes, David, ed. (1996) *Cross-Cultural Consumption: Global Markets, Local Realities.* New York: Routledge.

Hughes, Justin (1988) "The Philosophy of Intellectual Property," *Georgetown Law Journal* 77: 287–366.

Hughes, Roger (1992) *Hughes on Trademarks.* Toronto: Butterworths.

Hunt, Alan (1993) *Explorations in Law and Society: Toward a Constitutive Theory of Law.* New York: Routledge.

Hutcheon, Lynda (1989a) "Circling the Downspout of Empire: Post-Colonialism and Postmodernism," *Ariel* 20(4): 149–175.

——— (1989b) *The Politics of Postmodernism.* London: Routledge, Chapman and Hall.

Hutchinson, Alan (1989) "Talking the Good Life: From Free Speech to Democratic Dialogue," *Yale Journal of Law and Liberation* 1: 17–30.

Hyland, John F. and Linquist, Ted C., III (1993) "White v. Samsung Electronics America, Inc.: The Wheels of Justice Take an Unfortunate Turn," *Golden Gate University Law Review* 23: 299–338.

Jackson, Richard (1990) *Modernist and Postmodernist Inscriptions of Camp*. Paper presented at the Popular Culture meetings, 7–10 March.

Jacobson, Michael F. and Mazur, Laurie Ann (1995) *Marketing Madness: A Survival Guide for a Consumer Society*. Boulder, CO: Westview Press.

Jameson, Fredric (1981) *The Prisonhouse of Language: Narrative as a Socially Symbolic Act*. Ithaca: Cornell University Press.

——— (1984) "Postmodernism or the Cultural Logic of Late Capitalism," *New Left Review* 146: 53.

——— (1991) *Postmodernism, or, The Cultural Logic of Late Capitalism*. Durham, NC: Duke University Press.

Jaszi, Peter (1991) "Towards a Theory of Copyright: The Metamorphoses of 'Authorship,'" *Duke Law Journal* [1991]: 455–502.

——— (1992) "On the Author Effect: Contemporary Copyright and Collective Creativity," *Cardozo Arts & Entertainment Law Journal* 10: 293–320, reprinted in Woodmansee and Jaszi (1994), pp. 29–56.

——— (1996) "Goodbye to All That—A Reluctant (and Perhaps Premature) Adieu to a Constitutionally-Grounded Discourse of Public Interest in Copyright Law," *Vanderbilt Journal of Transnational Law* 29: 595–611.

——— (1996) "Caught in the Net of Copyright," *Oregon Law Review* 75: 299–308.

Jay, Martin (1993) "Unsympathetic Magic," *Visual Anthropology Review* 9(2): 79.

Jenkins, Henry, III (1988) "Star Trek Rerun, Reread, Rewritten: Fan Writing as Textual Poaching," *Critical Studies in Mass Communication* 5: 85–107.

——— (1992a) "'Strangers No More, We Sing': Filking and the Social Construction of the Science Fiction Fan Community," in L. A. Lewis (1992a), pp. 208–236.

——— (1992b) *Textual Poachers: Television Fans and Participatory Culture*. New York: Routledge, Chapman and Hall.

Jhally, Sut (1993) "Commercial Culture, Collective Values and the Future," *Texas Law Review* 71: 805–814.

Johnson, Barbara (1992) "The Postmodern in Feminism," *Harvard Law Review* 105: 1076–1083.

Johnson, Richard (1987) "What Is Cultural Studies Anyway?," *Social Text* 16: 38–80.

Jowett, Garth (1982) "The Emergence of Mass Society: The Standardization of American Culture 1830–1920," *Prospects* 7: 207–228.

Judovitz, Dalia (1995) *Unpacking Duchamp: Art in Transit*. Berkeley: University of California Press.

Jules-Rosette, Benetta (1990a) "Simulations of Postmodernity: Images of Technology in African Tourist and Popular Art," *Society for Visual Anthropology Review* 6: 29–37.

——— (1990b) *Terminal Signs: Computers and Social Change in Africa*. New York: Mouton.

Just, Peter (1992) "History, Power, Ideology, and Culture: Current Directions in the Anthropology of Law," *Law & Society Review* 26(2): 373–411.

Kahn, Ely. (1960) *The Big Drink: The Story of Coca-Cola*. New York: Random House.

Kairys, David (1982) "Freedom of Speech," in David Kairys, ed. *The Politics of Law: A Progressive Critique*. New York: Pantheon, pp. 237–272.

—— (1993) *With Liberty and Justice for Some: A Critique of the Conservative Supreme Court*. New York: New Press.

Kamuf, Peggy (1988) *Signature Pieces: On the Institution of Authorship*. Ithaca: Cornell University Press.

Kaplan, Benjamin (1967) *An Unhurried View of Copyright*. New York: Columbia University Press.

Karjala, Dennis S. (1992) "Copyright and Misappropriation," *University of Dayton Law Review* 17: 885–928.

Kearney, Michael (1996) *Reconceptualizing the Peasantry: Anthropology in Global Perspective*. Boulder, CO: Westview Press.

Kearney, Richard (1988) *The Wake of Imagination*. Minneapolis: University of Minnesota Press.

Keesing, Roger (1992) *Custom and Confrontation: The Kwaio Struggle for Cultural Autonomy*. Chicago: University of Chicago Press.

Kelber, Bruce C. (1994) "'Scalping the Redskins': Can Trademark Law Start Athletic Teams Bearing Native American Nicknames and Images on the Road to Racial Reform?," *Hamline Law Review* 17: 533–588.

Keller, Bruce and Bernstein, David (1995) "As Satiric as They Wanna Be: Parody Lawsuits under Copyright, Trademark, Dilution and Publicity Laws," *Trademark Reporter* 85: 239–262.

Kellner, Douglas (1988) "Postmodernism as Social Theory: Some Challenges and Problems," *Theory, Culture and Society* 5: 239–69.

—— (1989) *Jean Baudrillard: From Marxism to Postmodernism and Beyond*. Stanford: Stanford University Press.

—— (1992) "Popular Culture and the Construction of Postmodern Identities," in Lash and Friedman (1992), pp. 141–177.

Kelly, Daniel R. and Hartmann, Michael E. (1995) "Parody (of Celebrities, in Advertising), Parity (between Advertising and Other Types of Commercial Speech), and (the Property Right of) Publicity," *Hastings Communications & Entertainment Law Journal* 17: 633–698.

Keohane, Kieran (1992) "Symptoms of Canada: National Identity and the Theft of National Enjoyment," *Cineaction* 28: 20–33.

Kernan, Alvin (1990) *The Death of Literature*. New Haven, CT: Yale University Press.

Kester, Grant H. (1993) "Out of Sight Is Out of Mind: The Imaginary Space of Postindustrial Culture," *Social Text* 35: 72–92.

Knox, Paul L. and Taylor, Peter, eds. (1995) *World Cities in a World System*. Cambridge: Cambridge University Press.

Koenig, Dorean M. (1994) "Joe Camel and the First Amendment: The Dark Side of Copyrighted and Trademark-Protected Icons," *Thomas M. Cooley Law Review* 11: 803–838.

Koptiuch, Kristin (1996) "Cultural Defense and Criminological Displacements: Gender, Race, and (Trans)Nation in the Legal Surveillance of U.S. Diaspora Asians," In Smadar Lavie and Ted Swedenburg, eds., *Displacement, Diaspora and Geographies of Identity*. Durham, NC: Duke University Press, pp. 215–234.

—— (1997) "Third-Worlding at Home: Transforming New Frontiers in the Urban U.S.," in Gupta and Ferguson (1997b), pp. 234–248.

Kozinski, Alex (1993) "Trademarks Unplugged," *New York University Law Review* 68: 960–978.

——— (1994) "Mickey and Me," *University of Miami Entertainment & Sports Law Review* 11: 465.

——— and Volokh, Eugene (1993) "Lawsuit, Shmawsuit," *Yale Law Journal* 103: 463–467.

Krauss, Rosalind E. (1985) *The Originality of the Avante Garde and Other Modernist Myths*. Cambridge, MA: MIT Press.

Kravitz, Robert N. (1989) "Trademarks, Speech, and the *Gay Olympics* Case," *Boston University Law Review* 69: 131–184.

Krentz, Jayne Ann, ed. (1993) *Dangerous Men and Adventurous Women: Romance Writers on the Appeal of the Romance*. Philadelphia: University of Pennsylvania Press.

Kulzick, Kenneth E. and Hogue, Amy D. (1980) "Chilled Bird: Freedom of Expression in the Eighties," *Loyola of Los Angeles Law Review* 14: 57–78.

Kumar, Krishan (1995) *From Post-Industrial to Post-Modern Society: New Theories of the Contemporary World*. Oxford: Basil Blackwell.

Kurtz, L. (1994) "The Methuselah Factor: When Characters Outlive Their Copyrights," *University of Miami Entertainment & Sports Law Review* 11: 437–452.

Kwall, Roberta R. (1984) "Is Independence Day Dawning for the Right of Publicity?," *University of California-Davis Law Review* 17: 191–255.

——— (1989) "Governmental Use of Copyrighted Property: The Sovereign's Prerogative," *Texas Law Review* 67: 685–780.

——— (1994) "The Right of Publicity vs. the First Amendment: A Property and Liability Rule Analysis," *Indiana Law Journal* 70: 47–118.

Laclau, Ernesto (1993) "Power and Representation," in Mark Poster, ed. *Politics, Theory, and Contemporary Culture*. New York: Columbia University Press, pp. 277–296.

———, ed. (1994) *The Making of Political Identities*. London: Verso.

——— (1996) *Emancipation(s)*. London: Verso.

——— and Mouffe, Chantal (1985) *Hegemony and Socialist Strategy: Towards a Radical Democratic Politics*. London: Verso Books.

——— (1987) "PostMarxism without Apologies," *New Left Review* 166: 79–106.

Lacoue-Labarthe, Philippe (1989) "Transcendence Ends in Politics," in *Typography: Mimesis, Philosophy, Politics*. Cambridge, MA: Harvard University Press.

——— (1990) *Heidegger, Art and Politics: The Fiction of the Political*. Chris Turner, trans. London: Basil Blackwell.

La Duke, Winona (1991–92) "The Culture of Hydroelectric Power," *Borderlines* 23: 42–43.

Landes, Joan B. (1996) "The Performance of Citizenship: Democracy, Gender, and Difference in the French Revolution," in Seyla Benhabib, ed., *Democracy and Difference: Contesting the Boundaries of the Political*. Princeton: Princeton University Press, pp. 295–313.

Lange, David (1981) "Recognizing the Public Domain," *Law and Contemporary Problems* 44(4): 147–178.

——— (1992) "At Play in the Fields of the Word: Copyright and the Construction of Authorship in the Post-Literate Millennium," *Law and Contemporary Problems* 55: 139–151.

Langvardt, Arlen (1993) "Trademark Rights and First Amendment Wrongs: Protecting the Former without Committing the Latter," *Trademark Reporter* 83: 633–660.

Lansing, J. S. (1991) *Priests and Programmers: Technologies of Power in the Engineered Landscape of Bali*. Princeton: Princeton University Press.

Lash, Scott (1990) *Sociology of Postmodernism*. London: Routledge, Chapman and Hall.

———— and Friedman, Jonathan, eds. (1992) *Modernity and Identity*. Oxford: Basil Blackwell.

Latham, R. Brant (1985) "Explosion of Section 9(1)(n) Notices," *Patent and Trademark Institute of Canada Review* [1985]: 74–93.

La Valley, Al (1985) "The Great Escape," *American Film* 10(6): 29–34, 70–71.

Lawrence, Charles R., III (1990) "If He Hollers Let Him Go: Regulating Racist Speech on Campus," *Duke Law Journal* [1990]: 431–483.

Lawrence, Lisa (1987) "The Right of Publicity: A Research Guide," *Hastings Communications and Entertainment Law Journal* 10: 143–389.

Lazarus, Neil (1991) "Doubting the New World Order: Marxism, Realism, and the Claims of Postmodernist Social Theory," *Differences* 3(3): 94–138.

Lazarus-Black, Mindie and Susan Hirsch, eds. (1994) *Contested States: Law, Hegemony and Resistance*. New York: Routledge.

Leach, Edmund (1977) *Custom, Law and Terrorist Violence*. Edinburgh: Edinburgh University Press.

Leaffer, M. (1994) "Character Merchandising in the U.K., A Nostalgic Look," *University of Miami Entertainment & Sports Law Review* 11: 453–464.

Lears, T. Jackson (1994) *Fables of Abundance: A Cultural History of Advertising in America*. New York: Basic Books.

LeClair, T. (1988) Review of R. Hoban's *The Medusa Frequency. American Review of Books* 10(4): 4–5.

Lederman, Rena (1989) "Contested Order: Gender and Society in the Southern New Guinea Highlands," *American Ethnologist* 16: 230–247.

Lee, Benjamin (1993) "Going Public," *Public Culture* 5: 165–178.

Lees, Sue (1993) "Lawyers' Work as Constitutive of Gender Relations," in Cain and Harrington (1993), pp. 124–154.

LeFevre, Karen Burke (1992) "The Tell-Tale Heart: Determining 'Fair' Use of Unpublished Texts," *Law & Contemporary Problems* 55: 153–183.

Lefort, Claude (1988) *Democracy and Political Theory*. David Macey, trans. Cambridge: Polity Press.

Leonard, Jerry D., ed. (1995) *Legal Studies as Cultural Studies: A Reader in (Post)Modern Critical Theory*. Albany: State University of New York.

Leval, Pierre (1989) "Fair Use or Foul? The Nineteenth Donald C. Brace Memorial Lecture," *Journal of the Copyright Society* 36: 167–181.

———— (1990) "Toward a Fair Use Standard," *Harvard Law Review* 103: 1105–1136.

Lévi-Strauss, Claude (1985) "New York in 1941," in *The View from Afar*. New York: Basic Books, pp. 258–268.

Levinson, Marjorie et al., eds. (1989) *Rethinking Historicism: Critical Readings in Romantic History*. London: Basil Blackwell.

Levy, Sidney J. (1989) *Product and Brand Symbol Systems*, paper presented at The Marketing of Meaning: Toward a Better Understanding of Business Signs and Symbols, eleventh annual Summer Institute for Semiotic and Structural Studies, Indiana University–Purdue University at Indianapolis, 16–21 July. Proceedings available on cassette.

Lewis, Jon (1994) "Disney after Disney: Family Business and the Business of Family," in Smoodin (1994a), pp. 87–105.

Lewis, Lisa A., ed. (1992a) *The Adoring Audience: Fan Culture and Popular Media*. New York: Routledge, Chapman and Hall.

———— (1992b) Introduction, in L. A. Lewis (1992a), pp. 1–8.

Lifer, E. and Rogers, M. (1995) "NII White Paper Has Libraries Concerned About Copyright," *Library Journal News* 12 (October).

Limon, Jose E. (1994) "Dancing with the Devil: Society, Gender, and the Political Unconscious in Mexican-American South Texas," in Hector Calderon and Jose David Saldivar, eds. *Criticism in the Borderlands: Studies in Chicano Literature, Culture and Ideology*. Durham, NC: Duke University Press, pp. 221–259.

Lind, Christopher (1991) "The Idea of Capitalism or the Capitalism of Ideas? A Moral Critique of the Copyright Act," *Intellectual Property Journal* 7: 65–74.

Lipsitz, George (1990) *Time Passages: Collective Memory and American Popular Culture*. Minneapolis: University of Minnesota Press.

Litman, Jessica (1990) "The Public Domain," *Emory Law Journal* 39: 965–1023.

——— (1991) "Copyright as Myth," *University of Pittsburgh Law Review* 53: 235–249.

——— (1992) "Copyright and Information Policy," *Law & Contemporary Problems* 55: 185–209.

——— (1994a) "The Exclusive Right to Read," *Cardozo Arts and Entertainment Law Journal* 13: 29–54.

——— (1994b) "Mickey Mouse Emeritus: Character Protection and the Public Domain," *University of Miami Entertainment and Sports Law Review* 11: 429–436.

——— (1996) "Revising Copyright Law for the Information Age," *Oregon Law Review* 75: 19–48.

Locke, John (1978) *Second Treatise of Government* [1690]. New York: Wm. B. Eerdmans Publishing Co.

Lofgren, Orvar (1993) "Materializing the Nation in Sweden and America," *Ethnos* 58(3–4): 161–196.

Logan, Jim (1992) Untitled contribution in McMaster and Martin (1992a), pp. 142–147.

"Look Up in the Sky: It's the Flying Elvises, er, Elvi" (1995) *National Law Journal*, 17 April, p. A27.

Lord, M. G. (1994) *Forever Barbie: The Unauthorized Biography of a Real Doll*. New York: Avon Books.

Lott, Eric (1993) *Love and Theft: Blackface Minstrelsy and the American Working Class*. Oxford: Oxford University Press.

Lovell, Terry (1987) *Consuming Fiction*. London: Verso.

Loving, Paul E. (1992) "Native American Team Names in Athletics: It's Time to Trade These Marks," *Loyola of Los Angeles Entertainment Law Journal* 13: 1–44.

Lury, Celia (1993) *Cultural Rights: Technology, Legality and Personality*. London: Routledge, Chapman and Hall.

Lyotard, Jean-François (1984) *The Postmodern Condition: A Report on Knowledge*. Geoff Bennington and Brian Massumi, trans. Minneapolis: University of Minnesota Press.

——— (1992) *Explaining the Postmodern*. Minneapolis: University of Minnesota Press.

——— (1993) *The Postmodern Explained: Correspondence, 1982–1985*. Julian Pefanis and Morgan Thomas, eds. Don Barry et al., trans. Minneapolis: University of Minnesota Press.

MacCannell, Dean (1987) "Marilyn Monroe Was Not a Man," *Diacritics* 17: 114–127.

Macdonald, Bradley (1988) "Towards a Redemption of Politics," *Strategies* 1: 5–9.

MacDougall, David (1991) "Whose Story Is It?," *Visual Anthropology Review* 7(2): 2–10.

Mackey, Eva (1995) "Postmodernism and Cultural Politics in the Multicultural Nation: Contests over Truth in the *Into the Heart of Africa* Controversy," *Public Culture* 7(2): 403–432.

Macklem, Patrick (1991) "First Nations Self-Government and the Borders of the Canadian Legal Imagination," *McGill Law Journal* 36: 382–456.

——— (1993) "Distributing Sovereignty: Indian Nations and Equality of Peoples," *Stanford Law Review* 45: 1311–1367.

Macpherson, C. B. (1962) *The Political Theory of Possessive Individualism: Hobbes to Locke.* Oxford: Oxford University Press.

Madow, Michael (1993) "Private Ownership and Public Image: Popular Cuture and Publicity Rights," *California Law Review* 81: 127–240.

Manganaro, Marc, ed. (1990a) *Modernist Anthropology: From Fieldwork to Text.* Princeton, NJ: Princeton University Press.

——— (1990b) "Textual Play, Power, and Cultural Critique: An Orientation to Modernist Anthropology," in Manganaro (1990a), pp. 3–50.

Maracle, Lee (1989) "Native Myths: Trickster Alive and Crowing," *Fuse* (fall), pp. 29–31.

Marcus, George (1986) "Contemporary Problems of Ethnography in the Modern World System," in Clifford and Marcus (1986), pp. 165–193.

——— (1989) "The Debate over Parody in Copyright Law: An Experiment in Cultural Critique," *Yale Journal of Law and the Humanities* 1: 295–316.

——— (1992) "Past, Present and Emergent Identities: Requirements for Ethnographies of Late Twentieth-Century Modernity Worldwide," in Lash and Friedman (1992), pp. 309–330.

——— and Fischer, Michael (1985) *Anthropology as Cultural Critique: An Experimental Moment in the Human Sciences.* Chicago: University of Chicago Press.

Marcus, George and Myers, Fred R. (1995) "The Traffic in Art and Culture: An Introduction," in G. Marcus and F. R. Myers, eds. *The Traffic in Culture: Refiguring Art and Anthropology.* Berkeley: University of California Press, pp. 1–51.

Marincola, Paula (1982) *Image Scavengers: Photography.* Philadelphia: University of Pennsylvania Institute of Contemporary Art.

Marks, Kevin S. (1982) "An Assessment of the Copyright Model in Right of Publicity Cases," *California Law Review* 70: 786–815.

Marks, Richard D. (1994) "High Technology Legislation as an Eighteenth-Century Process," *Stanford Law & Policy Review* 6: 17–24.

Marling, Karal Ann (1984) *The Colossus of Roads: Myth and Symbol along the American Highway.* Minneapolis: University of Minnesota Press.

Marquette, Arthur F. (1966) *Brands, Trademarks and Goodwill: The Story of the Quaker Oats Company.* New York: McGraw-Hill.

Masquelier, Adeline (1992) "Encounter with a Road Sign: Machines, Bodies and Commodities in the Imagination of a Mawri Healer," *Visual Anthropology Review* 8: 56.

Matsuda, Mari J. (1989) "Public Response to Racist Speech: Considering the Victim's Story," *Michigan Law Review* 97: 2320–2381.

McCann, Graham (1988) *Marilyn Monroe.* New Brunswick, NJ: Rutgers University Press.

McCann, Michael (1994) *Rights at Work: Pay Equity Reform and the Politics of Legal Mobilization.* Chicago: University of Chicago Press.

McCarthy, J. Thomas (1987) *The Rights of Publicity and Privacy.* New York: Clark Boardman and Company.

——— (1984 and 1990 Supp.) *Trademarks and Unfair Competition.* 2 volumes. 2d ed. New York: Clark, Boardman and Company.

——— (1995a) *McCarthy on Trademarks and Unfair Competition*, 3d ed. New York: Clark, Boardman and Company.

———— (1995b) "Intellectual Property: America's Overlooked Export," *Dayton Law Review* 20: 809–819.

———— (1995c) "The Spring 1995 Horace S. Manges Lecture: The Human Persona as Commercial Property: The Right of Publicity," *Columbia-VLA Journal of Law and the Arts* 19: 129–148.

McClintock, Anne (1991) "The Angel of Progress: Pitfalls of the Term 'Post-Colonialism,'" *Social Text* 31/32: 84–98.

———— (1995) *Imperial Leather: Gender, Race, and Sexuality in the Colonial Contest.* London: Routledge.

McClure, Kirsty (1992) "On the Subject of Rights," in Mouffe (1992) pp. 108–127.

McEwen, Craig, Maiman, Richard and Mather, Lynn (1994) "Lawyers in Everyday Life: Mediation in Divorce Practice," *Law and Society Review* 28: 149–186.

McGann, Jerome (1983) *The Romantic Ideology.* Chicago: University of Chicago Press.

———— (1990) "My Brain Is Feminine: Byron and the Poetry of Deception," in A. Rutherford, ed. *Byron: Augustan and Romantic.* London: Macmillan, pp. 26–51.

McGrane, Bernard (1989) *Beyond Anthropology: Society and the Other.* New York: Columbia University Press.

McGuigan, Jim (1996) "Cultural Policy Studies—Or How to Be Useful and Critical," *Cultural Studies* 10: 185–190.

McHale, Brian (1987) *Postmodernist Fiction.* London: Methuen.

McKinney Adam E. (1984) *New York General Business Law.* New York: Mathew Bender.

———— (1988) *New York General Business Law.* New York: Mathew Bender.

McLean, Willajeanne F. (1993) "All's Not Fair in Art and War: A Look at the Fair Use Defense after *Rogers* v. *Koons*," *Brooklyn Law Review* 59: 373–421.

———— (1993) "The Birth, Death, and Renaissance of the Doctrine of Secondary Meaning in the Making," *American University Law Review* 42: 737–778.

McMaster, Gerald and Martin, Lee Ann, eds. (1992a) *Indigena: Contemporary Native Perspectives.* Vancouver: Douglas and McIntyre, Canadian Museum of Civilization.

———— (1992b) Introduction, in McMaster and Martin (1992a), pp. 11–23.

McRobbie, Angela (1989) "Postmodernism and Popular Culture," in Lisa Appignanesi, ed. *Postmodernism: ICA Documents.* London: Free Association Books, pp. 165–180.

———— (1994) *Postmodernism and Popular Culture.* London: Routledge.

Megill, Allan, ed. (1994) *Rethinking Objectivity.* Durham, NC: Duke University Press.

Mercer, Kobena (1990) "Welcome to the Jungle: Identity and Diversity in Postmodern Politics," in Jonathan Rutherford, ed. *Identity: Community, Culture, Difference.* London: Lawrence & Wishart, pp. 43–71.

Merry, Sally Engle (1990) *Getting Justice and Getting Even: Legal Consciousness among Working-Class Americans.* Chicago: University of Chicago Press.

———— (1995) "Resistance and the Cultural Power of Law," *Law & Society Review* 29(1): 11–26.

Merryman, John Henry (1986) "Two Ways of Thinking about Cultural Property," *American Journal of International Law* 80: 831–853.

———— (1989) "The Public Interest in Cultural Property," *California Law Review* 77: 339–364.

Mertz, Elizabeth (1994) "A New Social Constructionism for Sociolegal Studies," *Law and Society Review* 28: 1243–1265.

———— (1994) "Legal Loci and Places in the Heart: Community and Identity in Sociolegal Studies," *Law & Society Review* 28: 971–992.

Michaels, Walter Benn (1996) *Our America: Nativism, Modernism, Pluralism*. Durham, NC: Duke University Press.

Miklitsch, Robert (1995a) "News from Somewhere: Reading Raymond Williams' Readers," in Christopher Prendergast, ed. *Cultural Materialism*. Minneapolis: University of Minnesota Press, pp. 71–91.

——— (1995b) "The Rhetoric of Post-Marxism: Discourse and Institutionality in Laclau and Mouffe, Resnick and Wolff," *Social Text* 45: 167–196.

Miller, Daniel (1987) *Material Culture and Mass Consumption*. New York: Basil Blackwell.

——— (1994) *Modernity: An Ethnographic Approach*. Oxford: Berg.

——— (1997) *Capitalism: An Ethnographic Approach*. Oxford: Berg.

———, ed. (1995a) *Worlds Apart: Modernity through the Prism of the Local*. London: Routledge.

———, ed. (1995b) *Acknowledging Consumption*. London: Routledge.

Miller, J. R. (1989) *Skyscrapers Hide the Heavens: A History of Indian-White Relations in Canada*. Toronto: University of Toronto Press.

Miller, Toby (1993) *The Well-Tempered Self: Citizenship, Culture, and the Postmodern Subject*. Baltimore: Johns Hopkins University Press.

——— (1994a) "Introducing *Screening Cultural Studies*: Sister Morpheme (Clark Kent — Superman's Boyfriend)," *Continuum* 7(2): 11–44.

——— (1994b) "Culture with Power: The Present Moment in Cultural Policy Studies," *Southeast Asian Journal of Social Science* 22: 264–282.

Milrad, Aaron (1989) "The Cultural Property Export and Import Act," *Journal of Arts Management and Law* 19: 15–32.

Minda, Gary (1995) *Postmodern Legal Movements: Law and Jurisprudence at Century's End*. New York: New York University Press.

Minow, Martha (1991) "Identities," *Yale Journal of Law & the Humanities* 3: 97–103.

——— and Spelman, Elizabeth V. (1991) "In Context," in Mike Brant and William Weaver, eds. *Pragmatism in Law and Society*. Boulder, CO: Westview Press, pp. 247–273.

——— (1992) "Incomplete Correspondence: An Unsent Letter to Mary Joe Frug," *Harvard Law Review* 105: 1096–1105.

Mintz, Sidney W. (1985) *Sweetness and Power: The Place of Sugar in Modern History*. New York: Viking Penguin.

Mishra, Vijay and Hodge, Bob (1991) "What is Post(-) Colonialism?," *Textual Practice* 5(3): 399–414.

Mitchell, Timothy (1988) *Colonising Egypt*. Berkeley: University of California Press.

Modleski, Tania, ed. (1983) *Loving with a Vengeance*. Hamden, CT: Archon Books.

——— (1986) *Studies in Entertainment*. Bloomington: Indiana University Press.

Mohanty, Chandra (1990) "On Race and Voice: Challenges for Liberal Education in the 1990s," *Cultural Critique* 14: 179–208.

Monk, Philip (1988) *Struggles with the Image: Essays in Art Criticism*. Toronto: YYZ Books.

Moodley, Koglia (1983) "Canadian Multiculturalism as Ideology," *Ethnic and Racial Studies* 6: 320–331.

Moon, Richard (1985) "The Scope of Freedom of Expression," *Osgoode Hall Law Journal* 23: 331–357.

——— (1991) "Lifestyle Advertising and Classical Freedom of Expression Doctrine," *McGill Law Journal* 36: 76–129.

——— (1995) "The Supreme Court of Canada on the Structure of Freedom of Expression Adjudication" *University of Toronto Law Journal* 45: 419–470.

Moore, Henrietta (1994) *A Passion for Difference: Anthropology and Gender*. Indianapolis: Indiana University Press.

Morgan, Hal (1986) *Symbols of America*. New York: Viking.

Morley, David and Robins, Kevin (1995) *Spaces of Identity: Global Media, Electronic Landscapes and Cultural Boundaries*. New York: Routledge.

Mosher, Janet (1989) "Twentieth Century Music: The Impoverishment in Copyright Law of a Strategy of Forms," *Intellectual Property Journal* 5: 51–70.

Mouffe, Chantal (1988) "Radical Democracy: Modern or Postmodern?," in Ross (1988), pp. 31–45.

———— (1991a) "Democratic Citizenship and the Political Community," in Miami Theory Collective, ed. *Community at Loose Ends*. Minneapolis: University of Minnesota Press, pp. 70–82.

———— (1991b) "Pluralism and Modern Democracy: Around Carl Schmitt," *New Formations* 14: 1–16.

————, ed. (1992) *Dimensions of Radical Democracy: Pluralism, Citizenship, Community*. London: Verso.

————, ed. (1993) *The Return of the Political*. London: Verso.

———— (1995) "Democracy and Pluralism: A Critique of the Rationalist Approach," *Cardozo Law Review* 16(5): 1533–1546.

———— (1996) "Democracy, Power, and the 'Political'" in Seyla Benhabib, ed. *Democracy and Difference: Rethinking the Boundaries of the Political*. Princeton: Princeton University Press, pp. 245–256.

Moustakas, John (1989) "Group Rights in Cultural Property: Justifying Strict Inalienability," *Cornell Law Review* 74: 1179–1227.

Mukherjee, Arun P. (1990) "Whose Post-Colonialism and Whose Post-Modernism?," *World Literature Written in English* 30(2): 1–9.

Munger, Frank (1993) "Sociology of Law for a Postliberal Society," *Loyola of Los Angeles Law Review* 27: 89–25.

Murumba, Samuel K. (1986) *Commercial Exploitation of Personality*. Sidney: The Law Book Company Limited.

Musheno, Michael (1995) "Legal Consciousness on the Margins of Society," *Identities: Global Studies in Culture and Power* 2: 101–122.

Myers, Fred (1994) "A Note from the Journal Editor," *Cultural Anthropology* 9: 275.

Nader, Laura and Plowman, Timothy (1996) "Anthropology and Everyday Scholarship," *American Anthropologist* 98: 624–626.

Nancy, Jean-Luc (1991) *The Inoperative Community*. Minneapolis: University of Minnesota Press.

Nash, June (1979) *We Eat the Mines and the Mines Eat Us: Dependency and Exploitation in Bolivian Tin Mines*. New York: Columbia University.

———— and Kelly, P. F., eds. (1983) *Women, Men, and the International Division of Labor*. Albany: State University of New York Press.

Natter, Wolfgang, Schatzke, Theodore and Jones, John Paul, eds. (1995) *Objectivity and Its Other*. New York: Guilford Press.

Nederveen, Pieterse Jan (1992) *White on Black: Images of Africa and Blacks in Western Popular Culture*. New Haven, CT: Yale University Press.

Negt, Oskar and Kluge, Alexander (1993) *The Public Sphere and Experience*. Peter Labanyi, Jamie Daniel, and Assenka Oksiloff, trans. Minneapolis: University of Minnesota Press.

Nelson, Joyce (1990) *Sultans of Sleaze: Public Relations and the Media.* Toronto: Between the Lines Press.

Nevins, Francis (1991) "Availability: The Hidden Value in Copyright Law," *Columbia-VLA Journal of Law and the Arts* 15: 285–334.

"News Gathering, Intangible Property Rights and 900-Line Telephone Services: One Court Makes a Connection" (1991) *Loyola of Los Angeles Entertainment Law Review* 11: 535.

Newton, Esther (1979) *Mother Camp: Female Impersonators in America.* Chicago: University of Chicago Press.

Newton, Nell Jessop (1995) "Memory and Misrepresentation: Representing Crazy Horse," *Connecticut Law Review* 27: 1003–1054.

Nimmer, Melville (1954) "The Right of Publicity," *Law and Contemporary Problems* 19: 203–223.

Note, "Beyond *Rogers* v. *Koons*: A Fair Use Standard for Appropriation" (1993) *Columbia Law Review* 93: 1473–1526.

Note, "Copyright, Free Speech and the Visual Arts" (1989) *Yale Law Journal* 93: 1565–1585.

Note, "Copyright Infringement and the First Amendment" (1979) *Columbia Law Review* 79: 320–321.

Note, "A New Spin on Music Sampling" (1992) *Harvard Law Review* 105: 726–774.

Note, "The Parody Defense to Copyright Infringement" (1984) *Harvard Law Review* 97: 1395–1413.

Note, "Trademark Parodies and Free Speech: An Expansion of Parodists' First Amendment Rights in L.L. Bean, Inc. v. Drake Publishers, Inc." (1988) *Iowa Law Review* 73: 961.

O'Barr, William (1994) *Culture and the Ad: Exploring the World of Otherness in the World of Advertising.* Boulder, CO: Westview Press.

Ong, Aihwa (1987) *Spirits of Resistance and Capitalist Discipline: Factory Women in Malaysia.* Albany: State University of New York Press.

Ortner, Sherry (1973) "On Key Symbols," *American Anthropologist* 75: 1338–1346.

——— (1984) "Theory in Anthropology since the Sixties," *Comparative Studies in Society and History* 26: 126–166.

Orvell, Miles (1989) *The Real Thing: Imitation and Authenticity in American Culture 1880–1940.* Chapel Hill, NC: University of North Carolina Press.

Owens, Craig (1983) "The Discourse of Others: Feminists and Postmodernism," in H. Foster (1983a), pp. 57–82.

Owsley, Brian (1993) "Racist Speech and 'Reasonable People': A Proposal for a Tort Remedy," *Columbia Human Rights Law Review* 24: 323–367.

Pace, Kimberly A. (1994) "The Washington Redskins Case and the Doctrine of Disparagement: How Politically Correct Must a Trademark Be?," *Pepperdine Law Review* 22: 7–54.

Parameswaran, Uma (1996) "I See the Glass as Half Full" in Bahri and Vasudeva (1996b), pp. 351–367.

Parker, Andrew et al., eds. (1992) *Nationalisms and Sexualities.* New York: Routledge.

Parker, Patricia (1987) *Literary Fat Ladies: Rhetoric, Gender, Property.* London: Methuen.

Pask, Amanda (1993) "Making Connections: Intellectual Property, Cultural Property, and Sovereignty in the Debates Concerning the Appropriation of Native Cultures in Canada," *Intellectual Property Journal* 8: 57–86.

Patterson, Dennis (1992) "Postmodernism/Feminism/Law," *Cornell Law Review* 77: 254–317.

Patterson, L. Ray (1992) "Understanding Fair Use," *Law & Contemporary Problems* 55: 249–266.

––––– (1993) "Copyright and the 'Exclusive Right' of Authors," *Journal of Intellectual Property Law* 1: 1–48.

––––– and Lindberg, Stanley W. (1991) *The Nature of Copyright: A Law of User's Rights.* Athens: University of Georgia Press.

Pattishall, Beverly (1977) "The Dilution Rationale for Trademark–Trade Identity Protection, Its Progress and Prospects," *Northwestern University Law Review* 71: 618–633.

Pearce, Roy Harvey (1988) *Savagism and Civilization: A Study of the Indian and the American Mind.* Berkeley: University of California Press.

Pearson, Roberta E. and Uricchio, William, eds. (1991) *The Many Lives of the Batman: Critical Approaches to a Superhero and His Media.* New York: Routledge, Chapman and Hall.

Pease, Donald, ed. (1994a) *National Identities and Postnational Narratives.* Durham, NC: Duke University Press.

–––––, ed. (1994b) *Revisionary Interventions into the Americanist Canon.* Durham, NC: Duke University Press.

––––– (1994c) Introduction, in Pease (1994a), pp. 1–13.

––––– (1994d) "New Americanists: Revisionary Interventions into the Canon," in Pease (1994b), pp. 1–37.

––––– and Kaplan, Amy eds. (1993) *Cultures of American Imperialism.* Durham, NC: Duke University Press.

Pechey, Graham (1989) "On the Borders of Bakhtin: Dialogisation, Decolonisation," in Hirschkop and Shepherd (1989), pp. 39–67.

Peller, Gary (1985) "The Metaphysics of American Law," *California Law Review* 73: 1151–1290.

Pemberton, Gretchen A. (1993) "The Parodists's Claim to Fame: A Parody Exception to the Right of Publicity," *University of California-Davis Law Review* 27: 97–140.

Pendergrast, Mark (1993) *For God, Country, and Coca-Cola.* New York: Scribners.

Penley, Constance (1990) *To Boldly Go Where No Woman Has Gone Before: Feminism, Psychoanalysis, and Popular Culture*, lecture delivered at the Public Access Series Capital/Culture, Toronto, 24 April.

––––– (1991) "Brownian Motion: Women, Tactics and Technology," in Constance Penley and Andrew Ross, eds. *Technoculture.* Minneapolis: University of Minnesota Press, pp. 135–161.

––––– (1992) "Feminism, Psychoanalysis, and the Study of Popular Culture," in Lawrence Grossberg and Cary Nelson, eds. *Cultural Studies.* New York: Routledge, Chapman and Hall, pp. 479–500.

Perez, Steven M. (1995) "Confronting Biased Treatment of Trademark Parody under the Lanham Act," *Emory Law Journal* 44: 1451–1501.

Pesce, Christopher (1990) "The Likeness Monster: Should the Right of Publicity Protect against Imitation?," *New York University Law Review* 65: 782–824.

Peteet, Julie (1996) "The Writing on the Walls: The Graffiti of the Intifada," *Cultural Anthropology* 11: 139–159.

Peters, John Durham (1997) "Seeing Bifocally: Media, Place, Culture," in Gupta and Ferguson (1997b), pp. 75–92.

Pfau, Thomas (1992) "The Pragmatics of Genre: Moral Theory and Lyric Authorship in Hegel and Wordsworth," *Cardozo Arts & Entertainment Law Journal* 10: 397.

Philibert, Jean-Marc (1989) "Consuming Culture: A Study of Simple Commodity Consumption," in Henry J. Rutz and Benjamin S. Orlove, eds. *The Social Economy of Consumption*. Lanham, MD: Society for Economic Anthropology, University Press of America, pp. 59–84.

Plant, Sadie (1993) *The Situationist Internationale*. London: Routledge.

Platzman, Stephen (1992) "Objects of Controversy: The Native American Right to Repatriation," *American University Law Review* 41: 517–558.

Podlesney, Teresa (1991) "Blondes," in Arthur Kroker and Marilouise Kroker, eds. *The Hysterical Male: New Feminist Theory*. London: Macmillan, pp. 69–90.

Polan, Dana (1993) "The Public's Fear: or, Media as Monster in Habermas, Negt, and Kluge," in Robbins (1993b), pp. 33–41.

Polier, Nicole and Roseberry, William (1989) "Tristes Tropes: Postmodern Anthropologists Encounter the Other and Discover Themselves," *Economy & Society* 18: 245–264.

Pommersheim, Frank (1995) *Braid of Feathers: American Indian Law and Contemporary Tribal Life*. Berkeley: University of California Press.

Pope, Daniel (1983) *The Making of Modern Advertising*. New York: Basic Books.

Poster, Mark (1988a) Introduction, in Poster (1988b), pp. 1–9.

———, ed. (1988b) *Jean Baudrillard: Selected Writings*. Stanford: Stanford University Press.

Pottage, A. (1994) "The Law of the Father," in Douzinas et al. (1994).

Prager, E. A. (1996) "The Federal Trademark Dilution Act of 1995: Substantial Likelihood of Confusion," *Fordham Intellectual Property, Media and Entertainment Journal* 7: 121.

Pred, Allan and Watts, Michael John (1992) *Reworking Modernity: Capitalism and Symbolic Discontent*. New Brunswick, NJ: Rutgers University Press.

Price, Benjamin and Steuart, Arthur (1887) *American Trade-Mark Cases Decided by the Courts of the United States, Both State and Federal and by the Commissioner of Patents, and Reported between 1879 and 1887*. Baltimore: Cushings and Bailey.

Radin, Margaret (1982) "Property and Personhood," *Stanford Law Review* 34: 957–1015.

——— (1987) "Market Inalienability," *Harvard Law Review* 100: 1849–1937.

——— (1996) *Contested Commodities*. Cambridge, MA: Harvard University Press.

Radway, Janice (1984) *Reading the Romance*. Chapel Hill, NC: University of North Carolina Press.

Reddy, William M. (1992) "Postmodernism and the Public Sphere: Implications for an Historical Ethnography," *Cultural Anthropology* 7(2): 135–168.

Riles, Annelise (1994) "Representing In-Between: Law, Anthropology, and the Rhetoric of Interdisciplinarity," *University of Illinois Law Review* [1994]: 597–650.

Roach, Joseph (1996) *Cities of the Dead: Circum-Atlantic Performance*. New York: Columbia University Press.

Robbins, Bruce (1993a) "The Public as Phantom," in Robbins (1993b), pp. vii–xxvi.

———, ed. (1993b) *The Phantom Public Sphere*. Minneapolis: University of Minnesota Press.

——— (1995) "Some Versions of U.S. Internationalism," *Social Text* 45: 97–124.

Roberts, Diane (1994) *The Myth of Aunt Jemima: Representations of Race and Region*. London: Routledge.

Roediger, David R. (1991) *The Wages of Whiteness: Race and the American Working Class*. New York: Verso.

Rogin, Michael (1992) "Blackface, White Noise: The Jewish Jazz Singer Finds His Voice," *Critical Inquiry* 18: 425.

Root, Deborah (1996) *Cannibal Culture: Art, Appropriation, and the Commodification of Difference.* Boulder, CO: Westview Press.

Rorty, Richard (1979) *Philosophy and the Mirror of Nature.* Princeton, NJ: Princeton University Press.

Rosaldo, Renato (1989) *Culture and Truth: The Remaking of Social Analysis.* Boston: Beacon Press.

Rose, Gillian (1984) *Dialectic of Nihilism: Post-Structuralism and Law.* Minneapolis: University of Minnesota Press.

Rose, Mark (1988) "The Author as Proprietor: *Donaldson v. Beckett* and the Geneology of Modern Authorship," *Representations* 23: 51.

———— (1993) *Authors and Owners.* Cambridge, MA: Harvard University Press.

———— (1996) "Mothers and Authors: Johnson v. Calvert and the New Children of Our Imaginations," *Critical Inquiry* 22: 613–633.

———— (nd) *From Paternity to Property: The Remetaphorization of Writing.* Unpublished manuscript.

Roseberry, William (1989) *Anthropologies and Histories: Essays in Culture, History, and Political Economy.* New Brunswick, NJ: Rutgers University Press.

———— (1991) "Marxism and Culture," in B. Williams (1991b), pp. 19–43.

Rosenthal, Michael (1993) "What Was Postmodernism?," *Socialist Review* 22(3): 83–106.

Ross, Andrew, ed. (1988) *Universal Abandon? The Politics of Postmodernism.* Minneapolis: University of Minnesota Press.

———— (1989) *No Respect: Intellectuals and Popular Culture.* New York: Routledge, Chapman and Hall.

Ross, Marlon (1989) *The Contours of Masculine Desire: Romanticism and the Rise of Women's Poetry.* New York: Oxford University Press.

Roth, Lorna (1992) "Media and the Commodification of Crisis," in Marc Raboy and Bernard Dafenais, eds. *Media, Crisis and Democracy: Essays on Mass Communications and the Disruption of Social Order.* London: Sage Publications.

Rouse, Roger (1991) "Mexican Migration and the Social Space of Postmodernism," *Diaspora* 1: 8–23.

———— (1992) "Making Sense of Settlement: Class Transformation, Cultural Struggle, and Transnationalism among Mexican Migrants in the United States," *Towards a Transnational Perspective on Migration. Annals of the New York Academy of Sciences* 645: 25–52.

Rowe, John Carlos (1993) "The Writing Class," in Mark Poster, ed. *Politics, Theory, and Contemporary Culture.* New York: Columbia University Press, pp. 41–83.

Ruby, Jay (1991) "Speaking For, Speaking About, Speaking With, or Speaking Alongside: An Anthropological and Documentary Dilemma," *Visual Anthropology Review* 7(2): 50–67.

Ruddick, Susan (1990) "Heterotopias of the Homeless: Strategies and Tactics of Place-making in Los Angeles," *Strategies* 3: 184–201.

Russ, Joanna (1985) "Another Addict Raves about K/S," *Nome,* 8: 28–37.

Russell, Margaret (1992) "Entering Great America: Reflections on Race and the Convergence of Progressive Legal Theory and Practice," *Hastings Law Journal* 43: 749–767.

Rutherford, Jonathan (1990) "A Place Called Home: Identity and the Cultural Politics of Difference," in Jonathan Rutherford, ed. *Identity: Community, Culture, Difference.* London: Lawrence & Wishart, pp. 9–27.

Rydell, Robert (1984) *All the World's a Fair: Visions of Empire at American International Expositions, 1876–1916*. Chicago: University of Chicago Press.

Sahlins, Marshall (1976) *Culture and Practical Reason*. Chicago: University of Chicago Press.

——— (1985) *Islands of History*. Chicago: University of Chicago Press.

Said, Edward (1979) *Orientalism*. New York: Vintage Books.

——— (1986) "Orientalism Reconsidered," in Francis Barker, Peter Hulme, Margaret Iversen, and Diana Loxley, eds. *Literature, Politics and Theory: Papers from the Essex Conference 1976–1984*. London: Methuen, pp. 210–229.

——— (1989) "Representing the Colonized: Anthropology's Interlocutors," *Critical Inquiry* 15: 205–225.

Sampson, Edward (1993) *Celebrating the Other: A Dialogic Account of Human Nature*. Boulder, CO: Westview Press.

Samuels, Elizabeth I. (1995) "Ideology between Fiction and Fantasy," *Cardozo Law Review* 16(5): 1511–1532.

Samuelson, Pamela (1996a) "Legally Speaking: Intellectual Property Rights and the Global Information Economy," *Communications of the ACM* (January) 39: 23–28.

——— (1996b) "The Copyright Grab," *Wired* 4(1): 134–138.

——— (1996c) "Tightening the Copyright Noose: Why You Should Be Worried about the White Paper on Intellectual Property and the National Information Infrastructure," *Wired* 4(1).

Sangren, P. Steven (1988) "Rhetoric and the Authority of Ethnography: Postmodernism and the Social Reproduction of Texts," *Current Anthropology* 29: 405–424.

Sanjek, Roger, ed. (1990) *Fieldnotes: The Makings of Anthropology*. Ithaca: Cornell University Press.

Santos, Boaventura de Sousa (1995) "Three Metaphors for a New Conception of Law: The Frontier, the Baroque, and the South," *Law & Society Review* 29: 569.

Sarat, Austin (1989) "Lawyers and Legal Consciousness: Law Talk in the Divorce Lawyer's Office," *Yale Law Journal* 98: 1663–1698.

——— (1990) "'. . . The Law All Over': The Legal Consciousness of the Welfare Poor," *Yale Journal of Law and the Humanities* 2:343–381.

——— and Felstiner, William F. (1995) *Divorce Lawyers and Their Critics: Power and Meaning in the Legal Process*. New York: Oxford University Press.

Sarat, Autin and Kearns, Thomas R., eds. (1993) *Law in Everyday Life*. Ann Arbor: University of Michigan Press.

——— (1994) *The Rhetoric of Law*. Ann Arbor: University of Michigan Press.

——— (1998) *Law in the Domains of Culture*. Ann Arbor: University of Michigan Press.

Sassen, Saskia (1991) *The Global City: London, Tokyo, New York*. Princeton: Princeton University Press.

——— (1994) *Cities in a World Economy*. London: Pine Forge Press.

——— (1995) "When the State Encounters a New Space Economy: The Case of the Information Industries," *American University Journal of International Law and Policy* 10: 769–789.

Savan, Leslie (1994) *The Sponsored Life: Ads, TV, and American Culture*. Philadelphia: Temple University Press.

Schatzman, Morton, Sabbadini, Andrea and Forti, Laura (1976) "Coca and Cocaine: A Bibliography," *Journal of Psychedelic Drugs* 8: 95–128.

Schauer, Frederick (1993) "The Political Incidence of the Free Speech Principle," *University of Colorado Law Review* 64: 935–957.

——— (1982) *Free Speech: A Philosophical Inquiry.* New York: Cambridge University Press.

Schechter, Frank I. (1927) "The Rational Basis of Trademark Protection," *Harvard Law Review* 40: 813–833.

Schepple, Kim Lane (1991) "Facing Facts in Legal Interpretation," in Robert Post, ed. *Law and the Order of Culture.* Berkeley: University of California Press, pp. 42–77.

——— (1995) "Manners of Imagining the Real," *Law and Social Inquiry* 19: 995–1022.

Schickel, Richard (1985) *Intimate Strangers: The Culture of Celebrity, Where We Came In.* Garden City, NY: Doubleday.

Schiller, Herbert I. (1989) *Culture, Inc.: The Corporate Takeover of Public Expression.* Oxford: Oxford University Press.

——— (1996) *Information Inequality: The Deepening Social Crisis in America.* London: Routledge.

Schlag, Pierre (1987) "Fish v. Zapp: The Case of the Relatively Autonomous Self," *Georgetown Law Journal* 76: 37–52.

——— (1989) "Missing Pieces: A Cognitive Approach to Law," *Texas Law Review* 67: 1195–1250.

——— (1990) "Normative and Nowhere to Go," *Stanford Law Review* 43: 167–191.

——— (1991a) "The Problem of the Subject," *Texas Law Review* 69: 1627–1743.

——— (1991b) "Foreword: Postmodernism and Law," *University of Colorado Law Review* 62: 439–453.

Scott, David (1992) "Criticism and Culture: Theory and Post-Colonial Claims on Anthropological Disciplinarity," *Critique of Anthropology* 12(4): 371–394.

——— (1995) "A Note on the Demand of Criticism," *Public Culture* 8: 41.

Scott, Joan Wallach (1988) *Gender and the Politics of History.* New York: Columbia University Press.

Seed, Patricia (1991) "Colonial and Postcolonial Discourse," *Latin American Research Review* 26: 181–201.

Serequeberhan, Tsenay (1989) "The Idea of Colonialism in Hegel's Philosophy of Right," *International Philosophical Quarterly* 29: 301–318.

Sharpe, Robert (1987) "Commercial Expression and the Charter," *University of Toronto Law Journal* 37: 229–259.

Shaughnessy, Robert J. (1986) "Trademark Parody: A Fair Use and First Amendment Analysis," *Virginia Law Review* 72: 1079–1117.

Sheppard, Darren, Sparks, Simon and Colin Thomas (1997) *The Sense of Philosophy: On Jean-Luc Nancy.* London: Routledge.

Sherman, Brad (1994) "From the Non-original to the Ab-original: A History," in Brad Sherman and Alain Strowel, eds. *Of Authors and Origins.* Oxford: Oxford University Press, pp. 111–130.

Shiffrin, Steven H. (1994a) "The Politics of the Mass Media and the Free Speech Principle," *Indiana Law Journal* 69: 659–721.

——— (1994b) "Racist Speech, Outsider Jurisprudence, and the Meaning of America," *Cornell Law Review* 80: 43–103.

Shipton, Parker (1989) *Bitter Money: Cultural Economy and Some African Meanings of Forbidden Commodities.* Washington, DC: American Anthropological Association.

Shire, Howard J. (1987) "Dilution versus Deception: Are State Antidilution Laws an Appropriate Alternative to the Law of Infringement?," *Trademark Reporter* 77: 273–298.

Shohat, Ella (1991) "Notes on the 'Post-Colonial,'" *Social Text* 31/32: 99–113.

———— and Stam, Robert (1994) *Unthinking Eurocentrism: Multiculturalism and the Media.* New York: Routledge.

———— (1996) "From the Imperial Family to the Transnational Imaginary: Media Spectatorship in the Age of Globalization," in Wilson and Dissanakade (1996), pp. 145–172.

Shutz, Alfred (1970) *On Phenomenology and Social Relations.* Chicago: University of Chicago Press.

Shweder, Robin (1989) "Ad-Alterations as a Form of Cultural Interrogation," *Public Culture* 1(2): 80–83.

Silbey, Susan and Ewick, Patricia (1992) "Conformity, Contestation, and Resistance: An Account of Legal Consciousness," *New England Law Review* 26: 731.

Simon, Todd F. (1985) "Right of Publicity Reified: Fame as Business Asset," *New York Law School Review* 30: 699–755.

Singer, Barbara (1992) "Right of Publicity: Star Vehicle or Shooting Star?," *Cardozo Arts & Entertainment Law Journal* 10: 1–49.

Singer, Joseph William and Newton, Nell Jessup (1995) Law Professors Amicus Brief on Behalf of Petitioner, *In re Tasunke Witko,* Civ. No. 93-204 (Ct. App. Rosebud Sx. Tr., Mar. 10, 1995) (submitted by Singer and Newton).

Siskin, Clifford (1988) *The Historicity of Romantic Discourse.* New York: Oxford University Press.

Skuse, Dai and Kozzi, Kim (1992) Letter to the Editor, *Fuse* 15(6): 4.

Skuse, Dai, Kozzi, Kim and Brousseau, Napoleon (1989–90) Letter to the Editor, *Fuse* 13(3): 2.

Slotkin, Richard (1973) *Regeneration through Violence: The Mythology of the American Frontier.* Middletown, CT: Wesleyan University Press.

———— (1992) *Gunfighter Nation: The Myth of the Frontier in Twentieth-Century America.* New York: Harper Books.

Smith, Paul (1988) *Discerning the Subject.* Minneapolis: University of Minnesota Press.

———— (1991) "Laclau and Mouffe's Secret Agent," in Miami Theory Collective, ed. *Community at Loose Ends.* Minneapolis: University of Minnesota Press, pp. 99–111.

———— (1991-92) "Lost in America," *Borderlines* 17: 17.

Smoodin, Eric, ed. (1994a) *Disney Discourse: Producing the Magic Kingdom.* New York: Routledge.

———— (1994b) "Introduction: How to Read Walt Disney," in Smoodin (1994a), pp. 1–20.

Solway, Jackie and Lee, Richard (1990) "Foragers, Genuine or Spurious: Situating the Kalahari San in History," *Current Anthropology* 31: 109–146.

Spigel, Lynn (1990) "Communicating with the Dead: Elvis as Medium," *Camera Obscura* 23: 177–193.

Spillers, Hortense J. (1987) "Mama's Baby, Papa's Maybe: An American Grammar Book," *Diacritics* 17(2): 65–81.

Spivak, Gayatri Chakravorty (1988) "Subaltern Studies: Deconstructing Historiography," in Ranajit Guha and Gayatri Chakravorty Spivak, eds. *Selected Subaltern Studies.* Oxford: Oxford University Press, pp. 3–32.

———— (1990a) *The Postcolonial Critic: Interviews, Strategies, Dialogues.* New York: Routledge, Chapman and Hall.

————— (1990b) "Poststructuralism, Marginality, Postcoloniality, and Value," in Peter Collier and Helga Geyer-Ryan, eds. *Literary Theory Today*. Ithaca: Cornell University Press, pp. 219–244.

Spurr, David (1993) *Rhetorics of Empire: Colonial Discourse in Journalism and Travel Writing*. Durham, NC: Duke University Press.

Stack, Linda J. (1995) "White v. Samsung Electronics America, Inc.'s Expansion of the Right of Publicity: Enriching Celebrities at the Expense of Free Speech," *Northwestern University Law Review* 89: 1189–1226.

Staffin, Elliot B. (1995) "The Dilution Doctrine: Towards a Reconciliation with the Lanham Act," *Fordham Intellectual Property, Media, and Entertainment Law Journal* 6: 105–177.

Staiger Gooding, Susan (1994) "Place, Race, and Names: Layered Identites in *United States v. Oregon*, Confederated Tribes of the Colville Reservation, Plaintiff-Intervenor," *Law & Society Review* 28: 1181–1229.

Stallman, Richard (1996) "Re-evaluating Copyright: The Public Must Prevail," *Oregon Law Review* 75: 291–298.

Stallybrass, Peter and White, Allon (1986) *The Politics and Poetics of Transgression*. Ithaca: Cornell University Press.

Stambach, Amy (1996) *Curl Up and Dye*. Paper presented at the conference The Struggle for Civil Society in Postcolonial Africa, University of Chicago African Studies Conference, 31 May–1 June.

Starrett, Gregory (1995) "The Political Economy of Religious Commodities in Cairo," *American Anthropologist* 97(1): 51–68.

Stearns, Laurie (1992) "Copy Wrong: Plagiarism, Process, Property, and the Law," *California Law Review* 80: 513–553.

Stedman, Raymond William (1982) *Shadows of the Indian: Stereotypes in American Culture*. Norman: University of Oklahoma Press.

Stephens, Sharon (1989) *Anthropology since the 60's: Theory for the 90's*, University of Michigan CSST Working Paper Series Transformations, November.

Stewart, Susan (1991) *Crimes of Writing: Problems in the Containment of Representation*. Oxford: Oxford University Press.

Stocking, George, ed. (1983) *History of Anthropology, Vol. 1: Observers Observed: Essays on Ethnographic Fieldwork*. Madison: University of Wisconsin Press.

————— (1985) *History of Anthropology, Vol. 3: Objects and Others: Essays on Museums and Material Culture*. Madison: University of Wisconsin Press.

————— (1989) *History of Anthropology, Vol. 6: Romantic Motives: Essays on Anthropological Sensibility*. Madison: University of Wisconsin Press.

————— (1991) *History of Anthropology, Vol. 7: Colonial Situations: Essays on the Contextualization of Ethnographic Knowledge*. Madison: University of Wisconsin Press.

Stoller, Paul (1989a) "Speaking in the Name of the Real," *Cahiers d'Etudes Africaines* 29: 113–125.

————— (1989b) *The Taste of Ethnographic Things: The Senses in Anthropology*. Philadelphia: University of Pennsylvania Press.

————— (1994) "DoubleTakes on Jay on Taussig," *Visual Anthropology Review* 10.

Stone, Geoffrey, Epstein, Richard and Sunstein, Cass, eds. (1992) *The Bill of Rights in the Modern State*. Chicago: University of Chicago Press.

Strasser, Susan (1989) *Satisfaction Guaranteed: The Making of the American Mass Market*. New York: Pantheon Books.

Strategies Collective (1988) "Building a New Left: An Interview with Ernesto Laclau," *Strategies* 1: 10–25.

Streeter, Thomas (1992) "Broadcast Copyright and the Bureaucratization of Property," *Cardozo Arts & Entertainment Law Journal* 10: 567–590, reprinted in Woodmansee and Jaszi (1994), pp. 303–326.

———— (1996) *Selling the Air: A Critique of the Policy of Commercial Broadcasting in the United States.* Chicago: University of Chicago Press.

Stychin, Carl F. (1995) *Law's Desire: Sexuality and the Limits of Justice.* London: Routledge.

Sudjic, Deyan (1989) *Cult Heroes: How to Be Famous for More than Fifteen Minutes.* London: Andre Deutsch.

Sullivan, Kathleen M. (1995) "Free Speech and Unfree Markets," *U.C.L.A. Law Review* 42(4): 949–968.

Sullivan, Robert (1990) "Marxism and the 'Subject' of Anthropology," in Manganaro (1990a), pp. 243–265.

Sunstein, Cass R. (1993) *Democracy and the Problem of Free Speech.* New York: The Free Press.

Swann, Jerre B. and Davis, Theodore H., Jr. (1994) "Dilution, An Idea Whose Time Has Gone: Brand Equity as Protectable Property, the New/Old Paradigm," *Journal of Intellectual Property Law* 1: 219–257.

Swartz, R. G. (1989) "Patrimony and the Figuration of Authorship," *Works and Days* 7(2): 29.

Tannen, Deborah (1993) "Wears Jumpsuit. Sensible Shoes. Uses Husband's Last Name," *New York Times Magazine,* 20 June, pp. 18, 52, 54.

Taussig, Michael (1980) *The Devil and Commodity Fetishism in South America.* Chapel Hill, NC: University of North Carolina Press.

———— (1993) *Mimesis and Alterity: A Particular History of the Senses.* New York: Routledge, Chapman and Hall.

Taylor, Celeste J. (1994) "Know When to Say When: An Examination of the Tax Deduction for Alcohol Advertising That Targets Minorities," *Law & Inequality* 12: 573–612.

Taylor, Peter (1984) *The Smoke Ring: Tobacco, Money, and Multinational Politics.* New York: Pantheon.

Tedlow, Richard S. (1990) *New and Improved: The Story of Mass Marketing in America.* New York: Basic Books.

Thomas, Nicholas (1991) "Against Ethnography," *Cultural Anthropology* 6(3): 306–322.

———— (1994) *Colonialism's Culture: Anthropology, Travel, and Government.* Princeton, NJ: Princeton University Press.

Thomas, Richard M. (1991) "Milton and Mass Culture: Toward a Postmodernist Theory of Tolerance," *University of Colorado Law Review* 62: 525–575.

Thompson, E. P. (1971) "The Moral Economy of the English Crowd in the 18th Century," *Past and Present* 50: 76–136.

Thompson, John B. (1984) "Symbolic Violence: Language and Power in the Writings of Pierre Bourdieu," in John B. Thompson, ed. *Studies in the Theory of Ideology.* Berkeley: University of California Press, pp. 42–72.

Tiffin, Helen (1988) "Post-Colonialism, Post-Modernism, and the Rehabilitation of Post-Colonial History," *Journal of Commonwealth Literature* 23: 169–81.

Tobin, Joseph J. (1992a) "Introduction: Domesticating the West," in Tobin (1992b), pp. 1–41.

————, ed. (1992b) *Re-Made in Japan: Everyday Life and Consumer Taste in a Changing Society.* New Haven, CT: Yale University Press.

Tocqueville, Alexis de (1841) *Democracy in America*. H. Reeve, trans., 4th ed., revised and corrected from 18th Paris ed. New York: J. & H. G. Langley.

Todd, Loretta (1990) "Notes on Appropriation," *Parallelogramme* 16: 24–33.

——— (1992) "What More Do They Want?," in McMaster and Martin (1992a), pp. 71–79.

Todorov, Tzvetan (1984) *Mikhail Bakhtin: The Dialogical Principle*. Minneapolis: University of Minnesota Press.

Tomlinson, John (1991) *Cultural Imperialism*. Baltimore: Johns Hopkins University Press.

Trachtenberg, Alan (1982) *The Incorporation of America: Society and Culture in the Guilded Age*. New York: Hill and Wang.

"Trade-Marks" (1875) *Albany Law Journal*, reprinted in *Irish Law Times and Solicitor's Journal* 9 (April 4): 171–172.

Trager, Robert (1995) "Entangled Values: The First Amendment in the 1990's," *Journal of Communication* 45: 163–170.

Trask, Haunani-Kay (1991–92) "Lovely Hula Lands: Corporate Tourism and the Prostitution of Hawaiian Culture," *Border/lines* 23: 22–34.

——— (1993) *From a Native Daughter: Colonialism and Sovereignty in Hawai'i*. Bangor, ME: Common Courage Press.

Tremblay, Michel (1974) *Hosanna*. John Van Burek and Bill Glassco, trans. Vancouver: Talonbooks.

Treuttner, William H. (1991) *The West as America: Reinterpreting Images of the Frontier*. Washington, DC: Smithsonian Institution.

Trotter, David (1990) "Colonial Subjects," *Critical Quarterly* 32(3): 3–20.

Trouillot, Michel-Rolph (1991) "Anthropology and the Savage Slot: The Poetics and Politics of Otherness," in R. J. Fox (1991a), pp. 17–44.

Turner, Frederick (1980) *Beyond Geography: The Western Spirit against the Wilderness*. New York: Viking Press.

Turner, Patricia A. (1987) "Church's Fried Chicken and the Klan: A Rhetorical Analysis of Rumor in the Black Community," *Western Folklore* 46: 294–306.

——— (1992) "Ambivalent Patrons: The Role of Rumor and Contemporary Legends in African-American Consumer Decisions," *Journal of American Folklore* 105: 424–442.

——— (1993) *I Heard It through the Grapevine: Rumor in African-American Culture*. Berkeley: University of California Press.

——— (1994) *Ceramic Uncles and Celluloid Mammies: Black Images and Their Influence on Culture*. New York: Anchor Books.

Turner, Terence (1993) "Anthropology and Multiculturalism: What Is Anthropology That Multiculturalism Should Be Mindful of It?," *Cultural Anthropology* 8(4): 411–429.

Tyler, Parker (1968) "The Garbo Image" in Michael Conway, Dion McGregor, and Mark Ricci, eds. *The Films of Greta Garbo*. New York: Citadel Press, pp. 9–31.

Tyler, Stephen (1984) "The Poetic Turn in Postmodern Anthropology," *American Anthropologist* 86: 328–336.

——— (1986) "Postmodern Anthropology," in Phyllis Pease Chock and June R. Wyman, eds. *Discourse and the Social Life of Meaning*. Washington, DC: Smithsonian Institution Press, pp. 23–50.

Valencia-Weber, Gloria (1994) "Custom and Innovative Law," *New Mexico Law Review* 24: 225–263.

Vattimo, Gianni (1992) *The Transparent Society*. Baltimore: Johns Hopkins University Press.

Vaver, David (1981) "What's Mine Is Not Yours: Commercial Appropriation of Personality under the Privacy Acts of B.C., Manitoba and Saskatchewan," *University of British Columbia Law Review* 15: 241–340.

———— (1990) "Intellectual Property Today: Of Myths and Paradoxes," *Canadian Bar Review* 69: 98–128.

———— (1996) "Rejuvenating Copyright," *Canadian Bar Review* 75: 69.

Voloshinov, V. N. (1973) *Marxism and the Philosophy of Language.* New York: Seminar Press.

Wakankar, Milind (1995) "Body, Crowd, Identity: Genealogy of a Hindu Nationalist Ascetics," *Social Text* 14 (4): 45–73.

Walker, John A. (1994) *Art in the Age of Mass Media.* Boulder, CO: Westview Press.

Wall, David (1996) "Reconstructing the Soul of Elvis: The Social Development and Legal Maintenance of Elvis Presley as Intellectual Property [1]," *International Journal of the Sociology of Law* 24: 117–143.

Wallace, Michelle (1990) *Invisibility Blues: From Pop to Theory.* London: Verso Books.

Wang, Elizabeth H. (1990) "(Re)Productive Rights: Copyright and the Postmodern Artist," *Columbia-VLA Journal of Law & the Arts* 14: 261–281.

Warner, Michael, ed. (1993a) *Fear of a Queer Planet: Queer Politics and Social Theory.* Minneapolis: University of Minnesota Press.

———— (1993b) "The Mass Public and the Mass Subject," in Robbins (1993b), pp. 234–256.

———— (1994) "The *Res Publica* of Letters," in Pease (1994b), pp. 38–68.

Warren, Samuel D. and Brandeis, Louis D. (1890) "The Right to Privacy," *Harvard Law Review* 4: 193–220.

Warrior, Robert Allan (1992/92) "The Sweetgrass Meaning of Solidarity: 500 Years of Resistance," *Borderlines* 23: 35–37.

Watts, Michael J. (1991) "Mapping Meaning, Denoting Difference, Imagining Identity: Dialectical Images and Postmodern Geographies," *Geografiska Annaler* 73B: 7–16.

Webster, Gloria Cranmer (1992) "From Colonization to Repatriation," in McMaster and Martin (1992a), pp. 25–38.

Webster, Stephen (1990) "The Historical Materialist Critique of Surrealism and Postmodernist Ethnography," in Manganaro (1990a), pp. 266–299.

Weedon, Chris (1987) *Feminist Practice and Poststructuralist Theory.* London: Basil Blackwell.

Weiler, Fred M. (1994) "The Right of Publicity Gone Wrong: A Case for Privileged Appropriation of Identity," *Cardozo Arts & Entertainment Law Journal* 13: 223–273.

Weiner, Annette B. (1995) "Culture and Our Discontents," *American Anthropologist* 97(1): 14–26.

Weisman, Alisa M. (1982) "Publicity as an Aspect of Privacy and Personal Autonomy," *Southern California Law Review* 55: 727–768.

Weiss, Brad (1996) *The Making and Unmaking of the Haya Lived World: Consumption, Commoditization, and Everyday Practice.* Durham, NC: Duke University Press.

Wernick, Andrew (1991a) "Promotional Culture," *Canadian Journal of Political & Social Theory* 15: 260–284.

———— (1991b) *Promotional Culture: Advertising, Ideology, and Symbolic Expression.* London: Sage Publications.

Westberg, D. (1991) "Intellectual Property Law: New Kids on the Block v. News America Publishing, Inc.: New Nominative Use Defense Increases the Likelihood of Confusion Surrounding the Fair Use Defense to Trademark Infringement," *Golden Gate University Law Review* 24: 685.

White, Louise (1993) "Cars out of Place: Vampires, Technology, and Labor in East and Central Africa," *Representations* 27: 43.

Whitehead, Colson (1992) "Review of White on Black," *Voice Literary Supplement* (October), p. 25.

Wicke, Jennifer (1991) "Postmodern Identity and the Legal Subject," *University of Colorado Law Review* 62: 455–473.

Wildman, Stephanie M. (1996) *Privilege Revealed: How Invisible Preference Undermines America.* New York: New York University Press.

Williams, Brett (1991a) "Good Guys and Bad Toys: The Paradoxical World of Children's Cartoons," in B. Williams (1991b), pp. 109–132.

———, ed. (1991b) *The Politics of Culture.* Washington, DC: Smithsonian Institution.

Williams, Patrick and Chrisman, Laura (1994) *Colonial Discourse and Post-Colonial Theory: A Reader.* New York: Columbia University Press.

Williams, Raymond (1980) *Problems in Materialism and Culture.* London: Verso.

——— (1983a) *Culture and Society 1780–1950.* New York: Columbia University Press.

——— (1983b) *Keywords: A Vocabulary of Culture and Society,* 2d ed. New York: Oxford University Press.

Willis, Paul (1990) *Common Culture.* Boulder, CO: Westview Press.

Willis, Susan (1992) *A Primer for Everyday Life.* New York: Routledge, Chapman and Hall.

——— (1993) "Hardcore: Subculture American Style," *Critical Inquiry* 19: 365–383.

Wilson, Alexander (1991) *The Culture of Nature.* Toronto: Between the Lines Press.

Wilson, Rob (1994) "Goodbye Paradise: Global/Localism, Hawai'i, and Cultural Production in the American Pacific," *New Formations* 24: 35–50.

——— (1995) "Bloody Mary Meets Lois-Ann Yamanaka: Imagining Hawaiian Locality from *South Pacific* to Bamboo Ridge," *Public Culture* 8: 127–158.

——— and Wimal Dissanayake, eds. (1996) *Global/Local: Cultural Production and the Transnational Imaginary.* Durham, NC: Duke University Press.

Winter, Steven L. (1989a) "The Cognitive Dimension of the Agon between Legal Power and Narrative Meaning," *Michigan Law Review* 87: 2225–2279.

——— (1989b) "Transcendental Nonsense, Metaphoric Reasoning, and the Cognitive Stakes for Law," *University of Pennsylvania Law Review* 137: 1105–1237.

——— (1990) "Bull Durham and the Uses of Theory," *Stanford Law Review* 42: 639.

——— (1991) "Foreword: On Building Houses," *Texas Law Review* 69: 1595–1626.

——— (1993) "Fast Food and False Friends in the Shopping Mall of Ideas," *University of Colorado Law Review* 64: 965–974.

Wolf, Eric (1982) *Europe and the People without History.* Berkeley: University of California Press.

Wolff, Janet (1987) *The Social Production of Art.* New York: St Martin's Press.

Woodmansee, Martha (1984) "The Genius and the Copyright: Economic and Legal Conditions of the Emergence of the 'Author,'" *Eighteenth-Century Studies* 17: 425–448.

——— (1992) "On the Author Effect: Recovering Collectivity," *Cardozo Arts and Entertainment Law Journal* 10: 279–292, reprinted in Woodmansee and Jaszi (1994), pp. 15–28.

——— (1994) *The Author, Art, and the Market: Rereading the History of Aesthetics.* New York: Columbia University Press.

——— and Jaszi, Peter, eds. (1994) *The Construction of Authorship: Textual Appropriation in Law and Literature.* Durham, NC: Duke University Press.

Woolley, Benjamin (1992) *Virtual Worlds.* Oxford: Basil Blackwell.

Working Group on Intellectual Property Rights (1995) *Intellectual Property and the National Information Infrastructure: The Report of the Working Group on Intellectual Property Rights.* Bruce A. Lehman, Chair. Washington, DC: U.S. Government Printing Office.

Yen, Alfred C. (1990) "Restoring the Natural Law: Copyright as Labor and Possession," *Ohio State Law Journal* 51: 517–559.

—— (1992) "The Interdisciplinary Future of Copyright Theory," *Cardozo Arts and Entertainment Law Journal* 10: 423–438, reprinted in Woodmansee and Jaszi (1994), pp. 159–173.

Yonover, Geri J. (1995) "The 'Dissing' of Da Vinci: The Imaginary Case of Leonardo v. Duchamp: Moral Rights, Parody, and Fair Use," *Valparaiso University Law Review* 29: 935–1004.

Young, Iris Marion (1996) "Communication and the Other: Beyond Deliberative Democracy," in Seyla Benhabib, ed., *Democracy and Difference: Contesting the Boundaries of the Political.* Princeton: Princeton University Press.

Young, Robert (1990) *White Mythologies: Writing History and the West.* New York: Routledge, Chapman and Hall.

—— (1995) *Colonial Desire: Hybridity in Theory, Culture and Race.* New York: Routledge.

Young Man, Alfred (1992) "The Metaphysics of North American Art," in McMaster and Martin (1992a), pp. 81–99.

Yngvesson, Barbara (1993) *Virtuous Citizens, Disruptive Subjects: Order and Complaint in a New England Court.* New York: Routledge.

Yúdice, George (1995) "Civil Society, Consumption, and Governmentality in an Age of Global Restructuring," *Social Text* 45: 1–26.

Zerner, Charles (n.d.) *Metaphor Wars and Native Seeds: Contested Visions of the Extraction of Biological Resources from Tropical Countries.* Unpublished manuscript.

—— (1995) "Telling Stories about Biological Diversity," in Stephen Brush and G. Dubinsky, eds. *Valuing Local Knowledge: Indigenous People and Intellectual Property Rights.* Washington, DC: Island Press, pp. 68–102.

Ziff, Bruce and Pratima Rao, eds. (1997) *Borrowed Power: Essays in Cultural Appropriation.* New Brunswick, NJ: Rutgers University Press.

Zimmerman, Diane L. (1992) "Information as Speech, Information as Goods: Some Thoughts on the Marketplace and the Bill of Rights," *William and Mary Law Review* 33: 665–740.

Žižek, Slavoj (1991) *For They Know Not What They Do.* New York: Verso Books.

Zukin, Sharon (1995) *The Cultures of Cities.* London: Basil Blackwell.

Newspaper and Popular Magazine Articles

Brown, Fred (1990) "Collecting African American Images," *Globe and Mail*, 6 February, p. C5.

Burkhart, Dan (1991) "Turner Won't Change Braves' Name, but Wouldn't Mind Stopping the Chop," *Atlanta Journal*, 3 December, p. F8.

Campbell, Susan (1993) "Sculptor's Work Lives on in Monumental Tribute to a Chief," *Hartford Courant*, 12 July, p. A1.

Canedy, Dana (1997) "Advertising: After Two Decades and Counting, Procter & Gamble Is Still Trying to Exorcise Satanism Tales," *New York Times*, 29 July, p. C7.

Choate, Ed. (1995) "Mascots Not the Biggest Issue," *Times-Picayune*, 29 October, p. C3.

Cichowski, John (1996) "High School to Keep Team Name: Trustees Vote on Redskins Controversy," *The Bergen Record*, 3 May, p. NO1.

Clark, Sandra and Shepard, Paul (1993) "Trademark Makeovers Aim to Keep Image Hip," *Cleveland Plain Dealer*, 7 March, p. E1.

Clause, Lynda (1993) "Not an Honor, but an Insult," *Cleveland Plain Dealer*, 20 June, p. 3C.

Corbeil, Carole (1997) "Disney Gallops out to Trample Mountie T-shirt," *Toronto Star*, 8 February.

Dargis, Manohla (1990) "Being on the Lookout," *Village Voice*, 16 October, p. 51.

Dewar, Helen (1993) "Senate Bows to Braun on Symbol of Confederacy," *Washington Post*, 23 July, pp. A1, A10.

Dorris, Michael (1992) "Noble Savages? We'll Drink to That," *New York Times*, 21 April, p. A23.

Driedger, Bill (1992) Letter to the Editor, *Globe and Mail*, 28 March, p. D7.

Editorial, "Be Sensitive, but Don't Drop All Indian Names" *Seattle Times*, 28 Sept, p. B4.

Farnsworth, Clyde H. (1995) "For the Mounties, Justice Is Now a Licensing Fee," *New York Times*, 4 February, pp. 33, 45.

Findley, Timothy (1992) Letter to the Editor, *Globe and Mail*, 28 March, p. D7, reprinted in *OUT Magazine: Canada's National Gay Arts/Entertainment Monthly*, June 1992.

Giago, Tim (1994) "Drop the Chop! Indian Nicknames Just Aren't Right," *New York Times*, 13 March.

———— (1995) "Indian-Named Mascots Like Those in World Series Assault Self-Esteem," *Buffalo News*, 26 October, p. 3.

Godfrey, Stephen (1992) "Canada Council Asks Whose Voice Is It Anyway?" *Globe and Mail*, 21 March, pp. C1, C15.

———— (1991) "It May Be the Real Thing but Is It the Right Thing," *Globe and Mail*, 9 November, p. C1.

Goldstein, Richard (1990) "We So Horny: Sado Studs and Super Sluts: America's New Sex 'Tude," *Village Voice* 16 October, pp. 35–37, 160.

Grow, Doug (1992) "The Way to Redskins Owner's Heart Is through his Wallet," *Star Tribune* (Minneapolis), September 11 p. 3B.

———— (1995) "Relative of Crazy Horse Questions Brewer's 'Honor,'" *Star Tribune* (Minneapolis), 21 April, p. 3B.

Hays, Constance (1991) "Gay Patrol and MGM in a Battle over Name," *New York Times*, 27 May, p. 21(L).

Hirsley, Michael (1995) "Native American Sterotypes Live on in Sports Logos, Rituals," *Chicago Tribune*, 24 October, p. N1.

Hutchinson, Alan (1992) "Giving Smaller Voices a Chance to Be Heard," *Globe and Mail*, 14 April, p. A16.

Hutchinson, Joe P. (1995) "Nuances of a Nickname," *Arizona Republic*, 5 November, p. C5.

Jackson, Derrick Z. (1995) "Making Money by Any Means Necessary," *Boston Globe*, February 1, p. 13.

Jacoby, Joy Anne (1992) Letter to the Editor, *Globe and Mail*, 28 March, p. D7.

Jojola, Ted (1993) "Negative Image Exploited to Undercut Indian Self-Government," *Albuquerque Journal*, 27 June, p. B3.

Kaplan, David A. (1993) "I'd Like to Buy a Dollar: Vanna White's Lawsuit over an Ad Parody," *Newsweek*, 5 April, p. 54.

Keeshig-Tobias, Lenore (1990) "Stop Stealing Native Stories," *Globe and Mail*, 26 January, p. A8.

Key, Janet (1989) "At Age 100, a New Aunt Jemima," *Chicago Tribune*, 28 April, p. C1.

"Klan Rumor Helped Ruin Sport Clothing Firm" (1989) *San Francisco Chronicle*, 22 July.

Klawans, Stewart (1990) "American Notes," *Times Literary Supplement*, 20 July, p. 774.

Kruh, Nancy (1994) "Collecting Controversy: Evolving Images," *Dallas Morning News*, 13 February, p. 1f.

Lemay, J. J. (1995) "RCMP Has No Plans to Play Censor," *Toronto Star*, 23 August, p. A13 (Letter to the Editor).

Lippert, Barbara (1996) "Mrs. America," *New York Magazine*, July 22, pp. 34–39.

Marchand, Philip (1992) "When Appropriation Becomes Inappropriate," *Toronto Star*, 23 November, p. B5.

Marriott, M. (1990) "I'm Bart, I'm Black, and What about It?," *New York Times*, 19 September, p. B1.

McEwen, Bill (1995) "Great Scot! Nicknames Have Worth," *Fresno Bee*, 24 October, p. C1.

McLaughlin, Craig (1988) "The Walker Nomination: A Bork Style Battle in San Francisco," *San Francisco Bay Guardian*, 20 January, p. 7.

"Miami U. Abandon's 'Redskins' Name" (1996) *The Chronicle of Higher Education*, 4 October, p. A8.

Mihoces, Gary (1993) "Trying to Get a Handle: Possible Merchandise Bonanza Hinges on Selection," *USA Today*, 17 September.

Mills, D. (1990) "Bootleg Black Bart Simpson, the Hip-Hop T-Shirt Star," *Washington Post*, 28 June, p. D1.

Musto, M. (1990) "La Dolce Musto," *Village Voice*, 26 October, p. 44.

Neil, M. and Otey, A. (1995) All Shook Up: Two Skydiving Groups Try to Chute Each Other Down," *People*, 27 February, p. 50.

Outram, Richard (1992) Letter to the Editor, *Globe and Mail*, 28 March, p. D7.

"P & G Loses Campaign for the Moon and Stars" (1985) *Globe and Mail*, 26 April p. B6.

"P & G Signals Move to Acquire Existing Brands" (1985) *Montreal Gazette*, 3 October, p. E6.

Paris, Erna (1992) "A Letter to the Thought Police," *Globe and Mail*, 31 March, p. A16.

Pierson, Don (1992) "Redskins Nickname Will Be Protest Target," *Chicago Tribune*, 19 January, p. C2.

Prince, Greg (1994) "Tall Order: The Making and Marketing of Arizona Iced Tea," *Beverage World*, June, cover.

"Proctor and Gamble Lifts the Veil a Little" (1982) *Globe and Mail*, 15 March p. B1.

"Proctor and Gamble's Battles with Rumors" (1982) *New York Times*, 22 July, pp. D1, D10.

"A Professor's Class Video Runs into an MTV Protest" (1991) *New York Times*, 18 May, p. I46.

Ristich, Nada (1992) Letter to the Editor, *Saturday Night Magazine*, December, pp. 5, 14.

Shapiro, Leonard (1992) "Offensive Penalty Is Called on 'Redskins': Native Americans Protest the Name," *Washington Post*, 3 November, p. D1.

Shenon, Philip (1988) "Battle Looming over a Nominee for U.S. Court," *New York Times*, 14 January, p. A14.

Shuman, Mark (1996) "Native Voice," *Denver Post*, 28 January.

Smith, Russell (1992) Letter to the Editor, *Globe and Mail*, 3 April, p. A3.

"$2.4 Million for Singer Imitated in Ad" (1990) *Chicago Tribune*, 9 May, p. 5.

Vaillancourt, Meg (1994) "Big Crow's First Stand: Descendant of Crazy Horse Goes Public to Keep Legendary Warrior's Name off High-Octane Beer," *Boston Globe*, 4 December, p. A85.

Visser, Margaret (1992) "The Joy of Jelly," *Saturday Night*, September, p. 38.

Wheat, Jack (1993) "Real Seminoles Resent the Profits FSU Makes off Their Tribal Name," *Miami Herald*, 11 February, p. 7B.

Wilkerson, R. (1990) "Challenging Nike, Rights Group Takes a Risky Stand," *New York Times* 25 August, p. A10.

Winkler, Karen J. (1995) "An Anthropologist of Influence: Clifford Geertz Relishes Experimentation and Refuses to be Pigeonholed," *Chronicle of Higher Education*, 5 May, pp. A16, A23.

Cases

(1903) Bleistein v. Donaldson Lithographing Co., 188 U.S. 239 (U.S.S.C.).

(1917) Aunt Jemima Mills Co. v. Rigney & Co., 247 F.407 (2d Cir.).

(1928) Yale Electric Corp. v. Robertson, 26 F.2d 972 (2d Cir.).

(1930) Nichols v. Universal Pictures Corp., 45 F. 2d 119 (2d Cir.).

(1934) Waterman Co. v. Gordon, 72 F.2d 272 (2d Cir.).

(1942) Mishawaka Rubber & Woolen Mfg. Co. v. S. S. Kresge Co., 316 U.S. 203 (U.S.S.C.).

(1951) U.S. Life Insurance Co. v. Hamilton, S.W.2d 238 (289) (Tex. Civ. App.).

(1951) Garner v. Triangle Publications 97 F. Supp. 546 (S.D.N.Y.).

(1954) Warner Bros. Pictures, Inc. v. Columbia Broadcasting System, Inc., 216 F. 2d 945 (9th Cir.).

(1962) Lahr v. Adell Chemical Co., 300 F.2d 256 (1st Cir.).

(1964) Spahn v. Julian Messner, Inc., 43 Misc. 2d 219, 250 N.Y.S. 2d 529 (N.Y. County Ct.).

(1964) Tiffany & Co. v. Boston Club Inc., 231 F. Supp. 836, 844 (D. Mass.).

(1965) University of Notre Dame v. Twentieth Century Fox, 22 A.D. 2d 452, 256 N.Y.S. 2d 301 (N.Y. App. Div.).

(1968) Cepeda v. Swift & Co., 291 F. Supp. 242 (E.D. Mo.), (1969) 415 F.2d 1205 (8th Cir.).

(1968) Paulsen v. Personality Posers, 59 Misc. 2d 444, 299 N.Y.S. 2d 501 (N.Y. County Ct.).

(1972) Coca-Cola Co. v. Gemini Rising Inc., 346 F. Supp. 1183 (E.D.N.Y.).

(1973) Grant v. Esquire, Inc. 367 F. Supp. 876 (S.D.N.Y.).

(1974) Motschenbacher v. R. J. Reynolds Tobacco Co., 498 F.2d 821 (9th Cir.).

(1974) Rinaldi v. Village Voice 79 Misc. 2d 57, 359 N.Y.S. 2d 176 (N.Y. County Ct.), modified 47 A.D. 2d 180, 365 N.Y.S. 2d 199 (N.Y. App. Div.), (1975) cert. denied 423 U.S. 883.

(1975) Booth v. Colgate Palmolive Co., 362 F. Supp. 343 (S.D.N.Y.).

(1975) Boston Professional Hockey Ass'n. v. Dallas Cap & Emblem Mfg., Inc., 510 F.2d 1004 (5th Cir.).

(1975) Price v. Hal Roach Studios, Inc., 400 F.Supp. 836 (S.D.N.Y.).

(1976) Augusta National, Inc. v. Northwestern Mutual Life Inc. Co., 193 U.S.P.Q. (BNA) 210 (S.D. Ga.).

(1977) Athans v. Canadian Adventure Camps Ltd., 34 C.P.R.(2d) 126 (Ont. H.Ct.).

(1977) Factors Etc., Inc. v. Creative Card Co., 444 F. Supp. 279, 3 Media Law Reporter 1290 (S.D.N.Y.).

(1977) Ideal Toy Corp. v. Kenner Products, 443 F. Supp. 291 (S.D.N.Y.).

(1977) Lombardo v. Doyle, Dane & Bernback, Inc., 58 A.D. 2d 620, 396 N.Y.S. 2d 661 (N.Y. App. Div.).

(1977) Memphis Development Foundation v. Factors Etc., Inc., 441 F.Supp. 1323 (W.D. Tenn.), reversed and remanded (1980) 616 F.2d 956 (6th Cir.).

(1977) Reddy Communications, Inc. v. Environmental Action Foundation, Inc., 199 U.S.P.Q (BNA) 630, 631-32 (D.D.C.) (denying preliminary injunction); (1979) 477 F.Supp. 936 (D.D.C.) (denying permanent injunction).

(1977) Sid & Marty Kroft Television v. McDonald's Corp., 562 F. 2d 1157 (9th Cir.).

(1977) Zacchini v. Scripps-Howard Broadcasting Co., 433 U.S. 562 (S.C. Ohio).

(1978) Ali v. Playgirl, 447 F.Supp. 723, 3 Media Law Reporter (BNA) 2540, 206 U.S.P.Q. (BNA) 1021 (S.D.N.Y.).

(1978) Hicks v. Casablanca Records, 464 F. Supp. 426, 4 Media Law Reporter (BNA) (914970), 204 U.S.P.Q. (BNA) 126 (S.D.N.Y.).

(1978) Price v. Worldvision Enters., Inc., 455 F.Supp. 252 (S.D.N.Y.), aff'd (1979) 603 F.2d 214 (2d Cir.).

(1979) General Electric Co. v. Alumpa Coal Co., 205 U.S.P.Q. (BNA) 1036 (D. Mass.).

(1979) Hirsch v. S. C. Johnson & Son, 90 Wis.2d 379, 280 N.W.2d 129 (Wis. Sup. Ct.).

(1979) Lopez v. Triangle Communications, 70 A.D.2d 359, 421 N.Y.S. 2d 57, 5 Media Law Reporter (BNA) 2039 (N.Y. App. Div.).

(1979) Lugosi v. Universal Pictures, 160 Cal. Rptr. 323 (L.A. County Ct.).

(1980) Ann-Margret v. High Society Magazine, 498 F. Supp. 401, 6 Media Law Reporter (BNA) 1774 (S.D.N.Y.).

(1980) Hansen v. High Society Magazine, 5 Media Law Reporter (BNA) 2398 (N.Y. County Ct.), rev'd, 76 A.D. 2d 812, 429 N.Y.S. 2d 552, 6 Media Law Reporter (BNA) 1618 (N.Y. App. Div.).

(1981) Groucho Marx Productions, Inc. v. Day and Night Co., Inc., 523 F. Supp. 485 (S.D.N.Y.), (1982) 689 F.2d 317 (2d Cir.).

(1981) Loft v. Fuller So., 408 F.2d 619 (Fla. Dist. Ct. App.).

(1982) Atari Inc., v. North Am. Philips Consumer Elecs. Corp. 672 F. 2d 607 (7th Cir.).

(1982) Warner Bros. Inc. v. American Broadcasting Co., 530 F. Supp. 1187 (S.D.N.Y.).

(1983) Bi-Rite Enterprises, Inc., v. Button Master, 555 F. Supp. 1188 (S.D.N.Y.).

(1983) Canada Safeway Ltd. v. Manitoba Food and Chemical Workers, Local 832, 73 C.P.R. (2d) 234 (Man. Ct. App.).

(1983) Carson v. Here's Johnny Portable Toilets, Inc., 698 F.2d 831 (6th Cir.).

(1983) Exxon Corp. v. Exxene Corp., 696 F.2d 544, 550 (7th Cir.).

(1983) International Olympic Committee v. San Francisco Arts & Athletics, 219 U.S.P.Q. 982 (issuing preliminary injunction), affirmed (1983) 707 F.2d 517 (9th Cir.), (1987) 107 S.Ct. 2971.

(1983) Martin Luther King, Jr. Center for Social Change, Inc. v. American Heritage Products, 694 F.2d 674 (11th Cir.).

(1984) *Hollie Hobby* Trade Mark, [1984] R.P.C. 329, 350 (H.L.).

(1984) Lerman v. Flynt Distributing Co., 745 F. 2d 123, 10 Media Law Reporter (BNA) 2497 (2d Cir.), cert. denied 471 U.S. 1054.

(1985) Creel v. Crown Publishers, 115 A.D. 2d 414, 496, 219 N.Y.S. 2d, 12 Media Law Reporter (BNA) 1558 (N.Y. App. Div.).

(1985) Jordache Enterprises, Inc. v. Hogg Wyld, Ltd., 625 F. Supp. 48 (D.N.M.).

(1985) Lucasfilm Ltd. v. High Frontier, 622 F. Supp. 931 (D.D.C.).

(1986) Joseph v. Daniels, 11 C.P.R. (3d) 544 (B.C.S.C.).

(1986) Mutual of Omaha Ins. Co. v. Novak, 648 F. Supp. 905, 231 U.S.P.Q. (BNA) 963 (D. Neb.).

(1987) Ameritech, Inc., v. American Info. Technologies Corp., 811 F. 2d 960 (6th Cir.).

(1987) Elvis Presley International Memorial Foundation v. Crowell, 733 S.W.2d 89 (Tenn. Ct. App.).

(1987) Elvis Presley Enterprises v. Elvisly Yours, 817 F.2d. 104 (6th Cir.).

(1987) San Francisco Arts & Athletics Inc., v. United States Olympic Comm., 107 S. Ct. 2971.

(1988) Kamercorp Holdings Inc. v. 624564 Ontario Ltd., 23 C.P.R. (3d) 262 (F.T.D.).

(1988) Midler v. Ford Motor Co., 849 F.2d 460 (9th Cir.), cert. denied (1992) 117 L. Ed. 2d 650, 112 S.Ct. 1513, 112 S.Ct. 1514.

(1989) American Express Co. v. Vibra Approved Laboratories Corp., 1989 U.S. Dist. LEXIS 4377, 10 U.S.P.Q. 2d (BNA) 2006 (S.D.N.Y.).

(1989) Coca-Cola Co. v. Alma Leo U.S.A., Inc., 719 F. Supp. 725 (N.D. Ill.).

(1989) Irwin Toy v. Quebec (Attorney General) [1989] 1 S.C.R. 927 (S. Ct. Canada).

(1989) Mead Data Central, Inc. v. Toyota Motor Sales, U.S.A., Inc., 875 F.2d 1020 (2d Cir.).

(1989) Walt Disney Productions v. Air Pirates, 870 F. 2d 40 (2d Cir.).

(1990) In re Clarke 17 U.S.P.Q. 2d (BNA) 1238 (Trademark Trial & App. Bd).

(1990) Rocket v. Royal College of Dental Surgeons [1990] 2 S.C.R. 232 (S. Ct. Canada).

(1991) Feist Publications Inc. v. Rural Telephone Service Co., 111 S. Ct. 1282 (U.S.S.C.).

(1991) Rogers v. Koons, 960 F.2d 301 (2d Cir.), cert. denied (1992) 113 S. Ct. 365.

(1992) New Kids on the Block v. News America Publishing Inc. 971 F. 2d 302 (9th Cir.).

(1992) R. v. Butler, 89 D.L.R. (4th) 449 (S.C.C.).

(1992) White v. Samsung Electronics America, Inc. 971 F.2d 1395 (9th Cir.), rehearing en banc denied (1993) 989 F.2d 1512 (9th Cir.).

(1993) Hornell Brewing Co. v. Brady, 819 F. Supp. 1227 (E.D.N.Y.).

(1994) Anheuser-Busch, Inc. v. Balducci Publications, 28 F.3d 769, 31 U.S.P.Q. 2D (BNA) 1296 (8th Cir.).

(1994) Campbell v. Acuff-Rose Music, Inc., 114 S. Ct. 1164 (U.S.S.C).

(1994) Deere & Co. v. MTD Products Inc., 41 F. 3d 39 (2d Cir.).

(1994) Harjo v. Pro Football, Inc., 30 U.S.P.Q. 2d (BNA) 1828 (T.T.A.B.).

(1994) In re Tasunke Witko, Civ. No. 93-204 (Rosebud Sx. Tri. Ct.).

(1995) In re Tasunke Witco, Civ. No. 93-204 (Ct. App. Rosebud Sx. Tri., March 10).

(1995) R. J. R. MacDonald, Inc. v. Canada (Attorney General) [1995] 3 S.C.R. 199 (S. Court Canada).

(1996) Cie generale des establissements Michelin-Michelin & Cie v. National Automobile, Aerospace, Transportation and General Workers of Canada (CAW-Canada), [1996] F.C.J. No. 1685 QL.

(1996) Gould Estate v. Stoddart Publishing Co. [1996] O.J. NO. 3288 (Ont. Ct. Gen.)

Statutes, Canada

Act Respecting Indians. 1951 Statutes of Canada, 15 George VI, Chapter 29.

Act to Amend and Consolidate the Laws Repecting Indians. 1876 Statutes of Canada, 39 Victoria, Chapter 18.

An Act to Further Amend the "Indian Act, 1880." 1884 Statutes of Canada, 47 Victoria, Chapter 27.
Copyright Act, R.S.C. 1985, c.C-42.
The Intellectual Property Law Improvement Act, S.C. 1993 c.15.
Trade Marks Act R.S.C. 1985, c.T-13.

Statutes, United States

Amateur Sports Act 36 U.S.C. §371–396 (1988).
Copyright Act, 1976, 17 U.S.C. (1988 & Supp. V 1993).
Federal Trademark Dilution Act of 1995, 15 U.S.C 1051.
Lanham Act, 15 U.S.C.A.
Tennessee Code Annotated (1988).

Statutes, Great Britain

Trade Mark Act 1938.

International Treaties

The Convention for the Protection of Cultural Property in the event of armed conflict, enacted in the Hague on May 14, 1954 (249 U.N.T.S. 240).
The Convention on the Means of Prohibiting and Preventing the Illicit Import, Export, and Transfer of Ownership of Cultural Property of November 14, 1970, 823 U.N.T.S. 231, reprinted in (1971) INTERNATIONAL LEGAL MATERIALS 10: 289.

Index

Anheuser-Busch, Inc. v. Balducci Publications, 321 n.94
Ann-Margret, 262
Anti-aesthetic movement, 378 n.49
Antidilution statutes, 70, 71, 324 n.115, 325 n.119, 329 n.151
Anti-essentialism, 107, 227–28, 242
Antipotlatch laws, 236, 238
Anton Piller orders, 79, 331 n.164, 354 n.40
Aoki, Keith: on changes in trademark law, 61; on intellectual property and information technology, 364 n.81; on intellectual property laws privatizing the public domain, 53; and metaphor in intellectual property law, 326 n.131; on strategic defense initiative ad, 268
Appadurai, Arjun, 16–17, 31, 312 n.117, 346 n.84
Appropriation of personality, tort of, 90, 335 n.6
Art: advertising appropriated in, 73–76; artists addressing cultural appropriation, 244, 384 n.162; for art's sake, 381 n.102; European art-culture system, 216–25; identity in Native peoples', 381 n.102; Koons's *Banality* exhibition, 327 n.143; mass production destroying aura of works of, 101–2; multinational corporations as patrons of, 74; in politics of community, 290
Articulation: and alterity in the space of politics, 273–99; Laclau on, 294; of Native claims, 241–45; political articulations, 131–35; politics as, 132; of social world, 28, 295; utterances, 83
Athletic wear, 157–59
Atlanta Braves, 186, 187, 189
Audience, reading, 254–55, 256–57
Augusta National, Inc. v. Northwestern Mutual Life Ins. Co., 326 n.127
Aunt Jemima, 170, 185
Authentic artifacts, 218–19
Authenticity: authorial identity and, 214–15; logos as signatures of, 169; and mechanical reproduction, 101
Authentic masterpieces, 218–19
Authority: of anthropology, 251; as having to contend with alterity, 85; law as authoritative and pervasive discourse, 124; public authorities, 32, 135, 352 n.22
Authorship: as abstraction, 230; and alterity, 33–39, 85, 248–72; artists' critiques of, 73; authoring alterity, 18–29;

authoring culture, 1–39; the author in the bourgeois public sphere, 249–57; Barthes on death of the author, 284; as broker for management of textuality, 255; of celebrity, 92–100; as a commodity, 254; corporations as authors, 59–62; in films, 282–83; Foucault on the author, 59; in *Globe and Mail* debate, 210–15; interrogation of as crucial, 299; judiciary overestimating creativity of, 317 n.60; law as freezing signification in legitimating, 8; political role of bourgeois author, 277–78; postmodern challenge to, 284–85; Romantic individualist view of, 211–12, 219–20, 255, 283; the signature, 273, 283–89; and trademarks, 61, 62, 163; writing distinguished from the writer, 286

Bacon-Smith, Camille, 118–23, 124, 125, 351 n.204
Bakhtin, Mikhail, 82–85
Banality (Koons), 327 n.143
Barbie dolls, 66–67
Barnet, Richard, 143
Barthes, Roland, 284
Baudrillard, Jean: on brands, 56–57; on commodity culture as signifying culture, 55; on hermeneutics of suspicion, 308 n.81; on hyperreality, 360 n.138; paraphrased in alternative press, 2; on postmechanical reproduction, 107; on postmodern regime of signification, 133; on seduction, 360 n.139
Bellecourt, Vernon, 198
Belmore, Rebecca, 237
Bemidji, Minnesota, 178, 364 n.70
Benjamin, Walter, 101–2, 107, 150, 179, 242–43
Berkhofer, Robert, 188, 189
Berlant, Lauren, 170
Bhabha, Homi K.: on rumors, 143, 144, 145, 163; and Sikh Mountie controversy, 139; on stereotypes in colonial discourse, 190–91
Bickerton, Ashley, 73
Bidlo, Mike, 73
Big Crow, Seth, 202–3, 370 n.158, 372 n.182
Billie, James, 366 n.100
Birmingham school, 311 n.111
Bissoondath, Neil, 211
Blackface minstrelsy, 194–95, 196
Black Hills, 200, 201
Black Label beer, 2, 8

185, 187; and Redwood City Taco Bell, 181–83; term's origin, 180

Children: brand names on goods for, 52–53; rumors about trademarks, 358 n.81; trademarks as friends from childhood, 57; in turn-of-the-century imagery, 175

Chippewa peoples, 179

Chon, Margaret, 54

Churchill, Ward, 240, 366 n.98, 383 n.147

Church's Fried Chicken, 152–53, 162

Cifelli, Armand, 338 n.40

Citizenship: commodification of, 5; and consumption, 281; and mass media, 279; new concept required, 132; and transnational labor, 182

Civil society: and democracy, 396 n.114; Gramsci on, 396 n.114; Habermas on, 280, 392 n.18; in Laclau, 294; mass mediation and the publics of, 280–83; and textual forms, 257

Class: and access to media, 392 n.18; the ruling class and intellectual signs, 68. *See also* Working class

Clifford, James: on European art-culture system, 216–20, 378 n.49; on Lévi-Strauss's refugee period, 20–21; on realist ethnography, 36

Coca-Cola Company: and Burciaga's *Drink Cultura: Chicanismo*, 179, 181; logo's value to, 56, 318 n.64; losing its right to *cola*, 332 n.169; Santa Claus image, 313 n.5; trademark suits by, 72, 79–80, 332 n.168

Collage, 36, 86

Collective identities: active creation of, 29; cultural resources as required for constructing, 47–48; material objects epitomizing, 224

College sports, licensing revenues for, 365 n.96

Colonialism: intellectual property law in, 33; stereotypes in discourse of, 190–91. *See also* Native peoples; Postcolonialism

Commercial culture: academic attitude toward, 346 n.99; Indian imagery in, 232; intellectual properties' constitutive role in, 5

Commercial speech: defined, 268; fair use provision as devaluing, 267; protection for, 267–72, 390 n.116; public discourse compared with, 271

Commodified cultural forms: connotations exceeding those imagined at inception, 133–34; creating new relations of power

in cultural politics, 26; as generative and prohibitive, 89; as permeating experience, 57; political action requiring engagement with, 42; in proto-communities, 106; recoding of, 58, 248; ubiquity of, 21

Commodities: the author as, 254; black bodies as, 150–51, 207; commodity culture as signifying culture, 55; Indian spirituality as, 239–40; local cultural interpretations of foreign, 22–23

Commodity fetishism: legal endorsement of, 72; as shifting from product to sign, 56

Communities: advertising producing sense of belonging, 173; breakdown of traditional, 106; contingent visions of, 289–90; law as creating cultural spaces for formation of, 124; literature in politics of, 290–91, 395 n.100; proto-communities, 106; the unworked community, 289–97

Connolly, William, 132, 298–99, 397 n.123

Connor, Steven, 15, 105

Connotative value, 68

Constructionism. *See* Social (cultural) constructionism

Consumption: as active, 104; capitalism as culture of, 54; and citizenship, 281; consumers as audiences, 279; graffiti and tension in consumer culture, 184; marginality as pervasive in consumer society, 58; production of consumers as corporate goal, 56; as type of production, 27, 104

"Contesting Paternity: Histories of Authorship" (Coombe), 386 n.22

"Contesting the Self: Negotiating Subjectivities in Nineteenth-Century Ontario Defamation Trials" (Coombe), 347 n.104

Context: listening to Native claims in, 229–31, 241; signs existing in, 67

Contingency: attending to, 230; of communities, 289–90; in construction of identities, 132; cultural studies on, 24; of Enlightenment concepts, 292; an ethics of, 5, 274, 297–99; in just legal decisions, 299; postmodernist anthropology on, 34; of the social, 273; of those things we find natural, 45

"Contingent Articulations: A Critical Cultural Studies of Law" (Coombe), 303 n.8

ture, 16. *See also* Critical cultural legal studies

Culture: and anthropology's authorial dilemma, 250–51; as appropriated by other disciplines, 15–18; authoring culture, 1–39; as constructed, 242; contemporary properties of identity and, 226–29; cultural studies as writing against, 16; European art-culture system, 216–25; feminist anthropologists on, 14–15; as interdependence, 68; and law, 9, 10–11, 302 n.8; legal theorists as idealizing, 86, 334 n.202; as meaning-making, 82; as medium and consequence of social difference, 24; misgivings about concept of, 11–15; the objective world as cultural construction, 43–44; in orthodox cultural anthropology, 13–14; politics as cultural activity, 274; politics as separated from, 265; postmodern culture, 50–52; as process of constructing identity, 29; promotional culture, 261, 388 n.72; represented as homogenous and static, 226; slide to media from, 270; universalization and homogenization of, 22. *See also* Commercial culture; Cultural difference; Cultural identity; Cultural studies; Cultural nationalism; Mass culture; Popular culture; Subcultures

Curtis, Robin, 127

Dalton, David, 115

Davis, Bette, 110, 111

Day in Hollywood, a Night in the Ukraine, A (play), 96, 97

Dean, James: as the icon of our time, 115; lesbian refashionings of, 89, 115, 116; "Rebel" cologne, 340 n.54

Decentered subject, 42, 49, 315 n.35

De Certeau, Michel, 1, 104, 134

De Genova, Nick, 351 n.2

Democracy: civil society required in, 396 n.114; communicative democracy, 278; and contemporary theories of communication, 265; as dialogic, 129, 266, 271–72, 295–96; ethics of contingency for, 297–99; Habermas's discourse theory of, 276, 277, 278–79; in postmodern conditions, 273, 274; as tendency toward affirmation of "constitutive outside," 292

Denicola, Robert C., 325 n.116

Derrida, Jacques: on *différance*, 292; on postmodernism, 303 n.16; on writing, 46

Descriptive marks, 63, 197

Design patents, cultural power of, 6

Devil symbolism, 148–49

Dews, Peter, 392 n.18

Dialogue: communicative democracy as dialogic, 278; democratic politics as dialogic, 129, 266, 271–72, 295–96; dialogics of postmodern politics, 82–87; fans engaging in, 127; intellectual property laws affecting, 42, 50–51, 68–69, 86; as reciprocal, 85; as regulative ideal for political life, 46–47; social processes as stifling, 47

Diawara, Manthia, 156

Dietrich, Marlene, 110, 111

Différance, 292

Difference: as bracketed in public sphere, 276; capital appropriating indicia of national, 185; in construction of identities, 131, 132, 165, 295; mass-advertised trademarks and, 173; among Native peoples, 243; the signature occurring in a space of, 287; signification systems as systems of, 46. *See also* Cultural difference

Digital technologies, 249, 285

Dilution of a trademark, 70–73; antidilution statutes, 70, 71, 324 n.115, 325 n.119, 329 n.151; and Lanham Act, 319 n.82; Schechter on, 70; as strategy for Native peoples, 205; Trademark Dilution Act of 1995, 325 n.119; in twentieth-century law, 61, 68

Discipline and Punish (Foucault), 3

Dissonant cognitive frameworks, 313 n.6

Distinctiveness, 62, 175, 176

Dorris, Michael, 200

Dos Passos, John, 115, 178, 364 n.70

Doty, Alexander, 88, 345 n.63

Douzinas, Costas, 248, 299

Drag queens, 111, 113

Drescher, Thomas D., 68, 318 n.63

Dreyfuss, Rochelle: on case law tendency, 323 n.99; on consumer confusion requirement, 322 n.94; on equating value with right, 323 nn. 100, 106; on expressive genericity, 82, 269; on signaling functions and expressive capacity, 66–67

Driedger, Bill, 211

Drink Cultura: Chicanismo (Burciaga), 179–81

Dyer, Richard, 94

Elgin Marbles, 223

Embodiment, 166–207; bodily incorporation of advertising image, 206–7; commodification of bodies, 150–51, 207;

Embodiment (continued): contemporary contestations of embodied distinctions, 177–85; in liberal public sphere, 171; marked and unmarked bodies, 170–77; mimicry, alterity, and, 167–70

Enlightenment: authorial speech privileged by, 273; contingency of concepts of, 292; free speech grounded in concepts, 258; postmodern critique of, 303 n.16

Environmental Action Foundation, 69, 324 nn. 110, 111

Equality: contingency of, 292; law's commitment to abstract, 299

Errington, Frederick K., 20

Eskimos, 174, 175

Essentialism, 107, 132, 215, 227–28

Estoppel doctrine, 368 n.146

Ethics of contingency, 5, 274, 297–99

Ethnographic representation, 12, 304 n.17

Everard, John, 103

Ewen, Stewart, 103

Expressive genericity, 82, 269

Exxon Corp. v. Exxene Corp., 326 n.125

Fabo, Andy, 244

Fact/fiction dichotomy, 261–64

Fair use doctrine: and artistic appropriation of trademarks, 74, 75; in Canada, 324 n.115, 333 n.174, 371 n.163; commercial speech devalued by, 267; Kozinski's nominative fair use defense, 269; and publicity rights, 341 n.59; and scholarly use of copyrighted material, 81–82; in United States, 332 n.174, 371 n.163

Fandom: in gay camp subculture, 110–13; *Star Trek* fanzines, 117–23, 125–27; *Star Wars* fanzines, 128, 350 n.204; as vehicle for marginalized groups, 104

Farred, Grant, 153

Fast-food operations, 182, 357 n.81

Feather, John, 378 n.52

Feist Publications v. Rural Tel. Serv. Co., 317 n.59

Feminism: and Canadian obscenity law, 374 n.8; feminist anthropologists on culture, 14–15; Indian spiritual themes in, 239; on the legal subject, 314 n.22; on Marilyn Monroe image, 102–3, 345 n.72; on media use of female body, 73; the personal is the political, 108; poststructuralist, 107; poststructuralist challenges to, 108; sex and gender distinguished by, 109; on sexual identity, 107

Ferolito, Vultaggio & Sons, 200–202

Fictional characters: Canadian protection of, 78–79, 330 n.160; U.S. protection of, 60, 331 n.160

Fiction/fact dichotomy, 261–64

FILA sportswear, 130

Findley, Timothy, 210–11, 374 n.8

Fine, Gary Alan, 143, 147–48, 161, 356 n.71, 357 n.81

First Amendment. *See* Free speech

First contact, 20, 150

First Nations peoples: on Aboriginal Title, 245–47; in advertising, 4–5; articulating their claims in terms of possessive individualism, 241–42; artists appropriating from, 384 n.162; authentic identity rhetoric of, 214–15; consumer confusion doctrine and representations of, 381 n.103; representations of, 228–29; stereotypical images of, 197; values systems for works by, 381 n.101; and Western categories of property, 209–10. *See also* American Indians

Fishing rights, 384 n.164

Fiss, Owen, 258–60

"500 Years of Indian Resistance" meeting, 232

Florida State University Seminoles, 186, 366 n.100

Flying Elvi v. Flying Elvises, 350 n.194

Foster, Hal, 104–5

Foucault, Michel: on the author, 59; on disciplinary surveillance in construction of the subject, 45; *Discipline and Punish*, 3; on law, 350 n.191; on postmodernism, 303 n.16

Frankfurter, Justice Felix, 70

Fraser, Nancy, 171, 252, 276–77, 358 n.87

Freedom: contingency of, 292; and meaning, 334 n.195. *See also* Free speech

Free speech: for advertisers, 260–61; Canadian obscenity law, 374 n.8; and contemporary understanding of communication, 264–72; as defense for subcultural appropriation, 349 n.190; dissent model of, 267; Enlightenment foundations of, 258; as freedom from government interference, 259; in Gay Olympic Games suit, 137; Gordon's natural law defense of, 77–78; intellectual property laws ignoring, 54; legal theorists' materialist view of, 335 n.203; liberal model's shortcomings, 264–65, 387 n.56; as limited to the political,

274; and mass media, 258–60, 388 n.61; and parody of trademarks, 329 n.151; in postmodern conditions, 249, 257–64; property rights conflicting with, 259–64, 266; and publicity rights, 91–92, 261–64, 337 n.27; trademarks constraining, 69

Frito Bandito, 180, 185, 187

Frontier thesis, 177, 178

Frug, Mary Joe, 346 n.99

Fynsk, Christopher, 395 n.95

Gaines, Jane, 26, 60, 311 n.111

Garbo, Greta: in gay male subculture, 110, 111, 112; in Madonna's image, 97

Gardiner, Michael, 82

Garland, Judy: in Judith Butler fanzine, 123; in gay camp subculture, 110, 112–13

Garnham, Nicholas, 265, 267, 273, 279, 387 n.56

Gates, Henry Louis, Jr., 156

Gay camp subculture, 110–13; camp losing its appeal, 113; origins of, 110–11; Sontag on pastiche in, 105–6

Gay Olympic Games, 136–38, 353 nn. 28, 29, 354 n.35

Geertz, Clifford: on anthropology's identity crises, 1; on authorial dilemma of anthropology, 250, 385 n.8; on authorship in anthropology, 34–35; on the interpretive task, 14

Gender identities: androgyny, 117; bourgeois public sphere as gendered, 253; celebrity images in production of, 5, 31–32, 107–29; as culturally constructed, 109–10; marked and unmarked forms conveying, 172; as performative, 109, 112; racialized gender difference, 380 n.80; sex as distinguished from gender, 109. See also Queer identities; Women

General Electric, 72

General Foods, 81, 145, 356 n.68

Genericide, 79, 287, 344 n.59

Generic names, 79–82

Generic words, 62

Genius, 219, 255

Gewertz, Deborah B., 20

Giago, Tim, 366 n.104

Girl groups, 113

Glenbow Museum, 236, 237

Globe and Mail debate, 208, 210–15

Golding, Sue, 115–17

Golliwog, 166–67, 185, 361 n.6

Goodrich, Peter, 248, 299

Goodwill, 60, 64, 69, 174

Gordon, Wendy: on creation of meaning, 50–51; on deprivation of public domain as harm, 99; on free riding, 68; on intellectual property laws privatizing the public domain, 53–54, 317 n.59; natural law defense of free speech, 77–78; on reality as artifact, 41; on right following from value, 93

Gossip, 114–15

Gough, Robert, 371 n.170

Graffiti, 180, 183–84, 365 n.89

Gramsci, Antonio, 24, 82, 132, 294, 396 n.114

Greece, 379 n.71

Greenhouse, Carol, 29

Gregory, Steven, 358 n.87

Grieg, Noel, 88

Griffiths, Drew, 88

Griggers, Cathy, 107

Groening, Matt, 331 n.164

Groucho Marx Productions, Inc. v. Day and Night Co., Inc., 96

Group rights, 222–23

Haacke, Hans, 73, 74, 76

Habermas, Jürgen: on bourgeois public sphere, 171, 252, 258, 275, 278; on civil society, 280, 392 n.18; discourse theory of democracy, 276, 277, 278–79; on mass media, 278, 279, 392 n.18; on mechanisms of social spheres, 392 n.10; on postmodernism, 303 n.16; and slide from culture to media, 270; on subjectivity, 315 n.25

Hachamovitch, Yifat, 248, 299

Hachivi Edgar Heap of Birds, 236, 382 n.129

Hall, Stuart, 311 n.111

Hamlet (Shakespeare), 211, 213, 231

Handler, Richard, 223–25, 241–42

Hansen, Miriam, 281–82, 285

Hardt, Michael, 396 n.114

Harvey, David, 48

Hawaii, 174, 185

Hebdige, Dick, 105

Hegel, Georg Wilhelm Friedrich, 7, 220, 396 n.114

Heiferman, Marvin, 50

Hermaphrodism: biological, 116; lesbian, 115–17

Hermeneutics of suspicion, 308 n.81

Heterosexuality, denaturalization of, 110

Hettinger, Edwin, 94, 95

High culture: mass culture and high art, 58; and popular culture in postmodernism, 123

Hill, Richard, 384 n.162

Hirsch, Susan, 26

Hispanics (Latinos): brand names in gang profiles, 359 n.110; malt liquor marketed to, 200; tobacco advertising directed at, 160–61; Troop Sport clothing marketed to, 153. *See also* Chicanos

Historicism: consideration of context, 230; historicizing the subject, 47–50

Hoggart, William, 311 n.111

Hollie Hobby case, 320 n.91, 321 n.92

Homoerotic fiction: celebrities' response to, 127–28; fanzines for, 348 n.159; in *Star Trek* fanzines, 121–22

Homosexuals: Canadian obscenity law used against, 374 n.8; drag queens, 111, 113; gay caricatures of John Wayne, 289; Gay Olympic Games controversy, 136–38, 353 nn. 28, 29, 354 n.35; Stonewall riots, 112, 113. *See also* Gay camp subculture; Lesbians

Homosocial bonding in sports, 193–94

hooks, bell, 226, 227–28

Hornell Brewing Company, 371 n.162

Hosanna (Tremblay), 113

"Hurt/Comfort" stories, 121, 122, 349 n.182

Hutcheon, Lynda, 105, 377 n.37

Hutchinson, Alan, 214, 260, 265, 266, 270

Hybridity, 207, 285, 355 n.49

Hyperreality, 38, 163, 290, 360 n.138

Identities: American Indians in America, 192–93; Canadian crises of, 140–41; contemporary properties of culture and, 226–29; as contingent, 132; in cultural studies, 310 n.110; culture as process of constructing, 29; as dialectically created, 264–65; difference in construction of, 131, 132, 165, 295; the individual as having an identity, 223; legal treatment of, 226–27; mass media in construction of, 29–33, 105–7, 267; parody, pastiche, and irony in transitional, 105; surrogacy and effigy in creation of, 195; as temporary and uncertain, 28. *See also* Collective identities; Cultural identity; Gender identities; Race

Identity-based politics, 35, 227–28, 265

"If value then right" principle, 323 n.106

Incentive, property rights as, 340 n.59

Indian Affairs Acts (Canada), 234

Indian Affairs Department (Canada), 234–35

Individual, liberal, 44–45

Individual and society, Bakhtin on, 83

Individualism. *See* Possessive individualism; Romantic individualism

Information technology, 249, 285, 364 n.81

Inherently distinctive marks, 62, 64

Inkster, Norman, 354 n.38

Intangible interests: as accruing value in their own right, 144; increasing protection for, 54; misappropriation theory applied to, 68; and publicity rights, 341 n.59

Intellectual properties: constitutive role in commercial culture, 5; contemporary signifying practice threatened by, 26; as contingent on social responsibilities, 100; controversies over, 8; discursive properties of, 38; ethnographic approach to, 27; expansion of, 6–7; labor in value of, 94; literary property, 249, 273–74, 289, 395 n.93; natural law in justification of, 77–78; as not free, 344 n.60; and others, 129; in sports team images, 198; subalterns as doubly disadvantaged by, 276; subcultures mobilizing around, 31; value and, 323 n.106. *See also* Brand names; Copyright; Patents; Publicity rights; Trademarks

Intellectual property law: balances in, 344 n.60; creative worldmaking limited by, 226; and death of the author, 284; dialogic practice stifled by, 42, 50–51, 68–69, 86; discourses in public sphere affected by, 134; as going beyond rhetoric of rights, 27; in imperialism and colonialism, 33; language as viewed in, 46; law, culture, and interpretive agency intersecting in, 6; monologic forms privileged by, 86; Native Americans using, 204–6; paternity metaphors in, 326 n.131; political economy of mimesis constituted by, 169; as privatizing the public domain, 53–55; for protecting Native peoples' interests, 381 n.103; public interest as ignored by, 54–55, 317 n.60; scholarship on, 7, 302 n.7; the signature as propped up by, 287–88; and texts, 18. *See also* Intellectual properties

Intercultural, the, 140, 355 n.49

Internationalism, cultural, 220, 222, 237

Irony: in identity of marginalized groups, 105; and monologism of legal discourse, 68

Jackson, Jesse, 159
Jacoby, Joy Anne, 211
Jameson, Fredric, 2, 48
Jarmusch, Jim, 98, 339 n.53
Jaszi, Peter, 317 n.60
Jell-O, 80–81
Jenkins, Henry, III, 124, 125, 128
Jhally, Sut, 333 n.175
Joe Camel, 74–76, 261, 268, 329 n.152
Johnson, Richard, 17
Jordache Enterprises, Inc. v. Hogg Wyld, Ltd., 326 n.126
Jordan, Michael, 360 n.123
Judy (fanzine), 123
Just desserts, 323 n.106

Kamercorp Holdings Inc. v. 624564 Ontario Ltd, 321 n.92
Kamuf, Peggy, 283, 286–89, 290, 385 n.16
Kearns, Tom, 25
Keeshig-Tobias, Lenore, 240, 241
Kelber, Bruce C., 366 n.98
Kentucky Fried Chicken, 3, 162, 357 n.81
Keohane, Kieran, 140
Kester, Grant, 306 n.63
Key symbols, 132, 144, 351 n.4
King and I, The, 211, 213
Kleenex, 80
Kluge, Alexander, 252, 281–82
Koenig, Dorean M., 74–75, 261, 318 n.63
Koenig, Frederick, 163
Kool cigarettes, 159
Koons, Jeff, 327 n.143
Koptiuch, Kristin, 380 n.80
Kozinski, Judge Alex, 1, 66, 76, 137, 268–69, 322 n.98, 344 n.60
Kraft General Foods, 81, 145, 356 n.68
Kroc, Ray, 357 n.81
Kruger, Barbara, 73
Ku Klux Klan (KKK), 149–64; British Knights footwear rumor, 157; Brooklyn Bottling Company rumor, 152, 161–62; Church's Fried Chicken rumor, 152–53, 162; Kool cigarette rumor, 159; Marlboro cigarette rumor, 159–61; Reebok footwear rumor, 157–58; sexual metaphors in stories of, 151; sterilization rumors, 152; Troop Sport clothing rumor, 152, 153–57
Kwakiutl people, 238
Kwall, Roberta Rosenthal, 95, 338 n.46

La Bohème (Puccini), 211, 213
Lacan, Jacques, 140, 295
Laches doctrine, 368 n.146
Laclau, Ernesto, 290, 292–93, 294–95
La Duke, Winona, 246
Lahr v. Adell Chemical Co., 336 n.16
lang, k. d., 117
Lange, David, 97, 318 n.60
Language: Bakhtin on, 82–85; Gramsci on metaphoricality of, 82; as neutral medium in liberal theory, 264–65; ordinary language, 279, 392 n.10; ownership of, 46; women's use of, 278. *See also* Meaning; Metaphor; Signification; Writing
Language games, 303 n.16
Lanham Act, 319 n.82, 325 nn. 116, 119
Latham, R. Brant, 352 n.22
La Valley, Al, 113
Law: anthropological approach to, 39; as authoritative and pervasive discourse, 124; constitutive power of, 11; constitutive theories of, 25, 28; creating cultural spaces for community formation, 124; cultural studies as metaphorizing, 30–31; and culture, 9, 10–11, 302 n.8; enabling power of, 29; ethics as preceding, 299; hegemonic power of, 9–10; identity as constructed in contexts mediated by, 29; identity as treated in, 226–27; legal anthropology, 25; legal objectivists, 44; liberal premises of, 248–49; as medium and means of cultural politics, 28; as prohibitive and productive, 87, 350 n.191; as seeking to eliminate ambiguity, 1; signification frozen by, 8, 28–29; as social mediation, 25–26; sociolegal studies, 12, 25, 29, 303 n.10; textuality of, 30–31; universality and abstract equality in, 299. *See also* Critical cultural legal studies; Intellectual property law
"Lay" stories, 120–21
Lazarus, Charles, 52
Lazarus, Neil, 306 n.63
Lazarus-Black, Mindie, 26
Leach, Edmund, 1
Lederman, Rena, 304 n.27
Lee, Benjamin, 177
Lee, Spike, 360 n.123
Lefebvre, Henri, 133
Lefort, Claude, 290, 396 n.106
"Left Out on the Information Highway" (Coombe), 311 n.111, 364 n.81
Legal objectivists, 44

Lesbians: Canadian obscenity law used against, 374 n.8; and celebrity images, 113–17; James Dean as refashioned by, 89, 115, 116, 117; lesbian hermaphrodism, 115–17; "Lesbians fly Air Canada" message, 130–31; and Nancy Sinatra, 113, 348 n.138
Levinas, Emmanuel, 395 n.98
Levine, Sherry, 73
Lévi-Strauss, Claude, 20–21
Liberal individual, 44–45
Liberal model of free speech, 264–65, 387 n.56
Licensing arrangements: for celebrity images, 91, 343 n.59; character merchandising, 321 n.92; and consumer confusion, 65–66; Disney owning RCMP rights, 142; for sports team merchandise, 365 n.96. See also Merchandising rights
Likelihood of consumer confusion: in early trademark cases, 176; extension of principle, 322 n.96; in Flying Elvi v. Flying Elvises, 350 n.194; and official marks, 136; publicity rights as contributing to, 343 n.59; in representations of First Nations peoples, 381 n.103; in trademark protection, 64, 65–66, 70
Lipsitz, George, 215
Literary property, 249, 273–74, 289, 395 n.93
Literature: the novel, 255, 257; in politics of community, 290–91, 395 n.100; as problematic term, 291; the reading audience, 254–55, 256–57
Litman, Jessica, 317 n.60
Locke, John, 7, 67, 78, 94, 219, 223
Lott, Eric, 194–95
Lubicon Cree people, 236, 237
Lucasfilm Ltd., 128, 350 n.204
Lugosi v. Universal Pictures, 323 n.109, 336 n.15
Lury, Celia, 253–56, 282, 311 n.111, 387 nn. 52, 53
Lyotard, Jean-François, 290, 303 n.16

Macdonald, Sir John A., 233
Macpherson, C. B., 223
Madonna, 96–97, 98, 339 n.49
Madow, Michael, 88, 100
Magor, Liz, 384 n.162
Major League Baseball, licensing revenues for, 365 n.96
Maracle, Lee, 381 n.100
Mardi Gras Indians, 215

Marginality: celebrity images appropriated by marginal groups, 103–29; in classical concept of culture, 14; fandom as vehicle for marginalized groups, 104; as pervasive in consumer society, 58; as postmodern issue, 13; and subcultures, 31, 345 n.63
Marked and unmarked forms of words, 171–72
Marlboro cigarettes: Ku Klux Klan rumor, 159–61; the Marlboro Man, 74, 76, 143
Marling, Karal Ann, 177–78, 364 n.70
Martin, Emily, 3
Martin, Lee Ann, 241, 245
Marx Brothers, 95, 96, 97
"Mary Sue" stories, 119–20
Mass culture: central paradox of, 105; corporate hegemony over, 283; cultural studies approach to, 17; in everyday lives, 57; and high art, 58; in shaping politically salient forms of difference, 129; subcultures contrasted with, 345 n.63
Mass media: becoming mass through juridicalization, 31; celebrity images in, 92; as central in contemporary social theory, 265; and citizenship, 279; class and access to, 392 n.18; commodity culture as signifying culture, 55; corporate power as mass-mediated, 33; in cultural studies, 30; and emergence of trademark laws, 173; and free speech, 258–60, 388 n.61; Habermas on, 278, 279, 392 n.18; in identity construction, 29–33, 105–7, 267; the mediascape, 105, 164, 167, 346 n.84; opportunities afforded by, 100; ownership of, 52; postmodern concern with, 13; as privately controlled, 259; and the publics of civil society, 280–83; in public sphere's construction, 170–71; sign replacing product in, 56; slide from culture to, 270. See also Advertisements; Motion pictures; Television
Mass production: and emergence of trademark laws, 173; human fodder consumed in, 148; the signature in conditions of, 287; work of art's aura lost through, 101–2
Mattel, 66–67
McCarthy, J. Thomas, 352 n.19
McClure, Kirsty, 294
McDonald's, 4, 143, 357 n.81
McLean, Willajeanne, 63
McMaster, Gerald, 241, 245
McMurray, Walter, 338 n.40

National borders, 182, 289

National Football League, licensing revenues for, 365 n.96

National Hockey League, licensing revenues for, 365 n.96

Nationalist discourse, 139–40

Native peoples: on Aboriginal Title, 245–47; in advertising, 4–5, 186; articulating their claims in terms of possessive individualism, 241–45; bodies as marked by fetishism, 207; on cultural appropriation, 232–41; differences among, 243; double voiced rhetoric of, 242; identity in art of, 381 n.102; intellectual property laws for protecting interests of, 381 n.103; listening to claims of in context, 229–31, 241; multiculturalism and claims to self-determination by, 375 n.21; publishers on works by, 381 n.100; representations of, 227–29; and rights, 245, 384 n.164; stereotypes as more visible than their social existence, 288, 297; stereotypical commercial imagery of, 187; and Western categories of property, 209, 229. *See also* American Indians; First Nations peoples

Natural rights: and equating of value and right, 323 n.106; in Gordon's defense of free speech, 77–78

Navaho people, 205, 373 n.186

Negt, Oskar, 252, 281–82

New Age religions, 236, 239

Newsworthiness, 261–64

Newton, Esther, 111, 112

Newton, Nell Jessop, 372 nn. 182, 184

"Nigger-Hair Smoking Tobacco," 176–77

Nike footwear, 159, 359 n.123

Nimoy, Leonard, 127

Nominative fair use defense, 269

Normativity, 43, 313 n.10

Novel, the, 255, 257

Objectivists, legal, 44

Objects: of property and subjects of politics, 41–87; and subjects, 43–47, 264–72

Official marks, 135–43; Gay Olympic Games controversy, 136–38, 353 nn. 28, 29; as reified signifiers of power, 142; in Royal Canadian Mounted Police dress code controversy, 138–42; signifying power of, 32

Oka standoff, 369 n.150

Olivier, Laurence, 211, 213

Olympic Club, The, 137

Olympic Games, Gay, 136–38, 353 nn. 28, 29, 354 n.35

Oneida people, 170, 197, 205, 212

Ordinary language, 279, 392 n.10

Orientalism: in Canadian national consciousness, 141; in *Globe and Mail* debate, 210, 213; Said on, 376 n.23

Originality, 62, 219, 254, 283, 291

Outram, Richard, 211

Ownership: as abstraction, 230; concentration of, 266; of cultural properties, 222–23; fixing the signifier/owning the sign, 67–73; of language, 46; of mass media, 52; meaning as attached to, 8, 61, 71; as private, 276; of trademarks, 61, 71, 276, 325 n.116. *See also* Property

Paredes, Americo, 182

Paris, Erna, 211

Parody: *A Day in Hollywood* as, 97; in identity of marginalized groups, 105; and monologism of legal discourse, 68; in Rogers v. Koons, 328 n.143; of trademarks, 75–76, 328 n.151

Parthenon Marbles, 223

Particularity, 24, 275

Parton, Dolly, 114

Pask, Amanda, 228–29

Pastiche: in gay camp subculture, 105–6; in identity of marginalized groups, 105; in interculturalism, 140; mimetic juxtapositions of alterity, 206–7; and monologism of legal discourse, 68; in postcolonial Canadian identity, 140

Patents: design patents, 6; publicity rights compared with, 340 n.59

Penley, Constance, 124, 127, 348 n.159, 350 n.204

Pesce, Christopher, 335 n.8

Philip Morris Co.: advertising expenditures of, 318 n.63; blacks harvesting tobacco for, 160; Jell-O as trademark of, 81; Kraft General Foods acquired by, 81, 145, 356 n.68; as largest American advertiser, 145; satires of ads of, 74, 75–76. *See also* Marlboro cigarettes

Phillips, Lisa, 50

Photography, 101, 103

Picasso, Pablo, 217, 225

Pink Panther Patrol, 354 n.37

Pluralism, 132, 138, 141, 277

Podlesney, Teresa, 339 n.49

Polan, Dana, 270, 281

Polier, Nicole, 308 n.80

Politics: alterity and articulation in space of the political, 273–99; celebrity form and politics of postmodernism, 100–107; commodified cultural forms creating new relations of power in cultural, 26; of community, 290–91, 395 n.100; as cultural activity, 274; cultural appropriation as political, 132, 134, 285, 292; culture as separated from, 265; dialogics of postmodern, 82–87; dialogue as regulative ideal for, 46–47; of direct address, 294; identity-based politics, 35, 227–28, 265; imagery in postmodern, 142–43; law as medium and means of cultural, 28; objects of property and subjects of, 41–87; the personal as the political, 108; of the public sphere, 274–80; as signifying activity, 131–35; trademarks constraining political expression, 69–73. *See also* Citizenship; Democracy

Popular culture: conflicting interests in, 195; and high culture in postmodernism, 123; recoding cultural forms as essence of, 57; trademarks as invading, 76

Possessive individualism: cultural identity argument as extending, 225; in cultural nationalism, 223–24; Native peoples articulating their claims in terms of, 241–45; of opponents of cultural appropriation, 214; in Romantic view of authorship, 211–12; in Western categories of property, 209

Postcolonialism: Canada as postcolonial, 141, 355 n.53; colonialism's other still embodied in, 167; democracy in circumstances of, 274; and proprietary concept of culture, 215, 376 n.37

Postindustrial society: postmodernism associated with, 21, 48, 306 n.62, 355 n.61; Silicon Valley, 181–82; suspicion of corporate power in, 148; term's meaning, 355 n.61; Western societies becoming, 21

Postmodernism, 12–13; author-function challenged in, 284–85; the celebrity form and politics of, 100–107; and central paradox of mass culture, 105; and cultural anthropology, 12, 34–39, 303 n.16; culture of, 50–52; democracy in conditions of, 273, 274; dialogics of postmodern politics, 82–87; early employment of

concept, 303 n.16; on form's implications, 43, 313 n.9; free speech in conditions of, 249, 257–64; genres blurring in, 123; hermeneutic approaches distinguished from, 308 n.81; imagery in politics of, 142–43; jokes as element of, 58; as logic of late capitalism, 48–49, 51–52; Milton compared with, 315 n.35; and modernism contrasted, 273; political versus literary mode of, 304 n.19; and postindustrialism, 21, 48, 306 n.62, 355 n.61; postmodern goods, 55–58; poststructuralism as identified with, 12, 48; public sphere, 279; signification as proliferating in, 52, 133, 144; social constructionism of, 44, 242; and textuality, 18; on textual thickness of everyday life, 52; totalizing accounts rejected in, 15, 42–43; trademarks as key symbols in, 144

"Postmodernist Subject in Legal Theory, The" (Boyle), 49

Postmodernity: as defined in this study, 51. *See also* Postmodernism

Poststructuralism: authorship undermined by, 284; feminism challenged by, 108; as identified with postmodernism, 12, 48; poststructuralist feminists, 107; social constructionism in, 44

Potlatch, 236, 238

Power: constitutive power of the law, 11; cultural power of intellectual properties, 5, 6, 373 n.189; differential power of social agents, 47; free speech principle favoring those in, 266; hegemonic power of the law, 9–10; law as operation of, 28; law's enabling power, 29; mass-mediated nature of corporate, 33; official marks as reified signifiers of, 142; as producing its subjects, 108–9, 347 n.104; rumors making visible, 164–65; sexuality as constructed within existing relations of, 109–10; signs of the powerful as pervasive in capitalism, 271; trademarks as visual symbols of, 130. *See also* Politics

Powermaster Malt Liquor, 371 n.162

Presley, Elvis: cologne, 98, 339 n.54; Flying Elvi v. Flying Elvises, 350 n.194; images associated with, 102; "In Memoriam" picture, 263; in Jarmusch's *Mystery Train*, 98, 339 n.53; and lesbian hermaphrodism, 117; in Memphis redevelopment scheme, 98–99, 340 n.55; moral economies around images of, 350 n.194

Trademarks, 130–65; alterity and mimesis in, 167–70; and authorship, 61, 62, 163; in black public sphere, 23; brand-driven deals, 61, 318 n.63; capital's presence marked by, 164–65; as constitutive parts of public sphere, 170; cultural power of, 5, 6, 373 n.189; descriptive marks, 63; distinctiveness of, 62, 64, 175, 176; as distinguishing marker of origin, 60; embodied trademarks, 166–207; as favored form for protecting cultural texts, 62; fictional characters as, 60, 78–79, 331 n.163; as friends from childhood, 57; genericide, 79–82, 287, 344 n.59; inherently distinctive marks, 62, 64; as key symbols in postmodernity, 144; misappropriation rationale for, 61, 68, 319 n.82; nineteenth-century law of, 60; "our signs in their lives," 19–21, 373 n.189; owners of, 61, 71, 276, 325 n.116; as perpetual, 61; policing, 80; political expression constrained by, 69–73; as property, 61, 276; for protecting Native peoples' interests, 381 n.103; publicity rights compared with, 342 n.59; purely communicative uses as allowed, 268–69; rumors regarding, 22, 32, 33, 143–64, 287; secondary meaning in, 62, 63–64, 197; as self-referential signs, 55–56; *semiotics* as registered, 59; signaling and expressive functions of, 66–67; and the signature, 286; U.S. laws becoming federal, 173–77; in visual culture of the nation, 166–67; as visual symbols of power, 130. *See also* Dilution of a trademark; Likelihood of consumer confusion

Trager, Robert, 387 n.56

Tremblay, Michael, 113

Trips (Agreement on Trade-Related Aspects of Intellectual Property Rights), 325 n.119

Troop Sport clothing, 152, 153–57

Tropical Fantasy soft drink, 152, 161–62

Trouillot, Michel-Rolph, 19, 289

Turner, Frederick Jackson, 177, 178

Turner, Patricia, 149, 152–53, 155, 157–58, 162–63, 359 n.123

Turner, Terence, 16, 30

Tyler, Parker, 112

United States: *American* as pertaining to, 363 n.44; American Indians in American identity, 192–93; fair use doctrine in, 332 n.174, 371 n.163; fictional character protection in, 331 n.160; "melting pot" model of assimilation in, 142; official marks in, 135, 352 n.19; publicity rights in, 90; trademark laws becoming federal, 173–77; trademarks in, 64–65; violence in creation of, 196; visual display of excessive corporeality in, 172

United States Olympic Committee, 137–38, 353 nn. 28, 29, 354 n.35

Unmarked and marked forms of words, 171–72

Value: connotative value, 68; equating right with, 93, 323 nn. 100, 106; intangible interests accruing in their own right, 144; labor in intellectual properties', 94; market value arising after property rights, 93; trademark owners appropriating surplus, 66–67

Vierthaler, Bonnie, 76

Visser, Margaret, 80–81

Voloshinov, V. N.: and Bakhtin, 82, 85, 334 n.183; on consciousness as embodied in signs, 41; and politics as articulation, 132; on ruling class control of signs, 68

Wakankar, Milind, 193–94

Wallace, Michelle, 156

Walt Disney Co.: copyright suits by, 41, 53; *The Indian in the Closet,* 4; Royal Canadian Mounted Police licensing rights, 142

Warner, Michael, 170, 365 n.89

Warner Bros., 331 n.164

Warrior, Robert Allen, 233

Washington Redskins, 186, 189, 197, 198–99, 366 n.98, 369 n.155

Wayne, John, 289

Webster, Gloria Cranmer, 238, 383 n.139

Weiner, Annette, 13, 15–16, 304 n.19

Weinrich, Peter, 381 n.103

Welfare state: dismantling of, 4; state/market distinction collapsed by, 278

Wells, Chip, 339 n.49

Wernick, Andrew, 388 n.72

West, Cornell, 230

West, Mae, 110, 111

White, Allon, 195

White, Vanna, 90, 92

Whitehead, Colson, 166

Whites: formation of white working class, 194–95; Indians stereotyped by, 188; Nordics, 192; whiteness, 173–74, 193, 368 n.139

White v. Samsung Electronics, 1, 90, 344
n.60
Wicke, Jennifer, 48–49
Williams, Raymond, 24, 216, 311 n.111
Willis, Paul, 104, 106
Winnebago people, 170, 197, 205
Winter, Steven L., 44, 334 n.202
Women: the blonde, 339 n.49; bodies as
marked by fetishism, 207; as hermaphroditic, 116; Indian, 235–36; language use by,
278; Madonna's image of femininity, 96–
97; as readers, 257; and *Star Trek* fanzines,
117–23. *See also* Feminism; Lesbians
Woodmansee, Martha, 387 n.36
Working class: formation of white, 194–95;
as readers, 257
Writing: and modern notion of the author,
283; in politics of community, 290–91;
self and community as dependent on, 46;

as transcending its origins, 251; writer
distinguished from, 286. *See also*
Textuality

Xerox: and generic concept of photocopy,
79; rumors regarding, 357 n.81
"X Marks the Spot: The Ambiguities of African Trading in the Commerce of Black
Public Spheres" (Coombe and Stoller),
360 n.136

Young, Iris Marion, 275, 278
Young, Neil, 205
Yúdice, George, 280, 281

Zemans, Joyce, 214
Zipursky, Diane, 371 n.167
Žižek, Slavoj, 140